Lifespan Perspectives on Natural Disasters

Katie E. Cherry
Editor

Lifespan Perspectives on Natural Disasters

Coping with Katrina, Rita, and Other Storms

Springer

Editor
Katie E. Cherry
Department of Psychology
Louisiana State University
236 Audubon Hall
Baton Rouge LA 70803-5501
USA
pskatie@lsu.edu

ISBN 978-1-4419-0392-1 e-ISBN 978-1-4419-0393-8
DOI 10.1007/978-1-4419-0393-8
Springer Dordrecht Heidelberg London New York

Library of Congress Control Number: 2009929717

© Springer Science+Business Media, LLC 2009
All rights reserved. This work may not be translated or copied in whole or in part without the written permission of the publisher (Springer Science+Business Media, LLC, 233 Spring Street, New York, NY 10013, USA), except for brief excerpts in connection with reviews or scholarly analysis. Use in connection with any form of information storage and retrieval, electronic adaptation, computer software, or by similar or dissimilar methodology now known or hereafter developed is forbidden.
The use in this publication of trade names, trademarks, service marks, and similar terms, even if they are not identified as such, is not to be taken as an expression of opinion as to whether or not they are subject to proprietary rights.

Printed on acid-free paper

Springer is part of Springer Science+Business Media (www.springer.com)

Contents

Part I Children and Adolescents

1 Young Children's Demonstrated Understanding of Hurricanes . . .   3
  Teresa K. Buchanan, Renée M. Casbergue,
  and Jennifer J. Baumgartner

2 An Ecological-Needs-Based Perspective of Adolescent
  and Youth Emotional Development in the Context
  of Disaster: Lessons from Hurricane Katrina 27
  Carl F. Weems and Stacy Overstreet

3 Positive Adjustment in Youth Post-Katrina:
  The Impact of Child and Maternal Social Support and Coping . . 45
  Julia F. Vigna, Brittany C. Hernandez, Valerie Paasch,
  Arlene T. Gordon, and Mary L. Kelley

4 The Impact of Hurricane Katrina on Children
  and Adolescents: Conceptual and Methodological
  Implications for Assessment and Intervention 65
  Russell T. Jones, Kelly Dugan Burns, Christopher S. Immel,
  Rachel M. Moore, Kathryn Schwartz-Goel,
  and Bonnie Culpepper

Part II Young and Middle-Age Adults

5 The Psychological Impact of Hurricanes and Storms on Adults . . 97
  Thompson E. Davis III, Erin V. Tarcza, and Melissa S. Munson

6 Families and Disasters: Making Meaning out of Adversity 113
  M.E. Betsy Garrison and Diane D. Sasser

Part III Older Adults and the Oldest-Old

7 Encounters with Katrina: Dynamics of Older Adults'
  Social Support Networks 133
  Karen A. Roberto, Yoshinori Kamo, and Tammy Henderson

8 **Disaster Services with Frail Older Persons: From Preparation to Recovery** 153
Priscilla D. Allen and H. Wayne Nelson

9 **Natural Disasters and the Oldest-Old: A Psychological Perspective on Coping and Health in Late Life** 171
Katie E. Cherry, Jennifer L. Silva, and Sandro Galea

10 **Faith, Crisis, Coping, and Meaning Making After Katrina: A Qualitative, Cross-Cohort Examination** 195
Loren D. Marks, Katie E. Cherry, and Jennifer L. Silva

Part IV Special Topics

11 **The Psychology Behind Helping and Prosocial Behaviors: An Examination from Intention to Action** 219
Jennifer L. Silva, Loren D. Marks, and Katie E. Cherry

12 **Building a Disaster Mental Health Response to a Catastrophic Event: Louisiana and Hurricane Katrina** 241
Anthony H. Speier, Joy D. Osofsky, and Howard J. Osofsky

13 **Disaster Recovery in Workplace Organizations** 261
Tracey E. Rizzuto

14 **Disasters and Population Health** 281
Jennifer Johnson and Sandro Galea

Subject Index 327

Natural Disasters from a Life Span Developmental Perspective: An Introduction

Katie E. Cherry

Abstract This introduction was written to frame the intent of the book and set the stage for a discussion of disaster effects from a life span developmental perspective. The first part begins with a glimpse of the local experience of Hurricanes Katrina and Rita on the communities and people who lived in storm-affected areas during the hurricane season of 2005 and the years since then. The purpose and content of this book is presented next. A brief overview of Hurricanes Katrina and Rita characterizes these disasters and what happened in their aftermath, providing relevant background information for the chapters that follow. In the next part, developmental considerations in a disaster context are discussed and the individual chapters in this book are highlighted. The introduction concludes by underscoring the timeliness of considering natural disasters from a developmental perspective. The need for systematic research, clinical interventions, and thoughtful disaster planning is emphasized to increase the likelihood of effective preparation and management of future catastrophic hurricanes on local, state, and national levels.

Introduction

The hurricane season of 2005 brought profound and far-reaching changes to the physical, cultural, and spiritual landscape of South Louisiana, the Mississippi and Alabama coasts, and portions of southeast Texas (Alderman & Ward, 2008; Brinkley, 2005; Horne, 2006). For those of us who reside in the storm-affected areas, Hurricanes Katrina, Rita, and their aftermath have dominated our lives and brought numerous changes on every level imaginable. For instance, storm-related changes have affected our jobs, schools, and communities, as well as our families, friends, and routine ways of living. Whether directly exposed to the storms, such as those

K.E. Cherry (✉)
Department of Psychology, LSU Life Course and Aging Center, Louisiana State University, 236 Audubon Hall, Baton Rouge, LA 70803-5501, USA
e-mail: pskatie@lsu.edu

people who lost their homes, property, and possibly witnessed death, or indirectly exposed through storm-related disruptions and the influx of hundreds of thousands of evacuees into nearby cities and neighboring states, the hurricane season of 2005 has left deep and long-lasting marks on the face of our world.

In the months and years that have followed Hurricanes Katrina and Rita, local conversation related to the epic storms has run the gamut from stories of destruction and horror (e.g., homes under water, roof top rescues, a dead horse washed onto a carport) to complaints about storm-related frustrations (e.g., widespread power outages, increased traffic, felled trees, insurance claims) and shared concerns over long-term losses in the hardest hit areas (e.g., loss of neighborhoods, schools, public libraries, sports programs for youth, and other community-based recreation opportunities). Setbacks for local business and industries are another frequent topic of conversation (e.g., damage to refineries and offshore oil rigs, destruction of oyster beds, shrimping, fishing, timber and other agricultural industries, music and entertainment industry setbacks related to displaced performers). Local conversation with political commentary has been rich with opinion and accusatory fingers pointing, assigning blame to a variety of entities ranging from Mother Nature to local officials to the US Army Corps of Engineers to the Federal Government.

At the time of this writing (three-and-a-half years since the storms), reconstruction and rebuilding efforts have progressed noticeably. Blue tarps stretched tightly over damaged rooftops which had once dotted the skyline of houses across the Gulf Coast region are nearly all gone now. Many displaced residents have returned to their homes or relocated elsewhere and are settled in new areas. Most of the storm debris have been removed from sight, yet lingering and sometimes haunting images of storm-related devastation remain in our thoughts (i.e., ruined homes, churches and businesses, familiar landmarks destroyed, abandoned vehicles and neighborhoods, fishing boats blown miles ashore, storm-ravaged cemeteries with disturbed tombs, and unearthed coffins scattered widely). For some people, the storms have prompted deeper, philosophical thinking, occasionally interlaced with biblical reference (i.e., an act of cleansing, optimistic appraisals for rebuilding homes and lives). Other viewpoints on the storms invite sociological contemplation, such as the perceived racial inequities and the perennial question of where one draws the line between personal responsibility (listen to weather forecasts, heed the storm warnings, evacuate to safer ground before the storm) versus civic or institutional responsibility (local and federal governments should provide emergency transportation, safe refuge from the storms, adequate construction and maintenance of the levees that protect the city, effective emergency preparedness and response operations, etc.).

For this author, the fundamental question related to Hurricane Katrina was not what happened, why did it happen, or who is to blame for the misfortunes and suffering of many, or even what do we learn from our experiences of 2005. Rather, as a developmental psychologist, the one vexing question that surfaced initially for me and subsequently motivated this book was a seemingly simple question: who was more adversely affected by the Katrina and Rita disaster, children or elderly adults? There is no doubt that older adults perished during Katrina and the post-disaster period in far greater numbers than did children, youth, or any other age group combined (Johnson & Galea, Chapter 14 of this volume). Media coverage at the time of the storms also drew our attention to evacuation dilemmas which brought unspeakable suffering, such as medically compromised elderly persons dehydrated and dying in wheelchairs from heat exposure or running out of oxygen before help could arrive. Other horrors include the St. Rita's nursing home tragedy where 35 residents drowned and 24 survivors were left to suffer in the flooded facility in St. Bernard parish that did not evacuate (Cherry, Allen, & Galea, 2009; MSNBC, 2007; Schaefer, 2007). Four weeks after Katrina, residents from the Brighton Garden Home for the Aged in Texas were evacuating in preparation for Hurricane Rita when their bus caught fire. Tragically, oxygen tanks on the bus exploded and killed 23 of the residents (Gross, Griffin, Wilder, & Lyles, 2005; Horne, 2006).

If dying and death are the only indicators of storm impact, then one might quickly conclude that older adults were more affected by the storms than were children. On the other hand, new evidence has been revealed concerning the plight of children and youth. For instance, we now know about formaldehyde poisoning for those living in FEMA trailers (Sierra Club, 2008). Other evidence has shown that Katrina youth are among the sickest children in the nation, suffering from alarmingly high incidence of anemia, respiratory infections, and mental health problems (Carmichael, 2008; Redlener & Grant, 2008; Weems & Overstreet, 2008). Storm-displaced adolescents often endured multiple hardships, including relocation into strange and unfamiliar neighborhoods with a corresponding loss of structure, stability, and friendship networks. Displaced high school students were sometimes confronted with ridicule and torment by those in the host schools who resented their presence (Lussier, 2006). Other evidence has shown heightened emotional reactivity with a longer time to recover from emotional upsets among storm-displaced adolescents in their new schools (Nelson, 2008). From this vantage point, it is clear that children and youth were also deeply affected by Katrina and Rita and suffered greatly on many levels. Sadly, for some children and their families, the long-term negative consequences of these storms may have only just begun to be realized as the longevity of storm-related setbacks and threats to physical and mental health status have come to light.

At this juncture, the question of who was more affected by the storms, children or older adults, now seems overly simplistic and perhaps not the best question to ask. Rather, this fundamental question has evolved over time and now invites a comparative analysis: how were children and old people affected similarly and differently? Naturally, one must then wonder where these similarities and differences may lead us with respect to disaster planning and preparation, post-disaster interventions, long-term strategies for recovery, and policy considerations (see Dass-Brailsford, in press; Kilmer, Gil-Rivas, Tedeschi, & Calhoun, in press; Osofsky, Osofsky, & Harris, 2007).

Purpose and Content of this Book

The purpose of this book is to take a closer look at Hurricanes Katrina and Rita from a life span developmental perspective. In particular, the book was designed with two objectives in mind: (1) to provide data-based evidence about the Katrina and Rita experience at different points in the life span and (2) to increase awareness of the developmental relevance of practical matters related to the storms. The 14 chapters in this book were written by behavioral scientists in their areas of research expertise. In keeping with the stated objectives of this book, some chapters contain original data from recent Katrina studies, along with implications and recommendations for future research and theoretical development in the field. Other chapters review and synthesize the extant disaster research and literature, offering insight into best practice approaches with recommendations for planning and preparation, while illuminating gaps in existing disaster policy and practice. The intended audience is diverse, spanning the science to the service ends of the continuum. Those in the scientific community (e.g., social scientists, clinical teaching faculty, research associates, graduate students) may use this book for research and instructional purposes. Service providers among others in helping professions (e.g., school counselors, social workers, therapists, clergy or those in faith-based organizations) may find this book useful as a source of reference on the storms and related developmental issues. Given the complex and tragic nature of Katrina, the worst natural disaster in our nation's history, this book may also appeal to the general public.

This volume is divided into four parts. The first three parts are devoted to children and adolescents (Chapters 1, 2, 3, and 4), younger and middle-age adults (Chapters 5 and 6), and elderly adults (Chapters 7, 8, 9, and 10), respectively. A special topics part covers several spheres of influence on disaster-affected regions, from the individual responses of caring people (Chapter 11, the psychology of helping and volunteerism) to community-wide actions taken by first responders and mental health professionals (Chapter 12, emergency response and crisis intervention). Broader implications for business and industry (Chapter 13, workforce recovery) and public health (Chapter 14, short and long term population health) are also addressed in this part. The unifying theme is the Katrina and Rita experience, although other storms are mentioned in passing, including Hurricanes Betsy, Andrew, Floyd, Hugo, Ivan, Wilma, and the more recent 2008 hurricane season with Hurricanes Gustav and Ike. Man-made disasters and other catastrophic events are included in discussion, such as the 9/11 terrorist attacks, the Oklahoma City bombing, technological disasters, wildfires, earthquakes, and the Indian Ocean Tsunami of 2004. An overview of Hurricanes Katrina and Rita and their immediate aftermath is given next to provide a context for discussion for the chapters that follow.

Hurricanes Katrina and Rita: A Snapshot of the Disasters

On morning of August 29, 2005, Hurricane Katrina made landfall in the Gulf Coast region which includes the Mississippi coast and the lower Plaquemines and Orleans parishes in South Louisiana. Community destruction was widespread and loss of life has been considerable. Physicians, nurses, and other professionals flew in from all over the country to provide immediate assistance in the storm-ravaged areas. Local universities, schools, churches and faith-based organizations quickly stepped in, providing direct care and hands-on assistance with the relief effort (Cherry et al., 2009). In fact, Louisiana State University (LSU) in Baton Rouge established the largest disaster field hospital in US history in the Pete Maravich Assembly Center, which was used to treat and triage over 20,000 people. LSU also housed a Special Needs Shelter, an 800 bed field nursing home in the Maddox Fieldhouse (Allen, 2007). In the LSU field hospitals, 3,000 student, staff, and community members provided services for days and weeks following Katrina (Bacher, Devlin, Calongne, Duplechain, & Pertuit, 2005). Area churches and faith-based communities made substantial contributions to the relief effort, primarily through establishment of shelters that housed both storm victims and Red Cross volunteers, among others, some that operated for as long as 2-months after the hurricanes (Cain & Barthelemy, 2008).

Worldwide, people are familiar with Hurricane Katrina. Perhaps a lesser known fact is that much of the devastation in the greater New Orleans area was caused by the storm surge and levee failures. Sadly, many who survived Katrina's immediate impact perished in the record rising flood waters in the days that followed. The infamous 17th Street Canal breach, among other breaches that occurred shortly after, filled the low-lying areas of fragile and historic New Orleans with water, at times rising several feet in minutes. Levee failures sent a churning sea of water from Lake Pontchartrain across Lakeview and into Mid-City, Carrollton, Gentilly, City Park, and neighborhoods farther south and east. Hundreds of thousands either escaped the flood or were assisted into boats and airlifted to shelters. Storm victims made their way through the toxic and fetid waters or died in the aftermath.

On September 24, 2005, less than a month after Katrina, Hurricane Rita made landfall affecting primarily Calcasieu, Cameron, and Vermilion parishes on the western side of Louisiana and southeast Texas. With the destruction already apparent from Katrina, the American Red Cross established some 90 shelters throughout Louisiana to meet the needs of thousands of hurricane-impacted residents. In all, the Red Cross operated 149 shelters that served an estimated 93,000 residents in September, 2005 (American Red Cross, 2007). Rita, also a destructive Category 3 hurricane at landfall, only directly caused seven fatalities, yet property damage has reached 11.3 billion dollars (National Hurricane Center, 2007). Media coverage related to the storms has largely focused on Hurricane Katrina and the Lower 9th Ward and Lakeview areas of New Orleans. St. Bernard, St. Tammany, and Washington parishes were also severely affected by Katrina, although these parishes have received less attention. The disproportionate coverage of Hurricane Katrina has all but eclipsed Hurricane Rita which has led to the coining of the term *Rita Amnesia* (Hancock, 2006).

Developmental Considerations in a Disaster Context

Contemporary developmental psychology offers a research-based, scholarly perspective on a variety of real-life issues that affect our day-to-day lives under normal circumstances (Lerner, Easterbrooks, & Mistry, 2003; Fisher & Lerner, 1994). The traumatic stress or disruption of the developmental context associated with the disasters may have a substantial impact on some individuals or certain groups of people, altering normative developmental trajectories (see Weems et al., 2007, for discussion). Thus, awareness and sensitivity to fundamental developmental issues are of paramount importance, as such may become magnified in the face of a natural disaster or other catastrophic event. For instance, parental coping affects child outcomes in either a positive or a negative direction. Children and adolescents often face challenges in multiple environments (home, school, neighborhood, larger community) where disruption of established routines, conflict, and aggression may happen at times. Families function as a cohesive unit in daily life and in times of stress and crisis (or not). Intergenerational issues are yet another emerging concern, given the growing numbers of grandparents raising grandchildren and middle-age adults struggling with the ongoing demands of caring for dependent children while meeting the needs of aging parents.

Implicit in each of these examples is the notion of person–context relational processes which influence development in an individual over time. Historically, the assumption has been that developmental changes at any point in the life span are best understood in the context of a changing person in a changing world, where multiple levels of influence on the person and his/her environment are taken into account (e.g., Baltes, 1987; Bronfenbrenner, 1977; see also Chapter 2 of this volume). Generally speaking, most people recognize the synergy or interplay among various domains of life, where a significant change in one area may spill over to affect other areas of their lives. Experiencing a disaster may exacerbate ongoing (pre-disaster) burdens while creating yet an entirely new set of challenges and obstacles to be overcome for survivors, first responders, emergency personnel and local officials, among countless others in a disaster context. Several chapters in this volume speak directly to reciprocal influences of this nature in children (Buchanan, Casbergue, & Baumgartner), youth and adolescents (Vigna, Hernandez, Paasch, Gordon, & Kelley), and older adults (Cherry, Silva, & Galea). Reciprocal influence is also seen on an organizational level, such as in the workforce of the affected region (e.g., mental health service providers, Speier, Osofsky, & Osofsky; business and industry, Rizzuto). Together, the chapters in this volume bring to light the developmental significance of natural disasters for individuals, families, and communities. Individual chapters are highlighted next.

Chapter Highlights

The first part, children and adolescents, addresses the Katrina experience in early life, from preschool age children to high school age youth. Multiple contexts of development are brought into focus, including home, school, and community. Buchanan, Casbergue, and Baumgartner report data from an ambitious study conducted in the immediate impact period with samples drawn from four states that varied in geographic proximity to storm-ravaged areas (Louisiana, Georgia, Tennessee, and South Carolina). Young children's knowledge of hurricanes was assessed using play activities, writing, and interviews. Preschool and kindergarten teachers' activities in the classroom were also assessed. Based on these data, recommendations for social services and meeting the mental health needs of young children after a major disaster are considered. Weems and Overstreet review the literature on childhood and adolescent emotional development, emphasizing the critical role of hurricane exposure in development. They present an ecological, needs-based perspective of youth and adolescent emotional development and a new integrative framework designed to motivate research on the emotional consequences for youth in disaster contexts. Vigna, Hernandez, Paasch, Gordon, and Kelley consider the roles of parents and families in fostering post-trauma adjustment and positive adaptation in middle childhood and adolescence. Results of a study with 142 mother/child dyads who participated in two waves of testing are presented. Analyses of these longitudinal data confirm the beneficial role of social support in predicting positive outcomes in both the child-reported and the parent-reported data 25–28 months post-Katrina. Jones, Dugan Burns, Immel, Moore, Schwartz-Goel and Culpepper begin by describing his deployments to the devastated Gulf Coast region to assist state emergency personnel in coordinating the mental health response within weeks after Katrina made landfall. A critical review of assessment and intervention studies with children and adolescents in disaster contexts follows, which underscores the need for culturally sensitive and methodologically sound research in this area. Conceptual models of post-disaster functioning in children and youth are described. Recommendations for disaster management which emphasize cultural competence and disaster behavioral health follow.

The second part, young and middle-age adults, focuses on the Katrina experience in emerging adults, college students, and middle-age adults. Davis, Tarcza, and Munson consider the psychological effects of Katrina and other storms from an adult clinical perspective, noting that natural disasters can serve as psychological stressors that may trigger depressive episodes. They review the literature on post-disaster psychological sequalae (i.e., acute stress disorder, PTSD, generalized anxiety disorder) and discuss the problems that come with disruption in services and treatment. Risk factors and resiliency in a post-disaster context are considered. Garrison and Sasser bring a family science perspective to the disaster experience of middle-age adults and families, with special attention directed toward meaning making as a critical step in the post-disaster recovery process. Qualitative data are reported from an impressive study conducted in hurricane-ravaged areas in the immediate impact period and with a subsequent second wave assessment. Making sense of the storms and finding silver linings within, as well as maintaining a positive outlook and use of humor were several emergent themes found in their study.

The third part, older adults and the oldest old, focuses on the Katrina experience for storm-displaced older persons, frail elderly adults, and very old adults indirectly affected by the hurricanes. Roberto, Kamo, and Henderson focus on social support networks and faith-based community supports in relation to the emotional needs of storm-displaced older persons. Data are presented from an intriguing, mixed method study on older evacuees' storm experiences and relationships with social network members, beginning with their exodus from New Orleans across multiple moves that brought them to distant cities and states. These data are rich with local color and appeal, providing a collective voice for the many storm-displaced older adults who faced countless hardships in the post-disaster period. Allen and Nelson lend a social work perspective to disaster services with frail older persons, tracing the route from disaster preparation to recovery. These authors focus on frail and institutionalized older adults, the special needs designation and special needs shelters.

The last two chapters of this part focus on the oldest-old (i.e., persons 90 years of age and older). These chapters, as well as the first chapter in the next part (Silva, Marks, & Cherry), use data from the Louisiana Healthy Aging Study (LHAS) mixed method hurricane assessment study (Cherry et al., 2009). Cherry, Silva, and Galea review normative changes in physical, cognitive, and social functioning in late life and describe models of coping, stress, and resilience in late adulthood. They present data on self-reported health and well-being and a qualitative analysis of coping behaviors before and after the storms. Marks, Cherry, and Silva present three themes that emerged from a qualitative analysis of participants' responses concerning their use of religious beliefs and practices to help them cope with Hurricanes Katrina, Rita, and their aftermath. Points of similarity and difference among responses of the post-World War II "baby boomers" (cohorts 1 and 2) and the "great generation" older adults (cohorts 3 and 4) were noted.

The fourth part, special topics, extends the age-specific discussion to cover behaviors seen in people and organizations after a disaster. Silva, Marks, and Cherry consider natural disasters as they intersect with a fundamental human desire to help others in crisis. They review the literature on the development of helping, prosocial behaviors, and volunteerism. Qualitative data are presented that illustrate the variety of helping behaviors seen in the post-impact period by younger and older persons indirectly exposed to Katrina and Rita. Speier, Osofsky, and Osofsky focus on storm-related emergency preparation and response operations in New Orleans in the days and months following Katrina. These authors, themselves first responders, describe the chaos and deplorable conditions survivors faced in immediate impact period in vivid detail, along with the psychological interventions utilized to address their needs. Gaps in training and preparation for behavioral health personnel to meet the unique needs of people in crisis after a natural disaster are discussed.

Rizzuto focuses on the behavior of organizations after a disaster within an organizational change framework. Features of workplace disaster recovery are discussed, including social networking, survivor syndrome, and recovering the human structure of the organization. Johnson and Galea offer a comprehensive review of disaster population health effects across six topical areas (injury and mortality, health systems and infrastructure, mental health, infectious disease, chronic disease, and health behavior). They cover many catastrophic events, including natural (earthquakes, floods, hurricanes, tsunamis), technological (chemical exposures, radiological), and man-made disasters (9/11 terrorist attacks, Oklahoma City bombing). Short-term and long-term implications for individuals, communities, and cities are discussed.

Conclusion

The hurricane season of 2004, which brought four hurricanes (Charley, Frances, Ivan, Jeanne) slamming into the Florida coast within a 7-week period, raised our awareness of the destruction and costly nature of hurricanes. Hurricanes Katrina and Rita subsequently dealt a deadly and destructive blow to the entire Gulf Coast region that very next year. Together, these events have catapulted the study of natural disaster effects squarely into our collective conscious and demanded our attention as a nation. We are still processing the damage caused by Gustav and Ike in the 2008 hurricane season. As we consider the many and diverse implications of destructive hurricanes and other natural disasters as scholars and as a nation, the health status and psychological well-being of children, adolescents, emerging, and middle-aged adults, and elderly people must not be overlooked. Individual youth characteristics are important in shaping the developmental adaptation to disasters (Norris, Freedman, & Watson, 2002; Weems & Overstreet, Chapter 2 of this volume). As discussed in Allen and Wayne (Chapter 8 of this volume), health status and the availability of social services are critical to disaster survival for frail elderly adults. Catastrophic hurricanes have happened in recent years, yet more are expected in the future (Oriol, 1999). Understanding the protective factors that promote survival, recovery, and resilience in the face of a natural disaster may better prepare us for future storms as individuals and as a society (Chapter 5; Nelson, 2008). An analysis of natural disaster effects from a life span developmental perspective, then, would appear to be both a warranted and a timely endeavor.

References

Alderman, D. H., & Ward, H. (2008). Writing on the plywood: Toward an analysis of hurricane graffiti. *Coastal Management, 35*, 1–18.

Allen, P. D. (2007). Social work in the aftermath of disaster: Reflections from a special needs shelter on the LSU campus. *Reflections, 13*(3), 127–137.

American Red Cross (2007). Disaster FAQs. *Hurricane Katrina: Why is the Red Cross not in New Orleans?* [Posted Sept. 2, 2005] Retrieved December 29, 2008, from http://www.redcross.org/faq/0,1096,0_682_4524,00.html#4524

Brinkley, D. (2005). *The great deluge.* New York: Harper Collins Publishers.

Bacher, R., Devlin, T., Calongne, K., Duplechain, J., & Pertuit, S. (2005). *LSU in the eye of the storm: A university model for disaster response.* Retrieved from http://www.lsu.edu/pa/book/EYEofTheSTORMtxt.pdf

Baltes, P. B. (1987). Theoretical propositions on life-span developmental psychology: On the dynamics between growth and decline. *Developmental Psychology, 23*, 611–626.

Bronfenbrenner, U. (1977). Toward an experimental ecology of human development. *American Psychologist, 32*, 513–531.

Cain, D. S., & Barthelemy, J. (2008). Tangible and spiritual relief after the storm: The religious community responds to Katrina. *Journal of Social Service Research, 34*, 9–42.

Carmichael, M. (2008, December 1). Katrina kids: Sickest ever. *Newsweek*, 8.

Cherry, K. E., Allen, P. D., & Galea, S. (2009). Older adults and natural disasters: Lessons learned from Hurricanes Katrina and Rita. In P. Dass-Brailsford (Ed.), *Crisis and disaster counseling: Lessons learned from Hurricane Katrina and other disasters.* Thousand Oaks, CA: Sage. *Manuscript in press.*

Cherry, K. E., Galea, S., Su, L. J., Welsh, D. A., Jazwinski, S. M., Silva, et al. (2009). Cognitive and psychosocial consequences of Hurricanes Katrina and Rita on middle aged, older, and oldest-old adults in the Louisiana Healthy Aging Study (LHAS). *Journal of Applied Social Psychology* (in press).

Dass-Brailsford P., (Ed.). (2009). *Crisis and Disaster Counseling: Lessons Learned from Hurricane Katrina and other Disasters.* Thousand Oaks, CA: Sage (in press).

Fisher, C. B., & Lerner, R. M. (1994). *Applied developmental psychology.* New York: McGraw-Hill.

Gross, J., Griffin, L., Wilder, C., & Lyles, T. (2005). *Storm and crisis: The evacuation; luck and fate seated victims on a doomed bus.* The New York Times, Retrieved December 26, 2008, from http://select.nytimes.com/gst/abstract.html?res=F30E13F63B540C708CDDA90994DD404482&n=Top%2fReference%2fTimes%20Topics%2fSubjects%2fB%2fBuse

Hancock, M. (2006). *Many in Louisiana, Texas lament Rita 'amnesia'.* USA Today, Retrieved December 28, 2008, from http://www.usatoday.com/news/nation/2006-01-25-rita_x.htm

Horne, J. (2006). *Breach of faith: Hurricane Katrina and the near death of a great American city.* New York: Random House.

Kilmer, R. P., Gil-Rivas, V., Tedeschi, R. G., & Calhoun, L. G. (Eds.). (in press). *Meeting the needs of children, families, and communities post-disaster: Lessons learned from Hurricane Katrina and its aftermath.* Washington, DC: American Psychological Association.

Lerner, R. M., Easterbrooks, M. A, & Mistry, J. (2003). *Handbook of psychology: Developmental psychology.* Hoboken, NJ: John Wiley & Sons, Inc.

Lussier, C. (2006, September 19). Security beefed up at Tara. EBR school officials working on plans to defuse student tensions. *The Advocate,* B1.

MSNBC (2007). *Katrina nursing home operators acquitted.* Retrieved December 31, 2008, from http://www.msnbc.msn.com/id/20649744/

National Hurricane Center (2007, January 23). *November 2005 Atlantic tropical weather summary.* NOAA. Retrieved January 20, 2009, from http://www.nhc.noaa.gov/archive/2005/tws/MIATWSAT_nov_final.shtml

Nelson, L. P. (2008). A resiliency profile of Hurricane Katrina adolescents. *Canadian Journal of School Psychology, 23,* 57–69

Norris, F. H., Friedman, M. J., & Watson, P. J. (2002). 60,000 disaster victims speak: Part II. Summary and implications of the disaster mental health research. *Psychiatry, 65,* 240–260.

Oriol, W. (1999). Psychosocial issues for older adults in disasters. *Booklet SMA 99–3323.* Retrieved September 13, 2008, from http://download.ncadi.samhsa.gov/ken/pdf/SMA99-3323/99-821.pdf

Osofsky, J. D., Osofsky, H. J., & Harris, W. W. (2007). Katrina's children: Social policy considerations for children in disasters. *Social Policy Report, 21,* 3–18.

Redlener, I., & Grant, R. (2008). *Legacy of shame: The on-going public health disaster of children struggling in post-Katrina Louisiana.* Retrieved January 5, 2009, from http://www.childrenshealthfund.org/PDF/BR-WhitePaper_Final.pdf

Schaefer, M. (2007). *Lost in Katrina.* Gretna, LA: Pelican Publishing Company.

Sierra Club (2008, April). *Toxic trailers.* Retrieved January 5, 2009, from http://www.sierraclub.org/gulfcoast/downloads/formaldehyde_test.pdf

Weems, C. F., & Overstreet, S. (2008). Child and adolescent mental health research in the context of Hurricane Katrina: An ecological-needs-based perspective and introduction to the special section. *Journal of Clinical Child and Adolescent Psychology, 37,* 487–494.

Weems, C. F., Piña, A. A., Costa, N. M., Watts, S. E., Taylor, L. K., & Cannon, M. F. (2007). Pre-disaster trait anxiety and negative affect predict posttraumatic stress in youth after Hurricane Katrina. *Journal of Consulting and Clinical Psychology, 75,* 154–159.

About the Contributors

Priscilla D. Allen, MSW, Ph.D., Dr. Allen is an Associate Professor in the Louisiana State University (LSU) School of Social Work and the Associate Director of the LSU Life Course and Aging Center. Prior to her appointment at LSU, Dr. Allen worked in the nursing home setting for over 10 years as a social work practitioner, and later, as a Long-Term Care Ombudsman. During Hurricanes Katrina, Rita, Gustav and Ike, Allen provided social work services in the Special Needs Shelter on the LSU campus. Her research interest is long-term care and psychosocial intervention, culture change in the nursing home, and societal influence of ageism, pallen2@lsu.edu

Jennifer J. Baumgartner, Ph.D., Division of Family, Child, and Consumer Science; School of Human Ecology, LSU. Dr. Baumgartner's research examines issues of inter-contextual continuity among children's developmental contexts, specifically early care and the family and the connections between philosophy and practice among adults in children's lives. She has experience directing early child development laboratory schools and teaches critical perspectives in early childhood education, jbaum@lsu.edu

Teresa K. Buchanan, Ph.D., Educational Theory, Policy and Practice, LSU. Dr. Buchanan is an early childhood educator whose research focuses on the influence of context on educational practices. She has published in the area of developmentally appropriate teaching practices. She is the program leader for the PK-3 teacher certification program and was the lead investigator for this research project, tbuchan@lsu.edu

Kelly Dugan Burns, M.A., Department of Psychology, Virginia Polytechnic Institute and State University. Mrs. Burns is a PhD candidate in Clinical Psychology. Her research and clinical interests are in the area of child trauma. She spent 3 years working as a Clinical Research Coordinator for the Infant/Toddler/Preschool Post-9/11 project in New York City with Dr. Claude M. Chemtob and Dr. Robert Abramovitz. This project aimed to identify young children and their parents who continued to suffer significant mental health sequelae of exposure to the September 11, 2001 WTC attacks. Mrs. Burns has presented several posters addressing exposure to the 9/11 attacks, the effects of trauma on very young children, and the role of ethnicity and socio-economic status on trauma outcomes. She has also provided psychotherapy to several clients following the April 16, 2007 Virginia Tech shootings, kdugan@vt.edu

Renée M. Casbergue, Ph.D., Department of Educational Theory, Policy, and Practice, LSU. Dr. Casbergue is an early childhood literacy educator whose research focuses on the literacy development of young children with an emphasis on instructional practices and classroom environments that support language and literacy. She is director of a federally funded Early Reading First project devoted to creating centers of excellence for literacy learning in New Orleans preschool classrooms, rcasberg@lsu.edu

Katie E. Cherry, Ph.D., Department of Psychology, Louisiana State University (LSU). Dr. Cherry is a developmental psychologist whose research program focuses on memory aging in late adulthood. She is the Emogene Pliner Distinguished Professor of Aging Studies at LSU where she has published several papers that examine the psychosocial and cognitive consequences of Hurricanes Katrina and Rita on older adults in the Louisiana Healthy Aging Study. She is the Director of the LSU Life Course and Aging Center, pskatie@lsu.edu

Bonnie Culpepper, B.S., Department of Psychology, Virginia Polytechnic and State University. Ms. Culpepper graduated from the College of Science Summa Cum Laude with a major in Psychology. She has served as a member of the Recovery Efforts After Child Trauma (REACT) team for 2 years and is currently Team Leader of the undergraduate team. She has participated in a variety of disaster-related projects, including residential fire and Hurricane Katrina initiatives, bcpepper@vt.edu

Thompson E. Davis III, Ph.D., Department of Psychology, Louisiana State University (LSU). Dr. Davis is an assistant professor of clinical psychology whose research focuses on the assessment, treatment, and developmental psychopathology of anxiety disorders, particularly specific phobias. He is the founder and director of the Laboratory for Anxiety, Phobia, and Internalizing Disorders Studies (LAPIS) and co-director of child clinical services at the LSU Psychological Services Center. Dr. Davis has published studies and reviews on the effects and evidence-based treatment of anxiety disorders in children and young adults, ted@lsu.edu

Sandro Galea, MD, DrPH, School of Public Health, Institute for Social Research, and Center for Global Health, University of Michigan. Dr. Galea is an epidemiologist with an interest in the health consequences of conflict mass trauma. He has published extensively on the mental health effects of several mass traumas including the consequences of the terrorist attacks, including the September 11, 2001 terrorist attacks; the March 11, 2004 terrorist attacks in Madrid; and of conflict in Liberia, Ethiopia, and Israel. He has also studied the health consequences of Hurricane Katrina among other natural disasters, sgalea@umich.edu

M.E. Betsy Garrison, Ph.D., School of Human Ecology and Associate Dean, College of Agriculture, LSU and LSU AgCenter. As a family stress scholar, Garrison has authored more than 40 research publications. Along with Dr. Sasser, she is conducting a longitudinal research project (approved as CSREES project No. 93786) on families and disasters and is affiliated with the Disaster Science and Management (DSM) program at LSU, hcgarr@lsu.edu

Arlene T. Gordon, M.A., Department of Psychology, Louisiana State University. Ms. Gordon is a clinical psychology doctorate student whose research interests revolve around coping and psychological adjustment among children and families exposed to chronic stressors and traumatic events. Ms. Gordon has worked on studies exploring the after-affect of natural disasters such as Hurricane Katrina on children, agord11@lsu.edu

Tammy L. Henderson, Ph.D., Department of Human Development and Family Sciences, Oklahoma State University. Dr. Henderson conducts research in the area of policy, law, and diversity (e.g., grandparent rights and responsibilities, foster care, and diversity and law). She has conducted needs assessments and evaluation studies on faculty governance, faculty development, the capacity of faculty members at HBCU to address health disparities, and other policy concerns. Henderson also has served as a Co-Guest editor and Guest Editor of two special journal collections on family policy and law, tammy.henderson@okstate.edu

Brittany C. Hernandez, M.A., Department of Psychology, Louisiana State University. Ms. Hernandez is a Master's-level graduate student studying under Dr. Mary Lou Kelley at Louisiana State University. She is currently working toward her Doctor of Philosophy degree in clinical psychology. Her clinical interests include working with children and her main research interests lie in the areas of children's coping behaviors and spirituality, and the clinical implications of children's stress responses, bcorne2@lsu.edu

Christopher S. Immel, M.S., Department of Psychology, Virginia Polytechnic Institute and State University. Mr. Immel is a clinical psychology graduate student whose research focuses on trauma survivor's health risk behaviors and outcomes. Mr. Immel has worked in a research and/or practice capacity with survivors of Hurricanes Katrina and Rita, as well as the Virginia Tech Shootings. He also serves as a reviewer for a variety of trauma-related journals, csimmel@vt.edu

Jennifer Johnson, MPH., Center for Global Health, University of Michigan. Jennifer is an epidemiologist with an interest in the health impact of trauma and conflict on population health and health equity in the global context. She has published on the epidemiology of post-traumatic stress disorder and on disasters as a special challenge to resiliency. Jennifer has also studied the efficiency of data linkage techniques to improve data quality for minority populations in the United States, jennacj@umich.edu

Russell T. Jones, Ph.D., Department of Psychology, Virginia Polytechnic Institute and State University. Dr. Jones is a clinical psychologist with an extensive and federally funded (NIMH, FEMA) research program on the psychological effects of trauma and natural disasters on children. He was contacted by the White House to prepare Laura Bush for her visit with children displaced by Hurricane Katrina. He has made many trips to the Gulf Coast to assist in post-disaster relief efforts. He led the first crisis counseling team of its kind to the hardest hit regions of Mississippi, rtjones@vt.edu

Yoshinori Kamo, Ph.D., Department of Sociology and Life Course and Aging Center at Louisiana State University. Dr. Kamo's research covers the family division of labor, marital quality and disruption, minority families, and the living arrangement and caregiving of elderly people. He has been involved with a large research team to study the interplay between work and family in the United States, Japan, Korea, and China. Dr. Kamo's books include *Understanding Sociology* and *Eve of the Family Revolution* (in Japanese), kamo@lsu.edu

Mary L. Kelley, Ph.D., Department of Psychology, Louisiana State University. Dr. Kelley is a clinical psychologist whose research focuses on increasing parent involvement in promoting their children's academic success. More recently, she has focused on children's adjustment to disasters, especially post-Katrina. She has published extensively in the areas of child assessment and child behavioral interventions, mkelley@lsu.edu

Loren D. Marks, Ph.D., Division of Family, Child, and Consumer Science; School of Human Ecology, LSU. Dr. Marks is a qualitative, family studies researcher who examines faith and families and has authored or co-authored several related publications, lorenm@lsu.edu

Rachel M. Moore, M.S., Department of Psychology, Virginia Polytechnic Institute and State University. Ms. Moore is a graduate student in the Clinical Psychology doctoral program at Virginia Polytechnic Institute and State University. Ms. Moore's research focuses on coping strategies utilized following traumatic events, as well as pain management and health-related quality of life for chronically ill children and adolescents. She was the third author of a published study that focuses on recommendations for future disaster relief experiences following lessons learned from Hurricane Katrina in a special section of *Professional Psychology: Research and Practice*. She also recently completed her master's thesis which adapted the Transactional Stress and Coping Model to examine child and adolescent adjustment following residential fires, rmmoore@vt.edu

Melissa S. Munson, M.A., Department of Psychology, Louisiana State University (LSU). Melissa Munson is a doctoral student in clinical psychology at LSU. She earned her B.S. at the University of Florida. She is currently completing her thesis examining differences in intellectual ability between children with anxiety and those without. She also currently serves as the coordinator for the child and adolescent anxiety clinic. Her research interests include the assessment and treatment of child anxiety, with a specific interest in obsessive–compulsive disorder, mmunso6@lsu.edu

H. Wayne Nelson, Ph.D., Dr. Nelson is an Associate Professor at the Department of Health Science, Towson University, and is a Fellow of the Gerontological Society of America. Dr. Nelson is widely published in the field of aging and has decades of direct practice experience. He was in-state commander of a Medical Reserve Corps unit that treated over 6,000 patients in Jefferson Parish Louisiana during the Katrina relief effort and has published articles on the military aspects of disaster management. He is currently conducting research on the Long-Term Care Ombudsman Program's role in nursing home disaster readiness funded by the Borchard Foundation Center for Law and Aging, waynecol@comcast.net

Howard J. Osofsky, M.D., Ph.D., is a psychiatrist, psychologist, and psychoanalyst who is a Professor and Chair of the Department of Psychiatry at LSU Health Sciences Center and John and Kathleen Bricker Chair of Psychiatry. In the aftermath of Hurricane Katrina, he was asked to be Clinical Director for Louisiana Spirit and to provide services for first responders and their families in Metropolitan New Orleans. On August 29, 2006, he was honored with a Proclamation from the New Orleans City Council recognizing his work helping children and families in the aftermath of Hurricane Katrina. On March 18, 2007, he was recognized by the Superintendent of the New Orleans Fire Department as Honorary Deputy Chief for his efforts in the aftermath of Hurricane Katrina. In October 2007, he was recognized by Family Service of Greater New Orleans for outstanding service to the community. In November 2007, he received a proclamation from the St. Bernard Parish School Board for outstanding and continuing service to students and faculty of St. Bernard Parish Public Schools and also received the Sarah Haley Award for Clinical Excellence for work with trauma from the International Society for Traumatic Stress Studies, hosofs@lsuhsc.edu

Joy D. Osofsky, Ph.D., She is a psychologist and psychoanalyst and Professor of Pediatrics and Psychiatry at Louisiana State University Health Sciences Center in New Orleans. She is Head of the Division of Pediatric Mental Health. She is also an Adjunct Professor of Psychology at the University of New Orleans. Following Hurricane Katrina, Dr. Osofsky was asked to serve as Clinical Director for Child and Adolescent Initiatives for *Louisiana Spirit*, the Disaster Response Program, Department of Health and Human Services, Office of Mental Health. On August 29, 2006, she was honored with a Proclamation from the New Orleans City Council recognizing her work helping children and families in the aftermath of Hurricane Katrina. She was recognized in October 2007 by Family Service of Greater New Orleans for outstanding service to the community. In November 2007, she received a proclamation from the St. Bernard Parish School Board for outstanding and continuing service to students and faculty of St. Bernard Parish Public Schools. In November 2007, she received the Sarah Haley Award for Clinical Excellence for work with trauma from the International Society for Traumatic Stress Studies, jdosofsky@gmail.com

Stacy Overstreet, Ph.D., Department of Psychology, Tulane University. Dr. Overstreet is a school psychologist whose research program focuses on children at risk for maladjustment due to the presence of chronic stressors and trauma in their lives. Dr. Overstreet has published several studies examining the mental health effects of various types of traumatic experiences, including Hurricane Katrina. She directs the School Psychology Program at Tulane, soverst@tulane.edu

Valerie Paasch, M.A., Department of Psychology, Louisiana State University. Ms. Paasch is a graduate student completing her doctorate in clinical child psychology at LSU. Her previous research has focused on the effects of Hurricane Katrina on families, as well as homework interventions for ADHD adolescents, vpaasc1@lsu.edu

Tracey E. Rizzuto, Ph.D., Department of Psychology at Louisiana State University. Tracey is an I/O psychologist who had extensive involvement in Katrina Relief (KARE, a program of the Society for Industrial and Organizational Psychology). She has taken an active role in promoting I/O-related disaster service and research, trizzut@lsu.edu

Karen A. Roberto, Ph.D., Center for Gerontology and the Institute for Society, Culture and Environment, Virginia Polytechnic Institute and State University. Dr. Roberto's research examines the intersection of health and social support in late life. Her primary interests include older women's adaptation to chronic health conditions, family relationships and caregiving, health-care decisions making, and elder abuse and mistreatment. She is the author of over 100 scholarly articles and book chapters and the editor/author of seven books, kroberto@vt.edu

Diane D. Sasser, Ph.D., Professor and Extension Specialist, School of Human Ecology, LSU and LSU AgCenter. Her background is in Family Sciences with emphasis on adolescent development. Her primary research interests include family resiliency, maintaining relationships in marriage, and relationship formation and mate selection in adolescence, dsasser@agctr.lsu.edu

Kathryn Schwartz-Goel, B.A., Department of Psychology, Virginia Polytechnic Institute and State University. Mrs. Schwartz-Goel is currently a clinical psychology graduate student whose research focuses on children who have experienced residential fire. Specifically, she is interested in factors which contribute to resiliency following a traumatic event. She is also the coordinator of the Child Assessment Clinic at Virginia Tech, kjs@vt.edu.

Jennifer L. Silva, M.A., Department of Psychology, Louisiana State University (LSU). Jennifer is a doctoral student whose research interests include healthy aging, psychosocial stressors and resiliency in older adults. She is an author on several studies that examine health, well-being, and cognitive performance in older adults for the Louisiana Healthy Aging Study, jsilva6@lsu.edu

Anthony H. Speier, Ph.D., LSUHSC Department of Psychiatry. He is a licensed psychologist with specialization in Developmental Psychology and the Director of Disaster Mental Health Operations for the Louisiana Office of Mental Health. As such, Tony is the principal contact for all federally funded crisis counseling programs addressing the emotional impact of hurricanes Katrina on Louisiana residents. He is currently leading the LA Spirit Program, a mental health crisis counseling program for Katrina survivors, anthony.speier@la.gov

Erin V. Tarcza, M.A., Department of Psychology, Louisiana State University (LSU). Erin V. Tarcza, M.A. is a doctoral student in clinical psychology at LSU. She earned her B.S. at the University of Florida and her M.A. at Southeastern Louisiana University. She is currently the coordinator of a project examining massed and spaced exposure in the treatment of specific phobia in adults. Her current research interests include physiological correlates of anxiety, anxiety sensitivity, and the etiology and phenomenology of anxiety disorders in children and adults, etarcz1@lsu.edu

Julia F. Vigna, M.A., Department of Psychology, Louisiana State University. Ms. Vigna is working toward her Doctor of Philosophy degree in clinical psychology under Dr. Mary Lou Kelley at Louisiana State University. Ms. Vigna's research and clinical interests include the broad range of topics encompassed by the stress and trauma spectrum in both youth and adults, jvigna1@lsu.edu

Carl F. Weems, Ph.D., Department of Psychology, University of New Orleans (UNO). Dr. Weems is a developmental psychologist whose research focuses on the developmental psychopathology of anxiety and stress. He directs the Child and Family Stress Anxiety and Phobia Lab at UNO. He has published several studies on the mental health effects of Hurricane Katrina and edited a special section of the *Journal of Clinical Child and Adolescent Psychology* on Hurricane Katrina mental health research, cweems@uno.edu

Part I
Children and Adolescents

Chapter 1
Young Children's Demonstrated Understanding of Hurricanes

Teresa K. Buchanan, Renée M. Casbergue, and Jennifer J. Baumgartner

Abstract We examine young children's knowledge of disasters in the immediate aftermath of hurricanes, Katrina and Rita. Knowledge was measured by teacher reports of child-initiated spontaneous play in the classrooms and by children's responses to an interview designed to measure their knowledge of hurricanes in general and Katrina and Rita in particular. Findings indicated age-related differences, with older children demonstrating more knowledge than younger children. Analysis of teacher-reported specific activities indicated that children's demonstrated knowledge was different by region (with children more directly impacted by hurricanes demonstrating more knowledge of hurricanes than children less directly impacted) and seemed to reflect the stages of disasters: preparation, response, and recovery.

Introduction

Hurricanes Katrina and Rita struck the Gulf Coast in the Fall of 2005, bringing with them an unprecedented level of destruction. While many effects of the storms were immediately apparent, the deep and lasting impact of the storms on the lives of Louisiana and Mississippi residents is less evident. As these communities continue their struggle to recover, schools have had to either rebuild programs completely or adapt existing programs to serve new populations of displaced, often traumatized children. Many youngsters in these programs are at risk not just by virtue of their low socioeconomic status, but also by virtue of serious disruptions to their lives at home and at school.

In fact, health professionals have reported that children impacted by Katrina and Rita are experiencing severe health problems 3 years after the storms (Redlener,

---

T.K. Buchanan (✉)
Department of Educational Theory Policy and Practice and Life Course and Aging Center, Baton Rouge LA, USA
e-mail: tbuchan@lsu.edu

DeRosa, & Hut, 2008). The overall mental health of young children in affected areas was worse 2 years after the storm than it was in the immediate aftermath. Eaton (2007) cited statistics from the School of Public Health at Columbia University noting that more than 2 years following Katrina, over 46,000 children in the affected areas were still experiencing psychological distress, while Kessler et al. (2008) found that the rates of psychological disorders increased rather than decreased in the years following Katrina, with a significant increase in post-traumatic symptoms among children. These findings are perhaps due in part to continuing uncertainty and even hopelessness regarding permanent living conditions and the slow return of those neighborhoods that had served as supportive communities for families prior to the storm. That the landscape of schooling has shifted dramatically only exacerbates the difficulties families face in the storms' aftermath.

Destruction of Schools and the Effects on Developing Children

Of 2,000 primary schools in Louisiana at the start of the 2005–2006 school year, 1,500 were located within the parishes most impacted by the storms (Kent, 2006). Of those, Hurricane Katrina directly impacted 930 schools, affecting 480,000 students and teachers, while Rita impacted 515 schools with 235,000 students and teachers (Fig. 1.1). In some parishes and counties, schools were closed for a matter of days or weeks, reopening once initial cleanup of campuses and restoration of utilities were completed. In the most seriously impacted areas, over 835 schools were significantly damaged in Louisiana and 40 were completely destroyed. In Mississippi, 263 schools were damaged, with 16 destroyed (Louisiana Recovery Authority, 2006).

In the Louisiana parishes most affected by 2005 hurricanes, the number of displaced students was staggering. For example, 8,800 children were enrolled in schools in St. Bernard Parish, LA, in the 2004–2005 school year. One year after the hurricanes, only 3,750 children were enrolled in the school district. The Orleans Parish School District had enrolled over 60,000 children in 2004–2005 school year. In 2006–2007, there were 27,420 children enrolled in the district (Rowley, 2007). Thus, in the year after the storms, the population of public school students had decreased in the most severely affected parishes by nearly 60%. Districts in areas that were not as directly impacted by the storms absorbed the displaced students and saw enrollments increase. For example, the East Baton Rouge Parish public school enrollment went from 45,266 in 2004–2005 to 49,021 children in 2006–2007.

Three years after the storm, in the Fall of 2008, private and public school enrollments in the five parish New Orleans metropolitan area had rebounded to only 76% of pre-Katrina levels. In the city itself, the number of public school students had reached not quite half of its pre-Katrina level (Liu & Plyer, 2008). Equally important, public school families must now select the most promising placement for their

1 Young Children 5

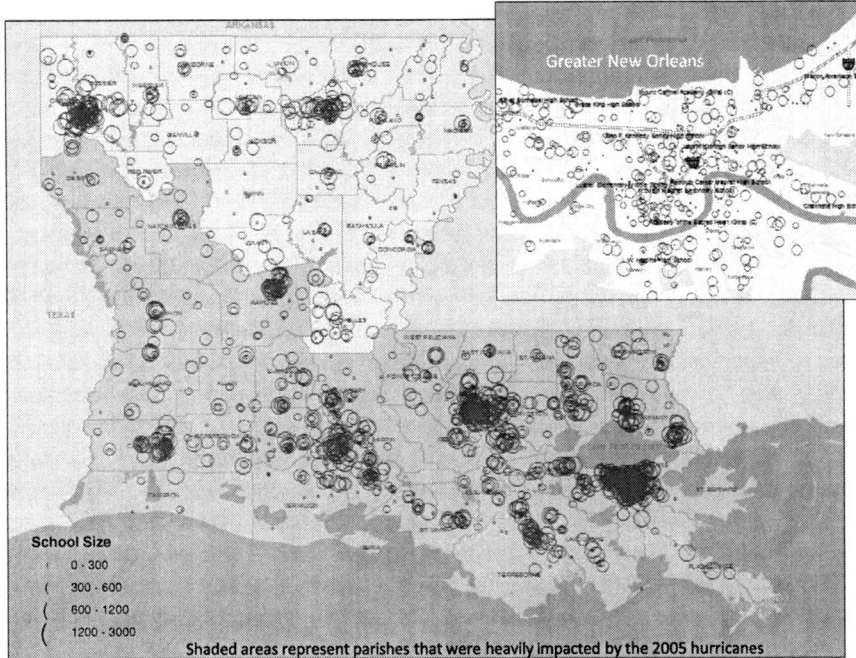

Fig. 1.1 From the 2005 Hurricane Atlas (lagic.lsu.edu) by the Louisiana Geographic Information Center (LAGIC) using data provided by Louisiana Department of Education (LDOE) and Louisiana Department of Social Services (LDSS). Reprinted with permission

children by navigating an entirely new labyrinth of independent citywide access charter schools, traditional schools run by the Orleans Parish School Board, and both charter and traditional schools run by the state's new Recovery School District. The dearth of traditional neighborhood schools with fixed geographic attendance boundaries has further fragmented already shattered communities. This chapter reports an investigation into the impact of those storms on young children.

Development of Young Children

Early childhood educators are interested in the unique developmental and educational needs of children from birth to 8 years of age. Several guiding principles from developmental science inform work with children in the context of early childhood classrooms (Bredekamp & Copple, 1997). First, development and the acquisition of knowledge predictably follow a path toward greater complexity. Children's cognitive processing of experiences, such as hurricanes, cannot be expected to equal most adults and younger children are expected to know less about things like natural disasters than older children. Early childhood educators typically assess children's current level of understanding and try to extend their knowledge and understanding of their world, considering what is appropriate for their stage of development.

Second, we know developmental domains are connected and related to one another. For example, physical development and language development are related. Research in language acquisition and the new use of sign language to communicate with typically developing infants demonstrates this principle (Bonvillian & Orlansky, 1983). Historically we have underestimated the ability of very young children to understand language and communicate because that ability develops more rapidly than the motor skills that control their voice. The relationship between emotional development and cognitive development is evidenced by our understanding that before learning and cognitive growth can occur, children must have met basic and minimum requirements for physical and emotional safety (Honig, 2005; Janson & King, 2006; Wolfe & Bell, 2007). Similarly, children who experience severe trauma or develop attachment disorders can experience developmental and academic delays later in life (Osofsky, 2007). Therefore, if young children are impacted emotionally by a disaster or crisis, it is likely that their cognitive development will also be impacted.

Third, children learn best when they make meaningful connections between prior experience or knowledge and new knowledge. Memory research has established that prior knowledge from direct experience can affect both the way in which information is remembered and how it is recalled (Elischberger, 2005; Bransford & Franks, 1971; McFarland & Ross, 1987). For example, Elischberger's work demonstrated that when 5- and 6-year-old children were asked to read a story and recall details, prior knowledge of the story impacted their recall (Elischberger, 2005). Children with direct experience of hurricanes would be more likely to demonstrate knowledge of hurricanes than children with no prior experience with hurricanes because experiences with the social and physical environment facilitate children's cognitive and language development as they process information (Bergen, 2008). Specifically, young children's direct interaction with people and materials can help facilitate gains in their attention and perception skills (Marti, 2003) leading to deeper understanding and longer retention of new concepts. In early childhood classrooms, we see this when children are engaged in meaningful and child-initiated play activities in which they act out and extend what they know.

Finally, we know children express their knowledge, development, and learning in a variety of ways. Broaders, Cook, Mitchell, and Goldin-Meadow (2007) found that when children who seemed unable to complete a math problem were told to gesture (instead of writing or speaking their answers), they were able to express through the gesture the correct problem-solving strategies. And while older children might demonstrate their understanding of a story by writing about it, younger children are more likely to demonstrate their knowledge by reenacting it in dramatic play activities. Any investigation of young children and disasters should use multiple strategies to assess that knowledge (Gurwitch, Sullivan, & Long, 1998).

Very young children are different from older children because of the unique and specific characteristics of their cognitive, language, moral, and emotional development (Charlesworth, 2008). Their pre-operational or concrete thinking means that they are egocentric and perception bound. While they have increasing capacities for mental representation, which aids in their development of the understanding of cause and effect, this is limited to familiar events or things they have actually experienced in some concrete way. Because they are less verbal than older children, very young children most clearly communicate their ideas, concerns, and needs through non-verbal communication and behaviors. Because they link unpleasant consequences with observable actions or behaviors, very young children may believe their own behaviors cause bad things to happen. And because of their stage of emotional development, it is very difficult for young children to understand or manage their own emotions or the emotions of others. These characteristics may cause young children to be more vulnerable to the effects of disasters than other groups (Gurwitch et al., 1998; Osofsky, 2007) or may promote resiliency (Saylor, Swenson, & Powell, 1992), but because of the scarcity of empirical research, the relationship between development and coping among young children is not clear (Anderson, 2005).

Young Children and Disasters

In addition to their developmental characteristics, young children are especially at risk during disasters because of their unique status in society. Peek (2008) explains that children's experiences are of particular interest to scholars because they are physically vulnerable, have special needs that may not be met after a disaster, and their personal growth and development can be affected in ways that have long-term implications. Additionally, according to Plummer (2008), children may be particularly vulnerable to disasters because the adults in their lives who typically care for them and meet their needs may not be reliable sources of care and because young children have little autonomy or control over where they go, what they do, or how they prepare or respond to the disaster.

Research on children and disasters has primarily focused on the emotional health and behaviors of children 8 years old and older (Anderson, 2005), possibly because by third grade children have developed to the point where surveys and interviews are effective research methods. That research has shown that older children experience significant post-traumatic stress (Gurwitch et al., 1998) and adults in the lives of children typically underestimate the stress their children are experiencing (Mercuri & Angelique, 2004; Zeece, 2001). Recent research has shown that children displaced by Katrina experienced a variety of mental and behavioral problems (Pane, McCaffrey, Kalra, & Zhou, 2008; Ward, Shelley, Kaase, & Pane, 2008). Studies have found the impact of disasters on children is mediated by a variety of factors (Vernberg, LaGreca, Silverman, & Prinstein, 1996), including family functioning and structure (Proctor et al., 2007; Swenson et al., 1996; Wasserstein & LaGreca, 1998), social support (Barrett, Ausbrooks, & Martinez-Coscio, 2008), and level of exposure to the event, although a meta-analysis of the research on children's responses to natural, technological, and natural–technological disasters by Mercuri and Angelique (2004) shows that the specific nature of the stressor does not appear to be as important as the amount of exposure to damage and destruction (see Russell et al., Chapter 4, for a related discussion).

While very little research has focused on children from birth through age 8, the existing studies of younger children and disasters demonstrate, contrary to early research using parental reports of children's reactions to disasters, young children do experience post-traumatic stress (Swenson et al., 1996; Gurwitch et al., 1998). This effect might be underestimated because either their reactions are not adequately measured with traditional methodologies (Saylor, Swenson, Reynolds, & Taylor, 1999; Scheeringa, Zeanah, Myers, & Putnam, 2003) or their natural response of post-traumatic play may help children process the trauma in ways that lead to healthy coping (Saylor et al., 1992). Gurwitch et al. (1998) explain that post-traumatic stress is most often seen in the play of young children through their "repeated acting out of what happened in the disaster during play" (p. 21). The phenomenon of young children using play to work through their responses to disaster offers one avenue for helping them cope. Following the 2004 Asian tsunami, for example, Canadian therapists effectively used sand play to help Asian immigrant children process strong emotions (Lacroix et al., 2007).

Early Childhood Education and Disasters

In his call for a focus on children in disaster research, Anderson (2005) suggests researchers study the impact of disasters on children, the actions taken to help children during disasters, and the actions taken by children to help prepare for and respond to disasters. He encourages researchers to examine the educational impact of disasters on things like children's school attendance and interruptions. We would add the importance of studying teacher's classroom response to disasters. There is very little research examining if or how teachers address children's emotional and behavioral needs in times of crisis, and less research examining how they use these opportunities to address children's knowledge about disaster agents.

Following Katrina we anecdotally observed classroom activities related to hurricanes. For example, in response to the children's obvious interest in hurricanes, teachers at the LSU Preschool guided children in a study of hurricanes that lasted several weeks (see Aghayan et al., 2005; Schellhaas, Burts, & Aghayan, 2007). Similarly, Metairie Park Country Day, a private K-12 school in the New Orleans metropolitan area, reopened for an abbreviated semester in November 2005 with a school-wide focus on defining and rebuilding a city. Children worked with teachers in multi-age teams to study the culture and architecture of different neighborhoods before the storm and created their ideal vision of what the city could be after recovery. Fothergill and Peek (2006) found that in one school near New Orleans, teachers directly addressed children's sense of loss and worked to help lessen the impacts of the disaster on children. Two new schools that opened specifically to take in Katrina and Rita evacuees did a great deal to welcome the new families and children (Paulson, 2005).

Other than those cases, we in Louisiana observed very little evidence that systematic attempts were made to assess the needs of children in the storms' immediate aftermath. Despite large numbers of displaced children enrolling in Baton Rouge schools immediately after Katrina, it was not until January, 2006 that the school system implemented a process to screen elementary school children for post-hurricane difficulties and advise teachers about referral options. In many schools during that Fall, there were no assemblies, no counseling sessions, and apparently no instruction regarding the hurricanes.

This was surprising, because it is clear that one important role of educators following a crisis is to provide children with accurate information and knowledge about the event (Brodkin & Coleman, 1994; Damiani, 2006) and very young children frequently display inaccurate understandings about the nature of disasters. For example, in their study of preschooler's play after Hurricane Hugo, Saylor et al. (1992) describe how young children personified Hugo. One mother of a 3-year-old girl said, "She put 'Hugo' in 'time out' many times for blowing her house away... she equated Hugo with the 'big bad wolf' from *The Three Little Pigs* who huffed and puffed and blew her house down..." (p. 145). The children at the LSU Preschool blamed missing puzzle pieces on bad Katrina. Alternatively, after Hurricane Andrew 3- and 4-year-old children accurately recalled information about a hurricane, especially when given specific prompts (Bahrick, Parker, Fivush, & Levitt, 1998). Further investigation is warranted to clarify our understanding of children's knowledge of disasters.

Most existing literature in this area tends to document examples of specific school activities in the aftermath of particular events or offer practical suggestions for educators but the ideas do not appear to be based on empirical findings. Researchers have investigated how schools can assist with children's emotional needs after disasters (e.g., Allen et al., 2002; Fairbrother, Stuber, Galea, Pfefferbaum, & Fleishman, 2004; Frost, 2005; Jimerson, Brock, & Pletcher, 2005; Mack & Smith, 1991; Miller, 1996; Pfefferbaum et al., 2004), and a number of authors offer recommendations for school system preparation before emergencies and disasters (Damiani, 2006; Jimerson et al., 2005; Klingman, 1978; Knox & Roberts, 2005).

However, there is very little research about what young children learn before, during, and after disasters. One exception is an investigation by Bahrick et al. (1998). They studied preschooler's memory about their experience with Hurricane Andrew and found that young children demonstrated accurate knowledge about the hurricane. Similarly, Zeece (2001) found preschoolers also knew about the Shuttle disaster, having learned about from news reports.

We were interested in finding out what children know about hurricanes because young children do not often have accurate information about these storms and because there is some evidence that suggests that accurate information can help reduce distress after traumatic events in children (Kenardy, Thompson, LeBrocque,

& Olsson, 2008) and adults (Kenardy et al., 2008; Kenardy & Piercy, 2006; Klein, 1982; Mills & Krantz, 1979; Shreve, Danbom, & Hanhan, 2002). Fothergill and Peek (2006) found that Katrina survivors reported that providing abundant and accurate information to children was one of the most helpful responses to children's emotional and mental health needs.

Young children are especially susceptible to the stress brought about by uncertainty and change in their lives. When their home lives are disrupted, the routines of school may provide comforting predictability in otherwise chaotic circumstances (see Garrison & Sasser, Chapter 6, for a related discussion). They may also provide opportunities for children to gain both factual knowledge and insight into feelings that restore some sense of control and confidence. The current study investigated children's knowledge about hurricanes and their impact as demonstrated through teacher reports of children's classroom activities, their play, and oral and written expressions of their hurricane experiences and through child interviews designed to measure their knowledge of hurricanes.

The Current Study

With help from the National Science Foundation, we first surveyed teachers in Louisiana and three other states to assess their response to the hurricanes and their observations of children's responses. We were interested in determining what children knew about hurricanes, as demonstrated by teacher reports of spontaneous play activities. To find out, we surveyed teachers in areas of Louisiana that had been impacted by Katrina and Rita. Because this was a national disaster observed by people all over the country, we also surveyed teachers from comparison sites. Those sites were southern states with geographic and demographic characteristics that matched the survey locations in Louisiana. We selected districts in Tennessee, a land-locked state, because the context was similar but the state was not prone to hurricanes. We selected districts in coastal South Carolina and Georgia that were also matched to the Louisiana school districts, but were prone to hurricanes. We expected that the teachers in South Carolina and Georgia would report more hurricane-related activities among their children than the teachers in Louisiana because we anticipated children in coastal areas would more strongly identify with the "victims of hurricanes" portrayed on national television. We also expected teachers in Louisiana to report more hurricane-related activities than all the other teachers.

Second, we conducted interviews with young children to assess their understanding of hurricanes as demonstrated by their responses to narrative story stems. Those children were from classrooms that were selected using stratified random sampling of teachers who completed the teacher survey. The sampling generated 15 classrooms that represented all the grade levels (pre-kindergarten, kindergarten, first, second, and third grades) and differential classroom attention to the hurricanes. Specifically, three teachers were selected from each grade level. One teacher reported doing a lot of hurricane-related activities, one reported doing some hurricane-related activities, and one reported doing no hurricane-related activities.

We expected older children and children in classrooms where teachers reported doing a lot of hurricane-related activities to demonstrate more knowledge about hurricanes than other children.

Teacher Survey

The teacher survey measured demographic characteristics of the sample, teacher responses to the hurricanes, and reported use of developmentally appropriate practices. The survey was sent the second week of November, 2005 to a total of 2,010 teachers: 1,155 in Louisiana (school districts outside the severely damaged area, yet heavily impacted by the hurricanes were over-sampled because we anticipated a lower-than-normal response rate from teachers in those areas), 560 to school districts in coastal South Carolina and Georgia, and 295 to southern districts in Tennessee. Teachers voluntarily chose to participate with no compensation.

The final survey sample consisted of 592 teachers. Those teachers were from Louisiana ($n = 344$), Tennessee ($n = 93$), coastal South Carolina ($n = 77$), and coastal Georgia ($n = 78$). The total response rate was 28%, with 30% of surveys in Louisiana returned and 27% of surveys returned from other states. A chi-square analysis shows the grade levels of the teachers (pre-kindergarten, 15%; kindergarten, 24%; first grade, 22%; second grade, 19%; and third grade, 19%) were not different by state ($\chi^2(12, n = 587) = 12.37$, ns). Results from a one-way analysis of variance (ANOVA) show the mean number of children per class on free or reduced-price lunch, an index of school poverty, was significantly different [$F(3,473) = 5.68, p < 0.01$], with Tennessee teachers reporting fewer children ($M = 9.69, SD = 5.24, n = 77$) in that category than teachers in Louisiana ($M = 12.81, SD = 6.26, n = 269$).

Teachers indicated (yes/no) if they had received training regarding (1) children's reactions to disasters and their aftermath and (2) how to help children and families after disasters. They were also asked if they would have liked additional training. If they responded in the affirmative, they were asked to describe (using an open-ended format) the training they thought they needed. Analysis indicated that 24% of the teachers in Louisiana had received training on children's reactions and 15% had received training on how to help children and families post-disaster, with nearly half (45%) reporting they would have liked to receive the latter training. Open-ended responses indicated they would have liked information about resources, how to talk to children and answer questions, how to help them cope, and literature to distribute to parents. The teachers also wanted information about offering emotional support to families and students, helping families and students adjust to changes, and helping them make transitions more easily.

Teachers reported on the *unplanned, spontaneous, or student-initiated activities* that had occurred in their classrooms following the hurricanes. They responded on a Likert scale of 0 (not at all) to 2 (a lot) to a 9-item measure that included items like "told stories about Katrina or hurricanes." The most common activities initiated by children were telling stories about Katrina or hurricanes ($n = 423$, 72%), discussing Katrina or hurricane-related events with the teacher ($n = 445$, 76%), and discussing

Table 1.1 Spontaneous student-initiated activities

	M	N	SD
Pre-kindergarten and kindergarten classrooms			
Told stories about Katrina or hurricanes	1.88	232	0.702
Discussed Katrina or hurricane-related events in the classroom with the teacher	1.87	231	0.677
Discussed Katrina or hurricane-related events in the classroom among themselves	1.74	231	0.679
Drew pictures about Katrina or hurricanes	1.61	231	0.670
Wrote stories, journal entries, or essays about Katrina or hurricanes	1.30	229	0.561
Selected a book to read about Katrina or hurricanes	1.15	231	0.367
Enacted Katrina or hurricane-related scenes in a dramatic play center	1.13	231	0.400
Enacted Katrina or hurricane-related scenes during outside play	1.11	231	0.343
Enacted Katrina or hurricane-related scenes at a sand or water table	1.06	231	0.249
Primary grade (first, second, and third) classrooms			
Discussed Katrina or hurricane-related events in the classroom with the teacher	2.04	353	0.671
Told stories about Katrina or hurricanes	1.96	353	0.694
Discussed Katrina or hurricane-related events in the classroom among themselves	1.91	350	0.668
Wrote stories, journal entries, or essays about Katrina or hurricanes	1.64	353	0.651
Drew pictures about Katrina or hurricanes	1.57	352	0.654
Selected a book to read about Katrina or hurricanes	1.21	351	0.429
Enacted Katrina or hurricane-related scenes in a dramatic play center	1.01	351	0.119
Enacted Katrina or hurricane-related scenes at a sand or water table	1.01	350	0.141
Enacted Katrina or hurricane-related scenes during outside play	1.03	350	0.198

Katrina or hurricane-related events with their peers ($n = 397$, 68%) (Table 1.1). Teachers reported that children in the primary grades did slightly more spontaneous hurricane-related activities than children in preschool or kindergarten [$F(1,585) = 3.83, p = 0.05$].

ANOVA results show that teachers in Louisiana reported that their students initiated significantly more ($M = 14.17$, $SD = 2.86$) hurricane-related activities than students in Tennessee ($M = 11.54$, $SD = 2.27$), South Carolina ($M = 11.67$, $SD = 2.59$), or Georgia ($M = 11.45$, $SD = 2.71$) [$F(3,590) = 44.77, p < 0.001$] (Table 1.2). Post hoc analysis using Schefeé comparisons showed teachers in Louisiana reported significantly more spontaneous journal entries about hurricanes [$F(3,586) = 17.15, p < 0.001$], telling of stories about hurricanes [$F(3,589) = 61.89, p < 0.001$], drawing of hurricane-related pictures [$F(3,587) = 32.89, p < 0.001$], and child-initiated discussions with their teacher [$F(3,588) = 19.40$, $p < 0.001$] and among themselves [$F(3, 585) = 29.64$, $p < 0.001$], than teachers in other states. Teacher reports from coastal South Carolina and Georgia did not significantly differ from reports of teachers in Tennessee.

If a teacher indicated children in her classroom did a particular activity by marking "some" or "a lot," the teacher was asked to give details about what the children were doing. That open-ended data were analyzed using constant comparative methodology (Glaser & Strauss, 1967) to create categories of responses across cases. Inductive analysis showed patterns and themes that emerged from repeated examination of the data. Two major themes emerged from this review of the teachers' responses regarding children's classroom activities. First, there were obvious geographical differences in the frequency and types of student-initiated activities. Second, children's actions in dramatic play, but not in other literacy and language activities, demonstrated knowledge about three stages of disasters: planning (how do we get ready), response (what happens during a hurricane), and recovery (what happens after a hurricane). Relationships between these themes also emerged. Each of these themes and relationships are described next.

Geographic Differences in Language, Literacy, and Play

Hurricane Stories

As expected, Louisiana teachers reported more instances of children telling stories, writing, and drawing about the hurricanes than did teachers in other states. Children in all four states sought opportunities to share stories about the storms, often as part of group activities like morning meetings or group discussions mediated by teachers. The content of the stories differed according to location, however, with teachers prompting Louisiana children to tell about their own evacuation and storm experiences and using group time to welcome and share information about evacuee children newly enrolled in their classrooms. Teachers in Georgia reported using discussion initiated by their children to compare experiences of Katrina and Rita to other hurricanes they had experienced and to extend children's understanding to broader themes such as needs versus wants, helping others, sharing, and people in need. Teachers in both South Carolina and Tennessee focused more on factual information about hurricanes, including the effect of Katrina on people and land along the Gulf Coast.

Teachers in all four states noticed children telling hurricane-related stories independent of planned group activities. Again, children in Louisiana were most likely to relate their firsthand experiences with the storms, with one teacher reporting that the evacuee children continued to tell hurricane stories for a longer period of time than children who had been enrolled in the school prior to the storm. The Louisiana children also shared stories of their current living situations and about the process of having their homes rebuilt. Those firsthand stories are in contrast to the stories reported by teachers in Georgia and Tennessee in which children related tales of

Table 1.2 Differences in classroom activities across States

	Louisiana			Georgia			South Carolina			Tennessee			Total		
	M	N	SD	M	N	SD	M	N	SD	M	N	SD	M	N	SD
Wrote stories, journal entries, or essays about Katrina or hurricanes	1.66	341	0.670	1.29	78	0.512	1.30	76	0.542	1.27	92	0.516	1.50	587	0.638
Told stories about Katrina or hurricanes	2.21	344	0.614	1.45	78	0.550	1.62	76	0.653	1.51	92	0.602	1.93	590	0.698
Drew pictures about Katrina or hurricanes	1.80	342	0.680	1.31	78	0.517	1.30	76	0.490	1.26	92	0.489	1.58	588	0.659
Selected a book to read about Katrina or hurricanes	1.19	342	0.398	1.18	78	0.448	1.16	75	0.369	1.20	92	0.426	1.18	587	0.405
Enacted Katrina or hurricane-related scenes in a dramatic play center	1.09	342	0.331	1.03	78	0.226	1.01	75	0.115	1.01	92	0.104	1.06	587	0.274
Enacted Katrina or hurricane-related scenes at a sand or water table	1.04	342	0.206	1.04	78	0.252	1.03	74	0.163	1.00	92	0.000	1.03	586	0.191
Enacted Katrina or hurricane-related scenes during outside play	1.09	341	0.317	1.04	78	0.252	1.03	75	0.162	1.00	92	0.000	1.06	586	0.267
Discussed Katrina or hurricane-related events in the classroom with the teacher	2.14	343	0.674	1.64	78	0.581	1.80	75	0.658	1.76	93	0.597	1.97	589	0.678
Discussed Katrina or hurricane-related events in the classroom among themselves	2.04	341	0.665	1.47	78	0.552	1.55	74	0.622	1.61	93	0.572	1.84	586	0.676

family members and friends from New Orleans – referred to as "my cousin stories" by one teacher. Whether children told stories of their own experiences or those they heard about family and friends, one source of stories was universal. Children in all four states were heard frequently repeating stories they heard from the news, with television coverage a significant source for children's stories about the hurricanes.

Writing About the Hurricanes

Children's writing revealed patterns of response to the storms similar to those reported for their stories. Journal writing routines offered children in Louisiana, Georgia, and Tennessee a possible outlet for writing about the storm. Children in Louisiana were often reported choosing to write about the storm itself and their evacuation experiences. They wrote about the damage they observed to homes and neighborhoods and about their new homes. Children in both Georgia and Louisiana chose to write journal entries about new children who enrolled in their schools after the storms. Children in Georgia also included in their journals ways they thought they could help those affected by the storm and information about hurricanes that they learned through news items and nonfiction books. They also used their journals to retell stories they saw on the news, expressing in their writing empathetic feelings of loss regarding destruction of homes and deaths brought about by the hurricanes.

Teachers in all three states except Louisiana reported children writing about the storms in response to class assignments. This writing ranged from assigned topics such as "how a city looks after a hurricane" and nonfiction about hurricanes or different kinds of weather, to letters to hurricane victims. It is likely that teachers in Louisiana did not feel the need to assign hurricane topics to children given how much writing about the storms children were doing on their own.

Drawing Hurricane Experiences

Younger children not yet able to write journal entries or essays on their own "wrote" about the hurricanes through pictures paired with oral dictation written down by their teachers. This experience was reported by teachers in Georgia and Louisiana, but not in South Carolina or Tennessee. Louisiana children drew pictures and dictated stories of storm damage, evacuation experiences, and activities with family and friends during days off from school. Children in Georgia drew more general pictures of weather, although one Georgia child drew a picture of "my dad helping in Louisiana." Even those children who were capable of writing on their own extended their writing with drawing. Teachers in all four states reported that children drew pictures on their own to accompany their journal entries.

Children in each state also took advantage of art centers during times when they had free choice of activities to produce drawings related to the hurricanes. Children with firsthand experience of the storms drew pictures of what their houses looked like or other destruction they saw in neighborhoods. Others drew pictures of what the storms looked like or what they saw during the hurricane and evacuation. One child in Tennessee drew a picture of "the policeman who saved my life."

Teachers in all four states reported that children engaged in storm-related drawing as part of assigned activities. In Louisiana, children made books and illustrated stories, including those that addressed how to prepare for a hurricane. In both Louisiana and South Carolina, children produced drawings in art classes that depicted different types of weather. Georgia teachers noticed children drawing victims of the storms and illustrating what they believed the storm looked like.

Using Books About Hurricanes

One surprising finding was how seldom teachers reported children using books about hurricanes or other weather phenomena, as compared to how often they told stories, wrote, and drew about the storms. One teacher in Georgia and one in South Carolina related how they selected nonfiction books about weather to read aloud to children. One Louisiana teacher mentioned reading the book *Hurricane Harry* (Caseley, 1994) to her class. This is a chapter book about a character by that name who has many adventures as he moves to a new town and goes to school for the first time. While it is not actually about a hurricane, children who had been through the storms as well as their classmates were likely to find much in common with the main character's experiences. One Georgia teacher reported reading an unspecified book aloud to answer children's questions about Katrina. Teachers in South Carolina referred generally to using books in their regular weather unit, although one teacher stated that she did not know of any hurricane books. Children in Louisiana appeared to be the most interested in reading about hurricanes on their own. While one teacher in Tennessee reported that she observed children choosing books and magazines about storms from the school library, children in Louisiana supplemented those same types of selections by purchasing their owns books using classroom order forms from Scholastic Publishers.

Play

Teachers were asked about children's activities in their dramatic play centers, water and sand table tables, and outside play time. Only teachers in Louisiana and Georgia responded that at least some children participated in hurricane play activities. Of those that described play activities, the types of play were different. Children in Louisiana engaged in play that dramatized things that happen during a storm ("students demonstrated trees falling and sound effects" or "hid under a table"), while children in Georgia discussed planning for hurricanes and what to do if a storm hit. One teacher in Georgia described an outside play activity as follows: "students demonstrated what to do when alarm sounds for bad weather (seek shelter, count to make sure all is accounted for)."

Conversations

Teachers reported that children engaged in conversations about hurricanes, both with teachers and with peers. Students initiated conversations with teachers in every site, but teachers from Georgia and Louisiana reported more of these conversations. Children in Tennessee and South Carolina were more likely to discuss the impact of hurricanes on the weather ("Discussed the states where the hurricanes occurred. How our city's weather was affected") or environment ("we discussed [as it relates to standards] wetlands and the destruction of wetlands contributing to the flooding of New Orleans"), while teacher–student conversations in Louisiana included specific impacts and responses to the storm: "we announce when someone has gotten their FEMA trailer and what work they are currently doing on their houses" or "how they felt about leaving [their homes]." Children in Louisiana were more likely to engage in conversation about the hurricane with their peers. Their conversations involved personal experience: "I overhear many discussions between the children about their experiences," "overheard many discussions of fallen trees, etc.," and "[evacuee] told others about their life in N.O. and what happened." Children in Georgia and Tennessee were reported to have different conversations that primarily focused on things children had seen on the news ("I overheard some of the children talk about the scenes on the news") or heard from others ("talked about flooding and houses lost").

Stages of Disasters Exhibited in Play and Conversations

Children's spontaneous play and conversations about hurricanes reflected the three stages of disasters. First, children showed interest in how to prepare for hurricanes. For example, in their play they practiced responses, hurricane drills, and responding to alarms. With their teachers, children discussed the path of the storms by tracking it on the weather channel and where to go and what not to do or not to do in case of a hurricane or a tornado. Second, children's play and conversations showed responses to a storm. In their play, children acted out what happens during a storm, either replicating their direct experiences or the things they saw happening during the storm around them or on the news. They hid under tables and pretended to be the storm, knocking things down. Teachers reported that while outside, some children pretended trees were falling and made sounds of a storm. In their conversations with children teachers "assured that their parents would make sure they would be safe if a hurricane came our way." Children also talked with their peers and teachers about what happened during the storm. Finally, children's play and conversations included descriptions of recovery efforts following a storm. Children talked with their peers "a lot about FEMA" and "why we were out [of school] for 2 days in September." Children discussed disaster recovery when they talked about the time it took for the school roof to be repaired and about the work being done on their homes. Children's play and conversations about the impact of disasters were informed by either direct experience (Louisiana) or, like Zeece's (1986) preschoolers, news media (Georgia and Tennessee).

Child Interviews

Although surveys, verbal interviews, and even tests might offer insight into the knowledge of older children, none of these methods are optimally effective in measuring what younger children know. As Gullo (2005) explains, formal testing is an ineffective way to evaluate young children's knowledge. Because of developmental characteristics, young children demonstrate their knowledge best through the things they say and do (Cohen, Stern, & Balaban, 1996). To meet the challenge of more directly assessing young children's knowledge, we adapted the narrative story stem technique (NSST) (Emde, Wolf, & Oppenheim, 2003; Page, 2001), a methodology that allowed us to quickly and accurately assess what very young children knew about hurricanes.

The NSST was created to examine the narrative structures with which young children organize their experience (Bretherton & Oppenheim, 2003; Page, 2001). It accomplishes this aim through a protocol of simple, semi-structured story stems the examiner introduces to the child using a set of family figures or dolls and simple play props. We modified this technique to observe and record children's knowledge about hurricanes in general and the 2005 Louisiana hurricanes in particular by developing story stems to generate relevant stories from the children (see Buchanan, Casbergue, & Baumgartner, 2009).

The sample for the interviews came from classrooms of 15 Louisiana teachers selected in a stratified random sample of those who had returned the teacher survey. Teachers who agreed to participate were mailed packets to distribute to their student's guardians. The survey included a section asking about the child's personal experiences with the hurricanes that included a 6-item measure of hurricane-related experiences (e.g., "My child had to evacuate as a result of Katrina") and a 9-item scale of personal loss associated with the hurricanes (e.g., "My child lost property due to Katrina"). We sent a total of 280 family packets home and, of those, 164 (43%) were returned with parental consent and 121 (43%) children were interviewed.

The final usable interview sample consisted of 84 children from six school districts in Louisiana. Forty-five percent of the parents had a high school education. The majority of children were from families with two biological parents living in their homes, and their parents reported annual incomes from $20,000 to $75,000. Fifty-two percent of the children had evacuated during the hurricanes, 25% were living in temporary housing or shelters, 25% had evacuees living with them, and 31% lost property.

For this activity, materials for the hurricane story stems were brought to a table and set in a standardized arrangement. The child was given a story stem and asked a standard set of prompts. For example, one story stem began "This is a family. They just found out that a big hurricane is coming. What are they going to do? Show me and tell me what the family will do now." The story stems were designed to measure children's knowledge about what happened to land and trees, animals, families, homes and property, urban communities during and after hurricanes, as well as who helps us after hurricanes (Fig. 1.2). After six stories were completed, a seventh scenario more directly assessed children's knowledge. In this scenario, the child pretended to tell a friend from another state all about hurricanes in general and what happened when Katrina or Rita came to Louisiana.

The interviews were videotaped and five coders were trained in four 2-h group sessions during which they watched a pilot video, coded it together, and then

Photograph by Angela Broussard

Fig. 1.2 This is a typical scene created by a child after the following story: "One day these animals were in their field. They were just eating and walking around (*indicate this by playing with the toys for a moment*). All of a sudden it got really dark. A great big hurricane came along. Show me and tell me what happened to the animals." Reprinted with permission

discussed each item. Over the course of the 7-day training period, an inter-rater reliability of 81% was achieved. A reliability judge re-coded 27% randomly sampled interviews ($n = 23$). The mean inter-rater reliability, calculated as percentage of agreement with number of identical codes divided by the total codes, was also 0.81.

The coding system scored each child's responses on a form with 69 statements about hurricanes. The statements were divided into five categories that included water/floods, property damage, effects on people, general scientific knowledge, and hurricane-related vocabulary. For example, under property damage one statement read, "Some trees fell down/broke/were damaged/fell on power lines/houses/cars/buildings/streets." If a child told a story that mentioned the trees falling down or being damaged, that statement was coded with either a 1 (some demonstration of understanding) or a 2 (clear demonstration of understanding by actions/examples/details). If the child never indicated with their words or actions some understanding of the item, it was coded as a 0.

The results show strong evidence that children understood the general effects of hurricanes and hurricane effects on people. As expected, older children ($M = 13.29$, $SD = 2.89$) demonstrated significantly more total knowledge of hurricanes than younger children ($M = 12.79$, $SD = 3.16$) [$F(1,72) = 34.11$, $p < 0.001$], a finding that was true for each category (Table 1.3). They knew that trees fell down or broke, people left their homes to evacuate, houses were damaged, and streets

Table 1.3 Children's demonstrated knowledge of hurricanes and hurricane effects

	Pre-kindergarten–kindergarten ($N = 35$)		Primary grades (first–third) ($N = 39$)			
	M	SD	M	SD	F	p
Hurricane effects	4.40	1.77	5.67	1.77	9.47	0.003
Property damage	2.83	1.18	3.79	1.58	8.77	0.004
Effects on people	5.60	1.99	8.18	2.49	23.87	<0.001
Effects on pets	3.57	2.08	4.74	2.05	5.96	0.017
Vocabulary	0.17	0.45	1.38	1.44	22.68	<0.001
Scientific knowledge	3.69	2.29	6.59	3.22	19.62	<0.001

and houses flooded. Many children indicated they understood that hurricanes are weather systems that can be destructive, are accompanied by power outages, and often have strong winds and heavy rain. Very few stories indicated knowledge of other characteristics or causes of hurricanes.

Demonstrated knowledge was negatively correlated with teachers' years experience [$r(84) = -0.25, p = 0.025$] and the total number of children in the classroom [$r(84) = -0.30, p = 0.006$]. Knowledge was also related to the age of the child [$r(74) = 0.56, p < 0.001$]. Knowledge was not significantly correlated with parental education, family income, or the child's experience with the hurricane, nor with hurricane-related teacher-planned classroom activities or with child-initiated activities.

Discussion

We surveyed teachers in school districts that were matched geographically with the Louisiana districts (i.e., southern, mostly rural with one suburban district) and compared responses of teachers in Louisiana with those in two hurricane-prone states (South Carolina and Georgia) and with teachers in a state rarely impacted by hurricanes (Tennessee). Results of the teachers' survey showed indirect evidence of children's knowledge through teacher reports. Teachers in all four states reported that young children engaged in spontaneous hurricane-related activities in their classrooms. Qualitative analysis of teacher reports about those activities indicates that the activities children initiated in the classrooms were different for different geographical locations and seemed to reflect the stages of disaster preparation, response, and recovery.

We also gathered more direct evidence of children's knowledge in a way that was appropriate for the age of these children. In particular, young children's stories in response to narrative story stems revealed they did have knowledge of hurricanes in general and of Katrina and Rita in particular. Older children, children in smaller classes, and children in classes with teachers with fewer years of experience demonstrated relatively more knowledge than other children.

The findings from this study are aligned with the developmental principles discussed in the introduction that inform the work of professionals in early childhood education. First, development moves toward greater complexity. Children were able to communicate some detailed and complex knowledge of hurricanes. This aspect of the data confirms the findings by Bahrick et al. (1998) and Zeece (1986) that very young children were able to accurately relate information about hurricanes. As expected, the knowledge of older children and those that were directly affected exhibited greater sophistication and depth. Second, developmental domains are interconnected. Although teachers reported that children in all four states demonstrated an impact of news reports on children's knowledge of hurricanes, children with direct experiences with hurricanes exhibited learning and knowledge that differed from those who did not experience the storms. The interconnection between the developmental domains was especially visible in children's discussions of the "my cousin" stories where their knowledge of hurricanes (cognition) was clearly informed by their social relationships and emotional connections.

Third, children learn by making meaningful connections. Children's spontaneous classroom activities moved from more personal (Louisiana) to more abstract (Tennessee) possibly as a result of the children's direct experiences with hurricanes. Different types of play and activities in the states highlighted the child's direct experiences with hurricanes. For example, like the children Saylor et al. (1992) studied after Hurricane Hugo, children in Louisiana played and acted out their own experiences during the hurricane. In Georgia, children connected the events of the hurricanes in Louisiana and Mississippi to their prior experiences and in Tennessee, the connection of the hurricane to weather in their state was highlighted. Thus, the children seemed to demonstrate they were making connections between the new knowledge of hurricanes and their previous experience and knowledge.

Fourth, children express their knowledge in a variety of ways. This was seen in the teacher observations and interviews. From the data about children's play involving hurricane knowledge, we know that children practiced and extended their learning about hurricanes through their play. Perhaps the children were processing post-traumatic stress (Gurwitch et al., 1998). Some children expressed knowledge through writing and others through play. Children also demonstrated knowledge about hurricanes in their verbal and nonverbal responses to the story stems, underscoring the importance of studying children's knowledge and experience using multiple methods. Children did show hurricane-related knowledge in their drawing, writing, and play like children in other studies (Fothergill & Peek, 2008; Saylor et al., 1992). Someone who did not see anything worrisome in a child's writing about disasters might conclude that the child had not experienced trauma, but a closer look at his/her play with multiple hurricane themes might offer a more detailed view of the child's actual knowledge and experience.

Fig. 1.3 The new sign of security, rooftops, drawn by an 8-year-old boy after Katrina. From http://www.katrinaexhibit.org ©2006 KTTEOC. Reprinted with permission

Conclusion and Future Directions

Children's emotional responses to disasters and how they organize and make sense of their experiences remain poorly understood today. When a group of therapists came to work with children in a large FEMA trailer park in Baton Rouge for several months after Katrina and Rita, they observed that instead of drawing houses (as most children do) the children were drawing triangle after triangle (Dewan, 2007). After observing this reoccurring many times, they realized the children were drawing roofs (Fig. 1.3). Roofs had replaced homes as a symbol of security and safety for these children.

There is a clear need for more attention to children and disasters. During the 2008 evacuation for Hurricanes Gustav and Ike, a reporter noted that children in a shelter were often left alone and no specialized services were being provided for young children (Kliff & Skipp, 2008). This prompted the established, but as yet inactive, National Commission on Children and Disasters to begin meeting 9 months after Congress formed the commission (What About the Children, 2008). The slow progress of this effort seems stark when contrasted with the quick action taken to provide disaster assistance for pets and their owners when, in the Fall of 2006, Congress passed the PETS act that authorized funding to help reimburse disaster-affected states for costs related to household pets and service animals (Case, 2008). It took another year to authorize a commission to make recommendations about how to help children and their families. It took another disaster for that commission to become active. When action is finally taken to help children and families, the results of this study suggest it will be important to give attention to the roles teachers and schools (the poorly prepared first responders for many children) should play in children's disaster preparation, response, and recovery.

Peek (2008) and Anderson (2005) offer thorough research agendas for future research on children and disasters. The results of this study suggest additional directions for future studies. First, further work should consider children's prior knowledge and investigate the growth and change of understanding following a natural disaster. Second, there is need for more comprehensive understanding of the effects of accurate knowledge on children's coping. If children have real and factual information about disasters, will that information reduce emotional trauma? An interesting finding from this study was the play activities involving hurricane themes in which children engaged during free-choice and recess times. Future research on children's responses to disaster should include documentation of play activities. Also, the NSST seems to be a promising methodology to use when assessing young children's knowledge. Finally, teachers' curricular responses to disasters should continue to be investigated. Does curricular response facilitate student learning following disasters, or does curricular attention to the crisis impair the "normalcy" sought by many after such an experience? We need to know more about what teachers do following natural disasters and how their actions impact children's knowledge and coping following disasters.

Acknowledgment This chapter is based on work supported by the National Science Foundation under Grant No. 0555387 and the Louisiana Board of Regents (PI: T. Buchanan). Any opinions, findings, conclusions, or recommendations expressed in this chapter are those of the authors and do not necessarily reflect the views of these organizations.

Diane C. Burts and Timothy Page were co-investigators on this project. Diane Burts' work on the materials and protocol as well as her work with Timothy Page to develop the stories for the interviews were critically important to this project. Virginia Gil-Rivas provided the tools used to measure teachers' psychological well-being, training, and teachers' and children's hurricane-related personal experiences. Ana Morales provided invaluable assistance throughout the entire project. We are grateful to these wonderful colleagues. We appreciate the hard work of research team members Rhonda Norwood, Susheel Brahmeshwarkar, Sharbari Dey, and Kyung-Ran Kim. We are deeply indebted to project consultant David Klahr who offered critically important support and insight and to the teachers and children who made this study possible.

References

Aghayan, C., Schellhaas, A., Wayne, A., Burts, D. C., Buchanan, T., & Benedict, J. (2005). Project Katrina. *Early childhood research and practice. 7*. Retrieved from http://ecrp.uiuc.edu/v7n2/aghayan.html

Allen, M., Jerome, A., White, A., Marston, S., Lamb, S., & Pope, D. (2002). The preparation of school psychologists for crisis intervention. *Psychology in the Schools, 39*, 427–439.

Anderson, W. A. (2005). Bringing children into focus on the social science disaster research agenda. *International Journal of Mass Emergencies and Disasters, 23*, 159–175.

Bahrick, L. E., Parker, J. F., Fivush, R., & Levitt, M. (1998). The effects of stress on young children's memory for a natural disaster. *Journal of Experimental Psychology: Applied, 4*, 308–331.

Barrett, E. J., Ausbrooks, C. Y. B., & Martinez-Coscio, M. (2008). The school as a source of support for Katrina-evacuated youth. *Children, Youth and Environments, 18*, 202–236.

Bergen, D. (2008). *Human development: Traditional and contemporary theories*. Upper Saddle River, NJ: Pearson Prentice Hall.
Bonvillian, J. D., & Orlansky, M. D. (1983). Developmental milestones: Sign language acquisition and motor development. *Child Development, 54*, 1435–1445.
Bransford, J. D., & Franks, J. J. (1971). The abstraction of linguistic ideas. *Cognitive Psychology, 2*, 331–350.
Bredekamp, S., & Copple, C. (Eds.). (1997). *Developmentally appropriate practice in early childhood programs*. Washington, DC: National Association for the Education of Young Children.
Bretherton, I., & Oppenheim, D. (2003). The MacArthur Story Stem Battery: Development, administration, reliability, validity and reflections about meaning. In R. N. Emde, D. P. Wolf, & D. Oppenheim (Eds.), *Revealing the inner worlds of young children: The MacArthur Story Stem Battery and parent-child narrative* (pp. 55–80). New York: Oxford University Press.
Broaders, S., Cook, S., Mitchell, Z., & Goldin-Meadow, S. (2007). Making children gesture brings out implicit knowledge and leads to learning. *Journal of Experimental Psychology, 136*, 539–550.
Brodkin, A. M., & Coleman, M. F. (1994). Equip kids to deal with disaster. *Instructor, 103*, 17–18.
Buchanan, T., Casbergue, R.M., & Baumgartner, J. (2009). Consequences for classroom environments and school personnel: Evaluating Katrina's effect on schools and system response. In R. P. Kilmer, V. Gil-Rivas, R. G. Tedeschi, & L. G. Calhoun (Eds.), *Meeting the needs of children, families, and communities post-disaster: Lessons learned from Hurricane Katrina and its aftermath*. Washington, DC: American Psychological Association (in press).
Case, H. (2008, November). Pets evacuation and transportation standards act (PETS act). *The American Veterinary Medical Association Advocate*, Retrieved from http://www.avma.org/advocacy/avma_advocate/nov08/aa_nov08d.asp
Caseley, J. (1994). *Hurricane Harry*. New York: Harper Collins.
Charlesworth, R. (2008). *Understanding child development*. Florence, KY: Delmar Cengage.
Cohen, D., Stern, V., & Balaban, N. (1996). *Observing and recording the behavior of young children*. New York: Teachers College Press.
Damiani, V. B. (2006). *Crisis prevention and intervention in the classroom: What teachers should know*. Lanham, MD: Rowman and Littlefield Publishing Group.
Dewan, S. (2007, September 17). Using crayons to exorcise Katrina. *The New York Times*.
Eaton, L. (2007, December 7). Many children struggling after '05 storms. *New York Times*, p. 24.
Elischberger, H.B. (2005). The effects of prior knowledge on children's memory and suggestibility. *Journal of Experimental Child Psychology, 92*, 2247–2275.
Emde, R. N., Wolf, D. P., & Oppenheim, D. (Eds.). (2003). *Revealing the inner worlds of young children: The MacArthur Story Stem Battery and parent-child narratives*. New York: Oxford University Press.
Fairbrother, G., Stuber, J., Galea, S., Pfefferbaum, B., & Fleishman, A. R. (2004). Unmet need for counseling services by children in New York City after the September 11th attacks on the World Trade Center: Implications for pediatricians. *Pediatrics, 113*, 1367–1374.
Fothergill, A., & Peek, L. (2006). Surviving catastrophe: A study of children in Hurricane Katrina. *Learning from catastrophe: Quick response research in the wake of Hurricane Katrina*. Boulder: Institute of Behavioral Science, University of Colorado, pp. 97–130.
Frost, J. L. (2005). Lessons from disasters: Play, work and the creative arts. *Childhood Education, 82*, 2–8.
Glaser, B., & Strauss, A. (1967). *The discovery of grounded theory*. Chicago: Aldine.
Gullo, D. F. (2005). *Understanding assessment and evaluation in early childhood education* (2nd ed.). New York: Teachers College Press.
Gurwitch, R. H., Sullivan, M. A., & Long, P. J. (1998). The impact of trauma and disaster on young children. *Child and Adolescent Psychiatric Clinics of North America, 7*, 19–32.
Honig, A. S. (2005). Emotional milestones and their link to learning. Infants & Toddlers. *Early Childhood Today, 20*, 30–32.

Janson, G. R., & King, M. A. (2006). Emotional security in the classroom: What works for young children. *Journal of Family and Consumer Sciences, 98*, 70–74.

Jimerson, S. R., Brock, S. E., & Pletcher, S. W. (2005). An integrated model of school crisis preparedness and intervention. *School Psychology International, 26*, 275–296.

Kessler, R., Galea, S., Gruber, M., Sampson, N., Ursano, R., & Wessley, S. (2008). Trends in mental illness and suicidality after Hurricane Katrina. *Molecular Psychiatry, 13*, 374–384.

Kenardy, J., & Piercy, J. A. (2006). Effect of information provision on trauma symptoms following therapeutic writing. *Australian Psychologist, 41*, 205–212.

Kenardy, J., Thompson, K., LeBrocque, R., & Olsson, K. (2008). Information-provision intervention for children and their parents following pediatric accidental injury. *European Child and Adolescent Psychiatry, 17*, 316–325.

Kent, J. D. (2006, May). *2005 Louisiana hurricane impact atlas, Vol. 1. Louisiana Geographic Information Center*. Retrieved May 29, 2007, from http://lagic.lsu.edu

Klein, K. (1982). Disconfirmed expectancies and imagined distress in a role-play of a visit to the dentist. *Motivation and Emotion, 6*, 181–192.

Kliff, S., & Skipp, C. (2008, October 6). Overlooked: The littlest evacuees. *Newsweek*. Retrieved from http://www.newsweek.com/id/161223/output/print

Klingman, A. (1978). Children in stress: Anticipatory guidance in the framework of the educational system. *Personnel and Guidance Journal, 57*, 22–26.

Knox, K. S., & Roberts, A. R. (2005). Crisis intervention and crisis team models in schools. *Children and Schools, 27*, 93–100.

Lacroix, L., Rousseau, C., Gauthier, M. F., Singh, A., Giguère, N., & Lemzoudi, Y. (2007). Immigrant and refugee preschoolers' sand-play representations of the tsunami. *The Arts in Psychotherapy, 34*, 99–113.

Liu, A., & Plyer, A. (2008). Summary of findings: The state of New Orleans three years after Hurricane Katrina: An overview. *The New Orleans Index*. Brookings Institution Metropolitan Policy Program & Greater New Orleans Community Data Center.

Louisiana Recovery Authority. (2006). *Initial quarterly report*. Retrieved May 31, 2007, from, http://www.lra.louisiana.gov/reports.html

Mack, C., & Smith, T. B. (1991). *Separation and loss: A handbook for early childhood professionals*. Pittsburgh, PA: Generations Together.

Marti, E. (2003). Strengths and weaknesses of cognition over preschool years. In J. Valsiner & K.J Connolly (Eds.), *Handbook of Developmental Psychology*. London: Sage Publications.

McFarland, C., & Ross, M. (1987). The relation between current impressions and memories of self and dating partners. *Personality and Social Psychology Bulletin, 13*, 228–238.

Mercuri, A., & Angelique, H. L. (2004). Children's responses to natural, technological, and na-tech disasters. *Community Mental Health Journal, 40*, 167–175.

Miller, K. (1996). *The crisis manual for early childhood teachers: How to handle the really difficult problems*. Beltsville, MD: Gryphon House, Inc.

Mills, R. T., & Krantz, D. S. (1979). Information, choice, and reactions to stress: A field experiment in a blood bank with laboratory analogue. *Journal of Personality and Social Psychology, 37*, 608–620.

Osofsky, J. D. (2007). *Young children and trauma: Intervention and trauma*. New York: Guilford Press.

Page, T. (2001). The social meaning of children's narratives: A review of the attachment-based narrative story stem technique. *Child and Adolescent Social Work Journal, 3*, 171–187.

Pane, J. F., McCaffrey, D. F., Kalra, N., & Zhou, A. J. (2008). Effects of student displacement in Louisiana during the first academic year after the hurricanes of 2005. *Journal of Education for Students Placed at Risk, 13*, 168–211.

Paulson, A. (2005, September 28). At school for storm evacuees, hugs before homework. *The Christian Science Monitor*, p 1.

Peek, L. (2008). Children and disasters: Understanding vulnerability, developing capacities, and promoting resilience – An introduction. *Children, Youth and Environments, 18*, 1–29.

Pfefferbaum, R. L., Fairbrother, G., Brandt, E. N., Robertson, M. J., Gurwitch, R. H., & Stuber, J. (2004). Teachers in the aftermath of terrorism: A case study of one New York City school. *Community Health, 27*, 250–259.

Plummer, C. (2008). *Understanding trauma and post-traumatic stress disorder*. Baton Rouge, LA: Author.

Proctor, L. J., Fauchier, A., Oliver, P. H., Ramos, M. C., Rios, M. A., & Margolin, G. (2007). Family context and young children's response to earthquake. *Journal of Child Psychology and Psychiatry, 48*, 941–949.

Redlener, I., DeRosa, C., & Hut, R. (2008). *Legacy of shame: The on-going public health disaster of children struggling in post-Katrina Louisiana*. New York: The Children's Health Fund and the National Center for Disaster Preparedness, Columbia University Mailman School of Public Health.

Rowley, K. (2007). *GulfGov reports: An examination of the impact of Hurricanes Katrina and Rita on the public school districts in 15 communities*. Baton Rouge, LA: Public Affairs Research Council of Louisiana and Albany, NY: The Nelson A. Rockefeller Institute of Government.

Saylor, C. F., Swenson, C. C., & Powell, P. (1992). Hurricane Hugo blows down the broccoli: Preschoolers' post-disaster play and adjustment. *Child Psychiatry and Human Development, 22*, 139–149.

Saylor, C. F., Swenson, C. C., Reynolds, S. S., & Taylor, M. (1999). The Pediatric Emotional Distress Scale: A brief screening measure for young children exposed to traumatic events. *Journal of Clinical Child Psychology, 28*, 70–81.

Scheeringa, M. S., Zeanah, C. H., Myers, L., & Putnam, F. W. (2003). New findings on alternative criteria for PTSD in preschool children. *Journal of American Academy of Child and Adolescent Psychiatry, 4*, 561–570.

Schellhaas, A., Burts, D. C., & Aghayan, C. (2007). Reflecting on "Project Katrina" and developmentally appropriate practices: A graduate student's perspective. *Journal of Early Childhood Teacher Education, 28*, 77–82.

Shreve, R., Danbom, K., & Hanhan, S. (2002). "Wen the Flood Km We Had to Lv": Children's understandings of disaster. *Language Arts, 80*, 100–108.

Swenson, C. C., Saylor, C. F., Powell, M. P., Stokes, S. J., Foster, K. Y., & Belter, R. W. (1996). Impact of a natural disaster on preschool children: Adjustment 14 months after a hurricane. *American Journal of Orthopsychiatry, 66*, 122–130.

Vernberg, E. M., LaGreca, A. M., Silverman, W. K., & Prinstein, M. J. (1996). Prediction of posttraumatic stress symptoms in children after Hurricane Andrew. *Journal of Abnormal Psychology, 105*, 237–248.

Ward, M. E., Shelley, K., Kaase, K., & Pane, J. F. (2008). Hurricane Katrina: A longitudinal study of the achievement and behavior of displaced students. *Journal of Education for Students Placed at Risk, 13*, 297–317.

Wasserstein, S. B., & LaGreca, A. M. (1998). Hurricane Drew: Parent conflict as a moderator of children's adjustment. *Hispanic Journal of Behavioral Sciences, 20*, 212–224.

What About the Children: A National Commission Starts Work to Make Sure the Young Aren't Forgotten During Disasters. (2008, October 14). *The Washington Post*, Retrieved from http://www.washingtonpost.com/wp-dyn/content/article/2008/10/13/AR2008101302279.html

Wolfe, C. D., & Bell, M. A. (2007). The integration of cognition and emotion during infancy and early childhood: Regulatory processes associated with the development of working memory. *Brain & Cognition, 65*, 3–13.

Zeece, P. D. (2001). Young children's understanding of the shuttle disaster (1986). *The Journal of Psychology, 124*, 591–593.

Chapter 2
An Ecological-Needs-Based Perspective of Adolescent and Youth Emotional Development in the Context of Disaster: Lessons from Hurricane Katrina

Carl F. Weems and Stacy Overstreet

Abstract This chapter reviews studies on the impact of natural disasters on childhood and adolescent emotional development with an emphasis on studies conducted with Hurricane Katrina samples. Special consideration is given to the role of exposure to disasters on adolescent emotional development. The findings are reviewed and presented within an integrative perspective (i.e., an ecological needs-based perspective) drawn from broad contextual theories of human development. The perspective emphasizes multiple levels of influence on emotional development through the interference of multiple human needs.

Introduction

Existing research on traumatic stress and post-traumatic stress disorder (PTSD) suggests that disasters like Hurricane Katrina can have profound effects on child and adolescent emotional development (see, e.g., La Greca, Silverman, Vernberg, & Roberts, 2002; Silverman & La Greca, 2002). In addition, research on traumatic stressors other than hurricane exposure has demonstrated that youth who have experienced severe stressors are more likely to display atypical brain development (Carrión et al., 2001; De Bellis et al., 1999) such as decreases in specific brain regions involved in cognitive emotional processing (e.g., the hippocampus, see Carrión, Weems, & Reiss, 2007). Traumatic stress can clearly impact emotional, behavioral, and cognitive development. However, the extent of the Katrina disaster forces us to look beyond individual responses and try to understand the individual child within multiple contexts.

The far-reaching effects of Katrina and its aftermath challenge the applicability of many specific theoretical models in psychology to capture the complexity of youth adaptation. For example, past mental health research has tended to focus on the impact of disasters on the functioning of the individual, and most

---

C.F. Weems (✉)
Department of Psychology, University of New Orleans, New Orleans, LA 70148, USA
e-mail: cweems@uno.edu

commonly in terms of PTSD symptoms (Norris, Friedman, & Watson, 2002). One of Katrina's lessons is that attempts to capture the entirety of the disaster's impact or the complexity of individual adaptation will require similarly complex integrative frameworks. For example, the massive scale of the Katrina disaster raised the question, "What are the social systems that are impacted and how does context play a role in shaping adaptation following catastrophe?"

To try to capture this breadth of influence, our writing and research on the Katrina disaster (Weems & Overstreet, 2008; Weems, Watts et al., 2007) has utilized broad contextual models of life span human development (e.g., Bronfenbrenner, 1977, 1979) and of risk and resilience to stress (e.g., Hobfoll, 1989; Sandler, 2001) within which to couch more specific theoretical models (such as those delineating specific predictors, moderators, and mediators of emotional disorder development following disaster, e.g., La Greca, Silverman, Vernberg, & Prinstein, 1996; Silverman & La Greca, 2002). Drawing from these theoretical models, we have termed our integrative framework an ecological needs-based perspective (Weems & Overstreet, 2008). The perspective helps show the interconnections among the diverse factors that influence youth adaptation following the experience of disasters. In the proceeding sections, we present an overview of the perspective and use it as a framework to review research on the impact of Hurricane Katrina among youth.

An Ecological Needs-Based Perspective

As noted, the perspective is based on contextual developmental theories, most directly Bronfenbrenner's ecological systems theory. This theory posits that individuals function within multiple contexts, or "ecologies", that influence each other and human development (Bronfenbrenner, 1977, 1979). These ecologies vary in their proximity to the individual (e.g., a child) and include the macrosystem, which is the most distal ecology and includes the government, culture, cultural values, and beliefs; the exosystem, which consists of processes taking place between two or more contexts, one of which does not directly involve the child, but has implications for the individual child (e.g., parent's workplace); the mesosystem, which represents the linkages between proximal ecologies (e.g., school and home, parental participation in the child's school); and the microsystem, which represents the proximal ecologies within which the child develops, including the family and school environments and peer relationships. The ontogenic level is the ecology of the individual and represents factors within the individual that influence developmental adaptation.

Our perspective also posits that disasters such as Hurricane Katrina impact emotional development by threatening basic human needs and goals (Hobfoll, 1989; Sandler, 2001). The basis of healthy emotional adaptation is the ability to meet basic needs. For example, Sandler's (2001) risk and resilience model suggests that there are four basic needs relevant to adaptation to severe stress including physical safety, self-worth, control/efficacy, and a sense of social relatedness. When these needs are met, an individual is more likely to be resilient in the face of adversity (see Sandler, 2001 for expanded discussion). Similarly, in Hobfoll's conservation of resources model (Hobfoll, 1989), stressors such as Katrina deplete the individual's financial, material, cognitive, and emotional resources. Disasters like Hurricane Katrina threaten these basic needs and resources and so challenge healthy emotional development and mental health.

Table 2.1 provides an overview of the various ecologies and examples of the salient needs that may influence youth adaptation following a disaster. The table is not a complete delineation of influences but is illustrative of salient needs that may

Table 2.1 Ecologies and salient needs that may influence youth adaptation following a disaster

Ecology	Salient needs affected	Examples of specific factors that may influence youth adaptation
Macrosystem	Physical safety	Geographic location and physical geography
	Self-worth	Societal prejudices
	Social relatedness	Community climate of support versus isolation
Exosystem	Physical safety	Evacuation policies and government infrastructure, community resources versus disadvantage (e.g., poverty)
	Self-worth	Parental loss of job/work
	Social relatedness	Disruptions in community infrastructure (e.g., school closures, changes in health care systems) lead to different teachers, classmates, doctors, etc.
Mesosystem	Physical safety	Referral systems for health care disrupted
	Social relatedness	Having to attend school outside the neighborhood
	Control/efficacy	Evacuation/relocations can foster a sense of lack of control over maintaining connections among microsystems
Microsystem	Physical safety	Family resources (e.g., home damaged/destroyed)
	Social relatedness	School disruption, loss of friendships/friend contacts
	Control/efficacy	Parental distress/psychopathology/mental health
Ontogenetic	Physical safety	Experiencing personal harm
	Control/efficacy	Perceptions of control, coping ability, pre-existing risk, anxiety sensitivity, developmental level
	Self-worth	Child mental health (or emotional reactions)

influence youth within various ecologies. It is incomplete because the "example needs" in the table are not a complete list and the needs may sometimes transcend specific ecologies. Moreover, the specific examples within the various needs may also affect or be related to other needs. However, the model and table highlights that in the case of Hurricane Katrina and its aftermath, threats to basic needs and the depletion of resources emanated from multiple ecologies, increasing the risk for negative emotional outcomes at many levels. Thus, an ecological needs-based perspective can be used to integrate data and knowledge by showing how various factors within different ecologies surrounding the child act alone and/or in conjunction with other ecologies to either impede or foster the child and family's ability to meet the child's basic needs.

Although broad in its framework, the perspective also allows us to focus in on more specific issues related to emotional development within various developmental periods, such as adolescence. Because of developmentally related biological, emotional, and psychosocial changes, disaster exposure may be particularly salient in certain facets of emotional development and emotional health for adolescents. For example, at the microsystem level for adolescents, there is a growing importance of social issues (e.g., peer groups, peer relations, social anxiety, see Weems & Costa, 2005; Weems, 2008). Natural disasters such as Hurricane Katrina may therefore make disruptions in peer relationships more emotionally taxing for adolescents or may make disruptions in peer relations more developmentally detrimental (e.g., disruptions in normal peer contact may interfere with normative social development). At the ontogenic level, pubertal transitions may make body sensations more salient for adolescents (see Warren & Sroufe, 2004). Exposure to anxiety provoking situations common in disasters may heighten these sensations thereby exacerbating normal body sensations (Hensley & Varela, 2008). In addition, due to their increased level of cognitive sophistication during this developmental period (e.g., Piaget, 1983) adolescents are also more likely to shift their focus internally in an introspective manner leading to increased rumination on internal mood states and sensations compared to younger children. Thus, while there is evidence that younger children may be at a generally increased risk for problems (Scheeringa & Zeanah, 2008; Weems et al., 2008) adolescents may be more susceptible to certain effects of disaster exposure or more susceptible in certain psychosocial domains. This possibility is noted further below as we review each of the ecological influences.

Research on the Effects of Katrina

Macrosystem Influences

As noted, macrosystem influences include cultural values as well as regional and national norms. Hurricane Katrina ignited a national discussion of societal prejudices toward people of color and people living in poverty (Bobo, 2006; Huddy & Feldman, 2006; Lieberman, 2006). Surveys of American citizens revealed that

Whites were more likely than Blacks to place some blame on Katrina victims for their plight and were less likely to be sympathetic toward those stranded in New Orleans (Huddy & Feldman, 2006).

Weems, Watts, et al. (2007) examined regional differences in the psychosocial impact of Hurricane Katrina. Participants ($N = 386$) were adults and emerging adults (i.e., late adolescents) recruited in the primary areas affected by Hurricane Katrina and included residents of metropolitan New Orleans (Orleans Parish, Louisiana), Greater New Orleans (i.e., Metairie, Kenner, Gretna), and the Mississippi Gulf Coast (i.e., cities along the coast from Waveland to Ocean Springs, Mississippi). Participants were assessed for post-traumatic stress disorder (PTSD) symptoms, other psychological symptoms, perceptions of discrimination, perceptions of social support, evacuation distance, and the extent to which they experienced hurricane-related stressful events. All data were collected between October, 2005 and January, 2006. The results of our survey study suggest that the residents of the areas impacted by Hurricane Katrina were subjected to a large number of traumatic events and experienced a number of psychological symptoms in the relatively immediate aftermath of the hurricane. These findings were consistent with Centers for Disease Control and Prevention reports on Hurricane Katrina (see Weisler, Barbee, & Townsend, 2006). Results are also consistent with previous research showing that the number of hurricane disaster events a person experiences is related to psychological symptoms (e.g., La Greca, Silverman, & Wasserstein, 1998; Sattler et al., 2002). Unfortunately, but consistent with the national trends noted previously, the survey indicated that ethnic minorities perceived more discrimination than non-minorities and that regardless of ethnicity, individuals living in New Orleans perceived less social support and more discrimination than those living along the Gulf Coast of Mississippi (Weems, Watts et al., 2007).

Prejudice, discrimination, and lack of social support represent factors within the macrosystem that pose a powerful threat to one's sense of physical safety, self-worth, self-efficacy, and social relatedness. The perception of prejudice or intergroup conflict can limit support seeking from others in the post-disaster environment (Norris et al., 2002; Rabalais, Ruggiero, & Scotti, 2002) and lead to feelings of low self-worth and poor self-efficacy (Greene, Way, & Pahl, 2006; Umaña-Taylor & Updegraff, 2006), all of which have negative implications for youths' ability to cope adaptively with a disaster. However, very few studies have empirically examined the impact of perceived discrimination on youth adaptation to disasters (Norris et al., 2002). Pina et al. (2008) addressed this in a study of youth ($n = 48$, mean age $= 11.4$ years) impacted by Katrina through an examination of whether perceived discrimination is related to post-traumatic stress reactions among youth survivors of Katrina. The results indicated that while African-American participants perceived more discrimination than White participants, it was only modestly and not statistically significantly associated with post-traumatic stress symptoms in the study ($r = 0.22$, $p > 0.05$). Importantly, Black participants in the sample also reported high levels of extra-familial social support. Such findings suggest that future research examine whether the potentially negative contextual effects of discrimination might be mitigated by a supportive proximal environment (see Jones et al., Chapter 4 of this volume, for a related discussion).

Returning to findings in Weems, Watts, et al. (2007) the residents of the Mississippi Gulf Coast also reported relatively more emotional symptoms, but they perceived a greater level of social support than those in metropolitan New Orleans. Such findings are consistent with the predictions we developed from theory and media coverage of the storm which depicted vast differences in the community atmosphere following the disaster. Moreover, social support was negatively related to emotional symptoms and a number of previous studies show that social support can be a protective factor (see Ozer & Weiss, 2004). Such conditions of positive social support would thus likely foster a quicker resolution of psychological problems. Although this conclusion cannot be drawn directly from the Weems, Watts et al. study alone, it is consistent with previous research on the role of social support (e.g., King, King, Fairbank, Keane, & Adams, 1998).

Developmentally, however, not all sources of social support are likely to be equally beneficial across the life span. We conducted some secondary analyses from the data in Weems, Watts et al. (2007) to examine differences in social support between late adolescents/emerging adults (Arnett, 2000) and older adults. The Family Support Scale (FSS; Dunst, Trivette, & Cross, 1986) was used to measure the helpfulness of 18 different sources of support. Descriptive analyses indicated that friends (66.5%), parents (63.6%), coworkers (37.9%), participants' own children (33.2%), and social groups (21.9%) were commonly reported as very helpful by Katrina survivors. However, chi-square analyses also suggest developmental differences consistent with our theorizing. For example, late adolescents/emerging adults (ages 18–25, $n = 159$) reported their parents as helpful (72%) more often than older adults (56%, $\chi^2 = 43.18$, $p < 0.005$), whereas older adults (ages 26–86, $n = 227$) more commonly reported their children (52%) and in-laws (37.4%) as helpful sources of support than late adolescents/emerging adults (8.7%; $\chi^2 = 117.11$, $p < 0.005$ and 25.4%; $\chi^2 = 9.81$, $p < 0.05$, respectively). Results thus point to potential developmental differences in beneficial forms of social support.

An additional broad influence that is important to note is the state and federal government response and the laws and policies that govern funding the mental health response. Drury, Scheeringa, and Zeanah (2008) have provided an insightful review of the federal laws governing the distribution of funds for mental services following Katrina. Drury et al. (2008) note that following the Katrina disaster, the Federal government allocated a large amount of funds (over 40 million dollars) to Louisiana for disaster-related mental health response through the Federal Emergency Management Agency (FEMA); however, the funds were not allocated to provide increased treatment services for individuals or to expand the training of clinicians in evidence-based approaches.

The Drury et al. (2008) policy analysis suggests that the reason for this was because the Stafford Disaster Relief and Emergency Assistance Act, which provides for federal assistance, describes the mental health response as "crisis counseling." The Substance Abuse and Mental Health Services Administration (SAMHSA) manages this FEMA mental health component and interprets the Stafford Act to mean that FEMA funds after disasters cannot be used for comprehensive mental health treatment. The SAMHSA Crisis Counseling Program is not mental health treatment in this regard; it is intended to be very short term (1–5 sessions) and is generally provided by non-licensed lay persons (Drury et al., 2008). For those who need treatment, the crisis counseling can function as a referral program; however, this is problematic if the community has few treatment providers in place or these services have been disrupted so that there is no one left to refer people to. Moreover, there is little evidence that short-term immediate crisis counseling helps people responding normally to recover more quickly or more fully and may even be detrimental for some (McNally, Bryant, & Ehlers, 2003). Resolving these and similar problematic policy issues is critical for improving future disaster response for youth (see Speier, Osofsky, & Osofsky, Chapter 12, for a related discussion).

A final potential influence worth noting at the macrosystem level is television viewing in a culture of continuous news cycles. Weems, Watts et al. (2007) found that 81–98% of the sample reported viewing some form of intense disaster-related traumatic events on TV, including death, human suffering, and violence following Katrina. Thus, in a culture of 24 h a day 7 days a week news cycles, even families who evacuated and did not experience the disaster first hand could not escape images of destruction on the TV. Comer and Kendall (2007) have recently developed a theoretical model of the potential for wide and insidious influence that events such as acts of terrorism can have on populations of youth via television viewing. While the empirical data are very limited, research aimed at clarifying the effect of horrific images repeatedly displayed on TV may be an important avenue for understanding the indirect effects of disasters on youth emotional development.

Exosystem Influences

Exosystem influences on child adaptation are indirect in nature; they originate in contexts that do not involve the child (e.g., parent's workplace, government agencies) and have their effects by creating disruptions in contexts that do involve the child (e.g., family, school). These indirect effects on the microsystems that surround the child are potentially potent risk factors for healthy youth adaptation. For example, the inadequate and inept governmental response to Katrina, in combination with the complete failure of communication systems, severely challenged the ability of families to communicate a sense of safety and control to their children (Bourque, Siegel, Kano, & Wood, 2006). In addition, the nature of the response called into question the worth of certain groups/communities and challenged feelings of social connectedness (Bourque et al., 2006; Huddy & Feldman, 2006).

Two studies on Katrina samples of youth have reported data relevant to exosystem influences on child mental health and both reveal surprising findings. First, Scheeringa and Zeanah (2008) found that workplace demands were the primary reason for parent–child separations during the evacuation and recovery periods following Katrina in their New Orleans sample of 70 preschool children aged 3–6 years. Although previous studies have found that parent–child separations during trauma present a risk factor for child mental health (Klingman, 2002; see also Osofsky, Osofsky, & Harris, 2007), Scheeringa and Zeanah found that parent–child separation during the evacuation period was associated with relatively fewer symptoms of PTSD for both the parent and the child. Given the chaotic and deplorable conditions in New Orleans in the immediate aftermath of the storm, parent–child separation during the evacuation period may have resulted in less trauma exposure for the child and less caregiver stress for the parent, which might have served to buffer against the development of PTSD symptoms.

In a second study, Scaramella, Sohr-Preston, Callahan, and Mirabile (2008) examined financial strain in two groups of mothers with a 2-year-old child and a child enrolled in Head Start. Before Hurricane Katrina struck, 55 mother–child dyads had participated (i.e., a pre-Katrina sample); after Katrina, 47 additional mother–child dyads were recruited and participated (i.e., a post-Katrina sample). Scaramella et al. (2008) found that the factors of financial strain and neighborhood violence created disturbances in the family environment which in turn were related to increased child emotional and behavioral problems. Interestingly, the authors did not find evidence that these particular risks were worsened by the post-Katrina environment. The authors speculate that for some families the chronic stress associated with extreme poverty may already be so pervasive that the incremental impact of the disaster on child functioning is difficult to detect (see also Aber, Gershoff, Ware, & Kotler, 2004; Steptoe & Hamer, 2007). Such findings may also represent ceiling or floor effects in symptom levels for the instruments used and so point to the need to develop methodological strategies in disaster research that are sensitive to testing incremental contextual impacts.

Mesosystem Influences

The mesosystem represents linkages between proximal (microsystem) ecologies (e.g., school and home, parental participation in the child's school). The immediate impact of Hurricane Katrina severed the ties (i.e., mesosystems) between the various microsystems in children's lives. Along the Gulf Coast, entire neighborhoods were swept away and in New Orleans, residents were under a forced evacuation for at least 5 weeks (DeSalvo et al., 2007). Hurricane Katrina and the failure of the levees in New Orleans displaced more than 2.5 million people throughout the United States (Larrance, Anastario, & Lawry, 2007). Children and their families were separated from peer groups, extended family networks, neighborhoods, schools, and day care centers and these separations tended to be extended. Up to 9 months after the disaster approximately 85,000 people remained housed in temporary FEMA trailer communities, resulting in continued separations from their original neighborhoods, schools, and extended family groups (Larrance et al., 2007). In the New Orleans area, 2 years after the disaster 55% of public schools were still closed, as were two-thirds of the city's child care centers (Liu & Plyer, 2007), forcing many families to enroll their children in new schools and day care centers. In contrast, many high school students returned to the city to complete the academic year at their former school, but at the cost of returning without their parents (Nossiter, 2006), resulting in obvious challenges to maintaining close ties between the home and the school environments.

Weak or disrupted mesosystem connections may result in a lack of congruency in the belief systems, expectations, and influences of the different microsystems, limiting the ability of these systems to act in concert to foster positive child adaptation. This lack of consistency and connectedness can challenge youths' sense of interrelatedness and self-efficacy as they attempt to navigate their various developmental challenges. A research study by Salloum and Overstreet (2008) illustrates the challenges to mesosystem connections in the post-Katrina environment and the potential of school-based mental health services to increase those connections in a sample of 58 second to sixth graders who received intervention services. Most parents of the children receiving the intervention in their study found it difficult to come to the school for a meeting, so the intervention incorporated a community-based parent meeting (i.e., at the parent's home or work) scheduled at the parent's convenience. This flexibility in service provision resulted in successful parent meetings for 73% of the sample, which allowed the opportunity to strengthen connections and ensure consistency between the home and the school environments. The study also shows the potential of interventions for improving child functioning. Youth in the intervention groups had statistically significant reductions in post-traumatic stress symptoms, depression, and traumatic grief.

Similarly, Weems et al. (2009) tested the effects of a school-based test anxiety intervention on reducing post-traumatic stress symptoms. Developmentally, most ninth grade youth are just beginning high school (i.e., the transition from junior high school to high school). Making this important transition immediately post-disaster could set a large number of youth on a path of academic failure because they are hampered by their anxiety. The study used a prospective intervention design with a sample of 94 ninth graders from New Orleans exposed to Hurricane Katrina and its aftermath. Thirty youth with elevated test anxiety completed a primarily behavioral group administered, test anxiety reduction intervention. Findings suggest a statistically significant positive effect of the intervention on test anxiety levels and academic performance with evidence of positive secondary effects on post-traumatic stress symptoms (PTS). Specifically, youth who received the intervention experienced a significant reduction in PTSD symptoms, change in test anxiety predicted change in PTSD symptoms, and there appeared to be no negative effects on natural PTSD symptom decline among those who received the intervention.

In sum, school-based interventions may help reconnect the ties (i.e., mesosystems) between the various microsystems in children's lives. In addition, ethnic minorities may be less likely to seek community treatment and perceive less potential benefit from clinic-based treatment for anxiety-related problems (Chavira, Stein, Bailey, & Stein, 2003; Mojtabai & Olfson, 2006) and so school-based interventions may be an important way to provide access to intervention and thus widen the benefit of important microsystems (like the school).

Microsystem Influences

The microsystem represents the proximal ecologies within which the child develops, including the family/home and school environments and peer relationships. Disasters also affect child adaptation by increasing risk in contexts proximal to the child, such as the family, school, and neighborhood environments. It is all too clear that disasters the scale of Hurricane Katrina create disruptions in all of the microsystems within which youth develop. However, research on the microsystems impacted by disaster has tended to focus on the family environment (Norris et al., 2002). For example, previous research has shown that marital stress, domestic violence, and parental psychopathology increase after disasters (Larrance et al., 2007; Norris et al., 2002), making it more difficult for youth to maintain their sense of safety, control, and interconnectedness (Sandler, 2001). Research by Scheeringa and Zeanah (2008) and Spell et al. (2008) speak about the importance of parental mental health for child functioning at two distinct developmental points. For preschool children, Scheeringa and Zeanah (2008) found that the onset of new mental health problems in preschool children was significantly correlated with the onset of new mental health problems in their caregivers. For school age children (8–16 years), Spell et al. (2008) obtained a similar finding among a sample of 260 displaced mother–child dyads recruited from primarily public schools within several of the main counties impacted by Katrina. Spell et al. reported that maternal psychological distress served as a significant predictor of child mental health following Hurricane Katrina. As noted by Scaramella et al. (2008), parental emotional distress and mental illness undermine parenting efficacy, resulting in increases in parental irritability and decreases in consistent discipline, both of which increase the risk for child mental health problems. In fact, Scaramella et al. found evidence for a mediating role of parenting efficacy in the relation between maternal depression and toddlers' internalizing and externalizing problems in Katrina-exposed families.

Community peer groups are another microsystem that can influence emotional development. Using the data set from Weems, Pina, et al. (2007) secondary data analyses were conducted to test the idea that natural disasters such as Katrina may make disruptions in peer relationships more emotionally taxing for adolescents. We examined the correlation between PTSD symptoms and a question which asked "Did you lose track of friends during the storm?" Correlations were examined for children aged 7–12 and adolescents aged 13–17. Both age groups reported similar rates of losing contact with friends, however, results indicated a moderate and significant association ($r = 0.46, p < 0.05$) in adolescents but a smaller non-significant correlation ($r = 0.20, p > 0.1$) in children.

Although disasters create disruptions within the microsystems surrounding the child, negative developmental outcomes are not always observed in youth exposed to disasters (see also Vigna, Hernandez, Paasch, Gordon & Kelley, Chapter 3 of this volume). The occurrence of negative outcomes depends on the balance between protective and vulnerability factors within the different contexts surrounding the child and factors within the child. For example, increased risk created by disasters within the family's broad environment can be offset by the presence of protective factors within the specific family context or within the other microsystems surrounding the child. School-based mental health services represent a protective factor within the school microsystem that can offset the negative developmental outcomes associated with disaster exposure (Abramason & Garfield, 2006; Pynoos, Goenijian, & Steinberg, 1998). In fact, Salloum and Overstreet (2008) and Weems et al. (2009) demonstrate the effectiveness of school-based interventions for children in post-disaster environments. Similarly, Pina et al. (2008) found that as perceived helpfulness from extra-familial sources of support (e.g., teachers, friends, church members) increased, post-traumatic stress reactions in youth (i.e., PTSD, anxiety, and depression) decreased.

Ontogenic Influences

The ontogenic level is the ecology of the individual and represents factors within the individual that influence developmental adaptation. Although disasters indirectly influence child adaptation through their impact on contexts, both proximal and distal to the child, they also have a direct impact on the child. A consistent relationship has been observed in which more severe and intense traumatic experiences during a disaster are associated with the development of more severe symptoms (La Greca et al., 1998; Weems, Pina, et al., 2007). For example, as perceived life threat during the disaster increases, the development of PTSD symptoms becomes more likely (La Greca et al., 1996; see also Jones et al., Chapter 4).

Disaster experiences that involve life threat can challenge one's sense of control and self-efficacy in containing the threat, leading to emotional reactions that may be difficult to regulate (Norris et al., 2002), ultimately increasing the risk for the development of psychopathology. Researchers have linked emotional dysregulation to conduct problems and aggression (Cole & Zahn-Waxler, 1992; Frick & Morris, 2004), as well as internalizing problems such as depression and anxiety (Suveg & Zeman, 2004). However, Marsee (2008) represents one of the first attempts to empirically test emotional dysregulation as a mediator of the relation between disaster exposure and aggression in adolescents.

Marsee (2008) has pointed out that while previous research has tended to focus on internalizing reactions to disaster such as depression and PTSD symptoms, specific types of aggressive responses (particularly those that involve poorly regulated emotion such as reactive aggression) may also follow disaster exposure in youth. Marsee (2008) found evidence for an indirect association between disaster exposure and reactive aggression in a sample of 166 adolescents recruited from high schools along the Gulf Coast of Mississippi following Katrina. Specifically, results of structural equation modeling indicated that level of hurricane exposure was related to reactive aggression via PTSD symptoms and poor emotion regulation. Results also indicated that hurricane exposure, PTSD symptoms, and poorly regulated emotion were associated with reactive aggression even after controlling for other forms of aggression (i.e., proactive aggression).

Research from additional Katrina-exposed samples of youth similarly suggests that disaster exposure may influence the development of many different forms of maladaptation. For example, Spell et al. (2008) reported that 13% of their school-aged sample of youth demonstrated clinically significant externalizing symptoms. Scheeringa and Zeanah (2008) found that PTSD in their preschool sample was comorbid with at least one of four other disorders in 88.6% of the sample. Hensley and Varela (2008) have further shown that disaster exposure may also have implications for physical adaptation. Their study moves the research on disaster reactions to new areas through their finding that hurricane exposure was also associated with somatic complaints such as headaches, gastrointestinal distress, and pain symptoms.

Individual youth characteristics are also important in shaping the developmental adaptation to disasters (La Greca et al., 2002; Norris et al., 2002). In support of this, research has consistently indicated that pre-existing characteristics of the child can determine the impact of disaster exposure on adaptation. For example, research has documented that pre-hurricane levels of trait anxiety predict PTSD symptoms above and beyond exposure to the trauma (La Greca et al., 1998; Weems, Pina, et al., 2007). For example, La Greca and colleagues examined stress reactions in a sample of children (fourth–sixth grade) assessed 3- ($n = 92$) and 7-months ($n = 74$) post-disaster (pre-trauma data were collected 15 months prior to Hurricane Andrew's landfall in South Florida) and found that trait anxiety was the strongest and most consistent predictor of youth's PTS reactions (e.g., trait anxiety predicted PTS symptoms even when controlling for level of exposure and demographic characteristics). These findings have also been replicated and extended in Katrina-exposed youth. Specifically, Weems, Pina, et al. (2007) found that both pre-disaster negative affect and trait anxiety predicted post-disaster PTS symptoms even when controlling for pre-disaster PTSD symptoms, level of exposure, and demographic characteristics. Theoretically, pre-existing trait anxiety is thought to impact the way children are able to cope with and process the traumatic event (La Greca et al., 1996; Vernberg, La Greca, Silverman, & Prinstein, 1996). Those with elevated trait anxiety are theorized to be less able to positively cope and are more likely to have elevated PTS symptoms even with relatively low exposure experiences (La Greca et al., 1998).

Hensley and Varela (2008) have extended this work on trait anxiety in a Hurricane Katrina sample by providing evidence that anxiety sensitivity moderated the relationship between trait anxiety and PTSD in a sample of sixth and seventh grade students exposed to Katrina. Anxiety sensitivity involves the expectancy that anxiety-related symptoms invariably lead to extremely negative consequences and is distinguished from trait anxiety, which is the propensity to experience anxiety sensations (i.e., anxiety sensitivity is a cognitive expectancy about anxiety sensations; trait anxiety is a propensity to experience anxiety sensations). Specifically, Hensley and Varela (2008) found that high trait anxiety coupled with high anxiety sensitivity is associated with the relatively highest PTSD symptoms. Their model suggests that anxiety sensitivity creates a cycle of anxiety amplification, resulting in extremely high levels of net anxiety that renders children less likely to adequately process and cope with the traumatic experience that is more than would occur with just high trait anxiety alone.

Another pre-existing factor that can shape adaptation to disaster exposure is developmental level (Salmon & Bryant, 2002). Although it is generally believed that children tend to be more severely affected by disasters than adults, no consensus has emerged regarding developmental differences in mental health problems prior to adulthood (Norris et al., 2002). Historically, researchers believed that preschool children were not highly affected by trauma exposure and our knowledge of how very young children respond to life-threatening traumatic events has lagged behind that of other age groups (Scheeringa & Zeanah, 2008; see also Buchanan, Casbergue, & Baumgartner, Chapter 1). Assessment of PTSD in preschool-aged children requires a developmentally sensitive approach. For example, Sprung (2008) demonstrated that young children's knowledge about the mind and its operations underlies their ability to monitor and report unwanted intrusive thoughts. Findings from the study by Sprung are consistent with the argument that certain symptoms of post-traumatic stress disorder (e.g., intrusive thinking, emotional numbing, and avoidance) can easily be overlooked in preschool children (Scheeringa, Zeanah, Myers, & Putnam, 2003). In fact, Scheeringa et al. (2003) have empirically validated alternative, developmentally sensitive diagnostic criteria for PTSD in young children. In their study of Katrina-exposed children, Scheeringa and Zeanah (2008) found that 50% of the children in their sample aged 3–6 years met criteria for PTSD following Katrina using the alternative criteria.

While there have been few longitudinal studies on the extended effects of Katrina that have appeared in the published literature to date, the first author (Weems et al., 2008) recently completed screening of a sample of over 200 New Orleans school children (grades 4 through 9) using the PTSD Reaction Index (Frederick, Pynoos, & Nadar, 1992) at two time points (Fall 2007 2 years post and Spring 2008 two-and-a-half years post). These youth were exposed to a number of Katrina-related traumatic experiences including losing contact with family and friends, having clothes and toys damaged, and temporary relocation to another city. In addition, as many as 68% had a home damaged or destroyed and 25% thought they might die at some point. In terms of PTSD symptoms, children were classified by severity of symptoms using the system developed by Frederick et al. (1992): Doubtful (score of 0–11), Mild (12–24), Moderate (25–39), Severe (40–59), and Very Severe (60–80). At time 1 sample reports indicated: "Doubtful" 26%, "Mild" 32%, "Moderate" 23%, "Severe" 16%, and "Very Severe" 5%. At time 2 the rates were highly similar: "Doubtful" 25%, "Mild" 36%, "Moderate" 23%, "Severe" 13%, and "Very Severe" 3%. Chi-square analyses indicated that youth were likely to retain their severity classification over time [$X^2(16) = 68.3$, $p < 0.001$]. Such findings point to the pervasive and chronic impact of Katrina given that the typical course of symptoms is usually one of remitting symptoms over time (La Greca et al., 2002). Moreover, the rates of at least "Severe" PTSD (i.e., a score of 40 or greater on the PTSD-RI) observed among samples of school-aged children exposed to Katrina and assessed much earlier were 12.6% (5–8 months following Hurricane Katrina; Hensley & Varela, 2008) and 11% (3–7 months following Hurricane Katrina; Spell et al., 2008).

Youth coping behaviors represent another potential moderator of psychological outcomes following natural disasters. For example, avoidant coping such as withdrawal is associated with greater PTSD symptoms (e.g., La Greca et al., 1996; Vernberg et al., 1996), while active coping such as problem-focused coping is associated with lower depression symptoms in youth hurricane survivors (e.g., Jeney-Gammon, Daugherty, Finch, Belter, & Foster, 1993). Pina et al. (2008) found that avoidant coping behaviors (i.e., repression, avoidant actions) predicted post-Katrina PTSD and anxiety symptoms, which is consistent with other research (Norris et al., 2002). However, they did not find evidence that active coping strategies (i.e., positive cognitive restructuring, problem focus coping) buffer youths' post-traumatic stress reactions. Terranova, Boxer, and Morris (in press) examined predictors of PTSD symptoms in a sample of 152 sixth grade school children from southeast Louisiana (neighboring Orleans parish) assessed at 1.5 months (time 1) and 8 months (time 2) after Katrina and found that negative coping (a combination of internalizing, externalizing and avoidant coping) was associated with PTSD at 1.5 months. Peer victimization (i.e., being bullied) was predictive of change in PTSD (PTSD symptoms at time 2 controlling for symptoms at time 1) and results further indicated that negative coping interacted with level of hurricane exposure to predict change in PTSD, such that high negative coping and high exposure were associated with the highest PTSD symptoms at time 2.

Conclusions

Research on Katrina-exposed samples of youth have added to the child and adolescent mental health knowledge at each level of influence posited by an ecological needs-based perspective. While research in this area still tends to focus on the individual child, the research to date does show that the impact of the Katrina disaster was felt at societal, community, family, and individual levels. Thus, one of the main lessons learned from the Katrina experience is that we must consider these multiple levels of impact when designing and implementing future research and prevention efforts. A very positive lesson is that interventions can be effective even in the wake of a disaster like Hurricane Katrina. The positive upshot of the ecological needs-based model is that while the model points to all the many potential negative influences on youth emotional development it also helps to show that there are just as many areas for intervention. Applying the extant empirical knowledge within the model we presented to the realm of policy suggests that efforts to prevent and minimize suffering in the wake of disaster will benefit from addressing each of these multiple levels of impact with interventions aimed at each of the ecologies (e.g., making sure government funding [macrosystem] is aimed at effective interventions [microsystem or ontogenic levels]). The perspective we have delineated and the data published to date on Katrina suggest that future researchers will benefit from considering in greater depth the contextual as well as individual influences on youth exposed to disaster.

References

Aber, J. L., Gershoff, E. T., Ware, A., & Kotler, J. A. (2004). Estimating the effects of September 11th and other forms of violence on the mental health and social development of New York City's youth: A matter of context. *Applied Developmental Science, 8*, 111–129.

Abramason, D., & Garfield, R. (2006). *On the edge – A report of the Louisiana child and family health study*. Retrieved from www.ncdp.mailman.columbia.edu/files/marshall_plan.pdf

Arnett, J. J. (2000). Emerging adulthood: A theory of development from the late teens through the twenties. *American Psychologist, 55*, 469–480.

Bobo, L. D. (2006). Katrina: Unmasking race, poverty, and politics in the 21st century. *Du Bois Review, 3*, 1–6.

Bourque, L. B., Siegel, J. M., Kano, M., & Wood, M. M. (2006). Weathering the storm: The impact of hurricanes on physical and mental health. *The Annals of the American Academy of Political and Social Science, 604*, 129–151.

Bronfenbrenner, U. (1977). Toward an experimental ecology of human development. *American Psychologist, 32*, 513–531.

Bronfenbrenner, U. (1979). *The ecology of human development*. Cambridge, MA: Harvard University Press.

Carrión, V. G., Weems, C. F., Eliez, S., Patwardhan, A., Brown, W., Ray R., et al. (2001). Attenuation of frontal lobe asymmetry in pediatric PTSD. *Biological Psychiatry, 50*, 943–951.

Carrión, V. G., Weems, C. F., & Reiss, A. L. (2007). Stress predicts brain changes in children: A pilot longitudinal study on youth stress, PTSD, and the hippocampus. *Pediatrics, 119*, 509–516.

Chavira, D. A., Stein, M. B., Bailey, K., & Stein, M. T. (2003). Parental opinions regarding treatment for social anxiety disorder in youth. *Journal of Developmental & Behavioral Pediatrics, 24*, 315–322.

Cole, P. M., & Zahn-Waxler, C. (1992). Emotional dysregulation in disruptive behavior disorders. In D. Cicchetti & S. L. Toth (Eds.), *Rochester symposium on developmental psychopathology: Vol. 4. Developmental perspectives on depression*(pp. 173–210). Rochester, NY: University of Rochester Press.

Comer, J. S., & Kendall, P. C. (2007). Terrorism: The psychological impact on youth. *Clinical Psychology: Science and Practice, 14*, 179–202.

De Bellis, M. D., Keshavan, M. S., Clark, D. B., Casey, B. J., Giedd, J. N., Boring, A. M., et al. (1999). Developmental traumatology: II. Brain development. *Biological Psychiatry, 45*, 1271–1284.

DeSalvo, K. B., Hyre, A. D., Ompad, D. C., Menke, A., Tynes, L. L., & Muntner, P. (2007). Symptoms of posttraumatic stress disorder in a New Orleans workforce following Hurricane Katrina. *Journal of Urban Health, 84*, 142–152.

Drury, S. S., Scheeringa, M. S., & Zeanah, C. H. (2008). The traumatic impact of Hurricane Katrina on children in New Orleans. *Child and Adolescent Psychiatric Clinics of North America, 17*, 685–702.

Dunst, C. J., Trivette, C. M., & Cross, A. H. (1986). Mediating influences of social support: Personal, family, and child outcomes. *American Journal of Mental Deficiency, 90*, 403–417.
Frederick, C. J., Pynoos, R. S., & Nadar, K. (1992). *Reaction index to psychic trauma Form C (Child)*. University of California, Los Angeles: Author.
Frick, P. J., & Morris, A. S. (2004). Temperament and developmental pathways to conduct problems. *Journal of Clinical Child and Adolescent Psychology, 33*, 54–68.
Greene, M. L., Way, N., & Pahl, K. (2006). Trajectories of perceived adult and peer discrimination among Black, Latino, and Asian American adolescents: Patterns and psychological correlates. *Developmental Psychology, 42*, 218–238.
Hensley, L., & Varela, R. E. (2008). PTSD symptoms and somatic complaints following Hurricane Katrina: The role of trait anxiety and anxiety sensitivity. *Journal of Clinical Child and Adolescent Psychology, 37*, 542–552.
Hobfoll, S. E. (1989). Conservation of resources: A new attempt at conceptualizing stress. *American Psychologist, 44*, 513–524.
Huddy, L., & Feldman, S. (2006). Worlds apart: Blacks and whites react to Hurricane Katrina. *Du Bois Review, 3*, 97–113.
Jeney-Gammon, P., Daugherty, T. K., Finch, A. J., Jr., Belter, R. W., & Foster, K. Y. (1993). Children's coping styles and report of depressive symptoms following a natural disaster. *The Journal of Genetic Psychology, 154*, 259–267.
King, L. A., King, D. W., Fairbank, J. A., Keane, T. M., & Adams, G. A. (1998). Resilience-recovery factors in post-traumatic stress disorder among female and male Vietnam veterans: Hardiness, postwar social support, and additional stressful life events. *Journal of Personality and Social Psychology, 74*, 420–434.
Klingman, A. (2002). Children under stress of war. In A. M. La Greca, W. K. Silverman, E. M. Vernberg, & M. C. Roberts (Eds.), *Helping children cope with disasters and terrorism* (pp. 359–380). Washington, DC: American Psychological Association.
La Greca, A. M., Silverman, W. K., Vernberg, E. M., & Prinstein, M. J. (1996). Symptoms of post-traumatic stress in children alter Hurricane Andrew: A prospective study. *Journal of Consulting and Clinical Psychology, 64*, 712–723.
La Greca, A. M., Silverman, W. K., Vernberg, E. M., & Roberts, M. C. (Eds.). (2002). *Helping children cope with disasters and terrorism*. Washington, DC: American Psychological Association.
La Greca, A. M., Silverman, W. K., & Wasserstein, S. B. (1998). Children's predisaster functioning as a predictor of posttraumatic stress following Hurricane Andrew. *Journal of Consulting and Clinical Psychology, 66*, 883–892.
Larrance, R., Anastario, M., & Lawry, L. (2007). Health status among internally displaced persons in Louisiana and Mississippi travel trailer parks. *Annals of Emergency Medicine, 49*, 590–601.
Lieberman, R. C. (2006). "The storm didn't discriminate." Katrina and the politics of color blindness. *Du Bois Review, 3*, 7–22.
Liu, A., & Plyer, A. (2007). *The New Orleans index*. Accessible at: http://www.gnocdc.org/KI/KatrinaIndex.pdf
Marsee, M. A. (2008). Reactive aggression and posttraumatic stress in adolescents affected by Hurricane Katrina. *Journal of Clinical Child and Adolescent Psychology, 39*, 519–529.
McNally, R. J., Bryant, R. A., & Ehlers, A. (2003). Does early psychological intervention promote recovery from posttraumatic stress? *Psychological Science in the Public Interest, 4*, 45–79.
Mojtabai, R., & Olfson, M. (2006). Treatment seeking for depression in Canada and the United States. *Psychiatric Services, 57*, 631–639.
Norris, F. H., Friedman, M. J., & Watson, P. J. (2002). 60,000 disaster victims speak: Part II. Summary and implications of the disaster mental health research. *Psychiatry, 65*, 240–260.
Nossiter, A. (2006, November 1). *After the storm, students left alone and angry*. New York Times, p. A1.
Osofsky, J. D., Osofsky, H. J., & Harris, W. W. (2007). Katrina's children: Social policy considerations for children in disasters. *Social Policy Report, 21*, 3–18.
Ozer, E. J., & Weiss, D. S. (2004). Who develops posttraumatic stress disorder? *Current Directions in Psychological Science, 13*, 169–172.

Piaget, J. (1983). Piaget's theory. In W. Kessen (Ed.), *Handbook of child psychology* (Vol. 1, pp. 103–128). New York: Wiley.

Pina, A. A., Villalta, I. K., Ortiz, C. D., Gottschall, A. C., Costa, N. M., & Weems, C. F. (2008). Social support, perceived discrimination, and coping as predictors of posttraumatic stress reactions in youth survivors of Hurricane Katrina. *Journal of Clinical Child and Adolescent Psychology, 37*, 564–574.

Pynoos, R. S., Goenijian, A. K., & Steinberg, A. M. (1998). A public mental health approach to post-disaster treatment of children and adolescents. *Child and Adolescent Psychiatry Clinics of North American, 7*, 195–210.

Rabalais, A. E., Ruggiero, K. J., & Scotti, J. R. (2002). Multicultural issues in the response of children to disasters. In A. M. La Greca, W. K. Silverman, E. M. Vernberg, & M. C. Roberts (Eds.), *Helping children cope with disasters and terrorism* (pp. 73–99). Washington, DC: American Psychological Association.

Salloum, A., & Overstreet, S. (2008). Evaluation of individual and group grief and trauma interventions for children post disaster. *Journal of Clinical Child and Adolescent Psychology, 37*, 495–507.

Salmon, K., & Bryant, R. A. (2002). Posttraumatic stress disorder in children: The influence of developmental factors. *Clinical Psychology Review, 22*, 163–188.

Sandler, I. (2001). Quality and ecology of adversity as common mechanisms of risk and resilience. *American Journal of Community Psychology, 29*, 19–61.

Sattler, D. N., Preston, A. J., Kaiser, C. F., Olivera, V. E., Valdez, J., & Schlueter, S. (2002). Hurricane Georges: A cross-national study examining preparedness, resource loss, and psychological distress in the U.S. Virgin Islands, Puerto Rico, Dominican Republic and the United States. *Journal of Traumatic Stress, 15*, 339–350.

Scaramella, L. V., Sohr-Preston, S. L., Callahan, K. L., & Mirabile, S. P. (2008). A test of the Family Stress Model on toddler-aged children's adjustment among Hurricane Katrina impacted and non-impacted low income families. *Journal of Clinical Child and Adolescent Psychology, 37*, 530–541.

Scheeringa, M. S., & Zeanah, C. H. (2008). Reconsideration of harm's way: Onsets and comorbidity patterns of disorders in preschool children and their caregivers following Hurricane Katrina. *Journal of Clinical Child and Adolescent Psychology, 37*, 508–518.

Scheeringa, M. S., Zeanah, C., Myers, L., & Putnam, F. (2003). New findings on alternative criteria for PTSD in preschool children. *Journal of the American Academy of Child and Adolescent Psychiatry, 42*, 561–570.

Silverman, W. K., & La Greca, A. M. (2002). Children experiencing disasters: Definitions, reactions, and predictors of outcomes. In A. M. La Greca, W. K. Silverman, E. M. Vernberg, & M. C. Roberts (Eds.), *Helping children cope with disasters* (pp. 11–34). Washington, DC: American Psychological Association.

Spell, A. W., Kelley, M. L., Self-Brown, S., Davidson, K., Pellegrin, A., Palcic, J., et al. (2008). The moderating effects of maternal psychopathology on children's adjustment post-Hurricane Katrina. *Journal of Clinical Child and Adolescent Psychology, 37*, 553–563.

Sprung, M. (2008). Unwanted intrusive thoughts and cognitive functioning and young elementary school children following Hurricane Katrina. *Journal of Clinical Child and Adolescent Psychology, 37*, 575–587.

Steptoe, A., & Hamer, M. (2007). Psychosocial determinants of the stress response. In M. Al'Absi (Ed.), *Stress and addiction: Biological and psychological mechanisms* (pp. 211–225). San Diego, CA: Elsevier.

Suveg, C., & Zeman, J. (2004). Emotion regulation in children with anxiety disorders. *Journal of Clinical Child and Adolescent Psychology, 33*, 750–759.

Terranova, A. M., Boxer, P., & Morris, A. S. (in press). Factors influencing the course of post traumatic stress following a natural disaster: Children's reactions to Hurricane Katrina. *Journal of Applied Developmental Psychology*.

Umaña-Taylor, A. J., & Updegraff, K. A. (2006). Latino adolescents' mental health: Exploring the interrelations among discrimination, ethnic identity, cultural orientation, self-esteem, and depressive symptoms. *Journal of Adolescence, 30*, 549–567.

Vernberg, E. M., La Greca, A. M., Silverman, W. K., & Prinstein, M. J. (1996). Prediction of posttraumatic stress symptoms in children after Hurricane Andrew. *Journal of Abnormal Psychology, 105*, 237–248.

Warren, S. L., & Sroufe, L. A. (2004). Developmental issues. In Ollendick, T. H. & March, J. S. (Eds), *Phobic and anxiety disorders in children and adolescents: A clinician's guide to effective psychosocial and pharmacological interventions* (pp. 92–115). New York: Oxford University Press.

Weems, C. F. (2008). Developmental trajectories of childhood anxiety: Identifying continuity and change in anxious emotion. *Developmental Review, 28*, 488–502.

Weems, C. F., & Costa, N. M. (2005). Developmental differences in the expression of childhood anxiety symptoms and fears. *Journal of the American Academy of Child and Adolescent Psychiatry, 44*, 656–663.

Weems, C. F., & Overstreet, S. (2008). Child and adolescent mental health research in the context of Hurricane Katrina: An ecological-needs-based perspective and introduction to the special section. *Journal of Clinical Child and Adolescent Psychology, 37*, 487–494.

Weems, C. F., Pina, A. A., Costa, N. M., Watts, S. E., Taylor, L. K., & Cannon, M. F. (2007). Predisaster trait anxiety and negative affect predict posttraumatic stress in youth after Hurricane Katrina. *Journal of Consulting and Clinical Psychology, 75*, 154–159.

Weems, C. F., Taylor, L. K., Costa, N. M., Marks, A. B., Romano, D. M., Verrett, S. L., et al. (2009). Effect of a school-based test anxiety intervention in ethnic minority youth exposed to Hurricane Katrina. *Journal of Applied Developmental Psychology, 30*, 218–226.

Weems, C. F., Taylor, L. K., Marks, A. B., Cannon, M. F., Ruiz, R., Romano, D. M., et al. (2008). *Post traumatic stress symptoms among New Orleans Public School youth exposed to Hurricane Katrina at two years and two and a half years post land-fall: A report on community need.* Louisiana: University of New Orleans.

Weems, C. F., Watts, S. E., Marsee, M. A., Taylor, L. K., Costa, N. M., Cannon, M. F., et al. (2007). The psychosocial impact of Hurricane Katrina: Contextual differences in psychological symptoms, social support, and discrimination. *Behaviour Research and Therapy, 45*, 2295–2306.

Weisler, R. H., Barbee, J. G., & Townsend, M. H. (2006). Mental health and recovery in the Gulf Coast after Hurricanes Katrina and Rita. *Journal of the American Medical Association, 296*, 585–588.

Chapter 3
Positive Adjustment in Youth Post-Katrina: The Impact of Child and Maternal Social Support and Coping

Julia F. Vigna, Brittany C. Hernandez, Valerie Paasch,
Arlene T. Gordon, and Mary L. Kelley

Abstract This chapter presents results of a longitudinal study conducted with youth and their parents post-Katrina. The study sought to identify both individual and family factors predictive of long-term positive adjustment in youth. Results indicated that family factors, such as parent-provided social support and coping through family routines and support, were paramount in predicting positive outcomes in youth 25–28 months post-Katrina. Youth with greater parent-provided support and who coped by relying on routines and support displayed greater long-term personal adjustment, as measured by interpersonal relations, self-reliance, and self-esteem.

Introduction

The profound effect of Hurricane Katrina penetrated family structure and dynamics, dividing households, and uprooting families and neighbors. However, many youth thrived despite this chaos. Some affected by the storm continued to have successful interpersonal relationships, academic success, and limited behavior problems. The focus of this chapter is on those disaster-exposed children and adolescents who displayed high levels of adjustment 25–28 months following Hurricane Katrina and the individual and family factors that may contribute to such positive outcomes. That many youths in this sample evidenced long-term positive outcomes is particularly noteworthy, considering the adverse living circumstances (e.g., pervasive violence exposure, low-income status, single-parent homes) that many of these southeastern Louisiana families faced daily.

Adjustment and Resilience Following Traumatic Events

There are many definitions of positive adjustment following a traumatic event, with resilience representing the most common conceptualization. Resilience has been defined as a dynamic process resulting in positive adaptation in the face of adversity

---

M.L. Kelley (✉)
Department of Psychology, Louisiana State University, Baton Rouge, LA 70803-5501, USA
e-mail: mkelley@lsu.edu

(Condly, 2006; Luthar, Cicchetti, & Becker, 2000; see also Chapter 9 of this volume). Although resilient individuals often experience mild, transient symptoms immediately following a stressor, they generally maintain pre-trauma levels of functioning (Bonanno, 2005; Williams, 2007). Researchers have identified three areas of functioning that reflect resilience or adaptive skills in youth: child individual factors, such as intellect and temperament; family factors, such as support and cohesion; and external factors, such as community, church, or school support (Garmezy, 1985, 1991; Werner, 1989). Importantly, Masten (2001) noted in her review of resilience literature that resilience is a common response that comprises ordinary processes. By this view, resilience results for most youth in the face of trauma, not just for a select few. Bonanno and others have echoed this perspective.

Resilience is multidimensional and can be differentially related to many areas of youth adjustment (Condly, 2006; Luthar et al., 2000). For example, Lipschitz-Elhawi and Itzhaky (2005) found specific family and child characteristics to be predictive of resilience in some areas, such as personal and academic adjustment, but not in others, such as interpersonal adjustment. To date, characteristics associated with positive adjustment post-trauma have been studied far less than variables related to maladjustment post-disaster. Nonetheless, resilience is now established as a vital area of study and provides a substantial literature base for drawing conclusions about factors related to positive outcomes post-trauma.

Another way in which positive adjustment post-trauma has been studied is through the construct of post-traumatic growth (PTG; Tedeschi & Calhoun, 1996, 2004). PTG is described as positive psychological growth in the aftermath of trauma and is conceptualized as growth in any of five areas: appreciation of life; meaningfulness of interpersonal relations; sense of personal strength; sense of new possibilities/change priorities; and spiritual growth. According to Tedeschi and Calhoun (2004), PTG results from the schema-disrupting quality of many traumas or crises and arises after extensive cognitive processing. That is, traumatic experiences often cause individuals to question their beliefs and views of the world, and it is through grappling with these challenges that trauma victims are somehow bettered in one or more of the aforementioned areas. The authors asserted that other factors, such as social support and self-disclosure (as through writing, talking, or praying), help forge the path of cognitive processing toward PTG. According to their theoretical model, automatic and intrusive rumination that is typically a proximal result of trauma develops into more deliberate cognitive processing and schema change (which then leads to growth) through self-disclosure, social support, and an eventual reduction in distress related to the rumination. Importantly, Tedeschi and Calhoun noted that PTG and psychological distress are not mutually exclusive and often coexist.

A fair amount of controversy has surrounded the concept of PTG. Hobfoll and colleagues (2007) argued against Tedeschi and Calhoun's (2004) conceptualization of PTG, stating that cognitive processing was not enough to produce benefits in the face of trauma. Instead, the authors argued, some sort of action or behavior related to newly acquired beliefs is necessary for an individual to derive benefits post-trauma. Hobfoll and colleagues also departed from Tedeschi and Calhoun with their suggestion that PTG cannot exist without a reduction in psychological symptomatology post-trauma. Finally, embedded within their argument is the notion that some aspects of PTG are "illusory" and that the idea of it can lead to negative consequences for some individuals (Hobfoll et al., 2007).

An important point in the study of positive adjustment post-trauma is that resilience and PTG are not synonymous. In a counter to Hobfoll and colleagues (2007), Westphal and Bonanno (2007) highlighted the differences between resilience and PTG, noting that "resilient outcomes typically provide little need or opportunity for PTG" (p. 419). That is, for individuals who maintain their existing levels of functioning following a potentially traumatic event, PTG is neither necessary nor a likely outcome because such individuals typically do not experience the same schema disruption that more traumatized individuals do. Thus, while PTG represents a provocative aspect of positive adjustment post-trauma, the construct has yet to be agreed upon or definitely described by empirical studies.

Although positive adjustment can be studied in the context of acute trauma, much consideration has been given to at-risk youth (e.g., those of low socioeconomic status or who are exposed to community violence) who confront chronic stressors. Researchers have identified assets that contributed to the success of urban African American children, including well-defined parent–child roles, a desire for education, prudence in behavior and decision making, good social skills, and positive self-esteem (Garmezy & Nuechterlain, 1972, *as cited in* Garmezy, 1991). In a study of South African youth exposed to chronic violence, Barbarin, Richter, and deWet (2001) found academic motivation to be related to family satisfaction and spirituality. In a sample of impoverished families, Wadsworth and Santiago (2008) found that coping through problem-solving and cognitive restructuring, a technique that involves critically evaluating and subsequently amending maladaptive thoughts, predicted reduced psychological symptoms in youth. Thus, youth exposed to chronic stressors may be resilient despite adverse circumstances, much like those who experience single traumas. The current study examines variables that may contribute to positive outcomes for youth exposed to both single-episode trauma (i.e., Hurricane Katrina) and chronic community violence.

Social Support and Adjustment

Social support has been defined as a multidimensional construct that includes physical and instrumental assistance, resource and information sharing, and emotional and psychological support (Lopez & Salas, 2006). Research has demonstrated that social support increases adults' ability to tolerate distressing life events (Norris & Kaniasty, 1996; Schumm, Briggs-Phillips, & Hobfoll, 2006). According to Vigil and Geary (2008), social support is among the strongest predictors of long-term mental health and physical functioning following a traumatic event. Cryder, Kilmer, Tedeschi, and Calhoun (2006) asserted that support aids in adaptive adjustment by encouraging expression of feelings, providing validation of event-related thoughts and feelings, and giving tangible assistance when needed.

Youth Social Support and Adjustment. As with adults, social support is related to positive adjustment in youth. Berman, Kurtines, Silverman, and Serafini (1996) found that social support buffered the effects of crime and violence exposure in youth; more social support was associated with the absence of post-traumatic stress disorder (PTSD), which is a disorder characterized by re-experiencing (such as through nightmares or flashbacks) of a traumatic event, along with avoidance of memories related to the event and hyperarousal, or feeling "keyed up" or "on edge" (see also Chapter 5 for discussion). In addition, perceived social support was a stronger predictor of positive outcomes than received social support. Likewise, Prevatt (2003) evaluated a model of children's adjustment with a focus on parenting practices and found family social support to predict better emotional functioning and higher academic achievement in youth.

Other evidence has shown that social support is related to positive adjustment following a natural disaster. For example, Cryder and colleagues (2006) found a positive relationship between supportive social environments and children's positive competency beliefs following a hurricane. Similarly, Vernberg, La Greca, Silverman, and Prinstein (1996) found that support from parents and classmates protected against the development of PTSD symptoms 7 months post-hurricane, while teacher support buffered adverse hurricane effects 10 months post-disaster. The current study evaluates longitudinally whether social support is related to positive outcomes in children following Hurricane Katrina.

Maternal Social Support and Youth Adjustment. Seldom, if ever, have researchers examined the relationship between maternal social support and youth adjustment following traumatic events. However, some research suggests that mothers with fewer and more negative social contacts parent more negatively than mothers with positive contacts, for example, using more coercion and responding less well to parenting treatment (Dumas & Wahler, 1983; Wahler, 1980). Furthermore, children behaved more negatively on days when their mothers experienced more negative contacts than on days with more positive contacts. In a longitudinal study of youth affected by Hurricane Katrina, Kelley and colleagues (2009) found that parents who reported lower levels of social support had children who endorsed significantly more PTSD symptoms 3–7 months following the storm, and this was significantly related to PTSD symptoms 14–17 months post-hurricane. The current study expands upon extant literature by examining the effect of maternal social support on the presence of positive attributes in youth post-hurricane.

Coping and Adjustment

Coping has been defined as actions and cognitions used to manage stressful demands (Lazarus & Folkman, 1984) and has been categorized in various ways (e.g., emotion focused vs. problem focused, approach vs. avoidant, escape oriented vs. control oriented; Chen & Chang, 2003; Folkman & Moskowitz, 2004; Lazarus & Folkman, 1984; Chapter 9 of this volume). Researchers have identified coping strategies related to adaptive vs. maladaptive outcomes following a traumatic event. For example, maladaptive coping strategies, such as blaming others and becoming angry, may affect adjustment more so than adaptive coping strategies, such as problem solving (Vernberg et al., 1996). However, research tends to inadequately describe specific coping strategies in relation to adjustment (Compas, 1987) and fails to employ psychometrically sound instruments for measuring coping (Vigna, Hernandez, Kelley, & Gresham, 2009).

Youth Coping and Adjustment. In general, problem solving, social support seeking, optimism, and active coping strategies appear to be related to higher levels of adjustment, while destructive or maladaptive coping is related to lower levels of adjustment (Brown, O'Keeffe, Sanders, & Baker, 1986; Jones & Ollendick, 2005). For example, in a review of the literature on youth coping and adjustment, Fields and Prinz (1997) found aggressive/destructive coping to be associated with poor adjustment while strategies such as problem solving, social support, approach coping, active coping, distraction, and positivity were generally related to better adjustment. Another study found that resilient children were more likely to employ coping strategies such as self-reliance and social support seeking and to be better problem solvers than their non-resilient counterparts (Parker, Cowen, Work, & Wyman, 1990). Through factor analysis, Hernandez, Vigna, and Kelley (2009) obtained a three-factor model of coping including diversion, ameliorative coping, and destructive coping, which was used in the current study. Diversion included strategies intended to turn one's attention away from distressing situations through reliance on family routines, spirituality, or overt distraction. Ameliorative coping included strategies intended to improve the situation through both problem-focused and emotion-focused techniques. Destructive coping included both destruction of property and self-destructive behaviors. The authors found that diversion was related to better personal adjustment in youth, while destructive behavior was related to increased distress.

Very few studies have examined the relation between youth coping and positive outcomes following a disaster. In one of the only studies to do so, Cryder and colleagues (2006) found that children's beliefs in their coping competency after Hurricane Floyd were positively related to PTG. The current study expands upon the scant body of literature on adjustment and resilience by examining coping behaviors related to long-term positive outcomes in youth exposed to Hurricane Katrina.

Parental Coping and Youth Adjustment. Research suggests that parental coping may influence children's adjustment. Bynum and Brody (2005) found that mothers who used problem-focused, rather than emotion-focused, coping had children who displayed greater self-control and less anger, which in turn resulted in fewer youth emotional and behavior problems. The relationship between maternal problem-focused coping and youth anger and self-control was mediated by an improved parent–child relationship. That is, an improved parent–child relationship was shown to be the mechanism through which maternal problem-focused coping attenuated anger symptoms and bolstered youth self-control. In a sample of asthmatic youth, mothers' use of active and cognitive coping was related to decreased anxiety and higher quality of life, whereas children whose mothers engaged in avoidant coping displayed greater anxiety and lower life quality (Sales, Fivush, & Teague, 2008).

Several studies suggest that the relationship between maternal coping and youth adjustment may be due to parental modeling. For example, Kliewer et al. (2006) found that caregiver modeling of and encouragement for using particular coping styles predicted youth coping. Likewise, Hoffman and Levy-Shiff (1994) found that adolescent boys' coping profiles matched those of their parents. The authors categorized youth and maternal coping as either emotionally, practically, or cognitively oriented and found that boys were more likely to use the same coping style as their mothers and less likely to use other styles. The relationship between parental coping and positive youth outcome is explored in the current study.

Current Study and Hypotheses

The adverse effects of disaster exposure on youth are well established (Kelley et al., in press; La Greca, Silverman, Vernberg, & Prinstein, 1996; Norris et al., 2002; Vernberg et al., 1996; see also Chapter 2 of this volume). However, factors contributing to positive outcomes for youth post-disaster remain unclear. The literature suggests that youth can experience positive adjustment in the face of chronic and acute stress. Parent and child social support has been shown to buffer against negative outcomes, such as PTSD, but their relation to positive outcomes is less certain. Likewise, more adaptive styles of parent and child coping have been shown to influence positive outcomes, while more maladaptive styles influence negative outcomes. However, little research has examined these influences in the context of a natural disaster. Furthermore, the widely accepted belief that parent attributes influence children's adjustment has not been empirically evaluated in a disaster-affected population. The present, longitudinal study addresses these shortcomings by examining the contributions of parent and youth social support and coping to the prediction of positive attributes in youth post-Hurricane Katrina.

A variety of maternal and youth experiences and behaviors were considered, and several hypotheses were tested. Table 3.1 presents information regarding measures used to assess all variables in the current study. Participants were 142 mother–child dyads recruited from various public and private elementary and middle schools in various "parishes" (i.e., counties) in southern Louisiana. Participants were recruited from Orleans Parish, Jefferson Parish (an immediate suburban county of New Orleans), and East Baton Rouge Parish (EBR; approximately 70 miles northwest of New Orleans). Although families in Orleans and Jefferson Parishes experienced more direct effects from Hurricane Katrina (e.g., being displaced), families from EBR also experienced wind damage and flooding. In addition, youth sampled from EBR were exposed to rates of community violence comparable to those of youth from New Orleans and surrounding areas, indicating that the groups were exposed to similar risk factors.

Youth who were suspected of having comprehension difficulties, such as children enrolled in special education for cognitive impairment or autism, were excluded from the study. At the time of recruitment, youth participants ranged in age from 8

3 Positive Adjustment in Youth

Table 3.1 Summary table of measures used

Variable	Measure and subscale(s) used in current study	Time of administration
Potential risk factors		
Hurricane exposure	*Hurricane-Related Traumatic Experiences* (HURTE; Vernberg et al., 1996)	Time 1[a]
	Life-threatening experiences ($\alpha = 0.58$)	
	Loss/disruption ($\alpha = 0.73$)	
Violence exposure	*Screen for Adolescent Violence Exposure* (SAVE; Hastings & Kelley, 1997)	Time 1
	Total score (z-score; $\alpha = 0.99$)	
	Kid-SAVE (Flowers, Hastings, & Kelley, 2000)	
	Total score (z-score; $\alpha = 0.97$)	
Potential protective factors		
Parent-provided social support to child	*Social Support Scale for Children* (SSSC; Harter, 1985)	Time 2[b]
	Parent support ($\alpha = 0.82$)>	
Youth coping	*Youth Coping Responses Inventory* (YCRI; Hernandez et al., 2009)	Time 2
	Diversion ($\alpha = 0.93$)	
	Ameliorative coping ($\alpha = 0.88$)	
	Destructive coping ($\alpha = 0.85$)	
Potential protective factors		
Parent received social support	*Interpersonal Support Evaluation List* (ISEL; Cohen & Hoberman, 1983)	Time 2
	Total score ($\alpha = 0.96$)	
Parent coping	*Brief COPE* (Carver, 1997)	Time 2
	Adaptive coping ($\alpha = 0.93$)[c]	
	Maladaptive coping ($\alpha = 0.85$)[c]	

Table 3.1 Continued

Variable	Measure and subscale(s) used in current study	Time of administration
Positive outcome variables		
Child-reported personal adjustment	*Behavioral Assessment System for Children, Second Edition, Self-Report of Personality-Child Version and Adolescent Version*(BASC-2 SRP; Reynolds & Kamphaus, 2004) Personal adjustment composite ($\alpha = 0.83$ for both versions)	Time 2
Parent-reported child adaptive skills	*Behavioral Assessment System for Children, Second Edition, Parent Report Scale-Child Version and Adolescent Version*(BASC-2 PRS; Reynolds & Kamphaus, 2004) Adaptive skills composite ($\alpha = 0.94$ for both versions)	Time 2

[a] Time 1: 4–7 months post-Katrina
[b] Time 2: 25–28 months post-Katrina
[c] Brief COPE factors derived from factor analysis of data gathered as part of the larger study from which this sample was taken
Note. All α's calculated using current sample.

to 15 with a mean age of 11.67 (*SD*= 1.51). The youth sample was 57.7% female, consisting of students enrolled in grades 4–8 (*M*= 6.06; *SD*= 1.34). The sample comprised predominantly African American families (59.3%). Family income ranged from $0 to over $100,000, with an average income between $15,000 and $24,999. More detailed demographic information is presented in Table 3.2.

Table 3.2 Demographic characteristics

	N	%
Child grade		
3	1	<1.0
4	21	14.8
5	31	21.8
6	28	19.7
7	38	26.8
8	23	16.2
Child sex		
Male	60	42.3
Female	82	57.7
Race/ethnicity		
African American	85	59.9
Caucasian	48	33.8
Asian American	5	3.5
Hispanic	4	2.8
Maternal marital status*		
Never married	44	31.7
Married	66	47.5
Previously married	29	20.9
Household type*		
Single parent	59	43.7
Two parent	76	56.3

*Indicates missing data

Participant evaluation took place in two phases: 3–7 months following Hurricane Katrina (referred to as Time 1 in this study) and 25–28 months following the hurricane (referred to as Time 2 in this study) as part of a larger grant funded research study (see Spell et al., 2008, for a detailed description). Most schools in Orleans Parish were closed for months following the storm (see Chapter 1). A few schools were open housing children from all over the district, which allowed for data collection from a range of students, despite the closure of most schools at Time 1. Information was obtained by youth self-report questionnaires as well as by parent self-report questionnaires.

Several hypotheses regarding maternal and youth risk and protective factors were tested.

Hypothesis 1. It was expected that heightened hurricane and community violence exposure would predict fewer positive outcomes, such as personal adjustment as measured by the BASC-2 Self-Report Profile.

Hypothesis 2. It was expected that youth endorsing more perceived social support from parents would display more positive adjustment on the BASC-2 Self-Report Profile 25–28 months post-Katrina than those endorsing less perceived social support from parents.

Hypothesis 3. It was predicted that positive youth coping strategies, such as diversion and ameliorative coping, would be associated with heightened adjustment in children and adolescents, while negative coping would be inversely related to positive outcome on the BASC-2.

Hypothesis 4. It was predicted that mothers reporting greater social support would have more well-adjusted children, while those reporting less social support would have children with fewer positive outcomes on the BASC-2.

Hypothesis 5. It was predicted that children whose mothers used more positive coping strategies would have more positive outcomes, while children whose mothers used negative coping strategies would display fewer positive outcomes on the BASC-2.

Results

Descriptive Statistics

Table 3.3 presents descriptive information for all continuous variables, including means, standard deviations, and minimum and maximum scores observed.

Hurricane Exposure. Frequency analyses were conducted for youths' reports of hurricane exposure at Time 1, including hurricane-related life threat and

Table 3.3 Means, standard deviations, and observed range for continuous variables

Variable	Mean	SD	Observed range	
			Minimum	Maximum
1. Child age	11.67	1.51	8.00	15.00
2. Hurricane life threat	0.61	0.73	0.00	3.00
3. Hurricane loss/disruption	2.89	2.25	0.00	8.00
4. Violence exposure (younger sample raw score)[a]	11.67	9.70	0.00	35.00
5. Violence exposure (older sample raw score)[a]	35.44	38.43	0.00	188.00
6. Child social support (parent provided)	3.60	0.52	1.00	4.00
7. Parent social support	89.01	22.40	15.00	120.00
8. Child coping (ameliorative)	2.03	0.60	1.00	3.64
9. Child coping (destructive)	1.55	0.48	1.00	3.79
10. Child coping (diversion	2.45	0.65	1.12	4.00
11. Parent adaptive coping	2.12	0.73	1.00	3.75
12. Parent maladaptive coping	1.33	0.47	1.00	3.22
13. Child-reported personal adjustment (T-score)	51.96	9.53	28	69
14. Parent-reported adaptive skills (T-score)	48.95	10.48	25	72

[a] Separate violence exposure measures exist for each age group

loss/disruption, on the HURTE. Many youth reported experiencing disruption and threat from the storm. For example, 43% of children reported that they were living in a house that still had damage 4–7 months after the hurricane, and 11% reported that their roof still leaked. When asked how scared or upset they were during the hurricane, 23% reported "a whole lot" and an additional 13% reported "a lot." Finally, 26% of children reported that they thought they might die at some point during the hurricane. The reports of damage found in this study are slightly greater than those found by La Greca and colleagues (1996), who reported that 27% of children still had damage to their homes 7 months after Hurricane Andrew. However, Vernberg and colleagues (1996) found that a greater number of children (60%) thought they might die during Hurricane Andrew.

Community Violence. Frequency analyses were conducted for children's reports of violence exposure in their homes, schools, or communities. Most youth tended to report some instances of witnessing, hearing about, or experiencing community violence. For example, 44% of youth reported seeing someone carry a gun either in their home, school, or neighborhood, and 70% reported seeing the police arrest someone in at least one of those three places. A sizeable minority of children (31%) reported that someone had threatened to beat them up at least once.

Youth and Parent Social Support. The parent-provided social support score was an average of scores on individual items. The mean score for this variable was 3.6 ($SD = 0.52$) out of a maximum score of 4, indicating that most children reported high levels of social support received from parents. The total scores for social support received by parents were much more variable ($M = 89.01$, $SD = 22.40$), but parents still tended to report receiving adequate social support.

Youth and Parent Coping. Youth reported using significantly more diversion than ameliorative coping [$t(141) = 8.46$, $p < 0.001$] and destructive coping [$t(141) = 16.62$, $p < 0.001$]. They also reported significantly more ameliorative coping than destructive coping [$t(141) = 9.48$, $p < 0.001$]. Similarly, parents tended to report higher use of adaptive coping than maladaptive coping [$t(141) = 12.90$, $p < 0.001$].

Positive Adjustment and Adaptive Skills. The BASC-2 measures are nationally normed measures intended to be interpreted in terms of T-scores (range of 0–100 with a mean of 50). According to children's reports of positive adjustment, only 1% reported clinically low levels of positive adjustment (i.e., T-scores 30 and below, as defined by BASC-2 manual), while there were no reports of very high levels of adjustment (i.e., T-scores 70 and above). High adjustment (i.e., T-scores between 60 and 69) was reported by 20% of youth. Most youth perceived themselves as being in the average range ($M = 51.96$, $SD = 9.53$). For parent-reported adaptive skills, only 3% reported clinically low levels of adaptive skills in their children, while 4% reported very high levels. High child adaptive skills were reported by 12% of parents ($M = 48.95$, $SD = 10.48$).

Regression Analyses

Hierarchical regression analyses were conducted to determine the roles of youth hurricane and violence exposure, youth and parental social support, and youth and parental coping in predicting positive outcomes in youth. Child-reported hurricane exposure (life threat and loss/disruption) and violence exposure were entered on the first step of the regression. Demographic variables (child sex and child age) were entered on step 2. Child social support (parent provided), child coping (ameliorative coping, destructive coping, and diversion), parental social support, and parental coping (adaptive and maladaptive) were entered on the final step.

Child-Reported Personal Adjustment. As shown in Table 3.4, the overall model predicting child-reported personal adjustment was significant [$F(12,129) = 6.39$, $p < 0.001$] and accounted for 37% of the variance. Results indicated that hurricane life threat was positively predictive of personal adjustment and uniquely accounted for 2% of the variance, as indicated by the sr^2 statistic, which represents the squared semipartial correlation and is an indication of unique variance or effect size (Tabachnik & Fidell, 2007; $B = 2.16$, $p = 0.036$, $sr^2 = 0.02$). Parent-provided social support was the greatest predictor of child-reported personal adjustment and uniquely accounted for 6% of the variance ($B = 5.16$, $p < 0.001$, $sr^2 = 0.06$). Child coping was the second greatest predictor of adjustment with diversion ($B = 5.01$, $p = 0.001$, $sr^2 = 0.05$) predicting adjustment in the positive direction (uniquely accounting for 5% of the variance) and destructive coping ($B = -4.26$, $p = 0.027$, $sr^2 = 0.02$) negatively predicting adjustment (uniquely accounting for 2% of the variance). In addition, child sex was predictive of adjustment such that females were more likely to show greater adjustment ($B = 3.11$, $p = 0.031$, $sr^2 = 0.02$). Child-reported hurricane loss/disruption, exposure to community violence, child age, parental social support, child ameliorative coping, and parental coping were not significantly predictive of child-reported personal adjustment in the final model.

Table 3.4 Regression analyses predicting child-reported personal adjustment

	R^2	ΔR^2	B	β	Sr^2	F model
Step 1	0.02					$F(3,138) = 0.91$
Hurricane loss/disruption			2.16*	0.17	0.02	
Hurricane loss/disruption			0.14	0.03	0.00	
Violence exposure			−1.01	−0.10	0.01	
Step 2	0.03	0.01				$F(5,136) = 0.93$
Child sex			3.11*	0.16	0.02	
Child age			0.14	0.02	0.00	
Step 3	0.37	0.34				$F(12,129) = 6.39**$
Child social support			5.16**	0.28	0.06	
Parent social support			0.04	0.10	0.01	
Child coping (ameliorative)			2.12	0.13	0.01	
Child coping (destructive)			−4.26*	−0.22	0.02	
Child coping (diversion)			5.01**	0.34	0.05	
Parent adaptive coping			0.99	0.08	0.00	
Parent maladaptive coping			0.86	0.04	0.00	

* Significant at the 0.05 level
** Significant at the 0.01 level

Table 3.5 Regression analyses predicting parent-reported adaptive skills

	R^2	ΔR^2	B	β	sr^2	F model
Step 1	0.04					$F(3,136) = 1.90$
Hurricane life threat			−1.45	−0.11	0.01	
Hurricane loss/disruption			0.71	0.15	0.02	
Violence exposure			−0.72	−0.06	0.00	
Step 2	0.06	0.02				$F(5,134) = 1.75$
Child sex			1.42	0.07	0.00	
Child age			−0.22	−0.03	0.00	
Step 3	0.37	0.31				$F(12,127) = 6.21^{**}$
Child social support			3.42*	0.18	0.03	
Parent social support			0.23**	0.49	0.15	
Child coping (ameliorative)			1.20	0.07	0.00	
Child coping (destructive)			−0.37	−0.02	0.00	
Child coping (diversion)			−0.05	−0.00	0.00	
Parent adaptive coping			1.41	0.10	0.01	
Parent maladaptive coping			−1.43	−0.07	0.00	

* Significant at the 0.05 level
** Significant at the 0.01 level

Parent-Reported Child Adaptive Skills. Regression analyses predicting parent-reported child adaptive skills were conducted to further elucidate the relation between positive youth outcomes and coping and social support. As indicated in Table 3.5, the final model was significant [$F(12,127) = 6.21$, $p < 0.001$] and accounted for 37% of the variance. Results indicated that social support received by the parent was the strongest predictor of parent-reported child adaptive skills and uniquely accounted for 15% of the variance ($B = 0.23$, $p < 0.001$, $sr^2 = 0.15$). Parent-provided social support to the child also significantly predicted child positive outcome and uniquely accounted for 3% of the variance ($B = 3.42$, $p = 0.026$, $sr^2 = 0.03$). Greater parent-received and parent-provided social support predicted greater adaptive skills in children. No other variables significantly predicted adaptive skills.

Discussion

The current study examined the roles of individual youth and family factors in predicting positive outcomes in youth following Hurricane Katrina. Previous research has examined the presence of negative symptoms post-hurricane (e.g., La Greca et al., 1996; Vernberg et al., 1996), but no literature exists that has studied longitudinally the presence of positive attributes in youth following a disaster. The current study tested a number of hypotheses regarding the roles of social support and coping in predicting youth adjustment, and the predictions were partially supported.

The hypothesis that hurricane and violence exposure would be inversely related to positive outcomes following Hurricane Katrina was not supported. Hurricane-related life-threatening experiences were positively related to personal adjustment, indicating that youth who experienced a greater degree of life threat during the storm also evidenced better adjustment 25–28 months post-hurricane. These findings may be surprising, considering past research that demonstrates a link between severity of disaster exposure and psychological distress (e.g., Asarnow et al., 1999), as well as a relationship between violence exposure and poor youth adjustment (e.g., Garbarino, 2002). However, the results of this study are consistent with the notion of PTG, which posits that individuals can develop positive attributes after experiencing a trauma (Tedeschi & Calhoun, 1996, 2004). It is possible that youth in this study who were faced with greater life-threatening experiences were forced to draw on their own strength of character, using attributes such as leadership or strong interpersonal skills, when faced with crisis situations during the storm. Nonetheless, definitive causal conclusions must not be drawn from a study of correlational nature, such as this one. It is also possible that surviving extreme disaster exposure gave youth in this study a better sense of self-reliance and self-esteem. Alternatively, it is possible that severity of hurricane exposure and prior violence exposure would have been negatively related to personal adjustment at an earlier point in time, closer to the actual experience of the hurricane.

The hypothesis that youth who received greater social support would evidence better outcomes post-Katrina was fully supported. Parent-provided social support was the strongest predictor of child-reported personal adjustment in children and adolescents, which points to the importance of parent support and involvement in a child's life post-disaster. That parent-provided support was of paramount importance to this sample of predominantly African American youth is logical, considering the importance of kinship support (i.e., support from family members and other adults) to coping ability and resilience in African American youth (see Jones, 2007; Chapter 7 of this volume).

It was also hypothesized that positive coping strategies such as diversion and ameliorative coping would be associated with greater personal adjustment, while destructive coping would predict poor outcomes post-Katrina. This hypothesis was partially supported. Diversion, which includes coping strategies such as blatant distraction (e.g., "played sports to forget") as well as more subtle forms of distraction (i.e., returning to family routines, drawing on social support, and relying on positivity and spirituality) significantly predicted positive outcome in youth. Each of the specific coping strategies subsumed by diversion has been shown to relate to decreased levels of distress or increased levels of adjustment (Jeney-Gammon, Daugherty, Finch, Belter, & Foster, 1993; La Greca et al., 1996; Salsman, Brown, Brechting, & Carlson, 2005). Ameliorative coping, which includes coping strategies that attempt to improve the problem either through problem solving or through attempts to express one's emotions about the problem, was not associated with positive outcomes after the storm, while destructive coping was inversely related with positive outcomes post-Katrina.

Diversion would likely be considered a problem-avoidant coping strategy based on existing classifications of coping (e.g., Altshuler & Ruble, 1989; Lazarus & Folkman, 1984), whereas ameliorative coping is generally problem focused.

Although problem-focused strategies are typically related to better adjustment (Brown et al., 1986; Fields & Prinz, 1997) and avoidant strategies are associated with greater distress (Blount, Davis, Powers, & Roberts, 1991; Jones & Ollendick, 2005; Tyc, Mulhern, Jayawardene, & Fairclough, 1995), some authors suggest that emotion focused or avoidant coping is more appropriate for uncontrollable circumstances (Altshuler & Ruble, 1989; Compas, Banez, Malcarne, & Worsham, 1991; Donaldson, Prinstein, Danovsky, & Spirito, 2000; Tyc et al., 1995). Thus, considering the uncontrollable nature of Hurricane Katrina and the chronic community violence to which this sample is exposed, it is not surprising that diversion from the stressor proved adaptive, while efforts to improve the problem were not predictive of positive outcomes. Nonetheless, this interpretation contradicts the findings of Pina and colleagues (2008), who found that avoidant coping was a positive predictor of PTSD symptoms in youth post-Katrina. Clearly, further research is warranted.

Destructive coping was a strong negative predictor of child-reported adaptive outcomes post-Katrina. Destructive coping includes behaviors such as the destruction of property (e.g., "destroyed things") as well as behaviors that can be considered self-destructive (e.g., "took it out on myself"). These findings are consistent with literature suggesting that behaviors such as social withdrawal and blaming others are detrimental to adjustment (e.g., Spirito, Francis, Overholser, & Frank, 1996; Stallard, Velleman, Langsford, & Baldwin 2001). The findings also align with those of Vernberg and colleagues (1996), who studied youth post-hurricane and found coping strategies such as blame and anger to be the most highly predictive of PTSD. The findings complement extant literature by demonstrating that negative, destructive coping behaviors are not only directly related to adverse outcomes (e.g., PTSD) but also inversely related to positive outcomes, such as effective interpersonal relations, self-reliance, and self-esteem.

The hypothesis that children of parents who received greater social support would themselves report greater personal adjustment post-Katrina was not supported. The amount of social support received by parents was not related to positive outcomes reported by youth. This finding is surprising considering Kelley and colleagues' (2009) finding that youth of parents reporting low levels of social support evidenced more PTSD symptoms than their counterparts. However, these findings emphasize the fact that positive outcomes do not represent merely the absence of negative symptoms, but rather the presence of positive attributes, such as self-reliance and high self-esteem.

Finally, it was hypothesized that children of mothers endorsing adaptive coping strategies would report better outcomes post-Katrina than children of mothers endorsing maladaptive coping strategies. This hypothesis was not supported, which is inconsistent with literature that documents a relation between maternal coping and youth outcome (e.g., Bynum & Brody, 2005). The results of this study seem to indicate that coping behaviors employed by youth themselves may be of greater importance than parental coping behavior.

Additional Findings

Results also indicated that girls reported better personal adjustment than boys, suggesting that girls may exhibit more self-reliance and better self-esteem and interpersonal relationships post-disaster than their male counterparts. These results are surprising considering literature which indicates that being a female is a risk factor for psychological distress following a disaster (Norris et al., 2002). However, the results may indicate that positive attributes and psychological symptoms can coexist and are not necessarily opposing ends of a continuum. More research is needed to further explicate such a relationship.

Additional analyses examined the roles of coping and social support in predicting parents' reports of youth adaptive skills, such as leadership, functional communication, and adaptability. Parents' received social support was the strongest predictor of parent-reported youth adaptive skills. This finding is consistent with literature demonstrating that mothers who have fewer social contacts parent more negatively and have more poorly behaved children. Alternatively, this finding may indicate that caregivers who receive adequate social support more readily recognize attributes such as leadership and adaptability in their children than their support-deficient counterparts. In addition, parent-provided social support significantly predicted youth's adaptive skills, which was consistent with the relation demonstrated between parent-provided social support and child-reported personal adjustment. Thus, it appears that parent-provided social support is associated with positive outcomes in youth from both the child and parent perspectives, and this finding is consistent with extant literature suggesting the importance of familial support (e.g., Prevatt, 2003).

Study Strengths and Limitations

This project represents the first longitudinal study to examine predictors of positive outcomes in youth post-disaster. In addition, the sample employed was heterogeneous in that it included participants with a range of family situations, incomes, and ethnicities in and surrounding New Orleans, which may permit broader generalizations. Though this study begins to fill a gap in the current literature, it has some important limitations to note. First, as this study is correlational in nature, causal conclusions cannot be drawn from the data. It is possible that the relations found in the study are bidirectional, or reciprocal, in nature, such that positive attributes like personal adjustment and adaptive skills may precipitate or work synergistically with particular coping styles or increased social support. In addition, baseline (i.e., pre-Katrina) data are not available on the current sample, so it is impossible to determine whether or not well-adjusted youth in this sample displayed positive attributes before the storm.

Conclusions, Implications, and Future Research

This study provides an important first step in longitudinal research examining positive outcomes post-trauma, but further research is needed to fully elucidate protective factors following a disaster. Future research should comprise prospective studies, thus allowing for baseline data to help clarify the role of disaster-related influences on behavior. Research related to PTG in youth post-disaster is currently lacking, and this represents another important future direction in the study of positive outcomes following a hurricane. In addition, it would be beneficial to identify varying trajectories of youth who evidence highly positive adjustment vs. those who suffer severe psychological symptoms post-disaster, as such information would be useful in planning individual and schoolwide interventions for youth. Finally, considering the gender difference found in this study, future research should consider whether gender moderates the relation between positive outcome and social support or coping.

Perhaps the single most important revelation of the current study is the dominance of parent-provided support in the long-term prediction of youth interpersonal skills, self-reliance, and self-esteem post-disaster. This finding supports research emphasizing the importance of familial support among youth and can guide parents in how best to assist their children in the aftermath of trauma. Moreover, it is fitting that coping through diversion was nearly as strong a predictor of child-reported positive outcomes as parent-provided support, given that this coping style relies heavily on returning to family routines and eliciting social support. This finding bolsters the importance of parents' and families' roles in post-trauma adjustment (see Chapter 7, for a related discussion). Taken together, these findings suggest that families, and parents in particular, are of paramount importance in the long-term development of positive attributes in youth following large-scale disaster exposure. Given this information, practitioners and policymakers should assist parents in recognizing the importance of their roles in their children's adjustment post-disaster, which in turn will help promote the development of positive personal attributes among youth in the face of adversity or traumatic experiences.

Acknowledgments Completion of this study was supported in part by a research grant from the National Institute of Mental Health (RMH-078148A).

References

Altshuler, J. L., & Ruble, D. N. (1989). Developmental changes in children's awareness of strategies for coping with uncontrollable stress. *Child Development, 60*, 1337–1349.

Asarnow, J., Glynn, S., Pynoos, R. S., Nahum, J., Guthrie, D., Cantwell, D. P., et al. (1999). When the earth stops shaking: Earthquake sequelae among children diagnosed for pre-earthquake psychopathology. *Journal of the American Academy of Child and Adolescent Psychiatry, 38*(8), 1016–1023.

Barbarin, O., Richter, L., & deWet, T. (2001). Exposure to violence, coping resources, & psychological adjustment of South African children. *American Journal of Orthopsychiatry, 71*, 16–25.

Berman, S. L., Kurtines, W. M., Silverman, W. K., & Serafini, L. T. (1996). The impact of exposure to crime and violence on urban youth. *American Journal of Orthopsychiatry, 66*, 329–336.

Blount, R. L., Davis, N., Powers, S. W., & Roberts, M. C. (1991). The influence of environmental factors and coping style on children's coping and distress. *Clinical Psychology Review, 11*, 93–116.

Bonanno, G. A. (2005). Resilience in the face of potential trauma. *Current Directions in Psychological Science, 14*, 135–138.

Brown, J. M., O'Keeffe, J., Sanders, S. H., & Baker, B. (1986). Developmental changes in children's cognition to stressful and painful situations. *Journal of Pediatric Psychology, 11*, 343–357.

Bynum, M. S., & Brody, G. H. (2005). Coping behaviors, parenting, and perceptions of children's internalizing and externalizing problems in rural African American mothers. *Family Relations, 54*, 58–71.

Carver, C. S. (1997). You want to measure coping but your protocol's too long: Consider the Brief COPE. *International Journal of Behavioral Medicine, 4*, 92–100.

Chen, S. T., & Chang, A. C. (2003). Factorial structure of the Kidcope in Hong Kong adolescents. *The Journal of Genetic Psychology, 164*, 261–266.

Cohen, S., & Hoberman, H. (1983). Positive events and social supports as buffers of life change stress. *Journal of Applied Social Psychology, 13*, 99–125.

Compas, B. E. (1987). Coping with stress during childhood and adolescence. *Psychological Bulletin, 101*, 393–403.

Compas, B. E., Banez, G. A., Malcarne, V., & Worsham, N. (1991). Perceived control and coping with stress: A developmental perspective. *Journal of Social Issues, 47*, 23–34.

Condly, S. (2006). Resilience in children: A review of the literature with implications for education. *Urban Education, 41*, 211–236.

Cryder, C. H., Kilmer, R. P., Tedeschi, R. G., & Calhoun, L. G. (2006). An exploratory study of posttraumatic growth in children following a natural disaster. *American Journal of Orthopsychiatry, 76*, 65–69.

Donaldson, D., Prinstein, M. J., Danovsky, M., & Spirito, A. (2000). Patterns of children's coping with life: Implications for clinicians. *American Journal of Orthopsychiatry, 70*, 351–359.

Dumas, J. E., & Wahler, R. G. (1983). Predictors of treatment outcome in parent training: Mother insularity and mother disadvantage. *Behavioral Assessment, 5*, 301–313.

Fields, L., & Prinz, R. J. (1997). Coping and adjustment during childhood and adolescence. *Clinical Psychology Review, 17*, 937–976.

Flowers, A. L., Hastings, T. L., & Kelley, M. L. (2000). Development of a screening instrument for exposure to violence in children: The KID-SAVE. *Journal of Psychopathology and Behavioral Assessment, 22*, 91–104.

Folkman, S., & Moskowitz, J. T. (2004). Coping: Pitfalls and promises. *Annual Review of Psychology, 55*, 745–774.

Garbarino, J. (2002). Pathways from childhood trauma to adolescent violence and delinquency. In R. Greenwald (Ed.), *Trauma and juvenile delinquency: Theory, research, and interventions* (pp. xix–xxv). New York: The Haworth Press, Inc.

Garmezy, N. (1985). Stress-resistant children: The search for protective factors. In J. E. Stevenson (Ed.), *Recent research in developmental psychopathology (Journal of Child Psychology and Psychiatry* Book Supp. No. 4, pp. 213–233). Oxford: Pergamon.

Garmezy, N. (1991). Resiliency and vulnerability to adverse developmental outcomes associated with poverty. *American Behavioral Scientist, 34*, 416–430.

Garmezy, N., & Neuchterlain, K. (1972, April). *Invulnerable children: The fact and fiction of competence and disadvantage.* Paper presented at the 49th Annual Meeting of the American Orthopsychiatric Association, Detroit, MI.

Harter, S. (1985). *Manual for the social support scale for children.* Denver: University of Denver.

Hastings, T. L., & Kelley, M. L. (1997). Development and validation of the Screen for Adolescent Violence Exposure (SAVE). *Journal of Abnormal Child Psychology, 25*, 511–520.

Hernandez, B. C., Vigna, J. F., & Kelley, M. L. (2009). The youth coping responses inventory: Development and initial validation. *Manuscript submitted for publication.*

Hobfoll, S. E., Hall, B. J., Canetti-Nisim, D., Galea, S., Johnson, R. J., & Palmieri, P. (2007). Refining our understanding of traumatic growth in the face of terrorism: Moving from meaning cognitions to doing what is meaningful. *Applied Psychology: An International Review, 56,* 345–366.

Hoffman, M. A., & Levy-Shiff, R. (1994). Coping and locus of control: Cross-generational transmission between mothers and adolescents. *The Journal of Early Adolescence, 14,* 391–405.

Jeney-Gammon, P., Daugherty, T. K., Finch, A. J., Belter, R. W., & Foster, K. Y. (1993). Children's coping styles and report of depressive symptoms following a natural disaster. *The Journal of Genetic Psychology, 154,* 259–267.

Jones, J. M. (2007). Exposure to chronic community violence: Resilience in African American children. *Journal of Black Psychology, 33,* 125–149.

Jones, R. T., & Ollendick, T. H. (2005). Risk factors for psychological adjustment following residential fire: The role of avoidant coping. *Journal of Trauma & Dissociation, 6,* 85–99.

Kelley, M. L., Palcic, J. L., Vigna, J. F., Spell, A. W., Pellegrin, A., Davidson, K. L., et al. (2009). The effects of parenting behavior on children's mental health post-Hurricane Katrina. In R. P. Kilmer, Gil-Rivas, V.,Tedeschi, R. G., & Calhoun, L. G. (Eds.), *Meeting the needs of children, families, and communities post-disaster: Lessons learned from Hurricane Katrina and its aftermath.* Washington, DC: American Psychological Association (in press).

Kelley, M. L., Self-Brown, S., Le, B., Vigna, J. F., Hernandez, B. C., & Gordon, A. T. (2009). Predicting posttraumatic stress symptoms in children following Hurricane Katrina: A longitudinal analysis of child and family variables. *Manuscript submitted for publication.*

Kliewer, W., Parrish, K. A., Taylor, K. W., Jackson, K., Walker, J. M., & Shivy, V. A. (2006). Socialization of coping with community violence: Influences of caregiver coaching, modeling, and family context. *Child Development, 77,* 605–623.

La Greca, A. M., Silverman, W. K., Vernberg, E. M., & Prinstein, M. J. (1996). Symptoms of posttraumatic stress after Hurricane Andrew: A prospective study. *Journal of Consulting and Clinical Psychology, 64,* 712–723.

Lazarus, R. S., & Folkman, S. (1984). *Stress appraisal and coping.* New York: Springer.

Lipschitz-Elhawi, R., & Itzhaky, H. (2005). Social support, mastery, self-esteem, and individual adjustment among at-risk youth. *Child and Youth Care Forum, 34,* 329–346.

Lopez, E. J., & Salas, L. (2006). Assessing social support in Mexican American high school students: A validity study. *Journal of Hispanic Higher Education, 5,* 97–106.

Luthar, S. S., Cicchetti, D., & Becker, B. (2000). The construct of resilience: A critical evaluation and guidelines for future work. *Child Development, 71,* 543–562.

Masten, A. S. (2001). Ordinary magic: Resilience processes in development. *American Psychologist, 56,* 227–238.

Norris, F. H., Friedman, M. J., Watson, P. J., Byrne, C. M., Diaz, E., & Kaniasty, K. (2002). 60,000 disaster victims speak, Part I: An empirical review of the empirical literature, 1981–2001. *Psychiatry, 65,* 207–239.

Norris, F. H., & Kaniasty, K. (1996). Received and perceived social support in times of stress: A test of the social support deterioration deterrence model. *Journal of Personality and Social Psychology, 71,* 498–511.

Parker, G. R.,Cowen, E. L.,Work, W. C., & Wyman, P. A. (1990). Test correlates of stress resilience among urban school children. *Journal of Primary Prevention, 11,* 19–35.

Pina, A. A., Villalta, I. K., Oritz, C. D., Gottschall, A. C., Costa, N. M., & Weems, C. F. (2008). Social support, discrimincation, and coping as predictors of posttraumatic stress reactions in youth survivors of Hurricane Katrina. *Journal of Clinical Child and Adolescent Psychology, 37,* 564–574.

Prevatt, F. F. (2003). The contribution of parenting practices in a risk and resiliency model of children's adjustment. *British Journal of Developmental Psychology, 21,* 469–480.

Reynolds, C. R., & Kamphaus, R. W. (2004). *Behavior assessment system for children* (2nd ed. manual). Circle Pines, MN: American Guidance Service.

Sales, J., Fivush, R., & Teague, G. W. (2008). The role of parental coping in children with asthma's psychological well-being and asthma-related quality of life. *Journal of Pediatric Psychology, 33*, 208–219.

Salsman, J. M., Brown, T. L., Brechting, E. H., & Carlson, C. R. (2005). The link between religion and spirituality and psychological adjustment: The mediating role of optimism and social support. *Personality and Social Psychology Bulletin, 31*, 522–535.

Schumm, J. A., Briggs-Phillips, M., & Hobfoll, S. E. (2006). Cumulative interpersonal traumas and social support as risk and resiliency factors in predicting PTSD and depression among inner-city women. *Journal of Traumatic Stress, 19*, 825–836.

Spell, A. W., Kelley, M. L., Wang, J., Self-Brown, S., Davidson, K. L., Pellegrin, A., et al. (2008). The moderating effects of maternal psychopathology on children's adjustment post-Hurricane Katrina. *Journal of Clinical Child and Adolescent Psychology, 37*, 553–563.

Spirito, A., Francis, G., Overholser, J., & Frank, N. (1996). Coping, depression, and adolescent suicide attempts. *Journal of Clinical Child Psychology, 25*, 147–155.

Stallard, P., Velleman, R., Langsford, J., & Baldwin, S. (2001). Coping and psychological distress in children involved in road traffic accidents. *British Journal of Clinical Psychology, 40*, 197–208.

Tabachnik, B. G., & Fidell, L. S. (2007). *Using multivariate statistics* (5th ed.). Boston: Pearson.

Tedeschi, R. G., & Calhoun, L. G. (2004). Posttraumatic growth: Conceptual foundations and empirical evidence. *Psychological Inquiry, 15*, 1–18.

Tedeschi, R. G., & Calhoun, L. G. (1996). The posttraumatic growth inventory: Measuring the positive legacy of trauma. *Journal of Traumatic Stress, 9*, 455–471.

Tyc, V. L., Mulhern, R. K., Jayawardene, D., & Fairclough, D. (1995). Chemotherapy-induced nausea and emesis in pediatric cancer patients: An analysis of coping strategies. *Journal of Pain and Symptom Management, 10*, 338–347.

Vernberg, E. M., La Greca, A. M., Silverman, W. K., & Prinstein, M. J. (1996). Prediction of posttraumatic stress symptoms in children after Hurricane Andrew. *Journal of Abnormal Psychology, 105*, 237–248.

Vigil, J. M., & Geary, D. C. (2008). A preliminary investigation of family coping styles and psychological well being among adolescent survivors of Hurricane Katrina. *Journal of Family Psychology, 22*, 176–180.

Vigna, J. F., Hernandez, B. C., Kelley, M. L., & Gresham, F. M. (2009). Coping behaviors in hurricane-affected African American youth: Psychometric properties of the Kidcope. *Journal of Black Psychology* (in press).

Wadsworth, M., & Santiago, C. (2008). Risk and resiliency processes in ethnically diverse families in poverty. *Journal of Family Psychology, 22*, 399–410.

Wahler, R. G. (1980). The insular mother: Her problems in parent–child treatment. *Journal of Applied Behavior Analysis, 13*, 207–219.

Werner, E. E. (1989). High-risk children in young adulthood: A longitudinal study from birth to 32 years. *American Journal of Orthopsychiatry, 59*, 72–81.

Westphal, M., & Bonanno, G. A. (2007). Posttraumatic growth: Different sides of the same coin or different coins? *Applied Psychology: An International Review, 56*, 417–427.

Williams, R. (2007). Psychosocial consequences for children of mass violence, terrorism, and disasters. *International Review of Psychiatry, 19*, 263–277.

Chapter 4
The Impact of Hurricane Katrina on Children and Adolescents: Conceptual and Methodological Implications for Assessment and Intervention

Russell T. Jones, Kelly Dugan Burns, Christopher S. Immel, Rachel M. Moore, Kathryn Schwartz-Goel, and Bonnie Culpepper

Abstract Hurricane Katrina was one of the most devastating natural disasters the United States has ever encountered. Although many were adversely affected by Hurricane Katrina, this chapter focuses on children and the role traumatic events can play on their mental health. The chapter begins with an overview of the immediate and ongoing efforts of the first author and his associates in the wake of Katrina. These efforts include deployments to the Gulf Coast and his briefing of the then First Lady, Laura Bush, on the psychological ramifications that traumatic events can have on children and adolescents. A review of the research literature regarding the impact of Hurricane Katrina on youth survivors follows. Recommendations for assessment and post-disaster intervention efforts are made within the context of the dose–response model. This conceptual model illustrates the roles of many risk and protective factors, including exposure, social support, coping, race/ethnicity, age, gender, parent–child interaction. The chapter concludes with recommendations for future clinical and research initiatives.

Introduction

> I've got a hole in my roof, but a greater hole in my heart because no one is looking out for the kids.
> —Jeanne Brooks (October 2006)

On August 29, 2005, Hurricane Katrina hit southeast Louisiana as a Category 3 hurricane, becoming the third most intense hurricane to make landfall in the United States. As it moved up the coast of Mississippi, its devastating winds and destructive powers resulted in Hurricane Katrina becoming the nation's most

---

R.T. Jones (✉)
Department of Psychology, Virginia Polytechnic Institute and State University, Blacksburg, VA 24061, USA
e-mail: rtjones@vt.edu

economically damaging storm in history (National Oceanic & Atmospheric Administration, 2006). Thousands lost their homes and loved ones, and relief efforts were made on a local, state, and national level. Although numerous relief efforts were activated, the enormity of the storms rendered many such efforts inadequate. Once again, clinical psychologists were called upon to aid our nation in the midst of yet another crisis. In terms of natural and technological disasters, this one proved to be the most challenging by far. Katrina was indeed a new benchmark for such natural disasters on American soil.

This chapter is organized as follows. The immediate and ongoing efforts of the first author and members of his team will be highlighted first. A review of available assessment and intervention research efforts targeting children and adolescents is presented next. The relative contribution of these scientific investigations to the growing literature, documenting the impact of disasters on the functioning of youths, is discussed. Recommendations for future research targeting the aftermath of disaster are discussed within the context of the dose–response model. The chapter concludes with recommendations for future clinical and research initiatives.

Clinical Initiatives and Deployments to the Gulf Coast

The first author's initial activities included consultation with local, state, and national agencies, advising the White House, and building capacity among mental health workers and volunteers living in the Gulf Coast in the domains of disaster behavioral health and cultural competence. During this time, a partnership with the lab in the Psychology Department at Virginia Tech and the Hurricane Katrina Community Advisory Group was forged with the purpose of assessing the impact of the storm on residents of the Gulf Coast. The first author's membership in the Disaster Technical Assistance Cadre (DTAC), sponsored by the Substance Abuse Mental Health Administration (SAMHSA, a division of the Department of Health and Human Services), facilitated several of these timely and innovative ventures. A brief overview of his deployments to cities in the Gulf Coast region is given next to contextualize the discussion and provide insight into active partnerships that may be useful for future disaster planning and management.

Deployments to the Gulf Coast

The first two deployments were to Baton Rouge, Louisiana, $2\frac{1}{2}$ weeks post-Katrina and Jackson, Mississippi, 6 weeks post-Katrina. The major objectives of these deployments were to assist state emergency directors in coordinating the mental health response to Hurricane Katrina. During this initial deployment, members of the mental health team toured New Orleans to get a firsthand view of the devastation wrought by the storm. Ongoing meetings were attended with mental and public health professionals, as well as with military personnel. Many of these meetings took place in temporary shelters, centers, and military command posts. Experts from organizations, including the Federal Emergency Management Agency (FEMA), the American Red Cross (ARC), and the Centers for Disease Control and Prevention (CDCP), provided input and guidance for several of our initial endeavors.

As team leader of the second deployment, the first author's primary goals were to provide guidance for team members' day-to-day activities and to ensure their overall safety and well-being. Too often mental heath workers have been guilty of taking care of others and not taking care of themselves. It was the first author's hope that this "practice" would not be repeated in this situation. An additional task was to establish parameters for clinical assessment in order to determine the extent of loss, displacement, and distress incurred by residents of the Gulf Coast. Furthermore, numerous efforts targeting screening, assessment, and intervention of impacted individuals and communities were discussed and implemented at varying levels.

An important effort at the national level was participation in workshops sponsored by the United States Department of Education. This effort, spearheaded by Secretary Margaret Spellings, was designed to educate school teachers and administrators about how to respond to the needs of students, who had been either directly or indirectly impacted by the storm. As a follow-up to this initiative, the first author is currently serving as a member of an advisory committee for the Department of Education, where issues related to the negative impact of a variety of traumas on students' academic and social functioning are being discussed. For example, prior to an event attended by children and their parents in Metairie, Louisiana, the first author briefed the First Lady, Laura Bush, on research findings pertaining to issues of loss, disruption, and how children best cope during recovery phases of disasters. This discussion provided an invaluable opportunity to share knowledge and expertise from the disciplines of clinical and community psychology, as well as principles of disaster behavioral health. Subsequent to this encounter, a discussion of related ventures with a member of her staff at her office in the White House ensued. Updates on various initiatives with children and their parents on the Gulf Coast have been made since that time.

Of particular interest to the first author, given his many years of research and clinical efforts in the area of minority mental health, were efforts targeting cultural competence and disaster behavioral health. The objective of these efforts was to enhance the skill sets and proficiency of indigenous mental health experts and volunteers within the domains of cultural competence and disaster behavioral health. While many of these individuals possessed varying levels of knowledge in these areas, given the massive needs of survivors, it was thought that additional training would be beneficial.

The first step in this process was to initiate focus groups with crisis counselors to determine their levels of proficiency in the areas of disaster mental health and cultural competence, as well as to determine the needs of their clients.

In March 2006, the Louisiana Department of Mental Health tasked four professionals with expertise in the areas of disaster behavioral mental health and cultural competency to develop and implement a training curriculum designed to enhance the skills of crisis workers in delivering effective and culturally and linguistically appropriate strategies and interventions (see Jones, Immel, Moore, & Hadder, 2008). The first author was a member of this team. Specific objectives of the focus groups were as follows: (a) to ascertain the degree to which survivors had received services and demonstrated progress toward recovery; (b) to identify the most salient concerns facing survivors; (c) to determine the types of assistance required by trainees to enhance their capacity to provide culturally and linguistically competent disaster behavioral health-care services; (d) to assess the demographics and cultural strengths of respondents; and (e) to determine the extent to which mental health crisis workers were to provide disaster behavioral health services within the context of the cultures of individuals served. During these focus groups, data were obtained by facilitators which were then used to develop a training manual. Training was guided by this manual during two, 2-day seminars presented in Baton Rouge and New Orleans, Louisiana, in 2006. Copies of the manual may be obtained from the first author upon request. In short, the above efforts exemplify how psychologists and other mental and public health professionals can apply their knowledge, expertise, and skills to challenges faced in the aftermath of disasters (see Chapter 12 for a related discussion).

With regard to research, a partnership between the Hurricane Katrina Community Advisory Group (spearheaded by Dr. Ronald Kessler at Harvard University) and the Recovery Effort After Child Trauma (R.E.A.C.T.) team was established in November 2005. The objective corollary of this collaboration was to carry out a series of studies assessing the short- and long-term mental health impacts of the storm on children and adults. While the child data are still being analyzed, two studies targeting adults have important implications for young children. The compelling results of the two products from this initiative will be discussed later.

Review of the Literature on Reactions to Katrina

A review of several assessment and intervention research efforts targeting children and adolescents will be presented. A total of 12 investigations (9 assessments and 3 interventions) are discussed below.

Assessment

Children. Scheeringa and Zeanah (2008) examined the psychological impact of Hurricane Katrina on preschool children and their caregivers in the New Orleans metropolitan area. Children between the ages of 3 and 6 and his/her primary female caregiver participated in the study. Ethnically, 57.1% of the participants were African American, 31.4% were white, 8.6% were "black–white mix," and 2.9% were "other." Using age-modified criteria, the participants were interviewed with the Diagnostic Interview Schedule for Children, the Preschool Age Psychiatric Assessment, and a disaster experiences questionnaire. Fifty percent of the children were diagnosed with posttraumatic stress disorder (PTSD), and 86.6% of those diagnosed with PTSD were also found to have at least one comorbid disorder, the most common of which were oppositional defiant disorder and separation anxiety. It was found that those who evacuated before the storm were just as likely to develop PTSD compared to those who were unable to leave the New Orleans area. Consistent with previous research (i.e., Laor et al., 1997), the children's new symptoms were also strongly correlated with their caregiver's new symptoms of PSTD.

Notwithstanding these findings, several shortcomings should be noted. It is not clear whether or not children's level of exposure was obtained. This has been found to be an important component for post-disaster investigations (Jones & Ollendick, 2002). There is no mention of the psychometrics of the instruments on this target sample. For example, no internal consistency was reported for the exposure measure. The relative impact of race on these findings was also not systematically explored. Additionally, as the author reported, the self-selected nature of participants may have led to an overestimate of psychopathology. The fact that self-selected participants are often more motivated than other participants may have also led to biases. Nonetheless, this study is valuable in that it examined that impact of Hurricane Katrina on young children via their caregivers. Relationships between parent and child interactions and psychopathology will be discussed in more detail later in this chapter.

In another study, Sprung (2008) examined 183 young children's cognitive reactions to Hurricane Katrina. Five- to eight-year-old children from the Mississippi area were questioned using a non-structured self-report interview to study the immediacy, persistency, frequency, and content of their intrusive thoughts, as well as their level of cognitive functioning, 7 months following the natural disaster. The sample consisted of both male and female participants who were categorized as "white," "black," or "other" ethnicity. Using children from Boston as a control group, hurricane-affected children experienced more negative intrusive thoughts (i.e., "didn't want to think about it"). In addition, children in the major loss–disruption group experienced more recurring negative intrusive thoughts and attempted to suppress these thoughts. A major shortcoming of this effort was that the children's subjective appraisal of the storms was not assessed. Additionally, the extent to which children's premorbid functioning may have impacted their degree of intrusive thoughts was not ascertained. While the impact of race was examined as a covariate, discussion of its potential unique impact on this target population may have been insightful given the dearth of consistent findings on race following disasters.

Cohen and colleagues (2008) assessed the impact of Hurricane Katrina 15 months post-disaster in children from the New Orleans area using a series of self-report questionnaires. The 195 boys and girls who participated were between fourth and eighth grades (with a mean age of 11.6) from New Orleans and Metairie, LA. Ethnically, the sample was 48% white, 46% African American, 5% Hispanic, and 2% were categorized as "other." This study measured hurricane exposure, lifetime trauma exposure, social support systems, and PTSD and depression symptoms. Teachers were also asked to report children's behavioral problems in school. The child's lifetime exposure to trauma was found to predict both PTSD and depression symptoms. Results revealed that both PTSD and depression were significant problems following this traumatic event; 23.6% of the participants had mild PTSD symptoms and 36.9% reported moderate to severe PTSD symptoms. One of the many strengths of this study, as opposed to similar studies, was that it examined lifetime exposure to trauma and both domestic and school violence across the lifespan.

Pina et al. (2008) examined several predictors of youth's posttraumatic stress reactions using several self-report assessment measures. Forty-six children completed a number of pre- and post-Katrina assessments, among whom 67% were European American and 33% were African American. First, social support was linked to mental health and was examined because the evacuation process likely disturbed the existing social network in the New Orleans area. Next, discrimination was studied in that perceived discrimination was elevated in the New Orleans area and has been found to lead to poor mental health in previous research. This research was significant in that it was one of the first to examine the role of discrimination among children following traumatic exposure. Lastly, coping strategies were examined in this empirical study. It was found that increased levels of social support resulted in fewer posttraumatic stress symptoms, signifying that extrafamilial social support served as a protective factor. Furthermore, children who engaged in avoidant coping were more likely to experience both PSTD and anxiety symptoms. Lastly, discrimination and active coping did not predict posttraumatic stress reactions. While the authors pointed out several shortcomings including children not being directly asked about the impact of social support and discrimination, an additional limitation was the absence of information on the role of resource loss on outcome. That is, while several studies measure the relative impact of exposure on outcome, they fail to mention the specific role of resource loss independent of exposure (Hobfoll, 1988). More research on the differentiation of these two overlapping constructs needs to be explored (see Hadder, 2008). Additionally, the relative moderational and mediation role of constructs explored was not examined.

Scaramella, Sohr-Preston, Callahan, and Mirabile (2008) assessed the impact of stress on low-income families, as well as any additional stress the hurricane may have added to the parents' and children's mood, behavior, and adjustment. Pairs of mothers and their 2-year-old child were recruited from the Head Start program in the New Orleans area pre- and post-Katrina and were assessed using a structured interview as well as several self-report surveys. Fifty-five mother–child pairs participated in the study prior to Hurricane Katrina, and an additional 47 pairs joined the study after Hurricane Katrina hit. The participants were mostly African American (about 80%) with mostly single mothers (average age of about 26 years); overall, 41 boys and 61 girls took part in the study. Surprisingly, no significant differences existed pre- and post-Katrina with perceived financial, social, or environmental stressors, indicating that the chronic stress of living in poverty was more substantial than the losses experienced from Hurricane Katrina. Results also indicated that family financial strain caused distress for the parents, weakening his/her parenting efforts, and the child is consequently more likely to exhibit behavioral problems. As pointed out by the authors, the need to actually obtain children's perceptions of the consequences of the disasters is essential for future research. The need for precise measures of social support is also in order. The validity of the family stress model in disaster situations should be explored at a more fine-grained level.

Weems et al. (2007) assessed the psychological impact on 52 children from the New Orleans area following Hurricane Katrina using a series of self-report questionnaires. Among the participants, 64% were European American, 29% were African American, and 7% were "other," with a mean age of 11.35. Each child's PTSD, trait anxiety, general anxiety, and depression symptoms were examined to determine pre- and post-Katrina mental health. Consistent with previous trauma literature, hurricane exposure predicted the number of PTSD symptoms. After controlling for hurricane exposure, trait anxiety and negative affect were found to be predictors of both PTSD symptoms and general anxiety symptoms following the disaster. Furthermore, females were more at risk for developing PTSD, general anxiety disorder, and depressive symptoms following a traumatic event. Shortcomings, including the reliance on youths' self-reports and the sole usage of self-report measures (rather than interviews), were aptly pointed out by the authors. Additionally, the need to determine the impact of varying time frames of data collections is essential to more clearly determine the impact of disasters on individuals' post-disaster functioning (see King et al., 2006).

To assess the impact of a mother's psychopathology on her child's distress following Hurricane Katrina, Spell and colleagues (2008) sampled 260 mother–child pairs who were displaced after the disaster with a series of self-report assessment tools. The children's ages ranged from 8 to 16 years of age, with 43% boys and 57% girls. Ethnically, 68% were African American, 24% were Caucasian, and 8% were categorized as other ethnicities (Asian, Hispanic, and Native American). Similar to other findings (Hensley & Varela, 2008), hurricane exposure, children's symptoms of posttraumatic stress disorder, and children's internalizing problems were related. Maternal psychological distress and PTSD were found to moderate the relationship between child hurricane exposure and mother-reported internalizing and externalizing problems. As alluded to earlier, a major shortcoming of this report was the lack of a more concise measure of loss and exposure. The advocacy for such a practice has been spelled by several authors (e.g., Jones & Ollendick, 2002; Hadder, 2008). Also, the importance of not over-generalizing these findings to non-Katrina samples is paramount.

Adolescents. Five to eight months following Hurricane Katrina, Hensley and Varela (2008) surveyed 302 sixth and seventh grade boys and girls in the New Orleans area with several self-report assessment measures. The sample consisted of 46% African Americans, 37% white, 8% Hispanic, 6% Asian/Pacific Islander, and 3% who chose not to respond. One of the major findings of this study was the impact of disaster on somatic complaints (e.g., headaches, dizziness, chest pain). Furthermore, anxiety sensitivity regarding social concerns moderated the relationship between symptoms of PTSD and trait anxiety, as well as the relationship between somatic symptoms and trait anxiety. While this is one of the few trauma-related studies examining the somatic complaints, as pointed by the authors, the use of self-report versus clinical interviews is essential to obtain more precise measures of functioning.

In a study examining the impact of Hurricane Katrina on adolescents in Mississippi, Marsee (2008) found associations between exposure, posttraumatic symptoms, and reactive aggression among 166 male and female students between 14 and 18 years of age using a series of self-report questionnaires. The sample consisted of 63% Caucasian, 30% African American, 2% Native American, 1% Hispanic, 1% Asian, and 2% other (the last 1% failed to disclose this information). Adolescents with increased exposure were more likely to exhibit symptoms for PTSD. Reactive aggression was also found to correlate with emotional dysregulation as well as symptoms of PTSD. Additionally, all minorities were more likely to experience emotional dysregulation when compared to Caucasians. The need to assess premorbid functioning, and to engagement in interviews rather than use self-report instruments, was aptly pointed out by these authors. However, the use of culturally competent clinicians and researchers in carrying out this study is not mentioned. The extent to which such individuals were not involved in this investigation may provide an explanation for the relatively low level of participation (see Jones, Hadder, Carvajal, Chapman, & Alexander, 2006).

Summary and Clinical Implications. While all of these studies represent pioneering efforts in the face of overwhelming challenges in the acute aftermath of the storm, there are several shortcomings. Specifically, many studies employed self-report instruments rather than structured diagnostic interviews and, hence, raise the possibility that participants could have been falsely diagnosed. Additionally, the possibility of attenuating the associations between risk factors and outcomes is greatly enhanced. The retrospective nature of the methods used to assess hurricane-related stressors may lead to subject recall bias. In the majority of studies reviewed, there was no differentiation made regarding the relative impact of the three storms (i.e., Katrina, Rita, and Wilma). Many of these studies failed to identify a conceptual model used to guide their efforts. The need to articulate the logical underpinnings for their thinking, as well as to develop testable hypotheses, is essential even under the most challenging conditions. Several studies failed to assess premorbid functioning and reactions over time. Despite the shortcomings, these studies provide important insights into our understanding of children's functioning following catastrophic natural disasters.

Interventions

Three studies that provided treatment for children and adolescents are discussed next.

Children. Scheeringa and colleagues (2007) reported two case studies in which cognitive–behavioral training was found to be successful in treating preschool children. One child was traumatized in an automobile accident and the other was a Hurricane Katrina survivor. Both children met the age-modified criteria for PTSD using the Diagnostic Interview Schedule and began cognitive–behavioral treatment, testing a 12-session manualized protocol for preschool children. During these sessions, the children were taught how to identify their feelings, practiced relaxation skills and exposure, techniques as well as learned relapse prevention techniques. Both cases indicate that preschool children possess the capability to engage in a structured therapy as well as learn and demonstrate relaxation techniques. While this intervention effort represents an important first step in assisting children to cope with the aftermath of Katrina, no threats to internal or external validity are mentioned.

Fifteen months following Katrina, an intervention study was implemented for children in the New Orleans area. Children who met criteria for PTSD using various self-report assessment tools were randomly selected to receive either group cognitive–behavioral interventions for trauma in school or individual trauma-focused, cognitive–behavioral therapy at a local mental health clinic. Both treatments included cognitive–behavioral strategies to deal with reexposure, anxiety symptoms, and negative mood symptoms, as well as to improve one's coping strategies. The in-school treatment, however, was less individually tailored than the mental health clinic intervention. The 195 boys and girls who participated were between fourth and eighth grades (with a mean age of 11.6) from New Orleans and Metairie, LA. Ethnically, the sample was 48% white, 46% African American, 5% Hispanic, and 2% were categorized as "other." Jaycox et al. (2005) discovered both treatments resulted in fewer PTSD symptoms at the 10-month follow-up; nonetheless, access to the mental health clinic was a significant conflict. It was shown that participants were more likely to seek out mental health services at school as opposed to traveling to the mental health clinic; 96% of students received treatment through the school, whereas only 35% of the children began treatment at the mental health clinic. In addition, family support and fewer new exposures during the in-school group therapy led to fewer PTSD symptoms at the 10-month follow-up. The overall findings suggest a need to implement a school-based intervention treatment following natural disasters. Among the shortcomings of this cleverly designed study was the lack of differentiation between loss and exposure, as mentioned earlier. Additionally, the race and ethnicity of therapists and assessors were not mentioned. Again, the extent of cultural sensitivity to this target population remains unknown. Participation rates by race may have been impacted by this lack of attention to cultural issues.

Adolescents. Weems et al. (in press) employed a school-based test anxiety intervention study to minority (African American, Asian American, Caribbean American, European American, and other) male and female ninth graders in New Orleans. Those students who reported high levels of test anxiety using self-report questionnaires received in-school group therapy. The treatment focused on improving self-efficacy, learning relaxation techniques, and hierarchy exposure to test anxiety. The intervention was found to lessen test anxiety, improve academic performance, and even yielded positive effects on posttraumatic stress symptoms. Results indicate that school-based test anxiety interventions can be used to lessen general anxiety, as well as trauma-based anxiety, which adds to the existing literature. Although this study targets skills to cope with trauma-based anxiety in minority children, the lack of randomization to groups and the sole reliance on self-report measures represent major shortcomings, as pointed out by the authors. While these early efforts are quite remarkable and add to our growing knowledge of the adequacy of cognitive–behavioral and school-based interventions following massive disasters, more evidence-informed and evidence-based research targeting intervention needs to be conducted.

Summary and Clinical Implications. A major shortcoming of several of the assessment and intervention studies was the relative lack of attention to issues related to culture, race, and ethnicity. A theme that resurfaced during deployments to the Gulf Coast was that culture, race, and ethnicity *count*. The necessity to consider issues related to these very important constructs is brought to attention by Jones et al. (2006). More specifically, (1) there is an insufficient number of ethnic and minority members represented in trauma-related research. Not only does this lessen the likelihood of gaining greater understanding and appreciation of these understudied target groups, sufficient power to ascertain their potentially unique reactions to disaster is obviated. (2) Data suggest that the prevalence of exposure to pre-disaster trauma is likely to be greater than the average among economically disadvantaged environments (see Breslau et al., 1998; Selner-O'Hagan, Kindlon, Buka, Raudenbush, & Earls, 1998). Hence, the greater likelihood of pre-disaster trauma-related psychopathology exists. (3) The underutilization of mental health services by members of minority and marginalized communities presents a need for further research investigation. Potential barriers, which include mistrust, racism, discrimination, and access to mental health services, should be examined in future ventures. (4) The effectiveness and efficacy of intervention strategies used with these target populations is virtually unknown. Future efforts should address issues related to treatment outcome. (5) Symptom expression of psychiatric disorders among ethnic and racial groups has seldom been addressed in disaster mental health research. A knowledge base discussing the intricacies of symptom presentation is sorely needed. Materials presented on the National Child Traumatic Stress web site that address issues of culture provide important guidelines for targeting several of these concerns.

What follows is a brief description of major conceptual models used to interpret children's post-disaster functioning. Of these models, the dose–response model will be advocated as the model of choice for future efforts given the bulk of empirical findings that support this approach. Previous studies identifying risk and protective factors advocated by this model will be briefly reviewed. Following this review will be a discussion of the relative contributions of these early studies to the existing literature.

Conceptualization of Children's Functioning Following Traumatic Experiences

While the dominant conceptual model on stress and mental illness is the diathesis–stress model, originated by Zubin and Spring (1977), the vulnerability–stress model has targeted the understanding and development of psychopathology (Ingram

& Luxton, 2005). Perhaps the most frequently employed and empirically supported model used to predict youth's functioning following traumatic events is the dose–response model (Green, Korol, Grace, & Vary, 1991; La Greca, Silverman, Vernberg, & Prinstein, 1996; Pynoos & Nader, 1988). Within this conceptualization, both risk and protective factors, as well as their relationship to outcomes, are described. More specifically, factors including preexisting characteristics (e.g., age, sex, race/ethnicity, socioeconomic status), exposure (e.g., life threat, disruption, chronic poverty, community/interpersonal violence), resource loss (e.g., condition, object, personal, energy), coping mechanisms (e.g., active, avoidant, distraction, social support seeking), previous life events (e.g., traumas), and social support (e.g., parent, peer, family members, teachers). The following section highlights the existing research examining mediators and moderators of children's mental health as well as other important factors that emerge in the wake of disaster. Additionally, the contributions of recent efforts targeting Hurricane Katrina are discussed.

Exposure. Exposure to a natural disaster has been conceptualized in two distinctive ways. The first definition examines the number of stressors experienced, as well as the relative severity of each stressor (Norris & Elrod, 2006). In general, research has supported the notion that as the number of stressors increase, so do an individual's symptoms of psychopathology. It has also been shown that certain factors predict greater psychological distress, such as bereavement, injury to self or family member, life threat, and panic, during the disaster (Norris & Elrod, 2006).

The second definition of exposure includes the presence of certain factors during a hurricane or other trauma that may lead to increased levels of psychopathology, such as thoughts that one might die, thoughts that another might die, or physical proximity to the event. A summary of several studies that examined the role of exposure following disasters follows.

Following Hurricane Hugo, La Greca et al. (1996) sought to determine the role of exposure in predicting PTSD in 442 children. These children were selected from three elementary schools located in Dade County, Florida, where the greatest levels of destruction from the Hurricane occurred. Exposure, defined as variables such as perceived life threat, and life-threatening events occurring during the hurricane, accounted for the greatest percentage of variance (15%) in PTSD symptoms of the variables assessed. Consistent with both definitions of exposure, the highest levels of distress were found in children who reported that they believed that their life was in danger, as well as those who reported the highest number of stressors as a result of the hurricane.

Exposure was also found to be the strongest predictor of PTSD symptoms in 558 ethnically diverse children following Hurricane Andrew (Vernberg, La Greca, Silverman, & Prinstein, 1996). Exposure variables predicted 35% of the variation in children's PTSD symptoms. Within exposure, it was found that loss–disruption variables accounted for the most unique variance (9%) and were related to greater numbers of PTSD symptoms.

Level of exposure was also found to be a major predictor of distress in children following a wildfire. In a study of 222 children, aged 8–18, all of whom had been exposed to a wildfire, the highest levels of distress were observed in those who thought they or a family member might die, who were within 50 m of the fire, who saw flames, or who were home alone during the fire (McDermott, Lee, Judd, & Gibbon, 2005). Once again, life-threatening variables such as the belief that they or a family member might die were found to predict the highest levels of distress. In addition, a measure of how frightening the day had been for the child was found to be significantly positively correlated ($r = 0.42$) with the development of PTSD symptoms.

Contribution. Several findings from the recent efforts described above confirm earlier findings. Specifically, Cohen and colleagues' (2008) finding that the child's lifetime exposure predicted both PTSD and depression symptoms partially replicate these conclusions. Similar findings were obtained by Hensley and Varela (2008), where it was found that immediate exposure also predicted PTSD. In addition, Marsee (2008) concludes that adolescents' increased exposure leads to symptoms of PTSD and reactive aggression. Exposure was also found to correlate with emotional dysregulation.

Social Support. Social support has been defined as social interactions or relationships that provide individuals with actual assistance or that embed individuals within a social system believed to provide love, care, or sense of attachment to a valued social group or dyad (Hobfoll & Stokes, 1988; see also Chapter 7). Social support has been found to be an important predictor of outcome following a disaster. Specifically, social support often acts as a protective factor; the higher the level of social support, the lower the levels of PTSD symptoms. Following a disaster such as Hurricane Andrew, Vernberg et al. (1996) found that social support variables (i.e., support from parents, friends, teachers, and classmates) each accounted for small but significant amounts of variance in symptoms in children. Specifically, children who perceived the highest level of support from others had the least amount of distress following the hurricane. Social support has also been shown to be a significant factor in predicting positive outcomes following a trauma. Specifically, in a study of 46 children following Hurricane Floyd, social support was found to be a significant contributor to positive outcomes (i.e., posttraumatic growth) (Cryder, Kilmer, Tedeschi, & Calhoun, 2006).

Social support also moderated the relationship of exposure and mental health outcomes (Hammack, Richards, Luo, Edlynn, & Roy, 2004; Pengilly & Dowd, 2000). For example, Hammack et al. (2004) found that social support served as a protective stabilizing factor when individuals were faced with the most severe levels of exposure to violence. It was found that there were no increases in psychopathology in the presence of social support, despite progressively higher levels of exposure. These support networks then lead to lower levels of psychological distress through their ability to help an individual deal with the accompanying emotions and challenges that one faces following a traumatic event.

Similarly, this construct was found to moderate the relationship between negative life events and mental health outcomes (Pengilly & Dowd, 2000). Specifically, for those with low support, high-stress individuals were found to be more depressed than low-stress individuals. The relationship between exposure and PTSD symptoms has also been found to be moderated by social support. Social support was found to moderate the relationship between trauma and PTSD, particularly for girls who had experienced high levels of distress during the Kuwait crisis (Llabre & Hadi, 1997). In fact, social support appeared to buffer the effects of stress. Results of this study indicated that, despite experiencing high levels of exposure, those with high levels of social support had comparable levels of PTSD to those in the control group who did not experience such trauma.

Contribution. Contributions from Hurricane Katrina dictated that extrafamilial support such as professional support services like social services and mental health professionals served as a protective factor following the disaster, but familial support did not. It is surprising that familial support was not a protective factor, but it is theorized that the severity of Hurricane Katrina negatively impacted the family as a whole, and thus the family was unable to serve as a source of help in the recovery process (Pina et al., 2008). These findings are a unique addition to the trauma literature, and further research regarding social support in the wake of massive traumatic events, such as Katrina, is indeed needed.

Coping. Coping can be defined as cognitive and behavioral efforts to manage environmental and internal demands that are appraised as taxing or exceeding personal resources (Folkman, Lazarus, Gruen, & DeLongis, 1986). Coping helps the individual deal with the problem that is causing the distress as well as aids in the regulation of the accompanying negative emotions that arise (Compas, Connor-Smith, Saltzman, Thomsen, & Wadsworth, 2001). Researchers have viewed coping as either active (i.e., seeking social support, problem solving) or avoidant (i.e., efforts to avoid the emotions associated with a stressor). Specifically, it has been found that engaging in avoidant coping behaviors is a major predictor of posttraumatic stress (Foa, Steketee, & Rothbaum, 1989), whereas those who engage in active coping strategies tend to experience less distress (Wadsworth et al., 2004). Other evidence has shown that those who utilize active coping strategies are more resilient in the aftermath of a traumatic event (Armstrong, Birnie-Lefcovitch, & Ungar, 2005; Walsh, Blaustein, Knight, Spinazzola, & van der Kolk, 2007).

In a study of 143 children and parents following the September 11, 2001 terrorist attacks, avoidant coping behaviors, specifically those related directly to the trauma, predicted greater posttraumatic stress (Lengua, Long, & Meltzoff, 2006). It is important to note, however, that while avoidant coping behaviors are most predictive of PTSD symptoms, they are often utilized the least (Russoniello et al., 2002). For example, following Hurricane Floyd, the least used coping strategies included "social withdrawal," "resignation," "blaming others," and "self-criticism," yet these coping strategies were most related to PTSD symptoms. In contrast, active coping strategies such as "cognitive restructuring" and "social support" were less likely to lead to PTSD.

Although avoidant coping behaviors often lead to PSTD, active coping behaviors have also been shown to contribute to negative outcomes. Following Hurricane Andrew, La Greca et al. (1996) found that higher levels of all types of coping (i.e., positive coping, blame/anger, and social withdrawal) were associated with the highest levels of distress. Although blame/anger contributed the greatest amount of variance in symptoms, there was also a strong relationship between positive coping behaviors and PTSD. Although counterintuitive, this relationship may exist because those children who experience the most severe levels of trauma must mobilize the greatest amount of coping behaviors. Therefore, despite engagement in positive coping behaviors the severity of the trauma overwhelms the child's ability to cope.

In addition to predicting levels of distress, coping may moderate the relationship between exposure and distress. For example, Haden, Scarpa, Jones, and Ollendick (2007) tested the hypothesis that active coping strategies, particularly interpersonal strategies, moderate the relationship between injury (i.e., perceived injury severity) and the development of PTSD. They found that for undergraduates who had all experienced a traumatic event, a stronger relationship existed between perceived trauma severity and PTSD for those who failed to utilize interpersonal coping strategies as compared to those who utilized these strategies. Those who perceived a severe injury and utilized few interpersonal coping strategies were most likely to develop PTSD. In sum, given the preceding findings, the potential mediating role of active and avoidant coping should be examined in a disaster context.

Lastly, Jones and Ollendick (2005) assessed the psychological well-being of 46 children and adolescents who experienced a residential fire using a series of self-report questionnaires. The participants were an average age of 11 years, 10 months, and were ethnically divided as follows: 52.2% Caucasian, 43.5% African American, 2.2% Hispanic, and 2.2% biracial. In this study, 41.3% of the mothers reported low education levels (seventh grade to high-school graduate), whereas 58.7% reported high education levels (college or graduate degree). Negative life events were related to children's level of fear for those whose mothers had lower education levels. On the other hand, avoidant coping and negative attributional styles were associated with levels of fear in children with mothers who had higher education levels. Thus, maternal education was found to play a moderating role in this study; having a higher level of education lessened the impact of negative life events.

Contribution. Only one study from the Katrina efforts examined avoidant coping. Consistent with previous findings, Pina et al. (2008) concluded that children who engaged in avoidant coping were more likely to experience both PSTD and anxiety symptoms, whereas active coping was not found to mediate psychological stress. Perhaps the severity of the storm and the traumatic stressors following it degraded the child's ability to cope. The need for further research on coping is needed.

Resource Loss. Resource loss can be defined as the loss of personal and social resources which results in diminished coping capacity and psychological distress (Freedy, Shaw, Jarrell, & Masters, 1992). According to the Conservation of Resources theory (Hobfoll, 1988), resources include objects (i.e., homes, physical possessions), conditions (i.e., health, employment, social support), personal characteristics (i.e., skills and personal traits), and energies (i.e., money, knowledge). All resources are valued for individual's survival although this relationship may be either direct or indirect. Resources fulfill both an individual's psychological and physical needs by allowing them to gain a sense of competence and mastery. As a result, it is suggested that the driving mechanism behind the psychological distress following a trauma is the loss of resources. Traumatic events, such as a natural disaster, often lead to a global loss of resources encompassing all four categories, which often leads to difficulties adjusting post-disaster. In addition, a loss of competency often occurs following a natural disaster as a result of this loss.

Overall, the literature has continued to support the influence of resource loss on psychological distress and development of PTSD following a disaster (Burke, Moccia, Borus, & Burns, 1986; Green et al., 1991; Lonigan, Shannon, Finch, & Daugherty, 1991).

The adult trauma literature has repeatedly supported the notion that resource loss is one of the strongest predictors of PTSD following a disaster (Freedy et al., 1992). Specifically, a loss of resources following a natural disaster has been found to be a major predictor of psychological distress and PTSD. Resource loss was found to have a significant positive correlation with psychological distress ($r = 0.64$) following Hurricane Hugo (Freedy et al., 1992). In order to assess functioning following the hurricane, 418 faculty and staff members at the Medical University of South Carolina in Charleston, South Carolina, were surveyed regarding their resource loss, coping behavior, and psychological distress after the hurricane. Resource loss was found to be the single, strongest predictor of distress after accounting for gender, age, ethnicity, income, previous trauma history, other life events, and life threat. Specifically, resource loss alone was found to contribute to 11% of the variance in psychological distress following the hurricane (Freedy, Saladin, Kilpatrick, & Resnick, 1994).

It appears that the effects of resource loss operate similarly in children. Following a wildfire in California, it was found that children, aged 7–12, who experienced high levels of loss experienced more distress than those in the low-loss group (Jones, Ribbe, Cunningham, Weddle, & Langley, 2002). Although the high-loss (HL) and low-loss (LL) groups were comparable on all major demographic variables, such as gender, income level, fire insurance, and age, PTSD symptoms were significantly more common in the HL group as compared to the LL group. Specifically, 92% of children who experienced high levels of loss were rated as having high PTSD symptom levels as compared to 56% of their peers who experienced lower levels of loss. In addition, there was a significant correlation between PTSD symptoms and resource loss ($r = 0.51$). Further supporting the importance of resource loss following Hurricane Floyd, loss, as measured by flooding in the home, was the variable that was found to be most related to severe symptomatology (Russoniello et al., 2002). Resource loss has also been found to be a greater predictor of distress than direct exposure following a severe earthquake in Southern California (Asarnow et al., 1999). This finding highlights the importance of both loss and the subjective evaluations of loss following a natural disaster.

Contributions. While no study of youth following Katrina examined factors related to resource loss, Galea et al. (2007) provide an excellent study demonstrating the impact of property loss on outcome. That is, in addition to physical illness, injury, and physical adversity, property loss was found to predict anxiety-mood disorders to residents in the New Orleans metropolitan area. The importance of differentiating exposure from resource loss is of paramount importance if the relative contribution of each construct is to be ascertained (see Hadder, 2008).

The Role of Ethnicity. Ethnicity is a complex variable which is thought to operate through a variety of proximal variables (i.e., minority status, SES) rather than having a unique affect on adaptation (Alvidrez, Azocar, & Miranda, 1996). However, ethnicity is often measured as a proximal variable and, following disasters, ethnic differences have emerged. It is generally supported that African-American children experience higher levels of psychological distress than Caucasian children. For example, following Hurricane Hugo, African-American youths reported more psychological distress, as measured by PTSD symptoms, than other minority youths or Caucasian youths (Lonigan et al., 1991; Lonigan, Shannon, Taylor, & Finch, 1994). In addition to experiencing higher levels of distress overall, it has also been found that, following Hurricane Andrew, minority youths were less likely to experience declines in levels of PTSD (La Greca et al., 1996).

Trauma literature has generally supported that African-American youths are more likely to develop PTSD, possibly due to higher levels of exposure to violence and psychological distress; however, it has also been found that they exhibit greater resilience in the face of these stressors (McLeod & Nonnemaker, 2000). This seemingly unexpected finding may be explained by greater access to more close-knit support systems which enables them to exhibit greater resilience in the face of stress (Wickrama, Noh, & Bryant, 2005) or perhaps that African-American families are better able to protect their members from the effects of outside stressors as compared to Caucasian families (Wadsworth & Santiago, 2008).

Contribution. These preexisting empirical findings may explain the Pina et al. (2008) findings where discrimination was not found to be a predictive factor of psychological distress following Hurricane Katrina among youths. However, it should be noted that Chia-Chen Chen, Keith, Airriess, Li, and Leong (2007) indicated that adult survivors experienced higher levels of racial discrimination during Katrina and higher levels of financial distress following the hurricane. These stressors were found to be associated with PTSD symptoms. It was also found that African-American females experienced more symptoms of PTSD compared to their male counterparts. Hence, both minorities and females seem to be at-risk populations and further research is needed to determine appropriate intervention strategies for these groups.

Age and Gender. Findings regarding age effects in PTSD are mixed. The majority of studies have found that younger children have a greater risk of developing PTSD symptoms following a disaster (Lonigan et al., 1991, 1994; McDermott et al., 2005; Stoppelbein & Greening, 2000). However, it has also been shown that those who are older are more likely to develop PTSD (Khamis, 2005). Other studies have failed to find a significant relationship between age and PTSD symptoms (Evans & Oehler-Stinnett, 2006; Green et al., 1991). Further research on the relationship between age and psychological distress is needed.

Despite the vast amount of research examining the influence of gender in the development of PTSD, no clear consensus has emerged. Although there appear to be differential effects in exposure to traumatic events, which would lead to a greater incidence of PTSD in boys (Khamis, 2005), many studies find that either girls are more likely to develop PTSD or that no significant gender differences exist. In studies of children following Hurricane Hugo, girls were significantly more likely to develop PTSD as compared to boys (Freedy et al., 1992; Russoniello et al., 2002). Specifically, being female was found to be the strongest predictor of PTSD, followed by loss incurred from the hurricane (Russoniello et al., 2002). Following the sinking of "Juniper," a cruise ship, girls were also more likely to develop PTSD symptoms (Udwin, Boyle, Yule, Bolton, & O'Ryan, 2000). Other research suggests that gender differences in the development of PTSD following a disaster do not exist. For example, following Hurricane Andrew, no gender differences were found (La Greca et al., 1996). Evans and Oehler-Stinnett (2006) also found no gender differences in PTSD symptoms in an ethnically diverse sample following a severe tornado in rural Oklahoma.

Several studies have implicated a child's gender as a potential moderator for psychological distress following a traumatic event (e.g., Mirza, Bhadrinath, Goodyer, & Gilmer, 1998; Stallard, Velleman, & Baldwin, 1998). The general consensus is that girls are more likely to develop subsequent psychopathology after experiencing a traumatic event; however, it is not clear as to why this occurs. For example, a prospective study (Stallard, Salter, & Velleman, 2004) found that girls were significantly more likely to develop PTSD following road traffic accidents compared to same-age boys. Similarly, the Board of Education study (Hoven et al., 2005) found that girls were at an increased risk for developing negative posttrauma symptomatology as compared to boys for many probable disorders beyond PTSD, such as generalized anxiety, separation anxiety, agoraphobia, and depressive disorders, with the exception of conduct and alcohol abuse/dependence problems. Further, Stallard and Smith (2007) found child gender to be the only non-cognitive variable that significantly predicted posttraumatic stress symptoms, explaining 5–6% of the variance.

In an effort to better understand these findings, Groome and Soureti (2004) theorized that girls might be more willing to report negative symptomatology, but they also implicate the role of cultural and/or biological reasons as to why girls appear to be more susceptible to disorders of posttraumatic stress and anxiety. Another possibility is that girls might adopt fatalistic attitudes and feelings of helplessness in response to a trauma when compared to the attitudes of boys, but the exact mechanisms for these responses are currently under dispute. Despite some uncertainties in the field, evidence continues to support this gender moderation.

Contribution. Following Hurricane Katrina and Hurricane Ivan, Lisa (2008) found that a child's cognitive age was correlated with the presence of PTSD symptoms. Weems et al. (2007) also determined that girls were at risk for having poor adaptive reactions following Hurricane Katrina. They were more likely to develop PTSD, generalized anxiety disorder, and depression following a traumatic event. These findings document the need to continue to examine the important role of age and gender following disaster.

Parent–Child Interaction. While the impact of a parent's behavior on their child's functioning has not been typically conceptualized as a formal risk or protective factor, it has been found to play a salient role in post-disaster environments (see Chapter 3 for a related discussion). Prior research in non-disaster contexts confirms the influence of parent–child interactions across the lifespan. For instance, children of depressed mothers are more likely to suffer from a variety of problems, such as psychological disturbances, social–emotional maladjustment, cognitive deficits, and neurological dysfunction (Gotlib & Goodman, 1999). Additionally, depressed mothers have impaired interactions with their children (Broth, Goodman, Hall, & Raynor, 2004; Zahn-Waxler & Wagner, 1993).

Disaster-specific investigations also document the negative impact that parents' post-disaster functioning can have on their offspring. For example, Laor et al. (1997) found that children's symptoms of PTSD were significantly correlated with their mothers' intrusive and avoidant symptomatology. More specifically, 3-year-old Israeli children appeared to model the anxiety symptoms of their mothers. Similarly, increases in mothers' depressive symptoms were found to correlate with declines in attentiveness, support, and positive emotions toward their children. Related findings were obtained when examining relationships between children and their parents following Katrina. For example, children between the ages of 3 and 6 who were not directly exposed to the storm exhibited symptoms of PTSD that were found to be highly correlated with their caregiver's (Scheeringa & Zeanah, 2008). In sum, these data attest to the fact that parental trauma reactions clearly affect child outcomes, especially for younger children.

Contributions. These findings become even more compelling in light of the documented impact of Katrina on adults following the storm. The next two studies from the Hurricane Katrina Advisory Group substantiate this claim. In assessing the prevalence of distress among a sample of 1043 adults following Hurricane Katrina, Kessler, Galea, Jones, and Parker (2006) found that the estimated prevalence of a serious mental illness increased from 6.1 to 11.3%, and mild to moderate mental illness increased from 9.7 to 19.9%. Similarly, in a follow-up study, exposure to trauma was strongly related to mental health. Adult residents from the New Orleans metropolitan area were estimated to have 49.1% prevalence of any *DSM-IV* anxiety–mood disorder with a 30.3% estimated prevalence of PTSD, while the remaining participants reported 26.4% estimated prevalence of an anxiety–mood disorder and a 12.5% estimated prevalence of PTSD (Galea et al., 2007). In sum, these findings point to the importance of examining the impact of parental functioning on children during the aftermath of disasters.

Future Research: Complimentary Models

While the utility of the dose–response model has been demonstrated in the above investigations, additional models may also be beneficial (see Chapter 2). What follows is a description of three complimentary models that may shed additional light on issues related to children and adolescents' post-disaster functioning.

A prominent example of a process-oriented model is the transactional stress and coping model(TSC), put forth by Thompson, Gustafon, Hamlett, and Spock (1992) and Thompson, Gil, Burbach, Keith, and Kinney (1993). The TSC model highlights the interaction of the person (e.g., demographic, cognitive, and coping processes) and situational variables (e.g., family environment/family functioning) related to adjustment (e.g., depression, anxiety, PTSD symptoms) following a stressor. Traditionally, trauma literature has followed Lazarus and Folkman's (1984) model to capture differences in child adjustment, while the TSC model has been utilized primarily within children's health literature to demonstrate the impact of family environment on child and family adjustment to a chronic illness.

In a recent application of this approach, Moore, Jones, and Ollendick (2008) applied the TSC model to understand child and adolescent adjustment outcomes following a residential fire. The sample in this study was comprised of 144 children and adolescents in the ages 12–18, 53% of whom were African American and 47% of whom were European American. Moore et al. (2008) found key relationships between family and child factors that support the transactional nature of child adjustment outcomes following trauma events. Higher levels of family conflict were predictive of higher levels of (parent-reported) later internalizing symptoms for children and adolescents. Children and adolescents' greater use of avoidant coping strategies was also found to predict higher levels of (self-reported) PTSD symptoms. In addition, an interaction was found between parent reports of children and adolescents' internalizing symptoms and children and adolescents' self-reports of religious avoidance. In other words, the positive relationship between internalizing symptoms and anxiety/depression is strongest for those children and adolescents who also reported high religious avoidance. A second moderation effect was found between children and adolescents' self-reports of their overall adjustment and self-reports of their active coping strategies. The positive relationship between internalizing symptoms and children and adolescents' overall adjustment is strongest for those who also reported a higher use of active coping strategies. Overall then, individual and contextual factors had an identifiable impact on individual adjustment outcomes.

These findings highlight the need to specifically consider individual and contextual factors in the research and treatment literature of psychological difficulties following residential fires. Investigations into the coping and adjustment processes of children and adolescents following residential fires remain in need of novel explorations. It is important for the field to continue to broaden the understanding of how children, adolescents, and their families adjust to trauma by testing innovative additions to current models. Another important area of investigation is the longitudinal psychological adjustment of children and adolescents following trauma. Empirical findings can be translated into greater practical utility with a deeper understanding of the timeline and composition of cognitive appraisal, coping methods, and the role of family processes and how these may impact adjustment over time.

Several possible targets for clinical intervention may include not only individual processes such as coping strategies but also contextual variables such as the family environment. As has been shown in the child chronic health literature, family-based cognitive–behavioral interventions and behavioral family systems therapy show promise in improving family communication, problem-solving strategies, and family and structural interventions (improvements in parent–child or parent–adolescent relationships) (Hocking & Lochman, 2005). These interventions may be equally promising strategies for children and families who have experienced trauma.

Furthermore, trauma-focused coping skills training that targets problem-solving, cognitive–behavioral modification, and conflict resolution may be other avenues to explore. While the TSC model shows utility in identifying the psychosocial processes comprising adaptive outcomes to trauma, a similar application to treatment processes remains unexplored. Relatively few studies have empirically tested the effects of interventions for children and adolescents following disasters. Future studies employing large sample sizes are needed to establish the treatment approaches that effectively improve adjustment to residential fire. Finally, these findings may have more broad-based implications for treatment and intervention efforts following other mass trauma experiences.

A second complimentary model is the Resilience model. By definition, resilience refers to positive patterns of functioning during or following an adversity (Masten, 2006). In order to fulfill this definition, two criteria must be met. First, an individual must be functioning at a level that is at or above what would be deemed developmentally appropriate for their age. The second criterion states that the individual must have been exposed to a threat or adversity. If an individual is functioning at an appropriate level but has not been faced with an adversity, they are considered competent or successful, rather than resilient (see also Chapter 9). A risk or adversity can range from a single event, such as a hurricane or fire, to ongoing stressors, including physical abuse or neglect. In addition, these stressors often occur in combinations, leading to increased overall stress levels.

Traditionally, the resilience literature has neglected to include mental health outcomes in the conceptualization of resilience. Although mental health measures were occasionally examined in addition to behavioral competence when studying resilience (Carle & Chassin, 2004; D'Imperio, Dubow, & Ippolito, 2000; Luthar, 1991; Luthar & Zigler, 1991), only recently have mental health outcomes been included in the conceptualization of resilience.

A recent study in our lab investigated the moderational role of competence in the link between overall loss following a residential fire and the development of PTSD. Competence is thought to operate as a protective factor following a trauma and may be an important variable constituting resiliency. The sample consisted of 64 children (42% Caucasian, 45% African American, and 13% "other") and their primary caregivers, all of whom had experienced a residential fire during which at least 15% of their house or belongings were lost. The children and adolescents were administered a combination of interviews and self-report questionnaires assessing loss following the fire, social support, coping mechanisms used, and basic demographic information. The findings of this study revealed that competence did not moderate the relationship between resource loss following the fire and PTSD. Implications for this study indicate that competence following a fire may not fully capture positive development following a trauma. When examining resiliency following a trauma, a more complete method of assessing positive adaptation may be needed.

A final model developed by Schnurr and Green (2004) may provide utility in explaining health outcomes following traumatic events. The model proposes that PTSD is the primary pathway by which trauma leads to negative health outcomes. It lists eight factors: trauma exposure, PTSD, biological alterations, psychological alterations, attentional processes, health risk behaviors, illness behaviors, and morbidity and mortality. For instance, given the physiological activation/deactivation of survivors both during and following a traumatic event, it is important to understand the biological alterations the body sustains following a traumatic event. In the literature review regarding biological abnormalities associated with PTSD, Yehuda and McFarlane (1997) and Friedman and McEwen (2004) noted several aversive alterations, particularly to the HPA axis system, which resulted in increases in the corticotropin-releasing factor, alterations in cortisol levels, and an increase in glucocorticoid receptors, which influence the regulation of cortisol. Influences on the sympathetic nervous system, arousal symptoms, including increased startle responses and disturbed sleep, were also cited.

Another recent study from our lab reported on a sample of 56 (48 women, 8 men) residential fire survivors, examining the mediating effect of PTSD between exposure and somatic symptoms. Participants were interviewed 4 months after a residential fire and were assessed on levels of exposure to the fire, PTSD symptomology, and somatic health complaints. Consistent with previous findings, PTSD was found to mediate the relationship between exposure to a traumatic event and reporting of somatic symptoms. Furthermore, increased arousal was found to mediate the aforementioned relationship, and avoidance symptoms were also found to partially mediate the same relationship between trauma exposure and the reporting of somatic symptoms. These results may have prominent implications for those who continue to experience distress, both somatic and otherwise, in the gulf region (Immel & Jones, 2009).

Current and Future Challenges

Several recommendations put forth by Jones et al. (2008) when discussing the role of psychologists following Hurricane Katrina are presented next.

Lessons Learned and Recommendations

Getting into the Field. Following a traumatic event, there are many obstacles and challenges mental health responders encounter as they begin to "enter the field." First, it is critical to facilitate rapid deployment in the wake of a natural disaster such as Katrina. A 3-day workshop such as the DTAC program for mental health professionals in May 2005 served as an enhancement tool for assisting them in such severe crisis situations. A lack of structure and coordination was seen following Hurricane Katrina, and perhaps, in the future, psychologists should contact whichever agency is responsible for deploying mental health professionals in order to be sent where assistance is needed most. Licensure, the impact of independent practice, and travel expenses are also challenges many psychologists will encounter in the face of a national crisis. Another lesson learned following Hurricane Katrina is the importance of communication systems. For example, the use of landlines and cell phones was impaired following the hurricane, so establishing more sophisticated and effective communication systems by collaborating with first responders is a recommendation to consider for future disasters.

Issues Related to Safety, General Well-Being, and Vicarious Traumatization. While psychologists are inspired to help others, it is critical to consider one's own safety when responding to any disaster. Health concerns, environmental toxins, and other dangers in affected areas can lead to sickness or disease. In addition to physical health, it is important to keep one's mental health in mind. Working with a community suffering from loss and distress can lead to "vicarious traumatization," also known as "burnout." It is critical for psychologists to engage in self-care while in the field in order to avoid negative results such as anxiety and depression.

Issues Related to Intervention. There are many factors which influence the reaction to a traumatic event. For example, both social support and coping strategies have been found to be protective factors following a traumatic event. Being familiar with these factors and existing literatures will assist in evaluating the impact following a natural disaster such as Katrina. It is also critical to consider the timing of intervention following a disaster. Even though many suffer negative consequences following a traumatic event, it is important to allow the community time to naturally heal before implementing psychological intervention strategies.

Cultural Sensitivity for Psychologists Working in Disaster Relief. Given that 67% of communities impacted by Hurricane Katrina were predominately African American, the need for cultural competence training is clear. Following the hurricane, issues of trust, access to resources, and cultural differences were present among many survivors. These issues, along with cultural differences across ethnicities, lead to the recommendation for psychologists to implement culturally sensitive screening and assessment instruments. Many individuals tend to feel more comfortable receiving assistance from someone they have already formed a relationship prior to the traumatic event. As a result, psychologists should consider collaborating with community organizations as well as other minority organizations such as the National Association of Black Psychologists to increase a sense of comfort for minority groups in the wake of a natural disaster.

The Social Sciences. The social sciences play a critical role in disaster relief efforts. After the first author's initial deployments to the Gulf Coast, he realized that "to achieve success with this daunting effort it will take our best science and utmost sensitivity." That is, the need to be culturally sensitive to target populations, as well as to integrate standards and guidelines based on our scientific clinical work and research, is essential. A complimentary set of recommendations incorporating aspects of the above-stated goals were developed by a group of national and international disaster mental health specialists, including the first author. This took place at a conference entitled "Mental Health and Mass Violence" in response to the September 11, 2001 terrorist attacks and was funded by the National Institute of Mental Health (NIMH). The recommendations are as follows: (a) mental health disaster response requires both research and program evaluation; (b) the scientific community has a responsibility to assess intervention efficiency; (c) there is a need to develop and employ a national strategy in order to guarantee systematic collection of data, evaluation, and research during and after traumatic events such as mass violence and disasters; (d) it is necessary to perform sound research and improve intervention strategies if the most favorable type of intervention is not yet known; (e) mental health professionals should be involved in systematic evaluation activities; (f) research needs to create a standard taxonomy; (g) there is a need to notify the broader research community concerning the magnitude of conducting research on disasters and mass violence; (h) empirically informed and evidence-based interventions are crucial; and (i) researchers are ethically responsible to discourage the use of ineffective or unsafe techniques (Friedman, 2006). It is our hope that these recommendations will continue to be followed by clinicians and researchers, as well as mental health and public health professionals.

The Breach

Following Hurricane Katrina, a literal and figurative breach unfolded. One ruptured the levee system of New Orleans, putting its inhabitants in grave danger, and another, perhaps more painful, breach emerged between the citizens' expectations and the somewhat disappointing realities of the government's short-term and long-term responses to this natural disaster and national tragedy (Carruthers & Jackson, 2006). Thus, several recommendations are discussed below to address current and future challenges resulting from traumatic experiences.

Disaster and Relief Issues. Those impacted by Hurricane Katrina need to share their stories of struggle and survival for others to hear and learn from. Such a tragedy should not be forgotten – being able to talk about a traumatic event can be painful, but it is a helpful coping strategy.

It is essential that national organizations such as FEMA coordinate emergency plans on local, state, and national levels, with an emphasis on the coastal areas that are most likely to be impacted by another natural disaster in the future (see Chapter 6 for a related discussion). Furthermore, this emergency plan, including evacuation procedures, must be made well known to the general public, especially to at-risk populations such as minority groups or those with low socioeconomic statuses. Organizations assisting with the recovery process should also improve their communication strategies with evacuees. For example, many reported having difficulty reaching FEMA operators or receiving helpful information in the wake of Hurricane Katrina.

Another recommendation is to begin forming new partnerships with churches and other community-based organizations; working within the confines of the community ensures more effective resource allocation as well as a potentially more ethnically diverse staff, giving survivors an elevated sense of connectedness and hope. Another policy to ensure an expedited reunification with family members is extremely important, especially for children; being separated from one's family for too long can lead to psychological discomfort.

Restoration Issues. The guidelines mentioned in the U.S. State Department for Internally Displaced Persons should be implemented for all Hurricane Katrina survivors; they should also be considered in all emergency planning committees throughout the nation. In addition, the Hurricane Katrina Recovery, Reclamation, Restoration, Reconstruction, and Reunion Act of 2005 should be passed, guaranteeing any evacuee from Hurricane Katrina who wishes to return can do so and be restored to their "status quo ante." The media also plays an important role in the recovery process and perceptions of a traumatic event, and their influence should be critically reviewed.

Public Policy Issues. Many legislation recommendations have been proposed, such as authority, accountability, and coordination procedures for future disasters, as well as initiatives that would ensure health care for every child in America, especially for minorities or those with parents in low socioeconomic status groups who cannot afford health care.

African-American Church and Community-Based Organizations Preparedness. Many sources recommend disaster mental health responders to receive cultural competence training in order to better understand the barriers minority groups face in recovering from a traumatic event. Similarly, training programs should be implemented in churches as well as other community-based organizations to emphasize the diversity present within communities, as well as to encourage the community to play a role in the restoration process following a disaster such as Hurricane Katrina. Churches and other organizations that survivors have established a relationship with prior to the disaster can play a tremendous role in coping with loss.

Recommendations for Interventions

Intervention following disasters is one of the many crucial yet understudied aspects of trauma. Thus, Hobfoll et al. (2007) recognized five evidence-informed principles to guide community and individual intervention. It is essential to promote a sense of safety, calming, a sense of self and community efficacy, hope, and connectedness following a traumatic event.

More specifically, in the wake of a disaster, children and their families are likely to experience a sense of threat or danger, disrupting their "protective shield" (Pynoos, Steinberg, & Wraith, 1995), which can lead to a variety of negative impacts for the family and surrounding community. It has been found that those who have rebuilt a sense of safety following a traumatic event, however, have a lower risk of developing PTSD than those who have not (Bleich, Gelkopf, & Solomon, 2003; Grieger, Fullerton, & Uranso, 2003). Similarly, promoting a sense of calmness is extremely important and has been found to be a protective factor for those recovering from a disaster; those who have failed to establish a sense of control or calmness are at higher risk of developing PSTD (McNally, Bryant, & Ehlers, 2003; Shalev & Freedman, 2005).

Another important principle to consider in intervention research is promoting a sense of self and collective efficacy. For example, Benight and Harper (2002) found it is advantageous to believe one can manage and solve trauma-related problems following disaster. Likewise, instilling hope in the aftermath of a disaster is essential to effective recovery after a traumatic event. Developing and maintaining an optimistic outlook among individuals and the community must take place in distressful situations. Lastly, Hagan (2005) recognizes the importance for children to form a connection with others and thus emphasizes the need for intervention strategies to reestablish connectedness between children and their families following a traumatic event. These five principles are critical factors for intervention and prevention strategies following a traumatic event on an individual and community-wide level. Thus, collaboration between mental health professionals, physicians, education and political systems, and many other gatekeepers must occur for successful intervention to help those recovering from traumatic events.

Conclusion

Hurricane Katrina was one of the most devastating natural disasters the United States has ever encountered. It tested the abilities of survivors and mental health professionals on local, state, and national levels. Although many were adversely affected by Hurricane Katrina in a myriad of ways, this chapter focused on children and the role traumatic events can play on their mental health. Recent empirical studies regarding the impact of Hurricane Katrina on youth survivors were reviewed and the contribution these scientific findings bring to the growing trauma literature was discussed. Although some studies contradict preexisting trauma literature, many support it, and some even bring new findings to the table of trauma research. The dose–response conceptual model emphasizes the roles of many risk and protective factors (i.e., exposure, social support, coping, race/ethnicity, age, gender, parent–child interaction), providing valuable insights for future direction for clinical and research initiatives.

Acknowledgments A special thanks is extended to first lady Laura Bush for the valuable contributions to the children affected by Hurricane Katrina. Thanks are also extended to the following individuals: Al Marie Ford, MSW (Mental Health Cultural Competence Office), Cheryll Bowers-Stephens, MD, MBA (Assistant Secretary for the Office of Mental Health), Gilda Armstrong-Butler, MSW (Assistant Director of Louisiana Spirit), Anthony Speier, PhD (Louisiana Office of Mental Health; Director of Disaster Services), and Jeanne Brooks, MA (Charles B. Murphy Middle School Teacher and Librarian).

References

Alvidrez, J., Azocar, F., & Miranda, J. (1996). Demystifying the concept of ethnicity for psychotherapy researchers. *Journal of Consulting and Clinical Psychology, 64*(5), 903–908.

Armstrong, M. I., Birnie-Lefcovitch, S., & Ungar, M. T. (2005). Pathways between social support, family well being, quality of parenting, and child resilience: What we know. *Journal of Child and Family Studies, 14*(2), 269–281.

Asarnow, J., Glynn, S., Pynoos, R. S., Nahum, J., Guthrie, D., Cantwell, D. P., et al. (1999). When the earth stops shaking: Earthquake sequelae among children diagnosed for pre-earthquake psychopathology. *Journal of the American Academy of Child & Adolescent Psychiatry, 38*(8), 1016–1023.

Benight, C. C., & Harper, M. L. (2002). Coping self-efficacy perceptions as a mediator between acute stress response and long-term distress following natural disasters. *Journal of Traumatic Stress, 15*(3), 177–186.

Bleich, A., Gelkopf, M., & Solomon, Z. (2003). Exposure to terrorism, stress-related mental health symptoms, and coping behaviors among a nationally representative sample in Israel. *Journal of the American Medical Association, 290*(5), 612–620.

Breslau, N., Kessler, R. C., Chilcoat, H. D., Schultz, L. R., Davis, G. C., & Andreski, P. (1998). Trauma and posttraumatic stress disorder in the community: The 1996 Detroit area survey of trauma. *Archives of General Psychiatry, 55*(7), 626–632.

Broth, M. R., Goodman, S. H., Hall, C., & Raynor, L. C. (2004). Depressed and well mothers' emotion interpretation accuracy and the quality of mother-infant interaction. *Infancy, 6,* 37–55.

Burke, J. D., Moccia, P., Borus, J. F., & Burns, B. J. (1986). Emotional distress in fifth-grade children ten months after a natural disaster. *Journal of the American Academy of Child Psychiatry, 25*(4), 536–541.

Carle, A. C., & Chassin, L. (2004). Resilience in a community sample of children of alcoholics: Its prevalence and relation to internalizing symptomatology and positive affect. *Journal of Applied Developmental Psychology, 25*(5), 577–595.

Carruthers, I. E., & Jackson, B. P. (Eds.). (2006, September). *The breach: Bearing witness.* Samuel DeWitt Proctor Conference, Inc. Retrieved February 14, 2009, from http://www.sdpconference.info/assets/downloads/breach.pdf

Chia-Chen Chen, A., Keith, V. M., Airriess, C., Li, W., & Leong, K. J. (2007). Economic vulnerability, discrimination, and Hurricane Katrina: Health among Black Katrina survivors in Eastern New Orleans. *Journal of the American Psychiatric Nurses Association, 13,* 257–266.

Cohen, J. A., Jaycox, L. H., Langley, A. K., Mannarino, A. P., Walker, D. W., Gegenheimer, K. L., et al. (2008, November). *Trauma exposure and mental health problems among school children 15 month post-Hurricane Katrina.* Paper presented at the International Society for Traumatic Stress Studies Annual Meeting, Chicago, IL.

Compas, B. E., Connor-Smith, J. K., Saltzman, H., Thomsen, A. H., & Wadsworth, M. E. (2001). Coping with stress during childhood and adolescence: Problems, progress, and potential in theory and research. *Psychological Bulletin, 127*(1), 87–127.

Cryder, C. H., Kilmer, R. P., Tedeschi, R. G., & Calhoun, L. G. (2006). An exploratory study of posttraumatic growth in children following a natural disaster. *American Journal of Orthopsychiatry, 76,* 65–69.

D'Imperio, R. L., Dubow, E. F., & Ippolito, M. F. (2000). Resilient and stress-affected adolescents in an urban setting. *Journal of Clinical Child Psychology, 29*(1), 129–142.

Evans, L. G., & Oehler-Stinnett, J. (2006). Structure and prevalence of PTSD symptomology in children who have experienced a severe tornado. *Psychology in the Schools, 43*(3), 283–295.

Foa, E. B., Steketee, G., & Rothbaum, B. O. (1989). Behavioral/cognitive conceptualizations of post-traumatic stress disorder. *Behavior Therapy, 20*(2), 155–176.

Folkman, S., Lazarus, R. S., Gruen, R. J., & DeLongis, A. (1986). Appraisal, coping, health status, and psychological symptoms. *Journal of Personality and Social Psychology, 50*(3), 571–579.

Freedy, J. R., Saladin, M. E., Kilpatrick, D. G., & Resnick, H. S. (1994). Understanding acute psychological distress following natural disaster. *Journal of Traumatic Stress, 7*(2), 257–273.

Freedy, J. R., Shaw, D. L., Jarrell, M. P., & Masters, C. R. (1992). Towards an understanding of the psychological impact of natural disasters: An application of the conservation resources stress model. *Journal of Traumatic Stress, 5*(3), 441–454.

Friedman, M. J. (2006). Disaster mental health research: Challenges for the future. In F. Norris, S. Galea, M. Friedman, & P. Watson (Eds.), *Research methods for studying mental health after disasters and terrorism* (pp. 265–277). New York: Guilford Press.

Friedman, M. J., & McEwen, B. S. (2004). Posttraumatic stress disorder, allostatic load, and medical illness. In P. P. Schnurr & B. L. Green (Eds.), *Trauma and health: Physical health consequences of exposure to extreme stress* (pp. 157–188). Washington, DC: American Psychological Association.

Galea, S., Brewin, C. R., Gruber, M., Jones, R. T., King, D. W., King, L. A., et al. (2007). Exposure to hurricane-related stressors and mental illness after Hurricane Katrina. *Archives of General Psychiatry, 64*, 1427–1434.

Gotlib, I. H., & Goodman, S. H. (1999). Children of parents with depression. In W. K. Silverman & T. H. Ollendick (Eds.), *Developmental issues in the clinical treatment of children* (pp. 415–432). Needham Heights, MA: Allyn & Backon.

Green, B. L., Korol, M., Grace, M. C., & Vary, M. G. (1991). Children and disaster: Age, gender, and parental effects on PTSD symptoms. *Journal of the American Academy of Child & Adolescent Psychiatry, 30*(6), 945–951.

Grieger, T. A., Fullerton, C. S., & Uranso, R. J. (2003). Posttraumatic stress disorder, alcohol use, and perceived safety after the terrorist attack on the Pentagon. *Psychiatric Services, 54*(10), 1380–1382.

Groome, D., & Soureti, A. (2004). Post-traumatic stress disorder and anxiety symptoms in children exposed to the 1999 Greek earthquake. *British Journal of Psychology, 95*, 387–397.

Hadder, J. M. (2008). *The meditational role of resource loss between residential fire exposure and psychological distress.* Unpublished master's thesis, Virginia Polytechnic and State University, Blacksburg.

Haden, S. C., Scarpa, A., Jones, R. T., & Ollendick, T. H. (2007). Posttraumatic stress disorder symptoms and injury: The moderating role of perceived social support and coping for young adults. *Personality and Individual Differences, 42*(7), 1187–1198.

Hagan, J. (2005). Committee on psychological aspects of child and family health and the task force on terrorism: Psychological implications of disaster or terrorism on children. A guide for the pediatrician. *Pediatrics, 116*, 787–795.

Hammack, P. L., Richards, M. H., Luo, Z., Edlynn, E. S., & Roy, K. (2004). Social support factors as moderators of community violence exposure among inner-city African American young adolescents. *Journal of Clinical Child and Adolescent Psychology, 33*(3), 450–462.

Hensley, L., & Varela, R. E. (2008). PTSD symptoms and somatic complaints following Hurricane Katrina: The roles of trait anxiety and anxiety sensitivity. *Journal of Clinical Child and Adolescent Psychology, 37*, 542–552.

Hobfoll, S. E. (1988). *The ecology of stress.* New York, NY: Hemisphere Publishing Corporation.

Hobfoll, S. E., & Stokes, J. P. (1988). The process and mechanics of social support. In S. Duck, D. F. Hay, S. E. Hobfoll, W. Ickes, & B. M. Montgomery (Eds.), *Handbook of personal relationships: Theory, research, and interventions.* (pp. 497–517). Oxford, England: John Wiley & Sons.

Hobfoll, S. E., Watson, P., Bell, C. C., Bryant, R. A., Brymer, M. J., Friedman, M. J., et al. (2007). Five essential elements of immediate and mid-term mass trauma intervention: Empirical evidence. *Psychiatry, 70*, 283–315.

Hocking, M. C., & Lochman, J. E. (2005). Applying the transactional stress and coping model to sickle cell disorder and insulin-dependent diabetes mellitus: Identifying psychosocial variables related to adjustment and intervention. *Clinical Child and Family Psychology Review, 8*, 221–246.

Hoven, C. W., Duarte, C. S., Lucas, C. P., Wu, P., Mandell, D. J., Goodwin, R. D., et al. (2005). Psychopathology among New York City public school children 6 months after September 11. *Archives of General Psychiatry, 62*, 545–552.

Immel, C. S., & Jones, R. T. (2009). Posttraumatic stress disorder and symptom subclusters symptoms as a mediator of self-reported somatic health distress among trauma survivors. Manuscript in preparation.

Ingram, R. E., & Luxton, D. D. (2005). Vulnerability-stress models. In: B. L. Hankin & J. R. Z. Abela (Eds.), *Development of psychopathology: A vulnerability-stress perspective* (pp. 32–46). Beverly Hills, CA: Sage Publications.

Jaycox, L. H., Cohen, J. A., Mannarino, A. P., Walker, D. W., Langley, A. K., Gegenheimer, K. L., et al. (2008, November). *Children's mental health care following Hurricane Katrina within a randomized field trial of trauma-focused psychotherapies.* Paper presented at the International Society for Traumatic Stress Studies Annual Meeting, Chicago, IL.

Jones, R. T., Hadder, J. M., Carvajal, F., Chapman, S., & Alexander, A. (2006). Conducting research in diverse, minority, and marginalized communities. In F. H. Norris, S. Galea, M. J. Friedman, & P. J. Watson (Eds.), *Methods for disaster mental health research* (pp. 265–266). New York: Guilford Press.

Jones, R. T., Immel, C. S., Moore, R. M., & Hadder, J. M. (2008). Hurricane Katrina: Experiences of psychologists and implications for future disaster response. *Professional Psychology: Research and Practice, 39,* 100–106.

Jones, R. T., & Ollendick, T. H. (2002). The impact of residential fire on children and their families. In A. La Greca, W. Sliverman, E. Vernberg, & M. Roberts (Eds.), *Helping children cope with disasters: Integrating research and practice* (pp. 175–202). Washington, DC: American Psychological Association Books.

Jones, R. T., & Ollendick, T. H. (2005). Risk factors for psychological adjustment following residential fire: The role of avoidant coping. *The Journal of Trauma and Dissociation, 6,* 85–99.

Jones, R. T., Ribbe, D. P., Cunningham, P. B., Weddle, J. D., & Langley, A. K. (2002). Psychological impact of fire disaster on children and their parents. *Behavior Modification, 26*(2), 163–186.

Kessler, R. C., Galea, S., Jones, R. T., & Parker, H. A. (2006). Mental illness and suicidality after Hurricane Katrina. *Bulletin of the World Health Organization, 84,* 930–939.

Khamis, V. (2005). Post-traumatic stress disorder among school age Palestinian children. *Child Abuse and Neglect, 29,* 81–95.

King, D. W., King, L. A., McArdle, J. J., Grimm, K., Jones, R. T., & Ollendick, T. H. (2006). Characterizing time in longitudinal trauma research. *Journal of Traumatic Stress, 19,* 205–215.

La Greca, A. M., Silverman, W. K., Vernberg, E. M., & Prinstein, M. J. (1996). Symptoms of post-traumatic stress in children after Hurricane Andrew: A prospective study. *Journal of Consulting and Clinical Psychology, 64*(4), 712–723.

Laor, N., Wolmer, L., Mayes, L. C., Gershon, A., Weizman, R., & Cohen, D. (1997). Israeli preschool children under scuds: A 30-month follow-up. *Journal of the American Academy of Child & Adolescent Psychiatry, 36,* 349–356.

Lazarus, R., & Folkman, S. (1984). *Stress, appraisal, and coping.* New York: Springer.

Lengua, L. J., Long, A. C., & Meltzoff, A. N. (2006). Pre-attack stress-load, appraisals, and coping in children's responses to the 9/11 terrorist attacks. *Journal of Child Psychology and Psychiatry, 47*(12), 1219–1227.

Lisa, J. (2008). The effects of mass trauma on children of different developmental stages: Examining PTSD in children affected by Hurricane Ivan and Hurricane Katrina. *Dissertation Abstracts International: Section B: The Sciences and Engineering, 69,* 681.

Llabre, M. M., & Hadi, F. (1997). Social support and psychological distress in Kuwaiti boys and girls exposed to the Gulf crisis. *Journal of Clinical Child Psychology, 26*(3), 247–255.

Lonigan, C. J., Shannon, M. P., Finch, A. J., & Daugherty, T. K. (1991). Children's reactions to a natural disaster: Symptom severity and degree of exposure. *Advances in Behavior Research & Therapy, 13*(3), 135–154.

Lonigan, C. J., Shannon, M. P., Taylor, C. M., & Finch, A. J. (1994). Children exposed to disaster: II. Risk factors for the development of post-traumatic symptomatology. *Journal of the American Academy of Child & Adolescent Psychiatry, 33*(1), 94–105.

Luthar, S. S. (1991). Vulnerability and resilience: A study of high-risk adolescents. *Child Development, 62*(3), 600–616.

Luthar, S. S., & Zigler, E. (1991). Vulnerability and competence: A review of research on resilience in childhood. *American Journal of Orthopsychiatry, 61*(1), 6–22.

Marsee, M. A. (2008). Reactive aggression and posttraumatic stress in adolescents affected by Hurricane Katrina. *Journal of Child and Adolescent Psychology, 37,* 519–529.

Masten, A. S. (2006). Developmental psychopathology: Pathways to the future. *International Journal of Behavioral Development, 30*(1), 47–54.

McDermott, B. M., Lee, E. M., Judd, M., & Gibbon, P. (2005). Posttraumatic stress disorder and general psychopathology in children and adolescents following a wildfire disaster. *Canadian Journal of Psychiatry, 50*(3), 137–143.

McLeod, J. D., & Nonnemaker, J. M. (2000). Poverty and child emotional and behavioral problems: Racial/ethnic differences in processes and effects. *Journal of Health and Social Behavior, 41*(2), 137–161.

McNally, R. J., Bryant, R. A., & Ehlers, A. (2003). Does early psychological intervention promote recovery from posttraumatic stress? *Psychological Science in the Public Interest, 4*(2), 45–79.

Mirza, K. A. H., Bhadrinath, B. R., Goodyer, I. M., & Gilmer, C. (1998). Post-traumatic stress disorder in children and adolescents following road traffic accidents. *British Journal of Psychiatry, 172*, 443–447.

Moore, R. M., Jones, R. T., & Ollendick, T. H. (2008, November). *Ecological approach to child outcomes following residential fire: Family processes and child coping*. Poster presented at the annual meeting of International Society of Traumatic Stress Studies, Chicago, IL.

National Oceanic & Atmospheric Administration. (2006). *Service assessment: Hurricane Katrina*. Retrieved January 30, 2008, from http://www.weather.gov/os/assessments/pdfs/Katrina/pdf

Norris, F. H., & Elrod, C. L. (2006). Psychosocial consequences of disaster: A review of past literature. In F. H. Norris, S. Galea, M. J. Friedman, & P. J. Watson (Eds.), *Methods for disaster mental health research*. New York: The Guildford Press.

Pengilly, J. W., & Dowd, E. T. (2000). Hardiness and social support as moderators of stress. *Journal of Clinical Psychology, 56*(6), 813–820.

Pina, A. A., Villalta, I. K., Ortiz, C. D., Gottschall, A. C., Costa, N. M., & Weems, C. F. (2008). Social support, discrimination, and coping as predictors of posttraumatic stress reactions in youth survivors of Hurricane Katrina. *Journal Clinical Child and Adolescent Psychology, 37*, 564–574.

Pynoos, R. S., & Nader, K. (1988). Psychological first aid and treatment approach to children exposed to community violence: Research implications. *Journal of Traumatic Stress, 1*, 445–473.

Pynoos, R. S., Steinberg, A. M., & Wraith, R. (1995). A developmental model of childhood traumatic stress. In D. Cicchetti, & D. J. Cohen (Eds.), *Developmental psychopathology, vol. 2: Risk, disorder, and adaptation* (pp. 72–95). Oxford, England: John Wiley & Sons,.

Russoniello, C. V., Skalko, T. K., O'Brien, K., McGhee, S. A., Bingham-Alexander, D., & Beatley, J. (2002). Childhood posttraumatic stress disorder and efforts to cope after Hurricane Floyd. *Behavioral Medicine, 28*(2), 61–70.

Scaramella, L. V., Sohr-Preston, S. L., Callahan, K. L., & Mirabile, S. P. (2008). A test of the family stress model on toddler-age children's adjustment among Hurricane Katrina impacted and nonimpacted low-income families. *Journal of Clinical Child and Adolescent Psychology, 37*, 530–541.

Scheeringa, M. S., Salloum, A., Arnberger, R. A., Weems, C. F., Lisa, A. J., & Cohen, J. A. (2007). Feasibility and effectiveness of cognitive–behavioral therapy for posttraumatic stress disorder in preschool children: Two case reports. *Journal of Traumatic Stress, 20*, 631–636.

Scheeringa, M. S., & Zeanah, C. H. (2008). Reconsideration of harm's way: Onsets and comorbidity patterns of disorders in preschool children and their caregivers following Hurricane Katrina. *Journal of Clinical Child and Adolescent Psychology, 37*, 508–518.

Schnurr, P. P., & Green, B. L. (2004). A context for understanding the physical health consequences of exposure to extreme stress. In P. P. Schnurr & B. L. Green (Eds.), *Trauma and health: Physical health consequences of exposure to extreme stress*, (pp. 3–10) Washington, DC: American Psychological Association.

Selner-O'Hagan, M. B., Kindlon, D. J., Buka, S. L., Raudenbush, S. W., & Earls, F. J. (1998). Assessing exposure to violence in urban youth. *Journal of Child Psychology, 39*, 215–224.

Shalev, A. Y., & Freedman, S. (2005). PTSD following terrorist attacks: A prospective evaluation. *American Journal of Psychiatry, 162*, 1188–1191.

Spell, A. W., Kelley, M. L., Wang, J., Self-Brown, S., Davidson, K. L., Pellegrin, A., et al. (2008). The moderating effects of maternal psychopathology on children's adjustment post-Hurricane Katrina. *Journal of Clinical Child and Adolescent Psychology, 37*, 553–563.

Sprung, M. (2008). Unwanted intrusive thoughts and cognitive functioning in kindergarten and young elementary school-age children following Hurricane Katrina. *Journal of Clinical Child and Adolescent Psychology, 37*, 575–587.

Stallard, P., & Smith, E. (2007). Appraisals and cognitive coping styles associated with chronic post-traumatic symptoms in child road traffic accident survivors. *Journal of Child Psychology and Psychiatry, 48*, 194–201.

Stallard, P., Salter, E., & Velleman, R. (2004). Posttraumatic stress disorder following road traffic accidents: A second prospective study. *European Child and Adolescent Psychiatry, 13*, 172–178.

Stallard, P., Velleman, R., & Baldwin, S. (1998). Prospective study of post-traumatic stress disorder in children involved in road traffic accidents. *British Medical Journal, 317*, 1619–1623.

Stoppelbein, L., & Greening, L. (2000). Posttraumatic stress symptoms in parentally bereaved children and adolescents. *Journal of the American Academy of Child & Adolescent Psychiatry, 39*(9), 1112–1119.

Thompson, R. J., Gil, K. M., Burbach, D. J., Keith, B. R., & Kinney, T. R. (1993). Psychological adjustment of mothers of children and adolescents with sickle cell disease: The roles of stress, coping methods, and family functioning. *Journal of Pediatric Psychology, 18*, 549–559.

Thompson, R. J., Jr., Gustafon, K. E., Hamlett, K. W., & Spock, A. (1992). Stress, coping, and family functioning in the psychological adjustment of mothers of children and adolescents with cystic fibrosis. *Journal of Pediatric Psychology, 17*, 741–755.

Udwin, O., Boyle, S., Yule, W., Bolton, D., & O'Ryan, D. (2000). Risk factors for long-term psychological effects of a disaster experienced in adolescence: Predictors of post traumatic stress disorder. *Journal of Child Psychology and Psychiatry, 41*(8), 969–979.

Vernberg, E. M., La Greca, A. M., Silverman, W. K., & Prinstein, M. J. (1996). Prediction of posttraumatic stress symptoms in children after Hurricane Andrew. *Journal of Abnormal Psychology, 105*(2), 237–248.

Wadsworth, M. E., Gudmundsen, G. R., Raviv, T., Ahlkvist, J. A., McIntosh, D. N., Kline, G. H., et al. (2004). Coping with terrorism: Age and gender differences in effortful and involuntary responses to September 11th. *Applied Developmental Science, 8*(3), 143–157.

Wadsworth, M. E., & Santiago, C. D. (2008). Risk and resiliency processes in ethnically diverse families in poverty. *Journal of Family Psychology, 22*, 399–410.

Walsh, K., Blaustein, M., Knight, W. G., Spinazzola, J., & van der Kolk, B. A. (2007). Resiliency factors in the relation between childhood sexual abuse and adulthood sexual assault in college-age women. *Journal of Child Sexual Abuse, 16*(1), 1–17.

Weems, C. F., Pina, A. A., Costa, N. M., Watts, S. E., Taylor, L. K., & Cannon, M. F. (2007). Pre-disaster trait anxiety and negative affect predict posttraumatic stress in youths after Hurricane Katrina. *Journal of Consulting and Clinical Psychology, 75*, 154–159.

Weems C. F.,, Taylor, L. K., Costa, N. M., Marks, A. B., Romano, D. M., Verrett, S. L., et al. (2009). Effect of a school-based test anxiety intervention in ethnic minority youth exposed to Hurricane Katrina. *Journal of Applied Developmental Psychology, 30*, 218–226.

Wickrama, K. A. S., Noh, S., & Bryant, C. M. (2005). Racial differences in adolescent distress: Differential effects of the family and community for Blacks and Whites. *Journal of Community Psychology, 33*(3), 261–282.

Yehuda, R., & McFarlane, A. C. (1997). Psychobiology of posttraumatic stress disorder. *Annals of the New York Academy of Sciences, 821*, 550.

Zahn-Waxler, C., & Wagner, E. (1993). Caregivers' interpretations of infant emotions: A comparison of depressed and well mothers. In R. N. Emdy, J. D. Osofsky, & P. M. Butterfield (Eds.), *The IFEEL pictures: A new instrument for interpreting emotions* (pp.175–184). Madison, CT: International Universities Press.

Zubin, J., & Spring, B. (1977). Vulnerability: A new view of schizophrenia. *Journal of Abnormal Psychology, 86*, 103–126.

Part II
Young and Middle-Age Adults

Chapter 5
The Psychological Impact of Hurricanes and Storms on Adults

Thompson E. Davis III, Erin V. Tarcza, and Melissa S. Munson

Abstract Almost immediately after making landfall, the psychological and physical impacts of Hurricane Katrina were evident. Thousands of people in the Gulf Coast endured countless stressors, hassles, financial crises, psychopathological symptoms, and fear, in addition to flooding, broken levees, lost homes, evacuations, and curfews. In this chapter, we review the literature specifically relevant to the impact that Hurricanes Katrina and Rita had on adults in the southern Louisiana area. In the first section, a ground work is laid for how hurricanes and natural disasters impact adults, including descriptions of relevant psychopathology, risk factors for developing psychopathology, and protective factors that lead to resiliency from psychopathology. In the next section, a review of findings from previous storms and hurricanes is given, followed by a review of the literature specific to Hurricanes Katrina and Rita. Implications for addressing the mental health needs of persons who reside in storm-prone areas are discussed. Future directions for private practitioners and researchers are considered.

Introduction

On August 29, 2005, Hurricane Katrina made landfall in Louisiana as a category 3 hurricane. The hurricane's impact on residents was severe—over 1800 lives lost (the third deadliest hurricane since 1900) and damage estimates around $125 billion (Graumann et al., 2005). While exposure to the hurricane itself was bad enough, the impact of Katrina was to be felt long after the winds and rain had passed. In the days following landfall problems worsened, leading fear to grip New Orleans, Baton Rouge, and surrounding areas. Compounding existing difficulties, rumors began to circulate wildly across the city, state, and country that included everything from

---

T.E. Davis III (✉)
Department of Psychology, Louisiana State University, 236 Audubon Hall, Baton Rouge, LA 70803-5501, USA
e-mail: ted@lsu.edu

the levees were destroyed purposely by the government (Cordasco, Eisenman, Glik, Golden, & Asch, 2007) to reports that those who evacuated to Baton Rouge from New Orleans were rioting, committing crimes, and looting stores (Clark, 2005; Thomas, 2007). Relief workers and those returning to their homes faced different difficulties. The Centers for Disease Control recorded 7543 nonfatal injuries among area residents and relief workers in the month following the hurricane as many returned to their homes and began the cleanup (Sullivent et al., 2006), and the murder rate in New Orleans in 2006 grew to be 69% higher than it was in 2004 (VanLandingham, 2007).

Months after the hurricane, workers in New Orleans were still under considerable stress with one quarter of workers "fairly often" or "often" feeling unable to control the important things in their lives (Leon, Hyre, Ompad, DeSalvo, & Munter, 2007). Long term, those residing in Federal Emergency Management Agency (FEMA) trailer parks would have to face scrutiny, avoidance, and stigma in addition to the loss of their homes (Lee, Weil, & Shihadeh, 2007). Overall, the psychological sequelae and phenomena experienced following Hurricane Katrina were varied, and the stress, impact, and trauma were experienced well beyond August 29, 2005. To make things worse, Katrina was quickly followed by Hurricane Rita which hit the Louisiana/Texas border on September 24, 2005 and further compounded the damage and impact.

As a result, this chapter reviews literature specifically relevant to the impact that Hurricanes Katrina and Rita had on adults in the southern Louisiana area. First, a ground work is laid for how hurricanes and natural disasters impact adults, including descriptions of relevant psychopathology, risk factors for developing psychopathology, and protective factors that lead to resiliency from psychopathology. This is followed by a review of findings from previous storms and hurricanes and a review of the literature specific to Hurricanes Katrina and Rita.

Diagnostic Considerations

Reactions to significant stressors such as natural disasters fall along a continuum ranging from short-term anxious responding to prolonged stress months or years following the event. These problems can interfere with many aspects of one's life including family and work, as well as cause psychosocial stressors, and impact social support, mental health, and physical health (Hochwarter, Laird, & Brouer, 2008; Weems et al., 2007). Although psychopathology resulting from exposure to traumatic events can take several forms, the more common reactions include acute stress disorder, posttraumatic stress disorder (PTSD), major depressive disorder, and other anxiety disorders such as generalized anxiety disorder (David et al., 1996; Shalev et al., 1998; Smith, North, McCool, & Shea, 1990).

Acute stress disorder describes extreme reactions to stressors that last 2 days to 1 month following the event (*DSM-IV-TR*; American Psychiatric Association, 2000). Criteria for acute stress disorder include exposure to a traumatic event and the experience of emotional numbing, reduced awareness of surroundings, derealization, depersonalization, and/or dissociative amnesia while the event was occurring. Additional criteria include interference following the event including reexperiencing the event through dreams, illusions, flashbacks, or intrusive thoughts; avoidance of reminders of the event; increased arousal; and significant interference or distress in social or occupational functioning (*DSM-IV-TR*). Among individuals exposed to traumatic events, approximately 14–33% develop acute stress disorder (*DSM-IV-TR*).

PTSD entails long-term symptoms that persist 1 month or more following a traumatic event. Criteria for PTSD include the experience of a traumatic event in which the person feels extreme helplessness or horror; reexperiencing of the traumatic event including intrusive thoughts, distressing dreams, and feeling as if the event is about to occur again; and distress when exposed to environmental or internal reminders of the event. Additional criteria include avoidance of reminders of the event, emotional numbing, and increased arousal including sleep problems, irritability, trouble concentrating, hypervigilance, and exaggerated startle response (*DSM-IV-TR*). Approximately 80% of individuals with acute stress disorder go on to develop PTSD; however, symptoms of PTSD can have a delayed onset in which the person does not experience symptoms until 6 months after the event (*DSM-IV-TR*). Epidemiology studies have found prevalence rates between 27 and 44% for PTSD among individuals who have been exposed to a natural disaster (Keane & Barlow, 2002).

Although acute stress disorder and PTSD are disorders that can occur following a traumatic event, other disorders such as depression and other anxiety disorders are often problematic for people as well. Individuals with major depressive disorder experience one or more depressive episodes. These depressive episodes are defined as 1 week or more of symptoms such as sadness, anhedonia, feelings of guilt, thoughts of death, and physical symptoms such as sleeping problems, weight changes, feeling fatigued, and psychomotor agitation or psychomotor retardation (*DSM-IV-TR*). Natural disasters such as Hurricane Katrina can serve as psychosocial stressors that can trigger depressive episodes. Also, the presence of comorbid diagnoses, such as PTSD and major depressive disorder, is related to poorer functioning and greater symptom severity (Shalev et al., 1998).

Another anxiety disorder that is often seen following traumatic events is generalized anxiety disorder (David et al., 1996; Smith et al., 1990). This disorder is characterized by pervasive worry about many different areas of one's life. Individuals with this disorder find it very difficult to control their worry, and they experience at least three other symptoms such as muscle tension, trouble sleeping, restlessness, irritability, or difficulty concentrating while they are worrying (*DSM-IV-TR*). The worry occurs more days than not throughout daily life and causes significant personal distress or impairment in social or occupational functioning (*DSM-IV-TR*). Overall, whether an individual eventually develops problematic symptoms following exposure to a hurricane (or any stressor for that matter) and which cluster of symptoms depends on a variety of individual characteristics, including risk and resiliency factors, described briefly next.

Risk and Resiliency

Some research has examined possible risk factors that would predispose an individual to developing one or more psychological problems following a disaster. Risk factors that increase the chance of developing PTSD following any type of trauma include a history of a psychological disorder prior to the event, being a woman, having a family history of psychological problems, and repeated exposure to multiple traumas over time (Fairbank, Ebert, & Caddell, 2004). Regarding disasters specifically, a history of a psychological disorder before the disaster and proximity to the disaster site are thought to be risk factors (Smith et al., 1990).

In addition to the research on risk factors for developing psychopathology, some researchers have begun to examine the qualities of resilient individuals (see Chapter 4 for a related discussion). This research focuses on the study of protective factors that prevent an individual from developing mental illness after exposure to a traumatic event (i.e., resiliency). Resiliency is an individual quality or set of qualities which prevent a person from developing psychopathology following a traumatic event (Mancini & Bonanno, 2006). It is different from recovery following a traumatic experience, in that resilient individuals do not experience significant distress at any point in time (Mancini & Bonanno, 2006). As a result, not everyone will need to undergo "grief work" after a traumatic experience as resilient individuals will not be distressed following an event (Bonanno, 2004). Resilient individuals would not have a need for debriefing or intervention following a potentially traumatic event. Resilience may also be more common than once thought; in a review, several studies show that many individuals exhibit resilience following multiple types of trauma including those involving natural or manmade disasters (cf. Bonanno, 2004; Masten, 2001).

There are also multiple pathways that are thought to lead to resilience, and these variables can sometimes be unexpected given they may or may not be adaptive in non-traumatic situations (Bonanno, 2004). Two such unexpected pathways are self-enhancement, which may not be adaptive in everyday interpersonal interactions, and repressive coping. Some individuals with a repressive coping style (i.e., giving little attention to the event and not going through a typical grieving process) do not experience grief later in life (Bonanno, 2004). Other qualities that lead to resilience are hardiness, positive emotion and laughter, optimism, and access to prompt intervention immediately following a disaster (Bonanno, 2004; Dougall, Hyman, Hayward, McFeeley, & Baum, 2001; Wang et al., 2000). Demographically, greater resiliency has been associated with being a man, having less than a college education, not experiencing income decline from a disaster, and having more social support (Bonanno, Galea, Bucciarelli, & Vlahov, 2007). Resiliency has also been found to decrease with more direct exposure impact, more immediate life stressors, and more past traumatic experiences (Bonanno et al., 2007).

Coping self-efficacy–the belief that one will be able to deal with trauma—has also been implicated as an important quality that leads to resiliency (Benight & Bandura, 2004; see also Chapter 9 of this volume). Coping self-efficacy is part of the social-cognitive theory of posttraumatic recovery. This theory is an "agentic" model, meaning that individuals are agents that act on their environments to produce the effect of resiliency (Benight & Bandura, 2004, p. 1133). In this way, protective factors do not serve as passive barriers to deflect distress reactions after a traumatic event; but rather, protective factors are actively produced by individuals which lead them to be more resilient than others exposed to the same event (Benight & Bandura, 2004). Coping self-efficacy, or perceived coping self-efficacy, has been found to mediate the relationship between exposure to a traumatic event and acute and long-term distress following the event (Benight & Harper, 2002; Benight, Swift, Sanger, Smith, & Zeppelin, 1999; Cieslak, Benight, & Lehman, 2008). For individuals exposed to Hurricane Opal in Florida (second landfall October 4, 1995), coping self-efficacy also served as a mediator of protective factors such as lost resources, optimism, and social support in addition to the amount of psychological distress experienced (Benight & Harper, 2002). Coping self-efficacy and coping behavior were also found to be significant predictors of distress following Hurricane Andrew; those losing more resources had poorer coping self-efficacy and more avoidant coping behaviors (Benight, Ironson, Klebe et al., 1999).

Findings from Previous Hurricanes and Storms

While research has recently been conducted on the impact of Hurricane Katrina (e.g., Wang et al., 2008; Galea et al., 2007; Weems et al., 2007), much less literature is available on the impact of other major storms. The following portion of this chapter will briefly highlight some of the findings that have been published on the psychological impact of other hurricanes and storms. The majority of the literature prior to Katrina focuses on the prevalence of and risk for the development of mental health problems following a storm or hurricane. Caldera, Palma, Penayo, and Kullgren (2001) examined the prevalence of PTSD symptoms following Hurricane Mitch in a low-income area of Nicaragua. They found the occurrence of PTSD ranged from 4.5% in the areas with the least damage to 9% in the most damaged areas. PTSD symptoms were associated with having a loved one pass away, having a house destroyed, being a woman, having previous mental health problems, and being illiterate. Other studies have examined similar issues specifically in older adults (Acierno, Ruggiero, Kilpatrick, Resnick, & Galea, 2006; Kohn, Levav, Garcia, Machuca, & Tamashiro, 2005). Older adults are a population that is of special interest because older age has actually been found to be a protective factor following natural disasters in some studies, with older individuals being at decreased risk of developing psychopathology (Acierno et al., 2002; Norris, 1992; see also Chapter 7). Similarly, Acierno et al. (2006) compared older adults (over 60 years) to younger adults living in places affected by the 2004 Florida hurricanes and found that older adults experienced fewer symptoms of PTSD, major depressive disorder, and generalized anxiety disorder. The specific demographic and storm-related risk factors that were associated with outcome varied by age group (i.e., income was not related to outcome for the younger group, but it was for the older group). Variables such as low social support, prior exposure to traumas, and poor health status were found to be universally predictive of psychopathology symptoms. Conversely, however, Kohn et al. (2005) looked at reactions of elderly adults following Hurricane Mitch and risk factors for psychopathology in that population. They found that these older adults did not differ significantly from younger people in their experience of PTSD or depression, and that risk factors for both groups included pre-hurricane psychopathology and the intensity of exposure.

Other studies have looked more generally at the variables associated with the experience of mental health symptoms following hurricanes. Victims of hurricanes have been shown to experience significant levels of depression, anxiety, somatization, general stress, and traumatic stress (Thompson, Norris, & Hanacek, 1993). Ethnic differences in mental health responses to Hurricane Andrew have also been explored (Perilla, Norris, & Lavizzo, 2002). Large differences in the prevalence of PTSD symptoms were found between ethnic groups, with only 15% of Caucasian participants experiencing these symptoms, while 23% of African Americans and 38% of Latinos experienced them. Sattler et al. (2002) looked at responses to Hurricane Georges in several different areas, including the U.S. Virgin Islands, Puerto Rico, the Dominican Republic, and the United States (U.S.). They found that those in the U.S. and the U.S. Virgin Islands had less damage and lost fewer resources than those in the other countries and also experienced fewer symptoms of acute stress disorder. Symptoms of acute stress disorder were associated with location, personal characteristic resource loss (i.e., locus of control, self-esteem, knowledge, skills), and low social support.

While it can clearly be seen that mental health difficulties exist for some individuals following the experience of a hurricane, other studies have looked at how these symptoms change over time. Norris, Perilla, Riad, Kaniasty, and Lavizzo (1999) found no difference in the percentage of people meeting criteria for depression and PTSD from 6 to 30 months following Hurricane Andrew. They did, however, find differences in the symptoms. Symptoms of intrusion and hyperarousal decreased over time, depressive symptoms remained stable, and avoidance/numbing symptoms increased. Interestingly, intrusion and hyperarousal were associated more strongly with pre-disaster (e.g., ethnicity, gender) and within-disaster (e.g., injury, property loss) variables than with post-disaster (e.g., stress, resources) variables, but the reverse was true for depression and avoidance (Norris et al., 1999).

Given the consistent finding that experiencing a hurricane leads to serious mental health symptoms and problems, it is not surprising that several studies have explored mental health service use following these storms. Bloch, Pandurangi, and Aderibigbe (2003) looked at help-seeking behaviors following Hurricane Floyd. They found that 83% of participants reported seeking help from a physician for physical symptoms such as headaches, dizziness, and racing heart, because they saw them as being better explained by somatic problems rather than psychological concerns. Even when no physical explanation could be found, participants were more likely to seek a second opinion from another physician rather than seeking help from a mental health professional (Bloch et al., 2003). Fried, Domino, and Shadle (2005) also looked at the use of mental health services following Hurricane Floyd and found that visits to psychologists, licensed clinical social workers, and physicians for mental health reasons were higher in affected areas after the hurricane. Inpatient admissions decreased, however, as did money spent on anti-anxiety medications, indicating that there were problems with service delivery for those that did seek help. Overall, those with higher education levels and previous mental health problems have been found to be the most likely to seek services following a hurricane (Caldera et al., 2001), though it seems that most individuals seek out primary medical care first.

Hurricane Katrina and Adults

Mental Illness, Prevalence Rates, and Associated Findings Following Katrina

Findings from the emerging literature on survivors of Hurricane Katrina have generally been consistent with those of previous storms and hurricanes. To date, the largest investigation of the effects of Hurricane Katrina has been based on 1043 adults (i.e., 18 years or older) from the Hurricane Katrina Community Advisory Group (CAG; Kessler, Galea, Jones, & Parker, 2006). The sample was targeted to be comparable to an earlier subsample of the National Comorbidity Survey-Replication (NCS-R) in what would become Katrina-affected areas years later (i.e., a new sample). Approximately 5–7 months after Katrina, CAG members participated in telephone screenings and surveys examining a variety of variables including mental illness, suicidality, and trauma exposure (Galea et al., 2007; Kessler et al., 2006, 2008). Results indicated most post-Katrina 30-day prevalence rates were nearly double the rates from the NCS-R assessment (Kessler et al., 2006). Rates for serious mental illness, mild–moderate mental illness, and any mental illness were 11.3, 19.9, and 31.2%, respectively, where they had previously been 6.1, 9.7, and 15.7% just 3–4 years before Katrina (Kessler et al., 2006). In addition, 30-day prevalence rates for PTSD were found to be 30.3 and 49.1% for any anxiety or mood disorder and were associated with trauma exposure, especially for New Orleans residents (Galea et al., 2007). Interestingly, the 12-month prevalence rate for suicidality decreased in those with suspected mental illness following Katrina. Rates for ideation went down from 8.4 to 0.7%, those with a plan went from 3.6 to 0.4%, and those who had attempted went from 2.3 to 0.8% (Kessler et al., 2006). It was concluded that these changes were associated with two areas of posttraumatic growth: faith in the ability to rebuild one's life and coming to a realization of one's inner strength (see Chapter 3, for a related discussion). Examinations of demographic characteristics suggested the increased rates of mental illness and suicidality were associated with being Caucasian, unmarried, and unemployed or disabled (Kessler et al., 2006); comparisons to the NCS-R sample, however, only revealed a significant association for being unmarried. A 1-year follow-up of 815 members of the CAG unfortunately revealed mental illness and suicidality remained and at rates which exceeded those from 1 year ago (Kessler et al., 2008). Rates for PTSD, serious mental illness, and having suicidal ideation and a plan to commit suicide all increased significantly.

Other researchers have examined the effects of Katrina as well. Weems et al. (2007) surveyed 401 adults from Katrina affected areas beginning a couple of months following the hurricane. Their findings suggested that the number of traumatic events one was exposed to was positively associated with other variables including PTSD and perceived discrimination and was negatively associated with evacuation distance. In addition, through a series of regression models the authors concluded that residing in Mississippi was associated with greater PTSD symptoms but also greater social support, while residing in New Orleans was associated with greater perceptions of discrimination (Weems et al., 2007). Examining outpatient adults in Mississippi 1 month before and after Katrina (i.e., differing samples), McLeish and Del Ben (2008) similarly found that depression increased following the hurricane though not PTSD. Depressive symptoms, however, were predicted by watching media coverage of the looting in New Orleans and the amount of time one was without power; symptoms of PTSD were predicted by using television viewing to cope. Using prayer to cope was associated with a decrease in PTSD (McLeish & Del Ben, 2008). Overall, similar findings have been made for those evacuated to other states including Oklahoma (Tucker et al., 2008) and Texas (Mollyann, Weltzien, Altman, Blendon, & Benson, 2006; North et al., 2008), though rates and results vary based on the sample, time of assessment, and methodology.

Findings from Young Adults

Davis and colleagues have also conducted a series of studies based on a survey of 827 young adults. In a series of four studies involving university students, they examined the effects of exposure to Hurricane Katrina, the effects of displacement from the Gulf Coast inland to Baton Rouge, the differences between African American and Caucasian experiences of and reactions to Katrina, and the effects of the storm on those with and without pre-existing storm fears. Three months immediately following Hurricane Katrina for a period of 1 month (mid-November to mid-December), students currently attending Louisiana State University (including those who had evacuated to Baton Rouge and enrolled/transferred to the university after the hurricane) participated in an online survey which contained a variety of psychometrically sound instruments to measure symptoms of anxiety, depression, and posttraumatic stress (e.g., the Depression, Anxiety, and Stress Scales, DASS; Lovibond & Lovibond, 1995; the Impact of Events Scale-Revised, IES-R; Weiss & Marmar, 1997). Participants also completed several other instruments including those measuring coping (e.g., Hurricane Coping Self-Efficacy Measure, HCSE, Benight, Ironson, & Durham, 1999), fear (e.g., Fear Survey Schedule-II, FSS-II, Geer, 1965), and traumatic exposure (Traumatic Exposure Severity Scale, TESS, Elal & Slade, 2005) among other things (e.g., fear of anxiety, quality of life, self-efficacy).

Effects of Exposure to Hurricane Katrina

Similar to those studies reviewed previously, exposure to Hurricane Katrina was associated with a variety of psychological difficulties. In an examination of 430 young adults, Davis, Grills-Taquechel, and Ollendick (2007, 2009a) examined differences between 215 adults reporting no hurricane exposure and the 215 reporting the most exposure on the TESS. The sample was 70% women with a mean age of 20.4 years ($SD = 2.4$ years). Subsequently, scores on the DASS, IES-R, and HCSE were examined. Significant differences were found on all of the instruments. As per hypotheses, those young adults exposed to the hurricane reported significantly more symptoms of depression, anxiety, and PTSD, as well as significantly poorer coping self-efficacy. Even so, the means for those exposed were consistent with only mild symptomatology, with the notable exception of coping self-efficacy. On the HCSE, the mean for those young adults not exposed was below the published means of those exposed to Hurricanes Andrew and Opal (i.e., higher scores indicate greater coping self-efficacy; cf. Benight, Ironson, Klebe et al., 1999; Benight, Swift et al., 1999); further, the mean for those young adults who were exposed was significantly less (i.e., poorer coping self-efficacy) than those not exposed. Overall, the researchers concluded that most of those with the most exposure to Hurricane Katrina and associated events generally suffered only mild psychological symptoms (i.e., most exhibited resiliency or recovery). This finding was not surprising given the presumably higher functioning of the participants (i.e., college students) and the extent to which the storm's impact may have been cushioned (i.e., students who were able to reenroll in a nearby university and quickly rejoin important routines, studies, university life, etc.). Even so, it is important to note that even these individuals experienced mild symptoms and, importantly, coping self-efficacy appeared to be particularly affected by exposure to Katrina—even more so than in Hurricane Opal or Hurricane Andrew.

Effects of Displacement from the Gulf Coast

Displacement due to Hurricane Katrina is a particularly important area of study; not only did people experience potentially traumatizing events but also had to contend with the loss of their homes, the dispersion of their families and friends, and the relocation and adjustment to an unfamiliar situation. In this study (Davis, Grills-Taquechel, & Ollendick, 2006, 2009b), 68 young adults indicating they had been displaced from the Gulf Coast due to Hurricane Katrina were matched on race, sex, and age to 68 young adults who were not displaced and resided at Louisiana State University immediately prior to, during, and after the hurricane (i.e., 136 total). Participants were 59% Caucasian (41% African American), 68% women, with a mean age of 20.8 years ($SD = 3.9$ years). Participants had similarly completed the DASS, IES-R, TESS, and HCSE. As expected, results indicated displaced young adults had more symptoms of depression and PTSD than non-displaced adults (though only in the mild range); however, the groups did not differ in their report of anxiety or coping self-efficacy—though coping was again below the means reported for previous hurricanes (cf. Benight, Ironson, Klebe et al., 1999; Benight, Swift et al., 1999). Consistent with expectations, young adults who were displaced from New Orleans and surrounding areas reported experiencing significantly more occurrences of trauma and distress from their traumatic exposure compared to those who were not displaced. Further, scores for both the occurrence of trauma and the subsequent distress from traumatic exposure were both found to mediate scores for depression: being displaced was associated with more traumatic exposure and more distress which was subsequently associated with higher depression scores.

Racial Differences in the Experience of Hurricane Katrina and Resulting Psychological Impact

The examination of experiences of Hurricane Katrina based on race has been a particularly controversial topic and one fraught with intense emotions and discussion (e.g., Cordasco et al., 2007). Davis et al. (2007) and Davis, Grills-Taquechel, and Ollendick (2009c) examined similarities and differences in African American and Caucasian young adults following Hurricane Katrina. Eighty-six African Americans were matched on sex and age to 86 Caucasians who were enrolled at Louisiana State University (77% women; mean age was 20.5 years, $SD = 3.4$ years). Examining the same measures mentioned previously, African Americans were found to have more symptoms of PTSD (though well below the clinical cutoff) and poorer coping self-efficacy, but understandably so as they also reported more occurrences of trauma and more distress from their exposure. Overall, the authors emphasized the strengths in the African American men and women as no differences were found on measures of anxiety or depression, and those differences which were found were at or below the cutoffs for mild symptoms even though African Americans experienced more trauma than their matched Caucasian counterparts.

Effects of Katrina on Those with Pre-hurricane Storm Fears

Very little research has been conducted examining the responses of those with pre-existing storm fears to hurricanes. Most of the literature that does exist on what has been termed "severe weather phobia" focuses on how these fears develop (Westefeld, 1996; Muris et al., 2002). In an attempt to expand on this area of research, Munson, Davis, Grills-Taquechel, and Zlomke (2009) examined the differences in how those with pre-hurricane storm fear experienced and coped with Hurricane Katrina as compared to those that did not report any fears of storms or otherwise before or after the hurricane.

Sixty-two women were included in the study, with 31 having indicated a fear of storms that began on average 120 months prior to Hurricane Katrina and 31 who reported no significant fears of any stimuli. Groups were matched on the occurrence of trauma from the hurricane based on their scores from the TESS. All participants were assessed on measures of exposure to and distress from the hurricane, coping, PTSD symptoms, and general fear (FSS-II, Geer, 1965). Results of the study indicated that despite controlling for any differences in the occurrence of trauma, those with storm fear experienced more distress from their exposure, particularly in regard to concern for others and exposure to the grotesque. This finding is consistent with prior studies that have found that people with phobias continue to report high levels of distress, even after the feared stimulus has been removed (Jones & Menzies, 2000). Consistent with the finding that previous psychopathology is a better predictor of distress from a traumatic event than level of exposure (McFarlane, 1989), pre-hurricane storm fear significantly predicted who would experience distress from the hurricane. The storm fearful group also reported significantly poorer coping self-efficacy and significantly higher levels of fear (i.e., more overall fear). Further, those who reported pre-hurricane storm fear also reported more concern for others and more distress related to that concern. While having more instances of being concerned for others significantly predicted distress from the concern, it was found to only be a partial mediator, suggesting that there is a unique component to being storm fearful. Overall the results of this study suggest that having a pre-existing fear of storms leads to more distress from hurricane exposure, which may make storm fearful individuals (as opposed to and in addition to those with PTSD) an underserved and under-recognized group following severe hurricanes.

Disruption to Service and Treatment

The psychological impact from Hurricane Katrina described earlier was further compounded by unmet treatment needs. Predicting the psychological need following a disaster is difficult, and following Hurricane Katrina needs assessments returned conservative estimates compared to subsequent post-Katrina published rates of PTSD and other disorders (Dalton, Scheeringa, & Zeanah, 2008). Studies have examined two important areas for future intervention research and post-disaster logistical planning: access to treatment following a disaster and continuation of any ongoing treatment following a disaster. Following telephone surveys conducted 8 months after Hurricane Katrina, Wang, Gruber et al. (2007) concluded almost a third of participants had a mood or anxiety disorder, but only a third of those had sought out mental health services for their difficulties (most commonly physicians and pharmacotherapy). Further, 60% had already discontinued treatment by the time of the interview. Wang et al. (2008) examined those who had been receiving treatment before the hurricane and those who sought it afterward. Following Katrina, 23% had to discontinue or curtail treatment and only 19% of those without pre-existing psychopathology but with new post-Katrina conditions had sought to initiate treatment. Barriers to the continuation of treatment reported by participants included a lack of the availability of services and financial and transportation needs.

The most common barrier among those with post-hurricane onset disorders was a simple failure to perceive a need for treatment.

Those with chronic medical conditions experienced serious disruption to their medical care as well. Wang, Kendrick et al. (2007) reported 20.6% of adults with serious, chronic conditions (e.g., cardiovascular, respiratory, digestive, and musculoskeletal problems) cut back on or discontinued treatment following the hurricane. The most common reasons people reported having to cut back were due to difficulty finding and accessing physicians, problems getting medications, and financial and transportation difficulties (Wang, Kendrick et al., 2007). The authors found treatment disruption was associated with a variety of variables including being a younger adult (less than 65 years), lacking health insurance, having poor or limited familial or social support, and having difficulty maintaining a residence. Overall, it seems access to treatment for both mental and medical health conditions was hampered following Hurricane Katrina. Most commonly, it appeared financial and transportation problems hampered obtaining assistance. Even so, there also seemed to be significant difficulties in accessing physicians and mental health professionals as well as disseminating information about who should seek treatment and for what symptoms.

Conclusions

Experiencing severe storms and hurricanes (e.g., Hurricanes Katrina and Rita) and the resulting stress and devastation can precipitate a number of different psychological reactions in adults—from brief, stressful adjustments to serious mental health concerns. Researchers have generally shown most individuals experiencing trauma from storms and hurricanes will be understandably stressed but resilient. Even so, there was a troubling increase in the prevalence of mental health issues following Hurricane Katrina with a concomitant reduction in the access to and the use of mental health and medical services. Additionally, displacement and evacuation also appear to be associated with poorer outcomes for adults, as well as having concomitant financial, transportation, residential, and social support difficulties. In addition, results seem, unfortunately, to indicate a variety of long-standing mental health difficulties for some following Hurricane Katrina.

Overall, the Gulf Coast region would seem to be a particularly important geographical area in which to concentrate mental health services and hurricane and trauma-related research. Given the frequency with which hurricanes and severe storms impact the region, there would surprisingly seem to be a relative lack of mental health services and research endeavors in that area. For example, most recently the region has again been struck by Hurricanes Gustav and Ike, just 3 years after Katrina and Rita. While ongoing research from Hurricane Katrina will likely be able to elucidate pre–post-changes from Gustav and Ike, the region would likely lend itself to more prospective approaches. In addition, the disturbing regularity of devastating storms would seem to indicate the need for better pre-disaster preparation and organization of practitioners in the area and some sort of broad-based training in evidence-based interventions for trauma recovery. Finally, while the research and treatment of PTSD is important during such disasters, investigators and practitioners should be encouraged to not overlook other psychopathologies (e.g., depression, phobias) which may be present as well.

Acknowledgment The participation of Thompson E. Davis III, Ph.D. was funded in part by an internal grant from the College of Arts and Sciences at Louisiana State University. This support is gratefully acknowledged.

References

Acierno, R., Brady, K., Gray, M., Kilpatrick, D. G., Resnick, H., & Best, C. L. (2002). Psychopathology following interpersonal violence: A comparison of risk factors in older and younger adults. *Journal of Clinical Geropsychology, 8*, 13–23.

Acierno, R., Ruggiero, K. J., Kilpatrick, D. G., Resnick, H. S., & Galea, S. (2006). Risk and protective factors for psychopathology among older versus younger adults after the 2004 Florida hurricanes. *American Journal of Geriatric Psychiatry, 14*, 1051–1059.

American Psychiatric Association. (2000). *Diagnostic and statistical manual of mental disorders – text revision* (4th ed.). Washington, DC: Author.

Benight, C. C., & Bandura, A. (2004). Social cognitive theory of posttraumatic recovery: The role of perceived self-efficacy. *Behaviour Research and Therapy, 42*, 1129–1148.

Benight, C. C., & Harper, M. L. (2002). Coping self-efficacy perceptions as a mediator between acute stress response and long-term distress following natural disasters. *Journal of Traumatic Stress, 15*, 177–186.

Benight, C. C., Ironson, G., & Durham, R. L. (1999). Psychometric properties of a hurricane coping self-efficacy measure. *Journal of Traumatic Stress, 12*, 379–386.

Benight, C. C., Ironson, G., Klebe, K., Carver, C. S., Wynings, C., Burnett, K., et al. (1999). Conservation of resources and coping self-efficacy predicting distress following a natural disaster: A causal model analysis where the environment meets the mind. *Anxiety, Stress, & Coping, 12*, 107–126.

Benight, C. C., Swift, E., Sanger, J., Smith, A., & Zeppelin, D. (1999). Coping self-efficacy as a mediator of distress following a natural disaster. *Journal of Applied Social Psychology, 29*, 2443–2464.

Bloch, R. M., Pandurangi, A., & Aderibigbe, Y. A. (2003). Emotional and somatic distress in eastern North Carolina: Help-seeking behaviors. *International Journal of Social Psychiatry, 49*, 126–141.

Bonanno, G. A. (2004). Loss, trauma, and human resilience: Have we underestimated the human capacity to thrive after extremely aversive events? *American Psychologist, 59*, 20–28.

Bonanno, G. A., Galea, S., Bucciarelli, A., & Vlahov, D. (2007). What predicts psychological resilience after disaster? The role of demographics, resources, and life stress. *Journal of Consulting and Clinical Psychology, 75*, 761–682.

Caldera, T., Palma, L., Penayo, U., & Kullgren, G. (2001). Psychological impact of the hurricane Mitch in Nicaragua in a one year perspective. *Social Psychiatry and Psychiatric Epidemiology, 36*, 108–114.

Cieslak, R., Benight, C. C., & Lehman, V. C. (2008). Coping self-efficacy mediates the effects of negative cognitions on posttraumatic distress. *Behaviour Research and Therapy, 46*, 788–798.

Clark, S. (2005, September 13). True crime? *Baton rouge business report*. Retrieved September 28, 2005, from http://www.allbusiness.com/legal/1126226-1.html

Cordasco, K., Eisenman, D., Glik, D., Golden, J., & Asch, S. (2007). "They blew the levee:" Distrust of authorities among Hurricane Katrina evacuees. *Journal of Health Care for the Poor and Underserved, 18*, 277–282.

Dalton, R., Scheeringa, M., & Zeanah, C. (2008). Did the prevalence of PTSD following Hurricane Katrina match a rapid needs assessment prediction: A template for future public planning after large-scale disasters. *Psychiatric Annals, 38*, 134–141.

David, D., Mellman, T. A., Mendoza, L. M., Kulick-Bell, R., Ironson, G., & Schneiderman, N. (1996). Psychiatric morbidity following Hurricane Andrew. *Journal of Traumatic Stress, 9*, 607–612.

Davis T. E., III, Grills-Taquechel, A. E., & Ollendick, T. H. (2006, November). *Displacement by Hurricane Katrina: Students' reaction to trauma.* Poster presented at the annual meetings of the Association for Behavioral and Cognitive Therapies, Chicago.

Davis T. E., III, Grills-Taquechel, A. E., & Ollendick, T. H. (2007, February). Hurricane Katrina: The psychological impact on young adults. In Katie E. Cherry (Chair), *Hurricane Katrina: Psychological impact and mental health issues across the lifespan.* Invited symposium presented at the annual meetings of the Southeastern Psychological Association, New Orleans, Louisiana.

Davis T. E., III, Grills-Taquechel, A. E., & Ollendick, T. H. (2009a). *Hurricane Katrina: The effects of exposure on young adults.* Manuscript in preparation.

Davis T. E., III, Grills-Taquechel, A. E., & Ollendick, T. H. (2009b). *The psychological impact from Hurricane Katrina: Effects of displacement on university students.* Manuscript submitted for publication.

Davis T. E., III, Grills-Taquechel, A. E., & Ollendick, T. H. (2009c). *Racial differences and similarities in the experience of and psychological impact from Hurricane Katrina.* Manuscript in preparation.

Dougall, A. L., Hyman, K. B., Hayward, M. C., McFeeley, S., & Baum, A. (2001). Optimism and traumatic stress: The importance of social support and coping. *Journal of Applied Social Psychology, 31*, 223–245.

Elal, G., & Slade, P. (2005). Traumatic Exposure Severity Scale (TESS): A measure of exposure to major disasters. *Journal of Traumatic Stress, 18*, 213–220.

Fairbank, J. A., Ebert, L., & Caddell, J. M. (2004). Posttraumatic stress disorder. In H. E. Adams & P. B. Sutker (Eds.), *Comprehensive handbook of psychopathology* (3rd ed., pp. 183–210). New York: Springer.

Fried, B. J., Domino, M. E., & Shadle, J. (2005). Use of mental health services after Hurricane Floyd in North Carolina. *Psychiatric Services, 56*, 1367–1373.

Galea, S., Brewin, C., Gruber, M., Jones, R. T., King, D., King, L., et al. (2007). Exposure to hurricane-related stressors and mental illness after Hurricane Katrina. *Archives of General Psychiatry, 64*, 1427–1434.

Geer, J. H. (1965). The development of a scale to measure fear. *Behaviour Research and Therapy, 3*, 45–53.

Graumann, A., Houston, T., Lawrimore, J., Levinson, D., Lott, N., McCown, S., et al. (2005; updated 2006). *Hurricane Katrina a climatological perspective: Preliminary report.* Retrieved November 8, 2007, from the National Oceanic and Atmospheric Administration's National Climatic Data Center, from http://www.ncdc.noaa.gov/oa/reports/tech-report-200501z.pdf

Hochwarter, W. A., Laird, M. D., & Brouer, R. L. (2008). Board up the windows: The interactive effects of hurricane-induced job stress and perceived resources on work outcomes. *Journal of Management, 34*, 263–289.

Jones, M. K., & Menzies, R. G. (2000). Danger expectancies, self-efficacy, and insight in spider phobia. *Behaviour Research and Therapy, 38*, 585–600.

Keane, T. M., & Barlow, D. H. (2002). Posttraumatic stress disorder. In D. Barlow (Ed.), *Anxiety and its disorders: The nature and treatment of anxiety and panic* (pp. 418–454). New York: The Guilford Press.

Kessler, R. C., Galea, S., Gruber, M., Sampson, N., Ursano, R., & Wessely, S. (2008). Trends in mental illness and suicidality after Hurricane Katrina. *Molecular Psychiatry, 13*, 374–384.

Kessler, R. C., Galea, S., Jones, R. T., & Parker, H. A. (2006). Mental illness and suicidality after Hurricane Katrina. *Bulletin of the World Health Organization, 84*, 930–939.

Kohn, R., Levav, I., Garcia, I. D., Machuca, M. E., & Tamashiro, R. (2005). Prevalence, risk factors and aging vulnerability for psychopathology following a natural disaster in a developing country. *International Journal of Geriatric Psychiatry, 20*, 835–841.

Lee, M., Weil, F., & Shihadeh, E. (2007). The FEMA trailer parks: Negative perceptions and the social structure of avoidance. *Sociological Spectrum, 27*, 741–766.

Leon, K., Hyre, A., Ompad, D., DeSalvo, K., & Munter, P. (2007). Perceived stress among a workforce 6 months following Katrina. *Social Psychiatry and Psychiatric Epidemiology, 42*, 1005–1011.

Lovibond, S. H., & Lovibond, P. F. (1995). *Manual for the depression anxiety stress scales.* (2nd ed.) Sydney: Psychology Foundation.

Mancini, A. D., & Bonanno, G. A. (2006). Resilience in the face of potential trauma: Clinical practices and illustrations. *Journal of Clinical Psychology: In Session, 62*, 971–985.

Masten, A. S. (2001). Ordinary magic: Resilience processes in development. *American Psychologist, 56*, 227–238.

McFarlane, A. C. (1989). The aetiology of post-traumatic morbidity: Predisposing, precipitating and perpetuating factors. *British Journal of Psychiatry, 154*, 221–228.

McLeish, A., & Del Ben, K. (2008). Symptoms of depression and posttraumatic stress disorder in an outpatient population before and after Hurricane Katrina. *Depression and Anxiety, 25*, 416–421.

Mollyann, B., Weltzien, E., Altman, D., Blendon, R., & Benson, J. (2006). Experiences of Hurricane Katrina evacuees in Houston shelters: Implications for future planning. *American Journal of Public Health, 96*, 1402–1408.

Munson, M., Davis T. E., III, Grills-Taquechel, A., & Zlomke, K. (2009). *The effects of Hurricane Katrina: How those who feared storms handled THE STORM.* Manuscript submitted for publication.

Muris, P., Meesters, C., Merckelbach, H., Verschuren, M., Geebelen, E., & Aleva, E. (2002). Fear of storms and hurricanes in Antillean and Belgian children. *Behaviour Research and Therapy, 40*, 459–569.

Norris, F. (1992). Epidemiology of trauma: Frequency and impact of different potentially traumatic events on different demographic groups. *Journal of Consulting and Clinical Psychology, 60*, 409–418.

Norris, F. H., Perilla, J. L., Riad, J. K., Kaniasty, K., & Lavizzo, E. A. (1999). Stability and change in stress, resources, and psychological distress following natural disaster: Findings from Hurricane Andrew. *Anxiety, Stress, and Coping, 12*, 363–396.

North, C., King, R., Fowler, R., Polatin, P., Smith, R., LaGrone, A., et al. (2008). Psychiatric disorders among transported hurricane evacuees: Acute-phase findings in a large receiving shelter site. *Psychiatric Annals, 38*, 104–113.

Perilla, J. L., Norris, F. H., & Lavizzo, E. A. (2002). Ethnicity, culture, and disaster response: Identifying and explaining ethnic differences in PTSD six months after Hurricane Andrew. *Journal of Social and Clinical Psychology, 21*, 20–45.

Sattler, D. N., Preston, A. J., Kaiser, C. F., Olivera, V. E., Valdez, J., & Schlueter, S. (2002). Hurricane Georges: A cross-national study examining preparedness, resource loss, and psychological distress in the U.S. Virgin Islands, Puerto Rico, Dominican Republic, and the United States. *Journal of Traumatic Stress, 15*, 339–350.

Shalev, A. Y., Freedman, S., Peri, T., Brandes, D., Sahar, T., Orr, S. P., et al. (1998). Prospective study of posttraumatic stress disorder and depression following trauma. *The American Journal of Psychiatry, 155*, 630–637.

Smith, E. M., North, C. S., McCool, R. E., & Shea, J. M. (1990). Acute postdisaster psychiatric disorders: Identification of persons at risk. *The American Journal of Psychiatry, 147*, 202–206.

Sullivent, E., West, C., Noe, R., Thomas, K., Wallace, D., & Leeb, R. (2006). Nonfatal injuries following Hurricane Katrina—New Orleans, Louisiana, 2005. *Journal of Safety Research, 37*, 213–217.

Thomas, S. (2007). Lies, damn lies, and rumors: An analysis of collective efficacy, rumors, and fear in the wake of Katrina. *Sociological Spectrum, 27*, 679–703.

Thompson, M., Norris, F., & Hanacek, B. (1993). Age differences in the psychological consequences of Hurricane Hugo. *Psychology and Aging, 8*, 606–616.

Tucker, P., Pfefferbaum, B., Khan, Q., Young, J., Aston, C., Holmes, J., et al. (2008). Katrina survivors relocated to Oklahoma: A talk of two cities. *Psychiatric Annals, 38*, 125–133.

VanLandingham, M. (2007). Murder rates in New Orleans, La, 2004–2006. *American Journal of Public Health, 97*, 1614–1616.

Wang, P., Gruber, M., Powers, R., Schoenbaum, M., Speier, A., Wells, K., et al. (2007). Mental health service use among Hurricane Katrina survivors in the eight months after the disaster. *Psychiatric Services, 58*, 1403–1411.

Wang, P., Gruber, M., Powers, R., Schoenbaum, M., Speier, A., Wells, K., et al. (2008). Disruption of existing mental health treatments and failure to initiate new treatment after Hurricane Katrina. *American Journal of Psychiatry, 165*, 34–41.

Wang, P., Kendrick, D., Lurie, N., Springgate, B., & Kessler, R. C. (2007). Hurricane Katrina's impact on the care of survivors with chronic medical conditions. *Journal of General Internal Medicine, 22*, 1225–1230.

Wang, X., Gao, L., Shinfuku, N., Zhang, H., Zhao, C., & Shen, Y. (2000). Longitudinal study of earthquake-related PTSD in a randomly selected community sample in North China. *The American Journal of Psychiatry, 157*, 1260–1266.

Weems, C. F., Watts, S. E., Marsee, M. A., Taylor, L. K., Costa, N. M., Cannon, M. F., et al. (2007). The psychosocial impact of Hurricane Katrina: Contextual differences in psychological symptoms, social support, and discrimination. *Behaviour Research and Therapy, 45*, 2295–2306.

Weiss, D., & Marmar, C. (1997). The impact of event scale -revised. In J. Wilson & T. Keane (Eds.), *Assessing psychological trauma and PTSD* (pp. 219–238). New York: Guildford.

Westefeld, J. S. (1996). Severe weather phobia: An exploratory study. *Journal of Clinical Psychology, 52*, 509–515.

Chapter 6
Families and Disasters: Making Meaning out of Adversity

M.E. Betsy Garrison and Diane D. Sasser

Abstract Based on Walsh's family resilience framework, the purpose of our chapter was to elucidate the manner in which families directly impacted by Hurricane Katrina have made meaning out of that traumatic event. We conducted in-depth semi-structured field interviews of south Louisiana families directly affected by Hurricane Katrina twice, in 2006 and again in 2007. Using Davis, Nolen-Hoeksema, and Larson's (*Journal of Personality and Social Psychology, 75,* 561–574, 1998) two-construct conceptualization of meaning making, three themes emerged about benefit finding: Improved relationships, prioritization and planning, and reappraisal; and four themes emerged about sense making: Order in social environment, attribution to a higher power, general acceptance, and old adages survive. An unexpected theme that emerged during data analyses was the use of humor. Besides discovering that families are resilient, our conclusions are as follows: Make people a priority, weather happens, hope rules, and humor helps. We recommend a bioecological and strength-based, multiple-level approach to all involved in the disaster and trauma arena, regardless of the nature of the crisis.

Introduction

In the last several years, the construct of *family* resilience, especially as a process, has gained prominence. In 2002, the two most influential family science journals, *Journal of Marriage and Family* (JMF) and *Family Relations* (FR), each published a special collection. The articles in JMF were both theoretical and empirical in nature and included topics such as economic hardship, gay and lesbian families, and families in poverty. The articles in FR, a more applied and practice-focused journal, were also both theoretical and empirical and included topics such as childhood cancer,

M.E.B. Garrison (✉)
Division of Family Science School of Human Ecology, LSU College of Agriculture Baton Rouge LA 70803 USA
e-mail: hcgarr@lsu.edu

post-welfare rural African-American single-mother-headed families, intervention-induced resilience from a preventive parenting program for divorced mothers, and practice applications of Walsh's family resilience framework. None of the articles mentioned natural disasters and non-natural ones, such as the 9/11 tragedy, were mentioned only in passing, indicating a realm understudied and possibly, at that time, overlooked. Beginning with the hurricanes that hit Florida in 2004, attention in this realm has mushroomed.

Pivotal to family resilience is the idea that a family has strengths or resources that allow it to overcome a challenging experience, trauma, or loss and to have thrived from that experience (Cowan, Cowan, & Shultz, 1996; Patterson, 2002; Walsh, 2003). Families who respond positively to adversity can become resilient. In some of our earlier works, we found that, although they "bounced back," families experienced a period of decreased functioning in the immediate aftermath of Katrina (Knowles, Sasser, & Garrison, 2009). A key aspect of resilience and recovering from loss is making meaning which usually involves acceptance and has also been referred to as "finding meaning," "explaining" the event, and "account making" (Davis et al., 1998). It is important to differentiate the process of making meaning from a traumatic experience from the search for meaning, typically considered a developmental task of adulthood, in a person's life (see Baumeister, 1991; Bruner, 1990; Frankl, 1985; King, Hicks, Krull, & Del Gaiso, 2006; Steger, Frazier, Oishi, & Kaler, 2006; Wong & Fry, 1998a, 1998b for a more general discussion of the latter). Within the context of family resilience, we decided to focus this work on meaning making and extend conceptual advances in this area beyond the bereavement, loss, illness, and disease literature into that of natural disasters. Thus, the purpose of our chapter is to elucidate the ways in which families directly impacted by hurricane Katrina made meaning out of that traumatic event.

Theoretical Background and Related Literature

Based on the bioecological model Bronfenbrenner (1977, 1986, see also 2005) and Walsh (2003) developed the family resilience framework that encompasses three areas of family functioning: belief systems, organizational patterns, and communication processes. Belief systems suggest that resilience is cultivated by a family's "shared facilitative beliefs" which help to create meaning in times of crisis, promote optimism, and provide connectedness through transcendence and spirituality. For a family to make meaning out of adversity it is necessary for the members within the family to rely on each other to overcome challenges. A resilient family remains hopeful, focuses on how their strengths can help them through the situation, adopts a "can-do" attitude, and accepts the aspects of the situation that are out of their control. Through transcendence and spirituality, the family is able to find connectedness through their value system, faith beliefs and practices, and their own personal transformation that comes from experiencing and working through adversity (Walsh, 2003, p. 407). Although not explicitly stated by Walsh, we assume that the listing of belief systems as the first component of resilience in her framework reflects its primacy in recovering and adaptation.

Meaning making plays a central role in adjustment to both loss and trauma (Davis & Nolen-Hoeksema, 2001; Krause, 2005; see also Chapter 10 in this volume) and has been deconstructed into two dimensions: benefit finding and sense making (Davis et al., 1998). Benefit finding has been linked to finding the "silver lining" and some typical responses included having a new appreciation for life, valuing current relationships more, or changing for the better. The process of sense making involves the development of a relatively benign explanation for the loss within an existing world view. In their seminal study of meaning making, Davis et al. (1998) found that sense making and benefit finding played independent roles in the adjustment process of people who have lost a family member due to a terminal illness. Unrelated to illness, they found six categories of sense making including predictability, acceptance, God/fate, just happens, expected/prepared for, and experienced growth and another six categories of benefit finding including growth in character, gained perspective, brought family together, positive support from others, others will benefit, and better that it is over. Using Davis et al.'s (1998) conceptualization, Pakenham, Sofronoff, and Samios (2004) in a study of 59 parents of children with Asperger syndrome found 8 benefit and 12 sense making themes. Of interest to the current work are the themes that are not closely related to the family's situation; in this case, parenting a child with a developmental disability. Benefit finding themes were positive personality change, positive effects of child on parent, change in life priority and/or goals, new opportunities, strengthening of relationships and growth in faith/spirituality. Sense making themes included changed perspective, acceptance, experienced growth, focus on parenting role, new life direction and priorities, similarity between child and self/others, and spiritual/faith interpretation.

Although not a study of meaning making per se, Curbow, Somerfield, Baker, Wingard, and Legro (1993) in a study of 135 bone marrow transplantation survivors found that positive changes were reported in plans for the future, sibling relationships, and beliefs about what is important in life. In separate studies, one of heart attack patients (Affleck, Tennen, Croog, & Levine, 1987) and/or one of HIV-seropositive men (Bower, Kemeny, Taylor, & Fahey, 1998), those study participants who mentioned benefits or found meaning, were physically healthier later in their lives. The perceived benefits cited, unrelated to their physical health, were (a) changes in philosophy of life, values, or religious views; (b) changes in family life and family relationships; (c) insight into the need for avoiding stress and conflict; and (d) changes in mode of life to increase enjoyment; and interestingly, they mentioned changes in philosophy of life, values, or religious views more frequently 8 years after a heart attack than 7 weeks after it (Affleck et al., 1987). Thus, empirical support for meaning making as an aspect of successful recovery from loss exists, although it has not been often been studied within the context of a natural disaster (see Chapter 10 for related discussion).

Current Study

Through qualitative methods, we investigated the salience of Davis et al.'s (1998) two-construct conceptualization of meaning making with families who were recovering from being directly impacted by a natural disaster. A priori we also included optimism as a construct as it is an aspect of Walsh's family resilience framework and considered a separate, but significant, construct by "meaning" and "bereavement" scholars (e.g., Davis et al., 1998; Davis & Nolen-Hoeksema, 2001; Walsh & McGoldrick, 2004).

Description of Targeted Study Site and Data Collection

Although not well recognized, one of the areas hard hit by Katrina was the St. Tammany parish area in Louisiana which is north of New Orleans. Within St. Tammany parish, the city of Slidell and its residents suffered major damage because of the proximity to Lake Pontchartrain (a body of water about half the size of Rhode Island). An estimated 4,000 out of 10,300 homes in Slidell sustained serious damage and it was estimated that 400–700 of the damaged houses would be complete losses. The estimated cost in business damage was $118,366,000 and 1,666 businesses in the St. Tammany region were destroyed, more than one out of every seven. Every school in the parish was either damaged or destroyed as were both universities in the parish (see Chapter 1 for discussion). Twenty-five percent of the staff in local hospitals has yet to return and the number of uninsured hospital patients has tripled (St. Tammany Parish Disaster Impact and Needs Assessment, 2006). Two years after the storm in 2007, contractors finished collecting debris and are in the process of removing 2,000 trees that died or are dying due to the saltwater intrusion from the hurricane's storm surge. The city's administrative center continues to operate out of temporary buildings, and the Slidell branch of the University of New Orleans has been closed permanently (Louisiana Speaks, 2006; City of Slidell Annual Report, 2007a; Update: City of Slidell Newsletter, 2007b).

The data for this study were collected in the first and second waves of a larger project on families and disasters. Prior to the beginning of the study, approval was granted from the institutional review board for the protection of human subjects at Louisiana State University. In early 2006, this project targeted for recruitment families who had returned to a residential area in southern Louisiana following Hurricane Katrina. Geographic information systems (GIS) was used to locate an area that had sustained wind damage or flooding. Respondents were recruited by door-to-door contact in the affected neighborhoods. In teams of two, semi-structured interviews were conducted over a 3-month period between February and April 2006. Most of the interviews took place in the participant's home or FEMA trailer. A few interviews were conducted at an elementary school in Slidell where several participants worked. Some respondents provided names and phone numbers of friends and family members who also qualified for the study. Prior to data collection, disaster mental health professionals were consulted and extensive interviewer training was conducted. The interview schedule for the larger project contained several assessments in addition to open-ended questions about family resilience (based on Walsh's framework) and was critiqued by two trauma experts as well as two accomplished qualitative researchers.

Method

Participants. The sample of wave 1 comprised 50 respondents living in St. Tammany Parish, Louisiana. Our sample was primarily middle aged ($M = 48$ years, $SD = 15.5$), married, employed Caucasians from middle-income families; 34% were male and 65% female. Approximately one-third of respondents reported that children were living in the household. In 2007, $1\frac{1}{2}$ years after Hurricane Katrina, 29 of the original respondents participated in the second wave of the study, after they were contacted by phone and door-to-door canvassing. Despite repeated attempts as many as eight and nine times, it was not possible to interview the remaining respondents from wave 1. Among those who did not take part in wave 2, 10 had moved, 5 passively declined, 3 actively declined, and 3 were not able to be contacted and as far as we knew had not moved (one person was not interviewed due to concerns about personal safety from the first wave). The findings reported here are from those respondents who participated in both waves of data collection.

Materials and procedure. A packet for each participant was prepared that included a list of local mental health professionals and agencies as well as some informational bulletins about coping published by the Louisiana Cooperative Extension Service. The packet also included a copy of the description of the larger longitudinal study as well as a blank consent form. A packet was left with each participant. The packet was updated for the second wave of data collection and informed consent was again obtained prior to interviewing in wave 2.

A digital voice recorder was used to record the entire interview. The interviews ranged from 30 min to 2 h with an average length of 60 min. During each interview, one of the interviewers logged notes as well as writing down comments about the veracity of the interview and participant at the end of interview. The narrative data were transcribed verbatim into Word documents.

Results

Overview of scoring and analyses. Data in the transcripts were closely scrutinized to identify themes or concepts established in the relevant literature suggested by Gilgun (1992). Open coding was also conducted to generate themes from questions in the interview protocol. Codes or concepts in each transcript were noted in a code book, and the number of times the themes appeared within the data was noted. Following the procedure for qualitative data analysis recommended in the grounded theory literature, a second deliberate pass through the data, or axial coding, was then conducted to organize themes or concepts into categories and sub-categories thus deepening the theoretical framework supporting the study (Neuman, 2006; Strauss & Corbin, 1990). The axial coding served to organize themes or concepts into categories and sub-categories thus deepening the theoretical framework underpinning the analysis (Neuman, 2006).

The line by line analysis recommended by Strauss and Corbin (1990) allowed comparisons of statements within each transcript. Considerations included the following: (a) Patterns and common themes that emerged in responses dealing with specific items and how those patterns (or lack thereof) helped to illuminate the broader study question or questions; (b) any possible deviations from these patterns which, if found, were examined for any factors that might explain these atypical responses; (c) interesting stories that emerged from the responses and how the stories could help to illuminate the broader study question or questions; and (d) whether the patterns that emerged corroborated the findings of any corresponding qualitative analyses that have been conducted. If not, the data were re-read to determine what might explain these discrepancies. Finally, selective coding was conducted so that the themes could be read again for a third time to confirm interpretations and look selectively for quotes or cases that illustrated the identified themes (Neuman, 2006). After coding them independently, the researchers discussed the core concepts and assigned the final themes after consensus was reached.

In terms of meaning making, both benefit finding and sense making were evident in the responses from 26 of the 29 survey participants in waves 1 and 2 of the study. Three of the 29 did not identify any benefits to the storms. However, all 29 attempted to make some sense of the storm even if it was a general acceptance. A wide range of benefits were found by the families in this study. Benefits were noted in both waves 1 and 2 of the study with a different emphasis each time. There did not appear to be a relationship between the benefits noted from wave 1 to wave 2. However, in making sense of the hurricane, the beliefs of most families about the root causes of the storm did not vary over time.

Three themes emerged about benefit finding: Improved relationships, prioritization and planning, and reappraisal. Four themes emerged about sense making: Order in social environment, attribution to a higher power, general acceptance, and old adages survive. These emergent themes will be discussed first. A discussion of the optimism, a construct that we a priori decided to study, will follow. Last, an unexpected theme that emerged during data analyses, use of humor, will be discussed. Where appropriate, representative quotes (with pseudonyms) from the participants themselves are integrated in the ensuing sections.

Benefit Finding

Improved relationships. Relationships were noted as a benefit by several participants. "You don't realize how much you love a person until they were gone," was Mrs. Riley's (*age 23*) expression of how the disaster helped her to gain a new appreciation for relationships (Janoff-Bulman, 1992). Likewise, the Martin family realized they were "more of a team than we ever were." Mr. Boudreaux (*age 50*)*broke* up the relationship with his fiancé and renewed his connection with his ex-wife after the storm. He views his ex-wife as the "angel who saved" him. His suggestion to others was "if you have your family, keep them close to you." "I have my friend with me," Mrs. Hebert (*age 70*) said about her husband," and I have my children around. I am blessed." "We were close anyway," Mr. Stephens (*age 67*) reported, "but it [the storm] brought us together." In wave 1 Ms. Smith (*age 33*) saw her grandparents as inspiration. "If they can do it, I can too," she remarked. By wave 2 she noticed her family "doesn't hold back as much as they did before. They are more emotional." This statement was in reference to the impression that her family had become better communicators after the storm, and they were more willing to tell each other how they felt toward each other (Janoff-Bulman & Frantz, 1997).

Prioritization and planning. "A wake-up call" was the benefit of the storm for many families. For some it was a reminder to be better prepared for an emergency. "We're gonna do better planning and have an evacuation plan in case there is a next time," according to Ms. Smith. She also shared recommendations for future shelters regarding the needs for individuals with medical problems or disabilities. She and her mother experienced several difficulties during their evacuation due to the lack of facilities and equipment for the disabled in the shelter where they were directed (see Chapter 8 for related discussion). Mr. Thibodeaux's (*age 59*) plan of action was to "not be around here the next time it directly comes at us." For other families the distinction between wants and needs changed dramatically as many pointed out their prior dependence on material goods or "things" and "stuff." "The things you have in your house are just things. They are replaceable, but your family and your faith are not," were comments made by Mrs. Hebert in wave 1. In wave 2 she remained adamant about her appreciation for simplicity. "You would be surprised how you learn to live with a lot less," she commented. "Why worry about stuff?" posed the Morgan family (*she at age 39 and he at age 25*). "You can't take it with you. All of my family is alive so I have no loss. You can't take anything with you but your memories. It is stuff and you can buy it again."

Reappraisal. Positive reinterpretations are noted in other studies as a response to stress (Park, Cohen, & Murch, 1996; Tedeschi & Calhoun, 1996). Rumors of the devastation and media coverage of the great losses that occurred served in some cases as a time of reappraisal for some families. "I think we faired a lot better than anyone I know or have heard of" were statements used by several families.

Sense Making

Order in social environment. "Everything happens for a reason," Mrs. Trahan (*age 54*) remarked in wave 2 mirroring the comments made by many participants in other studies indicating their need to frame the events into their concept that their environments must maintain a predictable, sensible order (Lerner, 1980; Janoff-Bulman,

1992). "It was meant to teach a lesson, to open a lot of people's eyes," she further explained again referring to the crimes she had heard reported in New Orleans even before the hurricanes. Further illustrating the need for some to have order are Mrs. Trahan's comments: "I think we have our lives all mapped out for us and that people who were forced to go into the superdome created their own problems. These people are on welfare and use that as a living and they don't want to get up and work for anything, they want it to be given to them and if not they become angry." To help frame some of the comments made, it is important to note at this juncture that the evacuation to the superdome was a source of national media attention immediately following Hurricane Katrina because of the controversy caused by reports of overcrowding, lack of resources, crime, and a sense of discrimination some evacuees felt by being evacuated to the superdome (Cherry, Allen, & Galea, 2009). The building suffered extensive damage to its roof causing rains to fall into the building and a loss of electrical power to the building leaving the evacuees in the dark and in standing water.

Ms. LeBlanc (*age 60*) recalled she had heard stories, through television and print media that the name "Katrina" meant "cleansing." "If so, we definitely needed that." She reflected further, "We have become so complacent and we can't see anything else."

Still others held the view that the storm had the purpose of focusing attention, be it local, state, or national attention, on government. "It's opened all this stuff up," said Mr. Albert about the image of corruption in Louisiana. "It's taken political pressure, federal pressure to get your acts together and start dealing with problems in a way that's structure and legal," was his message to local government officials. Louisiana "misspent tax dollars" was Mr. Broussard's (*age 58*) rationale for the devastation.

Attribution to a higher power. Remarks from several study participants recount their impression of the storms occurrence was that it was "time" or some kind of retribution. "Maybe God was trying to tell us all something, that maybe it's time for a lot of people to get their lives in order what with lots of crime in New Orleans," was the way Mrs. Riley made sense of the hurricanes and their destruction. "Sin," Mr. Stephens stated decidedly, "that's what causes [disasters]. Now I'm not saying God is punishing New Orleans or Slidell, but that's where all this came about." He further likened her statement to Biblical stories of the results of the sins of Adam and Eve. Mr. Morgan (*age 25*) felt that "I believe He (referring to God) has his reason and it is not for us to understand, it is for us to accept." This sense making was also supported by Ms. LeBlanc who said "God is the only One who knows for sure how to predict storms." Eleven of the 29 respondents interviewed in both waves 1 and 2 cited God or the Lord as either being responsible for or being aware of the storms.

"We've interfered with Mother Nature," was Mrs. Landry's (*age 40*) rationale. Nature appeared to be the controlling "entity" for eight respondents. Five of those eight referred to Mother Nature as having responsibility in the same way others credited God or the Lord with the storms. In a few cases, Mother Nature was using the storm as "pay back" for humans' contribution to global warming, building on beaches, and other activities deemed harmful to the environment. Similar sentiments have been found in other studies of trauma (Dull & Skokan, 1995; Smith, Pope, Rhodewalt, & Poulton, 1989; see also Furedi, 2007; Grandjean, Rendu, MacNamee, & Scherer, 2008).

General acceptance. Thirteen of the 29 study participants formed a general acceptance of the storms and their devastation in either wave 1 or 2 issuing responses to the specific question "How would you explain the storm to a young child if you had to?" "Storm effects are a matter of geology and geography," answered Mr. Boudreaux. "It was just one of those things," "Things happen," "It's how the earth reacts to things," and "weather phenomenon," were responses from others. Therefore, several storm survivors did not seem to need an explanation or to make sense of the storm as a coping strategy. This general acceptance could be attributed to other coping strategies such as faith or religious beliefs, social support or other positive means of coping. In fact 26 of the 29 respondents reported their faith or beliefs were the same or even stronger following the storms (see also Chapter 10).

Old adages survive. Study participants used decade old adages to summarize their outlook or sense of circumstances such as "There is always a light at the end of the tunnel. Behind every cloud is a silver lining. Take the good with the bad. Don't let it beat you down. Take one day at a time. Pick yourself up by the bootstraps. Life is short." Many of these adages were used definitively as if the phrase summed up life perspectives.

Optimism

Contrary to previous studies (e.g., Affleck & Tennen, 1996; Tedeschi & Calhoun, 1996), there appeared to be no definitive link between prior loss and optimism or pessimism. All 29 respondents had experienced prior loss before the hurricanes including but not limited to experiencing previous hurricanes and/or floods, loss of a loved one through death or divorce, or other stressful situations. There did appear to be some support, however, for the premise that pessimists are less inclined to seek the silver lining following adversity (Scheier, Carver, & Bridges, 1994; Smith et al., 1989).

Three of the 29 did not express optimism about their futures. Ms. Landry expressed disappointment and concern that things were getting worse for her and her family and concern that the government was not "reaching out" to her family. She gave no specific responses to questions about any change she may have experienced in her spirituality as a result of the storm. She reported her family had grown closer yet torn apart by the storm at the same time. However, she lived near an uncle who would grill each meal, whether breakfast, lunch, or dinner, and invite others over to share in the meal. Although she had experienced loss prior to the storm and after the storm, her losses did not appear to be to any greater degree than the losses suffered by other respondents who were more optimistic. It was difficult to determine the reason for her lack of optimism.

Mrs. Hannaman (*age 49*) reported she was very pessimistic by nature. She suffered from a medical disability and had experienced an attack by a person without a weapon but whose intent was to do harm to her, and she had experienced seeing someone seriously injured. She could not find benefit from the storms and made sense of the storm by stating only that it was an act of God.

Prior loss and aging appeared to contribute to Mr. Oglesby's (*age 75*) lack of optimism. He also seemed to be very worried that the "earth can't support the human race" due to decisions societies have made (or not made). His wife's son had lupus in wave 1 and his own son's wife had died several years prior to the storm. In wave 2 he reported his wife's son had died. In wave 2 he also reported he was not religious at all and his faith in the state and federal governments had been shaken by the devastation after Hurricane Katrina.

Humor

As previously mentioned, humor was an unexpected theme that emerged during data analysis. Mrs. Landry (*age 40*) may have used humor to relieve stress as she remembered her family's evacuation efforts to a special needs facility. "Next time we'll pack "bunny" ears for the TV in our care package," she said as she laughingly recounted her family's difficulty in getting word about the status of their home and their neighborhood. The "bunny ears" she spoke of was the term she used for an antenna for her analog television set. That sentiment may seem even funnier to her today as television stations will no longer be broadcasting via analog signals when the next hurricane hits.

Humor can contribute to spiritual growth as it helps people cope with adversity (Samra, 1986). In fact, when Mrs. Landry was asked if she relied on her faith to get her through the disaster she stated, "Mom thinks I relied on my faith too much because I didn't think we needed to evacuate. I guess I was waiting for the parting of the Red Sea!" (They had ended up in an evacuation shelter).

Ritz (1995, p. 198) described survivor humor as important in finding the absurdity in the adversity so that you will not lose hope in what feels like a hopeless situation. Mr. Trahan's (*age 59*) description of the large pine tree limb that pierced his daughter's trailer falls into the category of absurdity in the adversity. "One of those limbs had come off the pine tree and gone straight through the trailer down right through her couch. I'm sure y'all have never been to a strip club, but it looked like the pole the girls dance on at a strip club!" One wonders if Mr. Trahan would have made that comparison at other times.

As far back as Freud (1928), researchers have seen the benefits of humor. He was one of the first to recognize the role humor played as a mechanism that interrupted the "stress–worry cycle" (Pasquali, 2003). Freud noted gallows humor or dark humor while Nilsen (1993) later called it disaster humor after which it became known as survival humor. Thus when Mardi Gras parade floats, storefront displays and billboards depicted blue roofs on homes, mobile homes, and FEMA trailers, the humor poking fun at some of the macabre images after the storms brought comic relief to many survivors. Mr. Trahan's friend "Jack Daniels" [whiskey] was a droll proclamation that the tragedy was "driving him to drink." Mr. Stephens told a joke that included a local sheriff, Pat Canulette, who appeared to be well known in the region and spent many years before retirement as sheriff of St. Tammany parish. "There was a preacher," Mr. Stephens began, "who was living out in the boondocks. Parish law officers went out to his residence and told him he had to evacuate, that he was going to be flooded. He said "No, the Lord is going to take care of me." The authorities went back a second time and still he refused their help. The third time they went by boat to evacuate the preacher. He refused to leave and by then he was on his rooftop. He ended up drowning because he would not get into the boat. When he reached the pearly gates he asked the Lord, "Lord why didn't you take care of me?" The Lord responded "You big dummy, I sent Pat Canulette by three times to pick you up and you wouldn't get in the boat!" Mr. Stephens added "The Lord will provide a way, it's just that we have to open our eyes to see the way sometimes."

Our findings demonstrated that humor can play a role in meaning making (and recovery) because it affects various aspects of survival. While being thought of as an aid to heal the emotions of individuals, humor also helps to release chemicals in the body that are important to physical health as well as mental and spiritual health (Berk & Tau, 1989; Ruxton, 1988).

Discussion

Meaning making, therefore, appeared to be an aspect of resilience for the majority of the storm survivors in this study, although comments ran the gamut of benefit finding from closer relationships to a call to action for prioritization and planning for future storms. As in prior studies, survivors of crisis or disaster attempt to make sense of their situations very often by creating order out of chaos and/or being able to attribute the experience someone or something of with greater control or higher power. "Looking at things differently" and "opportunity to make things better" were phrases used by many families to report the benefits they were finding after the disaster that helped them to make meaning of what had happened in their lives. Attributing loss to "God's will," nature, or justice (because of all the "corruption") seemed to help others comes to grips with the devastation. For many, fitting the tragic events into predictable results helped them to make meaning of the disaster. Contrary to other studies, prior loss was not necessarily a predictor of lack of an optimistic view of the future, as all but one family noted prior loss before the storm. With the exception of three individuals, all the families noted they were hopeful about the future.

The present findings from a study of disaster survivors should be considered within the context of several limitations. Because the participants were able to return to their homes, they probably had more options and resources than those who were not able to return and as such experienced different levels of trauma and distress.

The people who did not return may have been a more appropriate sample for understanding how loss and trauma affect the family because they may have experienced more loss and greater trauma. Although the respondents were asked to provide a collective response that reflected the perceptions of their entire family, it should be acknowledged that the individual's experiences may have taken precedence over the entire family's collective experiences and we would have expected some differences in responses between and among members of the same family, particularly under such trying times. Last, as researchers close to the affected area, we may not be as impartial as those from outside of the affected area (see Chapter 10 for a related discussion).

Based on the findings of this particular work, we offer the following conclusions. One, "make people the priority." Material objects are more easily repaired or replaced than relationships (see also Morrow, 1997). As animal lovers, we would add another word to this conclusion which would be pets (Sasser, Navarre, & Garrison, 2005; see also Scott, 2008 and Chapter 8 of this volume). The inclusion of pets in evacuation procedures and shelters changed in the 3 weeks between Katrina and Rita in 2005 and less than a year later the Pets Evacuation and Transportation Standards (PETS) Act was signed into U.S. law by President Bush. As a result, the U.S. Department of Homeland Security now has a 16-page best practices piece about pet-friendly shelters (www.illis.gov).

Our second conclusion is that "weather happens." Although we are certainly not advocating a fatalistic agency, those of us who live or who have loved ones who live in disaster-prone areas, should expect (and be prepared) to have our lives and the lives of loved ones disrupted. Given the predicted increase in the frequency of natural disasters and an increased number of people susceptible to their impact (Cutter, 2003), these disruptions will not only continue but will increase. Across the world, disaster relief networks and agencies are making inroads, especially about including women and children and vulnerable and disenfranchised populations, in the entire emergency preparedness and disaster management arena. These groups include the United Nations International Strategy for Disaster Reduction (ISDR), Public Entity Risk Institute (PERI), Risk Reduction Education for Disasters, Skillshare International, and the Gender and Disaster Network (GDN). Even now at Disney World at the Epcot Center visitors have a chance to play Mother Nature at the new Storm Struck exhibit (www.stormstruck.com) and the characters from Sesame Street star in "Let's Get Ready: Preparing Together for Emergencies" (http://www.ready.gov/sesame).

Our third conclusion is that "hope rules and humor helps" (see also Walsh, 2007). It is probably no coincidence that the families we interviewed were by and large optimistic, especially as each of them was interviewed twice, in the approximate same location both times. Although not a theme we had anticipated would emerge, the role of humor in meaning making is certainly something we have observed in our own behavior, through our own work and through the work and behavior of others, including signage and debris-related art (see also Neff, 2007) and Zakin, McKibben, and Jordon, (2006) which is also referred to as hurricane graffiti (Alderman & Ward, 2008).

Recommendations and Future Directions

By in large, we have found families to be resilient (Knowles et al., 2009) and as such our implications follow accordingly. For researchers, it is important to capture data or interviews soon after the tragedy or disaster to get the most accurate recall. However, going in too soon after the tragedy may be viewed by the respondents as an infringement on their privacy, while they are looking for disaster relief. Be prepared with lists of resources for repairs to bricks and mortar as well as to the human spirit. The interview process is often cathartic for interview participants, particularly within the first few months after a tragedy. We received many apologies from interviewees for their tears and other reactions as they told their touching stories. By the second round of interviews, many had moved on with their lives and others may have moved away from the area. Some, we suspect, no longer wanted to look back by recounting their progress from the disaster. Others, however, wanted to have a voice in reminding the public that though the media was no longer focused on their tragedies, they continued to struggle with recovery.

The state of Louisiana, as well as many other governmental bodies worldwide, has an emergency plan in place with specifics on which agency or group is responsible for which piece before, during, and after storms (http://www.ohsep.louisiana.gov/). Families are encouraged to develop disaster plans and to practice them with their families. There are even suggestions on items to pack for extended evacuations (Tucker, 2008). However, once the basic needs for food, water, and shelter are met, individuals strive to satisfy their other needs, including physical and mental health. The Louisiana Cooperative Extension Service program, one of the partners in outreach education before and after storms, has done well in reaching families to help them recover after storms as has many other agencies, organizations, and institutions, including universities (for more information about LSU's immediate post-Katrina response, see Bacher, Devlin, Calongne, Duplechain, & Pertuit, 2005). Across the U.S., the Extension Service would better serve their clientele if they partnered more with mental health professionals to develop materials for individuals and families that tell them what to expect when loss is followed by grief, in addition to their current materials on storm recovery (see also http://www.eden.lsu.edu/). Individuals and families often do not realize what they are feeling is normal and what to expect they will feel after a tragedy.

Community and neighborhood leaders might consider organizing informal meeting areas where neighbors can meet and debrief after storms, exchanging information on available resources, how they fared after the storm, and to generally share experiences. When families are isolated, they may receive inaccurate information or no information. They may not be aware of what resources are available for them. Despite the best-laid plans, batteries in radios die out, too many sandwiches became boring fare for meal after meal and lack of human interaction has people hungry for contact.

These pieces appeared to be missing after hurricane Katrina. Strides were made to remedy these needs during Hurricanes Gustav and Ike, the storms of 2008 (see Chapter 8 for a related discussion) but were still below par in helping families know what to expect, such as their feelings after the loss of something as simple as their long-established route to the grocery store. The grocery store either no longer existed, had long lines if they were open, could not be reached because of fallen trees blocking routes, and a variety of other scenarios for that one task that caused frustration for many.

Educators and employers could veer from their routine when students and employees return from the disasters and allow time or even special activities to allow their students or employees to acknowledge their losses before attempting to put their focus into their tasks (see Chapter 1 and 13 for related discussions). Although returning to school or work aids in a return to normalcy, mental tip-toeing around problems may not be conducive to productivity and should be directly addressed.

As we wrap up this chapter, it is in the wake of Gustav and Ike, hurricanes eerily familiar to the 2005 season, but one in which we actually experienced greater personal loss (our communities shut down and curfews set, roads impassable and pitch-black, property damaged from either or both wind and rain, needs for water, food, and fuel unmet, and homes, neighborhoods, schools, churches, libraries, hospital, medical (and veterinary) clinics, agencies, and businesses closed – some for several days or without power and often limited generator power, as the mold and mildew multiplied and FEMA claims mounted). We kept finding ourselves coming back to previously drawn conclusions (Knowles et al., 2009). They were (a) "one size doesn't fit all" which also included cultural competence, (b) "life doesn't stop just because you've survived a disaster;" and (c) "do no harm." In addition to these we would today add two more. The first is "don't underestimate the sapping ability of heat and humidity." In the immediate aftermath of a disaster, of any kind, the effect of the current weather conditions is sometimes overlooked. We cannot help but think that the costs in terms of physical and mental health would be less if hurricanes occurred in cooler weather (see Klinenberg, 2002). During the 2003 European heat wave (a non-storm-related natural disaster), 3,000 people died in France alone. A further illustration of this point were the comparisons drawn in the media between Hurricane Katrina survivors who sweltered for days in the Superdome and wildfire evacuees sheltering in San Diego's Qualcomm stadium with its mild weather (and full utilities). Again, we recommend that policy makers and practitioners (and the media) take into account the full context of the disaster, including the effects of global warming and climate change.

A second conclusion is that "ripple effects are greater than storm surge." The full effect of a disaster is not limited to the directly affected area. First, we may not truly appreciate the entirety of the affected area. Those who live outside of the directly affected area are often unaware of all of the areas that were actually impacted because of how the media is covering any particular disaster. This lack of awareness seems to be particularly true in the case of hurricanes where the focus seems to be on the coast (landfall versus the projected path and warning areas) rather than inland where as much if not more damage can occur. We noticed this phenomenon in 2005 with Rita and again in September 2008 with Gustav and Ike. It is our understanding (since we did not have power) that Gustav received very little attention in the national news and we saw for ourselves how the coverage of

Ike seemed to be limited to Galveston and Houston and not heavily damaged areas of southern Louisiana, such as Calcasieu, Cameron, and Vermillion parishes in the southwest and Plaquemines, Terrebonne, and St. Mary parishes in the southeast or even the water and wind damage and power outages in the Ohio valley. In each Ohio and Kentucky 33 counties and in Arkansas 16 counties were declared disaster areas due to the remnants of Ike. In fact, the governor of Kentucky reported the storm to be the worst ever to hit his state.

An overlooked ripple effect would be the impact on those areas and peoples who take in (receive) evacuees (Cherry et al., 2009). This phenomenon was experienced in Baton Rouge during and after Katrina as well as in many others areas of the country, areas much farther away from New Orleans, such as Dallas, Denver, Atlanta, and Salt Lake City (as featured in the film Desert Bayou). In Baton Rouge, there were similar fuel and food shortages in the aftermath of both Katrina and Gustav. Another ripple effect would be the families of those called to the affected areas, such as members of the National Guard, employees of utilities companies (and tree services ones), health-care providers, and relief workers. In the case of the National Guard, a family's livelihood may be negatively impacted if the primary breadwinner's salary is more than what Guard pays (a related point could be made about the loss of enrollment status of college students). Job layoffs both within and outside the affected area may occur as supply and demand may be altered by a natural disaster.

We hope that others, especially researchers, extend and improve upon the work we have started here. In addition to what we have already mentioned, we recommend more research, as have others too numerous to mention here, on multiple levels and on multiple disasters. What are the nature of the relationships between families and communities? What is the impact of Gustav on Katrina survivors, like the families we interviewed from Slidell? What is the impact of Ike on Rita survivors? What impact, if any, do hurricanes have on the survivors of the summer 2008 floods in the midwestern part of the same country, a similar weather event? Do hurricanes have an indirect or secondary impact on the survivors of the California wildfires, a different type of natural disaster in the same country? And last, what will the impact be of a global crisis, such as an economic one, on family resilience, and how similar is it going to be to recovering from a natural disaster, even one where the levees failed?

It is sometimes said that families are the bedrock of society. If that is true, then strengthening families should diminish the effect of catastrophe on the world. As family scientists, we advocate for a bioecological and strength-based, multiple-level approach, irrespective of nationality, creed, governmental, or family structure.

Acknowledgments The research was supported in part by the School of Human Ecology, the College of Agriculture, Louisiana State University and the Louisiana State University Agricultural Center. This support is gratefully acknowledged.

We would like to thank the participants of our research, as well as Vicky Tiller, Research Associate, and Robin Knowles, Graduate Assistant, without whom this project would not have been possible.

Approved for publication by the Director of the Louisiana Agricultural Experiment Station as manuscript number 2008-239-1936.

References

Affleck, G., & Tennen, H. (1996). Constructing benefits from adversity: Adaptational significance and dispositional underpinnings. *Journal of Personality, 64*, 899–922.

Affleck, G., Tennen, H., Croog, S., & Levine, S. (1987). Causal attributes, perceived benefits, and morbidity after a heart attack: An 8 year study. *Journal of Consulting and Clinical Psychology, 55*, 29–35.

Alderman, D. H., & Ward, H. (2008). Writing on the plywood: Toward an analysis of hurricane graffiti. *Coastal Management, 35*, 1–18.

Bacher, R., Devlin, T., Calongne, K., Duplechain, J., & Pertuit, S. (2005). LSU in the eye of the storm: A university model for disaster response. Retrieved from http://www.lsu.edu/pa/book/EYEofTheSTORMtxt.pdf.

Baumeister, R. F. (1991). *Meanings of life*. New York: Guilford Press.

Bower, J. E., Kemeny, M. E., Taylor, S. E., & Fahey, J. L. (1998). Cognitive processing, discovery of meaning, CD 4 decline, and AIDS-related mortality among bereaved HIV-seropositive men. *Journal of Consulting and Clinical Psychology, 66*, 979–986.

Bronfenbrenner, U. (1977). Toward an experimental ecology of human development. *American Psychologist, 32*, 513–531.

Bronfenbrenner, U. (1979). *The ecology of human development*. Cambridge, MA: Harvard University Press.

Bronfenbrenner, U. (1986). Ecology of the family as a context for human development: Research perspectives. *Developmental Psychology, 22*, 723–742.

Bronfenbrenner, U. (Ed.). (2005). *Making human beings human: Bioecological perspectives on human development*. Thousand Oaks, CA: Sage.

Bruner, J. (1990). *Acts of meaning*. Cambridge, MA: Harvard University Press.

Berk, L. S., & Tau, S. A. (1989). Neuroendocrine influences of mirthful laughter. *American Journal of the Medical Sciences, 298*, 390–396.

Cherry, K. E., Allen, P. D., & Galea, S. (2009). Older adults and natural disasters: Lessons learned from hurricanes Katrina and Rita. In P. Dass-Brailsford (Ed.), *Crisis and disaster counseling: Lessons learned from Hurricane Katrina and other disasters*. Thousand Oaks, CA: Sage (in press).

City of Slidell (2007a) *Annual report*. Retrieved October 15, 2007, from http://www.slidell.la.us/files/annualreportwebsite.pdf.

City of Slidell (2007b). Financial fuss over city rebuilding costs resolved. *Update: City of slidell newsletter*. Retrieved October 15, 2007, from http://www.slidell.la.us/files/CityofSlidellUpdateJulyAugustgSept2007web.pdf.

Cowan, P. A., Cowan, C. P., & Shultz, M. S. (1996). Thinking about risk and resilience in families. In E. M. Hetherington & E. A. Blachman (Eds.), *Stress, coping and resiliency in children and families* (pp. 1–38). Mahwah, NJ: Lawrence Erlbaum.

Curbow, B., Somerfield, M. R., Baker, F., Wingard, J. R., & Legro, M. W. (1993). Personal changes, dispositional optimism, and psychological adjustment to bone marrow transplantation. *Journal of Behavioral Medicine, 16*, 423–443.

Cutter, S. (2003). The changing nature of risks and hazards. In S. Cutter (Ed.), *American hazardscapes: The regionalization of hazards and disasters* (pp. 1–12). Washington, DC: Joseph Henry Press.

Davis, C. G., & Nolen-Hoeksema, S. (2001). Loss and meaning: How do people make sense of loss? *American Behavioral Scientist, 44*, 726–741.

Davis, C. G., Nolen-Hoeksema, S., & Larson, J. (1998). Making sense of loss and benefiting from the experience: Two construals of meaning. *Journal of Personality and Social Psychology, 75*, 561–574.

Dull, V. T., & Skokan, L. A. (1995). A cognitive model of religion's influence on health. *Journal of Social Issues, 51*, 49–64.

Frankl, V. E. (1985). *Man's search for meaning*. New York: First Washington Square.

Freud, S. (1928). Humor. *International Journal of Psychoanalysis, 9*, 1–6.
Furedi, F. (2007). The changing meaning of disaster. *Area, 39*, 482–489.
Gilgun, J. F. (1992). Definitions, methodologies, and methods in qualitative family research. In J. F Gilgun, K. Daly, & G. Handel (Eds.), *Qualitative methods in family research* (pp. 22–39). Newbury Park, CA: Sage.
Grandjean, D., Rendu, A., MacNamee, T., & Scherer, K. R. (2008). The wrath of the gods: Appraising the meaning of disaster. *Social Science Information, 47*, 187–204.
Janoff-Bulman, R. (1992). *Shattered assumptions: Towards a new psychology of trauma*. New York: Free Press.
Janoff-Bulman, R., & Frantz, C.M. (1997). The impact of trauma on meaning: From meaningless world to meaningful life. In M. Power & C. R. Brewin (Eds.), *The transformation of meaning in psychological therapies* (pp. 91–106). New York: Wiley.
King, L. A., Hicks, J. A., Krull, J. L., & del Gaiso, A. K. (2006). Positive affect and the experience of meaning in life. *Journal of Personality and Social Psychology, 90*, 179–196.
Klinenberg, E. (2002). *Heat wave: A social autopsy of disaster in Chicago*. Chicago: The University of Chicago Press.
Knowles, R., Sasser, D. D., & Garrison, M. E. B. (2009). Family resilience and resiliency following Hurricane Katrina. In R. P. Kilmer, V. Gil-Rivas, R. G. Tedeschi, & L. G. Calhoun (Eds.), *Meeting the needs of children, families, and communities post-disaster: Lessons learned from Hurricane Katrina and its Aftermath*. Washington DC: American Psychological Association (in press).
Krause, N. (2005). Traumatic events and meaning in life: Exploring variations in three age cohorts. *Ageing and Society, 25*, 501–524.
Lerner, M. J. (1980). *The belief in a just world*. New York: Plenum.
Louisiana Speaks. (2006). *St. Tammany parish goals: Long-term community recovery planning*. Retrieved October 15, 2007, from http://www.louisianaspeaks-parishplans.org/IndParishHomepage_RecoveryGoals.cfm?EntID=16
Morrow, B. H. (1997). Stretching the bonds: The families of Andrew. In W. G. Peacock, B. H. Morrow, & H. Gladwin (Eds.), *Hurricane Andrew: Ethnicity, gender and the sociology of disasters*(pp. 141–170). London: Routledge.
Neff, T. (2007). *Holding out and hanging on: Surviving Hurricane Katrina*. Columbia, MO: University of Missouri Press.
Neuman, W. L. (2006). *Social research methods: Qualitative and quantitative approaches*, (6th Ed.), Boston: Pearson Education.
Nilsen, D. L. F. (1993). *Humor scholarship: A research bibliography*. Westport, CN: Greenwood Press.
Pakenham, K. I., Sofronoff, K., & Samios, C. (2004). Finding meaning in parenting a child with Asperger syndrome: Correlates of sense making and benefit finding. *Research in Developmental Disabilities, 25*, 245–264.
Park, C. L., Cohen, L. H., & Murch, R. L. (1996). Assessment and prediction of stress-related growth. *Journal of Personality, 64*, 71–105.
Pasquali, E. A. (2003). Humor: An antidote for terrorism. *Journal of Holistic Nursing, 21*, 398–414.
Patterson, J. M. (2002). Integrating family resilience and family stress theory. *Journal of Marriage and Family, 64*, 349–360.
Ritz, S. E. (1995). Survivor humor and disaster nursing, In K. Buxman & A. Lemoine (Eds.), *Nursing perspectives on humor* (pp. 197–216). Staten Island: Power Publications.
Ruxton, J. P. (1998). Humor deserves our attention. *Holistic Nursing Practice, 2(3)*, 45–62.
Samra, C. (1986). *Aspects of internalization*. New York: International Universities Press.
Sasser, D., Navarre, C., & Garrison, M. E. (2005). Do you have a disaster plan for your pets? *News you can use*. Baton Rouge, LA: Louisiana State University Agricultural Center, Louisiana State University.
Scott, C. (2008). *Pawprints of Katrina: Pets saved and lessons learned*. Hoboken, NJ: Wiley & Sons.

Scheier, M. F., Carver, C. S., & Bridges, M. (1994). Distinguishing optimism from neuroticism (and trait anxiety, self-mastery, and self-esteem): A reevaluation of the Life Orientation Test. *Journal of Personality and Social Psychology, 67*, 1063–1078.

Smith, T. W., Pope, M. K., Rhodewalt, F. L., & Poulton, J. L. (1989). Optimism, neuroticism, coping and symptom reports: An alternative interpretation of the Life Orientation Test. *Journal of Personality and Social Psychology, 56*, 640–648.

Steger, M.F., Frazier, P., Oishi, S., & Kaler, M. (2006). The meaning in life questionnaire: Assessing the presence of and search for meaning in life. *Journal of Counseling Psychology, 53*, 80–93.

Strauss, A., & Corbin, J. (1990). *Basics of qualitative research: Grounded theory procedures and techniques*. Newbury Park, CA: Sage.

St. Tammany Parish Disaster Impact and Needs Assessment (2006). Retrieved June 7, 2007, from http://www.louisianaspeaks-parishplans.org/IndParishHomepage_BaselineNeedsAssessment.cfm?EntID=16

Tedeschi, R. G., & Calhoun, L. G. (1996). The posttraumatic growth inventory: Measuring the positive legacy of trauma. *Journal of Traumatic Stress, 9*, 455–471.

Tucker, J. (2008). *Pack evacuation box now in case you need to 'grab and go.'* Retrieved November 11, 2008, from http://www.lsuagcenter.com/en/communications/news/storm+flood+news/pack+evacuation+box+now+in+case+you+need+to+grab+and+go.htm

Walsh, F. (2003). Family resilience: Strengths forged through adversity. In F. Walsh (Ed.), *Normal family processes* (3rd ed., pp. 399–423), New York: Guildford Press.

Walsh, F. (2007). Traumatic loss and major disasters: Strengthening family and community resilience. *Family Process, 46*, 207–337.

Walsh, F., & McGoldrick, M. (2004). *Living beyond loss: Death in the family*. New York: Norton.

Wong, P. T. P., & Fry, P. S. (Eds.). (1998a). *Handbook of personal meaning: Theory, research, and application*. Mahwah, NJ: Erlbaum.

Wong, P. T. P., & Fry, P. S. (Eds.). (1998b). *The human quest for meaning*. Mahwah, NJ: Erlbaum.

Zakin, S., McKibben, B., & Jordon, C. (2006). *In Katrina's wake: Portraits of loss from an unnatural disaster*. New York: Princeton Architectural Press.

Part III
Older Adults and the Oldest-Old

Chapter 7
Encounters with Katrina: Dynamics of Older Adults' Social Support Networks

Karen A. Roberto, Yoshinori Kamo, and Tammy Henderson

Abstract Hurricane Katrina forced the evacuation of thousands of people from the storm-ravaged Gulf Coast. Storm-displaced older adults faced many challenges during the evacuation process and in the months that followed. In this chapter we examine the dynamics of displaced older adults' social networks during the evacuation and post-Katrina events. We begin with a brief review of the literature on social support in late life, with emphasis on social support in times of disaster. In the next section, we present findings from a mixed method study conducted in the post-Katrina immediate impact period. Qualitative analyses of interviews with storm-displaced older persons provide new evidence concerning reliance on others for help and emotional support as they faced the aftermath of the storm. We also examined their perceptions of the availability of network members to provide future assistance and support as they rebuild their lives. Implications of these findings for developing effective evacuation strategies and meeting the social and emotional needs of storm-displaced older adults during the recovery period are considered.

Introduction

In the years following Hurricane Katrina, much discourse has been generated about the impact of the disaster on older adults. Over 70% of deaths related to Hurricane Katrina were among adults over the age of 75 (Benson & Aldrich, 2007; Gibson, 2006). Reports suggested that, in general, the older population was reluctant to evacuate, often because they were limited by physical and cognitive impairments (Arbore, 2007; Fairchild, Colgrove, & Jones, 2006; Gibson, 2006; U.S. Senate Committee on Aging, 2006; Zakour, 2008). Anecdotal information from survivors of the

K.A. Roberto (✉)
Center for Gerontology and Institute for Society, Culture and Environment Virginia Polytechnic Institute and State University, Blacksburg, VA 24061, USA
e-mail: kroberto@vt.edu

hurricane suggested that family members often had to plead with and prod ablebodied as well as frail older adults to leave their homes and communities. Older adults without family and friends nearby often relied upon the formal service sector and religious organizations for help with evacuating and advocating for their needs in the immediate aftermath of Katrina (Benson & Aldrich, 2007; Dyer et al., 2006; Kaiser Family Foundation [KFF], 2006).

Recent research has suggested that community-dwelling older adults with prior disaster experience tend to be more resilient during disaster situations than other age groups (Knight, Gatz, Heller, & Bengtson, 2000; Norris, Byrne, Diaz, & Kaniasty, 2007; Watanabe, Okumura, Chiu, & Wakai, 2004; Weintraub & Ruskin, 1999). For example, Cherry, Galea, and Silva (2008) found minimal differences among middle-aged (aged 45–64), young-old (aged 65–89), and oldest-old (aged 90+) adults on self-reported measures of health, depression, and health-related quality of life (e.g., physical functioning, social functioning, role limitations) pre- and post-Hurricanes Katrina and Rita. Though age may be a protective factor in helping older adults cope with disaster, gender, race, class, and health of individual survivors complicate the issue. For example, older, poor African-American women were disproportionately negatively affected by Hurricane Katrina (Dyer et al., 2006). As noted in a report issued by the KFF (2007), "[t]hose who were most likely to report being less well off than before the storm were those who [could] least afford it: the poor, the unemployed and those heavily reliant on social services" (p. 8). In spite of this bleak picture, many older individuals, with assistance from their social networks, showed their resilience during these troubled times. In this chapter we examine the dynamics of displaced older adults' social networks during the evacuation and post-Katrina events. Specifically, we explore older adults' reliance on others for help and emotional support as they face the aftermath of the storm and their perceptions of the availability of network members to provide future assistance and support as they rebuild their lives.

Social Support in Late Life

Older adults participate in complex social support networks consisting of relatives, friends, neighbors, and other nonprofessional members of the community. Network members provide older adults with companionship (Rook, 1987) and social support, including information, help with personal tasks, and emotional support (Barrera, 1986). The type, frequency, and amount of support provided and received vary depending on individual needs and abilities, the type of relationship, and personal resources (Antonucci, 2001; Antonucci & Akiyama, 1995; Roberto & Husser, 2007). Social and cultural norms or beliefs also strongly influence the extent and type of support and assistance provided by family members. In contrast with the majority White American culture, which emphasizes democracy and individuality, the needs and well-being of the family unit are of utmost importance and a driving influence in the lives of many diverse families in late life (Baldwin & Hopkins, 1990). Even so, findings from a national study indicated that African Americans are no more likely than White Americans to either give or receive tangible assistance or emotional support (Silverstein & Waite, 1993).

When the needs of older adults exceed the capacity of their families and friends, or if informal network members are not available, they may seek formal support from professionals employed by local governments, nonprofit agencies, and private enterprises. The church also serves as a significant source of support for many older adults. Krause (2002) reported racial differences in church-related support. Specifically, older African Americans give and receive more social support in church than their White counterparts. For the majority of older adults, the assistance received from formal networks supplements, but does not replace the social support received from members of their informal networks.

Support for Older Adults in Times of Disasters

When large-scale disasters hit, such as Hurricane Katrina, informal and formal support networks quickly congeal to ensure the safety and well-being of their older members. However, the nature and scope of the disaster influences the actual availability of support. Data from a panel study of older adults that began 3 months prior to the 1981 floods in Kentucky revealed that pre-flood expectations of help in hypothetical crises were about three times higher than the amount of support actually received from family members following the disaster (Cherry et al., 2008; Kaniasty & Norris, 1993). Both personal loss and community destruction were associated with declines in the older victims' perceptions of the availability of support. The authors speculated that the decline in expectations of help may have constituted a veridical assessment of the capability of victims' social networks to provide support at that time.

In extended crises situations, lingering and profound needs, chronic familial and social stress, ongoing community disruption, and progressive psychological fatigue can quickly deplete initial support and resources provided to persons in need (Norris & Kaniasty, 1996). However, the initial amount of help received may have long-term psychological benefits. A longitudinal study of adult survivors of Hurricanes Hugo and Andrew revealed that high levels of help received immediately after the hurricanes had positive and lasting effects on perceptions of social support (Norris & Kaniasty, 1996). The receipt of help at the time of the crises served a protective function against the erosion of support received over time.

Racial differences emerged when researchers examined sources of support relied upon in the aftermath of Hurricane Katrina. Among adults aged 18 and older who had registered with the Red Cross, White residents reported getting more emotional support from family and friends whereas African-American residents reported getting more emotional support from religious faith (Elliott & Pais, 2006). Although the African-American respondents received emotional support from friends and family, they believed that God was responsible for the emotional support they received from members of their social network. This finding endorses Lee and Sharpe's (2007) discovery that older African Americans, in general, tend to name God as their primary source of social support even when they have high levels of support from the community.

When individuals are strongly embedded and connected within their communities, as is often the case for African Americans, communities act as sites of sanctuary and empowerment for many individuals and their families (Collins, 1991). This is especially true for older women. In her review of the literature from the 1990s on kinship networks, Johnson (2000) noted that older African-American women seem to perceive, get, and give high levels of social support. These findings support earlier theorizing about African-American families (Collins, 1991; hooks, 1984; Stack, 1974) that suggested many African-American communities use complex social networks as an adaptive response to stressful events (e.g., parental death and illness, migration, economic, and social injustice) and other positive and negative concerns (Franklin, 2007; Stack & Burton, 1993; Sudarkasa, 2007). Although the development and reliance on extended kin (e.g., nieces, nephews, cousins) and fictive kin (i.e., nonrelatives considered to be "like" family) networks are strengths of African-American communities (Chatters, Taylor, & Jayakody, 1994; Johnson, 1999), these networks may be vulnerable in times of disaster because such ties may not be recognized by authorities who direct and organize relief efforts. When these networks are locally based, the entire network can be uprooted to lose its strength. Thus, community-wide loss, as was the case with Hurricane Katrina, may be even more stressful than personal loss (Green et al., 1990; Kaniasty & Norris, 1993; Watanabe et al., 2004).

Older Adults in the Aftermath of Hurricane Katrina

Study Participants

As part of a larger study of aging families in the aftermath of Hurricane Katrina, we interviewed 122 older adults who relocated from the New Orleans metropolitan area to the Baton Rouge metropolitan area. Baton Rouge is located approximately 80 miles from New Orleans. They ranged in age from 60 to 97 ($M = 72$ years; $SD = 9.0$) and were most commonly African American (73%), Protestant (67%), women (67%), retired workers (57%), and widowed (42%). The majority of older adults reported an annual income of $16,600 or less (78%). A little more than one-half of the older adults were homeowners (57%) and had resided in their community for more than 30 years (52%).

Procedures

The institutional review boards of the participating universities approved this research. We gained access to potential sample members with assistance from local organizations, churches, aging agencies, and other senior groups. Staff members obtained permission from their clients for a member of the research team to contact them. We also recruited participants from the trailer communities constructed by the Federal Emergency Management Agency (FEMA) to provide temporary housing for individuals displaced by Hurricane Katrina. Officials managing the trailer communities granted the research team permission to conduct interviews on site. We posted flyers with information about the project, time, and place of the interviews in key locations (e.g., community room, laundry room, and mailboxes). The authors, graduate students, and local professionals (employees of the state office on aging and area senior centers) conducted face-to-face interviews with aging adults between January and June of 2006. The interviews took place at the older adults' home or in a designated site, often within the trailer communities. Interviews took 60–90 minutes to complete, and each older adult received a $25 Wal-Mart gift card in appreciation of their participation.

Questions and Measures

The survey was comprised of open- and close-ended questions informed by the general aging literature and constructs from two theoretical frameworks underpinning the research – the life course perspective and the ecological model of human development. The life course perspective (Elder, 1977) provided a broad-based analytical foundation for studying older adults coping with a disaster within the context of their immediate lives and the broader society. It recognizes that aging reflects a lifetime accumulation of interacting social, behavioral, and biomedical processes that shape personal decision making, response to stress, and reliance on family and formal service systems. The life course perspective, as well as the ecological model (Bronfenbrenner, 1986), acknowledges the salience of individual, as well as family, community, and social contexts that influence how older people behave, think, and feel when faced with the daily realities involved in reestablishing their families in the aftermath of a natural disaster. We designed our survey focusing upon these multiple layers of contexts. Areas covered included demographic information, health and well-being, individual decision-making styles, coping strategies, family structure, community involvement, social and community support, and family functioning (i.e., family cohesion, communication, allocation of resources, and dynamics). For the purposes of this chapter, we focused on the older adults' responses to questions about the evacuation, including the type of help and support received from individuals and other types of community services, and beliefs about the kinds of support available if needed, including who would provide the support.

To obtain information about the evacuation experience, we presented the participants with a calendar noting August 29, 2005, as the day Hurricane Katrina hit New Orleans and then asked them to describe when they left their home, where they went first, who went with them, how long they stayed, and so forth. Questions were repeated for each move they made until they reached their place of residence at the time of the interview. We also asked a set of forced-choice questions to identify the type of assistance the older adults received during the evacuation process and who provided the help. These 11 items were developed in consultation with professional service providers who assisted persons as they evacuated from New Orleans and during their stay in the temporary shelters.

To assess the older adults' reliance on members of their social network, we modified the *Medical Outcomes Study Social Support Survey* (MOS-SSS; Sherbourne & Stewart, 1991). The 19-item scale measures four dimensions of support: emotional and informational support (8 items; $\alpha = 0.92$), tangible support (4 items; $\alpha = 0.87$), affectionate support (3 items; $\alpha = 0.78$), and positive social interactions (3 items; $\alpha = 0.80$). To reduce participants burden, we changed the five-option response set [(1) none of the time to (5) all of the time] to dichotomous (1) yes or (0) no responses. In addition, for each positive response, we asked the older adults who they would turn to for such support, (1) family, (2) non-family, or (3) both.

Coding and Analyses

We computed descriptive statistics for the demographic variables, the MOS-SSS, and other structured items related to social support. The open-ended portions of all interviews were transcribed verbatim by a professional transcriber, and transcripts were compared with the tapes by research team members to ensure accuracy. The first author and a team of students coded the timeline data. For each participant, we used a standard template to record the number of moves, the location of each move, the reason for each move, how they made the move (i.e., transportation), who, if anyone, traveled with them, the type of residence, and the length of stay. Using content analysis, a method of dividing text into meaningful units (Lincoln & Guba, 1985), we coded the older adults' descriptions of the effect of Hurricane Katrina on them and their families, their relationships with others, and how they spend their day. We subjected these codes to an interactive process over three waves of coding. In each wave, one team member coded the responses; then the coded responses were reviewed by a second member of the team. Coders discussed and resolved any coding discrepancies. This coding approach yielded 100% agreement in the development and application of the coding scheme, which enhanced the rigor of the analysis and the dependability of the findings (Anfara, Brown, & Mangione, 2002).

Study Findings

The Journey out of New Orleans

It took the older adults an average of 63.5 days ($SD = 52.28$; *Range* $= 1-240$ days) and between one and nine moves ($M = 3.94$, $SD = 1.72$, *Range* $= 1-9$) to arrive at their residence in Baton Rouge. They typically left New Orleans either with family members (68%; $n = 83$) or friends (11%; $n = 13$); others traveled alone (18%; $n = 22$). For example, one woman (P134E) described how she did not intend to leave her home until her daughter called and insisted that they leave town together. The daughter had heard from a weather-reporter friend that the storm was expected to be severe. The mother then agreed to evacuate. Another man (P235E) decided to join others nearby as the storm became more severe. He stayed at a friend's house during the night Katrina hit, intending to return home the next day. However, the next day he evacuated with his friends by boat to the freeway where they were taken to the Super Dome. A male respondent (P199E) said that he intended to stay in his home but his daughter "kept calling and calling" that he finally evacuated to put her mind at ease.

Over one-half (55%) moved four or more times. Common reasons given for the multiple moves included the initial move being to a temporary shelter, the initial shelter or home being too crowded, family or relationship conflicts, and wanting to have their own place. For example, a 75-year-old African-American woman (P135E) who moved five times related that she left New Orleans in a caravan with her friends. This group of women took turns sleeping and driving during the first few days of evacuation trying to get out of harm's way. They then attempted to go back to check on their homes, but were directed to a shelter before entering the city. She moved through two shelters, trying to contact her daughter. From the last shelter, she moved to her daughter's home. A 68-year-old African-American man (P103E) made seven moves with his family in less than 2 months during and after Hurricane Katrina. His family moved once in New Orleans to a hotel, then moved through two shelters, two more hotels, and a relative's home, before settling into a trailer community in Baton Rouge.

Immediacy of Support: The Days Following Hurricane Katrina

The majority of older adults received support from FEMA (93%) or the Red Cross (83%); approximately 78% received aid from both sources. When asked about specific types of assistance, a greater percentage of older adults received assistance from community services than from individuals except for the areas of completing paper work, washing clothes, and housing (see Table 7.1). More respondents relied on individuals for temporary housing (46.6%) than any other type of assistance. Less than one-sixth of the older adults received financial support from either individuals or community services (13.8% and 15.1%, respectively).

Demographic comparisons revealed that overall, older females received more types of support from individuals than their male counterparts ($M = 2.90$ vs. 1.88; $t = 2.46, p = 0.02$). Compared to older men, a greater percentage of older women received fellowship (33% vs.15%; $\chi^2 = 4.06, p = 0.04$) and help locating temporary housing (57% vs. 26%; $\chi^2 = 10.29, p = 0.001$) from individuals and food and water (74% vs. 56%; $\chi^2 = 3.80, p = 0.05$) from community services. Conversely, a greater percentage of older men than women received help in completing paperwork (34% vs. 13%; $\chi^2 = 7.35, p = 0.01$) and finding temporary housing (48% vs. 23%; $\chi^2 = 7.33, p = 0.01$) from community services rather than individuals. We found no difference in the number of different types of assistance the older men and women received from community organizations or both sources combined.

Table 7.1 Help and support older adults received from individuals and community services in the aftermath of Hurricane Katrina

Type of help or support received	Individual		Community services	
	No.	%	No.	%
Food/water	31	26.5	82	68.3
Clothes	31	27.0	73	61.9
Furniture	8	6.9	14	11.8
Transportation	29	25.4	37	31.6
Money	16	13.8	18	15.1
Completing paperwork	34	29.1	23	19.8
Locating health care	20	17.2	34	29.1
Washed clothes	33	28.2	15	12.8
Temporary housing	55	46.6	37	31.4
Permanent housing	15	12.7	13	11.0
Fellowship	32	27.1	38	32.8
Other	3	2.7	6	5.4

There were only two notable differences in the type and number of supports received by race. White older adults were more likely to receive furniture from individuals (16% vs. 4%; $\chi^2 = 4.04$, $p = 0.05$) than Black respondents. Black older adults were more likely to receive help in locating health care from community services (34% vs. 12%, $\chi^2 = 4.98$, $p = 0.03$) than White older adults. There was no difference by race of respondent in the total number of types of help received from individuals, community services, or both combined.

Although the respondents' age was not associated with the type of help received from individuals, advanced age was associated with the type of help received from community organizations. Older respondents were less likely to receive clothes ($r = -0.27$, $p = 0.01$), help completing paperwork ($r = -0.22$, $p = 0.02$), and fellowship ($r = -0.20$, $p = 0.03$) compared with younger aged respondents. The total number of help received from community services was also negatively related with the respondents' age ($r = -0.20$, $p = 0.03$).

Persons who rated their health more positively were less likely to have received help with washing clothes ($r = -0.29$, $p = 0.01$) from individuals than those who rated their health more negatively. Similarly, fewer healthier older adults received help from community services with transportation ($r = -0.20$, $p = 0.04$), completing paperwork ($r = -0.26$, $p = 0.01$), and locating health-care services ($r = -0.28$, $p = 0.01$) than those with poorer health.

Having a higher income was associated with receiving temporary housing ($r = 0.21$, $p = 0.03$) from individuals. Conversely, older adults with higher incomes were less likely to have received help from community organizations with transportation ($r = -0.24$, $p = 0.01$). However, older persons with higher incomes were more likely to receive "other" types of help from community services than those with lower income ($r = 0.21$, $p = 0.04$).

Informal Support: Relationships and Interactions

The majority of older adults (84%) described how family or friends helped them evacuate from New Orleans and supported them throughout the aftermath of the hurricane. Four types of relationships emerged from our qualitative analyses of the older adults' responses to questions about the evacuation process and time thereafter that characterized the nature of their interactions with members of their social support networks: ambivalent ($n = 38$), positive ($n = 35$), neutral ($n = 20$), and negative ($n = 9$). Eleven older adults reported receiving minimal help from members of their social networks during the evacuation process and afterward. We viewed these individuals as being more "alone" than others we interviewed and did not include them in the analysis. For example, one 68-year-old African-American woman (P101E) who lived alone was rescued by her neighbor after the levees broke, but moved through the shelters alone, making "new friends" each time she moved. Other individuals described themselves as loners and did not mention any help from social network members. Nine respondents did not provide specific information about their relationships with others and were not included in the analyses.

Ambivalent Relationships. Older adults whose relationships were depicted as ambivalent noted both positive and negative aspects of their interactions with others. Three themes emerged that differentiated the respondents' ambivalent feelings about their relationships: encountering situational stress ($n = 17$), maintaining independence ($n = 15$), and experiencing despair ($n = 6$). Normally strong family relationships experienced stress and strain in the aftermath of Hurricane Katrina. The older adults depended on their family and friends for support, but felt that the pressures of evacuation and rebuilding negatively impacted the amount of support they received as well as gave to others. A typical response came from a 72-year-old African-American woman (P231E) who voiced frustration that she was unable to help her grown children rebuild, and that they were unable to help her, because there was too much work to do. She noted that normally they helped one another, but the amount of rebuilding that needed to be done meant that they were not able to help as much as usual. Comments from a 74-year-old White woman (P176E) who depended on her daughter and son-in-law for help and support illustrate the continuum of positive and negative emotions and interactions older adults experienced within their relationships. When asked about the evacuation process, she reported moving around a lot largely because members of the households had difficulty getting along within the confines of limited personal space and stretched resources. But when asked how she spent her time since the hurricane, she said she "enjoyed being with friends and family." The aftermath of the hurricane put social support networks under unusual stress that participants had to negotiate in order to maintain their connections to one another.

For some, maintaining connections with family and friends ironically meant that they asserted their independence. "Independent" older adults had strong relationships with friends and family, but either liked living alone, did not want to impose too much on others, or both. These relationships differed from those who experienced situational stress in that their responses highlighted not just a desire for personal space, but that their independence was important to the health of their networks. One 60-year-old African-American woman (P102E) who lived with her mother, children, and grandchildren during the evacuation captured the sentiments of many individuals when she told the interviewer that it was both like "hell" and "nice": hell in that there were so many people in one house, but nice in that people tried to be kind and help one another. As soon as she was able to move into her own FEMA trailer, she did so and continued to rely on her children for emotional and instrumental support as she made decisions about her property in New Orleans. For her, living alone relieved some of the day-to-day burden of being another body in an over-crowded house without weakening family ties.

A small number of older adults either explicitly stated that they felt depressed or revealed information that would suggest symptoms of depression. Their responses suggested that the experience had a more negative impact on their emotional well-being than the other respondents. For example, a 76-year-old African-American woman (P154E), who lived with her husband and was in contact with many of her family members, reported that she cried often because she misses her home and her church community greatly. Like most other respondents, she said that even though she wanted to go home, she felt sick to see the devastation in New Orleans. Although she had family she could turn to for help and support, she grieved for the part of her support network that was lost. A 61-year-old African-American man (P238E), dependent on his extended family and neighbors for support of himself and his wife, revealed that he lost 10 pounds since evacuating and spent much of his free time sleeping and smoking. This man grieved not only for the health of his wife, who had recently lost one of her legs [does not reveal reason], but also for their lost home as he believed that it was unlikely that they would ever be able to return. Overall, the older adults experiencing emotional despair found it difficult to be positive about their relationships with others.

Positive Relationships. Older adults, who depicted their relationships as positive ($n = 35$), used affirmative language when describing their relationships. However, the context of their language revealed different emphases for different participants. Specifically, some older adults believed that Hurricane Katrina brought their family closer together emotionally ($n = 17$); others positively described the companionship provided by friends and family in the aftermath of the storm ($n = 13$) and a few respondents consistently referred to their belief in being positive thinkers, thus, reading their relationships in an optimistic light ($n = 5$).

Those who believed that the aftermath of Hurricane Katrina brought their families closer emotionally used comparative language to assess their social support networks before and after the storm. These respondents acknowledged stress in their relationships, but believed that the hard times had made their relationships stronger. When asked about the effect Hurricane Katrina has had on her family, a 61-year-old African-American woman (P161E) who lived with her two daughters at different times during in the aftermath of Hurricane Katrina noted that their family appreciated one another more than before the storm. She felt blessed to be able to have her children in her life. Another respondent (P233) also said that she felt blessed to have her family, but was glad that they had moved on since the hurricane. This 67-year-old African-American woman said that Hurricane Katrina was a "wake-up call" to their family, spurring positive changes in the lives of her children. Her children had relocated for employment in other states after the storm and were rebuilding their lives in a way that obviously pleased their mother. She explained that before the hurricane her children, and others in their network, had at times been overly dependent on her hospitality. She saw the changes that the hurricane brought as an opportunity for her family and friends to "reinvent" themselves.

Other respondents were less reflective about their relationships and more focused on how network members contributed to their personal sense of well-being. All of these participants mentioned that their friends and family provided companionship. For example, one 70-year-old White man (P199E) said his friends enjoyed cooking and eating lunch together to take their minds off all they had lost. He mentioned that his sons visited him often and that he did not have to worry about them. A 74-year-old African-American woman (P244E) invoked the importance of companionship in her life. She said the storm and its aftermath gave her an opportunity to spend an extended period of time with her sister and daughter. She made clear that she was upset by the storm at first, but felt that moving in with her sister compensated for what she had lost because it allowed her to continue socializing at the senior center she attended prior to the storm.

Though all respondents who spoke of their social support networks in positive terms tried to make the most of their situation, some respondents were especially reluctant to say anything negative about their situation. These "positive thinkers" frequently prefaced their comments by saying they had faith that God would restore their lives and did not believe in dwelling on their problems (also see Chapter 10). In these interviews, the older adults consistently referred to their belief in looking at the bright side of things. A 71-year-old woman (P213E) [race missing] who reported a monthly income of $630, called herself poor. Although she had lost everything but the shell of her house, she consistently sandwiched her description of difficult realities with positive religious interpretations. She said that she did not believe that God rewarded those who complained, and resisted talking about how hard it was for her to lose all her books from water damage. When asked what made her happy – her response captured the sentiments of other positive thinkers – she emphasized that she loved to see people get along with one another and believed that New Orleans needed God-fearing politicians to fix the educational system. Unlike those who talked about their networks in positive terms in the context of emotional closeness or companionship, these respondents tended to reiterate that they felt that the cause of unhappiness in general, and problems related to Katrina in particular, was the result of a faithless society that did not live a godly life.

Neutral Relationships. Respondents who used neutral language to describe their relationships were similar to the small group of positive thinkers in that they were focused on bigger issues. They had family or friends present in their narratives, but did not reveal the quality of the relationships; instead, they had some other major concerns that dominated the trajectory of their responses such as an illness ($n = 10$) or on returning home ($n = 10$). The older adults depended on others for help and support, but were not forthcoming in how they felt about these relationships. They simply commented on the presences of significant others in their lives.

Although they were not the only respondents to mention an illness affecting their lives, some older adults who spoke of their family and friends in neutral terms appeared preoccupied with their own or a significant other's illness. For an 80-year-old African-American woman (P131E), avoiding illness was the focus of her story. She noted that she was treated well in the shelters, but that one place in particular was very cold and she spent much of her time there wrapped up in blankets. When asked how the hurricane affected her and her family, she commented on her physical limitations. Similarly, a 64-year-old African-American man (P147E) commented that he did not want to interact with others and that his wife's heart trouble worried him throughout their evacuation process. He said that though some people at the shelters were nice and helpful, he felt uncomfortable and wanted to get his bed-bound wife back home.

Others who spoke in neutral terms about their social support networks focused on obstacles that prevented them from living in their former residences or finding a new home. A 69-year-old African-American man (P122E) mentioned how his family worked together, but the focus was on rebuilding their home; he did not comment on the nature of these relationships except that they provide instrumental support. Likewise, at the time of the interview, an 80-year-old African-American woman (P138E) commented that she was looking for a new place to settle because New Orleans had become an unpleasant place to live even before the storm. She relied on her family for shelter and transportation during the evacuation, and reported being in contact with them still, but did not comment on the quality of their relationships except to say that "Hurricane Katrina made a difference." Without explaining what difference it made, she said that it didn't really matter since she was leaving New Orleans anyway, changing the subject to her perceptions of problems in her New Orleans community.

Negative Relationships. Respondents who shared negative stories about their relationships ($n = 9$) implied that lifestyle differences accounted for their unpleasant interactions with their loved ones. For some, these differences became apparent once they were forced to live together; for others differences had already compromised the strength of their network. A 76-year-old White man (P139E) initially went to his son's home, but felt compelled to leave because he believed his son lived an immoral life. Though he settled in with friends, he confessed that his experience with his son made him feel depressed for a long time afterward. Conversely, an 80-year-old White man (P169E) fled his niece's home because she tried to boss him around. He indicated that he was much happier once he left her residence and her rules. A 78-year-old Latina woman (P172E) reported feeling unwelcome in her son's home. At first she had stayed with a group of friends for a month in Shreveport, LA, until they were evicted. She realized then that she needed to be closer to New Orleans. One of her sons said she could come to his home on the condition that it would be temporary. After a few days he told her that she had to leave even though she had nowhere to go. Finally, she was able to locate herself in a FEMA trailer community where she was happy to be on her own.

Rebuilding Relationships

Coping with the aftermath of Hurricane Katrina placed significant strain on the older adults' informal social networks. More than three-fourths of the respondents (76%; $n = 93$) discussed how they were rebuilding their social lives. Respondents visited senior centers, invited others to their homes, attended church as often as possible, sought companionship from family and friends, and provided care for family members.

About one-third of the respondents ($n = 36$) explained that connections with family and old friends were important in their daily lives post-Katrina. For example, an 80-year-old African-American woman (P143E) described how her children who lived in other towns visited her often to make sure she was well. In addition to doing grocery shopping and laundry, they organized holiday and birthday celebrations that made her feel connected to the whole family. A 62-year-old African-American man (P128E) reflected traditional male and female gender roles when he commented that he found joy in working so that his family would have their material needs met. Being able to successfully perform his "provider" role was how he interpreted rebuilding his relationships. Other respondents maintained contact with intimate family members and friends, but also attempted to build relationships in their new communities ($n = 31$). They described a need to "stay active" to stave off despair, and did so by spending time with others. The response of one 62-year-old African-American man who shared a home with his parents (P124E) was typical of most others – he liked to spend his free time socializing with other displaced persons.

One-fourth of the older adults ($n = 26$) discussed the role religion played in rebuilding their lives and social relationships. Those who attended religious services were part of large Christian denominations that had congregations in multiple cities. They were integrated into the religious communities of their new homes, often with other family members. A 68-year-old African-American woman demonstrated the complexities of participating in her new religious community. She noted that her daughter had found a community that she enjoyed. However, she commented that her participation was limited because she was the caregiver for her frail mother. She could only attend day services, as she did not want her mother to walk in the dark for evening services. It is important to note that others who were rebuilding relationships also may have attended church services but did not mention it during our interviews.

Older adults who had not attempted to rebuild their informal networks (14%, $n = 16$) reported feeling isolated, fearful, or too stressed by their personal situation to engage with others. For those who reported being isolated and fearful, lack of transportation prohibited their social involvement. A 67-year-old African-American woman (P132E) reported feeling unsafe walking around in her new neighborhood. She said that insufficient public transportation virtually imprisoned her inside her new home. An 80-year-old African-American woman (P187E) was representative of others when she said that she could not socialize because caring for her husband with Alzheimer's disease took all her time and energy. Other respondents lacked agency (i.e., ability to act in one's own interest or in accordance with one's own desires) due to limited material and social resources. However, they expressed hope that once they moved into their old communities or found permanent new communities their situation would improve. Only three respondents stated that they had no wish to be with others. One 75-year-old African-American man (P235E) echoed the two others by saying he spent his days in his home and did not want to make friends with anyone in his new neighborhood.

Perceptions of Support

At least 85% of older adults perceived that they had support in all domains of help assessed (see Table 7.2). The most common types of perceived available support were affective support, particularly love and affection (94.9%), and emotional/informational support, with 94% of the older adults indicating that they had someone they could count on to listen to them. Generally, the older adults reported that they would seek support from family members more so than non-family. For example, 47% of the older adults indicated that family members would provide love and affection, whereas 16.2% perceived this type of support coming from non-family only and 31.6% indicated both family and non-family members. Similarly, 44.1% of the older adults expected that family members would be there to listen to them when they needed to talk, 20.3% indicated non-family, and 29.7% reported they could depend on both family and non-family. This mix of "family," "both," then "non-family" held for all types of support assessed, except for perceived help if "confined to bed." The older adults reported that this type of help would come from either family members or non-family more so than both.

Approximately 64% of the older adults perceived having all 19 types of support available to them. The average number of available supports was 17.05. Differences in perceived available support were found between male and female respondents. Overall, older women perceived having significantly more types of support available to them than older men ($M = 17.6$ vs. 16.0; $t = 2.08$, $p = 0.04$). This difference existed in the number of emotional/informational supports available ($M = 7.4$ vs. 6.6; $t = 2.18$, $p = 0.03$), affectionate support ($M = 2.9$ vs. 2.5; $t = 2.77$, $p = 0.01$), and positive interaction ($M = 2.8$ vs. 2.5; $t = 2.08$, $p = 0.04$). No significant sex differences were found for the number of tangible support items.

Other demographic characteristics, including race, income, and health status, were not associated with the perceived availability of each type of support. The lack of significant findings is at least partially due to highly skewed distributions of the perceived support items.

Conclusions and Implications

Study findings contribute to previous disaster research as they revealed the complex situations older adults navigated as they evacuated and reestablished some sense of normalcy in their daily lives. Assistance from intact support networks as well

Table 7.2 Older adults' perceptions of the available and source of support

Someone (to/who) ...	Available		Family		Non-family		Both	
	No.	%	No.	%	No.	%	No.	%
Emotional/information support								
Count on to listen to you when you need to talk	111	94.1	52	44.1	24	20.3	35	29.7
Give you information to help you understand a situation	107	90.7	40	34.2	29	24.8	37	31.6
Give you good advice about a crisis	106	89.8	40	33.9	30	25.4	36	30.5
Confide in or talk to about yourself or your problems	107	90.7	44	37.3	28	23.7	35	29.7
Advice you really want	102	87.2	43	36.8	27	23.1	32	27.4
Share your most private worries and fears with	104	88.9	52	44.4	24	20.5	28	23.9
Turn to for suggestions about a personal problem	105	89.0	47	39.8	28	23.7	30	25.4
Understands your problems	105	89.0	49	41.5	23	19.5	33	28.0
Tangible support								
Help you if you were confined to bed	101	86.3	64	54.7	20	17.1	17	14.5
Take you to the doctor if you needed it	110	93.2	59	50.0	25	21.2	26	22.0
Prepare your meals if you were unable to do it yourself	101	85.6	53	44.9	22	18.8	24	20.5
Help with daily chores if you were sick	103	87.3	54	45.8	21	17.8	28	23.7
Affectionate support								
Shows you love and affection	112	94.9	55	47.0	19	16.2	37	31.6
Love you and make you feel wanted	112	94.9	56	47.5	19	16.1	37	31.4
Hugs you	103	87.3	47	39.8	21	17.8	35	29.7
Positive social interaction								
Have a good time with	106	89.8	37	31.4	32	27.1	37	31.4
Get together with for relaxation	108	91.5	43	36.4	29	24.6	36	30.5
Do something enjoyable with	106	90.6	37	31.6	26	22.0	42	35.6
Other support								
Do things with you to help you get your mind off things	103	87.3	37	31.6	26	22.2	39	33.3

as from other individuals and community organizations was essential to ensuring the older adults' safety and addressing their care needs in the aftermath of Katrina. Thus, professionals and others who work with older adults must further develop and continue to advocate evacuation strategies that address the unique needs and concerns of older adults and that connect with their support network of family and friends (Arbore, 2007).

As the older adults left New Orleans they relied on the assistance of family members, friends, and neighbors to make their ways to safer locations. Similar to the findings of other studies, even in situations of substantial need, informal supports are most often the main source of help for older adults (Davey et al., 2005). Often reluctant to leave their homes, it was the encouragement, particularly of family members and neighbors that ultimately influenced the older adults' decision to evacuate. In many cases, members of their informal support network provided them transportation away from New Orleans and a safer haven for them to stay.

Individuals and community organizations banded together to address the initial care needs of the displaced older adults. Support received differed by type, sex, race, income, and health status. In general, older women received more forms of assistance than older men, and these supports typically came from individuals rather than community services. Although we do not know who comprised the "individual" category, it appeared that the older women were equipped with a large amount of informal social capital (Hurlbert, Beggs, & Haines, 2000). That is, older women were well embedded in a knowledgeable and trustworthy social network and received various types of assistance from individuals, most likely from family members and friends. These gender differences were most clearly shown in housing. While over one-half of older women found their temporary housing through individuals, only about one-fourth of older men did the same. Conversely, almost one-half of older men depended on community services to find temporary housing compared to about one-fourth of older women. Age, health, and income also distinguished patterns of initial support received by the older adults. Fewer types of support from community organizations were received as the age of participants increased. Similarly, fewer healthier older adults, and those with higher incomes, received help from community services than those with poorer health and with lower income. However, receiving more types of help from individuals did not mean the older adults did not receive support from formal sources, suggesting a complementary relationship (Bronfenbrenner, 1986; Miner, 1995). These findings indicate that reliance on informal assistance does not negate the need for formal support, particularly in times of crisis. Future research on how disasters impact individuals and communities, particularly those that are diverse or socioeconomically marginalized, needs to be mindful of the important role of social capital and networks in the development of theories and best practices of disaster evacuation, relocation, and personal recovery. Further understanding of the influence of background characteristics and personal resources embedded in social networks on the type of assistance and support needed and received from both informal and formal networks will help facilitate a greater understanding of the response and recovery process.

Informal relationships played a pivotal role in the lives of the older adults as they responded to this stressful life event. As we analyzed the older adults' responses to questions about their personal situations, the influence of Hurricane Katrina on relationship dynamics and interactions became apparent quickly. Four types of relationships emerged in the data: ambivalent, positive, neutral, and negative relationships. The relationship between perceived support and perceived relationship quality revealed that most people expected relatively high levels of social support as well as saw their relations in positive or ambivalent terms. Even those with negative familial relationships believed they would have support from family or friends if needed. This suggests that relationship quality may not influence perceived support except in the most extreme cases (Krause, 2001). All of the older adults who expressed ambivalence about their relationships continued to maintain those relationships. Even when the older adults felt conflicted about giving or receiving support, they did not withdraw from their relationships. Rather, most negotiated the strains on their relationships by limiting the amount of support they were willing to accept.

The findings regarding perceived support suggest that older adults may draw boundaries that limit the support they are willing to accept or would be available to them (see Chapter 8). Fewer people perceived the availability of time-intensive, work-like tangible support, in contrast with emotionally satisfying, but less time-intensive emotional support. These findings support other studies that reported a relationship between perceived support and comfort with receiving support (Norris & Kaniasty, 1996). As a result of Katrina, many of the older adults were physically distanced from their family and community networks; thus, they may have believed that it was unrealistic for family and friends to be available or able to provide tangible day-to-day support. The aging and social support literature shows that perceived availability of support and quality interactions with family and friends are strong predictors of well-being in late life (George, 2006). Researchers need to pay greater attention to the cognitive (e.g., beliefs about the role of families and friends), affective (e.g., emotional reaction to family support), and behavioral (e.g., communication between family members) processes that influence reliance on informal networks during and following periods of extreme distress.

Rebuilding one's life requires support on multiple levels. Because disasters disrupt and destroy physical places as well as relationships, we also encourage researchers to continue exploring how "belonging" (Campbell, 2006) is constructed through interpersonal relationships. Recall the woman (P134E) whose daughter urged her leave New Orleans because she had heard that the storm was going to be particularly bad. This same woman also told how she stayed with her daughter in a motel for a few days before moving to stay with her son in California. Although she enjoyed living with her son, she decided to move to her other son's house in Baton Rouge so that she could be nearer her home. For her, home was New Orleans. Like so many others, her reluctance to leave New Orleans before the hurricane and her desire to come back to New Orleans and rebuild demonstrate the power of "place," of home, and the importance of community support for many older adults.

Professional support and intervention may be needed as older adults move through the phases of rebuilding their lives and relationships.

In conclusion, both researchers and practitioners recognize informal networks as the first and often most effective support that older adults turn to in times of need. However, in times of extreme duress, like that brought on by Hurricane Katrina, there is likely to be a deficit of informal resources and potential unmet need. Professionals working with older adults need to inquire directly about the availability and quality of interactions with support of both family and friends and, where appropriate, seek to develop partnerships with these informal networks prior to being faced with a catastrophic event. Such alliances will help ensure that older adults have adequate access to and knowledge about where to turn and are able to maintain vital connections with key family members and friends whom they regularly rely upon for assistance and emotional support.

Acknowledgments The authors gratefully acknowledge funding from the National Science Foundation (Grant # 0650909), cooperation by local churches, New Orleans Council on Aging, East Baton Rouge Council on Aging, Council on Aging in St. Tammany, and the Governor's Office on Elderly Affairs, and the assistance of numerous students at each of our respective universities.

References

Anfara, V. A., Brown, K. M., & Mangione, T. L. (2002). Qualitative analysis on stage: Making the research process more public. *Educational Researcher, 31*, 28–38.

Antonucci, T. C. (2001). Social relations: An examination of social networks, social support, and sense of control. In J. E. Birren & K. W. Schaie (Eds.), *Handbook of the psychology of aging* (5th ed., pp. 427–453). San Diego, CA: Academic Press.

Antonucci, T. C., & Akiyama, H. (1995). Convoys of social relations: Family and friendships within a life span context. In R. Blieszner & V. H. Bedford (Eds.), *Handbook of aging and the family* (pp. 355–371). Westport, Connecticut: Greenwood Press.

Arbore, P. (2007). Why do elders resist evacuation when natural disasters strike? *Healthcare and aging.* Retrieved August 25, 2008, from http://www.asaging.org/asav2/han/enews/07winter/psych_issues.cfm

Baldwin, J. A., & Hopkins, R. (1990). African-American and European-American cultural differences as assessed by the Worldviews Paradigm: An empirical analysis. *Western Journal of Black Studies, 14*, 38–52.

Barrera, M. (1986). Distinctions between social support concepts, measures, and models. *American Journal of Community Psychology, 14*, 413–445.

Benson, W. F., & Aldrich, N. (2007). *CDC's disaster planning goal: Protect vulnerable older adults.* Washington, DC: CDC Healthy Aging Program.

Bronfenbrenner, U. (1986). Ecology of the family as a context for human development: Research perspectives. *Developmental Psychology, 22*, 723–742.

Campbell, J. (2006). On belonging and belongings: Older adults, Katrina, and lessons learned. *Generations, 31*, 75–78.

Chatters, L. M., Taylor, R. J., & Jayakody, R. (1994). Fictive kinship relations in Black extended families. *Journal of Comparative Family Studies, 25*, 297–312.

Cherry, K. E., Galea, S., & Silva, J. L. (2008). Successful aging in very old adults: Resiliency in the face of natural disaster. In M. Hersen & A. M. Gross (Eds.), *Handbook of Clinical Psychology: Volume 1* (pp. 810–833). Hoboken, NJ: John Wiley & Sons.

Collins, P. H. (1991). *Black feminist thought: Knowledge, consciousness, and the politics of empowerment.* New York: Routledge.

Davey, A., Femia, E. F., Zarit, S. H., Shea, D. G., Sundström, G., Berg, S., et al. (2005). Life on the edge: Patterns of formal and informal help to older adults in the United States and Sweden. *Journal of Gerontology: Social Sciences, 60,* S281–S288.

Dyer, C., Festa, N. A., Cloyd, B., Regev, M., Schwartzberg, J. G., James, J., et al. (2006). *Recommendation for best practices in the management of elderly disaster victims.* Houston: Baylor College of Medicine and the American Medical Association.

Elder, G. (1977). Family history and the life course. *Journal of Family History, 2,* 279–304.

Elliott, J. R., & Pais, J. (2006). Race, class, and Hurricane Katrina: Social differences in human responses to disaster. *Social Science Research, 35,* 295–321.

Fairchild, A. L., Colgrove, J., & Jones, M. M. (2006). The challenge of mandatory evacuation: Providing for and deciding for. *Health Affairs, 25*(4), 958–967.

Franklin, J. H. (2007). A historical note on Black families. In H. P. McAdoo (Ed.), *Black families* (4th ed., pp. 3–6). Thousand Oaks, CA: Sage.

George, L. K. (2006). Perceived quality of life. In R. H. Binstock & L. K. George (Eds.), *Handbook of aging and the social sciences* (6th ed., pp. 321–336). New York: Academic Press.

Gibson, M. J. (2006). *We can do better: Lessons learned for protecting older persons in disasters.* Washington, DC: American Association of Retired Persons.

Green, B. L., Lindy, J. D., Grace, M. C., Gleser, G. C., Leonard, A. C., Korol, M., et al. (1990). Buffalo Creek survivors in the second decade: Stability of stress symptoms. *American Journal of Orthopsychiatry, 60,* 43–55.

hooks, B. (1984). *Feminist theory: From margin to center.* Cambridge, MA: South End Press.

Hurlbert, J., Beggs, J., & Haines, V. (2000). Social networks and social capital in extreme environments. In N. Lin, K. Cook, & R. Burt (Eds.), *Social capital: Theory and research* (pp. 209–231). New York: Aldine DeGruyter.

Johnson, C. L. (1999). Fictive kin among oldest old African Americans in the San Francisco Bay area. *Journal of Gerontology: Social Sciences, 54B,* S368–S375.

Johnson, C. L. (2000). Perspectives on American kinship in the later 1990s. *Journal of Marriage and the Family, 62,* 623–639.

Kaiser Family Foundation. (2006). *Voices of the storm: Health experiences of low-income Katrina survivors.* Retrieved October 31, 2008, from, http://www.kff.org/uninsured/7538.cfm

Kaiser Family Foundation. (2007). *Giving voice to the people of New Orleans: The Kaiser Post-Katrina baseline survey.* Retrieved October 31, 2008, from, http://www.kff.org/kaiserpolls/7631.cfm

Kaniasty, K., & Norris, F. H. (1993). A test of the social support deterioration model in the context of a natural disaster. *Journal of Personality and Social Psychology, 64,* 395–408.

Knight, B. G., Gatz, M., Heller, K., & Bengtson V. L. (2000). Age and emotional response to the Northridge earthquake: A longitudinal analysis. *Psychology and Aging, 15,* 627–634.

Krause, N. (2001). Social support. In R. H. Binstock & L. K. George (Eds.), *Handbook of aging and the social sciences* (5th ed., pp. 273–294). New York: Academic Press.

Krause, N. (2002). Exploring race differences in a comprehensive battery of church-based social support measures. *Review of Religious Research, 44,* 126–149.

Lee, E.-K. O. L., & Sharpe, T. (2007). Understanding religious/spiritual coping and support resources among African American older adults: A mixed-method approach. *Journal of Religion, Spirituality, and Aging, 19*(3), 55–75.

Lincoln, Y. S., & Guba, E. G. (1985). *Naturalistic inquiry.* Beverly Hills, CA: Sage.

Miner, S. (1995). Racial differences in family support and formal service utilization among older persons: A nonrecursive model. *Journal of Gerontology: Social Sciences, 50B,* S143–S153.

Norris, F. H., Byrne, C. M., Diaz, E., & Kaniasty, K. (2007). *Psychosocial resources in the aftermath of natural and human-caused disasters: A review of the empirical literature, with implications for intervention.* Retrieved August 25, 2008, from, http://www.ncptsd.va.gov/ncmain/ncdocs/fact_shts/fs_resources.html?printable-template=factsheet

Norris, F. H., & Kaniasty, K. (1996). Received and perceived social support in times of stress: A test of the social support deterioration deterrence model. *Journal of Personality and Social Psychology, 71*, 498–511.

Roberto, K. A., & Husser, E. K. (2007). Social relationships: Resources and obstacles to older women's health adaptations and well-being. In T. J. Owens & J. J. Suitor (Eds.), *Advances in life course research, Vol. 12: Interpersonal relations across the life course* (pp. 383–410). New York: Elsevier Science.

Rook, K. S. (1987). Social support versus companionship: Effects on life stress, loneliness, and evaluations of others. *Journal of Personality and Social Psychology, 52*, 1132–1147.

Sherbourne, C. D., & Stewart, A. L. (1991). The MOS social support survey. *Social Science & Medicine, 32*, 705–714.

Silverstein, M., & Waite, L. J. (1993). Are Blacks more likely than Whites to receive and provide social support in middle and old age? Yes, no, and maybe. *Journal of Gerontology: Social Sciences, 48*, S212–S222.

Stack, C. B. (1974). *All our kin: Strategies for survival in a Black community*. New York: Harper & Row.

Stack, C. B., & Burton, L. M. (1993). Kinscripts. *Journal of Comparative Family Studies, 24*, 157–170.

Sudarkasa, N. (2007). Interpreting the African heritage in Afro-American family organization. In H. P. McAdoo (Ed.), *Black families* (4th ed., pp. 29–48). Thousand Oaks, CA: Sage.

U.S. Senate Committee on Aging. (2006). *Caring for seniors in a national emergency: Can we do better?* (pp. 109–123). Washington, DC: Author.

Watanabe, C., Okumura, J., Chiu, T.-Y., & Wakai, S. (2004). Social support and depressive symptoms among displaced older adults following the 1999 Taiwan earthquake. *Journal of Traumatic Stress, 17*(1), 63–67.

Weintraub, D., & Ruskin, P. E. (1999). Posttraumatic stress disorder in the elderly: A review. *Harvard Review Psychiatry, 7*(3), 144–152.

Zakour, M. J. (2008). Social capital and increased organizational capacity for evacuation in natural disasters. *Social Development Issues, 30*(1), 13–28.

Chapter 8
Disaster Services with Frail Older Persons: From Preparation to Recovery

Priscilla D. Allen and H. Wayne Nelson

Abstract Hurricanes claim the lives of the frail elderly more than any other age group due to this population's reduced health status and heightened dependence, especially for those institutionalized. Social workers are obligated and ethically compelled (NASW, 1996, Code of ethics of the National Association of Social Workers. Washington, DC: NASW) to meet this high-risk group's disaster readiness and recovery needs as posed to them by unexpected meteorological crises like Hurricanes Katrina, Rita, Gustav, and Ike. This chapter critically assesses social works' tested but largely unheralded traditional disaster roles, as well as new ones that are emerging in the wake of Katrina and in light of recent developments in the field of emergency preparedness. These mandate that the social work profession boost its capacity and capability to provide competent emergency services to ease the suffering of older individuals before, during, and after a crisis. Recommendations by the AMA, The American Red Cross, AARP, and various disaster and gerontological scholars are synthesized.

Introduction

As is now widely recognized, older people and institutionalized elders in particular are often hit the hardest by meteorological disasters, especially hurricanes (Yeoman, 2007, p. 73). Hurricanes Katrina and Rita killed older people in numbers far in excess of any other age group, including any other special needs population (persons with disabilities, single mothers, children, infants, and the hearing and vision impaired). The majority of older people who died were medically compromised, disproportionately black, and, in the case of Katrina, were more likely to have resided in vulnerable flood basins in New Orleans (Landesman, 2005, p.194;

P.D. Allen (✉)
LSU Life Course and Aging Center, School of Social Work, Louisiana State University, 311 Huey P. Long Fieldhouse, Baton Rouge, LA 70803-5501, USA
e-mail: pallen2@lsu.edu

Sharkey, 2007). Their reduced health status, mobility, self-sufficiency, and greater isolation, among many other risk factors, sharply spiked their risks for mortality, morbidity, and psychological trauma during Katrina's, acute, immediate post-acute, and longer term recovery phases.

Social workers have a long and critical legacy of serving the victims of events like Katrina, dating back to the profession's early roots in the Civil War (Zakour, 1996). Their efforts have traditionally included line crisis intervention, case management, and counseling. Although many social workers ply these disaster skills as a part of their employing agencies' normal protective response and relief efforts, many more perform disaster work simply because they showed up to help. Regardless, most social workers are probably unfamiliar with contemporary disaster management protocols and best practices that are designed to facilitate optimal functioning of older individuals as they begin their often long and dangerous journeys back to pre-incident living conditions, or better (Zakour).

This chapter analyzes the critical skills that social workers brought to bear during the Katrina catastrophe, and to a lesser extent Hurricanes Rita, Gustav, and Ike. It is our position that these crises have sharply increased the social work profession's awareness of the need for increased disaster preparedness within the profession generally, and for special populations in particular.

In this connection, two realities bear attention: First, more hundred-year-type hurricanes are impacting coastal areas at increased rates, and second, the oldest-old, i.e., those aged 85 and older, who are the fastest growing segment of the population, are migrating in disproportionate numbers to retirement homes, condominiums, and a host of elder care facilities that have been built in invitingly warm, but deceptively dangerous flood- and typhoon-prone coastal zones (Marscher, 2004). To assess the risks, we review disaster literature both generally, and specifically as it sheds light on how hurricanes have affected older persons in order to (1) assess disaster recovery best-practice standards and to identify any gaps, trends, and opportunities in the disaster aspects of the profession's clinical/private and mental practice domains; (2) improve social work emergency relief planning, education, and practice; (3) promote the improved integration of the social work profession with state, regional, and national emergency management planning and response entities; and (4) increase social work advocacy for state and federal policy and regulations that better safeguard the elderly in the event of a disaster.

Hurricane Aftereffects and the Elderly

On the one hand, age in and of itself does not necessarily indicate a poor outcome to disaster. Older persons, i.e., those over the age of 65, reflect a sizeable range of functional ability. Many are active and engaged. Much evidence shows that they provide support to citizens of all ages during crisis (Cherry, Allen, & Galea, In Press; Dyer et al., 2006). Older persons have long volunteered at higher rates than younger persons and currently provide a reliable pool of volunteer disaster force in a range of disaster planning, support, and recovery efforts (see Chapter 11). Their participation in Area Agency on Aging disaster support opportunities, for example, includes training, serving, and leading local Community Emergency Response Teams (CERT), participating in the Retired Senior Volunteer Program Homeland Security Initiative, and volunteering for a range of local Citizen Corps Council disaster readiness efforts, such as coordinating or volunteering for a local medical reserve corps or other community preparedness efforts (Western Illinois Area Agency on Aging, August 26, 2007).

On the other hand, it is also obvious that advanced age coupled with social isolation and the existence of chronic health conditions place a significant segment of the elderly population at high risk for adverse effects during and after a disaster (Faffer, 2007; Fernandez, Byard, Lin, Benson, & Barberam, 2002; Torgusen & Kosberg, 2006; Zakour & Harrell, 2003). These are often referred to as the "frail elderly" who comprise virtually all nursing home residents. And although there is some variability on defining this group, Fernandez et al. (2002) provide a comprehensive definition of frail elderly as "Individuals aged 65 years or older with physical, cognitive, social, psychological, and/or economic circumstances that will likely limit their ability to perform, or have performed for them, one or more of Activities of Daily Living (ADLs) or Instrumental Activities" (p. 71).

As Cherry, Silva and Galea have discussed in Chapter 9, many age-related changes occur in physical, cognitive, and social functioning in late life. Although particular age-related deficits are too numerous to list here, suffice it to say that the frail elderly experience some functional decline in all bodily systems over time which can make it harder to recover from injury or extreme stress. This is far truer for nursing home residents, over half of whom in 1997 were over age 85, over two-thirds female, required assistance with an average of 4.4 daily living tasks and of whom, fully 65% were incontinent (Sahyoun, Pratt, Lentzner, Dey, & Robinson, 2001). The most common medical conditions include "congestive heart failure, coronary artery disease, degenerative joint disease, diabetes mellitus, hypertension, obstructive lung disease, renal failure" among a host of other problems (Ouslander, cited in Hazzard, Blass, Ettinger, Halter, & Ouslander, 1999, p. 514).

Cognitive impairment is a leading reason that older individuals are institutionalized (Sahyoun et al., 2001). In fact, fully 48% of nursing home patients, for example, suffer mild to severe degenerative dementia (McCarthy, Blow, & Kales, 2004) (which ties with incontinence as two leading impairments for this group [Senior Journal, April 30, 2008]). The dementia factor alone, depending on its severity, can rob an elder of any meaningful fate control in the best of circumstances (Blau cited in Huber, Nelson, Netting, & Borders, 2007) and subjects them to much worse, if they are abandoned to the deadly hurricane's harshest effects. The increased risks faced by nursing home residents and the elderly generally are perhaps no better illustrated than by the disproportionate mortality rates they suffered during the Katrina crises. The exact numbers vary slightly from source to source and will remain imprecise as no formal body is responsible for an aggregate count (Knowles, 2007). A growing body of evidence estimates that while only 15% of New Orleans' population was aged 60 or older, fully 74% of those who died were of this age group and

50% were older than age of 75 (Simerman, Ott, & Mellnik as cited in Dyer et al., 2006). Of the approximately 1,500 bodies recovered, 215 were found in or around nursing homes and hospitals (Mead, 2006). Forty-nine percent of all victims were older than age 75 regardless of where they died (Brunkard, Namulanda, & Ratard, 2008; Senior Journal, April 30, 2008; Sharkey, 2007). The majority of recovered bodies proved to be of the elderly as evidenced by a report from the Louisiana Department of Health and Hospitals that detailed how "584 out of 853 bodies discovered by St. Gabriel and Carville Morgues were over 60 years old" (Knowles & Garrison, 2006, n.p).

Flooding caused by the levee breaches in lower New Orleans is but one of the causes of death, but was by no means the leading one. Even when an older individual survived Katrina's initial onslaught, failure to receive needed care too often spelled doom. In fact, a far greater proportion of death resulted from complications of chronic conditions that could not be adequately treated during the evacuation and recovery phase. Most of the frail elders perished after the storm in the sweltering heat, or in transit or as a combination of factors. Lack of services and medical care made surviving serious pre-existing medical conditions tenuous or impossible for many of the frail elderly (Mead, 2006). For example, a list from the Harris County deaths (in Dyer et al., 2006) identifies causes of death for evacuees relocated to Houston, from August 27 to October 30, 2005. Chronic conditions were far more likely for those over the age of 65 (i.e., congestive heart failure, cancer, complications of dementia, leukemia, cirrhosis, and atherosclerotic cardiovascular disease).

The Effects of Evacuation and Transfer

Evacuation is the most basic means to protect the general public from the deadly effects a hurricane's high winds and floods. Effective evacuations were undoubtedly the hallmark of the successful emergency prevention efforts like those associated with the 2008 hurricanes, Gustav and Ike (see also Garrison & Sasser, Chapter 6). But when planning whether or not to evacuate older people, even assuming that adequate transportation exists or that people can be found, or reached, if found, few will agree to leave. Emergency planners must undertake a careful risk–benefit analysis, as moving them always entails calculated peril. The determination of whether to stay or evacuate can have dire ramifications as was seen in the extreme case of St. Rita, where 35 nursing home residents died as a result of not evacuating (Cherry et al., In Press). If the benefits of removal outweigh the risks of staying, and adequate resources are available, then evacuation is justified. However, if the risks of transfer outweigh the risks of staying, then sheltering in place "may be the only choice" (McGlown, 2004, p. 135). Of course, sheltering in place is no option for those who are too isolated, or who lack structural supports to see them safely through (Browning, Wallace, Feinberg, & Cagney, 2006). They may be left to fend for themselves.

But even for those who must and can be evacuated, the odds of survival vary greatly depending on the evacuee's health status. The odds of perishing during evacuation can be higher for the frail elderly in general and extremely high for nursing home residents. This is due to the severely disorienting and sometimes deadly effects of "transfer trauma" which is a severe form of emotional relocation stress that affects many older people when they are suddenly moved. The resulting fear and anxiety induce stress which can overtax a vulnerable elder's already diminished mental and emotional stamina often leading to depression, confusion, and other disturbances that ultimately risk sickness and death (Spader, 2005).

Special Needs Shelters and Transportation Issues

After being evacuated as a cause of Katrina, most frail older persons required some special accommodation. This requirement cast them into the disaster management classification of being a "special needs" group. Kailes (2005), a disability advocate, feels that this term is not only pejorative but is vaguely inclusive which she supports by the fact that potentially 50% of all people could require special accommodation at any given point in their lives which would qualify them for inclusion in the special needs group. Nevertheless, *special needs* is the term used by disaster planners to refer to individuals who are unsuitable for placement in a public shelter due to their medical care needs or because they require monitoring or assistance with one or more of their activities of daily living (Landesman, 2005). Special Needs Shelters (SNS) are typically area buildings of opportunity that have been staffed and equipped to meet the health needs of special populations. During the Katrina relief effort, shelters were organized by the Capital Area Mental Health District, monitored by Louisiana Department of Health and Hospitals, Department of Social Services. The most vulnerable included persons receiving dialysis, with advanced dementia, requiring sustenance through the use of a feeding tube, suffering from obesity, paralysis, or stroke, requiring use of oxygen, breathing treatments, and were incontinent (Clinton, Hagebak, Sirmons, & Brennan, 1995).

Following Hurricanes Katrina and Rita, the largest area Special Needs Shelters in the state were set up in two large sports complexes at Louisiana State University (LSU), the Pete Maravich Center – approximately 70 miles from New Orleans (which provided acute triage to over 10,000 evacuees) and the next door Maddox Fieldhouse (a 400-bed SNS) (Allen, 2007). Another facility, more widely reported on was the Reliant Astrodome Complex (see Dyer et al., 2006; James & Scantlebury, 2007). Countless hospitals and emergency rooms were overwhelmed by homeless, mentally ill, and otherwise dislocated individuals. Churches and shelters providing non-medical care also found themselves with frail elders who required more assistance than their volunteers were prepared to provide. The city of New Orleans outlined criteria for occupants of Special Needs Shelters. These shelters are reserved for persons who "have no other resources and who need assistance that cannot be guaranteed in a regular shelter, i.e., medication that requires refrigeration, oxygen equipment, etc., clear language that specifies in capital letters, "IT IS NOT INTENDED AS A GUARANTEE OF SAFETY (City of New Orleans Office of Emergency Preparedness, n.d., p. 1)."

Transport to these shelters involved an array of often poorly coordinated and spontaneously tagged cars, ambulances, civil and military aircraft and perhaps, most commonly buses, including the one that exploded in flames burning 23 older patients to death on a lonely Texas highway (MSNBC, September 30, 2005). One police report detailed how another resident died during a non-air-conditioned bus trip. The others "received no medicine, food, or water, [and] most of them had to urinate on themselves and defecate" (Mead, 2006, n.p.).Some bussed residents may have been tied to the seats to keep them from tumbling about and falling (personal communication L. Sadden, November, 2005).

The Hurricanes of 2008: Gustav and Ike

Just prior to Hurricane Gustav, roughly 3 years after Katrina, LSU in Baton Rouge reopened the two sports facilities as Special Needs Shelters. What was not known at the time of designated shelter status was that Baton Rouge was directly in the path of the storm which yielded up to 90 miles per hour winds and devastated parts of the flagship campus resulting in over 350 million in damages (Personal communication, LSU Chancellor Michael Martin). Fortunately, planning had begun early enough with vulnerable seniors already identified and placed in the shelter prior to Gustav hitting land.

There are always a few problems or close calls in SNS activity, i.e., citizens rerouted to the wrong facility while caregivers waited, some miscounts in food, where the vendor did not have enough for the staff who were working 12 h and over shifts. One memorable and too common case was a situation of a botched, but remedied transport. An older man arrived (via ambulation) in a highly distraught status. He had taken care of his wife for the past 10 years, and did not know where she was, although she was slated to arrive at the LSU SNS by 9:30 am. He waited for 8 h while wringing his hands, convincing himself that his wife was dead. The patient's paid caregiver was also present, and near hysterical, feeling that the person she called her "pride and joy" was left into the hands of incapable people. The transport employees did not possess the phone numbers of the responsible parties, and the woman, who suffered from end-stage Alzheimer's, out of her home, without her caregivers, was unable to provide information. The first author had the opportunity to work with this man, and of utmost importance was listening to him, providing solace while working with the team to identify which ambulance company had transported her and to finally learn that she was on her way. When she arrived, the husband was beyond relief, but it seems there are still some uncoordinated planning concerns.

Aside from workers restricted from leaving the shelters, which caused some stress about not being able to monitor the storm, and a brief, but scary episode with a generator failure, the LSU SNS shelter ran much smoother than it did after Katrina, although the comparison is not a fair one. There were far fewer evacuees and the health severity was less extreme given the advanced planning and enhanced transportation, health services, nutrition and hydration, etc. Far more nursing home residents were transferred to the SNS shelter on the LSU campus for Katrina and Rita in 2005 than for Gustav and Ike in 2008, demonstrating that transfer plans were in place and implemented prior to the evacuation. Another fundamental difference is that during Gustav, nursing homes did not evacuate to the SNS as some did during Katrina and Rita. Plans were enforced that an SNS transfer from nursing homes did not meet the emergency preparation regulated by the Department of Health and Hospitals.

In contrast to Katrina and Rita, Gustav responses were more organized. Planners had learned vital lessons and prepared for the worst. Some scholars called the approach used following Katrina and Rita a "seat-of-the-pants" approach, which was necessary given the immediacy and magnitude of the evacuees. Yet such chaos can be destructive, not only to the evacuees but also to the elders who require care, and to the staff supplying support and intervention (Dyer et al., 2006). Post-Gustav, social workers were far more prepared to conduct needs assessments, conduct discharge planning, and reconnect citizens with family and pets.

The relationship people have with their pets has a tremendous impact on their mental health and stability, perhaps even more demonstrated with elders (Torgusen & Kosberg, 2006; see also Chapter 6 of this volume). It is well known that many people will risk their lives in order to stay with their animals, essentially putting both the resident and their pet in harm's way. Gustav evacuees arrived at LSU's SNS with wrist bands identifying that they had a pet in a shelter nearby. Often, they would request to call the shelter to make sure their pet was safe and sheltered. This was, by far, an enormous improvement over procedures during Katrina and Rita, although thanks to the LSU Vet students, the largest pet shelter was operating and they saved and placed thousands of pets after Katrina. The same shelter did not operate during Gustav, likely because the recovery plans were not as dramatic and planning was in place prior to the storm.

If there is a silver lining in the epic Katrina disaster, it may be that nursing homes and other LTC facilities, state agencies, as well as organizations serving older persons have improved disaster planning and preparation. Nursing homes, for example, must have adequate food and water on hand for a least 3-day sustainability. They must also have electric generators and are required to at least annually test their emergency plans through a disaster drill. Laditka reports that among the key lessons learned after Katrina is the need for facilities to develop alternative modes of communication in order to keep in contact with emergency planners, families, staff, transportation services, and other support agencies (Laditka, n.d.). They should also identify both primary and alternate transportation routes in the event of involuntary closures and evacuations and execute memoranda of understanding with designated sheltering facilities. Facilities must also be integrated with local- or county-level disaster response systems and identify government agencies that can provide resources and other assistance during a disaster (Laditka, n.d.).

Since Katrina, the CDC has published several emergency checklists, not only for community-dwelling older individuals but also for nursing homes, elder service agencies, and "persons in long-term care facilities (LTC) and their family members, friends, personal, caregivers, guardians & long-term care ombudsmen" (CDC, September, 2007). These lists are posed on the web site of the National Long Term Care Ombudsman Resource Center for use by LTC ombudsmen to assist facilities in their disaster preparations. Evidence suggests that since Katrina, many state-level LTC ombudsmen programs have improved their emergency preparedness capabilities by providing disaster training to their regional coordinators and volunteers and have improved their linkages to local and state disaster planners (Nelson, Borders, Huber, & Netting, F. E., 2008). One telephone survey found that fully 70% of the 42 responding state LTC Ombudsmen felt fairly well to moderately/adequately prepare to help their regional and local programs and volunteers assist residents during disaster (Nelson et. al., 2008).

Despite these improvements, inconsistencies in preparation exist and depending on the level of care a facility provides. Varied approaches occur, such as some charge advanced payment to cover housing and care in another facility. Facilities caring for older persons have better standards in terms of signing agreements in advance so as to reduce the risk of persons refusing to relocate during times of mandatory evacuations. Social workers can help to assure that plans are in line with maximizing the highest self-determination and well-being of residents.

Disaster Preparation from a Social Work Perspective

Emergency Preparedness

Social work disaster preparation gaps are not unique to social work. Despite recent advancements in emergency preparedness generally, readiness deficits are common to all health, medical, and human service specialties and to disaster science generally. Many social workers new to emergency work find the disaster management field to be just as alien as the language used in it, "vulnerability assessment, National Incident Management System (NIMS), an all-hazards approach, pre- and post incident mitigation, field treatment sight, and countless acronyms like "SEMO," state emergency planning office," "MRC," medical reserve corps, "HEICS," "Hospital emergency incident command system, " and "CCP," casualty collection point, are among the countless terms abbreviations that can quickly confuse the neophyte (Landesman, 2005).

But failure to grasp the concepts behind this jargon suggests a deficit in social work disaster education and preparation. The exact extent of this deficit is hard to assess, but it seems safe to assume that outside the areas of disaster mental health, the traditional social work core area of disaster practice falls short of what is needed (Wallace, 2005). Social work graduates receive no more, and often less than the 4 h of disaster readiness education that nurses receive during their schooling (International Nursing Coalition for Mass Casualty Education cited in Weiner, Irwin, Trangenstein, & Gordon, 2005). Moreover, Social Work Faculty on average are also probably no better prepared in disaster management than their nursing faculty peers, even if they themselves have already rushed to disasters to ply their professional skills. "Just in time" field training is still common to many disaster health and relief workers. These education and concomitant practice gaps have been the concern of social work dating back to Freidsam who addressed this issue back in 1960 with continued, albeit, limited growth until it was greatly accelerated by the horrors of Hurricane Katrina in 2005 (Dyer et al., 2006; Friedsam, 1960; Mellor, 2003; Puig & Glynn, 2003; Torgusen & Kosberg, 2006; Zakour & Harrell, 2003).

Disaster practice is now becoming a fast growing area of specialization supported a growing literature, with seminars and classes cropping up with some frequency. This growth is exactly consistent with the four-decade-old issue-attention cycle (Bellavita, 2005; Downes cited Sylves, 2008). This four-decade-old model reliably predicts how the concern about a specific emergency threat among disaster planners, practitioners, and scholars and the public will unfold in five stages: (1) the pre-problem phase, where the threat remains hidden or neglected; (2) the alarmed discovery stage which sees a sharp surge in research, funding, regulation, planning, and development; (3) the growing awareness stage where concern about the costs or the sheer institutional difficulties problem solution dominate; (4) the interest decline phase of diminished interest and commitment; and (5) the "post-problem stage" which characterized by general apathy (Bellavita, 2005).

The hurricane preparedness alarmed discovery stage was perhaps best exemplified by the 2005 the White House Conference on Aging which stressed the necessity for a systematic, coordinated national response to meeting the needs of elderly disaster victims (Dyer et al., 2006). The participant's alarm was expressed in their vivid assessment that

> No formal mechanism existed to ensure that frail elders were assisted with eating, bathing, toileting, or other activities of daily living. There were no formal means to ensure that they received needed medical treatments or medication, although both were available on site. Many frail elders in couples or alone without family could not function in the shelter and needed placement in settings that could provide for their needs, such as personal care homes or nursing facilities (Dyer et al., 2006, p. 8).

Along with fate and improved preparations based on lessons learned from Katrina, many residents dodged the twin blasts of Gustav and Ike in 2008. But luck would not always hold. Other catastrophes will surely hit somewhere and relatively soon, although they will probably not be as ruinous as either Katrina, which killed nearly 2,000 people. What seems certain is that the elderly will remain at disproportionately at higher mortality risks of all Mass Casualty Indexes even when compared to infants and children (Landesman, 2005). Finally, if Katrina remains a reliable guide the institutionalized elderly who are the most vulnerable and dependent on the infrastructure, those in nursing homes should be a primary concern of our national public health system, or more will unnecessarily perish (Elder Law Answers, 2008).

Nevertheless, hurricanes and other natural disasters kill far fewer people than say a typical seasonal flu outbreak, which kills about 36,000 people each year and sickens many more (Center for Disease and Control and Prevention, [CDC], 2007). These numbers pale in comparison to a runaway horror like the Spanish influenza of 1918–1919 which killed more than 20 million people worldwide (Louisiana Public Broadcast, 1998). Although vastly different in scope, one striking similarity between hurricanes and influenza is that they both pose starkly disproportionate threats to the elderly, killing more frail elders than any other age group (Landesman, 2005).

Older Persons' Resilience and Exposure to Hurricanes

Prior exposure to an event may serve as a predictor to improved coping and resilience among older persons (see Chapter 9). Social support can also boost resilience as discussed in Chapter 7. Both can be devastated in times of natural disaster. Although resilience may enhance well-being, it may in fact put an elder in danger of sheltering in place and not recognizing the implications of a natural disaster. In terms of success of making it through a hurricane unharmed, the safety net for elders must be reinforced. Likewise, if those on whom an older person is relying on are in harm's way themselves, the potential for risk is amplified. Just imagine the responsibility of the family members who live outside of New Orleans or another vulnerable area in the anticipation of disaster.

Many persons, including older persons, had a change of heart regarding whether to stay or leave after the Katrina experience. Even the heartiest that experienced the wrath of Betsy, Camille, Andrew, and Katrina have shifted their position about not evacuating in the threat of an impending hurricane. One family member described his spirited, New Orleans' mother's change of heart with this anecdote,

> "Before Katrina, I called my 97 year-old mother in New Orleans to tell her I was picking her up and bringing her to my home in Baton Rouge, and she stated an adamant, *"Oh, no you're not, I'm not leaving!"* She did, however, which was a good thing as her house took in six feet of water. When Gustav hit, and she was back in her home, I called to tell her I was picking her up, and she inquired – what time?"

As noted earlier the low casualty impacts of Gustav and Ike may provide only illusory assurance that advances in post-Katrina disaster planning significantly mitigate future risks for older persons in south Louisiana. Such improvements, while significant, will easily be offset by the exploding numbers of elderly, both in aggregate and in proportion to the general population continue to move to flood- and hurricane-prone zones (Knowles & Garrison, 2006). Geographic realities place a huge burden on emergency preparedness and relief planners either to protect these seniors or safely vacate and care for them should disaster strike (Torgusen & Kosberg, 2006). And this burden may even be more challenging as some evidence suggests that the elderly are less disposed than others seek or accept help in the face of need (Lamb, O'Brien, & Fenza, 2008). This tendency pushes the load more squarely on the shoulders of health and human service workers, including social workers, who must sharply hone their outreach skills if they are to protect the elderly before a disaster or meet their health, safety, and welfare needs afterward. But evidence shows that they still are not (Nelson & Arday, 2007). In fact, it is fully accepted that for most elements the emergency response system suffer serious inadequacies including the preparation and training of its personnel (Nelson & Arday). This is far less true for first responders, but holds for surge medical responders as well as the full array of public and private relief workers.

Disaster Planning Teams and Partnerships

All participating NASW members are required to complete the Red Cross disaster mental health services course as a result of the partnership established between NASW and the American Red Cross at the 1996 NASW Delegate Assembly (Webb, 2000). The statement reads, "NASW supports participation in and advocates for programs and policies that service individuals and communities in the wake of disaster" (NASW, 2000, p. 71). The partnership is viewed as a constructive and successful agreement. "Social workers make up 40 percent, psychologists 22 percent, nurses 14 percent, counselors 18 percent, marriage and family therapists 5 percent, and physicians and psychiatrists 1 percent of the trained American Red Cross disaster mental health volunteers" (NASW, 2000, p. 71). As important as the partnership between Red Cross and NASW is, training remains generic. With a crisis in the numbers of social workers who enter the field of gerontology, more needs to be done to cross-train all social workers with aging members. If a social worker is to do any disaster work at all, unless they are in a shelter or area segregated by age, and are only working with pediatrics, for example, they will come into contact with older persons with medical, psychosocial, and resource needs. Particularly since more and more elders are caring for their grandchildren and the more geographically disenfranchised a person is, the more reliant on emergency support services they are. Therefore, a call to action related to older persons and social work must be heeded.

Identifying High-Risk Elders

For decades, it has been recorded that older people are less likely to ask for help before or after a disaster (Cherry et al., In Press; Friedsam, 1950). In emergency planning, identifying the needs of the elderly, whether at home or in other community settings or in nursing homes constitute what is known as a *vulnerability analysis*.

Although the U.S. Department of Health and Human Services is tasked with involving every arm of federal government, including the Administration on Aging, in disaster preparation, the old adage that all disasters are local, still dominates American disaster planning. This entrenched model holds that effective preparation is "one that starts at the local level and grows with the support of surrounding communities, the state and then the federal government. The bottom-up approach yields the best and quickest results in saving lives" (Carafano, 2007, p. 4). Those most vulnerable in the community setting are identified by various agencies charged for meeting the needs of older adults including Agencies on Aging and Councils on Aging. Additionally, programs such as Meals on Wheels and Protective Services and Senior Rx Programs provide information and register those most vulnerable to organizations including the Red Cross so as to synthesize and coordinate response efforts (American Red Cross, 2000). Katrina taught us that one of the most important tools is to centrally identify where older persons are after disaster. The Red Cross established a Safe and Well List, and the Louisiana Nursing Home Association posted a web site where people could search for an elder and it would identify if they had been placed in a nursing facility. Likewise, churches and local voluntary organizations are essential in identifying and meeting the needs of older persons.

As a response to the immediate need to screen especially frail elders, the response team in Houston the Reliant Astrodome Complex (RAC) developed an instrument to screen and intervene with the most vulnerable elders. The tool, called the Seniors Without Families Triage (SWiFT) is to be used in the post-disaster phase, primarily within shelters, and has three levels, from requiring maximum services, i.e., nursing home or hospital placement to referring to a rescue organization service (see Dyer et al., 2006 for a full explanation and example of the instrument). The assessment level 1 explains the shelter occupant "Cannot perform at least on basic ADL: (eating, bathing, dressing, toileting, walking, continence) without assistance." For these persons, the post-disaster action includes "Immediate transfer to a location that can provide skilled or personal care (i.e., assisted living facility, nursing home, hospital)." Level 2 explains the criteria as "Trouble with instrumental activities of daily living (i.e., finances, benefits management, assessing resources)." The action plan for level 2 is "connecting the citizen with a local aging services manager." Level 3 denotes those elders who are the most independent, with the actions "Needs to be connected to a rescue organization service (i.e., Red Cross)." The SWiFT tool was quickly developed and implemented in the RAC, assisting hundreds of people who may have otherwise "languished on their cots" (Dyer et al., 2006, p. 1).

Social Work Roles and Risks – Freelancing and Credentialing Issues

A rapidly developing disaster management literature discusses the concern of people showing up without any familiarity with disaster response, noting that this can be a serious liability for the integrity of the profession, a risk to the elders, and cause conflict in the shelters and communities, and organizations poised to respond (Dyer et al., 2006; Torgusen & Kosberg, 2006; see also Chapter 13 of this volume). The literature classifies these workers as freelancers be they doctors, social workers, paramedics, or any others, as *unaffiliated* spontaneously *converging* volunteers

(Campos-Outcalt, 2006). These unpaid workers flock to the scene to help, and some will find a role, but this activity will be less likely in the future if professional emergency managers have their way – thanks to Katrina. This is because many freelancers, especially during the chaotic acute and immediate post-acute phases, are actually useless or even burdensome. On site emergency managers did not have the time to credential them, assess their capabilities, or to track and control them (Campos-Outcalt, 2006). Nor did they have the time to feed, lead, transport, shelter, or otherwise provide them with the minimal amenities of life. Not all these professional volunteers are medically or psychologically fit, or in any way prepared or suited to the extreme stress of emergency operations. Liability coverage is also a concern, as was security, both after 9/11 and Katrina (Nelson & Arday, 2007).

Prospects for affiliated social workers (organizationally sponsored) who were pushed through Katrina through by FEMA or associated with the Red Cross, for example, do not present these problems. Furthermore, the difficulties associated with this threat diminishes markedly during the longer term recovery phase where the more traditional social work advocacy, resource brokering, and service coordination roles play out in an increasingly stable environment.

Regardless, social workers have an ethical obligation to *provide appropriate professional services in public emergencies to the greatest extent possible* (NASW, 1996). It has been estimated that social work disaster and recovery efforts should prioritize practice in three stages: (1) planning for disaster prevention, (2) working on procedures during a disaster, and (3) conducting interventions following disaster (Torgusen & Kosberg, 2006). Torgusen and Kosberg also identify several broad imperatives for gerontological social workers in terms of disaster response with frail elders, to promote public awareness, to increase standards in education, and to provide training to other professionals and students, to encourage use of telecommunication (i.e., equipment/devices to call for help or to report an emergency), to promote planning efforts, such as conducting mock disasters drills to identify readiness, problems, and to forge local and regional disaster preparedness partnerships.

Whether they are fully ready for these roles or not, affiliated social workers who have actually engaged in emergency field work have typically done so under the auspices of the American Red Cross, which in a declared emergency, becomes the federal agency, legally responsible organization. Pursuant to the National Response Plan, for Emergency Support Function (ESF) 6: "Mass Care, Housing, and Human Services" the Red Cross sets responsibilities for sheltering, feeding, and general care of victims (Nelson & Arday, 2007). ESF 6 responsibilities additionally include client access to a host of government services ranging from food stamps to providing Women, Infants and Children (WIC) services. For the elderly, any number of state and local, private, and public agencies instrumental to the daunting resettlement tasks are involved with the diverse needs of an especially frail and population (Nelson & Arday).

Other social workers are involved in Emergency Support Function # 8 which concerns "Public Health Medical Services" wherein many hospital and nursing home social workers as part of their normal work roles, shift gears and ramp up to evacuate their own clients, as in Katrina, or will work with medical staff to assess the surge inflow of victims who will often need to be transferred out again to overflow shelters, light surge field treatment sites, and/or other available receiving facilities (Landesman, 2005). It also encompasses the social workers mental health roles.

At the management level, social workers broker partnerships with disaster management agencies across disciplines in order to extend meaningful relief efforts via "community development, program development, and service coordination, and community liaison, all of which are major practice domains of community social work practice" (Taylor & Roberts, 1985 as cited in Wallace, 2005, n. p.).

Conclusions and Implications

Hurricanes displace a higher proportion of the frail elderly in a radically compressed time frame in a delimited geographic area. This process, in turn places a strain on response and recovery resources that are easily stressed and overwhelmed particularly when workers themselves are impacted by the storm. With fewer persons entering the aging field, added pressure is put on individual workers and their own families who carry the burden and leave a skeleton crew during times of crisis.

With what seems to be increasing hurricane activity, it seems advisable that priorities need to be reexamined, establishing partnerships with other state agencies that are not nearly as taxed as those that live in places more prone to hurricanes and other disaster. What may be the most demanding role of social workers and other health and mental health-care providers is responding to the chronic, enduring postdisaster care of older persons. However, with fewer gerontological social workers and fewer social workers showing up to help during and after disaster (Wallace, 2005), we are in a worrisome time, as if the impending needs of frail elders are heading toward us like a category 5 hurricane. The field of aging must reexamine the necessary workforce for the increasing needs in the years ahead (see Chapter 13 for a related discussion).

Hurricanes and other natural disasters can have long-range, even lifetime effects. Social workers are likely to be on the scene long after the event occurred, tending to such lingering realities as posttraumatic stress among first responders and survivors, relocation and resource linkage, and mental health needs of mental health issues, loss, and transition. Social workers tend to the needs of older citizens who have faced disaster long after the media has disappeared (Padgett, 2002).

Families and informal caregivers are often the unsung heroes in the response of frail older persons in disaster. Families unquestionably provide the less visible, but herculean support in times of disaster (see Garrison & Sasser, Chapter 6 for discussion). Integrating social work with emergency preparedness could enhance our nation's all-discipline/all-hazards approach to emergency preparedness which is imperative if the well-being of the nation's elders is to be protected at meaningfully improved levels. Literature highlighting the strengths of family, resilience, and social support, such as discussions found in Chapter 7 add to the knowledge to better prepare all persons to better respond to older members, and to understand and maximize mitigating factors when disaster strikes.

References

Allen, P. D. (2007). Social work in the aftermath of disaster: Reflections from a special needs shelter on the LSU campus. *Reflections, 13*(3), 127–137.
American Red Cross. (2000). The American Red Cross Disaster Mental Health Services: Development of a cooperative, single function, multidisciplinary service model. *The Journal of Behavioral Health Services and* Research, *27*(3), 314–320.
Bellavita, C. (2005). Changing homeland security: The issue-attention cycle. *Homeland Security Affairs, 1*(1), 1–6, Retrieved October 17, 2008, from http://www.hsaj.org/pages/volume1/issue1/pdfs/1.1.1.pdf
Browning, C. R., Wallace, D., Feinberg, S. L., & Cagney, K. A. (2006, August). Neighborhood social processes, physical conditions, and disaster-related mortality: The case of the 1995 Chicago heat wave. *American Sociological Review, 71*, 661–678.
Brunkard, J., Namulanda, G., & Ratard, R. (2008). Hurricane Katrina deaths, Louisiana, 2005. *Disaster medicine and public health preparedness*. Retrieved October 11, 2008, from http://www.dmphp.org/cgi/content/abstract/DMP.0b013e31818aaf55v1
Campos-Outcalt, D. (2006). Disaster medical response: Maximizing your effectiveness. *The Journal of Family Practice, 55*(2), 113–116.
Carafano, J. J. (2007). *FEMA and federalism: Washington is moving in the wrong direction*, The Heritage Foundation. Retrieved July 2, 2007, from http://www.heritage.org/Research/HomelandDefense/bg2032.cfm
Centers for Disease Control and Prevention. (2007). *Health information for older adults*. Retrieved on July 16, 2008, from http://www.cdc.gov/aging/info.htm#2
Cherry, K. E., Allen, P. D., & Galea, S. (In Press). Older adults and natural disasters: Lessons learned from Hurricanes Katrina and Rita. In P. Dass-Brailsford (Ed.), *Crisis and disaster counseling: Lessons learned from Hurricane Katrina and other disasters*. Thousand Oaks, CA: Sage.
City of New Orleans. (n.d.). Office of Emergency Preparedness. *Comprehensive emergency management plan*. Retrieved September 28, 2005, from http://www.cityofno.com/pg- 46-26-hurricanes.aspx
Clinton, J. J., Hagebak, B. R., Sirmons, J. G., & Brennan, J. A. (1995). Lessons learned from the Georgia floods, *Public Health Reports, 110*, 684–688.
Dyer, C., Festa, N. A., Cloyd, B., Regev, M., Schwartzberg, J. G., James, J., et al. (2006). *Recommendations for best practices in the management of elderly disaster victims*. Baylor College of Medicine and the American Medical Association. Retrieved July 16, 2008, from http://www.bcm.edu/pdf/bestpractices.pdf
Elder Law Answers. (2008). *Nursing home residents among last to be evacuated; Many die* Retrieved June 6, 2008, from http://www.elderlawanswers.com/resources/article.asp?id=4903&section=4
Faffer, J. I. (2007). In the eye of the storm: Responding to senior needs before, during, and after. *Journal of Jewish Communal Service, 83*(1), 70–74.
Fernandez, L. S., Byard, D., Lin, C. C., Benson, S., & Barbera, J. A. (2002, April–June). Frail elderly as disaster victims: Emergency management strategies. *Prehospital and Disaster Medicine*. Retrieved October 16, 2008, from http://www.gwu.edu/~icdrm/publications/67-74_fernandez.pdf
Friedsam, H. J. (1960, Winter). Older persons as disaster casualties. *Journal of Health and Human Behavior, 1*, 267–278
Hazzard, W. R., Blass, J. P., Ettinger, W. H., Halter, J. B., & Ouslander, J. G. (1999). *Principles of geriatric medicine and gerontology* (4th ed.). New York: McGraw-Hill.

Huber, R., Nelson, H. W., Netting, F. E., & Borders, K. (2007). *Elder advocacy: Essential knowledge and skills across settings*. Belmont, CA: Thomson, Brooks Cole.

James, C. H., & Scantlebury, C. (2007, Winter). After the storm: When Houston becomes home. *Generations, 31*(4), 55–56.

Kailes, J. I. (2005). *Disaster services and "special needs": Term of art or meaningless term?* Retrieved July 8, 2007, from http://www2.ku.edu/˜rrtcpbs/findings/pdfs/SpecialsNeeds.pdf

Knowles, R. M. (2007). *Family resiliency among hurricane survivors: Resource loss, prior traumatic events, and cumulative stress*. Unpublished thesis, Louisiana State University, Baton Rouge. Retrieved December 3, 2008, from http://etd.lsu.edu/docs/available/etd- 07112007-150118/unrestricted/RobinKnowlesThesis.pdf

Knowles, R. M., & Garrison, B. (2006). Planning for elderly in natural disasters. *Disaster Recovery Journal, 19*(4), n.p. Retrieved on December 4, 2008, from http://www.drj.com/articles/fall06/1904-07p.html

Laditka, S. (n.d.). *Protecting our most vulnerable citizens: Lessons learned from Katrina to improve readiness in nursing homes*. University of South Carolina. Retrieved October 27, 2008, from http://www.sc.edu/katrinacrisis/laditka.shtml

Lamb, K. V., O'Brien, C., & Fenza, P. J. Elders at risk during disasters. *Home Healthcare Nurse, 26*(1), 30–8.

Landesman, L. Y. (2005). *Public health management of disasters: A practice guide* (2nd ed.). Washington, DC: American Public Health Association.

Louisiana Public Broadcast. (1998). A Science Odyssey. *A worldwide flu pandemic strikes, 1918–1919*. Retrieved October 10, 2008, from http://www.pbs.org/wgbh/aso/databank/entries/dm18fl.html

Marscher, F. (2004). *Elderly in Florida at risk in every hurricane season*. BNET. Retrieved October 8, 2008, from http://findarticles.com/p/articles/mi_qn4188/is_/ai_n11475506

McCarthy, J. F., Blow, F. C., & Kales, H. C. (2004). Disruptive behaviors in veterans affairs nursing home residents: How different are residents with serious mental illness? *Journal of the American Geriatrics Society, 52*(12), 2031–2038.

McGlown, K. J. (2004). *Terrorism and disaster management: Preparing healthcare leaders for the new reality*. Chicago: Health Administration Press.

Mead, R. A. (2006, Spring). St. Rita's and lost causes: Improving nursing home emergency preparedness. *7 Marquette Elder's Advisor, 2*, 153–201.

Mellor, M. J. (2003). From the editor. *Journal of Gerontological Social Work, 40*(4), 1–2.

MSNBC (2005, September 30). *Officials deny responsibility for evacuee bus fires*. Retrieved October 3, 2008, from http://www.msnbc.msn.com/id/9547486

National Association of Social Workers (NASW). (1996). *Code of ethics of the National Association of Social Workers*. Washington, DC: NASW.

National Association of Social Workers. (2000). Disasters. In*Social work speaks, National Association of Social Workers policy statements, 2000–2003* (pp. 67–77). Washington, DC: NASW Press.

National Long Term Care Ombudsman Resource Center. (n.d.). *Center emergency procedures from the CDC*. Retrieved October 6, 2008, from http://www.ltcombudsman.org/ombpublic/49_369_4543.cfm.

Nelson, H. W., & Arday, D. (2007). Medical aspects of disaster preparedness and response: A system overview of civil and military resources and new potential. *Joint Center for Operational Analysis Journal, 9*(2), 42–55.

Nelson, H. W., Borders, K., Huber, R., & Netting, F. E. (2008). Assessing long term care ombudsman program readiness to assist long term care facilities in the event of a disaster. Unpublished raw data.

Padgett, D. (2002). Social work research on disasters in the aftermath of the September 11 tragedies. *Social Work Research, 26*(3), 185–192.

Puig, M. E., & Glynn, J. B. (2003). Disaster responders: A cross-cultural approach to recovery and relief work. *Journal of Social Service Research, 30*(2), 55–66.

Sahyoun, N. R., Pratt, L. A., Lentzner, H., Dey, A., & Robinson, K. N. (2001). *The changing profile of nursing home residents: 1985–1997.* Aging Trends No. 4. Retrieved October 28, 2008, from http://www.cdc.gov/nchs/data/ahcd/agingtrends/04nursin.pdf

Senior Journal (2008, April 30). *Alzheimer's, dementia & mental health.* Retrieved October 27, 2008, from http://seniorjournal.com/NEWS/Alzheimers/2008/8-04-30-SeniorDementia.htm

Sharkey, P. (2007). Survival and death in New Orleans: An empirical look at the human impact of Katrina. *Journal of Black Studies 37*(4), 482–501.

Spader, C. (2005). Understanding transfer trauma. *Nurse Week.* Retrieved October 28, 2008, from http://www2.nursingspectrum.com/articles/article.cfm?aid=18535

Sylves, R. (2008). *Disaster policy and politics: Emergency management and homeland security.* Washington, DC: University of Delaware.

Torgusen, B. L., & Kosberg, J. I. (2006). Assisting older victims of disasters: Roles and responsibilities for social workers. *Journal of Gerontological Social Work, 47*(1/2), 27–44.

Wallace, J. R. (2005). Social work management in an age of terrorism. *The national network for social work managers.* Retrieved October 10, 2008, from https://www.socialworkmanager.org/articles.php?id=article0

Webb, R. (2000). *NASW and the American Red Cross partners in disaster mental health.* Retrieved September 15, 2008, from http://www.socialworkers.org/practice/health/redcross.asp

Weiner, E., Irwin, M., Trangenstein, P., & Gordon, J. (2005). Emergency preparedness curriculum in nursing schools in the United States. *Nursing Education Perspectives, 26* (6), 334–339.

Western Illinois Area Agency on Aging. *A guide to the basics of disaster preparedness.* Retrieved October 19, 2008, from http://www.wiaaa.org/rsvp/basic_disaster_preparedness.htm

Yeoman, B. (2007, September). Katrina: The untold story. *AARP, The Magazine,* 72–79. Retrieved on October 28, 2008, from http://www.aarpmagazine.org/people/Katrina_untold_story.html

Zakour, M. (1996). Disaster research in social work. In C. L. Streeter & S. A. Murty (Eds.), *Research on social work and disasters* (pp. 7–25). Philadelphia: Haworth Press.

Zakour, M. J., & Harrell, E. B. (2003). Access to disaster services: Social work interventions for vulnerable populations. *Journal of Social Service Research, 30*(2), 27–54.

Chapter 9
Natural Disasters and the Oldest-Old: A Psychological Perspective on Coping and Health in Late Life

Katie E. Cherry, Jennifer L. Silva, and Sandro Galea

Abstract Hurricanes Katrina and Rita caused unprecedented destruction and disruption in the lives of thousands of people. In times of such intense stress and uncertainty, older adults have historically been considered an at-risk group. In this chapter, we focus on health and well-being in a disaster context. We begin by reviewing normative age-related changes in physical, cognitive, and social functioning. Next, we discuss resilience and coping and as they relate to adaptation to stressful situations in adulthood. We present select data from the Louisiana Healthy Aging Study (LHAS) that examined the impact of the storms on psychosocial indices of health and well-being in adults who varied in age from mid-twenties to ninety years and older. Results yielded comparable self-reported health and well-being across the pre- and post-hurricane assessments. A qualitative analysis of coping strategies before and after the storms revealed similar types and reported frequencies of coping behaviors among the age groups. Implications of these findings for disaster preparedness in late adulthood are discussed.

Introduction

National demographic trends show increasing numbers of older adults in society as the post-World War II baby boom generation (i.e., the 76 million people born between 1946 and 1964) approaches late adulthood. These trends have drawn attention to the issues and challenges associated with aging society. By the year 2030, current estimates hold that one-fifth of the US population or 70 million Americans will be 65 years of age and older. The majority of those age 65 years and older are relatively healthy and live independently in the community. However, the probability of illness or chronic condition that leads to disability, immobility, or chronic pain increases with age (Administration on Aging, 2007). Critically, the "oldest-old" (i.e., people 85 years of age and older) are the fastest growing segment of the

---

K.E. Cherry (✉)
Department of Psychology, Louisiana State University, Baton Rouge, LA 70803-5501, USA
e-mail: pskatie@lsu.edu

population, also having the greatest health-care needs. Careful consideration of the social, economic, and political ramifications of an aging population, with special attention to the oldest-old, is an important challenge for the social sciences (Suzman, Harris, Hadley, Kovar, & Weindruch, 1992).

For the most part, the scientific literature on catastrophic disasters and trauma exposure has focused on adults younger than age 65. Given the changing demographic trends, interest in understanding the influence of disaster and trauma-related distress on older persons is growing among researchers and clinicians today (Cook & Niederehe, 2007). There are many reasons why older adults warrant special consideration in disaster planning and after a disaster has happened. For instance, older people may process storm warnings differently compared to their younger counterparts and they may be slower to respond when a natural disaster occurs (Perry & Lindell, 1997). Older people may also seek post-disaster assistance and financial support less often than younger people do (Kilijanek & Drabek, 1979). As discussed in Chapter 14, mortality rates in the wake of Hurricane Katrina favored older adults who perished in the storm more often than any other age group combined. Chapter 7 describes many sources of vulnerability that older adults in the storm-impacted areas faced in preparation for and after Hurricane Katrina, including reluctance in leaving their home, lack of transportation, evacuation dilemmas and multiple moves on route to safer locations, declining physical health, and limited resources. Thus, it is not surprising that older adults are generally considered a special risk group for post-disaster distress (Massey, 1997). On the contrary, findings from the disaster research literature yield a complicated picture of disaster impact on elderly persons. Some have found a significant influence of natural disasters on older adults' physical health (Phifer, Kaniasty, & Norris, 1988) and psychological symptoms (Phifer & Norris, 1989; Phifer, 1990). Others have found that older adults appear less vulnerable and better able to cope with post-disaster stress than are younger people (Cherry, Galea, et al., 2009; Knight, Gatz, Heller, & Bengtson, 2000; Thompson, Norris, & Hanacek, 1993; Tracy & Galea, 2006).

In this chapter, we examine the impact of natural disasters on coping strategies and health in very old adults. We begin with an overview of age-related physical, cognitive, and social changes that commonly occur in adulthood. Understanding the developmental trajectories of late life senescence under ordinary circumstances is important, as the sudden occurrence of a hurricane or other natural disaster constitutes a significant environmental event that may threaten the health and wellness balance of older persons who are aging in place. Cherry, Galea, and Silva (2008) have made the point that natural disasters provide a context to study adaptation, resilience, and successful aging in later life. Accordingly, we review select models and findings related to resilience and coping to characterize normative development and lay a foundation for looking at adaptation to post-disaster stress in late adulthood. In the next section, we present select data from the Louisiana Health Aging Study (LHAS), a multidisciplinary study of the determinants of longevity and healthy aging in the oldest-old. Specifically, we describe the LHAS hurricane assessment study that examined Katrina and Rita's impact on several psychosocial indicators of health and well-being in younger, middle age, older, and oldest-old adults. We conclude by considering the implications of the LHAS hurricane study findings for future disaster planning and preparation for healthy older adults.

The Older Adult Population: A Snapshot of Late Life

The growing numbers of older persons in society today have sparked scientific interest in longevity and steps to promote healthy aging (Bradshaw & Klein, 2007; Winerman, 2006). Understanding factors that contribute to successful aging, such as one's genetic constitution, nutrition, exercise habits, social relations, and dispositional traits, is important for improving quality of life and decreasing the financial burden associated with medical treatment and long care in adulthood (Suzman et al., 1992). In this section, we describe select aspects of physical, cognitive, and social functioning in late adulthood to illustrate the many age-related changes that occur under ordinary circumstances.

Three Domains of Age-Related Change

Age-Related Changes in Physical Health. Age-related changes in health status and physical functioning are common in adulthood. Prevalence for chronic conditions, such as arthritis, hypertension, hearing impairment, heart disease, and cataracts, increases with age. To illustrate, an average 75-year-old has been diagnosed with three different chronic conditions and is taking five different prescription medications (Center for Disease Control and Prevention, 2007). For many older persons, the onset of age-related chronic conditions brings numerous challenges and implications for everyday living. For example, older adults may experience difficulties in performing activities of daily living (ADLs), including self-care and routine tasks such as grocery shopping, cooking, and performing basic household chores. Debilitating chronic conditions, such as heart disease, cancer, stroke and diabetes, may threaten independent living and are also major causes of death for older persons (Administration on Aging, 2007). A poor diet, sedentary lifestyle, and other health risks such as smoking and obesity may also promote the occurrence of age-related diseases that contribute to disability and death in adulthood (Reynolds, Saito, & Crimmins, 2005).

Fortunately, the health benefits of proper diet, nutrition, and exercise for well-being in later life are widely recognized today (Bradshaw & Klein, 2007). Proper diet and adequate physical activity can lead to a number of different health benefits, such as reduced chronic disability, enhanced immune, cardiovascular and muscular functioning, and improved emotional status (U.S. Department of Health and Human Services, 1996). Even among the oldest-old, therapeutic interventions such as cataract surgery and geriatric rehabilitation have been shown to be effective, implying that late life frailty and disability may be more modifiable than previously assumed (Suzman et al., 1992). Furthermore, the increasing emphasis on disability prevention, healthy lifestyles, and avoiding health risks has significantly prolonged active life expectancy, defined as the average number of years older persons can expect to live without disability (Crimmins, Haywood, & Saito, 1996). Understanding the dynamics of disability, such as risk and prevention, as well as retention and recovery of functional capacities in older persons, is an important direction for future research (Suzman et al., 1992).

Age-Related Changes in Cognition. Broadly defined, cognition refers to mental processes, such as attention, memory, decision making, problem solving, and language. Cognition plays a vital role in healthy aging, independent living, and quality of life. As Allen and Wayne note in Chapter 8, cognitive deficits are the primary reason for institutionalization of elderly persons. For first responders, service providers, and others who interact with elderly clientele, understanding the cognitive competencies of elderly persons is especially critical, as cognitive decrements in late life may affect interpersonal communication and exchange of information.

Ample experimental evidence has shown that cognition declines with age (Craik & Salthouse, 2008). For example, lapses of attention and memory in daily life occur with greater frequency for healthy older adults compared to younger adults (Reese & Cherry, 2004). Emotional and physiological states may also contribute to momentary forgetfulness for older persons. Age-related cognitive deficits are also noticeable to older adults who may complain or joke about their declining memory abilities. Heightened sensitivity to cognitive functionality is certainly understandable, given the increased public awareness of memory impairment associated with Alzheimer's disease (AD) and related dementias. A critical point for consideration, however, concerns the difference between memory problems of normal aging from those that may be due to underlying physiological or psychopathological factors. For instance, people of all ages experience lapses of memory that may be due to internal states (e.g., inattention, interference, fatigue), external factors (e.g., inadequate retrieval cues, information overload), or both. On the other hand, forgetting names of family members or close friends, confusion in space and time, and difficulties with simple motor tasks (e.g., unlocking a door with a key) are behaviors that could be signaling a serious health condition, such as dementia (Cherry & Smith, 1998).

It is widely recognized that changes in health are often accompanied by changes in cognition (Siegler, Bosworth, & Poon, 2003). Thus, accurate diagnosis of the underlying conditions producing serious cognitive problems is critical. In some cases, cognitive deficits may be responsive to treatment, although deficits such as those observed in the adult dementias are irreversible. Nonetheless, early intervention efforts remain vitally important for effective case management and to foster adaptive coping strategies for caregivers, family members, and individuals suffering from cognitive impairments (Cherry & Plauche, 1996).

Age-Related Changes in Social Relations. Family and friends can provide companionship, as well as social and emotional support, which contribute positively to well-being in adulthood (Adams & Blieszner, 1995; see also Chapter 7 of this volume). Interestingly, friends are generally considered more important to the psychological well-being of older adults than family members (Antonucci & Akiyama, 1995). This trend is probably related to the fact that older people are more likely to confide in age peers, and there is a greater likelihood of friends involving the older person with the larger society (Adams & Blieszner, 1995). Supportive family members and friends increase the variety of skills and resources that can be brought to bear when an older person needs help or assistance.

Other evidence confirms a strong association between social relations and health. Social relations, such as family, friends, and others important to the individual, may boost one's feelings of self-worth and mastery which are needed for health maintenance and well-being (Antonucci, 2001). These persons may also assist in the attainment of health-related goals (VonDras & Madey, 2004) or help to promote healthy lifestyles and discourage unhealthy behaviors (Tucker, Klein, & Elliott, 2004). Note, however, that social relations may not always be beneficial. In some cases, social relations may have negative consequences for the individual (for reviews, see Burg & Seeman, 1994; Rook, 1990). Prior findings have shown that negative social exchanges with family, friends, and neighbors may have a detrimental effect on emotional well-being (e.g., Rook, 2001) and physical health (Newsome, Mahan, Rook, & Krause, 2008). Thus, the influence of social relations in late life may depend importantly on the circumstances and qualities of these relationships.

Summary and Developmental Implications

Age-related changes in physical, cognitive, and social functioning and the interplay among these domains of life appear to be the norm rather than the exception for most old people today. Demographic trends confirm that a substantial number of individuals are living to advanced ages, which implies that greater functional deficits also accumulate in late life. Freund and Riediger (2003) have made the point that declines in physical and cognitive functioning are more pronounced in very old age (85 years and older) compared to adults in their sixties and seventies. Consequently, they underscore the value and need to distinguish between *young-old* and *oldest-old* adults, a conceptual distinction which traces its historical roots to Bernice Neugarten (1974) who coined the descriptive terms, "young-old" and "old-old," in reference to subgroups of older adults (i.e., those 55–75 years versus those older than 75 years).

Where the line is drawn with respect to the precise chronological ages that delimit subgroups within the older population is fundamentally arbitrary and likely to change in future generations. Our interest concerns potential differences in health status, functional abilities, and adaptive capacities of young-old compared to oldest-old adults. This question warrants special consideration because a hurricane or other disaster may differentially affect these two cohorts of older people, relative to their middle age or younger reference groups. Given the striking diversity among adults over age 65, sweeping generalizations about elderly adults as a single demographic classification group are simply not warranted, especially in a disaster context. Physically frail and medically compromised older persons may not survive the evacuation process or may die in the aftermath (see Chapter 8). In contrast, healthy older adults with a lifetime of experience and rich, factual knowledge of the storm affected area may be a tremendous asset to the relief and recovery process (see Chapter 11). Even very old adults may show remarkable adaptation and resilience in the face of a natural disaster. As a case in point, Cherry, Galea et al. (2009) found that oldest-old adults were not directly involved in disaster relief assistance, yet one community-dwelling 95-year-old prepared and sent a pot full of red beans and rice to feed Katrina evacuees who were sheltered at her church. Remembering the remarkable adaptive capacities and strengths of some older individuals while acknowledging the vulnerabilities of others is a critical consideration for those personnel involved in disaster relief work (Oriol, 1999).

In sum, very old adults may have more health issues and functional limitations compared to younger persons, yet they cope with these difficulties and find joy in their lives, despite the changing life circumstances that occur with aging. Rowe and Kahn (1997) have defined successful aging as avoiding disease and disability, maintaining high levels of physical and cognitive functioning, and remaining engaged in social and productive activities. Others suggest that successful aging should be conceptualized in terms of the processes of developmental regulation in late life, with emphasis on regulatory processes such as control over one's affairs and coping strategies (see Freund & Riediger, 2003, for discussion). Adaptation and coping with changes in later life can take many forms, including modifying the environment to adapt to physical changes, drawing strength from family and friends, and cultivating optimism, a positive outlook, and hope (Baltes & Baltes, 1990). Based on the assumption that natural disasters offer a context to study adaptation and resilience in the face of a significant environmental stressor (cf. Cherry et al., 2008), we review select models and related findings on resilience and coping from a developmental perspective in the next section.

Resilience and Coping in Late Adulthood

The terms *stress* and *coping* are often paired with the concept of *resilience*. Most agree that adaptive coping can be efficacious against stress (Folkman, 1984; see also Chapter 3 of this volume). Resilience, however, is conceptually distinct from coping. Coping is a behavioral process directed at the source of stress and is typically a temporary phenomenon during stress exposure. In contrast, resilience is an outcome that is observed or inferred after a stressful event. Resilience is often linked with a lack of psychopathology, as indexed through behavioral and physical measures, following exposure to a traumatic event (Masten, 2001; Rutter, 2006; see also Chapter 4 of this volume).

Review of Resilience

Resilience has been defined in similar ways across the literature, usually as successful adaptation in the face of an adversity that is typically associated with a negative outcome (Bonanno, 2004; Masten, 2001; Rutter, 2006). Specifically, resilience is postulated to be the "maintenance, recovery, or improvement in mental and physical health following change" (Bar-Tur & Levy-Shiff, 2000, pp. 263–264). Typically perceived as an outcome, resilience becomes evident over time and is not immediately associated with a negative event, risk, or threat (Bonanno, Galea, Bucciarelli, & Vlahov, 2007; Rutter, 2006). To observe or infer resilience, one must meet two main distinct criteria (Masten, 2001). The first criterion is the presence of obvious risk. The lack of risk simply cannot lead to resilience. A person who has not experienced any risk should not be identified as resilient. Also, the threat alone is necessary but not sufficient enough to infer or observe resilience. The second criterion is that an individual must attempt to cope or withstand the risk/threat, and not actively avoid it.

The concept of resilience was initially identified in longitudinal studies that examined the psychopathology and behavioral outcomes of children exposed to traumatic or other risk experiences, such as death of a parent or having a low socioeconomic status (for review, see Masten, 2001). This early approach was *deficit focused* and sought to identify all of the negative experiences and characteristics (i.e., deficits) associated with long-term, adverse outcomes, such as mental illness, delinquency, and distress. Those experiencing negative outcomes were assumed to have encountered a deficiency or risk at some point in their lifetime. Thus, resilience was viewed as the avoidance or simple lack of risk exposure. Consequently, it was believed that in order to promote positive outcomes and resilience, one should actively attempt to avoid risk.

Findings from these early investigations produced a result contrary to the deficit-focused hypothesis. Werner and Smith (1989, 1992, 2001) conducted a 40-year longitudinal investigation of 698 children born in 1955 in Kauai, Hawaii. These authors followed participants from birth to maturity in order to determine the impact of biological and environmental risk factors on development. By age 2, one-third of surveyed children were exposed to various familial risks, such as poverty, violence, mental illness, prenatal problems, instability/discord, and alcoholism. By age 18, these two-thirds of these "high-risk" children had gone on to develop behavioral problems. However, by mid-adulthood (32–40 years of age) the vast majority (about 80%) had gone on to live stable lives and did not show evidence of behavioral problems or mental illness. Werner and Smith concluded that both internal and external factors worked concurrently to impact an individual's development and further promote resilience. Internal factors were identified as autonomy, ability to problem solve, social competence, and having a sense of future. External or environmental factors were seen as strong familial relationships that promoted active participation and behavioral standards or expectations.

As resilience research progressed, there was a shift from viewing resilience as deficit focused to *strength focused* (Benard, 1991; Howard, Dryden, & Johnson, 1999; Rutter, 2006). This new approach assumed that some persons might have some additional strength or protective factors which buffer risk in light of a negative experience (Rutter, 1985, 1990). To promote resilience in risk-exposed youth, one should attempt to minimize risk/threat characteristics and maximize these protective factors. Benard (1991) defined protective factors as those "traits, conditions, situations, and episodes that appear to alter (or even reverse) predictions of negative outcome and enable the individual to circumvent life stressors" (p. 3). Protective factors identified in the literature include having a social support network, using adaptive coping mechanisms, and possessing an easy temperament (see Vance & Sanchez, 1998, for review).

Review of Coping

Resilience concerns the behavioral and psychological outcomes following a negative life event/experience, whereas coping is considered a temporary response to something an individual perceives as threatening, harmful, or challenging (Lazarus & Folkman, 1984). Coping is more of a temporary adaptation, which if successful, may reduce distress and foster resilience over time. The transactional theory (Folkman & Lazarus, 1988; Lazarus & Folkman, 1984) views coping as a process that has a bidirectional relationship with emotion. In other words, not only can an emotional reaction influence a chosen coping strategy but coping may in turn mediate an individual's current emotional state. Coping decisions are usually made after an initial appraisal of the situation, because one must determine the exact nature of a potential threat.

Coping can be influenced by a variety of antecedent variables that include personal traits, perceived capabilities, and past experiences, all of which affect appraisal of a stressful situation. For example, upon a stressful encounter there is an appraisal process each person goes through. During primary appraisal one may ask the question, what is at stake for me? If a person assumes that his/her safety is at jeopardy, this will impact how threatening, harmful, or challenging the situation is perceived. Secondary appraisal poses the question, what can I do about this? This is when one reflects upon his/her own unique capabilities, factoring in goal importance as well. If a person believes he/she can manage the situation effectively and has the necessary capabilities, or if the goal (or situation) is highly important, one would most likely engage in *problem-focused coping* (e.g., confrontational strategies). While, if the person feels as if there is not much that can be done with the situation, he/she would most likely engage in *emotion-focused coping*, such as denial, self-blame, or positivity (Folkman & Lazarus, 1988; Lazarus & Folkman, 1984).

Determinants of Adaptive Behavior in Older Adults

Older adulthood is often characterized by losses and deterioration, as indexed by declines in physical health (Brandstadter, Wentura, & Greve, 1993; Rowe & Kahn, 1997). Brandstadter and colleagues have shown that despite systematic increases in losses and declines, older adults have comparable self-esteem and life-satisfaction rates as their younger counterparts. Further, younger and older adults also report similar levels perceived control scores, suggesting that while older adults encounter more losses, they do not show a loss of perceived control over life events. It has been documented that older cohorts have lower prevalence of psychological disorders, such as depression and anxiety, compared to younger cohorts (Carstensen & Freund, 1994; Cook & Niederehe, 2007). From these observations, researchers have asked, "How to older people, faced with losses in many domains, maintain a positive sense of well being?" (Carstensen & Freund, 1994, p. 82).

According to Brandstadter et al. (1993), older persons may engage in two distinct coping processes, namely assimilation and accommodation. Assimilation coping occurs when one directly alters the situation so that it meets ones personal goals. Accommodation is when a person restructures his/her goals or preferences, so that the events lose their aversive or threatening meaning. These two processes are conceptually similar to Lazarus and Folkman's (1984) *problem-* and *emotion-focused* coping strategies. The majority of individuals will use assimilative strategies. However, if a situation appears to be overtaxing or unchangeable, then accommodative strategies may predominate. As individuals age, they tend to participate less in assimilative strategies and engage more in accommodative approaches, implying a systematic change in coping behaviors occurs across the lifespan (Brandstadter et al., 1993; Slangen-de Kort, Midden, Aarts, & van Wagenberg, 2001). That is, older adults adapt themselves rather than their environment in order to cope with problems.

Brandstadter and colleagues examined this age-related shift hypothesis by measuring preferred coping strategy and two dispositional characteristics linked with goal adherence, flexibility, and tenaciousness. Prior research showed that those who choose assimilation strategies were likely to be tenacious and not give up their goals. In contrast, those with accommodative strategies were more flexible with their goals and are more likely (or able) to reformulate their attitudes. Results demonstrated that flexibility and tenaciousness scores held opposite patterns for each age cohort, with older adults exhibiting higher flexible scores and engaging in more accommodative strategies. In sum, identifying persons as either flexible or tenacious predicted what type of coping method chosen and older adults consistently demonstrated more accommodative coping style.

Subsequent research conducted by Slangen-de Kort et al. (2001) also utilized an older adult population. Their participants completed disposition assessments and were presented with various problem scenarios. One such scenario states, "Your daughter lives 3000 miles away in California and you don't see her a lot. You talk to her on the phone everyday, but recently your hearing has become worse and you are unable to understand her. What would you do?" These participants were then prompted to choose among potential accommodative and assimilative coping strategies. Flexible persons viewed accommodative strategies as more efficacious and were most likely to adopt those. Overall, accommodative coping strategies were identified as emotion focused, because there was usually a change in attitude. Conversely, tenacious individuals reported accommodative strategies to be less efficacious and were more likely to choose an assimilative strategy.

In sum, our review of the coping literature points to the existence of a hypothesized shift in coping strategies with age, where older adults are more likely adapt themselves rather than their environment in response to a stressful situation. A variety of disaster-specific stressors may challenge people of all ages in a disaster context. For older persons, these challenges may be particularly taxing, given normative declines in physical health and stamina (Oriol, 1999). As discussed in Chapter 6, maintaining an optimistic attitude and a sense of humor are effective coping strategies in times of disaster. Although Brandstadter et al. (1993) did not specifically address coping with natural disasters, one could argue that optimism and humor, among other more positive emotional reactions, represent accommodative coping strategies that may be seen among older adults in the wake of disaster.

In the next section, we present select data from the Louisiana Healthy Aging Study (LHAS) to illustrate the effects of Hurricanes Katrina and Rita on self-reported health and coping behaviors in the months following the storms. The LHAS hurricane study used a mixed method design with pre- and post-hurricane quantitative measures (on select psychosocial indicators of well-being) and qualitative open-ended questions to allow an in-depth examination of participants' reactions to the storms and their coping behaviors before and after the storms.

Coping with Katrina and Rita: LHAS Hurricane Study

The LHAS is a multidisciplinary study of the determinants of longevity and healthy aging which began in January of 2002. When Hurricanes Katrina and Rita (HK/R) struck the Gulf Coast in 2005, we had a unique opportunity to examine the influence of a natural disaster on several domains of cognitive and psychosocial functioning with a prospective research design. We utilized a subset of the LHAS individual difference measures to permit pre- and post-hurricane comparisons by age group. Our primary interest concerned the impact of the storms on the oldest-old, defined as persons 90 years of age and older, and their younger counterparts. Our secondary aim was to gain new evidence of storm impact, coping, and resilience using open-ended questions and other mental health measures new to the LHAS protocol to account for possible psychological distress due to the storms and their aftermath (see Cherry et al., 2008, for description).

The LHAS study sample resides within approximately a 40-mile radius of Baton Rouge, Louisiana, outside of the severely affected areas. While direct trauma exposure was minimal for most of these participants, virtually all had children, grandchildren, and in some cases, great grandchildren, as well as nieces, nephews, and other family members and close friends in the affected areas at the time of the storms. LHAS participants' family members, friends and acquaintances from the affected areas evacuated to Baton Rouge and frequently stayed in their homes in the wake of the storms. Most would agree that witnessing property damage and community destruction experienced by loved ones and friends is disturbing, having the potential for threats to health and/or lingering psychological effects. Understanding the influence of how family members and friends may have fared in the storms on LHAS participants' emotional state and sense of well-being during the post-disaster recovery period was also a significant motivation for this study.

Overview of Method

Wave 1 data were collected between October 2005 and January 2006 to assess immediate impact of the storms. Three age groups were included in wave 1 testing: middle age adults (45–64 years), older adults (65–89 years), and the oldest-old adults (90 years and older). The first findings of wave 1 are reported elsewhere (Cherry et al., 2008; Cherry, Galea, et al., 2009). Wave 2 data were collected between March and November of 2006 to examine storm impact 6–14 months post-disaster. Most of the original participants in wave 1 (89%) were retested in wave 2. We added a comparison group of young adults (20–44 years) in wave 2 to increase the breadth of inferences warranted regarding lifespan differences in post-hurricane psychological reactions. Two measures of religious coping were added to the wave 2 protocol because faith and religious beliefs were mentioned by some as a form of coping in wave 1. Participants completed a structured religious beliefs and practices questionnaire (not reported here). They also answered an open-ended question concerning their use of religious coping strategies with the storms and their aftermath. Emergent themes from the religious coping question are presented in two other chapters (i.e., Chapters 10 and 11).

Results and Discussion

LHAS Individual Difference Measures. Table 9.1 presents mean responses to three self-perceived health questions from the Older American Resources and Services questionnaire (OARS; Duke University Center for the Study of Aging and Human Development, 1975), the Geriatric Depression Scale (GDS; Sheikh & Yesavage, 1986), and the Medical Outcomes Study Short Form-36 (SF-36; Ware & Sherbourne, 1992) physical and mental component scores (PCS, MCS) that measure health-related quality of life. In the analyses that follow, we examined middle age, older, and oldest-old adults' responses at pre-HK/R, wave 1, and wave 2 testings because these age groups participated in all three assessments. Follow-up analyses at pre-HK/R and wave 2 testings included the younger adults to permit greater insight into response differences across a comparatively broader range of ages.

As can be seen in Table 9.1, most respondents had a positive appraisal of their health. Analyses of ratings for health at the present time and health prevents activities yielded no significant age group or time of testing effects. For health compared to others, analyses of the older age groups' ratings at 3 times of testing yielded a significant age group main effect, $F(2, 55) = 13.65, p < 0.001$. Middle age adults rated their health compared to their age mates ($M = 1.63$) less favorably than did the older ($M = 1.16$) and oldest-old adults ($M = 1.01$) who rated their health as better than their age mates, replicating Cherry et al.'s (2008) first findings and extending them across wave 2 testing. Follow-up analyses with the younger adult group confirmed the significant age effect for health compared to others, $F(3, 67) = 15.89$, $p < 0.001$. Younger adults ($M = 1.96$) and middle age adults ($M = 1.71$) rated

Table 9.1 Self-perceived health and health-related quality of life before and after the storms

	Age group			
	Younger adults	Middle-aged adults	Older adults	Oldest-old adults
	M (SD)			
Health at the present time[a]				
Pre-HK/R	2.00 (0.41)	2.00 (0.61)	1.63 (0.68)	1.74 (0.54)
Post-test wave 1	– –	1.88 (0.70)	1.79 (0.63)	1.96 (0.56)
Post-test wave 2	1.85 (0.69)	1.94 (0.66)	1.63 (0.76)	1.91 (0.60)
Health prevents activities[b]				
Pre-HK/R	1.38 (0.51)	1.65 (0.70)	1.58 (0.51)	1.48 (0.67)
Post-test wave 1	– –	1.53 (0.62)	1.58 (0.69)	1.78 (0.74)
Post-test wave 2	1.46 (0.52)	1.65 (0.61)	1.58 (0.51)	2.00 (0.74)
Health compared to others[c]				
Pre-HK/R	1.92 (0.64)	1.76 (0.75)	1.16 (0.37)	1.04 (0.21)
Post-test wave 1	– –	1.47 (0.62)	1.16 (0.37)	1.00 (0.00)
Post-test wave 2	2.00 (0.71)	1.65 (0.70)	1.17 (0.38)	1.00 (0.00)
GDS[d]				
Pre-HK/R	1.69 (1.80)	1.18 (1.33)	1.00 (1.15)	1.52 (1.62)
Post-test wave 1	– –	1.29 (1.31)	0.68 (0.89)	1.48 (1.31)
Post-test wave 2	1.92 (2.02)	0.82 (1.74)	0.63 (0.83)	1.78 (1.73)
SF-36 PCS[e]				
Pre-HK/R	52.64 (5.49)	47.53 (11.89)	47.76 (8.28)	44.91 (7.87)
Post-test wave 1	– –	48.14 (8.97)	46.97 (7.91)	44.22 (8.75)
Post-test wave 2	48.87 (8.57)	47.99 (11.90)	43.79 (10.64)	38.24 (9.62)
SF-36 MCS[e]				
Pre-HK/R	48.35 (9.51)	54.80 (5.61)	57.53 (6.57)	58.95 (5.22)
Post-test wave 1	– –	56.90 (4.06)	57.64 (5.50)	58.55 (5.63)
Post-test wave 2	48.94 (10.77)	56.88 (5.46)	57.49 (7.44)	58.84 (6.58)

[a]Health at the present time on a 4-point Likert scale (1 = excellent to 4 = poor). [b]Health prevents activities (1 = not at all to 3 = a great deal). [c]Health compared to others (1 = better to 3 = poorer). [d]Geriatric Depression Scale (GDS, Sheikh & Yesavage, 1986). [e]SF-36 Physical Health Composite Score (PCS) and Mental Health Composite Score (MCS) from the SF-36 (Ware & Sherbourne, 1992). SF-36 scores range from 0 (lowest functioning) to 100 (highest functioning).

their health less favorably compared to their age mates, whereas older adults ($M = 1.17$) and oldest-old adults ($M = 1.02$) rated their health as better than their age mates. Importantly, the time of testing effects was non-significant in these analyses of self-rated health, confirming that the hurricanes had no appreciable effect of LHAS participants' perceptions of their health.

Participants were asked whether they had experienced a change in health status, medications, and life circumstances since their pre-hurricane research participation (8 months or less before the storms). As can be seen in Figs. 9.1 and 9.2, the proportion of persons who reported changes in health status, medications, and life circumstances increased from wave 1 to wave 2 testings, respectively. Analyses of the three older age groups' responses yielded only a significant time of testing effect,

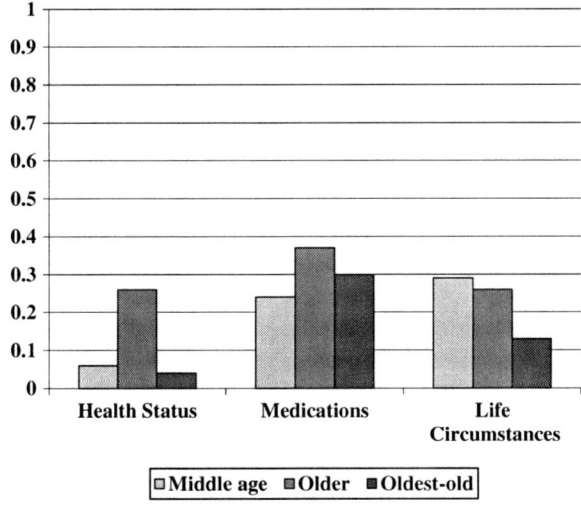

Fig. 9.1 Self-reported changes in health status, medications, and life circumstances at wave 1

$F(1, 56) = 17.11$, $p < 0.001$, confirming greater changes in health status at wave 2 compared to wave 1. There were no significant effects for changes in medications and life circumstances. Although the proportion of persons who reported a change in life circumstances at wave 2 relative to pre-hurricane testing was numerically higher for the younger and oldest-old adults (see Fig. 9.2), one-way analyses with age group as a factor yielded no statistically significant effects.

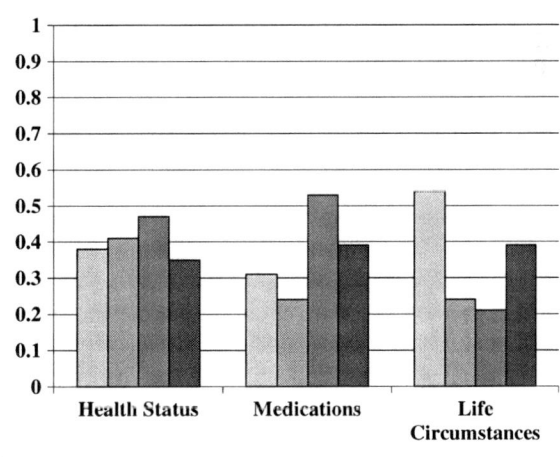

Fig. 9.2 Self-reported changes in health status, medications, and life circumstances at wave 2

Most participants' scores on the GDS were within the normal range, below the cutoff score of 6 considered to be indicative of mild depression (see Table 9.1). Analyses of the GDS scores yielded no significant age group or time of testing effects. While most did not appear to be suffering from depression, one younger and one oldest-old adult had a GDS score suggestive of mild depression at pre-HK/R testing. No one had a GDS score of 6 or higher at wave 1 testing, yet three persons did at wave 2 testing (one younger, one middle age, and one oldest-old adult).

Analyses of the SF-36 PCS scores for the three older age groups at the three assessments yielded only a significant time of testing effect, $F(2, 106) = 6.35$, $p = 0.002$. Means for pre-HK/R, wave 1, and wave 2, were 46.73, 46.44, and 43.34, respectively. Analyses of the MCS scores yielded non-significant effects. Follow-up analyses of the PCS scores with the younger adults at pre-HK/R and wave 2 testings confirmed a significant age group effect, $F(3, 65) = 3.19$, $p = 0.03$. As expected, younger adults' mean score (50.76) exceeded the middle (47.76), older (45.76), and oldest-old adults' (41.58) scores. The time of testing effect was also significant, $F(1, 65) = 11.68$, $p = 0.001$, owing to the drop in mean PCS scores from pre-HK/R (48.21) to wave 2 testing (44.72). Analyses of the MCS scores yielded only a significant age group effect, favoring the oldest-old adults, $F(3, 65) = 7.44$, $p < 0.001$. Interestingly, the mean MCS score was lowest for the younger adults (48.65), followed by the middle (55.84), older (57.51), and oldest-old adults (58.90). This was an unexpected but nevertheless intriguing finding, implying that very old adults have higher perceptions of mental health than do their younger counterparts. It is possible that the MCS scores are serving as a proxy variable for well-being or interpersonal happiness. Indeed, prior research has shown that a majority of older people are happy (e.g., Mroczek & Kolarz, 1998) and experience more positive and less negative emotion that one might expect given the losses associated with age in other life domains (see Bertrand & Lachman, 2003, for discussion). Future studies that examine the dynamic relationships among happiness, well-being, and health-related quality of life seem warranted.

Mental Health Measures. Table 9.2 presents the findings for the mental health measures new to the LHAS protocol (see Cherry et al., 2008). Symptoms of post-traumatic stress disorder were assessed using the PTSD Checklist, because this measure is often used in health settings when a clinically administered diagnostic interview is not possible (Blanchard, Jones-Alexander, Buckley, & Forneris, 1996; Weathers, Litz, Herman, Huska, & Keane, 1993). Symptoms of major depression and generalized anxiety disorder were assessed using the PHQ-9 and GAD-7 portions of the Patient Health Questionnaire, respectively. Both were adapted from the PRIME-MD (Primary Care Evaluation of Mental Disorders). The PHQ-9 contains nine items and has been validated as a screen for depression (Spitzer, Kroenke, & Williams, 1999). The GAD-7 has seven items and is a validated screen for general anxiety disorder (Spitzer, Kroenke, Williams, & Löwe, 2006). These measures were originally intended for primary care settings, but are widely used based on their specificity and sensitivity.

As can be seen in Table 9.2, only one person in the sample met the clinical criterion for a diagnosis of PTSD (a younger adult at wave 2). The PTSD Checklist total scores ranged from 17 to 41 ($M = 22.32$, $SD = 5.28$). Only one person met

Table 9.2 Mental health characteristics of the sample

	Wave 1[a]		Wave 2		Wave 2[b]	
	N (%)					
Total	59		59		13	
PTSD[c]						
No	59	(100.00)	59	(100.00)	12	(92.31)
Yes	0	(0.00)	0	(0.00)	1	(7.69)
Major depression[d]						
No	58	(98.31)	59	(100.00)	13	(100.00)
Yes	1	(1.69)	0	(0.00)	0	(0.00)
Severity of depression[d]						
Minimal (0–4)	46	(77.97)	46	(77.97)	8	(61.54)
Mild (5–9)	12	(20.34)	13	(22.03)	2	(15.38)
Moderate (10–14)	1	(1.69)	0	(0.00)	3	(23.08)
Moderately severe (15–19)	0	(0.00)	0	(0.00)	0	(0.00)
Severe (20–27)	0	(0.00)	0	(0.00)	0	(0.00)
Generalized anxiety disorder[e]						
No	59	(100.00)	58	(98.31)	12	(92.31)
Yes	0	(0.00)	1	(1.69)	1	(7.69)

[a]Includes participants from wave 1 ($N = 66$) who were tested in wave 2 ($N = 59$).
[b]Younger adults were tested in wave 2 only. [c]PTSD symptoms were assessed using the PTSD Checklist (civilian version, PCL-C; Weathers et al., 1993). Ratings reflect how often they were bothered by 17 items on a 5-point scale. Anchors for the severity rating scale ranged from "not at all" to "extremely." The overall PTSD score reflects the sum of scores across all items. [d]Major depression and severity were assessed using the PHQ-9 (Spitzer et al., 1999). [e]Generalized anxiety disorder was assessed using the GAD-7 (Spitzer et al., 2006).

the criterion for major depression. The PHQ-9 depression total scores ranged from 0 to 12 ($M = 2.82$, $SD = 2.79$). For depression severity, 75.00% of the sample were considered minimal, 20.83% were mild, and only 4.17% (three people) were moderately depressed. The GAD-7 generalized anxiety disorder total scores ranged from 0 to 9 ($M = 2.79$, $SD = 2.36$). Two people in the sample met the clinical criterion for generalized anxiety disorder at wave 2.

The outcomes of the mental health measures (Table 9.2) imply that psychological distress due to the storms and their aftermath was minimal for the majority of the LHAS participants. These mental health measures were added to the LHAS protocol to provide a broader assessment of post-disaster health outcomes and psychological well-being than would be possible had we only included the GDS and self-reported health measures. The present findings of minimal mental health problems in the post-disaster period compliment those of Melick and Logue (1985–1986) who found no evidence of elevated anxiety and depression in a sample of elderly flood victims compared to a non-victim sample.

Qualitative Measures. To fully understand the impact of disaster on well-being in late life, six open-ended questions were included in wave 1 and 2 testings to permit a wide range of responses concerning prior flood and hurricane experience, reactions to the storm, coping strategies, and perceived storm outcomes. We developed a scoring key to categorize participants' responses to the six open-ended questions in wave 1 testing (Denver & Cherry, 2007). In brief, the first author and a graduate student reviewed select protocols randomly drawn from each of the three age groups to identify prominent themes and develop conceptual category codes. The research team (one professor, two graduate and two undergraduate students) refined the category codes and piloted the key on a new set of wave 1 protocols. Based on the outcomes of the pilot testing, a final key was developed and used to code all of the wave 1 protocols. A second team of seven raters (one graduate and six undergraduate students) coded subsets of protocols according to a plan so that every protocol was independently coded three times and no two raters coded the same protocol twice. Discrepancies were resolved by an independent fourth rater to achieve 100% agreement. In this chapter, we focus on participants' responses to the two questions that assessed coping behaviors before and immediately after the storms (wave 1 only). Results are given in Table 9.3.

Inspection of Table 9.3 reveals three interesting observations. First, the types and reported frequencies of coping behaviors were quite similar across age groups, both before and after the storms. While the proportion of oldest-old adults who reported instrumental coping behaviors was somewhat lower than the other age groups, it is nonetheless striking that 80.8% of those age 90 years and older mentioned instrumental coping activities, such as securing outside furniture and stockpiling food, water, and supplies in preparation for the storms. This same general pattern was

Table 9.3 Coping before and coping after the storms

	Age group					
	Middle-aged adults		Older adults		Oldest-old adults	
	N (%)					
Coping before the storm[a]						
Instrumental coping	18	(100.0)	18	(94.7)	21	(80.8)
Emotional coping	9	(50.0)	9	(47.4)	14	(53.8)
Spiritual coping	0	(0)	2	(10.5)	3	(11.5)
Coping after the storm[b]						
Instrumental	17	(94.4)	19	(100.0)	20	(76.9)
Cognitive/emotional	10	(55.6)	10	(52.6)	13	(50.0)
Spiritual	1	(5.6)	3	(15.8)	3	(11.5)
Other	1	(5.6)	1	(5.3)	4	(15.4)

Notes. Entries reflect wave 1 testing.
[a]Participants responded to these questions: Think about how you coped with Hurricanes Katrina/Rita. Did you take any actions *before* the storm(s) to prepare for it? If so, what steps did you take? In what other ways did you cope with the hurricane before it happened? [b]Participants answered this question: Think about how you coped with Hurricanes Katrina/Rita. What did you do after the storm(s) had passed through your area to help you cope with the hurricane *after* it happened?

also evident after the storms, with nearly all of the middle age adults, all of the older adults, and 76.9% of the oldest-old adults reporting instrumental coping behaviors after the storms, such as checking on their property, picking up debris from their yards, and tending to storm-related damage to their vehicles or homes (i.e., initiating insurance claims, contracting repair work, covering damaged rooftops with blue tarp). This aspect of the data was not surprising in that most of the sample were storm experienced and perhaps accustomed to "riding out the storm," which is fundamental to the culture of south Louisiana. The second observation was that only about half of the persons in each age group reported emotional coping behaviors, such as communicating with their family and friends before and after the storms. The third observation was only the older and oldest-old adults reported using spiritual forms of coping, such as prayer, before and after the storms. The finding that some older people spontaneously discussed prayer, their faith, and attending religious services in the immediate impact period prompted us to add a question that specifically assessed the use of religious beliefs and practices as an aid to coping with the storms and their aftermath in the wave 2 assessment. Analyses of participants' responses to the religious coping question are discussed in Chapters 10 and 11.

Conclusion and Implications

We began this chapter with an overview of normative changes in physical, cognitive, and social domains of life to establish a context for looking at natural disaster effects in late life. We briefly reviewed the literature on resilience and coping. Our focus on determinants of adaptive behavior featured a conceptual model describing an age-related shift in coping strategies across the lifespan. Specifically, Brandstadter et al. (1993) propose that as individuals age, they shift from problem-focused coping that alters the source of the stress to more emotion-focused strategies that foster perceptual or attitudinal change so that stressful events lose their aversive or threatening meaning over time. This literature also tells us that despite the losses and deterioration commonly linked with aging, some older people are resilient to these declines and continue to thrive during their advanced years. The LHAS hurricane study findings are largely consistent with this view. Our findings provide new and exciting evidence that the oldest-old may have a rich repertoire of coping responses that promote adaptation and resilience in the aftermath of natural disasters of the worse kind, Katrina and Rita. We close this chapter by noting psychological and practical implications that emerge from the LHAS hurricane study for disaster preparedness with very old adults.

Psychological Implications

The results of the LHAS hurricane study showed that nonagenarians were not so different from their younger counterparts in the months following Hurricanes Katrina and Rita. Ratings for health at the present time and health prevents activities did not differ by age group or times of testing. However, self-reported changes in health status from pre-HK/R testing were significantly greater at wave 2 compared to wave 1 (see Figs. 9.1 and 9.2). Similarly, the PCS scores of the SF-36, an index of everyday functioning and health-related quality of life, were lower at wave 2 compared to wave 1 and pre-HK/R participations (see Table 9.1). The finding that the SF-36 PCS scores, which reflect physical health, were lower across assessments for all age groups is not surprising and most likely reflects normative declines in physical functioning in adulthood. The more interesting aspect of these data was that the MCS scores of the SF-36, which reflect mental health, showed the opposite pattern where the mean was highest for the oldest-old adults, followed by the older adults, middle age adults, and younger adults with the lowest score. This finding is generally compatible with the lower prevalence of psychological disorders for older compared to younger adults, with the exception of dementia (Oriol, 1999). Interpretive caution should be exercised, however, as older adults may underreport psychological symptoms based on perceived stigma or they may misinterpret psychological symptoms as physical problems (Cook & Niederehe, 2007). Nonetheless, the finding that the oldest-old had the highest mean MCS score in this study is intriguing and suggestive of psychological well-being and successful aging despite the significant environmental stresses imposed by Hurricanes Katrina and Rita (see Cherry et al., 2008, for a related discussion).

Taken as a whole, the largely parallel results from these different age groups support two primary possibilities. First, LHAS participants, regardless of age, coped successfully in the days, weeks, and months following Hurricanes Katrina and Rita. Second, the majority did not exhibit psychopathology or significant declines in self-reported health, which can be linked to the concept of resilience. Although the LHAS study findings are suggestive of long-term resilience (e.g., lack of physical and mental decline, psychopathology symptoms), interpretative caution is warranted because we did not include an objective measure of resilience in the study. Two other methodological limitations should be noted. First, those who participate in a multidisciplinary study of healthy aging may be unusually high functioning at the outset. The finding that the hurricanes appeared to have relatively little influence on the self-reported health, among other psychosocial indicators of well-being, may reflect selectivity in the direction of successful aging. That is, the LHAS sample may be rich with individuals who adapt and overcome adversity, and handle environmental stressors well, which limits the generalizability of the findings. Second, the storm-related environmental stressors for people in this study were modest compared to New Orleans proper and surrounding areas where flooding resulted in roof top rescues for some and loss of property and homes for many. In the greater Baton Rouge area, most experienced loss of power for a period of days (or weeks for some) which resulted in cold water for bathing, no air conditioning, spoiled food, and other inconveniences, as well as limited access to resources outside of the home due to gasoline shortages, increased traffic, and other discomforts (Cherry, Galea, et al., 2009). Conceivably, a different pattern of outcomes would have been obtained had the participants lived in the hardest hit areas of south Louisiana and the Mississippi Coast.

Practical Implications

The US population is aging and the increasing numbers of older adults today bring many issues and challenges for individuals, families, and society. Older persons were less likely to survive Katrina, although the greater death toll may possibly reflect failed attempts to shelter in place rather than differential vulnerability of older people generally. Nevertheless, it is critical to remember that predisposing medical, physical, and cognitive conditions may affect certain segments of the older adult population and shape their recovery from disaster. We must also remember that healthy older adults can be an asset to the relief and recovery efforts of local and national agencies. As noted in Chapter 11, society must not neglect the multifaceted and unique contributions that older cohorts can provide in times of great need, especially after a natural disaster. Disaster planning for the older population should include the modification of evacuation procedures and relief efforts, which can be tailored to the unique needs of older adults (see Chapter 8 for discussion). Recognizing the heterogeneity of young-old and oldest-old adults is an important step toward effective disaster planning and preparation on individual, community, and federal levels (Cherry, Allen, & Galea, 2009).

Louisiana Healthy Aging Study: [†]Meghan B. Allen, BS; Gloria Anderson, BS; Iina E. Antikainen, BS; Arturo M. Arce, MD; Jennifer Arceneaux, RN; Mark A. Batzer, PhD; Emily O. Boudreaux, MA; Lauri Byerley, PhD; Catherine M. Champagne PhD, RD; Katie E. Cherry, PhD; Liliana Cosenza, BS; M. Elaine Cress, PhD-Consultant; Jenny Y. Denver, MS; Andy Deutsch, PhD; Devon A. Dobrosielski, MS; Rebecca Ellis, PhD; Marla J. Erwin, MA; Mark Erwin, MA; Jennifer Fabre, MPT; Elizabeth T. Fontham, PhD; Madlyn Frisard, PhD; Paula Geiselman, PhD; Lindsey Goodwin; Tiffany Hall; Scott W. Herke, PhD; Jennifer Hayden, MS; Kristi Hebert; Fernanda Holton; Hui-Chen Hsu, PhD; S. Michal Jazwinski, PhD; Sangkyu Kim, PhD; Beth G. Kimball, BS; Christina King-Rowley, MS; Kim Landry; Carl Lavie, MD-Consultant; Daniel LaVie; Matthew Leblanc; Christina M. Lefante, MPH; Li Li, MD; Hui-Yi Lin, PhD, MSPH; Kay Lopez, DSN; John D. Mountz, MD PhD; Jennifer Owens, BA; Kim B. Pedersen, PhD; Andrew Pellett, PhD; Eric Ravussin, PhD; Paul Remedios; Yolanda Robertson, NP; Jennifer Rood, PhD; Henry Rothschild, MD, PhD; Ryan A. Russell, BS; Erin Sandifer; Beth Schmidt, MS; Robert Schwartz, MD – Consultant; Donald K. Scott, PhD; Mandy Shipp, RD; Jennifer L. Silva, MA; L. Joseph Su, PhD MPH; Jessica Thomson, PhD; Valerie Toups, LPN; Crystal Traylor, APRN, MSN, WHNP; Cruz Velasco-Gonzalez, PhD; Julia Volaufova, PhD; Celeste Waguespack, BSN, RN; Jerilyn A. Walker, MS; David A. Welsh, MD; Michael A. Welsch, PhD; Robert H. Wood, PhD; Sarah Zehr, PhD; Pili Zhang, PhD (Louisiana State University, Baton Rouge; Pennington Biomedical Research Center, Baton Rouge; Louisiana State University Health Sciences Center, New Orleans; Tulane University, New Orleans; University of Alabama, Birmingham).

Acknowledgments We thank Annie Crapanzano, Patricia Fraser, Marla Erwin, and Mark Erwin for their help with wave 1 testing and Erin Jackson, Emily Smitherman, and Robert Smith for their assistance in wave 2 testing. We are grateful to Jenny Denver, Brittany Ostarly, Lauren Sherrer, Priscilla Hurd, Sarah Brent, Tracey Frias, and Miranda Melancon for audiotape transcriptions, coding, and entering and checking qualitative data in wave 1. We also thank Mary Robichaux, Tia Bradley, Marisa Sullivan for help with data scoring and Miranda Melancon and Zia McWilliams for audiotape transcriptions in wave 2. We also thank Karen Roberto for her helpful comments on an earlier draft of this chapter.

This research was supported by grants from the Louisiana Board of Regents through the Millennium Trust Health Excellence Fund [HEF(2001-06)-02] and the National Institute on Aging P01 AG022064. This support is gratefully acknowledged.

References

Administration on Aging, U.S. Department of Health and Human Services. (2007). *Profiles of older Americans*. Retrieved January 8, 2008, from, www.aarp.org/research/reference/statistics/aresearch-import-519.html

Adams, R. G., & Blieszner, R. (1995). Aging well with friends and family. *American Behavioral Scientist, 39*, 209–224.

Antonucci, T. C. (2001). Social relations: An examination of social networks, social support, and sense of control. In J. E. Birren, & K. W. Schaie (Eds.), *Handbook of the psychology of aging* (5th ed., pp. 427–453). San Diego, CA: Academic Press.

Antonucci, T. C., & Akiyama, H. (1995). Convoys of social relations: Family and friendships within a life span context. In R. Blieszner & V. H. Bedford (Eds.), *Handbook of aging and the family* (pp. 355–371). Westport, CF: Greenwood.

Baltes, P. B., & Baltes, M. M. (1990). *Successful aging: Perspectives from the behavioral sciences*. Cambridge, UK: University Press.

Bar-Tur, L., & Levy-Shiff, R. (2000). Coping with losses and past trauma in old age: The separation-individuation perspective. *Journal of Personal and Interpersonal Loss, 5*, 263–281.

Benard, B. (1991). *Fostering resiliency in kids: Protective factors in the family, school, and community*. Portland, OR: Western Center for Drug-Free Schools and Communities.

Bertrand, R. M., & Lachman, M. E. (2003). Personality development in adulthood and old age. In R. M. Lerner, M. A. Easterbrooks, & J. Mistry (Eds.), *Handbook of psychology: Developmental psychology* (Vol. 6, pp. 463–485). New York: Wiley.

Blanchard, E. B., Jones-Alexander, J., Buckley, T. C., Forneris, C. A. (1996). Psychometric properties of the PTSD Checklist (PCL). *Behaviour Research and Therapy, 34*, 669–673.

Bonanno, G. A. (2004). Loss, trauma, and human resilience have we underestimated the human capacity to thrive after extremely aversive events? *American Psychologist, 59*, 20–28.

Bonanno, G. A., Galea, S., Bucciarelli, A., & Vlahov, D. (2007). What predicts psychological resilience after disaster? The role of demographics, resources, and life stress. *Journal of Consulting and Clinical Psychology, 75*, 671–682.

Bradshaw, J., & Klein, W. O. (2007). Health promotion. In J. A. Blackburn & C. N. Dulmus (Eds.), *Handbook of gerontology: Evidence-based approaches to theory, practice, and policy* (pp. 171–200). Hoboken, NJ: John Wiley & Sons, Inc.

Brandstadter, J., Wentura, D., & Greve, W. (1993). Adoptive resources of the aging self: Outlines of an emergent perspective. *International Journal of Behavioural Development, 16*, 323–349.

Burg, M. M., & Seeman, T. L. (1994). Families and health: The negative side of social ties. *Annals of Behavioral Medicine, 16*, 109–115.

Carstensen, L. L., & Freund, A. (1994). The resilience of the aging self. *Developmental Review, 14*, 81–92.

Centers for Disease Control and Prevention and The Merck Company Foundation. *The State of Aging and Health in America 2007*. Retrieved November 1, 2008, from, www.cdc.gov/aging/saha.htm

Cherry, K. E., Allen, P. D., & Galea, S. (2009). Older adults and natural disasters: Lessons learned from Hurricanes Katrina and Rita. In P. Dass-Brailsford (Ed.), *Crisis and disaster counseling: Lessons learned from Hurricane Katrina and other disasters*. Thousand Oaks, CA: Sage (in press).

Cherry, K. E., Galea, S., & Silva, J. L. (2008). Successful aging and natural disasters: Role of adaptation and resiliency in late life. In M. Hersen & A. M. Gross (Eds.), *Handbook of clinical psychology* (Vol. 1, pp. 810–833). NJ: John Wiley & Sons, Inc.

Cherry, K. E., Galea, S., Su, L. J., Welsh, D. A., Jazwinski, S. M., Silva, J. L., et al. (2009). Cognitive and psychosocial consequences of Hurricanes Katrina and Rita on middle aged, older, and oldest-old adults in the Louisiana Healthy Aging Study (LHAS). *Journal of Applied Social Psychology* (in press).

Cherry, K. E., & Plauche, M. F. (1996). Memory impairment in Alzheimer's disease: Findings, interventions, and implications. *Journal of Clinical Geropsychology, 2*, 263–296.

Cherry, K. E., & Smith, A. D. (1998). Normal memory aging. In M. Hersen & V. B. Van Hasselt (Eds.), *Handbook of clinical geropsychology* (pp. 87–110). New York: Plenum Press.

Cook, J. M., & Niederehe, G. (2007). Trauma in older adults. In M. J. Friedman, T. M. Keane, & P. A. Resick (Eds.), *Handbook of PTSD* (pp. 252–276). New York: Guilford Press.

Craik, F. I. M., & Salthouse, T. A. (2008). *The handbook of aging and cognition* (3rd ed.). New York: Psychology Press.

Crimmins, E. M., Haywood, M. D., & Saito, Y. (1996). Differentials in active life expectancy in the older population of the United States. *Journal of Gerontology: Social Sciences, 51B*, S111–S120.

Denver, J. Y., & Cherry, K. E. (2007, February). Prior hurricane experience, coping and resiliency following Hurricanes Katrina/Rita in the oldest-old. In K. E. Cherry (Chair), *Hurricane Katrina: Psychological impact and mental health issues across the lifespan*. Invited symposium presented at the annual meetings of the Southeastern Psychological Association, New Orleans, Louisiana.

Duke University Center for the Study of Aging and Human Development. (1975). *OARS: Multidimensional functional assessment questionnaire*. Durham, NC: Author.

Folkman, S. (1984). Personal control and stress and coping processes: A theoretical analysis. *Journal of Personal and Social Psychology, 46*, 839–852.

Folkman, S., & Lazarus, R. S. (1988). Coping as a mediator of emotion. *Journal of Personality and Social Psychology, 54*, 466–475.

Freund, A. M., & Riediger, M. (2003). Successful aging. In R. M. Lerner, M. A. Easterbrooks, & J. Mistry (Eds.), *Handbook of psychology: Developmental psychology* (Vol. 6, pp. 601–628). New York: Wiley.

Howard, S., Dryden, J., & Johnson, B. (1999). Childhood resilience: Review and critique of literature. *Oxford Review of Education, 25*, 307–323.

Kilijanek, T. S., & Drabek, T. E. (1979). Assessing long-term impacts of a natural disaster: A focus on the elderly. *The Gerontologist, 6*, 555–566.

Knight, B. G., Gatz, M., Heller, K., & Bengtson, V. L. (2000). Age and emotional response to the Northridge earthquake: A longitudinal analysis. *Psychology and Aging, 15*, 627–634.

Lazarus, R. S., & Folkman, S. (1984). *Stress, appraisal, and coping*. New York: Springer.

Massey, B. A. (1997). Victims or survivors? A three-part approach to working with older adults in disaster. *Journal of Geriatric Psychiatry, 3*, 193–202.

Masten, A. S. (2001). Ordinary magic: Resilience processes in development. *American Psychologist, 56*, 227–238.

Melick, M. E., & Logue, J. N. (1985–1986). The effect of disaster on the health and well-being of older women. *International Journal of Aging and Human Development, 21*, 27–38.

Mroczek, D. K., & Kolarz, C. M. (1998). The effect of age on positive and negative affect: A developmental perspective on happiness. *Journal of Personality and Social Psychology, 75*, 1333–1349.

Neugarten, B. L. (1974). Age groups in American society and the rise of the young old. *Annals of the American Academy of Political and Social Science, 415*, 187–198.

Newsome, J. T., Mahan, T. L., Rook, K. S., & Krause, N. (2008). Stable negative social exchanges and health. *Health Psychology, 27*, 78–86.

Oriol, W. (1999). Psychosocial issues for older adults in disasters. *Booklet SMA 99-3323*. Retrieved March 5, 2006, from, media.shs.net/ken/pdf/SMA99-3323/99-821.pdf

Perry, R. W., & Lindell, M. K. (1997). Aged citizens in the warning phase of disasters: Re-examining the evidence. *International Journal of Aging and Human Development, 44*, 257–267.

Phifer, J. F. (1990). Psychological distress and somatic symptoms after natural disaster: Differential vulnerability among older adults. *Psychology and Aging, 5*, 412–420.

Phifer, J. F., & Norris, F. N. (1989). Psychological symptoms in older adults following a natural disaster: Nature, timing, duration, and course. *Journal of Gerontology: Social Sciences, 44*, S207–S217.

Phifer, J. F., Kaniasty, K. Z., & Norris, F. H. (1988). The impact of natural disaster on the health of older adults: A multiwave prospective study. *Journal of Health and Social Behavior, 29*, 65–78.

Reese, C. M., & Cherry, K. E. (2004). Practical memory concerns across the lifespan. *International Journal of Aging and Human Development, 59*, 237–255.

Reynolds, S. L., Saito, Y., & Crimmins, E. M. (2005). The impact of obesity on active life expectancy in older American men and women. *The Gerontologist, 45*, 438–444.

Rook, K. S. (1990). Stressful aspects of older adults' social relationships: Current theory and research. In M. A. Parris Stephens, J. H. Crowther, S. E. Hobfoll, & D. L. Tennenbaum (Eds.), *Stress and coping in later-life families* (pp. 173–192). New York: Hemisphere Publishing Corporation.

Rook, K. S. (2001). Emotional health and positive versus negative social exchanges: A daily diary analysis. *Applied Developmental Science, 5*, 86–97.

Rowe, J. W., & Kahn, R. L. (1997). Successful aging. *The Gerontologist, 37*, 433–440.

Rutter, M. (1985). Resilience in the face of adversity: Protective factors and resistance to psychiatric disorder. *British Journal of Psychiatry, 147*, 598–611.

Rutter, M. (1990). Psychosocial resilience and protective mechanisms. In J. Rolf, A. Masten, D. Cicchetti, K. Neuchterlein, & S. Weintraub (Eds.), *Risk and protective factors in the development of psychopathology*. New York: Cambridge University Press.

Rutter, M. (2006). Implications of resilience concepts for scientific understanding. *Annals of the New York Academy of Science, 1094*, 1–12.

Sheikh, J. L., & Yesavage, J. A. (1986). Geriatric depression scale (GDS): Recent evidence and development of a shorter version. In T. L. Brink (Ed.), *Clinical gerontology: A guide to assessment and intervention* (pp. 165–173). New York: Haworth Press.

Siegler, I. C., Bosworth, H. B., & Poon, L. W. (2003). Disease, health, and aging. In R. M. Lerner, M. A. Easterbrooks, & J. Mistry (Eds.), *Handbook of psychology: Developmental psychology* (Vol. 6, pp. 423–442). New York: Wiley.

Slangen-de Kort, Y. A. W., Midden, C. J. H., Aarts, H., van Wagenberg, A. F. (2001). Determinants of adaptive behavior among older persons: Self-efficacy, importance and personal dispositions as directive mechanisms. *International Journal of Aging and Human Development, 53*, 263–278.

Spitzer, R. L., Kroenke, K., & Williams, J. B. W. (1999). Patient Health Questionnaire Primary Care Study Group. Validation and utility of a self-report version of PRIME-MD: The PHQ Primary Care Study. *JAMA, 292* (18), 1737–1744.

Spitzer, R. L., Kroenke, K., Williams, J. B., & Löwe, B. (2006). A brief measure for assessing generalized anxiety disorder: The GAD-7. *Archives of Internal Medicine, 166* (10), 1092–1097.

Suzman, R. M., Harris, T., Hadley, E. C., Kovar, M. G., & Weindruch, R. (1992). The robust oldest old: Optimistic perspectives for increasing healthy life expectancy. In R. M. Suzman, D. P. Willis, & K. G. Manton (Eds.), *The oldest old* (pp. 341–358). New York: Oxford University Press.

Thompson, M. P., Norris, F. H., & Hanacek, B. (1993). Age differences in the psychological consequences of hurricane Hugo. *Psychology and Aging, 8*, 606–616.
Tracy, M., & Galea, S. (2006). Post-traumatic stress disorder and depression among older adults after a disaster: The role of ongoing trauma and stressors. *Public Policy & Aging Report, 16*(2), 16–19.
Tucker, J. S., Klein, D. J., & Elliott, M. N. (2004). Social control of health behaviors: A comparison of young, middle-aged and older adults. *Journal of Gerontology: Psychological Sciences, 59B*, P147–P150.
U.S. Department of Health and Human Services. (1996). *Physical activity and health: A report of the surgeon general*. Atlanta, GA: Centers for Disease Control and Prevention, National Center for Chronic Disease Prevention and Health Promotion. Retrieved January 30, 2007, from, www.cdc.gov/nccdphp/sgr/intro.htm
Vance, E., & Sanchez, H. (1998). *Creating a service system that builds resiliency*. North Carolina Division of Mental Health, Developmental Disabilities and Substance Abuse Services. Retrieved on October 16, 2008, from, www.ncdhhs.gov/mhddsas/childandfamily/bestpractice/risk-resiliency-vance.doc
VonDras, D. D., & Madey, S. F. (2004). The attainment of important health goals throughout adulthood: An integration of the theory of planned behavior and aspects of social support. *International Journal of Aging and Human Development, 59*, 205–234.
Ware, J. E., & Sherbourne, C. D. (1992). The MOS 36 item short-form health survey (SF-36): I. Conceptual framework and item selection. *Medical Care, 30*, 473–483.
Weathers, F. W., Litz, B. T., Herman, D. S., Huska, J. A., & Keane, T. M. (1993, October). *The PTSD checklist: Reliability, validity, and diagnostic utility*. Presented at the Annual Meeting of the International Society for Traumatic Stress Studies, San Antonio, TX.
Winerman, L. (2006, November). Keys to longevity and well-being. *American Psychological Association Monitor*, Vol. 37, No. 10, 42–44.
Werner, E. E., & Smith, R. S. (1989). *Vulnerable but invincible: A longitudinal study of resilient children and youth*. New York: Adams, Bannister, and Cox.
Werner, E. E., & Smith, R. S. (1992). *Overcoming the odds: High-risk children from birth to adulthood*. New York: Cornell University Press.
Werner, E. E., & Smith, R. S. (2001). *Journeys from childhood to midlife: Risk, resilience, and recovery*. Ithaca, NY: Cornell University Press.

Chapter 10
Faith, Crisis, Coping, and Meaning Making After Katrina: A Qualitative, Cross-Cohort Examination

Loren D. Marks, Katie E. Cherry, and Jennifer L. Silva

Abstract Very few studies in the disaster literature include elderly adults, whose life experiences, perceptions, and spiritual needs in the post-disaster period may markedly differ in comparison to younger cohorts. In this chapter, we address the topic of how young, middle age, older, and oldest-old adults coped with and made meaning of Hurricanes Katrina and Rita during the storms and their aftermath. The individuals who provided the qualitative interviews upon which this chapter is based were enrolled in the *Louisiana Healthy Aging Study* (LHAS), a multidisciplinary study of the determinants of longevity and healthy aging (see Cherry, Silva, & Galea, Chapter 9 of this volume). We begin this chapter by presenting three central themes to contextualize our findings. These themes include (1) *crisis*, in the sense of a significant, developmental turning point (cf. Erikson E.H., 1998); (2) *coping*, a behavioral response to stressful events; and (3) *meaning making*, which pertains to an individual's unique interpretation of an event and attributions for why it happened. We describe the sample, interview procedures, coding process, and emergent themes arising from the qualitative interviews. Implications for adjustment, acceptance, and personal growth in the post-disaster period are considered.

Introduction

Hurricanes Katrina and Rita have brought unparalleled destruction and immeasurable losses to the people of South Louisiana and the Gulf Coast region. Both the media and the popular press have riveted our attention to the catastrophic losses and suffering of hundreds of thousands of people in the storm-ravaged Gulf Coast. It is important to realize that the influence of these treacherous storms has been felt widely by countless numbers of people, including those who live outside of the severely storm-damaged areas. In this chapter, we focus on the experience of a

L.D. Marks (✉)
Division of Family, Child and Consumer Sciences; School of Human Ecology; and Life Course and Aging Center, Louisiana State University, Baton Rouge, LA 70803-5501, USA
e-mail: lorenm@lsu.edu

sample of adults in South Louisiana who ranged in age from early 20s to 90 years and older. These persons were enrolled in the *Louisiana Healthy Aging Study* (LHAS), a multidisciplinary study of the determinants of longevity and healthy aging (see Cherry et al., Chapter 9). They reside in greater Baton Rouge, outside of the areas severely impacted by Katrina and Rita. Few evacuated at the time of the storms, yet nearly all had family and close friends who lived in the more heavily storm-damaged areas. Many LHAS participants sheltered displaced family and friends in their homes for days and weeks on end during the post-impact period (see Cherry, Galea, & Silva, 2008 for discussion).

Our central mission in this chapter is to allow LHAS participants' voices to be heard. Emergent themes arising from their qualitative interviews are rich with local and historical color, as well as having noteworthy implications for successful aging. We begin by presenting an overview of the three central issues of this chapter, crisis, coping, and meaning making, to contextualize our later discussion of the findings. In light of our objective to focus on LHAS participant voices, a brief overview of core concepts that emerged in the research project will supplant an extended traditional review of literature. In the next section, we describe our qualitative research methods. All of our participants were affected by Hurricanes Katrina and/or Rita (HK/R) but were kind enough to share their stories and thoughts with us. The breadth of experience in the LHAS study sample is astonishing, with stories that ranged from early recollections of the outbreak of the flu epidemic of 1918 (see also Allen & Wayne, Chapter 8) and unnamed storms of the late teens and early 1920s, to the Flood of 1927, to more recent storms, including Hurricanes Audrey in 1957, Betsy in 1965, Camille in 1969, and Andrew in 1992 (Cherry, 2006). In the last section, we present three emergent themes which constitute the major findings of this portion of the study. This chapter is based solely on the qualitative interviews conducted shortly after the hurricanes struck in late August and September of 2005. We conclude by considering the emergent themes identified here in relation to psychological well-being and personal growth in the post-disaster period.

Three Central Issues in Overview

Crisis

In his psychological theory, Erik Erikson (1998) introduces eight stages of development, each of which is characterized by a *crisis* or central struggle (e.g., the struggle between identity and identity confusion during adolescence). Joan Erikson (1998) added a ninth stage, *gerotranscendence*, to address the growing 90+ years old population that both she and her late husband lived long enough to join. This ninth stage of 90+ years is especially relevant to our chapter because this population is represented in our study by Cohort 4 (as we will discuss later). Although all of the Eriksonian stages involve a crisis, for Erikson crisis is not synonymous with tragedy. Instead, a crisis is a developmental point where an individual is confronted by a specific challenge. If one is successful in overcoming the crisis, the individual progresses to the next stage. If the crisis is not resolved, development stagnates. However, whether progression or stagnation occurs, it is not possible to simply return to pre-crisis life. Crises are not singular events, but challenges that recur in each of the nine stages across the life span.

Hurricanes Katrina and Rita (HK/R) presented South Louisiana with natural disasters unparalleled in her modern history, but the hurricanes did more than this. For many of Louisiana's sons and daughters, the hurricanes served as crises in the Eriksonian sense. For the participants who were interviewed and hundreds of thousands like them, pre-HK/R life is irretrievably gone. Perhaps no extant research captures this reality as richly, or as bleakly, as Pulitzer-nominated journalist Chris Rose's (2007) documentary volume *1 Dead in attic*. In his book, Rose captures New Orleans in the Katrina aftermath with a poignant depth and feel. An overriding theme is that of a city (and individuals) in crisis. Consistent with Erik Erikson's work, Rose portrays the duality of crisis in a way that captures hope and despair—generativity and stagnation.

Pauline Boss (2002), arguably the nation's leading scholar of family stress, has added her reminder that crisis is not inherently and absolutely negative, and even argues that crisis presents opportunity. Similarly, *Webster's New World Dictionary* (1991, 3rd ed.) defines *crisis* as "the turning point...for better or worse" (p. 328). Finally, the late psychiatrist Viktor Frankl (1984) has extended this line of thinking even further by arguing that meaning is often found *in* the struggle. Frankl's argument is captured in his statement that

> What man actually needs is not a tensionless state but rather the striving and struggling for a worthwhile goal, a freely chosen task.... If architects want to strengthen a decrepit arch, they *increase* the load which is laid upon it, for thereby the parts are joined more firmly together (pp. 127–128, emphasis in original).

The above perspectives on crisis are relatively positive and optimistic; certainly crisis can be viewed in more malignant ways. However, this brief overview is a generally appropriate fit for the participants in our study. We next turn to a discussion of coping, a process that may lessen the challenges and assist in crisis resolution with potential for positive growth and personal development.

Coping

Coping is broad term that comprises a wide range of variables (e.g., Menaghan, 1983; Nesteruk & Garrison, 2005). It is generally defined as the process by which resources are used to respond to stressor events (Garrison, Malia, & Molgaard, 1991; see also Silva, Marks, & Cherry, Chapter 11).

Coping, like crisis, is inherently dualistic. Crisis typically holds a negative connotation but involves positive potential as well (Boss, 2002). Similarly, coping can be negative and/or positive. While coping frequently carries a positive and resilient connotation, there are negative or "red flag" approaches to coping as well, such as coping by turning to alcohol and drug abuse (Marks, Swanson, Nesteruk, & Hopkins-Williams, 2006; Pargament, 1997) or by being primarily reactive instead of proactive (Garrison et al., 1991). In this chapter, however, we will focus on positive coping.

To offer a historical glance, nearly 60 years ago Reuben Hill (1949) developed the "roller-coaster profile of adjustment to crisis" in the wake of post-World War II family dissolution (p. 14; see also Koos, 1946). In this early view of coping, families go through four stages: "crisis, disorganization, recovery, and reorganization" (Ingoldsby, Smith, & Miller, 2004, p. 138). Hill (1949) also developed the ABC-X model of family stress wherein A represents a stressor event, B represents available family resources and strengths, and C represents the family's definition of the situation. X represents the resulting stress and crisis; in other words, the outcome of how the family responds to and defines the initial stressor. Although the ABC-X model has received several modifications by other scholars, these basic concepts still serve as the foundation for much of the current research on family stress and coping (Ingoldsby et al., 2004).

In the present study, Hurricanes Katrina and Rita serve as the initial stressors ("A") that provide a rich (although tragic) context for examining key resources and strengths ("B"), and individual and family definitions ("C") that exacerbated or minimized personal and familial crises ("X"). In this chapter, our findings will focus particularly on key coping resources and approaches. Having briefly overviewed coping, we turn to the third central concept of meaning making.

Meaning Making

Psychiatry's most influential work on meaning making is arguably Viktor Frankl's (1984) *Man's Search for Meaning*. The body of this work is largely comprised of a section entitled "Experiences in a Concentration Camp," in which Frankl describes his accompanying struggle and search for meaning. Near the conclusion of his autobiographical notes, Frankl states, "Everything can be taken from a man but one thing: the last of human freedoms—to choose one's attitude in any given set of circumstances, to choose one's own way" (p. 104). While it is certainly not our intent to compare the thousands of people in the Gulf Coast region who survived Katrina to those from Auschwitz or Dachau, the profound physical losses suffered by many in South Louisiana and Mississippi remind us that much (if not "everything") *can* be taken from a person in the tangible sense. In spite of heartbreaking losses such as these, Nietzsche has argued that "he who has a *why* to live for can bear with almost any *how*" (cf. Frankl, 1984, p. 97). The hurricane survivors [many dislike being referred to as "victims," (Rose, 2007)] were forced to answer some pressing why and how questions, not just intellectually but pragmatically. The following statement from H. E. Fosdick seems to capture the struggle faced by our participants:

> We must believe that there is a purpose running through the stern, forbidding process. What men have needed most of all in suffering, is not to know the explanation, but *to know that*

there is an explanation....[We need] confidence that human tragedy is *not* the meaningless sport of physical forces, making our life what Voltaire called it, 'a bad joke' (Fosdick, 1918, p. 20, emphasis added)

As we will illustrate later, this struggle for meaning, explanation, and purpose was salient and pervasive among our participants. We now turn to a discussion of the qualitative method we used in our efforts to better understand crisis, coping, and meaning making among those participants in our sample.

Method

Sample and Interview Procedures

The study sample consisted of 72 predominantly Caucasian adults who were enrolled in the *Louisiana Healthy Aging Study* (LHAS) with four age groups: younger adults ($M = 37.7$ years, $SD = 5.3$ years, 2 males, 11 females), middle-aged adults ($M = 54.0$ years, $SD = 5.7$ years, 10 males, 7 females), older ($M = 74.3$ years, $SD = 7.0$ years, 8 males, 11 females), and oldest-old adults ($M = 91.9$ years, $SD = 1.2$ years, 10 males, 13 females). All were free of neurologic impairment due to stroke or adult dementia. Participants were tested individually in their home or in the laboratory at Louisiana State University (LSU) across two sessions that lasted approximately an hour to 1 h and 30 min each. Younger participants were tested in a single session, if desired. On the first day, informed consent was obtained and the quantitative measures were administered (see Cherry et al., Chapter 9, for a description). Next, participants were given a list of seven open-ended questions to read during a break period for those tested in a single session and to take home and consider for those tested across two sessions. On the second day (or second half of a single session), participants answered the questions and their responses were tape recorded. Audiotapes were transcribed for the purpose of qualitative coding (described next). In this chapter, we focus on their responses to the religious coping question, as follows: "In times of trouble, people often turn to their religion and spiritual beliefs to help them cope with life stresses. Have your religious beliefs and practices helped you cope with Hurricanes Katrina and Rita. If so, in what way? Please tell us about how your beliefs helped you cope when the storms first hit and also cope with the challenging times after the hurricanes." Following the open-ended questions, remaining quantitative measures (not addressed in this chapter) were administered and debriefing followed.

Analysis and Coding

The qualitative interview data were analyzed in a manner consistent with grounded theory methodology (Strauss & Corbin, 1998). Open coding (identifying themes and concepts in the interview data) was performed independently by five members of our research team on an interview-by-interview basis. We met once a week for several months to discuss, compare, and contrast our independent open coding from the previous week on a line-by-line, page-by-page basis, with each member alternatively "leading out" by discussing her/his personal open coding of a given page. Following presentation of one's independent coding of a given page, the other four members would discuss similarities and differences from their coding. Researchers also did content analyses of their open coding for each interview, similar to Miles and Huberman's (1994) "data accounting sheet" (p. 80). At the conclusion of the coding, researchers' content analyses for each interview were collected and compared, offering five "at-a-glance" perspectives of the concepts and themes expressed in each of the interviews (cf. Marks, Nesteruk, Swanson, Garrison, & Davis, 2005). Next, the central themes were identified based on two factors: prevalence (within and across interviews) and salience.

To ensure that each of these themes were verifiable and clearly supported by the data, each member was assigned one theme which they were asked to confirm. Team members then revisited all of the interviews and copied and pasted all data that had been directly identified with the theme. The result was that each theme had several pages of supporting data—consistent with Patton's (2002) suggestion of creating a data "audit trail" (p. 93).

In a final exercise to increase rigor, we then worked through a triple-check reliability assurance process. In overview, this process included the following steps:

1. Each team member composed a file that included all of the excerpts coded in connection with that code/theme.
2. Each team member was assigned to review another member's file as a double check. She looked for any data segments that related to the theme that were overlooked or missed—as well as looking for excerpts that were "a stretch."
3. A third team member then repeated the check procedure, so that each of the themes (and the supporting data) were triple checked to ensure inter-rater reliability and to minimize idiosyncratic bias.

Having discussed our attempts to be methodologically systematic and rigorous, we now turn to a note on reflexivity.

Reflexivity

Reflexivity involves discussing how personal experience and biases might color one's collection, analysis, and reporting of the data. Accordingly, we note that living through Hurricanes Katrina and Rita in Baton Rouge (where all of the authors resided) was somewhat surreal (see Cherry, Allen, & Galea, 2009, for discussion). At LSU, the Pete Maravich Assembly Center (home to basketball games and commencement exercises) became a hospital/triage center run largely through the volunteer efforts of LSU students (Bacher, Devlin, Calongne, Duplechain, & Pertuit,

2005). By some estimates, Baton Rouge's population doubled almost overnight. In addition to the destruction and several days of power outage, there was scarcity. It is difficult to capture the eerie feeling of seeing nothing but bare shelves on the bread aisle at the grocery store, or the sinking realization that there is no more gasoline at your corner pump—or in your vehicle. Many of us in Baton Rouge had friends, family, or former strangers from flooded areas living under our roofs. We, however, were only grazed by comparison to those from New Orleans, Slidell, and the other decimated areas. Here in Baton Rouge, we had no power and precious little gas or food...but we had our families, our homes, our jobs, our belongings, and our photo albums—those precious books that research indicates are the one tangible item most of us would grab first in the event of home destruction (Gilbert, 2006). For us to pretend that we understand what those from the flooded areas experienced would be dishonest. Yet, we do have a desire to report what our participants told us to the best of our ability. Our hope is that our HK/R experiences have softened us enough to be subjective in a sensitive and positive way—while still maintaining sufficient objectivity.

Findings

In the paragraphs that follow, we discuss three of the major themes that emerged from our team-based analysis of the qualitative interviews. The themes include (1) *Crisis: Tragedy, Opportunity, or Simply "Part of Life"?*; (2) *Approaches to Coping: Comparison, Gratitude, Optimism, and Personal Strength*; and (3) *Meaning Making: "God is in Control...Right?"* In connection with each of these three major themes, we provide illustrative and supportive excerpts from the participants' interviews. Consistent with our desire to allow LHAS participants' voices to be heard, we have tried to keep our explanations and interpretations at a functional but minimal level, in order to allow the reader to construct his/her own meanings. The first theme we will highlight is that of *crisis*—which Erik Erikson (1998), Boss (2002), and Webster (1991) all define as a developmental turning point.

Theme 1—Crisis: Tragedy, Opportunity, or Simply "Part of Life"?

The definitions of, and the responses to, Katrina and Rita as crises were diverse—not only across the state, but in our sample. Many viewed the time of crisis as a time for re-evaluation. A 42-year-old man reported:

> HKR 3: A lot of things are [not that important]...[the hurricane gets you] re-evaluating where you are in your life, what you're doing, what is important to you.... I am Christian...but I would think that even the atheist, after Hurricane Katrina, would have to sit down and...not suddenly believe in God, but they would have to sit back and re-evaluate where they are in life and realize how precious life is.

An African American woman (age 39) similarly discussed her re-evaluated and altered perspective:

> **HKR 15:** [Going through Katrina and the aftermath] has been a humbling experience and it has changed my life in a way that I really can't even explain. [H]elping people, that helped me to cope. [I] couldn't remember any problems that I had prior to Katrina, because I took on so much other stuff, helping other people...[it] drowned out what I was going through and God fixed [those other problems].

The participants' reflections regarding re-evaluation often included notes on personal religious revival, as the following four examples illustrate:

> **HKR 4,** *35 years:* I think [an] event like this it makes you...if you are religious person and spiritual, then I think it brings you back [to God]. I think that's why things [like Katrina] happen...not that God wants everybody to be devastated...but... I think that different things happen to make people realize what is important, to come back and find Him and know that He is going to be there for you.... I think it just reminds you how important it is to have [God] in your life.... You kind of get relaxed about looking to God...and when something like this happens...right there in your face [it brings you back].
> **HKR 7,** *38 years:* I think [Katrina] affected me and our family in wanting to know more about the Lord and his words.... To actually go back to the [Bible] and read...that helped us.... I realized that in times of trouble, [we] go back to that.
> **HKR 112,** *54 years:* Hurricane[s] Rita and Katrina...made a couple people...go to church to thank the good Lord that they [are] still here [and breathing].
> **HKR 105,** *48 years:* Right after [Katrina and Rita] hit, I think that people [did] turn to their spiritual beliefs and (go back to God).

Although little previous research has examined religion and spirituality in the aftermath of natural disasters, the above statements resonate with previous research conducted on the East Coast in the months following the 9/11 attacks on the Twin Towers and the Pentagon (Marks, 2002). In that study, a Jewish mother reflected:

> I mean, it was just an automatic thing to go to synagogue and to look at death from a Jewish perspective.... I think that after September 11, with the [terrorist] attack, we instinctively went to synagogue the next Friday night, and it was packed. I think that's just how we cope (p. 47).

As we see above, traumatic events like 9/11, Katrina, and Rita can stimulate actions including re-evaluation, revival, and a search for deeper purpose—at least for some. Indeed, the interviews of several of our participants called to mind the quip that some of us spend our lives "climbing the ladder of success only to discover [that the ladder is] leaning against the wrong wall" (Covey, 2004, p. 98).

The above excerpts, however, represent only a portion of the story behind the first theme of crisis. Our study covered four major cohorts (20–44 years, 45–64 years, 65–89 years, and 90 years and over). For all in this study, hurricane damage and losses were relatively minimal compared to other areas of the state as reported elsewhere (see Cherry, Galea, et al., 2009). Overall, the four cohorts were largely comparable in terms of storm exposure and impact. It is important to note, however, that *all* of the above excerpts portraying HKR as a crisis are from the two younger cohorts. In the Eriksonian sense outlined at the beginning of this theme, the two younger (under age 65) cohorts generally viewed the hurricanes as life-altering *crises* and discussed the disasters and their aftermath in relatively dramatic terms. By comparison, many of the individuals in the older two cohorts were almost sanguine—especially by comparison with the younger cohorts. Consider the following six examples, all of which are drawn from the two older (65 years and up) cohorts:

> **HKR 212**, *65 years:* [I try to] just to keep on keeping on. That is all you can do.
> **HKR 301**, *91 years*: I just don't have any terrified feelings.... I really don't (worry).... Like I say, one of these days [it'll be my time]...but I'm not going to go...until it comes.
> **HKR 308**, *91 years*: You just do what you can to.... It'll settle down. We'll live through it and wait for the next one. [You know], water seeks its level, and that's what's going to happen to everybody. We'll manage.
> **HKR 315**, *93 years*: I think that I have a satisfactory relation with God and [so] I am comfortable... whatever [the] outcome.
> **HKR 316**, *91 years*: I think things will be alright.
> **HKR 320**, *91 years*: All my life, I've been well taken care of, so I'm...just thankful and feel blessed.... I [have] been taken care of all these ninety-one years and I just [feel fortunate].

The above responses are not only qualitatively different in terms of the level of (or lack of) dramatic intensity they convey, the responses are also brief and direct, almost laconic. More detailed comments from the two senior cohorts included the following:

> **HKR 308**, *91 years*: I'm older. I['ve] had a lot of experience. I've been through stresses so much, I'm used to it. I'm hardened by it. I can take it.... We'll live through it and wait for the next one....Time heals...
> **HKR 301**, *91 years*: When you look at something and it looks pretty dark...there's got to be a light behind it somewhere.... Maybe you kind of give in to [darkness] for a while, but you know that it's going to change. I just think, "I'm going to get out of it"...and here I am.
> **HKR 218**, *66 years*: I just...have a trust that things will work out one way or the other, and whatever works out, there's a final lesson, a blessing, or something to be gained [from] it.

Some participants, like the latter (HKR 218), used the spiritual terms "blessing" and "blessed," even during the hurricanes' aftermath. Others tended to be more specific in their religious references, choosing to discuss God and their sense of relationship with the divine. The following two quotations are representative:

> **HKR 219**, *86 years*: I am not saying this for anyone to think that I am not a sinner because I am a sinner. We all know that that we are sinners, but there is always hope, there is always a new day, there is always a call in God.
> **HKR 207**, *89 years*: I don't dwell on [Katrina] because it's something that I cannot do anything about, other than feeling like the Lord will give me the protection I need....[Often in life, it] look[s] like everything goes wrong, but right behind that, everything come[s] out alright. [I feel that eventually] everything's going to be alright.

In some instances, a participant's sense of a personal relationship with God was captured in portions of conversations with the divine that he or she shared with the interviewer. HKR 306, age 91, was one such individual. She explained:

> I said, "Lord, You've always kept a roof over my head, given me food to eat, and taken care of me. And I know you will [get me] through this in some way."

As our qualitative research team coded, analyzed, and discussed the interviews, we compared and contrasted key findings, themes, and tendencies across cohorts. Those members of the research team who were less familiar with gerontology and with cross-cohort studies of later adulthood were struck by some of the differences between the age-graded emotional and the psychological differences manifested in the interviews. As discussed previously, our coding procedures were highly democratic, with every member having an opportunity to weigh in on each page of interview data. Predictably, there were occasional points of difference. However, points of unanimous consent included the team's conclusions that (a) In many ways, Cohorts 1 and 2 resembled each other, while Cohorts 3 and 4 also resembled each other; and (b) In many ways, Cohorts 1 and 2 were distinctly different from Cohorts 3 and 4, in that the two younger cohorts (1 and 2) seemed to view and portray the hurricanes and their aftermath as *crises*, while the senior cohorts seemed to view them as additional experiences.

As mentioned earlier in the paper, if crises are turning points, then coping is the process through which we determine whether our subsequent trajectory is downward or upward. It is to this process of coping that we turn in theme 2.

Theme 2—Approaches to Coping: Comparison, Gratitude, Optimism, and Personal Strength

During our analyses of our participants' interviews, references to coping were abundantly coded. Nearly all of our participants discussed coping at some level. Additional coding of the data that related specifically to coping identified at least four major approaches to coping. These are not pure types; indeed, they often overlapped. Nevertheless, these approaches to coping were distinguishable and salient. These approaches included (a) *beneficial comparison*, (b) *gratitude*, (c) *optimism*, and (d) *personal strength*. Each approach to coping is addressed and illustrated next.

Sub-theme 1: Beneficial comparison as a coping strategy. Many of our participants suffered personal, familial, and property-related losses during Katrina and Rita that are reported elsewhere (Cherry, Galea, et al., 2009). Even so, most chose not to delineate or bemoan their losses during their interviews. It was quite common, however, for participants to comment on others whose losses were far more severe—even if these people were only passing or casual acquaintances or "people on TV." These comparative references recurred frequently enough to establish this tendency as an important and often valuable coping approach. One participant mentioned "helping other people...[and seeing their problems] drowned out what I was going through" (see also Silva et al., Chapter 11). Although no interview question asked them to do so, many participants explicitly compared their own post-HKR circumstances favorably with others, as the following three statements reflect:

> **HKR 104**, *60 years*: I'm just fortunate I don't have as much [repair] work to do as some of the people.

HKR 302, *93 years*: Well, when the storm hit, . . .[I was] thanking God that we weren't hit [as bad as some people].

HKR 116, *52 years*: [I quit feeling so bad for myself] once I realized that there would be people that would never find their family members, you know. When you go to those [relief] sites and see how many people were looking for people, and how many of those people were looking for [their family members]. . .so many people that cannot afford [much of anything]. . .[it makes you slower to complain].

One participant (HKR 305), age 93, similarly commented:

[W]hen I think of those people who had lost everything, I realized how blessed I am.. . . . [I also think of poor] people in other parts of the world. . .[and] the people living right here in our own country who have been victims of all these tornados, up in Tennessee. . .. I feel like I [have] be[en] so blessed to be able to have what I have and be as safe as I am.

Another older participant (HKR 312), age 91, said:

[I] stop and think that so many don't have [a thing in the world]. [Now], I ain't got [hardly] nothing, but so many people don't have what I got. . .. I [say to myself], "Well, I got those old scraps. I think I'll wear them." If anybody don't like them, they don't have to come see me.

A vivid and concluding example of the power of coping through beneficial comparison was offered by a participant (HKR 7), age 38, who reported that a New Orleans woman who had lost her home and everything in it visited the church where our participant attended shortly after Katrina hit. The visiting woman asked permission to sing a solo hymn of praise for the congregation, a gesture that profoundly affected our participant. She (HKR 7) reflected:

Still to this day, she just made me feel so [much]. . .. I was [thinking], "We just lost [electrical] power [for a few days and had relatively minor damage], you know. And you are here and you lost *everything* and you are singing praises to the Lord."

As we see from the above statements, favorable comparison of one's own circumstances with those of others in more dire straits was reported as a helpful and sometimes even transformative approach to coping used by many participants, whether they were consciously aware of this coping strategy or not. A second approach to coping is discussed next.

Sub-theme 2: Gratitude in the face of loss. The field of positive psychology has grown in recent years and focuses on the pursuit of optimal human functioning by developing specific inner strengths, such as optimism, courage, hope, and honesty (Seligman, 2004; Seligman & Csikszentmihalyi, 2000). It is believed that individuals can enjoy a fulfilling life and thrive if these internal characteristics are fostered. In this positive psychology literature, there is little extant research which examines the mental and emotional states of individuals following catastrophic events. Furthermore, there have been even fewer studies in contextual settings that compare with the real-world laboratory of post-HKR South Louisiana. As a result of the novel context, we knew little about what to expect in terms of the participants' psychological states. As a research team, we were struck by how frequently the participants' responses exuded health, optimism, and a generally positive approach to coping. Some of our participants even expressed *gratitude* and a conviction that they would avoid taking life for granted, as the following three excerpts illustrate:

> **HKR 9**, *42 years*: [I was reminded] that we shouldn't take for granted what we have. [...] I realize how good we have it and I'm very grateful, thankful...and I thank Him [God] for that on a daily basis. I don't take for granted that I've got a good life...
>
> **HKR 305**, *93 years*: I was blessed, and I have been blessed through all these ninety, almost ninety-four years. [I] was not unfortunate in having to cope with the hurricanes personally. You know, [by comparison to some] I didn't have...problem[s] at all. I was blessed.
>
> **HKR 306**, *91 years*: [For now, I am grateful to be staying with family]. I enjoy being here. I enjoy [and] love my family and I like to be with them. ...[Unlike many, I made it through this but] I know that when I [die], I'll go to a better place.

In terms of positive psychology, one participant (HKR 9) framed Katrina as a reminder that she "shouldn't take for granted" what she has, and went on to call herself "very grateful." HKR 305 referred to herself as "blessed" and "not unfortunate"—but it is probable that these are euphemistic terms for losing less than everything. Indeed, the latter participant (HKR 306) was without her home, perhaps permanently, but she still focused on the joy she felt in being with her family. Simple phrases of gratitude such as these are not uncommon to hear in daily life from the more positive persons around us—but against an oppressively dark backdrop of Katrina-induced loss, statements like "I enjoy [and] love my family and I like to be with them" are made striking by effect of contrast.

Sub-theme 3: Optimism as a coping resource. Many participants did not go so far as to express gratitude but still exuded an optimism—an optimism that in spite of the natural disasters they would cope well and come out strong, maybe even stronger (see Garrison & Sasser, Chapter 6, for a related discussion). Some individuals invoked timeworn but optimistic phrases, as reflected in the following three comments:

> **HKR 9**, *42 years*: I'm trying to look at my glass as half-full not half-empty. I'm trying to look on the optimistic side here.
>
> **HKR 105**, *48 years*: A lot of times there is a silver cloud, a silver lining behind every dark cloud, and I think that people's faith was tested in a lot of ways [during Katrina]...but I think that people, including myself, [are] generally optimistic that things [are] going to get better...that there are better times ahead.
>
> **HKR 305**, *93 years*: I do think that every cloud does have a silver lining, and that all of these things when they happen to us, there is a reason.

Other participants like HKR 15, age 39, drew analogies. She stated:

> I just know that in spite of what I go through or may face even in future life, it's just for a season, and we do know that storms come in seasons, you know, it's hurricane season so storms come in your nature life as well as your spiritual life.

Others, like the following two participants, offered their personal philosophies:

> **HKR 105**, *48 years*: I...just have an optimism and faith that things will get better and that there is maybe even a reason, I hate to say a reason, [that Katrina] happened. But we can learn and benefit from even something so awful as this, and look to the positive end of it.
>
> **HKR 207**, *89 years*: [Sometimes it] look[s] like everything goes wrong, but right behind that, everything come[s] out all right. [...]Everything's going to be all right.

Having addressed the third psychological coping resource of optimism, we now turn to a final related sub-theme.

Sub-theme 4: Personal psychological strength. Many participants' comments, like those above, conveyed an optimism that "things will get better." A handful of others did not explicitly express optimism (much less gratitude), but nevertheless offered comments that addressed more internal, personal psychological qualities or characteristics that seemed to serve as coping resources for them. The following three statements are representative of this group:

> **HKR 108**, *47 years*: It's not that I am naive or that I am just that I am [too] ignorant to know that bad things happen to good people. It's just, I have never been a depressed, stressed out person...
> **HKR 202**, *70 years*: Being the [strong] type [of] personality that I am, I had no problem.
> **HKR 315**, *93 years*: Under the circumstances, ...I just accepted things the way they were. ...I think things will be alright. I just accept them the way they are. That [part of my personality] didn't change. I still do the same thing, [I accept things and move on].

It might be said that in terms of coping, we had a grateful group, an optimistic group, and an accepting but strong group. Some individuals, however, had a flair of their own. One participant (HKR 104), age 60, a colorful character with some New Orleans swagger, offered one of the most memorable lines of our project:

> Like I [have] always said, "*Life's a bitch and it has puppies.*" So whatever He (God) throws you...[it may be tough now, but something good will come of it].

To summarize our overall findings on approaches to coping, there were several facilitative processes exemplified by our participants. Some used a beneficial comparison approach that involved focusing on those who were relatively less fortunate, thereby curbing tendencies toward self-pity. Others, in spite of tangible and intangible losses, focused on what they still had and expressed gratitude for these things. For others, optimism seemed key. Finally, some participants focused on personal psychological strengths as a resource that helped them cope. Taken as a whole, these coping approaches offered a varied array of positive psychological approaches that helped our participants as they coped with the worst natural disasters in their state's history. Having discussed two of the three central themes of this paper, we now turn to the final theme of meaning making.

Theme 3—Meaning Making: "God is in Control...Right?"

In this theme we seek to convey how participants struggled to find meaning in the wake of catastrophic carnage and loss. One approach to "explain" and make meaning out of Hurricane Katrina was to view it as the result of divine wrath over the sexual activities in New Orleans' French Quarter. A local reverend, Bill Shanks, represented this view in a widely distributed Internet message, a portion of which read:

> New Orleans now is Mardi Gras free. New Orleans now is free of Southern Decadence and the sodomites, the witchcraft workers, false religion—it's free of all those things now. God simply, I believe, in His mercy, purged all of that stuff out of there... (cf. Rose, 2007, p. 29).

Although none of our participants explicitly endorsed this view, the view was prevalent enough in local conversations to enter into our participants' consciousness. Several spontaneously drew attention to these views and then offered their rebuttals. Some participants, like the following three, simply rejected the notion that Katrina was a divine wake-up call or punishment.

> **HKR 220**, *77 years*: I heard a comment made that the Lord [sent] the hurricanes [to tell us] we have to change our ways and things like that. [Some say that] He is giving us these things because we're not living the way we should. [...] That's really not true.
>
> **HKR 111**, *53 years*: I do not believe that this was...a sign of God, or a punishment from God, but I do believe that God can help us cope and can help give us strength.... [What did Katrina mean?] I think it was a hurricane (Laughs). That is all I think it was. [...] God is not a hateful, vengeful God that is striking us like this because of too many gays in New Orleans...
>
> **HKR 202**, *70 years*: I think that those that feel God is punishing [us in] some way [are] ridiculous. I don't think it's the act of God or punishment. It's nature, actually.

Other participants also offered rejections of the "Katrina as punishment" concept but continued further to point out inconsistencies and contradictions they saw in this view. The following two insights were among the more cogent arguments presented by participants:

> **HKR 2**, *32 years*: I didn't see it as God coming after us.... God didn't do this to us...to punish us. I heard that so much, that God just took out New Orleans because it was such a sinful place. No...Mother Nature took New Orleans out—and it would have taken out anything that was there, whether it was New Orleans or a little podunk town.... You know, [Katrina] took out Slidell too and that's a suburban area.
>
> **HKR 210**, *67 years*: I heard somebody say that because New Orleans was a sin city, God cause[d] it (Katrina). I don't believe God causes things. I don't believe He causes cancer in children. I don't believe He causes these [hurricanes]. For one thing, Bourbon Street [in the heart of the French Quarter] was not really damaged and some churches *were* damaged. So, I mean I [don't think] that God would save...the "bad people" and ruin the churches. I mean God didn't have anything to do with it.

Both of the above rejections resonate with those of New Orleans' social chronicler Chris Rose (2007) who remarked:

> [T]ry telling some poor sap...who has never heard of Southern Decadence and who goes to Bible study every Wednesday night that he lost his house and his job and [that] his grandmother died in a flooded nursing home because God was angry at a bunch of bearded guys in dresses over on Dumaine Street. [...] How come Plaquemines, St. Bernard, the East, and Lakeview are gone but the French Quarter is still standing? (p. 29).

From a psychological standpoint, these participants were engaged in a process that might be called *negating*. Although most of the aforementioned persons do not attempt to explain or verbalize what Hurricane Katrina meant, these participants were passionate in expressing what the hurricane did *not* mean to them—namely, Katrina did not mean that God wanted to destroy New Orleans.

Erik Erikson's (1998) theory of development includes a focus on the development of psychological identity during adolescence. A primary task in identity development involves "the selective affirmation and *repudiation* of an individual's [early] identifications" (p. 72, emphasis added). In other words, adolescents make key decisions about who they are by rejecting or repudiating who they are not. Erik Erikson posits that "later an *existential identity* [forms] which...transcends the psychological one" (p. 73). In this quest, "defiance" and "negative identity" are again integrals, just as they are during early identity formation. In short, as we struggle to find and create existential meaning and identity, we selectively repudiate and affirm identifications in ways that define us. At some level, a similar exercise was seemingly undertaken by many in our sample.

Continuing on this theme, we noted that several participants not only stated their existential beliefs—they also implicitly disparaged those who held opposing beliefs. Examples of this approach included the two following, non-religious participants:

> **HKR 215**, *70 years*: I don't...rely on religious beliefs and practices to help me cope with Katrina and Rita. *I'm more pragmatic than that.*
> **HKR 308**, *91 years*: No...I don't [rely on religion]. No, [religious beliefs] did not [help me cope]. *I'm mature enough to know [better].*...I think I've had enough experience that I can see the thing as it is and live with it. You have to live with it in your own way.

In both of these cases, the participants are not content to simply state their non-religious stance. They both speak further and offer comments such as "I'm more pragmatic than that" and "I'm mature enough to know [better]"—comments that may be interpreted not only as self-reflection, but also as a jabs at those who invoke religion in their coping and meaning making.

While both of the above comments have an agnostic or atheistic timbre to them, this tendency to implicitly disparage those who saw the world differently was also manifested by some religious persons as well. Two representative statements included:

> **HKR 206**, *73 years*: You have faith in God to provide and keep you out of harm's way. *If you've got brains enough to listen [to Him]...*
> **HKR 211**, *67 years*: [Faith] has a calming effect, and if you are religious, it's ... I don't know, it's a strength that it brings out in you. *I feel sorry for people that don't [have it].*

As before, in both cases a statement of personal beliefs is followed by implicit condescension of those with contrary beliefs. Two more statements, both from faith-based perspectives, seem to offer additional examples of this point:

> **HKR 309**, *93 years*: People who are deeply religious are prone not to worry as much as other people do. Th[ose with faith] say, "Well, we put it into the hands of the Lord. And if it happens, it happens." [Other] people who worry a lot, generally do not live as long as other people do.... I didn't have any fear.
> **HKR 325**, *92 years*: [My religion] helps because I know that God can do stuff that we can't do.... The ones that don't believe in God and that have no prayer or don't have nothing at all, I don't know how they [cope] when they get in a tight spot.

Hurricanes Katrina and Rita were, for many, crises. A crisis, as discussed at the outset of this chapter, is a profound developmental challenge or even a turning point. In several of the previous examples, we seem to see persons in crisis who are struggling for their personal existential identities by affirming their own beliefs and repudiating beliefs that are different. Perhaps many of the persons in our study, like the elderly Jews studied by the late ethnographer Barbara Myerhoff (1980), "fight [in order] to keep warm" (p. 153).

Most of our South Louisiana sample were at least nominally religious and many were highly so, consistent with research on the high religiosity of the South as a region (Silk & Walsh, 2006). We now turn to an examination of participants' meaning-making efforts at explaining God's involvement (or lack of involvement) in Katrina and Rita. As mentioned earlier, none of our participants explicitly stated that the hurricanes were divine retribution. However, some participants did state that the disasters were "the Lord's will" or "His plan" without much further explanation. The following five quotes are illustrative:

> **HKR 16**, *43 years*: He still performs miracles and He is still on the throne. It does not matter what is going on in this world today, He is still on the throne...this is just part of His plan.
> **HKR 207**, *89 years*: [T]he Lord will give me the protection I need....And if it's the Lord's will, I can't have anything to worry about... Certain things are out of our hands...
> **HKR 218**, *66 years*: [I heard this quote that said], "Your level of stress will go down significantly when you give up your position as general manager of the universe." I just love that! So, I try to remind myself that I am not in control of most of these things... Because I have an abiding trust that things will work out the way the Lord wants them to, and they're not for me to decide....I'm just ...Those are things are beyond my control, and I know they're not in my control, so I don't worry about them. I don't.
> **HKR 104**, *60 years*: Well, I believe there's a God, and I believe God does everything for a reason....So we just got to put our faith in God and go by what He tells us. ... Whatever He throws at us, we got to accept. Lot of times we don't like it, but sometimes we have to accept it.
> **HKR 206**, *73 years*: Sometimes (chuckles)...[God's] got His own ideas.

For these participants and many others, the meaning-making effort seemed to be a fairly straightforward affair. Things go "the way the Lord wants them to." They may not understand why, but they accept it, because it is out of their hands anyway.

Others took different approaches in explaining the hurricanes. Some of those approaches involved establishing varying degrees of separation between God and Nature. Some wanted to place some exceptions or limitations on God's control. One said, "I know that God is in control of *almost* everything that happens..." Other participants believed that God "puts certain rules on Mother Nature" but that He does not exercise (or choose to exercise) absolute control over Nature. One participant (HKR 13), age 46, explained:

> [I] had a lot of my young nieces and nephews ask why... why did God do this? It was the opportunity for me to explain how I've been taught that God...He puts certain rules [on] Mother Nature...[but] that this is something that Mother Nature did. [...] He [God] didn't bring it there, it just happened.

For both of the above participants, God is still benevolent and powerful, but perhaps He does not possess or at least exercise all control. The inference from both statements is that there are *some* bad things that happen, that God does not control. One example of meaning making, from participant, HKR 110 (age 49) seemed to combine elements of divine control with a view of Nature as a separate hostile entity. He said:

> People may not believe it, but God was merciful in where he had Katrina hit because he did move it to the East. If Katrina would've kept going in the path it was headed, [the eye of the hurricane] would've went right over New Orleans then New Orleans would not be there now.

The collection of participants represented above seemed to draw lines of varying thickness between God and Nature, making statements that imply a less than absolute power by God [e.g., that God is in control of "almost everything", that "this is something that Mother Nature did", and that God moved Katrina to the east (but did not obliterate it)]. Unlike the previous group we presented, this group's approaches to meaning making do not insist that the hurricanes were God's will or plan. Further, for some there was passing of hurricane-related blame from God to a (somewhat independent) Mother Nature.

We now turn to another tendency among the interviewed participants. This tendency was not necessarily to identify the causes of the hurricanes, but to offer post hoc explanations rooted in lessons learned. One prevalent explanation was that the hurricanes served as a primer in humility, a reminder that "you're not in control." The following four statements convey this notion:

> **HKR 115**, *51 years*: The interesting thing about a hurricane...is there's nothing you can do about it, and for once the world can see that they can't control [things]. This is definitely God. This is a God thing. Not that he is punishing [us] or anything, but it lets you have a perspective of who you really are, that *you're not in control*. And this is where Katrina [gives us the] right perspective, that God's in control...
> **HKR 203**, *82 years*: [Katrina is a reminder that] we need to understand that there always is that power in charge.
> **HKR 218**, *66 years*: I [was reminded], you are not in control of the things.... A lot of these things that happen, *you're not in control* of them.
> **HKR 101**, *62 years*: You just have to learn that God can do all things..... We can build walls and house[s] that [we think] the storms can't tear down but when it is time for these things to happen there is nothing we can do.

As indicated above, some participants saw the hurricane experience as a type of divine reminder that we are not in control, while God is. Others emerged with yet another take on the experience.

The last group that will be represented ranged from atheistic to highly religious but shared a central similarity—instead of spending emotional and psychological energy trying to define or explain the hurricanes they had endured, they seemed to strive to make meaning through doing their best in present, at-hand struggles. One highly religious participant (HKR 218) explained:

> [I just say], "His will be done." And then [I say], "Give me the strength to handle whatever that will is." ...[My prayer has been], "Your will be done.. *just give me the strength to handle it.*"

Participant HKR 9, age 42, also a person of faith, similarly expressed:

> I just don't think I could have made it through without knowing that He's there.... [W]hatever happens is going to happen, but *He's going to see us through it.*

Another reflection was offered by non-religious participant that seemed to richly capture the sum of meaning making for many of those we interviewed. One participant (HKR 111), age 53, summarized:

> Do I think everything happens for the best? No. Do I think we [should try to] make the best out of everything that happens? Yes. That's basically what I believe right there, that *we make the best out of what happens*.

Despite varying degrees of religiosity and fatalism, these three participants (and many others from our study) shared two central commonalities. First, instead of focusing on the past, they shared a present/future orientation, as illustrated by such statements as "[God is] going to see us through it" and "We [will] make the best out of what happens." The second commonality in their meaning-making perspective is a capabilities-focused paradigm. These are not sheltered and starry-eyed Pollyannas but individuals who have weathered two of the worst natural disasters in Louisiana's history. Still, at the risk of sounding triumphalistic, they manifest an apparent toughness and resilience. What did Katrina "mean"? To many of these participants, it meant (and still means) there is much hard work ahead—work that they will strive to "make the best of."

Discussion

Each of the three themes discussed in this chapter captures a piece of the participants' collective story of life in the Katrina/Rita aftermath. The first theme (Crisis: Tragedy, Opportunity, or Simply "Part of Life") reflects our participants' experiences of Katrina and Rita as *crises* in the Eriksonian sense. For some in the sample, the challenges and losses associated with these historic storms made pre-hurricane life as irretrievable as the flooded and now razed homes in the devastated regions of the Gulf Coast. However, these crises were not solely negative. Some individuals reported emerging from the storm with a renewed sense of commitment to "what matters most" and a deeper appreciation for "how precious life is."

The crisis-related analyses in theme 1 offered the most striking cross-cohort finding of our study. Namely, Hurricanes Katrina and Rita were portrayed as crises for most individuals in the two younger (under age 65) cohorts we interviewed, while the hurricanes were typically discussed in more temperate ways by the two senior (over age 65) cohorts. We want to avoid overstating the contrast between the older and the younger cohorts and note that there were one or two individual exceptions (e.g., younger participants who were more stoic). Even so, the overall cohort-based differences were pronounced enough to be identified by all members of the research team. We note that from a historical vantage, the timeframe that separated Cohorts 1 and 2 from 3 and 4 was 1940/1941—the years immediately preceding the United States' involvement in World War II. Phrased differently, most of Cohorts 1 and 2 were "Baby Boomers," while most members of Cohorts 3 and 4 belonged to what Tom Brokaw (2004) has chronicled as "The Greatest Generation." Whether the relative tendency of the two senior cohorts to minimize the personal influence of HK/R is more a function of specific cohort experiences (e.g., the Great Depression and/or World War II years), or whether it is influenced more by age itself, we cannot say. What we *can* state is that there were cohort differences with respect to whether individuals defined Hurricanes Katrina and Rita as crises or not.

The second theme, "Approaches to Coping," did not reflect cross-cohort differences like theme 1. However, a variety of coping approaches and resources did emerge, including *gratitude in the face of loss*, *optimism as a coping resource*, and *personal psychological strength*. A fourth coping approach, *beneficial comparison*, was evident as many participants favorably contrasted their situation with persons in worse circumstances. This coping approach meshes with previous research that has found that people "with life-threatening illnesses are likely to compare themselves with those who are in worse shape" (Wood, Taylor, & Lichtman, 1985; cf. Gilbert, 2006, p. 183) and that 96% of cancer patients in one classic study self-reported that they were better off than "the average patient" with cancer (Taylor, Falke, Shoptaw, & Lichtman, 1986). This coping method of selectively focusing on individuals who are worse off, en route to beneficial comparison, might be criticized as pointless self-deception, were it not for the salutary influence of positive reframing and positive perception (Gilbert, 2006). Indeed, a host of symbolic interaction theorists have argued that "perception *is* reality" and that, as the Thomas Theorem states, "If people define situations as real, they are real in their consequences" (Thomas & Znaniecki, 1920; cf. LaRossa & Reitzes, 1993, p. 140). In short, people who see themselves as doing relatively well are more likely to adjust in healthy ways than those who see themselves as failing—as supported by research on the psychology of coping (Pargament, 1997). As a result, in the hurricane aftermath, a critical concern from a psychological perspective is how the affected individuals and families view and define their present situation and their prospective futures. This issue closely relates to the final theme of meaning making.

In connection with meaning making, one of the generally accepted truisms in psychology, family counseling, and human services work is the potency of the "Pygmalion effect" or self-fulfilling prophecy—namely, that our beliefs regarding what will happen to us tend to drive our behaviors in directions that significantly increase the likelihood of the predicted outcome (Corey & Corey, 2003; Covey, 2004). In light of this point, after the immediate crises have passed, after different coping strategies have been adopted with varying degrees of success, and after meanings have been attributed, it may be that beliefs such as *"we make the best out of what happens"* will have significant influence in the lives of these survivors. Their individual and collective belief, desire, and effort to prove such "prophecies" true may provide the meaning and thrust necessary to see those visions realized. In conclusion, we come full circle and again hear Frankl's (1984, p. 104) words, "Everything can be taken from a man but one thing: the last of human freedoms—to choose one's attitude in any given set of circumstances, to choose one's own way."

Acknowledgment We thank Tracey Frias, Miranda Melancon, and Zia McWilliams for their assistance with data summary and qualitative analyses. We also thank M.E. Betsy Garrison for her helpful comments on an earlier version of this manuscript.

References

Bacher, R., Devlin, T., Calongne, K., Duplechain, J., & Pertuit, S. (2005). *LSU in the eye of the storm: A university model for disaster response.* Available at http://www.lsu.edu/pa/book/EYEofTheSTORMtxt.pdf

Boss, P. (2002). *Family stress management.* Thousand Oaks, CA: Sage.

Brokaw, T. (2004). *The greatest generation.* New York: Random House.

Cherry, K. E. (2006, August). Effects of hurricanes Katrina/Rita on the oldest-old. In P. Dass-Brailsford (Chair), *Intersecting dimensions of multicultural issues in disaster response: Aging, disability, ethnicity and SES.* Invited symposium presented at the annual meetings of the American Psychological Association, New Orleans, Louisiana.

Cherry, K. E., Allen, P. D., & Galea, S. (2009). Older adults and natural disasters: Lessons learned from Hurricanes Katrina and Rita. In P. Dass-Brailsford (Ed.), *Crisis and disaster counseling: Lessons learned from Hurricane Katrina and other disasters.* Thousand Oaks, CA: Sage (in press).

Cherry, K. E., Galea, S., & Silva, J. L. (2008). Successful aging and natural disasters: Role of adaptation and resiliency in late life. In M. Hersen & A. M. Gross (Eds.), *Handbook of clinical psychology* (Vol. 1, pp. 810–833). New Jersey: John Wiley & Sons, Inc.

Cherry, K. E., Galea, S., Su, L. J., Welsh, D. A., Jazwinski, S. M., Silva, J. L., et al. (2009). *Cognitive and psychosocial consequences of Hurricanes Katrina and Rita on middle aged, older, and oldest-old adults in the Louisiana Healthy Aging Study (LHAS)* (in press).

Corey, M. S., & Corey, G. (2003). *Becoming a helper* (4th ed.). Pacific Grove, CA: Brooks/Cole.

Covey, S. R. (2004). *The 7 habits of highly effective people.* New York: Free Press.

Erikson, E. H. (1998). *The life cycle completed.* New York: Norton.

Erikson, J. M. (1998). Gerotranscendence. In E. H. Erikson (Ed.), *The life cycle completed* (pp. 123–129). New York: Norton.

Fosdick, H. E. (1918). *The meaning of faith.* New York: Association Press.

Frankl, V. (1984). *Man's search for meaning.* New York: Washington Street Press.

Garrison, M. E., Malia, J. A., & Molgaard, V. K. (1991). Conceptual and theoretical integration of family resource management theory and family stress theory. *Themis: Journal of Theory in Home Economics, 1,* 1–17.

Gilbert, D. (2006). *Stumbling on happiness.* New York: Vintage.

Hill, R. (1949). *Families under stress: Adjustment to the crisis of war separation and reunion.* New York: Harper and Brothers.

Ingoldsby, B., Smith, S., & Miller, J. E. (2004). *Exploring family theories.* New York: Roxbury.

Koos, E. L. (1946). *Families in trouble.* New York: Kings Crown Press.

LaRossa, R., & Reitzes, D. C. (1993). Symbolic interactionism and family studies. In P. G. Boss, W. J. Doherty, R. LaRossa, W. R. Schumm, & S. K. Steinmetz (Eds.), *Sourcebook of family theories and methods: A contextual approach* (pp. 135–163). New York: Plenum Press.

Marks, L. D. (2002). *Illuminating the interface between families and face.* Unpublished doctoral dissertation, University of Delaware, Newark.

Marks, L. D., Nesteruk, O., Swanson, M., Garrison, M. E. B., & Davis, T. (2005). Religion and health among African Americans: A qualitative examination. *Research on Aging, 27,* 447–474.

Marks, L. D., Swanson, M., Nesteruk, O., & Hopkins-Williams, K. (2006). Stressors in African American marriages and families: A qualitative study. *Stress, Trauma, and Crisis: An International Journal, 9,* 203–225.

Menaghan, E. G. (1983). Individual coping efforts: Moderators of the relationship between life stress and mental health outcomes. In H. B. Kaplan (Ed.), *Psychosocial stress: Trends in theory and research* (pp. 157–192). New York: Academic Press.

Miles, M. B., & Huberman, A. M. (1994). *Qualitative data analysis: An expanded sourcebook.* Thousand Oaks, CA: Sage.

Myerhoff, B. (1980). *Number our days.* New York: Touchstone.

Nesteruk, O., & Garrison, M. E. B. (2005). An exploratory study of the relationship between family daily hassles and family coping and managing strategies. *Family and Consumer Sciences Research Journal, 34,* 140–152.

Pargament, K. I. (1997). *The psychology of religion and coping: Theory, research, and practice.* New York: Guilford.

Patton, M. Q. (2002). *Qualitative research & evaluation methods* (3rd ed.). Thousand Oaks, CA: Sage.

Rose, C. (2007). *1 dead in attic: After Katrina.* New York: Simon & Schuster.

Seligman, M. E. P. (2004). *Authentic happiness: Using the new positive psychology to realize your potential for lasting fulfillment.* New York: Free Press.

Seligman, M. E. P., & Csikszentmihalyi, M. (2000). Positive psychology: An introduction. *American Psychologist, 55,* 5–14.

Silk, M., & Walsh, A. (2006). *Religion by region: Religion and public life in the United States.* Blue Ridge Summit, PA: AltaMira.

Strauss, A., & Corbin, J. (1998). *Basics of qualitative research: Techniques and procedures for developing grounded theory.* Thousand Oaks, CA: Sage.

Taylor, S. E., Falke, R. L., Shoptaw, S. J., & Lichtman, R. R. (1986). Social support, support groups, and the cancer patient. *Journal of Consulting and Clinical Psychology, 54,* 608–615.

Thomas, W. I., & Zaniecki, F. (1920). *The Polish peasant in Europe and America.* Boston, MA: Badger.

Webster's New World Dictionary. (1991, 3rd ed.). New York: Simon & Schuster.

Wood, J. V., Taylor, S. E., & Lichtman (1985). Social comparison and adjustment to breast cancer. *Journal of Personality and Social Psychology, 49,* 1169–1183.

Part IV
Special Topics

Chapter 11
The Psychology Behind Helping and Prosocial Behaviors: An Examination from Intention to Action

Jennifer L. Silva, Loren D. Marks, and Katie E. Cherry

Abstract When disasters strike, many people rise to the challenge of providing immediate assistance to those whose lives are in peril. The spectrum of helping behaviors to counter the devastating effects of a natural disaster is vast and can be seen on many levels, from concerned individuals and community groups to volunteer organizations and larger civic entities. In this chapter, we examine the psychology of helping in relation to natural disasters. Definitions of helping behaviors, why we help, and risks of helping others are discussed first. Next, we discuss issues specific to natural disasters and life span considerations, noting the developmental progression of age-related, altruistic motivations. We present a qualitative analysis of helping behaviors based on interviews with participants in the *Louisiana Healthy Aging Study* (LHAS; see Cherry, Silva, & Galea, Chapter 9). These data show that some people directly engaged in helping behaviors to further the relief effort after Hurricanes Katrina and Rita, while others spoke of helping indirectly through their associations with local churches and faith-based organizations that provided storm relief. Implications for helping behaviors and intentions to help in a post-disaster situation are considered.

Introduction

In the wake of one of the largest natural disasters in United States history, persons from across the globe opened their homes, hearts, and wallets to those affected by Hurricanes Katrina and Rita. In 2006 it was reported that citizens and humanitarian organizations had contributed a combined total of 3 billion dollars to relief efforts (Indiana University Center on Philanthropy, 2007). This same organization also reported that a majority of surveyed US households provided monetary donations for victims of the Gulf Coast storms. While financial assistance was a prominent form of aid, it was not the only manner of aid exhibited. There were

K.E. Cherry (✉)
Department of Psychology, Louisiana State University, Baton Rouge, LA 70803-5501, USA
e-mail: pskatie@lsu.edu

many persons who traveled to the devastated regions of Louisiana and Mississippi to donate their time and services. Many worked tirelessly by handing out food and clothing, locating missing persons, rescuing those stranded in their houses, organizing relief efforts, and counseling persons who lost their homes and possessions (see Allen and Wayne, Chapter 8). In addition, those not able to travel to disaster areas may have held community bake sales or collected canned goods in order to make their own donation to the Gulf Coast recovery. All of these described actions can be defined as *prosocial behaviors*, which are those actions that help or benefit another individual or group (Eisenberg & Fabes, 1998). Furthermore, these behaviors may result from some level of concern or empathy on the part of the helper and provide a benefit to the recipient (Dovidio, Palivan, Schroeder, & Penner, 2006; Eisenberg & Fabes, 1998).

In recent years, the demonstration of prosocial behaviors has increased and was especially evident after the attacks of 9/11 (Pyszczynski, Solomon, & Greenburg, 2003). People from across the country flocked to blood centers to give blood to the survivors. Some established trust funds for the children of those who perished in the twin towers. Millions in donations poured into the various humanitarian organizations across the nation. In the days and weeks following the attacks of 9/11, the United States of America became the face of humanity, compassion, and camaraderie.

The outpouring of these helping behaviors prompted psychologists to investigate those factors that motivate individuals to help one another during or following a catastrophic event. The origins of these behaviors have sparked scientific interest for decades and have led to a variety of hypotheses that are discussed in this chapter (see also Dovidio et al., 2006). We adopt a life span perspective by examining how an individual's age can influence the manner in which he/she can make unique contributions to their local community. In particular, we present data from the Louisiana Healthy Aging Study (LHAS), which has examined the impact of Hurricanes Katrina and Rita on its participants (see Cherry et al., Chapter 9). During interviews with a sample of LHAS participants, it became clear that many had either directly or indirectly helped those affected by Hurricanes Katrina and Rita, and others had received storm-related assistance. While investigating the presence/impact of helping behaviors was not an initial target of the LHAS investigation, participant reports provided a clear rationale for further investigation.

Why Do We Help?

The reason behind why individuals help one another is not as straightforward as some might predict. Many factors have been identified that may influence prosocial behaviors. For instance, biological theories of helping behavior consider the role of genetics, evolution, and survival of the fittest. Internal factors like empathetic responses, a negative personal state, and other personal motivations may also be involved. Individual differences in personality, current mood, and results from an internal cost–benefit analysis may impact ones' decision to help (for a review, see Dovidio et al., 2006). These different views are discussed next to offer insight into the fundamentals of prosocial behaviors and provide a context for understanding the psychology of helping as it applies to post-disaster reactions.

Kin Selection View of Prosocial Behavior

One of the more naturalistic explanations for prosocial behavior branches from evolutionary psychology and early experiments examining genetics and species survival (Hamilton, 1963, 1964). Early research documented basic helping behaviors in non-human species, which many assume to have a limited (or non-existent) emotional relationship with other members of their species. From these observations, Hamilton was the first to theorize that prosocial behavior could possess some genetic origin. This rationale stemmed from the idea that prosocial behaviors could lead to species fitness. Hamilton hypothesized that without help between cohort members, species survival would be in jeopardy and extinction would become eminent. Consequently those members who actively engage in and receive prosocial behaviors are those most likely to survive, pass on their genes to future generations, and ultimately contribute to species development.

Using Hamilton's rationale, helping is thought to be a genetically programmed, innate behavior. For instance, visualize a young mother and her newly born child. Across many species, the mother commonly reduces the level of attention and help devoted to older offspring, in order to attend to younger and less self-sufficient ones. Hamilton (1963, 1964) assumes this is done because older offspring are more capable, due to their acquisition of survival skills. The mother chooses the younger offspring to ensure their survival. They not only receive more attention and care from their mother, but a mother may forgo her own physiological and safety needs to provide for her young. In contrast, mothers who fail to care for their young are those least likely to pass their genetic code and ensure species survival. Thus, the *kin selection theory* (Hamilton, 1963, 1964) assumes that members of the species who possess a genetic *code* for prosocial behavior will be the most likely to reproduce.

The *kin selection theory* branch of evolutionary theories relates to John Bowlby's attachment theory (Bowlby, 1969, 1988). Attachment theory offers psychological and evolutionary explanations for human relationships. Bowlby's early work centered on the strong, stable, and secure bond between an infant and a caregiver, but his conclusions were eventually applied to adult relationships. According to attachment theory, infants are thought to be dependent for the sole purpose of survival, and thus need a safe and strong relationship with their caregiver (usually their mother). Infants will eventually use their caregiver as a secure base from which they explore the world. Some researchers have argued that Hamilton's *kin selection theory* cannot be distinguished from Bowlby's attachment theory, since both reflect the fundamental nature of the relationship between a mother and her child (Hood, Greenberg, & Tobach, 1995). In both theories, a strong attachment is presumed to exist between a parent and the child from birth, and this relationship becomes stronger as the child demonstrates their complete dependence.

Research has also demonstrated that helping occurs between members of the kinship other than just the mother and child. To test the *kin selection theory* in an adult population, Burnstein, Crandall, and Kitayama (1994) examined the role of kinship in prosocial behaviors. During their experiments, participants were presented with a scenario such as *three people need you to run an errand: your sister, your cousin, and an acquaintance, however you only have time to complete an errand for one person*. Participants were instructed to make a choice and results consistently demonstrated a strong association to kin, where the closest individual would be chosen first (e.g., the sister, then the cousin, and the acquaintance last). This trend was consistent across everyday situations, such as running errands, but was even more pronounced in a *life or death* situation, like choosing one individual to rescue from a burning building. Cunningham, Jegerski, Gruder, and Barbee (1995) verified these results by showing that the percentage of prosocial behavior exhibited is positively correlated with the degree of relatedness. Furthermore, Madsen et al. (2007) have suggested that kinship level is simply a baseline category from which subsequent factors about prosocial behavior are compared (e.g., personal obligation and sense of morals).

Another theory associated with the evolutionary perspective of prosocial behavior is *reciprocal altruism*. Reciprocal altruism occurs when one engages in a prosocial behavior in order to assist another, however, this is done under the assumption that this help will later be returned. Furthermore, these prosocial actions may decrease the helper's own chances of survival (Trivers, 1971). Trivers explains that one may be more willing to help a non-relative if a better chance of survival is possible. This behavior has been well documented in bats, non-human primates, and humans (Brosnan & de Waal, 2002; Rapoport & Chammah, 1965; Wilkinson, 1984). Wilkinson has provided unique evidence and has documented this reciprocal helping behavior in vampire bats. Each evening these bats require a blood meal to keep them satisfied for the night. However, members of this bat species are not always successful at obtaining their nightly meal and death soon becomes a possibility for those with empty stomachs. As a result, this species engages in reciprocal altruism behavior, where one bat will regurgitate their meal in order to feed another starving member. This prosocial behavior ensures the survival of other members, yet is done at the cost of those helping since the helpers will go hungry for the night. From the assumption that these animals do not possess empathy, guilt, or views of morality, one can theorize that these behaviors are biological in origin and can be programmed into ones genetic code.

Reciprocal altruism is also evident in every day human behavior. We all do favors or run errands on the behalf of friends and neighbors, and we do so on the presumption that this favor will one day be returned. In contrast, some may argue that we lend a hand out of genuine kindness and that people do not care if the favor is returned. However, some individuals may not continue to provide favors for an individual that never returns or acknowledges their efforts. Trivers (1983) has identified situations that promote reciprocal altruism. Typically, individuals must live in a society where they cannot remain anonymous. Reciprocal altruism is common in communities where "free-loaders" are detected with ease. Furthermore, research has shown that those persons living in rural areas and small towns are more likely to help than individuals who reside in more urban environments (Hedge & Yousif, 1992).

Additional investigations into the *reciprocal altruism* hypothesis have been conducted using the *prisoners' dilemma* task (Axelrod, 1984; Rapoport & Chammah, 1965). In the classic form of this paradigm, two suspected criminals are placed under arrest and locked in separate holding cells. The police do not have enough evidence to charge them and thus both suspects are offered an identical deal. If one testifies against the other, this prisoner will be released while the other prisoner is given a 10-year jail sentence (called *defection*). If neither talks, both will receive lighter sentences of 6 months in jail (*cooperation*). However, if each incriminates the other then both will receive 5 years imprisonment for the crime. Therefore, a strong dilemma is presented: *Would you lessen your own punishment at the expense of another? Or do you say nothing in the hopes that your counterpart also remains quiet?* Rationally, participants would initially want to defect in order to gain the benefit of release. But most quickly realize that if both prisoners incriminate one another, then the consequences will be severely worse than if they both said nothing. This paradigm is based on the fact that one is unaware of their partner's actions. The prisoners' dilemma game is played over a series of trials and an individual can quickly gauge their partner's tendency to cooperate. This paradigm is highly comparable to the reciprocal altruism theory, which poses a similar question: *do you help another in the hopes that he/she will return the favor?* The unknown is a hallmark feature within both of these concepts, which subsequently impacts the decision to help. Furthermore, many reciprocal behaviors require a sacrifice on the part of the helper, and thus the rewards are not immediately evident. The prisoners' dilemma is analogous in that participants do not know their partners actions until the games end and therefore are initially unaware if their help (or lack of) was reciprocated.

Empathy–Altruism Hypothesis and Relief of Negative State

Genetics are only half of the nature–nurture debate, which theorizes that genes may not be the sole contributor to behavior, but that ones' environment and social encounters may possess an equally strong influence (Ridley, 2003). The *empathy–altruism hypothesis* states that individuals act in a prosocial manner due to internal feelings of empathy toward others (Coke, Batson, & McDavis, 1978; Batson & Coke, 1981; Toi & Batson, 1982). Batson and Coke define empathy as a matching emotional reaction with those persons experiencing the situation; it is also similar to feelings of sympathy, compassion, and tenderness. It is possible that feeling empathy for another is a genetic dispositional trait, although emotional reactions of empathy can instilled in an individual from their environmental encounters. Despite the outcome of this debate, the empathy–altruism hypothesis suggests that an empathetic reaction is primarily responsible for helping behaviors. Coke et al.

(1978) presented a stage model with two key components to prosocial behavior. First, one must successfully take the perspective of the individual in need. Consequently, taking this perspective will directly increase the emotional response within the observer. Second, an emotional, empathetic response will subsequently lead to prosocial behaviors. Overall, this theory proposes that those who have an authentic concern for the well-being of others are most likely to help. In support of this view, numerous studies have demonstrated that a highly empathetic response is positively associated with helping behaviors (Coke et al., 1978; Toi & Batson, 1982; Fultz, Bateon, Fortenbach, McCarthy, & Varoey, 1986; Batson, Duncan, Ackerman, Buckley, & Birch, 1981). For example, Toi and Batson had participants listen to a radio advertisement of a student who was in an accident, broke both legs, and as a result was now behind in their classes. Participants were then asked how likely they were to help the injured student. Two primary factors were manipulated: the empathy of the radio presentation (high versus low) and the overall cost associated with helping (indexed by the amount of time required to help). Their findings confirmed that empathy was associated with helping. Specifically, those in the high-empathy condition were most likely to help and did so regardless of the cost, while those in the low-empathy condition only helped if the cost was minimal.

Producing an empathetic response is not the only possibility set forth by Batson and colleagues. They also presented the notion that those who help do not do so for self-gratification (Batson, Fultz, & Schoenrade, 1987). Therefore, bystander actions cannot be interpreted as selfish or egoist in motive. To clarify this hallmark feature, Batson stated that two distinct emotional responses are possible: empathy toward the victim and personal negative distress. As stated previously, by producing an empathetic response one would help in order to alleviate the victim's distress. This is the primary feature of the empathy–altruism hypothesis—that an individual's empathetic concern will lead to altruistic behavior. Conversely, it is also possible that by taking the victim's perspective, one would generate his or her own personal distress (alarm, fear, or anxiety). In this case, the bystander will only help after he/she believes it is the most effective means available to alleviate their own personal suffering. In this situation, help is egoist in nature and is provided purely for self-satisfaction and relief of a personal negative state.

Consequently, the *relief of negative state view* directly contradicts the assumptions put forth by the empathy–altruism hypothesis (Cialdini, Baumann, & Kenrick, 1981). Proponents of this theory argue that helping behavior is selfish in nature (Cialdini et al., 1981; Cialdini et al., 1987; Harris, Benson, & Hall, 1975; Schaller & Cialdini, 1988; Wallach & Wallach, 1983). These authors reasoned that prosocial behaviors are expressed mostly due to intrinsic desires to gain self-gratification. For example, as children we are taught to share our toys, play nicely with others in the playground, and to help mom clean up the mess in the living room. When children engage in these helping behaviors without being prompted, they are commonly rewarded and praised by their parents. As children get older, helping behaviors become more complex and parents (and others) still provide rewards. As these prosocial actions are regularly rewarded, they are said to become a conditioned stimulus that increases self-esteem and personal gratification. Thus, when bystanders view another person in distress it produces a negative emotional reaction, such as sadness, and most bystanders may help in order to relieve the negative induced state. Cialdini et al. (1987) propose that helping a victim restores the original mood of the bystander, and this happens since most adults have been conditioned to perceive helping as a rewarding stimuli. Thus, these authors conclude that most individuals engage in altruistic behaviors for "an entirely egoistic reason: personal mood management" (p. 750).

Harris et al. (1975) conducted a classic pseudo-investigation into the *negative state relief* hypothesis of altruistic behavior. These authors requested monetary donations (for a worthy cause) from Roman Catholic parishioners while they were either entering or leaving weekly confession. The donation of money was identified as a measure of altruistic behavior, since the donations were to be sent to those less fortunate. Harris and colleagues discovered that the frequency and the amount of donations were greater from those individuals entering church compared to those persons leaving. Their conclusion pointed to the notion that persons leaving confession were presumed to be absolved on their sins and consequently possessed lesser intrinsic guilt compared to those entering the church. Therefore, the decease in exit donations could primarily be attributed to lessened guilt and relief of a negative internal state. Harris and colleagues conclude that altruistic behaviors could be associated to a current negative self-concept or mood. In summary, a negative mood will most likely lead to helping and altruistic behaviors if the one assumes that this course of action will relieve this distress.

Cost–Reward Model

While many individuals have a strong empathetic reaction toward those in need of help, there are some who make the decision to not come to the assistance of another. Thus, the empathy–altruism hypothesis may not be fully prepared to explain why this segment of the population fails to provide assistance. Piliavin, Dovidio, Gaertner, and Clark (1981) proposed a simple economic view of prosocial behavior which may account for those individuals who fail to act. These authors posed the assumption that all people have the common goal of maximizing their rewards and minimizing their costs. From this statement, one can presume that individuals undergo an internal *cost–reward analysis*, where they weigh the costs and benefits associated with helping. There are two broad categories of costs and rewards—those linked with helping and those associated with not helping. Using the cost–reward approach, one can see that most individuals may look at the benefits and penalties of their potential actions. Dovidio et al. (2006) suggest that costs associated with helping may include time, money, danger, embarrassment, and interruption of current activities. In contrast, rewards were identified as money, thankfulness of the victim, praise, fame, and intrinsic pleasure. To summarize, the *cost–reward model* assumes that as costs increase, helping decreases; and as rewards increase, helping behavior also increases.

The cost–reward model of altruistic behavior can be linked with Latané and Darley's (1970) stage model of bystander intervention. These researchers hypothesized that there are five fundamental decisions that an individual must make during an emergency. Each of these decisions will eventually lead to one of two opposing outcomes, helping or not. The first of these stages is simple: *does an individual notice the event is happening?* While it is obvious that emergencies cannot be predicted, a person may not realize that an emergency is occurring. This may be due to proximity and/or the fact that persons are too preoccupied to notice and are therefore not attentive to the situation. On the other hand, others may choose to not pay attention to the event, such as not wanting to get involved in a husband and wife dispute. This first stage assumes that a bystander must recognize an emergency.

Second, an individual must *determine if the event is a true emergency*. We are not always aware all of the facts surrounding an event. For example, one may see a parked car on the interstate and assume he/she is having car trouble. However, that person may be stopping to take a nap, talk on a cell phone, or be checking a map for directions. It is not always easy to make the determination if there is an emergency. Latané and Darley (1970) hypothesize that if there is an inclination that a situation is a non-emergency, the frequency of helping behavior will drastically be reduced.

The third stage is when *a person must assume that it is his/her responsibility to help*. Not all individuals feel that it is their responsibility to help out another in need. This personal variable has become a main factor in differentiating those who help and those who remain bystanders to the situation. Latané and Darley (1970) provide additional insight into person's failure to act. They hypothesize two contributors to non-action: *diffusion of responsibility* and *pluralistic ignorance*. According to their *diffusion of responsibility theory*, persons are presumed not to help because they feel like another person has (or will) come to the aid of those in need. Consequently, it is assumed that as the number of bystanders increases, the likelihood that someone will help decreases. *Pluralistic ignorance* occurs when individuals do not want to make an inappropriate response. For example, one may be reluctant to yell "fire" when they smell smoke in case it may be a false alarm. This stems from the assumption that some individuals would rather not risk embarrassing themselves than initiate help.

The last two factors determine if an individual will engage in helping behavior and may subsequently include the internal *cost–reward analysis* (Piliavin et al., 1981). The fourth stage is determining if you *know what to do* and the fifth is *making the decision to help*. People are less inclined to help if they do not know how to handle the situation. One would most likely not attempt to provide CPR to a choking individual unless they had at least minimal training. Subsequently, he/she must make the final decision: *do I help or do I do nothing?* This final decision may often times be the most difficult, since there are commonly risks associated with engaging in prosocial behavior. This is where one could engage in a *cost–reward analysis* as previously described. Dovidio et al. (2006) propose that the degree of help is commonly associated with the outcome of this internal analysis. For example, individuals may realize that sometimes victims may refuse the assistance of others, or bystanders may even be assaulted if they attempt to assist another. These unpleasant consequences and concerns may overshadow perceived benefits. These factors may also weigh heavily on a bystander's conscience and he/she may ultimately choose to do nothing.

Belief in a Just World

The preceding theories of helping behavior relate to the biological and social determinants of helping. However, personal beliefs and assumptions may also play a critical role in one's decision to help following an emergency or natural disaster. In the days following Hurricanes Katrina and Rita, there were many online forums, discussions, television interviews, and web pages that were devoted to how the victims *affected by the storms had asked for it*. Proponents stated that these victims had chosen to live in neighborhoods that were below sea level, so they were deserving of this destruction in light of their choices. More stated that the government warranted the destruction because they were too incompetent to produce effective levees. Others suggested that New Orleans' nickname *The Big Easy* implied the residents lived in sin and consequently God wanted the fun-loving, free-spirited, sin-filled city to be destroyed.

These drastic views reflect a belief in a just world, or the conviction that in an orderly and fair world people should get what they rightly deserve (Lerner & Simmons, 1966; Lerner, 1980). Believers in a just world perceive that good individuals are rewarded and the bad suffer negative consequences. Furthermore, these punishments and rewards are not simply random acts of fate, but are directed towards those who warrant these outcomes. These persons may see victims of emergencies, disasters, and other misfortunes as deserving of their fate. Extreme views suggest that victims may have brought the negative consequences upon themselves.

Justice as a motivator is qualitatively different than other prosocial motivators (Tyler, Boeckmann, Smith, & Huo, 1997; Blader & Tyler, 2001). According to Blader and Tyler, the concept of justice prompts an individual to help in order to alleviate injustice, while empathy leads one to help when their emotions and psychological perspective match those of the victim(s). Justice and empathy are usually viewed as a two individual concepts that exert their own unique influence on prosocial behavior (Blader & Tyler, 2001). Empathetic responses are typically viewed on an individual level, where persons are finding connections and an emotional linkage between themselves and the victim. Justice commonly examines group-fairness and is usually identified as a motivator when the victim is perceived as a collective group of individuals rather than one person.

Consequently, the question exists as to why people are inclined to believe in a just world and use justice as a prosocial motivator? Lerner (1997) has associated belief in a just world to religiosity and views of immortality. The title of his manuscript appropriately addresses the fundamentals of this issue, *What does the belief in a just world protect us from: The dread of death or the fear of undeserved suffering?* One prominent Christian belief is that a life free of sin will be rewarded with an eternal life in heaven after death with God. This can be evidenced with the verse,*"For he wages of sin is death; but the gift of God is eternal life through Jesus Christ our Lord"*(Romans 6:23, KJV).

Conversely, others who support the view of a just world may simply believe in cause and effect relationships. For example, many persons have a difficult time perceiving their fate as a series of random events (Lerner & Simmons, 1966; Rubin & Peplau, 1975). These authors theorize that most find it hard to believe they have no control over the events in their lives; most want to assume that we have some command over our destiny. Therefore, people may presume that if they are good citizens their behavior will be rewarded. Others may trust that those who choose negligence and recklessness will be disciplined and given a punishment. Those who oppose this view may see these negative outcomes as unreasonable and undeserved (Rubin & Peplau, 1975). These individuals may actually perceive the world as being unjust and as a random series of events; they believe in the possibility that bad things happen to good people.

In sum, these theories just described make an attempt to provide a rational explanation for why people engage in prosocial, altruistic, helping behaviors. The previous section reviewed a variety of questions that all eventually lead to the same fundamental end point of helping. Is there a genetic code programmed into our DNA that elicits prosocial behavior? Is helping the product of an empathetic emotional reaction or is it the result of our own egotistic motives? Do we weigh the pros and cons of helping against one another to determine our actions? Or lastly, do we help because we hold the belief that the world is a fair and just place? All of these questions present probable explanations and but there is one clear fact: people do help. There is a portion of the population that makes the leap from intention to action, and ultimately reaches out to help.

Crossing the Barrier from Intention to Action

Life Span Development View

Theories of prosocial behaviors may be useful for understanding helping behaviors generally, but they do not consider an individual's age as a salient characteristic. Perhaps the motivation behind helping varies throughout the life span. Indeed, it seems likely that the motivations of a child may differ compared to those of an adolescent and older adult. This section focuses on age-related changes in helping and prosocial behaviors. Developmental theories associated with helping and other behaviors, such as short-term and long-term volunteering, are also discussed. We address the motivations and patterns of helping prominent in each age cohort. We also outline ways in which volunteer and other humanitarian organizations can increase prosocial activity across each age group.

It has been proposed that there is a cognitive or perceptual switch of helping behaviors from childhood to early adolescence. Cialdini, Kenriek, and Baumann

(1982) proposed a socialization model that can be applied to the psychology of helping. Cialdini and colleagues suggest that children go through a variety of stages, all of which can influence their motivations and their perceived value of helping. There are three primary stages that children go through, presocialization, awareness, and internalization. *Presocialization* is when children are simply not aware of the value of helping, nor do they realize that helping is associated with positive reinforcement. Young children may help purely as a way to spend time with their parent or a relative. Children during this period are can be considered passive helpers, meaning that they will act if prompted but helping will most likely not occur spontaneously. As a result, children under age 10 must usually be reminded to pick up their toys, clean their rooms, and help set the table for dinner. Positive associations with these helping behaviors are usually not acknowledged until they transition into the second stage of *awareness*. Cialdini and colleagues hypothesize that children transition to this stage between the ages of 10 and 12. During this awareness stage, children become increasingly aware that their parents, teachers, friends, and society value helping behavior. These pre-teenagers are more likely to initiate helping their parents, teachers, or friends, but only do so because they are eager to please. Children at this age clean their rooms so their father does not get mad, or may help put the groceries away in order to put a smile on their mother's face. They may also begin to realize that association between helping and reinforcements, such as allowance or various privileges. On the other hand, helping still appears to have no intrinsic reward during this stage; all of the benefits are primarily associated with outside reinforcements. Lastly, children are thought to transition to the *internalization* stage at around 15 or 16 years old. These adolescents help in order to gain self-satisfaction. Their motivation is internal and they usually help to satisfy a personal need, such as feeling good about themselves or gaining self-confidence.

Development of empathetic responses in second, fourth, and sixth grade children has been examined (Litvack-Miller, McDougall, & Romney, 1997). During their investigation, the researchers administered altruism questionnaires and a measure to assess each student's level of empathetic concern. The altruism questionnaires provided students with a vignette such as this abbreviated version, *One morning Chris was so late getting ready for school that he forgot to eat breakfast...he was really hungry at lunchtime...as he unwrapped his sandwich, he noticed a student sitting alone, who looked sad and hungry....he must have forgot his sandwich.* Students had to subsequently choose from three potential courses of action. Furthermore, they were provided actual opportunities to make monetary donations or to volunteer for a worthy cause. Results supported the view that those students with a greater empathetic concern were those most likely to help during both the altruism questionnaire and the real life opportunity. Second, this behavior increased with age, where the older students were significantly more likely to help and have empathetic concern than their younger counterparts.

From these views it can be assumed that as children mature there is a gradual change in their motivation for helping. Younger children appear to lack spontaneous motivations to help; they help when ordered and do not recognize external or internal rewards from their actions. Older children progressively realize the external associations with helping, such as pleasure and rewards from their parents. Eventually, children not only learn that their helping actions have external rewards but gain an internal benefit as well. These children realize that their actions impact their personal pride, confidence, and pleasure. Consequently, many adolescents engage in long-term helping behaviors, such as volunteering, in order to promote positive growth and reduce juvenile delinquency (Yates & Youniss, 1996). Previous researchers have further examined the relationship between self-perception and helping, and their results suggest that those adolescents who volunteer on a consistent basis show higher levels on confidence and self-esteem measures (Johnson, Beebe, Mortimer, & Snyder, 1998; Moore & Allen, 1996). A similar pattern of results is evident in middle-aged adult populations (Park, 2002). In sum, beginning in early adolescence and continuing on to middle adulthood, the general consensus is that prosocial behaviors are completed because of personal motives, such as self-improvement and self-esteem (Black & Kovacs, 1999; Omoto, Synder, & Martino, 2000).

Research into the motivations of volunteerism does not show a strong disparity across age until one reaches older adulthood. For older adults, the motivation behind helping appears to be more about remaining physically active while *doing good* for society, and less about satisfying their own personal needs (Choi, 2003; Tang, 2006). Twenty-three percent of older adults (65+) contribute to various humanitarian organizations (Bureau of Labor Statistics, 2007). It has been estimated that adults aged 65–74 volunteer approximately 6 hours per week, while those above age 75 average 4.4 hours (Fryock & Dorton, 1994; Kouri, 1990). Furthermore, when one directly compares the volunteer behavior of both younger and older adults, it is realized that while younger adults (25–36 years) may represent a larger segment of the volunteering population, older adults (65+ years) appear to be the more committed segment since they produce the most annual hours (Bureau of Labor Statistics, 2007). This finding may indicate that older adults, while only a small section of the volunteer population, are the most invested, reliable, and stable of all volunteer populations.

Hertzog and Morgan (1993) provide a comprehensive overview of the various predictors significantly associated with volunteerism and prosocial behavior in older adults. These factors include diverse demographic variables and resources such as religion, age, gender, income, educational attainment, marital status, and current level of physical functioning. In recent research paradigms, these factors were analyzed in two distinct populations of 6,465 and 3,617 older adults (Choi, 2003; Tang, 2006). Both of these research paradigms used a predictor model, which wanted to determine those factors most predictive of volunteerism in an older population. Results indicated that *importance of religion* and *church attendance* were prominent predictors of volunteerism in older adults. In addition, these results are related to similar research showing that older adults are more likely to act as mentors and counselors in religious organizations compared to younger adults (Morrow-Howell & Tang, 2003). *Physical health*, such as presence of chronic diseases and self-reported functioning, was also strongly associated with and predictive of volunteerism in older adults. This is highly important, since those most likely to volunteer are also probably the healthiest. *Education* and *income* served as additional predictors, where an increase in income and education levels was associated with an increase in volunteerism (Choi, 2003; Tang, 2006).

In sum, this literature provides important insight into the factors associated with prosocial behavior in older adults. This segment of the population appears to be a well-equipped and untapped resource for volunteer organizations. Despite the fact that older adults represent a smaller proportion of national volunteers, they appear to be among the most committed to and invested in prosocial efforts. In the future, organizations should make more of an effort to utilize this segment of the population. Tang (2006) presents some considerations and incentives that volunteer communities should offer in order to not only recruit but also ensure the safety of their older adult volunteers. First, it should be recognized that communities will benefit from these older adult volunteers, and thus barriers should be removed or minimized that inhibit this population from engaging in volunteer efforts. Tang further identifies these barriers as such factors like transportation and expenses incurred. Older adults may not be able to drive or lack the necessary funds to pay for the commute. It is also recommended that volunteer organizations should provide transportation vouchers, tax credits, as well as education credits for those older adults who consistently volunteer their time. Offering these rewards and being knowledgeable of age-related concerns may help eliminate factors that may initially prevent one from volunteering.

Disaster Helping Literature

Disasters bring out demonstrations of humanity in many individuals. Fritz and Williams (1957) state, "During the first few days or weeks following a major community-wide disaster, persons tend to act toward one another spontaneously, sympathetically, and sentimentally, on the basis of common needs rather than in terms of pre-disaster differences in social and economic status" (p. 48). Displays of altruistic behaviors become a prominent response following a disaster—communities come together, neighbors may meet one another for the first time. As Fritz and Williams imply, these humanitarian actions may transcend socioeconomic, age, gender, religious, and racial ties. However, there are several questions that researchers have attempted to answer during the time following a disaster. First, how do individuals personally change in response to a disaster? Second, what factors prompt a sizable portion of the population to help following a community-wide disaster? The answers to these questions provide insight into not only helping behaviors, but the uniqueness associated with a disaster, such as the events of September 11, 2001, the Asian Tsunamis of 2004, and the Gulf Coast storms in 2005.

Peterson and Seligman (2003) investigated personal character changes in individuals following the 9/11 terrorist attacks. Their research addressed the question, of whether there is any change on a personal level in response to a large scale, community disasters. While the attacks of 9/11 were associated to distinct communities, its effects were spread across the nation and worldwide. Researchers could not anticipate the onset of this event, and therefore those with pre-disaster data are highly limited. Peterson and Seligman (2003) had previously recruited 4,817 participants from across the United States (87%) and worldwide (13%) to complete a character measure, the VIA Inventory of Strengths (VIA-IS). Thus, their research population was not solely limited to participants in directly impacted regions. The VIA-IS is a measurement that assesses personal character strengths, such as hope, kindness, and persistence. The VIA-IS was completed 2 months prior to 9/11. Peterson and Seligman also asked participants to re-complete those measures in the months following the attacks. From the pre- and post-disaster scores, the authors were able to determine any character changes in their population. They found seven primary character strength increases in their population: gratitude, hope, kindness, leadership, love, spirituality, and teamwork. These strengths demonstrated a significant increase across participants in the 2 months following 9/11 and were still elevated (to a lesser extent) during the 10-month follow-up assessment. These results provide insight into the motives behind why people may help in the aftermath of significant disasters. Petersen and Seligman did not assess levels of prosocial behaviors, but one may conclude that an increase in volunteerism could be related to personal character changes.

Further research into the motives behind helping following 9/11 has also been conducted and results have linked altruism with personal identification to the victims (Beyerlein & Sikkink, 2008). These findings appear to be consistent with the empathy–altruism view of prosocial behavior, where those most likely to help are those who develop an empathetic response toward the victim. Beyerlein and Sikkink demonstrated that their participants formed a personal connection with the victims in drastically different ways. Some individuals felt a strong connection because they actually knew someone who was killed or in danger of being killed during the attacks. Others identified with the victims through media coverage and social events, like candlelight vigils and community prayer sessions. The authors put forth the notion that the emotions expressed following 9/11 prompted individuals to reflect upon their lives and develop a strong connection to the victims, which eventually lead to volunteering for 9/11 relief efforts. In sum, these authors conclude that a strong emotional reaction was likely the key component to altruistic behavior following this specific disaster.

While the circumstances behind 9/11 were fundamentally different than those surrounding Hurricanes Katrina and Rita, there are some underlying similarities between the two events. Both produced extreme levels of devastation and led to an overwhelming emergence of prosocial behavior. In accordance with the majority of disasters, neither of these events was completely anticipated and each received dramatic national coverage. The mass media portrayed both events as utterly devastating and dominated news outlets for significant periods of time. Although the causes of disasters were diverse (man-made versus naturalistic), these disasters produced dramatic destruction and impacted sizeable number of communities. Based on these factors, one should presume that investigations into prosocial behavior after disasters follow one comprehensive and unified set of goals.

Research following Hurricane Katrina has identified *personal responsibility* as a major factor linked with volunteerism (Michel, 2007). This research recruited participants from areas near the capitol of Baton Rouge, which is approximately 80 miles from New Orleans. Baton Rouge was a major triage center following the landfall of Hurricane Katrina (see Cherry, Chapter 9). Approximately 204 participants were asked to complete a personal responsibility assessment by providing a Likert scale answer to the question,"*I have a responsibility to use my time to help those affected by Hurricane Katrina.*" Michel (2007) also assessed the volunteer activity in response to Hurricane Katrina. Using a regression analysis, Michel's study examined the link between personal responsibility and actual volunteer hours. Almost 93% of persons stated that they felt some level of personal responsibility to use their time to help those affected by the disaster. After controlling for demographic variables such as age, gender, educational attainment, and religion, the results produced a significant link between perceived level of personal responsibility, religious attendance, and volunteer hours in the days following Hurricane Katrina. Therefore, this study provides evidence suggesting that personal attributes, such as feeling personally responsible, can accurately predict altruistic behaviors. These results relate with those provided by Peterson and Seligman (2003) following the attacks of 9/11.

In sum, research following a disaster can be highly difficult to conduct due to the unpredictability of the event and the chaos of the aftermath. Those researchers that have carried out such investigations have consistently found that helping behaviors are apparent in the days and weeks following the event. Even so, there is much we do not about when and why individuals help or do not help following a disaster.

Helping Others in the Aftermath of a Natural Disaster: Findings from the Louisiana Healthy Aging Study

When Hurricanes Katrina and Rita hit the Gulf Coast region in 2005, the Louisiana Healthy Aging Study (LHAS) had a rare opportunity to assess the influence of the storms on cognitive and physical functioning in adults who ranged in age from their twenties to over ninety years old. The first findings from the LHAS hurricane study are reported elsewhere (see Cherry, Galea, & Silva, 2008; Cherry, et al., 2009; Cherry et al., Chapter 9). Marks, Cherry, and Silva (Chapter 10) report initial findings from qualitative analyses of responses concerning how participants' religious beliefs and practices helped them cope with Hurricanes Katrina and Rita and their aftermath. We found that "Helping Others" was clearly a dominant theme in this team-based qualitative analysis, which prompted our in-depth focus on the individual level psychology of helping. In the sections that follow, we discuss four data-based themes which relate to the central concern of "helping others." The themes are presented in turn, along with primary data excerpts from the participants' interviews for illustration.

Theme 1: Reports of "Being Helped"

Very few participants discussed help they received, so this first theme has less supporting data than the other themes. Thus, it is listed as a counterpoint, a striking non-finding. Perhaps in a country that values independence above almost all else, it can be highly difficult to discuss receiving assistance. This may be even more so when dealing particularly with life's basic needs, such as food, water, shelter, or clothing. Two of the rare narratives that *were* shared with us by one woman involved being helped in emotional and spiritual ways versus receiving tangible assistance. She first recalled:

> **HKR 7**, *38 years:* I just vividly [remember] in my mind…a family from one of the hardest hit areas outside of Grand Isle….. They came…about a week or two after the hurricane and sang at our church….. [T]hey lost everything. I mean they lost every picture…*everything*. I am going to cry just thinking about because it makes me feel [so sad for them]…[but] she was there trying to make us feel better and she had nothing….. Still to this day, [I remember thinking that day], "You are here and you lost everything and you are singing praises to the Lord."

The same woman also reported an experience during the Katrina aftermath that she interpreted in a way that meant a great deal to her.

> **HKR 7**, *38 years*: I just felt like the Lord lead me to this little old lady who was waiting in line [at the store] and she had her grandson [with her]. She had lost her home…she was from New Orleans and lost her home. And in 1994, [she] lost her husband…[but] she said, with joy in her heart, "God closes one door and opens another." [S]he said, " Now I am blessed everyday day to be with my [two-year old] grandson…I am home with him everyday…" [I]t was just a real testament to her strength. [Also, when he was still a little boy] her [now grown] son…was in coma and…there was nothing [they could] do, [but] her son ended up living and now is…the head of [a department] at [a large hospital]. [The lady said], "God saved him so that he can save all these others." …It was just a real dramatic thing just in the grocery store…God led me to her.

In both of the above narratives, this woman describes being lifted and helped by the example and attitude of persons who had lost far more than she did in Katrina. However, similar stories of being "helped" were exceptionally rare among our participants.

Theme 2: Pride Through Association with a Faith Community

One recurring theme in our data was the tendency of participants to express pride in their specific church's involvement in helping those affected by Hurricane Katrina. Of these participants, many offered the specific names of their faith communities.

Interestingly, most of those who explicitly drew attention to their faith communities also admitted that they were not involved in assisting in a hands-on manner. (Related statements are italicized for emphasis.)

> **HKR 111**, *53 years:* My church played a very active role [helping Katrina victims]. It's [church name and denomination] downtown.... My church played a very active role in feeding, clothing and housing and they were a distribution point for a lot of FEMA supplies coming in. They were kind of the central point for trucks coming and other trucks coming out. *I did not participate in that...but I was very proud to know that was happening.* Then they also used a lot of the Sunday school classrooms for schooling for the evacuees so I just thought [that] was just fabulous. *So I was very proud of my church. Even though I had nothing to do with it.*
> **HKR 2**, *32 years:* I was very...happy with my church's response to the situation. My husband and I were both just (so involved) with our jobs...that *we weren't really able to volunteer but it helped to know that the church that we belong to, that we give money to, [was] helping....* They housed different people at the church, so it helped to know that we were a part of that...
> **HKR 9**, *42 years:* I just don't know how people could get through that without his help. That's all I can say.... I know that the church that we are members of, *they* were very helpful with people who needed help and that sort of thing.
> **HKR 11**, *27 years:* [My] church was very supportive, collecting clothes, and food, and giving shelter and offering prayer services...and they had a blood drive.
> **HKR 13**, *46 years:* [T]he young men [from my church] would go out there [to the hard hit areas], and they would...pick a neighborhood, go down the street, cut trees down off people's houses. And [people would] say, "Let us pay you." "No," the young men said, "We're doing God's work." And they would just go through [and help] and people were just amazed. [S]o our church really did [a lot]...

One person who referred to her specific church, also readily acknowledged the efforts of other churches as well. She reported:

> **HKR 118**, *49 years:* Well, I am [denomination] and the church we belong to helped out. [But]...it [was] all the churches; it wasn't just ours. All the churches opened the churches and their families and their houses if they could. Everything was opened up to everybody. Almost all the churches around here [helped out].

Individuals are often deemed "guilty by association" due to questionable company they keep. It seems that we are seeing a converse principle in action, a kind of "exoneration by association." Exonerated from what?: the charge of doing nothing to help those who desperately needed it. From a psychological vantage, the pattern in the above statements is an interesting one. Although no questions explicitly addressed the question, participants repeatedly reported the involvement and efforts of "their" churches and the pride and happiness they took in this involvement, in spite of a lack of personal, firsthand contribution. This pattern leads us to a closely related theme, that of ethics and intentions.

Theme 3: The Road Paved with Good Intentions, Noble Phrases, and Ethics

Some of our participants referred specifically to their desire to help. Likewise, many of our participants pontificated on what we "should" and "ought" to do in situations like Hurricanes Katrina and Rita. Here are several examples:

> **HKR 203**, *82 years:* ...[We need] to be caring individuals, to love one another, and to also try to help take care of one another. And I think when...you have people who care, then that helps you through these trying times. Now we have brought that [kind of spirit] together into organizations—our institutions of churches. And [because of] them, we have better unified, organized [ways] to help people out....
>
> **HKR 303**, *92 years:* [You should] be willing and able to help your neighbor if he's in trouble or needs help. Share what you have.... It's the old saying, "You are your brother's keeper."
>
> **HKR 109**, *59 years:* My personal philosophy is that each of us is suppose to live with virtue for virtue's sake, and try to do the best you can and help your fellow man when you can and do what is right.
>
> **HKR 118**, *49 years*: [M]y beliefs were always...help when you can help. Always help others and we have always done that. I guess you do it more when there is a disaster.
>
> **HKR 212**, *65 years:* My religion has taught me to help people [and that] you are supposed to help people no matter what or what circumstances.
>
> **HKR 213**, *78 years:* I think that as humans on this earth, we are to help our fellow men...when and where we can.

With these things noted, we move to the final theme—one that focuses on those who *did* cross the canyon, so to speak, to offer their tangible assistance.

Theme 4: Bridging the Belief-to-Behavior Gap

We now turn our attention to some individuals who did bridge the "belief-to-behavior gap" by converting positive ethics and intentions into action.

> **HKR 2**, *32 years:* I had always wondered what difference one person could make and in this situation it showed me that I do have some impact on other people. And it was very strange because I would get up in the mornings and I thought, "Oh gosh. I have got to find housing for this person and this person and this person. I can't do this by myself! No one else has a clue. Nobody has a clue. The State doesn't have a clue. What am I supposed to do?" [But things seemed to work out]...So it strengthened me.
>
> **HKR 5**, *31 years:* In situations like Hurricane Katrina, [that's] where the rubber meets the road. You either say what you believe and then do something to show [it and] your actions meet up with that—or you just say a bunch of stuff and do the opposite. And I think that knowing what I believe and the hope that I have, it kind of just makes you only want to share that and give that hope to someone else. I feel like we didn't have a whole lot of damage to our house so we were able to not have to spend any time fixing up our stuff and taking care of our needs. *We were able to just go right out and help others and minister to them.*
>
> **HKR 15**, *39 years:* [A]fter the storms...the main thing that I can see that actually has come out of it for me is...it has been a humbling experience and it has changed my life in a way that I really can't even explain. [H]elping [other] people, that [is what] helped me to cope.... I took on so much other stuff helping other people [that] it kind of drowned out what I was going through and God fixed it. So while I was trying to fix somebody else['s

situation], God was fixing *mine*. I...just continued to stay in prayer and helped those that needed help [and in the process, God helped me].

HKR 116, *52 years:* [After Katrina] I realized that there would be people that would never find their family members, you know. When you go to those [emergency] sites and see how many people were looking for [family and loved ones]... and the more that you talk to people at the shelters and see their eyes and [and their faces] and [see] what they are going through, [the less you think about your own worries].

HKR 213, *78 years:* I tried to help people, those people who were hurting. The most...the thing that I felt that I could do at my stage in life was to help them through feeding them and helping to clothe them. I sorted clothes by sizes, and then I served them..... I felt that I...I felt that I was contributing.

HKR 312, *91 years:* I [gave] them the last dollar I had to buy food. It was even more than what I got in the house. I don't want to see them hungry. That's the only thing I know to do. That's the only [help I could give]....People can help you, but they can't do for you what God can do.

We suspect that some of the more dramatic stories of human kindness were ***not*** told. Perhaps, such stories are veiled by simple, laconic phrases like these two:

HKR 101, *62 years:* [We] do the best we can to help...each other.
HKR 110, *49 years:* We have done what we can to try to help people...and that's pretty much it.

In summary, we learned a handful of lessons from our participants. First, these people were not anxious to discuss ways in which they had received assistance. Second, many participants were anxious to express pride through association with their churches—even when they had little or no firsthand role personally. Third, many participants spontaneously discussed the abstract importance of helping "brothers and sisters." Fourth, most struggled to convert their personal ethics and intentions into deliberate action. Those of us on-site in Louisiana who lived through that time will not judge them too harshly, as we recollect our own pain, grief, and disbelief in the aftermath of Hurricanes Katrina and Rita. Finally, while we must acknowledge that while most of our participants were not heroic in the face of these challenges, a select few *were* remarkable helpers. As a group of participants from across the adult life span, there is much we can learn, both in terms of human tendency and in terms of human potential in the face of a natural disaster.

Conclusion

We opened this chapter with a selective literature review of the psychology of helping with coverage of topics and theories of the origins of prosocial behaviors. This chapter also documented the gradual, developmental progression of age-related, altruistic motivations. We addressed issues specific to a disaster by discussing prospective studies from 9/11 and Hurricanes Katrina and Rita. Qualitative data from LHAS participants who experienced the aftermath of Hurricanes Katrina and Rita yielded four central lessons, as follows. From Theme 1, we learned that the participants in our study were reluctant to mention, much less discuss, receiving assistance in the aftermath of the hurricanes. In Theme 2, we were reminded that faith communities and organizations were active players in post-hurricane help efforts. Most of the LHAS participants reported a religious affiliation and many of those were quick to draw attention to help that their church had provided, while confessing that they had done little or nothing themselves—a pattern we called "exoneration by association." In Theme 3, we illustrated that many of the participants spontaneously addressed the ethic of helping others, as well as their intentions to put those ethics into action—indicating that the psychological dilemmas regarding who, how, and when to help (as discussed in our review of literature) were very real to them. Theme 4 illustrated two realities. First, that most of the ethics and intentions aimed at helping others were not converted into action. Second, however, a few persons did bridge the belief-to-behavior gap by helping in significant ways—even to the point of a woman giving her last dollar. In closing, we learn from our participants that people often fail to meet their own standards in helping after a crisis. Yet, if some are not as noble as we might hope…some exceed our expectations and present new possibilities.

Acknowledgment We thank Tracey Frias, Miranda Melancon, and Zia McWilliams for their assistance with data summary and qualitative analyses. We also thank Erin C. Goforth for her helpful comments on an earlier version of this manuscript.

This research was supported by grants from the Louisiana Board of Regents through the Millennium Trust Health Excellence Fund (HEF[2001-06]-02) and the National Institute on Aging P01 AG022064. This support is gratefully acknowledged.

References

Axelrod, R. (1984). *The evolution of cooperation*. New York: Basic Books.
Batson, C. D., & Coke, J. S. (1981). Empathy: A source of altruistic motivation for helping? In P. Rushton & R. M. Sorrentino (Eds.), *Altruism and helping behavior: Social, personality, and developmental perspectives* (pp. 167–187). Hillsdale, NJ: Erlbaum.
Batson, C. D., Duncan, B. D., Ackerman, P., Buckley, T., & Birch, K. (1981). Is empathic emotion a source of altruistic motivation? *Journal of Personality and Social Psychology, 40*, 290–302.
Batson, C. D., Fultz, J., & Schoenrade, P. (1987). Distress and empathy: Two qualitatively distinct vicarious emotions with different motivational consequences. *Journal of Personality, 55*, 19–39.
Beyerlein, K., & Sikkink, D. (2008). Sorrow and solidarity: Why Americans volunteered for 9/11 relief efforts. *Social Problems, 55*, 190–215.
Black, B., & Kovacs, P. J. (1999). Age-related variation in roles performed by hospice volunteers. *Journal of Applied Gerontology, 18*, 479–497.
Blader, S. L., & Tyler, T. R. (2001). Justice and empathy: What motivates people to help others? In M. Ross & D. T. Miller (Eds.), *The justice motive in everyday life* (pp. 226–250). New York: Cambridge University Press.
Bowlby, J. (1969). *Attachment and loss* (Vol. I). London: Hogarth.
Bowlby, J. (1988). *A secure base: Clinical applications of attachment theory*. London: Routledge Press.
Brosnan, S. F., & de Waal, F. B. M. (2002). Approximate perspective on reciprocal altruism. *Human Nature, 13*, 129–152.
Bureau of Labor Statistics. (2007). *Volunteering in the United States, 2007*. Retrieved September 30, 2008, from, http://www.bls.gov/news.release/volun.nr0.htm
Burnstein, E., Crandall, C., & Kitayama, S. (1994). Some neo-Darwinian decision rules for altruism: Weighing cues for inclusive fitness as a function of the biological importance of the decision. *Journal of Personality and Social Psychology, 67*, 773–789.

Cherry, K. E., Galea, S., & Silva, J. L. (2008). Successful aging and natural disasters: Role of adaptation and resiliency in late life. In M. Hersen & A. M. Gross (Eds.), *Handbook of clinical psychology* (Vol. 1, pp 810–833). New Jersey: John Wiley & Sons, Inc.

Cherry, K. E., Galea, S., Su, L. J., Welsh, D. A., Jazwinski, S. M., Silva, J. L., et al. (2009). Cognitive and psychosocial consequences of Hurricanes Katrina and Rita on middle aged, older, and oldest-old adults in the Louisiana Healthy Aging Study (LHAS). *Journal of Applied Social Psychology* (in press).

Choi, L. H. (2003). Factors affecting volunteerism among older adults. *The Journal of Applied Gerontology, 22,* 179–196.

Cialdini, R. B., Baumann, D. J., & Kenrick, D. T. (1981). Insights from sadness: A three-step model of the development of altruism as hedonism. *Developmental Review, 1,* 207–223.

Cialdini, R. B., Kenriek, D. X., & Baumann, D. J. (1982). Effects of mood on prosocial behavior in children and adults. In N. Eisenberg (Ed.), *The development of prosocial behavior* (pp.339–359). New York: Academic Press.

Cialdini, R. B., Schaller, M., Houlihan, D., Arps, K., Fultz, J., & Beaman, A. (1987). Empathy-based helping: Is it selflessly or selfishly motivated? *Journal of Personality and Social Psychology, 52,* 749–758.

Coke, J. S., Batson, C. D., & McDavis, K. (1978). Empathic mediation of helping: A two-stage model. *Journal of Personality and Social Psychology, 36,* 752–766.

Cunningham, M. R., Jegerski, J., Gruder, C. L., & Barbee, A. P. (1995). *Helping in different social relationships: Charity begins at home.* Unpublished manuscript, University of Louisville.

Dovidio, J. F., Piliavin, J. A., Schroeder, D. A., & Penner, L. A. (2006). *The social psychology of prosocial behavior.* New Jersey: Lawrence Erlbaum.

Eisenberg, N., & Fabes, R. A. (1998). Prosocial development. *Handbook of child psychology* (5th ed., Vol. 3, pp. 701–778). New York: Wiley and Sons.

Fryock, C. D., & Dorton, A. M. (1994). *Unretirement: A career guide for the retired...the soon-to be retired...the never-want-to-be retired.* New York: American Management Assoc.

Fultz, J., Bateon, C. D., Fortenbach, V. A., McCarthy, P. M., & Varoey, L. L. (1986). Social evaluation and the empathy-altruism hypothesis. *Journal of Personality and Social Psychology, 50,* 761–769.

Fritz, C., & Williams, H. 1957. The human being in disasters: A research perspective. *Annals of the American Academy of Political and Social Science, 309,* 42–51.

Hamilton, W. D. (1963). The evolution of altruistic behavior. *American Naturalist, 97,* 354–356.

Hamilton, W. D. (1964). The genetical evolution of social behaviour: I and II. *Journal of Theoretical Biology, 7,* 1–16 and 17–52.

Harris, M. B., Benson, S. B., & Hall, C. L. (1975). The effects of confession on altruism. *Journal of Social Psychology, 96,* 187–192.

Hedge, A., & Yousif, Y. H. (1992). Effects of urban size, urgency, and cost on helpfulness: A cross-cultural comparison between the United Kingdom and the Sudan. *Journal of Cross-Cultural Psychology, 23,* 107–115.

Hertzog, A. R., & Morgan, J. S. (1993). Formal volunteer work among older Americans. In S. A. Bass, F. G. Caro, & Y. P. Chen (Eds.), *Achieving a productive aging society* (pp. 119–12). Westport, CT: Auburn House Press.

Hood, K. E., Greenberg, G., & Tobach, E. (1995). *Behavioral development: Concepts of approach-withdrawal and integrative levels. The T. C. Schneirla Conference Series,* Vol. 5. New York: Garland.

Indiana University Center on Philanthropy. (2007). Giving in the aftermath of the gulf coast hurricanes. Retrieved on September 29, 2008, from, http://foundationcenter.org/gainknowledge/research/pdf/katrina_report_2007.pdf

Johnson, K., Beebe, M. T., Mortimer, J. T., & Snyder, M. (1998). Volunteerism in adolescence: A process perspective. *Journal of Research on Adolescence, 8,* 309–332.

Kouri, M. K. (1990). *Volunteerism and older adults.* Santa Barbara, CA: ABC-CLIO Press.

Latané, B., & Darley, J. (1970). *The unresponsive bystander: Why doesn't he help?* New York: Appleton-Century-Crofts Press.

Lerner, M. J. (1980). *The belief in a just world: A fundamental delusion.* New York: Plenum.
Lerner, M. J. (1997). What does the belief in a just world protect us from: The dread of death or the fear of understanding suffering? *Psychological Inquiry, 8,* 29.
Lerner, M. J., & Simmons, C. H. (1966). The observer's reaction to the 'innocent victim': Compassion or rejection? *Journal of Personality and Social Psychology, 4,* 203–210.
Litvack-Miller, W., McDougall, D., & Romney, D. M. (1997). The structure of empathy during middle childhood and its relationship to prosocial behaviour. *Genetic, Social and General Psychology Monographs, 123,* 303–325.
Madsen, E. A., Richard, J., Fieldman, G., Plotkin, H. C., Dunbar, R. I. M., Richardson, J., et al. (2007). Kinship and altruism: A cross-cultural study. *British Journal of Psychology, 98,* 339–359.
Michel, L. (2007). Personal responsibility and volunteering after a natural disaster: The case of hurricane Katrina. *Sociological Spectrum, 27,* 633–652.
Moore, C. W., & Allen, J. P. (1996). The effects of volunteering on the young volunteer. *The Journal of Primary Prevention, 17,* 231–258.
Morrow-Howell, N., & Tang, F. (2003). *Elder service and youth service in comparative perspective: Nature, activities, and impacts.* St. Louis, MO: Washington University, Center for Social Development [Working paper].
Omoto, A. M., Synder, M., & Martino, S. C. (2000). Volunteerism and the life course: Investing age-related agendas for action. *Basic and Applied Social Psychology, 22,* 181–197.
Park, G. J. (2002). Factors influencing the meaning of life for middle-aged women. *Korean Journal of Women's Health Nursing, 2,* 232–243.
Peterson, C., & Seligman, M. E. P. (2003). Character strengths before and after September 11. *Psychological Science, 14,* 381–384.
Piliavin, J., Dovidio, J. F., Gaertner, S. L., & Clark, R. (1981). *Emergency intervention.* New York: Academic Press.
Pyszczynski, T., Solomon, S., & Greenburg, J. (2003). *In the wake of 9/11: The psychology of terror.* Washington, DC: American Psychological Association.
Rapoport, A., & Chammah, A. M. (1965). *Prisoner's dilemma.* Ann Arbor: University of Michigan Press.
Ridley, M. (2003). *Nature via nurture: Genes, experience, and what makes us human.* New York: Harper Collins Press.
Rubin, Z., & Peplau, L. A. (1975). Who believes in a just world? *Journal of Social Issues, 31,* 65–89.
Schaller, M., & Cialdini, R. B. (1988). The economics of empathic helping: Support for a mood management motive. *Journal of Experimental Social Psychology, 24,* 163–181.
Tang, F. (2006). What resources are needed for volunteerism? A life course perspective. *The Journal of Applied Gerontology, 25,* 375–390.
Toi, M., & Batson, C. D. (1982). More evidence that empathy is a source of altruistic motivation. *Journal of Personality and Social Psychology, 43,* 281–292.
Trivers, R. L. (1971). The evolution of reciprocal altruism. *Quarterly Review of Biology, 46,* 35–57.
Trivers, R. L. (1983). The evolution of cooperation. In D. L. Bridgeman (Ed.), *The nature of prosocial development.* New York: Academic Press.
Tyler, T. R., Boeckmann, R. J., Smith, H. J., & Huo, Y. J. (1997). *Social justice in a diverse society.* Boulder: Westview.
Wallach, M. A., & Wallach, L. (1983). *Psychology is sanction for selfishness: The error of egoism in theory and therapy.* New York: W.H. Freeman and Company.
Wilkinson, G. S. (1984). Reciprocal food sharing in the vampire bat. *Nature, 308,* 181–184.
Yates, M., & Youniss, J. (1996). A developmental perspective on community service in adolescence. *Social Development, 5,* 85–115.

Chapter 12
Building a Disaster Mental Health Response to a Catastrophic Event: Louisiana and Hurricane Katrina

Anthony H. Speier, Joy D. Osofsky, and Howard J. Osofsky

Abstract The psychological impact of a catastrophic event is complex and is often not well understood by either response personnel or persons directly impacted by the incident. Catastrophic events by their very nature are outside of normal experience and thus, their psychological force is often miscalculated. This miscalculation can directly influence how behavioral health personnel are utilized in disaster response operations. This chapter examines the preparation for natural disasters (hurricanes) in Louisiana since 1992 (Hurricane Andrew) through the more recent emergency planning and response activities associated with Hurricane Katrina. The role of behavioral health agencies and professionals in becoming an integral component of the emergency response infrastructure is examined within the context of the Hurricane Katrina emergency response operations. Our experience delivering crisis interventions services to first responders, children, and survivors in a variety of settings underscores the importance of preparing behavioral health workers with the skills for utilizing standard crisis response protocols including the ability to recognize the symptoms of psychological trauma. Behavioral health disaster operations planning represents an ongoing strategy which is now emerging as a core component of state and national planning, response, and deployment tactics.

Introduction

In the best of literary tradition, the phrase often associated with New Orleans is "the City that Care Forgot" (Tinker, 1953). This phrase certainly engenders a somewhat romantic notion associated with a sense of invulnerability, an acceptance of life as is, and where the best of all solutions to life's adversities may, for some, be found in the drink made famous in New Orleans, The Hurricane.

A.H. Speier (✉)
Deputy Assistant Secretary, Quality and Accountability, Office of Mental Health, Baton Rouge, LA 70821, USA
e-mail: anthony.speier@la.gov

Implicit in this fictional response strategy is the timing of response...slow and easy... things happen, all can be taken care of in its own good time. Romantic fantasy where the world moves at the pace we desire and consequences are not to be taken too seriously. An excerpt from a newspaper article preceding the arrival of Hurricane Georges in 1998 illustrates the point:

> New Orleans knows what a direct hit means. In 1969, Hurricane Camille swept through the region, taking 30 or so lives, and everyone here is talking about Camille and Betsy, her equally destructive sister.
> But life goes on. The hotel bar is packed ahead of the 6 p.m. curfew and the hotel notice board announces that a wedding was due to take place yesterday night.
> People are getting used to Georges. My wife even wants to name our unborn child after him. (Thornton, 1998).

The above notion of a slow and stress-free hurricane response strategy makes for great fiction. Fortunately, it represents a very different reality than our actual hurricane response. The acknowledging and acting on the distinction between what we may wish or hope happens and what, in the light of day, is the harsh reality of physical destruction, trauma, and catastrophic loss is the universal challenge facing emergency response authorities throughout the nation.

Throughout this chapter we will attempt to illustrate through our experiences in state-level and community-level disaster planning a variety of roles which behavioral health agencies and mental health professionals may be called upon to perform during a disaster response operation. Emergency response planning is a broad topic, which encompasses just about every aspect of government at the local, state, and federal levels. Traditionally, behavioral health interventions occur sometime after the initial disaster incident as survivors of the incident begin having symptoms associated with difficulty coping with the aftermath of the disaster and recovery process. As mental health professionals living and working within an area of the United States at high risk for numerous natural disasters, we have normalized disaster preparedness and response within our routine repertoire of professional and personal activities. However, all disaster incidents are unique and bring their own set of situational demands. Hurricane Katrina as a catastrophic event demonstrated how intense can be the immediate need for a broad spectrum of immediate behavioral health interventions. The typical "response" time associated with a disaster incident is 72 h, after which emergency operations evolve into a "recovery" operations. Throughout this chapter we will illustrate a broad spectrum of emergency "response" operations when the "response" phase of the disaster involves mass casualties, mass trauma exposure, and an incident duration of months instead of days.

Preparation and Response

The importance of preparing behavioral health workers with trauma-focused knowledge and skills for intervening with standard crisis response protocols, the ability to recognize the signs and symptoms of reactions to significant trauma exposure, knowledge of when to obtain consultation and/or referral for additional services, establishment of needed referrals and communication links, and staying "mission-focused" in the here and now represented the basic elements of mounting a successful response strategy. The uniqueness of the incident results in the necessity of responding to unexpected situations, each with its own challenges and exposure risks.

Building an effective response strategy is a long-term endeavor. In Louisiana, hurricane response planning has been ongoing for many years. Behavioral health response planning began as a serious enterprise with the aftermath of Hurricane Andrew, 1992, but really gained full governmental support following the massive evacuations associated with Hurricane Georges, 1998. Louisiana was fortunate as Georges skirted the edge of the state making landfall on the Mississippi coast as a Category 2 storm. The state had mounted a successful evacuation at many levels, but lessons learned from the incident indicated the need for more effective evacuation strategies, especially for those with need for medical and ongoing caregiver support. Many residents experienced 12 h evacuation trips from New Orleans to Baton Rouge, these long trips to travel less than 100 miles were particularly difficult for the frail elderly causing undue hardships, two deaths, and seriously compromised the health of many evacuees. The City (New Orleans) did survive a direct hit, making it even more difficult for emergency response personnel to convince residents to evacuate. In 1999, the State initiated emergency planning strategies for activating the 12,000 employees of the Department of Health and Hospitals to assist with the health care of evacuees in what has become known today as Medical Special Needs Shelters (MSNS). Louisiana was hurricane free until October 3, 2002 when Hurricane Lilli hit the coast. The storm, predicted to be of Category 4 intensity, made landfall along the central Louisiana coast as a Category 2 storm. Again the residents of New Orleans felt that they had dodged another major storm, and while the threat was acknowledged, the city would yet again, survive.

In the ensuing years between Hurricanes Georges, Lilli, and Katrina, the state mounted a persistent effort in emergency response preparation. Working in partnership with federal agencies evacuation, transportation, sheltering and health-care plans were developed and practiced. In the year prior to the arrival of Hurricane Katrina, State and Federal authorities implemented a massive planning effort named Hurricane Pam. (Innovative Emergency Management, 2004). With respect to the National Response Plan Emergency Support Function#8– Public Health and Medical Services Annex, the Louisiana Department of Health and Hospitals trained its 12,000 employees as an emergency response workforce for duty in a variety of response and relief roles, most notably supporting mass evacuation and medical special needs sheltering duties. The behavioral health response organized the resources of the office of addictive disorders, developmental disabilities, and mental health. Staff were trained in basic supportive counseling techniques and stress management strategies. Each office developed "call-list" organizing the workforce into response teams with specific duties which could be mobilized to different response sites and shelters as needed

During the 2005 hurricane season, the State Mental Health Authority was ready to evacuate state hospitals in response to Hurricane Dennis in July, 2005 and had activated disaster response plans several times in recent months. As discussed above, in the week preceding Hurricane Katrina, State and Federal agencies completed a simulation exercise, "Hurricane Pam" which involved the evacuation and sheltering of 300,000 residents of the greater New Orleans area. The exercise included many of the strategies utilized in the evacuation and rescue operations implemented in response to Hurricane Katrina. These included the activation of Search and Rescues Operations Bases (SARBOs), Temporary Medical Observation Staging Areas (TMOSA), and a network of general and special needs shelters. The simulated evacuation strategies included the systematic search and removal of persons from New Orleans who did not evacuate before the storm and the systematic triage and deployment to either general or special needs shelters. Behavioral health staff performed roles throughout the exercise as shelter staff and crisis counselors at all of the disaster response sites. Additional roles played by behavioral health staff included an operational presence at the various command centers operated by the Office of Emergency Preparedness and the Office of Public Health. Primary behavioral health duties included supportive counseling, resource management, staff and patient evacuation, resource deployment and consultation to disaster operations at the state, regional, and local levels throughout this disaster incident.

The limitations of disaster preparedness exercises and planning strategies are the absence of the actual disaster incident. Although well planned, the exercises cannot approximate the intensity, uncertainty, and emotional upheaval of the actual event. Planning only exposes staff in a general sense, to the types of locations and intervention strategies that will in most cases be experienced.

With respect to Hurricane Katrina, the hurricane was not the initial problem. It seemed as if it were a "normal" storm, it was the levies breaking and the ensuing flooding of the city that overwhelmed our response capabilities. No one could imagine the massive devastation that was to follow. Hurricane Katrina made landfall east of Plaquemines parish around 6:49 a.m. as a Category 4 storm. Below is a description of the strength of Hurricane Katrina from a national weather advisory at 6:00 a.m., minutes before the storm made landfall;

> ...EXTREMELY DANGEROUS CATEGORY FOUR HURRICANE KATRINA PREPARING TO MOVE ONSHORE NEAR SOUTHERN PLAQUEMINES PARISH LOUISIANA......HURRICANE-FORCE WIND GUSTS OCCURRING OVER MOST OF SOUTHEASTERN LOUISIANA...IN THE NEW ORLEANS METROPOLITAN AREA...AND AS FAR EAST AS THE CHANDELEUR ISLANDS... (National Weather Service, 2007)

Initial Response: The First Wave of Emergency Responding

Within hours following landfall, emergency operations staff were told to expect numerous helicopters and ambulances transporting nursing home residents who had been rescued from flooded facilities. The federal resources were still 24 h away and we (local triage response staff) were just a few Office of Public Health and Office of Mental Health workers trying to craft together a Temporary Medical Operations and Staging Area (TMOSA), which is a temporary shelter/medical triage center for an unknown number of evacuees. We had only a few cots, secured 70 mattresses from a state hospital over 100 miles away, and bedding and towels from a forensic facility 40 miles away. Our other resource was card board flats for people to lie on. Once survivors began arriving in the early morning hours we were quickly overwhelmed with survivors, nursing home staff, and other caregivers who had been in flood waters and in transport for many hours. The survivors were exhausted, weak, and many in shock. The medical teams did an extraordinary job attending to survivor needs. The minimal number of behavioral health staff began organizing volunteers and provided services based on an adaptation of Psychological First Aid (Brymer et al., 2006; Vernberg et al., 2008) to hundreds of persons within the first 24 h. Over the next 48 h the original makeshift site was rapidly transformed into a first-class triage and receiving center. Various federal medical teams and the National Guard established order and a standard routine for admitting, screening, and treating the survivors.

It was in this collegiate basketball arena, where almost all who were now present as workers or volunteers, had spent many an exciting time cheering the LSU basketball teams, that thousands of evacuees were brought from across South Louisiana and the New Orleans area, to be triaged, then admitted to the floor or assigned to other shelters or hospitals throughout Louisiana and neighboring states (see Cherry, Chapter 9). Most of these citizens were transported by coach or helicopter, while others were brought by family members and left at the facility so that other family members could evacuate more easily to their intended destinations. During the days that the LSU PMAC served as a TMOSA, over 40,000 people were seen, and about 5,000 were admitted to the facility. Some stays were for a few hours, while others were in the facility for several days before a suitable placement could be found. Ultimately, various newspaper and federal reports indicated that over 270,000 persons were housed in shelter setting and an additional 616,000 were temporarily placed in hotels (Special Report of the Senate Committee on Homeland Security and Governmental Affairs, 2006; U.S. Department of Homeland Security, 2008; Wolf, 2005).

Numerous "After-Action-Reviews" have also identified the broad-reaching consequences and readiness issues associated with massive internal population displacements (Kromm & Sturgis, 2008; Vest & Valadez, 2006; White, Fox, Rooney, & Cahill, 2007).

From a command center perspective, the emergency response operations activities involved responding to numerous crises and emerging situations. At the Emergency Operations Center (EOC), we were constantly receiving messages via cell phones of persons trapped in their attics with rising flood water threatening their survival, incredibly hot weather, and hospitals with patients, staff, and no power facing rapidly deteriorating situations. The response staff was beyond exhausted as the events continued to become more complicated over the next week. The Coast Guard teams were valiant in their rescue efforts which resulted in people being rescued from their roof tops and placed on interstate overpasses, again without any or minimal water and food. A location referred to as the Search and Rescue Base of Operations (SARBO) was established as a staging area at I-10 and Causeway Boulevard on the outskirts of New Orleans. Rioting and looting within the City were rampant as survivors became more desperate. The medically fragile were collected and placed on the interstate with minimal medical resources in the early stages of the response. From there they were transported to makeshift disaster medical stations at the New Orleans International Airport awaiting transport to Baton Rouge or if able to cities out of state. All of these locations were filled with thousands of persons separated from family members and not knowing where they were going or who was going to bring them to safety. Uniformed soldiers patrolled the areas with automatic weapons trying to keep order in a rapidly deteriorating environment. Residents who had fled the area where arriving at shelter sites throughout Louisiana and neighboring states. Calls were coming into the EOC from people frantic to find their missing loved ones, report of people drowning, or pleading for an emergency rescue. The magnitude of requests for assistance and emergency response roles required health and behavioral health officials to rapidly design, staff, and deploy workers into disaster response roles they had never before encountered

The behavioral health staff responding to Hurricane Katrina were required to apply their training in a number of novel venues. Many of the duties staff were asked to perform required them to generalize the application of basic response skills within the context of unique and stressful environments. The impact of the sights, sounds, smells, and pace of a disaster response environment cannot be fully appreciated until experienced. Many of the behavioral health staff deployed had very limited emergency response experience. The vast majority of staff experience was limited to participation in training exercise or didactic presentations on crisis counseling and working within a disaster setting. The principle disaster operations sites where staff were deployed included (a) Medical Special Needs Shelters, (b) Temporary Medical Operations and Staging Areas, (c) Search and Rescue Base of Operations, (d) General Needs Shelter and mobile crisis teams, and (e) Community Mental Health Center crisis units. Below is a brief description of the activities associated with each of these locations, and the type of duty staff was asked to perform within each of the disaster response sites in which staff were deployed

Medical Special Needs Shelters: OMH Staff provided 24/7 coverage at the 5 Medical Special Needs Shelters (MSNSs) located in the designated parishes. Services include grief counseling, support counseling, basic social support, information and referral, and formal and informal stress reduction interventions for shelter leadership, staff, and volunteers. During the height of the evacuation over 795 buses were running 24 h/day carrying survivors from the incident area. Hundreds of Emergency Medical Staff (EMS) personnel and ambulances from across the country also delivered patients into shelter sites and required behavioral health support. Statewide, behavioral health staff provided 350–400 h per day of services to the medical special needs shelter evacuees which included over 1000 persons per day at the height and averaged 650–700 evacuees per day. Crisis counseling and support to special needs shelters began Saturday August 27th, as voluntary and mandatory evacuations from the southeastern parishes went into effect. The enormity of the evacuation operation resulted in several hundred nursing home patients as well as persons from supported living environments being abandoned at shelter sites with minimal to no staff coverage from the nursing facilities. The majority of interventions included both crisis intervention and grief counseling services as a number of evacuees placed in the MSNS did not survive the evacuation process.

TMOSA-Baton Rouge: The Temporary Medical Observation and Staging Area (TMOSA) field hospital setting in Baton Rouge was a primary evacuation triage site where workers provided 24/7 mental health coverage. The 200 bed capacity of this critical care hospital expanded to a population of 270 at its height. The TMOSA triaged well over 40,000 people and admitted 5,000 during its time of operation. Behavioral Health staff continually monitored the emotional level of TMOSA leadership, medical and non-medical staff, EMS Teams, ambulance and bus drivers, and volunteers, offering spontaneous one-to-one opportunities for expressing emotions as well as regularly scheduled stress group discussions. Additional and extensive crisis counseling services were provided to the caretakers and family members who accompanied their loved ones to the TMOSA. Mental health evaluations and psychiatric consults were also provided. Mental Health staff teamed with the EMS triage teams to detect persons with only mental health problems so they could be diverted directly to appropriate shelter sites.

SARBO – I-10 & Causeway Blvd and TMOSA – New Orleans Airport

Once the levees were breached and the greater New Orleans metroplex became inundated with water, mass-forced evacuation and rescue efforts were initiated. The Search and Rescue Base of Operations (SARBO) for these efforts was located at the first available non-flooded area in Jefferson Parish about 8 miles from the center of New Orleans at Interstate 10 and Causeway Boulevard. At this location search and rescue boats and helicopters transported evacuees from the flooded areas to waiting busses or ambulances for evacuation to the TMOSA located at the New Orleans airport, the TMOSA in Baton Rouge, or general shelter sites throughout Louisiana and Texas.

The SARBO site was overwhelmed with thousands of persons waiting transport to shelter sites. Transport delays resulted in many persons standing in the heat for hours with minimal supports. In addition, the SARBO site provided minimal triage services for injured and medically fragile persons who required further medical assistance at the TMOSA sites in Baton Rouge or the New Orleans Airport. Due to sniper fire directed at the transport buses, ambulances, and other support personnel, operations sending people away from the SARBO were curtailed at nightfall. However, evacuees from New Orleans continued to arrive at the I–10/Causeway site. The need for mental health services at this site and the New Orleans Airport

TMOSA (which still did not have any electrical power beyond minimal generator coverage) was extreme.

A team of behavioral health professionals was placed with the triage unit at I-10 and Causeway on the evening of August 31, 2005. The team remained on location until about 1:00 p.m. on Thursday September 1. At the team's arrival, approximately 200 individuals requiring or receiving medical care were in the medical area. Throughout the next 24 h period, the number of evacuees arriving at the SARBO in need of medical and mental health care continued to increase several times over.

Behavioral health crisis response teams were continuously and fully engaged in providing spur-of-the-moment stress management supports one to one for medical personnel as well as very basic supportive intervention to disaster victims. The team also provided administrative and communications supports to medical personnel by establishing a patient sorting system and maintaining contact with the State Command Center regarding urgent medical and transportation needs at the location. Upon arrival of relief teams from Texas, the I-10 and Causeway team was folded into the New Orleans Airport TMOSA teams. Estimates of numbers of evacuees, medical cases, and interventions provided cannot be accurately reported due to the extreme nature of the situation and minimal access to electronic equipment.

General Needs Shelters and Mobile Crisis Teams: The demand for crisis counseling and social services in various general needs shelters for the first 3 days after the Hurricane required the redeployment of staff from MSNS to general shelter sites until the American Red Cross (ARC) was able to secure out of state volunteers. By the second week after the Hurricane, staff had established relationships with ARC and continued augmenting ARC services, including provision of crisis counseling, psychiatric evaluations, and medication. The evacuation of hundreds of thousands of people throughout the State resulted in the opening of hundreds of temporary shelter sites and a constant demand for behavioral health consultation as well as direct services. The state again reassigned staff as necessary into five member mobile response teams operating on a 24 h basis.

Extended Community Mental Health Center Hours: The hours of operation of 10 Community Mental Health Centers throughout the state were increased to offer crisis and support counseling, psychiatric treatment, and medications for displaced clients of the public mental health system displaced by the hurricane. Many of these individuals evacuated with only the clothes on their back and had no medications or access to medical records.

First-Responder Intervention

First-Responder Crisis Counseling: The Office of Public Health, Emergency Operations Center was the base of operations for all EMS services related to the evacuation of persons from New Orleans and the surrounding areas impacted by Hurricane

Katrina. Behavioral health staff provided 24 h crisis counseling to the command center staff and EMS workers returning from various life-support missions. These workers participated in hundreds of shift debriefings and ad hoc crisis counseling activities with first-responder personnel. Examples of special crisis response missions in which behavioral health workers had been deployed include the following: The New Orleans Police Department 1st through 8th District Police, 17th Street Canal site, Convention Center, St Gabriel Morgue, Sheraton Hotel (housing first responders), Plaquemine EMS, Staging Center by Harrah's Casino, State Police Troop B, Louisiana State Police Headquarters, Louisiana State University Special Needs Shelter, DCON at 900 Loyola in New Orleans, the New Orleans Airport Shelter site, DCON St Bernard Parish, State Police Troop L, the Kenner body recovery site, and the Covington Medical Complex. Other first-responder groups to whom services have been provided include bus drivers transporting evacuees, Coast Guard Search and Rescue personnel, fire services, wildlife, and fisheries personnel who have provided search and rescue, security services and operated boat fleets used to rescue survivors, as well as law enforcement personnel throughout the declared parishes.

The level of destruction, loss, and death that these workers were constantly exposed to became more and more difficult for individual responders to manage. Over 33% of the New Orleans Police Department (500 officers) were initially missing and within the first week of the response, the NOPD had experienced two suicides by uniform officers overwhelmed by personal loss. One of the major sources of unresolved stress for city personnel and community residents was the inability to grasp the enormity of loss to the community and individuals, and how this inextricable loss changed their lives, hopes, and expectations forever.

Emergency Response and Employee Stress Management: Louisiana has a relatively small number of personnel to meet the demands of the state during non-disaster times. The disaster response demands brought on by Hurricane Katrina was of such magnitude that the state's personnel resources were multi-tasked and worked 12–18 h days. As the disaster continued to escalate, in scope and complexity, staff continued to be needed to operate at these excessive levels of on-duty hours. The long duty hours, excessive fatigue, sustained exposure to a rapidly changing and highly charged work environment, and exposure to the immensity of human suffering resulted in the emergence of a wide range of negative stress reactions within the workforce. To help keep these essential workers fit for active duty, behavioral health staff provided continuous informal opportunities for these employees to discuss what they have seen, done, and heard since the incident and their associated complex emotional and physical reactions.

Mass Casualty Identification

The National Find Family Call Center was established to provide a focal point of service to support exchange of information and compassionately address needs of families who had lost a loved one (either missing or deceased) in Hurricane Katrina. The FAC was a joint effort of the Louisiana Department of Health and Hospitals, FEMA, and the National Medical Disaster Services Disaster Mortuary Operations Response Team (NDMS/DMORT), with expert consultation from the US Northern Command and the American Red Cross. Lead responsibility for all activities related to body recovery and identification rests with DMORT and the State Medical Training Director. Behavioral health personnel were tasked with the development and implementation of the critical mental health and emotional components of the operation (Disaster Mortuary Operational Response Team, 2006; Louisiana Department of Health and Hospitals, 2006).

The role of crisis counseling involved supporting call center staff and volunteers, mandatory debriefings as staff go off shift, ad hoc support and stress management counseling as indicated during a shift, and grief and loss counseling to support callers who request services or who were identified to be in need of services by the intake managers. Many individuals searching for relatives were frustrated by the limited information available to them and the need for additional documentation and possible DNA samples in order to identify their deceased family members. Behavioral health staff-assisted spiritual counselors in their support to callers and provided "just-in-time" telephone counseling training to volunteers and others assigned to take calls from the public.

Summary of Behavioral Health Activities

The above descriptions of locations and services provided in the days and weeks following the landfall of Hurricane Katrina illustrate the mounting psychological distress that was present among both survivors and responders. When one reflects on the demands made on individual responders and the roles required of behavioral health personnel, one is truly amazed by the heroic actions of these individuals in service of their fellow man (see Silva, Marks, & Cherry, Chapter 11, for a related discussion). The physical and psychological challenges associated with providing such a broad-based and diverse level of emergency response creates an environment where the skills of well-prepared behavioral health workers are a great asset to the overall incident response. When responding to a major incident with rapidly changing demands, it is essential that these workers maintain awareness of the following features of the response environment:

1. The "emotional temperature" of the response environment in which they are assigned.
2. The sights, sounds, and smells of a disaster/response setting impact worker performance, and sustainability.
3. The demand for rapid-fire decision making.
4. The need for "Just-in-Time" training and support of volunteer personnel.

5. Physical and emotional exhaustion and its impact on processing information.
6. The importance of brief non-therapeutic intervention strategies such as psychological first aid.
(See U.S. Department of Health and Human Services, 2004 for a more comprehensive discussion.)

Initial Response: The Second Wave of Assistance to First Responders

The second wave of "initial" response activities to Hurricane Katrina occurred during the first few weeks and months following the inception of the incident. Prior to Katrina, most reports of disaster response activities are described as the range of actions initiated by responders to stabilize the impact of the immediate impact of the disaster. This period typically lasts for 3–5 days. By that time survivors have returned to their communities, and essential infrastructure such as schools, housing, and public services are in the process of being restored. This restoration process and the return to pre-disaster status is known as the recovery phase of the disaster (U.S. Department of Health and Human Services, 1994; Federal Emergency Management Agency, 2008a.).

Recovery from this hurricane is distinguished by the protracted response phase of the incident. The massive flooding of approximately 80% of Orleans, Plaquemines, and St. Bernard parishes, accompanied by the slow process of draining the area of water resulted in situations where persons were displaced for an unusually long period from their communities. Additionally, the almost total destruction of the area left little or nothing in the way of homes and personal belongings to return to.

The immediate psychological impact of this degree of trauma exposure, of being in a continuous response mode, with little to no psycho-social supports is exemplified through the experiences of first responders, specifically New Orleans Fire and Police personnel who remained in the city. The brave men and women had lost all their homes and personal possessions were separated from their families and were working under extreme conditions. We have recounted the experiences of the Louisiana State University Health Sciences Center, Department of Psychiatry staff as they intervened with first-responder personnel.

In New Orleans, our Trauma Team from Louisiana State University Health Sciences Center (LSUHSC) had worked for 12 years with first-responder agencies in providing recruitment assessments, education on community and family needs, and responding in emergencies. With the New Orleans Police Department as well as the New Orleans Fire Department and Emergency Medical Services, we had many pre-existing trusting relationships. Mayor Nagin asked the Department of Psychiatry to provide support to first responders and their families, 80% of whom had lost their homes in the flooding; his request was then followed by one from the devastated neighboring St. Bernard Parish.

Beginning in those early days, we together with teams of professionals from LSUHSC Department of Psychiatry met with New Orleans Police Officers, New Orleans Firefighters, and New Orleans Emergency Medical technicians on a daily basis. Meetings took place on the ninth floor of City Hall while water still surrounded that area, at Harrah's Casino, a central staging area for NOPD and other first responders, at the Sheraton Hotel, out of which displaced first responders were working and housed following Hurricane Katrina, at displaced police districts, at the Royal Sonesta Hotel which became the Command Center for NOPD, and at Woodlands, a meeting and living area for first responders, including firefighters and EMS. Meetings took place with first responders individually and in groups. In general, they took place where the responders were – often on the street – and dealt with psychologically important and real issues for the officers. Consistent with the principles of Psychological First Aid, discussions revolved around the extreme stress of the work that was required during Hurricane Katrina and its aftermath, the high percentage of loss of homes, the trauma of displacement of children, economic problems, and difficulties in achieving reunions with families.

The first issue that was brought up for the police when we saw them during the week after the hurricane was the two suicides of officers during the hurricane. They needed to talk about the suicides, circumstances around them, their wishes that they could have been prevented, and, in some cases, guilt with worries they could have done more to anticipate and prevent them. We were able to provide support and allow them to grieve and work through their feelings.

For the first 2 weeks after the hurricane, it was very clear, in providing psychological first aid, that we were dealing with a hierarchy of needs. There was much focus on working with first-responder agencies in helping to meet "basic needs" for first responders such as housing, food, water, clothes, and safety for self and family. Major concerns then turned to trying to figure out how to reunite with family members and how to re-establish some "normal" necessary parts of life such as where to live, where their children would go to school, and the displacement of family members to many different areas of the country. Many families in New Orleans and the surrounding parishes have strong extended family and neighborhood ties. Thus, the displacement of family members to other states was particularly wrenching for many individuals, both first responders and citizens. These issues emerged with particular poignancy for citizens who lived in the 9th Ward and in St. Bernard parish, areas that were underwater for weeks.

Work on the Cruise Ships with First Responders and their Families

On September 14, cruise ships were provided in New Orleans by FEMA to help first responders and essential city employees reunite with their still displaced families – their homes still being uninhabitable. Another cruise ship was docked in the almost totally devastated St. Bernard Parish to provide temporary housing for first responders. From the outset, our trauma team members who could return worked with the first responders and their returning families. We and our team provided awareness training about the effects of trauma on children, adolescents, and families, psychological first aid, crisis intervention, consultations, evaluations, and services. Together with colleagues and SAMHSA volunteers, we were able to provide immediate support for the traumatized children and families. The experiences and concerns that the displaced children shared in groups and with counselors were "eye opening." Most often, they talked about missing their friends, not being able to communicate by cell phone or e-mail, and feeling isolated. Together with the mental health professionals who were able to return, we provided additional training, collaborated with SAMHSA volunteers, and as they re-opened, helped the schools accommodate the significant temporary influx of new families.

Our team (consisting of psychiatrists, psychologists, and social workers) made contact with many hundreds of NOPD officers, firefighters, and EMS personnel. Confidentiality was important to them. They described the events of the hurricane and, at times, their sense of futility, the events at the Superdome and Convention Center, the trauma of being unable to achieve security, difficulties in evacuation and being unable to rescue citizens, having to decide in numerous situations who they could save and who would be left to die, being frustrated by the loss of equipment and cars, not having boats to be able to operate in an effective way with the flooding, and having very limited resources and support. They described the long days, inability to shower, continually wet with no change of clothes for days, having limited food and water supplies, and heroic attempts to keep the city safe with little outside and needed support. They described worries about job security (with few citizens in the city, how many police would be needed), limited family economics, separation from families and worries about their children being dispersed, and overall instability and uncertainty. They emphasized concerns about economic insecurity and, at times, difficulties in negotiating with FEMA and the Red Cross. Some commented that they believed FEMA and others did not care about them. Many officers shared specific concerns. One was on a waiting list for a heart transplant and due to the stress of the hurricane started smoking again. He asked us if we could help him stop smoking so that he could be put on the heart transplant list again. Another officer expressed extreme frustration and anger in not having equipment that they needed to fight the violence and crime, such as cars, guns. Many complained about feeling very alone without support and guidance during the hurricane and immediate aftermath when the entire communications system was down. Many were extremely frustrated by being isolated and trapped by the flood waters, needing to be evacuated, or not being able to get to their districts to report and do their work. Four weeks after the hurricane, one evening on the boat when we were talking and someone asked the date, replied, "Every day is the day after the hurricane!" Utilizing psychological first aid allowed them to share their stories of the traumatic events and helped support some sense of stability in their lives despite the continuing stress and uncertainty. On those few occasions when a serious mental health issue was identified or when an officer was feeling desperate, an immediate referral and intervention took place.

Two of us (HJO and JDO) and a senior social worker were quartered together with first responders; other available faculty, often in shorts and sandals, worked tirelessly in providing services. Our team, together with SAMHSA volunteers and other colleagues provided psychological first aid. We worked to help unite families by providing local, easy accessible education for their children now that schools had opened in nearby parishes, provided some respite and day care for stressed families, and provided activity groups for older children so they could play, make friends, and also give their parents some relief and time to themselves. On the boat, supportive interventions were provided. The activities that were set up for children on the boat included a daily 2 h day care center for the children that also provided respite for the parents, and a weekly activity time with our staff for the older children to play and make new friends.

We saw smiles on the initially dispirited children's and parents' faces as more activities were developed for the children that contributed to greater support and a sense of community. Staff spent much time with children and families, for example, during and after meal times and offered more services and support as needed. Much energy was placed on services enhancing family cohesion. Focus was placed on concerns related to economic uncertainty, need for permanent housing, displacement of families with children in school in other cities where extended family may live or where they evacuated, and other uncertainties continue. While the cruise ships provided housing, food, clothing, and some stability for the lives of the first responders, living on a boat is not home. Seeing homes destroyed and dealing with citizens who return and who see the destruction of their property raises tensions. We knew that the risk of posttraumatic stress symptoms, depression and potentially even suicide would be increased over time for many people displaced from heavily devastated areas and for those returning (Assanangkornchai, Tangboonngam, & Edwards, 2004; Briere & Elliot, 2000; Davis, Tarcza, & Munson, Chapter 5 of this volume; Fullerton & Ursano, 2005; Gittelman, 2003; LaGreca, Silverman, Vernberg, & Prinstein, 1996; North, Kawasaki, Spitznagel, & Hong, 2004; Norris, Murphy, Baker, & Perilla, 2004; Osofsky, Osofsky, & Harris, 2007; Shelby & Tredinnick, 1995; Smith & Freedy, 2000; Sutker, Corrigan, Sundgaard-Riise, Uddo, & Allain, 2002; Vernberg, La Greca, Silverman, & Prinstein, 1996).

Initial Response: Assistance to Children and Schools

The impact of such a horrific series of events associated with mass evacuation, threat to one's life, exposure to intense traumatic material coupled with the absolute dissolution of the very fabric of one's home, school, and community will leave a lasting mark on the children and youth of Katrina. Today many of these children who are experiencing developmental and emotional problems 3 years after the "storm" are referred to in the common vernacular as "Katrina" children. During the early weeks following the landfall of Hurricane Katrina, members of the LSUHSC Department of Psychiatry faculty and other behavioral health volunteers provided a wide range of behavioral health interventions to children in a diverse array of non-traditional and traditional settings. Below is an example of the work these behavioral health personnel delivered within the struggling communities.

In collaboration with the State Department of Education, Jefferson Parish School District, the Louisiana Department of Social Services, and Access II, children living on the cruise ships were enrolled in and transported to schools. Full services were developed and offered to all school children including after school activities, interactive wireless computer tutoring, and other age appropriate activities being available. Respite and child care services were offered with active parent participation. Using the NCTSN Hurricane Assessment and Referral Tool (NCTSN, 2005) a needs assessment and evaluation of post-traumatic symptoms was carried out with 61 children and families of first responders initially returning on the cruise ship in order to guide service development. Fifty-four percent of these children met the cut-off on the measure for referral for additional mental health evaluation which is not unexpected considering the traumatic events these children including being displaced (93%), seeing hurricane damage (85%), having their home destroyed (83%), losing their personal belongings (73%), and being separated from a caregiver (44%).

Work with Re-opening Schools

Based on a long-standing collaborative relationship, during the weeks immediately following Hurricane Katrina, the late Cecil Picard, Superintendent of the Louisiana State Board of Education, requested the we (JDO and HJO) help in meeting the needs of students, parents, and school personnel in devastated parishes as well as work with the Department of Education in developing a mental health component for School Emergency Response to Violence (Project SERV).

In October 2005, we established an extremely meaningful relationship with the newly established post-Katrina St. Bernard Unified School District. St. Bernard Parish was the most heavily impacted parish, almost completely destroyed by flooding. All of the schools were flooded and most were totally destroyed (see Buchanan, Casbergue, and Baumgartner, Chapter 1). A toxic oil spill led to further questions about whether the parish could be resettled. Doris Votier, Superintendent of the St. Bernard School System, (honored in 2007 with the John F. Kennedy Profile in Courage) believed that the school system should serve as the center of rebuilding and recovery of the community and that there must be a functioning school system if people were to return to the parish. We and the other LSUHSC faculty volunteered to work together with Superintendent Votier and Associate Superintendent Beverly Lawrason as they re-opened their school in temporary modular trailers and classrooms. We all agreed that more mental health support would be very important since so many children and families had experienced much trauma. Initially the Unified

School System expected about 150 students to return, instead 350 returned. From the beginning, Superintendent Votier and Associate Superintendent Lawrason and the teachers worried about their students and families, how much they had lost, and how they were currently living. Administrators, teachers, and other school employees, all of whom were living in trailers, worried that at the end of the day, students would leave school buses and go into darkened areas as power and light had not yet returned to the parish. Utilizing temporary structures, they provided hot lunches to returning students knowing that this might be their only hot meal. One child said when served hot spaghetti and meatballs for lunch, "We had real food!" The Superintendent's office asked that we collaborate with them to screen all students returning to the school to identify services needs as well as provide services to students having difficulties.

The LSUHSC Department of Psychiatry's Trauma Team simultaneously reached out to Orleans and Plaquemines Parishes. The then President of the Orleans Parish School Board, Reverend Torin Sanders, asked for help in October 2005. Because of the already failing schools, after Hurricane Katrina, the State Legislature placed most of the schools in the New Orleans Parish School System into a new Recovery School District under the Louisiana State Board of Education. The remaining New Orleans Schools System (NOPS) lost key administrative and school facilities in the flooding but planned to re-open five schools initially followed by others.

Many other schools throughout the region turned to LSUHSC for support and services as they re-opened. For example, In January 2006, the Sisters of the Holy Family opened the MAX school. Numerous families who evacuated from New Orleans because of the hurricane frequently had no home or job to which they could return. When these families returned to New Orleans in spite of difficulties, they cited allowing their child to return to their pre-Katrina school as a primary reason for returning to the city. Though the area was devastated, schools served as a safe haven in the midst of the crisis. The children were able to reconnect with their friends and have a sense of normalcy when they were in school. Many families reported that their children were happier when they returned to New Orleans and their schools; the children no longer felt like outsiders. They shared stories reflecting their difficulties and strengths. They poignantly shared being teased as "trailer trash" and missing the culture including the food in New Orleans when living as evacuees in unfamiliar locations within Louisiana or neighboring states.. While they were appreciative to those schools that took them in, many did not feel accepted in the communities.

Unfortunately, some adolescents were living on their own with very little supervision due to family circumstances, crowding in trailers, and few options for still displaced families. Counselors and teachers describe worrisome behaviors in elementary-age children as well as older students, including an inability to pay attention in class, disruptive behaviors, risk taking, changes in their behaviors and friendships. They mentioned adolescents being unable to talk with their parents because of the parents' traumatization and stress interfering with their being emotionally available to listen to their children and adolescents. Schools recognized that they needed additional support for their students, teachers, and families in order to address the stresses created by the traumatic experiences as well as the ongoing recovery process. Older children had little to do after school, and substance use and risky sexual behaviors were more common. Younger children were more likely to engage in disruptive and aggressive behaviors, symptoms of emotional withdrawal, inability to concentrate, and depression were frequently observed in these children. Training school personnel, local providers, and others to recognize "red flag" behaviors indicative of trauma was a primary focus of our team.

Summary

The role of the LSUHSC Department of Psychiatry faculty and other behavioral health staff was crucial from the first weeks after the hurricane in providing psychological first aid, crisis counseling, and other trauma-focused essential interventions which would hopefully foster the personal resiliency within first-responder personnel, their families and children as they moved forward on their journey of recovery. This needed outreach to police, firefighters, and EMS provided support for maintaining a "staying within the present" orientation as these individuals struggled to maintain their job readiness and ability to successfully cope with the simple tasks of daily survival.

As one would expect many of the first responders we interacted with were traumatized by the events they had to experience and respond to during and in the immediate aftermath of Katrina. Skilled behavioral health response strategies were needed even in casual encounters to recognize and prevent more serious problems. Issues included their own difficulties in trying to protect the city and rescue those remaining after Hurricane Katrina and the subsequent flooding, painful sights and decisions in triaging and rescuing efforts, the suicide of two police officers, financial losses, loss of homes, displacement of families and meeting the needs of displaced family members, hardships in living situations, and conflicts between commitment to duties and family needs. The trauma team also was instrumental in helping provide support to decrease the impact of the expected vicarious traumatization resulting from situations they encountered and continually were repeated in setting where first responders and/or their families would gather.

Our team provided important outreach to children and families, at first on the cruise ships and later in school settings. Because of the many losses, separation from parents, caregivers and community, destruction of their homes and displacement, children needed much support. Confidential evidence-based screenings and ongoing collaboration with the re-opening schools allowed for needed school-based services and resilience building programs. Intervention strategies were used adjusted for the developmental age of the survivor and consistent with initial drafts of the methods finalized and recommended in Field Operations Guide for Psychological First Aid (Brymer et al., 2006). The interventions provided essential support to individuals as they coped with the basics of surviving in the early weeks of post-Katrina existence.

Behavioral health teams relied on implementation of an adaptation of Psychological First Aid (PFA) as a primary intervention on the flooded streets of New Orleans with distraught residents and with first responders and their families living within the surreal setting of vacation cruise ships as temporary living quarters. The behavioral health interventions we used allow us to assess the situation, gather information, provide support, problem-solve with the individuals or families, connect them with the limited resources that were available, and help them cope with the immediate impact of this catastrophic event.

The basis for interventions within schools was guided by first gathering an understanding of the children and their perception of their experiences. The availability of a screening instrument which had been used in prior disasters allowed us to quickly build a screening and assessment model within a devastated school system with few resources. The National Child Traumatic Stress Network Hurricane Assessment and Referral Tool for Children and Adolescents (2005), modified for both cultural sensitivity and accessibility for students, helped us to use what we learned about the experiences and reactions of the returning children and adolescents to build culturally relevant interventions. The data gathered (reported elsewhere) represented the response of a cross section of all children affected, primarily those returning to the most heavily impacted areas. This assessment process help direct immediate intervention strategies as well as respond to needs and aid in the development of services to support the children and adolescents both in promoting resilience and in providing psychotherapeutic interventions when needed.

Conclusion

National disaster response efforts following the catastrophic events of September 11, 2001, and the devastating hurricanes along the Gulf Coast in 2004 and 2005 have resulted in a revised national strategy for disaster response planning and implementation. The National Response Framework (FEMA, 2008b) is the basis for building an emergency response strategy. Response is defined in the documents as "immediate actions to save lives, protect property and the environment, and meet basic human needs. Response also includes the execution of emergency plans and actions to support short-term recovery." The National Incident Management System (FEMA, 2008a) is a companion strategy to the National Response Framework and is currently the primary strategy used by national, state, and local emergency response units for managing a disaster incident.

This national framework is based on many of the lessons learned from hurricane Katrina. This chapter illustrates activities associated specifically with building and initiating a behavioral health emergency response strategy prior to the catastrophic events of 2005, and the immediate implementation of response activities over the initial weeks and months of a protracted response phase of emergency services. The unique and exceptional features of the nation's largest catastrophic event required a sustained level of intervention previously not experienced by response agencies or behavioral health personnel.

Traditionally, from a behavioral health perspective, most disaster response plans heretofore, provide limited detail as to the role of behavioral health professionals, usually limited to support functions and a brief nod to crisis counseling. The response activities associated with Hurricane Katrina, an event of unprecedented destruction and mass trauma exposure demonstrated the essential role of behavioral health agencies and professionals in disaster response. Collaborative planning between emergency response agencies and behavioral health agencies has been demonstrated to have numerous benefits resulting in the building of professionals relationships, trust and respect among responders and behavioral health staff, and the normalization of psychological fatigue, and trauma exposure as anticipated aspects of disaster response activities for responders and survivors.

References

Assanangkornchai, S., Tangboonngam, S., & Edwards, J. (2004). The flooding of Hai Tai: Predictors of adverse emotional responses to a natural disaster. *Stress and Health, 20,* 81–89.

Briere, J., & Elliot, D. (2000). Prevalence, characteristics, and long-term sequelae of natural disaster exposure in the general population. *Journal of Traumatic Stress, 13,* 661–679.

Brymer, M., Jacobs, A., Layne, C., Pynoos, R., Ruzek, J., Steinberg, A., et al. (July 2006). *Psychological first aid: Field operations guide*(2nded.). Retrieved October 7, 2007, from https://www.nctsn.org and https://www.ncptsd.va.gov

Disaster Mortuary Operational Response Team. (2006). *DMORT mass fatality assistance.* Retrieved, January 24, 2009 from: http://www.dmort.org/

FEMA. (2006) Recovery Division Policy No. 9523.9. Retrieved February 1, 2009, from http://www.fema.gov/government/grant/pa/9523_9.shtm

FEMA. (2008a). *Federal Emergency Management Agency*. Retrieved November 30, 2008, from http://www.fema.gov/emergency/nims/index.shtm

FEMA. (2008b). *National Response Framework, Resource Center*. Retrieved November 30, 2008, from http://www.fema.gov/emergency/nrf/

Fullerton, C. S., & Ursano, R. J. (2005). Psychological and psychopathological consequences of disasters. In J. J. Lopez-Ibor, G. Christodoulou, M. Mai, N. Satorius, & A. Okasha (Eds.), *Disasters and mental health* (pp. 13–36). New York: John Wiley and Sons.

Gittelman, M. (2003). Disasters and psychosocial rehabilitation. *International Journal of Mental Health, 32,* 51–69.

Innovative Emergency Management. (2004). *Southeast Louisiana Catastrophic Hurricane Functional Plan* (IEM, No. TEC04-070).

Kromm, C., & Sturgis, S. (2008). *Hurricane Katrina and the Guiding Principles on Internal Displacement*. Institute for Southern Studies, Durham, NC. Special Report Vol. XXXVI, No. 1 & 2. Retrieved January 2, 2009, from http://www.southernstudies.org/iss/4

LaGreca, A., Silverman, W., Vernberg, E., & Prinstein, M. (1996). Symptoms of posttraumatic stress in children after Hurricane Andrew: A prospective study. *Journal of Consulting and Clinical Psychology, 64,* 712–723.

Louisiana Department of Health and Hospitals. (2006). *DHH Emergency news*. Retrieved November 30, 2008, from http://www.dhh.louisiana.gov/offices/?ID=145

National Child Traumatic Stress Network (2005). *Hurricane Assessment and Referral Tool for children and Adolescents*. [Electronic version]. Retrieved September 15, 2005, from http://www.nctsnet.org/nctsn_assets/pdfs/intervention_manuals/referraltool.pdf

National Weather Service. (2007). *2005 Tropical Cyclone Advisory Archive*. Retrieved November 30, 2008, from http://www.nhc.noaa.gov/archive/2005/

Norris, F., Murphy, A., Baker, C. K., & Perilla, J. L. (2004). Postdisaster PTSD over four waves of a panel study of Mexico's 1999 flood. *Journal of Traumatic Stress, 17*, 283–292.

North, C. S., Kawasaki, A., Spitznagel, E. L., & Hong, B. A. (2004). The course of PTSD, major depression, substance abuse, and somatization after a natural disaster. *The Journal of Nervous and Mental Disease, 192*, 823–829.

Osofsky, J. D., Osofsky, H. J., & Harris, W. W. (2007). Katrina's children: Social policy considerations for children in disasters [Electronic version]. *Social Policy Reports, 21*, 1–20. Retrieved November 20, 2008 from http://www.srcd.org/spr.html

Shelby, J. S., & Tredinnick, M. G. (1995). Crisis interventions with survivors of natural disaster: Lessons from Hurricane Andrew. *Journal of Counseling and Development, 73*, 491–497.

Smith, B. W., & Freedy, J. R. (2000). Psychosocial resource loss as a mediator of the effects of flood exposure on psychological distress and physical symptoms. *Journal of Traumatic Stress, 13*, 349–357.

Special Report of the Senate Committee on Homeland Security and Governmental Affairs. (2006). *Hurricane Katrina: A nation still unprepared* (U.S. Senate, S. Rept. 109–322). Retrieved November 30, 2008, from the GPO Access Web site: http://www.gpoaccess.gov/serialset/creports/katrinanation.html

Sutker, P. B., Corrigan, S. A., Sundgaard-Riise, K., Uddo, M., & Allain, A. N. (2002). Exposure to war trauma, war-related PTSD, and psychological impact of subsequent hurricane. *Journal of Psychopathology and Behavioral Assessment, 24*, 25–37.

Thornton, P. (1998, September 28). New Orleans empties as Hurricane Georges heads for the mainland [Electronic version]. *The Independent (London)*. Retrieved November 30, 2008, from http://findarticles.com/p/articles/mi_qn4158/is_19980928/ai_n14182423/pg_2?tag=art Body;col1

Tinker, E.L. (1953). *Creole City The Past and its People* New York, Longmans, Green & Co. 1953, p. 347.) Retrieved 12-12-08, from http://nutrias.org/facts/careforgot.htm#_ftnref15

U.S. Department of Health and Human Services, (1994) *Disaster Response and Recovery: A Handbook for Mental Health Professionals*. DHHS Pub. No. SMA 94-3010. Rockville, MD. Center for Mental Health Services, Substance Abuse and Mental Health Services Administration.

U. S. Department of Health and Human Services. (2004) *Mental Health Response to Mass Violence and Terrorism: A Training Manual*. DHHS Pub. No. SMA 3959. Rockville, MD: Center for Mental Health Services, Substance Abuse and Mental Health Services Administration.

U.S. Department of Homeland Security. (2008). *FEMA's sheltering and transitional housing activities after Hurricane Katrina* (Office of Inspector General, No. OIG-08-93). Retrieved November 30, 2008, from http://www.dhs.gov/xoig/assets/mgmtrpts/OIG_08-93_Sep08.pdf

Vernberg, E., La Greca, A., Silverman, W., & Prinstein, M. (1996). Prediction of posttraumatic stress symptoms in children after Hurricane Andrew. *Journal of Abnormal Psychology, 105*, 237–248.

Vernberg, E., Steinberg, A., Jacobs, A., Brymer, M., Watson, P., Osofsky, J., et al. (2008). Innovations in disaster mental health: Psychological first aid. *Professional Psychology: Research and Practice, 39*, 381–388.

Vest, J. R, & Valadez, A.M. (2006). Health conditions and risk factors of sheltered persons displaced by Hurricane Katrina. *Prehospital and Disaster Medicine, 21*, 55–58.

White, G. W., Fox, M. H., Rooney, C., & Cahill, A. (2007). Assessing the impact of Hurricane Katrina on persons with disabilities. Lawrence, KS: The University of Kansas, The Research and Training Center on Independent Living.

Wolf, R. (2005, October 10). Baton Rouge shelter that aided 6.720 evacuees will close Friday [Electronic version]. *USA Today*. Retrieved January 24, 2009, from http://www.usatoday.com/news/nation/2005-10-13-shelter-closing_x.htm

Chapter 13
Disaster Recovery in Workplace Organizations

Tracey E. Rizzuto

Abstract Not only do large-scale disasters disrupt the personal lives of individuals, they also disrupt work lives and workplaces. Much has been written about organizational changes associated with common occurrences, like leadership transitions, competitive adaptations, and mergers and acquisitions. Less is known about how people and workplaces cope with and recover from extraordinary circumstances, like the Hurricane Katrina disaster. This chapter discusses features of catastrophic disaster recovery that distinguish it from traditional approaches to organizational change and describes the recovery processes of organizational workplaces and individual employees in response to Hurricane Katrina. Scientific and practical implications for workplace recovery and rebuilding in the wake of disaster are discussed.

Introduction

Throughout history, individuals and organizations have shown remarkable resilience in their abilities to recover and rebuild from disasters. With crises increasing in occurrence, severity, and diversity in our society (Hart, Heyse, & Boin, 2001; Quarantelli, 2001; Riebeek, 2005; Robert & Lajtha, 2002), academics and practitioners across disciplines are turning to the organizational disaster and change literatures to develop workplace strategies for crisis prevention and disaster recovery (Lalonde, 2007; Rosenthal, Boin, & Comfort, 2001). However, 3 years into the Hurricane Katrina recovery process, two facts are clear (1) the organizational development (OD) literature does not satisfactorily address workplace needs and circumstances in the disaster context and (2) Hurricane Katrina was not a "normal" disaster. It was a "catastrophic" disaster that created extraordinary circumstances for workplace recovery (Carafano, 2005; Piotrowski, 2006; Quarantelli, 2005). This

---

T.E. Rizzuto (✉)
Department of Psychology, Louisiana State University, Baton Rouge, LA 70803-55501, USA
e-mail: trizzut@lsu.edu

chapter describes the unique challenge of workplace recovery in response to catastrophic disaster, like Hurricane Katrina. It begins with a look at typical approaches to OD under ordinary circumstances, and an analysis of key features that differentiate catastrophic disasters from other change contexts, making it an interesting subject for OD interventions. Next, reactions to disaster are explored as a developmental human process and with regard to three components of an organizational system. Last, this chapter provides practical suggestions and research directions for establishing an OD model for catastrophic disaster recovery that rebuilds lives and businesses.

Workplace Recovery in Overview

Just as a healthy personal life can help to diffuse workplace stressors, one's work life can be a sanctuary for stability, social support, and personal accomplishment during times of personal crisis (Barnett & Hyde, 2001; Hulin, 2002). Personal identity is threatened when disaster events result in the loss of familiar surroundings, homes, jobs, and social networks (Hawkins, 2005). Not only does the restoration of normalcy and stability in the personal and family life domains enhance the productivity and well-being of working adults but also normalcy and stability in the work domain translates into greater economic stability, self-confidence, resources, and support for bread-winners who must provide for their families. Therefore, disaster recovery is an important topic, not only because of the economic implications for communities but also because of the optimism that workplace normalcy offers other life domains (see Garrison & Sasser, Chapter 6, for a related discussion).

The actions organizational leaders take in response to, and in the aftermath of, a disaster can help return businesses to normal operations (Junglas & Ives, 2007). Despite the need to understand science and practice of workplace recovery, very little is written from the organizational perspective about disaster management, the discipline of dealing with and avoiding risks through preparation, disaster response, and rebuilding after disasters have occurred (Haddow & Bullock, 2004). Rather, much of the disaster literature focuses on individual-level clinical interventions and community-level policies and programs (e.g., Comfort et al., 1991), and most of the crisis management research is comprised of case studies that make knowledge synthesis across events difficult or impossible (Lalonde, 2007). Further, although traditional OD practices have improved the management of ordinary workplace change (e.g., leadership transitions), the magnitude of a catastrophe makes typical OD practices difficult to apply in workplaces recovering from disasters like Hurricane Katrina. Therefore, due to our lack of a solid research knowledge on the topic of organizational workplace disaster recovery, this chapter is an effort to compile documentation to assist and to achieve a preliminary approach to help OD specialists, as well as business and community leaders, in their disaster recovery efforts.

A Look at the Norm: Ordinary Disaster and Typical Approaches to OD

Ordinary Disasters Versus Catastrophic Disasters

A number of features differentiate Hurricane Katrina, a catastrophic disaster event, from a non-catastrophic or "ordinary" disaster event (Quarantelli, 2005). Unlike ordinary disasters that have relatively isolated targets and limited scopes, catastrophic disasters are multiple stressor events that put tens-of-thousands of lives at risk, disable multiple tiers of support (local, state, and federal), and disrupt both work and personal life domains. Specifically, in the case of Hurricane Katrina, storm winds, tidal surge, broken levees, and poor coordination and management across response units wreaked havoc on 1.2 million people (Appleseed, 2006). It created struggles to secure community infrastructure and normalize work and personal lives that are still on-going today. Because of its complexity and magnitude, Hurricane Katrina is a catastrophic disaster with unique qualities that differentiate it from other disasters like 9/11, destructive tornados, and snowstorms where the event is more regionally contained and where local leaders are able to turn to state resources when they are exhausted (Carafano, 2005). For these reasons, catastrophic disasters present unique challenges to workplace disaster recovery (Quarantelli, 2005).

Typical OD in Normal Circumstances

OD is defined as the science and practice of educational strategies designed to bring about planned organizational change among relatively healthy individuals in controlled workplace settings (Kotter & Schlesinger, 1979). Traditional approaches to OD interventions are carried out in controlled, planned steps that begin with the establishment of a relationship between the organization personnel and OD specialists, research and evaluation of the system's functioning, identification and application of approaches to improve organizational effectiveness, and an evaluation of the intervention effect on the organization (Neilsen, 1984). Although the OD literature is vast, very little research addresses organizational change as the result of a disaster. Unfortunately, from a practitioner's perspective, the conditions of most businesses immediately following the storm defied the foundational assumptions for implementing traditional OD practices. In contrast to disaster contexts, Babad and Saloman (1978) note that classical OD practices should occur with (1) sufficient time to systematically advance change as opposed to just-in-time interventions; (2) regard for all relevant parts of the organizational system instead of targeted subunits of the organization; (3) a client that is emotionally balanced and able to change, and not experiencing extreme stress and trauma; (4) consultants who are able to maintain emotional distance from clients, and not subject to notable guilt and stress; and

(5) with regular intervention evaluation as opposed to unique situations that preclude comparative benchmarks. Rather, the post-crisis organizational environment has been described as "chaotic" with intense stressors being introduced in unpredictable circumstances that evade the control of traditional OD approaches (Dolan, Garcia, & Auberbach, 2003; Piotrowski, 2006).

Furthermore, traditional OD tools and interventions are designed and validated for use in ordinary contexts, such as leadership transitions and company mergers, not for crisis situations where OD needs-assessments are conducted using traumatized populations who are dealing with highly intense stressors from both personal and professional realms of their lives (Babad & Salomon, 1978; Piotrowski, 2006; Rizzuto, 2008). Research shows that individuals who undergo emotional experiences often record incredibly detailed "flashbulb" memories; however, the narrowing of attention to peripheral events also simultaneously introduces informational biases or inaccuracies (Easterbrook, 1959). As a result, the data captured by traditional OD assessments may potentially skew the perceptions and inferences OD specialists use to develop workplace interventions. That is, while Katrina survivors may be able to share their personal storm experiences in vivid detail, the ability to accurately assess the current state of workplace affairs post-disaster may be hindered by situational complexity, uncertainty about the status and developments occurring across organizational units, and extensive demands on one's cognitive ability to attend to professional matters amidst personal crisis.

Traditional OD practices are further complicated by the fact that organizational experiences of catastrophic disaster and recovery are often nested within contexts of broader, large-scale disasters. During many types of workplace calamities, organizations can rely upon other groups and organizations in the local community to provide stability and resources (Carafano, 2005; Rizzuto & Maloney, 2008). However, catastrophic disasters that afflict large geographic regions, like Hurricane Katrina, overwhelm state and local resources, and in some cases negative spillover effects impact other industry organizations (Yu, Insead, & Lester, 2008). For example, Entergy Corporation has had to recall utility crews brought to disaster-affected areas from other communities when those locations faced the threat of their own crises (Burns, 2008). In sum, these features make workplace recovery from catastrophic disasters like Hurricane Katrina unchartered territory for establishing OD practices and guidelines.

OD in Extraordinary Circumstances: Rebuilding Workplaces After Hurricane Katrina

To understand how OD practices can be adapted and applied to aid organizational recovery in extraordinary circumstances, it is helpful to understand human reactions to traumatic events from the perspective of individual employees and the organizational system within which they work. Then, we will identify the organizational components that are most vulnerable to disasters and have the greatest need for OD support.

Developmental Stages of Disaster Response

Although disasters leave distinct footprints along their paths of destruction, there are often recognizable patterns in how individuals and organizations react to them. These reactions are thought to unfold over time and can be considered "isomorphic" in that they reflect similar and/or parallel processes between humans and collective systems. These reactions to uncontrollable and devastating change have been documented by both crisis management and traumatic stress researchers (e.g., Cohen, 2002; Smith, 1990). Both disciplines describe three stages of disaster response that include pre-period, during-period, and post-period. Together, these stages provide a framework for understanding how organizations and the people within them react to disasters, and how OD interventions may support recovery (Cohen, 2002; Smith, 1990).

In theory, disasters are thought to unfold in linear progression with an ultimate return to equilibrium (Raphael, 1986). However, given the complexity and cacophony surrounding real catastrophic disasters, iterative loops are suggested to emerge and cause organizations to oscillate between during-crisis and post-crisis circumstances and to alternate strategies that target short-term fixes, intermediate steps, and long-term solutions (Fleming, 2006; Rizzuto & Maloney, 2008). Each developmental stage is described below to depict typical human (individual and organizational) reactions to disaster.

Pre-stage Crisis

Smith's (1990) organizational crisis management stages and Cohen's (2002) framework of post-traumatic human reactions to disaster both begin before disaster strikes and as the threat of the event becomes imminent. From an individual perspective, the pre-crisis period is characterized by information gathering and a variety of adaptive defenses that include denial, repression of fright, and reaction-formation (e.g., paradoxical behavior, such as planning or attending a "hurricane parties"). Although individuals respond to disasters differently depending on personality, demographic status, coping style, and the availability of support; regardless of one's personal degree of pre-crisis reactivity, people live, work, and operate in interconnected social systems. Social relationships begin to converge around "worry work" (Janis, 1958) where friends and family begin to contact each other regarding plans and preparations for the event, and nervous tensions pervade as people adopt different coping patterns (Cohen, 2002). From an organizational perspective, how business leaders react prior to a crisis is thought to mitigate or exacerbate failure (Smith, 1990). The accurate detection of crisis signals is critical to ensuring an effective and responsible organizational response, while overlooking signals and hyper-vigilant reactivity to signals set the organization for failure (Pearson & Clair, 1998).

During-Stage Emergency

During an emergency and in the hours and days that follow, neurological changes introduce fatigue, restlessness, and changes to appetite and sleep and are often accompanied by emotional expressions of fear, worry, shame, and guilt. Cohen (1999) notes "cognitive clouding" that leads to disorientation and disorganization. Moreover, interpersonal behaviors can vacillate broadly from isolation, rigidity, helplessness, and acquiescence. The efficacy of organizational leaders to maintain intra- and interpersonal stability, and make smart business decisions amidst uncertainty, can strengthen the organization's internal support and trust in management or dissolve it into search for culpability (Smith, 1990).

Post-stage Disaster

The final stage in disaster response occurs once risks subside and as individuals and organizations initiate steps toward intermediate and long-term rebuilding. It is optimal for OD intervention because it marks a time when individuals and organizations can turn attention to higher-order goals and needs (Maslow, 1998). For this reason, the post-stage is also the central focus of this chapter.

As people begin to pick-up the pieces of their work and family lives and put the disaster behind them, some will struggle with symptoms associated with post-traumatic stress disorder (PTSD; see also Davis, Tarcza & Munson, Chapter). According to the *Diagnostic and Statistical Manual of Mental Health Disorders*, the American Psychiatric Association defines PTSD as the development of characteristic symptoms involving re-experiencing the traumatic event, dysphoria, and the numbing of the responsiveness to, or reduced involvement with, the external world as the result of a psychologically traumatic event (APA, 1994). Given the prevalent rates of PTSD following a disaster, some reported at high as 22% in the New Orleans population 2 years after Hurricane Katrina (Galea, Tracy, Norris, & Coffey, 2008), OD interventions introduced in the post-stage cannot consider recovery of the technical and operational workplace functions without considering the impact of traumatic stress on the human workplace structures.

As time passes, individuals who have experienced extreme stress and trauma begin to assess, react to, and process their losses, often giving rise to an increase in somatic complaints and psychosomatic conditions (Cohen, 1999). Struggles to cope with personal emotions, interpersonal relationship, and the demands of daily living can lead to feelings of helplessness as usual defense mechanisms, at times, fail and decision-making demands increase as people begin to reconstruct their lives (Cohen, 1999). Interpersonal behaviors become erratic and paradoxical as individuals who once sought social interaction and support may begin to express irritability, frustration, and demonstrate social avoidance since involvement with and dependence upon others may be viewed as a loss of control (Cohen, 1999). Withdrawal from one's social support creates heightened risk for mental health challenges (e.g., depression) and diminishes opportunities to interchange relief efforts and resources (Aneshensel & Stone, 1982). From a workplace perspective, business leaders must help employees cope with these intra- and interpersonal challenges and lead them to re-invest confidence in managerial capacities to restore the human, operational, and technical structures of the organization.

Restoring Human, Operational, and Technical Organizational Structures

When a catastrophic event occurs, waves of disruption ripple through three structural components of a workplace: the human, operational, and technical structures. The human structure of an organization dictates the manner with which work is conducted (e.g., efficiently, cohesively), while the operational structure refers to what job tasks, roles, and functions are fulfilled (e.g., administration, production). The technical components refer to the facilities, tools, and materials needed to carry out the core operational functions of a business. The following section reviews the typical vulnerabilities and impairments to these structures that were sustained by Gulf Coast businesses as a result of Hurricane Katrina. It will also discuss the OD practices that were effective for protecting and repairing damage to these vital workplace structures.

Recovering the Human Structure of an Organization

Much of the crisis management literature focuses on the protection and recovery of the technical aspects of work (e.g., Fleming, 2006; Smith, 1990; Turner, 2007), while the human structures relating to employee health and organizational well-being are often overlooked. Employees who experience personal loss or safety violations as the result of a disaster can experience debilitating and enduring negative emotions and behaviors that hold consequences for their personal well-being, interpersonal relationships, and job performance (e.g., Baker, Dwight, & Chapman, 1962). Catastrophic disasters, in particular, upend multiple life domains and deplete the psychological resources that can buoy individuals during difficult times. Indeed, "bleed over" effects from crises have been shown to permeate and transfer from one life domain to another (Barnett & Hyde, 2001), compounding negative disaster effects on individuals. In fact, Galea and colleagues (2008) found that people who faced economic and employment instabilities in addition to lacking social support were more prone to PTSD 2 years after Hurricane Katrina. Employees who endure personal losses and injuries as the result of a disaster are likely to experience high stress and time pressure across personal, work, and family life domains, and therefore, are at an increased risk for PTSD, burnout, lower job satisfaction, role conflict, and other precursors that ultimately lead to job turnover (Milano, 2005). Successful OD interventions for the human structural components in a workplace must acknowledge the strain of this inter-domain interference on employees as they rebuild their lives. Organizations can provide timely and tangible relief services (Sanchez, Korbin, & Viscarra, 1995), such as housing, transportation, and flextime that may not only improve organizational functioning but also remove obstacles to establishing workplace routines and alleviate inter-domain conflicts (Rizzuto & Maloney, 2008).

Healthy social relationships among co-workers and a satisfying work life can help employees manage inter-domain stress (Hulin, 2002). Examples of workplace collegiality and demonstrations of co-worker support are common (e.g., workplace sympathy card). Such gestures are relatively easy to coordinate for a single individual or a small number of people, as in the case of ordinary disasters (e.g., house fire, illness). In contrast, entire employment communities sustained injuries and losses during Hurricane Katrina. The scope of catastrophic disaster make coordinating such efforts and displays of support a challenge—and even draining—particularly for employees who play dual-roles as "supportive colleague" and "disaster-affected employee." Furthermore, from a systems thinking perspective, organizations are organic and dynamic networks of interconnected relationships wherein severe stress and trauma experienced in one part of the system ripples throughout the system (Senge, 1990). These interconnected human structures offer another unique feature of workplace disaster recovery: whether directly or indirectly affected by hardship, virtually no employee remains untouched by catastrophe. Everyone in the organizational system feels the impact of the disaster, even to the extent that indirectly affected individuals approximate PTSD symptoms in a phenomenon referred to as "survivor syndrome" (Wilson & Raphael, 1993).

As a result, aggregated effects of stress and trauma within the human structure of a workplace have compounded and interactive effects on employees in both positive and negative ways. Not only do individual employees experience their own personal psychological discomforts, the organization as a whole experiences increased levels of stress and anxiety that exacerbate interpersonal interactions and emotions among employees (e.g., Rizzuto, 2007). Yet, at the same time, a common disaster experience creates the opportunity to share struggles and seek sympathetic comfort. Therefore, Green and Soloman (1995) advocate using formal and informal social networks to provide support and to disseminate resources about mental health challenges and effective coping strategies for dealing with difficult circumstances. This approach relies on the identification of individuals who may be exhibiting ineffective coping behaviors and reaching out to at-risk populations (e.g., elderly, poor) who are particularly vulnerable to illness and employment challenges after disasters (Zotterelli, 2008).

The use of formal and informal social networks within the work environment to help employees heal and face hardships is a deviation from traditional approaches to delivering mental health services and counseling through employee assistance programs (EAP). Given the scope of catastrophic disaster and the vulnerabilities and complexities of the human structure operating in the workplace, OD interventions should work with an organization's EAP to ensure an approach to recovering the human structure that is pervasive enough to reach all employees in need, systemic and seen as an essential facet to restoring work life, sustained over time, and not too taxing or time consuming. One such example is the combined individual and organizational stress intervention approach (Kohler & Munz, 2006). Unlike traditional EAP service delivery approaches, it draws on individual and group counseling concepts to facilitate skills development for diffusing stress. It teaches individuals strategies for identifying and managing intrapersonal symptoms associated with PTSD, such as guilt, depression, persistent anxiety, and emotional numbness (Cohen, 2002), helps employees anticipate and manage interpersonal stress-related conflicts with colleagues, and in some post-Katrina work environments been shown to reduce organizational stress levels during the recovery process (e.g., Rizzuto & Maloney, 2008).

Researchers note varying disaster reactions and mental health outcomes depending on whether events are perceived to be natural or technological (i.e., man-made) (Baum, Flemings, & Davidson, 1983). Baum and colleagues (1983) attribute these differences to perceived beliefs about an individual or community's ability to anticipate and control future crises. Employees with an external locus of control who believe that future crises cannot be mitigated display more negative coping behaviors (e.g., stress and anxiety) and job-related counterproductivity (e.g., poor job performance and task focus) than those who believe crises can be anticipated and managed (e.g., Anderson, 1977). Although as with Hurricane Katrina, the distinction between natural and technological disaster may not be clear, or may be an unfortunate cataclysm of both. Regardless of the cause, the two disaster types both have in common immediate threat, danger, and the potential for ongoing destruction (Green & Soloman, 1995). Therefore, another priority for recovering human structures is to restore a sense of security and confidence in the leadership of the organization, and its ability to protect the workplace from future crises. According to Pearson and Clair (1998), leaders can reinstate confidence after disaster by demonstrating the ability to reflect and learn from past events. Similarly, best practices for change management frequently advocate employee participation in knowledge-capturing activities that can increase access to valuable information to aid crisis planning and prevention and build confidence and trust in the managerial leadership (Rizzuto & Reeves, 2007; Shrivastava & Shaw, 2003).

The final challenge for restoring the human structure of an organization is to build a workplace culture that is adaptive to change, compassionate to hardships, yet robust and resilient during crisis (Rizzuto & Maloney, 2008). Employees within a workplace collectively share the disaster experiences and beliefs that ultimately shape the normative influences that guide workplaces through disaster recovery. Theories of social behavior have been used to describe how collective behaviors and attitudes develop and cohere under stress (Barton, 1969; Bankoff, 2002). They suggest that "individuals attach meanings to and interpret the environment within which they work. These meanings and perceptions then influence the way in which individuals behave within the organization" (Hofmann & Stetzer, 1996, p. 314). For this reason, the OD literature views workplace culture as an important factor that can facilitate organizational change (Karaevli & Hall, 2003; Stock & McDermott, 2001).

Cultural norms in a workplace dictate the extent to which disaster experiences are discussed and support offered to those struggling with the personal, work-family, and emotional consequences of a disaster. Additionally, workplace culture influences how employees respond operational changes in the organization, such as how they respond to newcomers to the organization. When changes occur quickly and unexpectedly, rumors and false information can heighten emotional reactivity in highly stressed individuals, and in some cases result in fractured "camps" that each adhere to very different organizational perceptions and beliefs (Bordia, Jones, Gallois, Callan, & Difonzo, 2006). Disaster "survivors" that remain with an organization may come to view post-crisis new hires as different, untested in their loyalty, and limited in their understanding of organizational operations and institutional history. Similarly, new staff entering the post-disaster workplace may view "survivors" as clique-ish, resistant to innovation, and opposed to change (e.g., Rizzuto & Maloney, 2008). OD interventions should maximize information sharing across hierarchical levels in an organization to build trust and shared understandings about workplace changes (Bordia et al., 2006). Moreover, OD efforts should also strengthen the communication, leadership, and managerial skills of organizational leaders so that they have the capacity to build and reinforce a healthy workplace culture for dealing with change.

Recovering the Operational Structure of an Organization

Just as the human structure characterizes *how* work gets done, the operational structure dictates *what* work is done. The operational structure of an organization refers to the job roles, tasks, procedures, and policies that guide workplace coordination, communication, and workflow. Disruptions to an organization's operational structure often have consequences for workplace procedures and staffing, particularly when organizations experience significant turnover and technical impairments that mandate job redesign and/or training to carry-out new work processes. In the months following Hurricane Katrina, job turnover rates soared among New Orleans businesses due to large waves of population displacement and uncertainties surrounding the safety and economic sustainability of a city so devastated (Kates, Colten, Laska, & Leatherman, 2006). As a result, many organizations were challenged to perform without enough adequate personnel to fill operational positions and complement needed competencies, and with little time for leadership development and succession planning (e.g., Rizzuto & Maloney, 2008).

The dire staffing situation led organizations to adapt their operational strategies, rely on internally available resources, and seek external assets from other organizations. First, some organizations temporarily suspended or scaled-back services and/or production, particularly when the markets they served indicated poor health, their client/customer base was diminished, and/or when staffing inadequacies disabled core business functions. For example, one New Orleans animal shelter whose mission is to protect animals and to educate the public about animal health and well-being lost nearly 80% of its staff after the storm. The shelter temporarily suspended its educational projects and programs; and in doing so, they were able to successfully sustain their shelter's core function (i.e., animal protections) until more staff could be trained and hired (Rizzuto & Maloney, 2008).

Still, other organizations looked to internal staffing solutions by examining the obstacles to job stability that their employees faced. It has been widely noted that federal programs for post-disaster recovery do not adequately address housing needs that emerge during catastrophic disasters in large metropolitan areas (Kamel & Loukaitou-Sideris, 2004). Organizations that made attempts to secure or provide temporary housing solutions to staff (e.g., allowing employees and their families personal access to work facilities) were able to retain experienced and highly skilled staff. In addition, job incentives such as higher salaries, signing bonuses, housing vouchers, and advanced-level entry jobs were also used to recruit labor in economically robust industries (Ewing & Kruse, 2003).[1]

Traditional OD personnel selection practices advise person-job-organization fit strategies for recruiting and selecting employees (e.g., Holland, 1997; Schneider, 1987; Edwards, 1991). The months following Hurricane Katrina, organizations had limited opportunities to so selectively hire staff, but instead relied upon internal promotion strategies and internal training and development to fill positions requiring greater skill and more experience. As a result, "instant training" had to be far more directive and prescriptive than typical OD training where knowledge and skill development is allowed to process over time (Babad & Soloman, 1978).

Such rapid rates of hiring and promotion put a strain on succession planning practices in organizations, and left little time to assess long-term development needs and procedural changes to reflect new operational structures put in place. While tradition OD practices for workplace procedures and staffing often advocate long-term development strategies, the post-disaster operational recovery necessitates just-in-time fixes to short-term needs without the luxury to learn from and adapt the practices over time. Babad and Soloman (1978) refer to this as an *adaptive* approach to OD, which is geared toward immediate solutions and mitigations of problems, while the traditional *adoptive* approach assumes iterative feedback and adjustments to develop and inform the change process.

External resources contributed by other groups, businesses, and organizations can also provide relief to organizations struggling to recover operational structures after disaster. To address the need for fast-track coaching and leadership development, some business leaders sought free organizational management services offered by the Katrina Aid and Relief Effort (KARE), an interdivisional volunteer effort of the American Psychological Association (Rizzuto, 2008). Others sought staffing resources from industry partners. Kendra and Wachtendorf (2003) emphasize the importance of forging relationships with other local organizations and community groups that can offer staffing solutions in times of crisis. These relations proved essential to the resilience of the New York City Emergency Operations Centre (EOC) during and after the World Trade Center attacks and allowed key positions within the operational structure to be filled by trained and qualified personnel from other EOC units (Kendra & Wachtendorf, 2003). However, given the broad regional impact that catastrophic disasters may have national (as opposed to regional) industry ties may be a more reliable source of assistance since, as seen during Hurricane Katrina, many local organizations and groups were rendered helpless as they reeled from their own disaster-related struggles.

Volunteers also serve as an important staffing source for organizations. The National and Community Service Organization logged millions of hours of services

---

[1] Industrial sectors within a disaster-affected region show different degrees of vulnerability (Ewing & Kruse, 2003); however, the ability to regain stability after a disaster is largely dependent upon the magnitude of the disaster to infrastructure and natural resources in the affected area (Rose & Lim, 2002).

by volunteers within the first 2 years of Katrina (National Service Organization, 2007). While volunteer service is invaluable to organizations, it does present some operational challenges. First, organizational recovery does not begin immediately. Rather, depending on the extent of damage, it may take businesses weeks, months, or even years before they begin to rebuild. Meanwhile, the greatest volunteer interest occurs in the immediate aftermath of a disaster and wanes over time. Second, some staff position needs require job-relevant experience and/or specific skill and knowledge sets that cannot easily be filled by volunteers. Furthermore, occupation type and credentialing can also pose problems (see Allen & Wayne, Chapter 8 of this volume, for a related discussion). As noted in a post-Katrina research report presented by the Heritage Foundation (2006), no standards exist for credentialing "first responder" personnel across regional jurisdictions. Therefore, external staffing solutions, whether they are sourced by other organizations or by individual volunteers, need to consider the legal and contractual environment surrounding these arrangements.

The viability of the different staffing solutions may depend on organization size and industry type. External staffing may work best for large organizations composed of, or affiliated with, regional "branch" offices that have similar operational structures and staffing competencies. Smaller businesses, on the other hand, may benefit from having a simpler organizational structure with positions to staff; however, they are also vulnerable to cash flow interruptions, typically have poor crisis plans, and often lack access to federal assistance and capital for recovery (Runyan, 2006). Steps can be taken in advance of a disaster to anticipate staffing options and to identify the essential personnel, competencies, and credentials needed to restore an organization's core function. Likewise, regional and national partnerships can be forged to aid and secure redundant operational structures and to establish memoranda of agreement with other groups and organizations to outline expectations for resource sharing in the event of a disaster (Seville et al., 2007). Finally, business leaders may also find helpful feedback and support from other organizations that have shared similar experiences (Fleming, 2006).

Despite efforts to prepare for crisis, many organizational leaders at the helm during Hurricane Katrina bemoaned the same fact: "no blueprints for response, no established procedures, and no policies existed for a disaster of this magnitude" (Dowell, 2008, p. 1). As staff changes occur in an organization, so must the procedural operations that coordinate and communicate the workflow process. In some cases, jobs are redesigned to reflect the new (and often reduced) function of the organization and/or the skill and knowledge sets of existing staff. For example, in dire staffing circumstances, the inability to fill a position may lead to the organization to merge job roles and responsibility to create a new job title, thus resulting in increased workload and role ambiguity as the operational structure adjusts to the change. Such operational changes require clear communication and alignment with formal training and performance appraisal practices as well as with incentive structure to support behavioral adherence to the new job roles and responsibilities (Miles & Snow, 2003).

Hurricane Katrina introduced vast developmental needs for the recovery of workplace operational structures. The figure below depicts a range of organizational

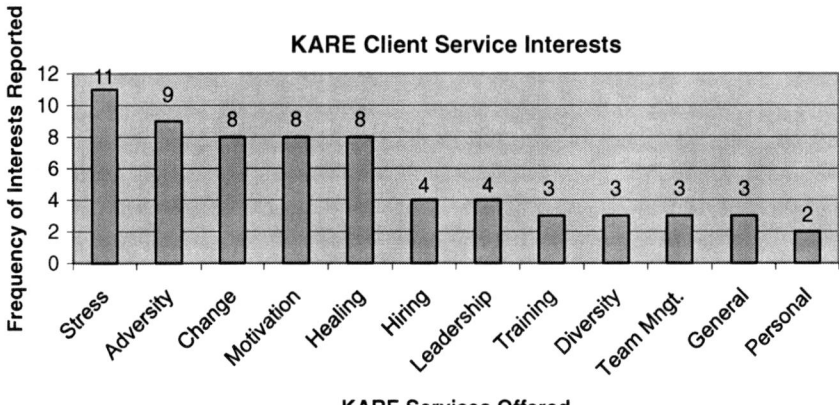

Fig. 13.1 Organizational recovery needs reported by storm-affected businesses one year after Hurricane Katrina. Reprinted from Rizzuto (2008), with permission from the Society for Industrial and Organizational Psychology, Inc.

recovery needs reported by a sample of New Orleans businesses during an intake assessment conducted by the KARE group 1 year after the storm. Stress, change, and adversity management ranked among the most frequently reported OD recovery needs reflecting both operational and human structural workplace components (Rizzuto, 2008) (Fig. 13.1).

Recovering the Technical Structure of an Organization

Damage to facilities, tools, equipment, as well as hardware and software associated with the technical infrastructure of an organization may need to be restored or replaced before basic business operations can resume. Sadly, the extensive wind and flood damage to the Gulf Coast region caused by Hurricane Katrina rendered many workspaces uninhabitable and left tools and materials in short supply. Furthermore, longitudinal analysis shows that disaster impediments to city residential areas and public systems (e.g., bridges, roadways, electrical grids) stunt the economic and employment recovery in disaster-affected regions and create tremendous difficulties for business organizations (Kates et al., 2006). Delays in the rebuilding of an organization's technical infrastructure create frustration and financial uncertainty. In many cases, businesses must re-evaluate basic organizational strategies for carrying out work functions. Toward this end, the owner of Silk Road in New Orleans successfully converted his brick and mortar artisan shop to e-commerce when local tourism was slow to return (Iwata, 2008).

Another important feature of a workplace's technical structure is the system and tools for managing and storing valuable organizational knowledge. Workplace technologies, software, and computer equipment are relied upon heavily to document, store, and manage essential organizational data (Turner, 2007). Damage to the systems that manage organizational data and knowledge creates particular challenges to business recovery because both public and private sector organizations depend on data documentation, organization, and dissemination to function effectively. For example, the Federal Emergency Management Agency (FEMA) and private insurance companies require documentation of workplace insurance policies, purchases, certificates, and contracts to establish rights and to validate ownership of property, facilities, and equipment that may be damaged or no longer exist due to a disaster. Previous research that documents disaster recovery processes in local government organizations suggests that an "immense" effort is required to document and track data to merely receive assistance for recovery (Fleming, 2006). Furthermore, rebuilding the technical infrastructure that manages knowledge for an organization also means missed business opportunities, market losses to competitors, and lost revenue that can never be recovered (Pasek, 2002).

Although some losses to technical infrastructure may be unavoidable, the identification of technical systems (and personnel needed to operate them) that are critical to central business functions may help mitigate damage and expedite recovery (Hunton, 2002). In addition, crisis preparations that protect the organization's technical infrastructure should include provisions for the safe storage, maintenance, and duplication of information that is vital to the organization. Other strategies include storing electronic documents on servers housed in geographically distant locations that are unlikely be threatened by the same catastrophic event and appointing temporary staff to help manage the paper and documentation needs that will emerge afterward (Hunton, 2002; Fleming, 2006). Finally, while technology provides businesses a foundation for recovery plans and data storage, the technical infrastructure cannot operate effectively without practice and participation of people (Mathews, 2005). Crisis preparation and evacuation drills can improve the efficiency and completeness with which the protection of people and property can be executed during an emergency (Lindell & Prater, 2003).

Practical and Scientific Suggestions for Workplace Disaster Recovery

Workplace Preparation and Planning

Among the numerous changes to the human, operational, and technical structures in organizations during times of disaster, the role of crisis planning and prevention is often foremost on the minds of organizational leaders. A great deal of loss and damage can be mitigated by prior organizational planning and quick recovery achieved with the implementation of management procedures to help businesses prepare for and rebuild from disaster (Fink, 1986; Ives & Junglas, 2006). Crisis planning intersects all three workplace structures in that it often creates the needs for new technical equipment (e.g., back-up server, duplicate tools) and new staff to oversee the planning operations. In addition, workplaces must strike a precarious balance between crisis preparation and crisis pre-occupation, which is particularly challenging for post-stage employees still tending the emotional wounds to the human structures within their places of work (e.g., Rizzuto & Maloney, 2008). Bankoff (2002) finds that people in communities where the threats are constant come to integrate disasters into the scheme of daily life such that expectations and beliefs about how the community will respond to disaster forms a "culture of disaster." Strong leadership can help cultivate a workplace "culture of disaster" that is prepared for, but not pre-occupied with, disaster.

Future Research Directions

While disaster relief is typically delivered through clinical interventions, research and community responses are also needed to manage disasters (Galambos, 2005). From a scientific perspective, research on disasters and workplace recovery is difficult to study and results in a number of practical and scientific limitations (Dynes & Drabek, 1994). To start, disasters can occur randomly or with little forewarning to allow researchers time to react; some research contexts are difficult to access and risky to observe. In addition, workplace disaster recovery is complex topic that demands multiple skill and knowledge sets. Therefore, collaborations between academics and practitioners from a wide variety of disciplines (e.g., business, sociology, psychology) are needed to develop best practices for crisis management and OD practices to aid workplace recovery. Given these considerations, it is not surprising that a dearth of research limits our knowledge of OD practices for disaster recovery.

A number of research avenues would help to move the science and practices forward. First of all, most workplace recovery practices are based on traditional OD that occurs in ordinary change contexts, but the effectiveness of practices applied to disaster contexts has not been empirically and systematically investigated. More research is needed to examine the validity and utility of traditional OD needs-assessments in large-scale, unplanned, and highly emotional change settings. Future research may also explore the extent to which the practice of replicating needs-assessments at multiple time periods across different hierarchical organizational levels improves data reliability and accuracy in complex and dynamic post-stage work environments.

Second, more research is needed on the employees and organizations who play vital occupational roles in protecting and rebuilding lives, businesses, and communities. Occupational groups whose mission it is to protect and service during crises, like military, rescue and emergency crews, and first responders of varying types provide vital services to people and communities. Despite the awareness of the considerable stress experienced by people in these occupations (e.g., Douglas, Blanks, Crowther, & Scott, 1988; James, 1988; Kamarck, 2007), little is known about the impact of disaster on their own occupational, health, and well-being outcomes. Some research suggests that first responders who experience their own negative life changes are more likely to experience depression, post-traumatic stress, and anxiety in the year following a disaster (McCaslin et al., 2005). Emotional reactions to disaster are also shown to amplify when individuals are separated from their family members (Fritz & Marks, 1954), yet this circumstance is a reality for many first responders who serve during disasters. Furthermore, research also suggests gender differences with regard to disaster planning and disaster responses in households and in organizations (Enarson, 1998). Research might also explore demographic differences in inter-domain conflicts that first responders face when protecting their families and fulfilling service responsibilities during disasters. Investigations into these topics will help us understand how disaster relief organizations may better protect the employees and volunteers whose communities rely upon so desperately during disaster.

Finally, from an applied perspective, a wealth of advice has been offered to guide organizations through the disaster prevention, preparation, and recovery process. A few summary points are as follows:

- *Workplace disaster recovery begins with multi-structure crisis planning.* Organizational leaders should anticipate human, operational, and technical workplace needs. Do not overlook the human aspects, as is so commonly done. Organizations should help employees navigate personal, mental health, and work–family conflicts by taking non-traditional approaches to EAP and work incentives (e.g., flextime, housing/transportation resources).
- *Make formal and informal social networks WORK.* Organizations should use workplace relationships to bolster social support, disseminate resources, and facilitate the development of a healthy organizational culture.
- *Build a community of interest.*Draw on volunteer groups, industry partners, and community leaders to form a community of interest around crisis management issues. External resources and national partnerships can be a source of support during disaster. Learn from the disaster experiences of other businesses and offer support to other organizations in times of need.
- *Necessity is the mother of invention.* Dire times call for creative and innovative solutions tohuman, operational, and technical workplace needs. Recovery may require the novel reinvention of workplace structures and practices.

As New Orlean historian and storm survivor, Brinkley (2005), points out in his chronicle of Hurricane Katrina, the Louisiana SPCA New Orleans animal shelter and other organizations were able to aid the city in its disaster recovery because of their preparedness and proactivity. Workplace recovery brings hope and stability to individuals whose lives are chaotically upended and provides a tremendous resource to communities responding to and recovering from catastrophic disaster (Brinkley, 2005).

References

American Psychiatric Association. (1994). *Diagnostic and statistical manual of mental disorders* (4th ed.). Washington, DC: American Psychiatric Association.
Anderson, C. R. (1977). Locus of control, coping behaviors, and performance in a stress setting: A longitudinal study. *Journal of Applied Psychology, 62*, 446–451.
Aneshensel, C. S., & Stone, J. D. (1982). Stress and depression: A test of the buffering model of social support. *Archives of General Psychiatry, 39*, 1392–1396.

Appleseed (2006). *A continuing storm: The on-going struggles of Hurricane Katrina Evacuees* (pp. 20–36). Washington, D.C.: The Appleseed Foundation.

Babad, E. Y., & Salomon, G. (1978). Professional dilemmas of the psychologist in an organizational emergency. *American Psychologist, 33*, 840–846.

Baker, G. W., Dwight, W., & Chapman, E. (1962). *Man and society in disaster*. New York: Basic Books, Inc.

Bankoff, G. (2002). *Cultures of disaster*. Richmond, VA: Curzon Press.

Barnett, R. C., & Hyde, J. S. (2001). Women, men, work, and family: An expansionist theory. *American Psychologist, 56*, 781–796.

Barton, A. H. (1969). *Communities in disaster*. Garden City, NY: Doubleday & Company, Inc.

Baum, A., Fleming, R., & Davidson, L. (1983). Natural disaster and technological catastrophe. *Environment and Behavior, 13*, 533–354.

Bordia, P., Jones, E., Gallois, C., Callan, V. J., & Difonzo, N. (2006). Management are aliens! Rumors and stress during organizational change. *Group & Organization Management, 31*, 601–621.

Brinkley, D. (2005). *The great deluge*. New York: HarperCollins Publishers.

Burns, M. (2008). Entergy utilizes working to restore power on three fronts after Ike. *Reuters Newswire*. Retrieved from http://www.reuters.com/article/pressRelease/idUS236140+15-Sep-2008+PRN20080915

Carafano, J. J. (2005, September 15). *Improving the national response to catastrophic disaster (Testimony)*. Statement before the Committee on Government Reform House of Representatives, Washington, D.C.

Cohen, R. E. (1999). *Mental health services in disasters: Instructor's guide*. Washington, DC: Pananmerican Health Organization.

Cohen, R. E. (2002). Mental health services for victims of disaster. *World Psychiatry, 1*(3), 149–152.

Comfort, L., Wisner, B., Cutter, S., Pulwarty, R., Hewitt, K., Oliver-Smith, A., et al. (1991). Reframing disaster policy: The global evolution of vulnerable communities. *Environmental Hazards, 1*, 39–44.

Dolan, S. L., Garcia, S., & Auberbach, A. (2003). Understanding and managing chaos in organizations. *International Journal of Management, 20*, 23–35.

Douglas, R. B., Blanks, R., Crowther, A., & Scott, G. (1988). A study of stress in West Midlands firemen using ambulatory electrocardiograms. *Work and Stress, 2*, 309–318.

Dowell, M. S. (2008). Overcoming overwhelmed and reinventing normal: A district administrator's account of living in Hurricane Katrina's aftermath. *Journal of Education for Students Placed at Risk, 13*, 135–167.

Dynes, R. R., & Drabek, T. E. (1994). The structure of disaster research: Its policy and disciplinary implications. *International Journal of Mass Emergencies and Disasters, 12*, 5–23.

Easterbrook, J. A. (1959). The effect of emotion on cue utilization and the organization of behavior. *Psychological Review, 66*, 183–201.

Edwards, J. R. (1991). Person-job fit: A conceptual integration, literature review, and methodological critique. In C. L. Cooper & L. T. Robertson (Eds.), *International review of industrial and organizational psychology, 6*, 283–357. New York: Wiley.

Enarson, E. (1998). Through women's eyes: A gendered research agenda for disaster social science. *Disasters, 22*(2), 157.

Ewing, B. T., & Kruse, J. B. (2003). A comparison of employment growth and stability before and after the Fort Worth tornado. *Global Environmental Change Part B: Environmental Hazards, 5*(3/4), 83–91.

Fink, S. (1986). *Crisis management: Planning for the inevitable*. New York: American Management Association press.

Fleming, C. (2006). After the rescue workers go home. *Public Management, 88*(4), 6–10.

Fritz, C. E., & Marks, E. S. (1954). The NORC studies of human behavior in disaster. *Journal of Social Issues, 10*(3), 26–41.

Galambos, C. M. (2005). Natural disasters: Health and mental health considerations. *Health and Social Work, 30*, 83–86.

Galea, S., Tracy, M., Norris, F., & Coffey, S. F. (2008). Financial and social circumstances and the incidence and course of PTSD in Mississippi during the first two years after Hurricane Katrina. *Journal of Traumatic Stress, 21*, 357–368.

Green, B. L., & Solomon, S. D. (1995) The mental health impact of natural and technological disasters. In J. R. Freedy & S. E. Hobfoll's (Eds.) *Traumatic stress: From theory to ractice.* New York: Plenum Publishing Corporation.

Haddow, G. D., & Bullock, J. A. (2004). *Introduction to emergency management.* Amsterdam: Butterworth-Heinemann.

Hart, P., Heyse, L., & Boin, A. (2001). Guest editorial introduction. New trends in crisis management practice and crisis management research: Setting the agenda. *Journal of Contingencies and Crisis Management, 9*, 181–188.

Hawkins, B. D. (2005, October 20). The road to psychological recovery. *Diverse Issues in Higher Education, 22*(18), 7–8.

Heritage Foundation (2006). Homeland Security Special Report #6: Empowering America: A proposal for enhancing regional preparedness. Retrieved from: http://www.heritage.org/Research/HomelandSecurity/SR06.cfm

Hofmann, D., & Stetzer, A. (1996). A cross-level investigation of factors influencing unsafe behaviors and accidents. *Personnel Psychology, 49*, 307–339.

Holland, J. L. (1997). *Making vocational choices: A theory of vocational personalities and work environments* (3rd ed.). Odessa, FL: Psychological Assessment Resources, Inc.

Hulin, C. L. (2002). Lessons from industrial and organizational psychology. In J. M. Herman & F. Drasgow (Eds.), *The psychology of work* (pp. 3–22). Mahwah, NJ: Erlbaum.

Hunton, J. E. (2002). Backup your data to survive a disaster. *Journal of Accountancy, 4*, 65–69.

Ives, B., & Junglas, I. (2006). Information systems in Northrop Grumman ships sector: The Hurricane Katrina recovery. *Communications of the AIS, 18*, 27.

Iwata, L. (2008, May 8). Tech tools bring big success for small firms. *USA Today*, 01b.

James, A. (1988). Perceptions of stress in British ambulance personnel. *Work and Stress, 2*, 319–326.

Janis, I. L. (1958). *Psychological stress.* London: Chapman Hall.

Junglas, I., & Ives, B. (2007). Recovering IT in a disaster: Lessons from Hurricane Katrina. *MIS Quarterly Executive, 6*, 39–51.

Kamarck, E. C. (2007, February). When first responders are victims: Rethinking emergency response. *Harvard Law & Policy Review Online.* Retrieved from www.hlpronline.com/2007/02/book_kamarck_01.html

Kamel, N. M. O., & Loukaitou-Sideris, A. (2004). Residential assistance and recovery following the Northridge earthquake. *Urban Studies, 41*, 533–562.

Karaevli, A., & Hall, D. (2003). Growing leaders for turbulent times: Is succession planning up to the challenge? *Organizational Dynamics, 32*(1), 62–79.

Kates, R. W., Colten, C. E., Laska, S., & Leatherman, S. P. (2006). Reconstruction of New Orleans after Hurricane Katrina: A research perspective. *Proceedings of the National Academy of Sciences of the United States of America (Special Feature), 103*(40), 14653–14660.

Kendra, J. M., & Wachtendorf, T. (2003). Elements of resilience after the World Trade center disaster: Reconstituting New York City's Emergency Operations Centre. *Disasters, 27*, 37–53.

Kohler, J. M., & Munz, D. C. (2006). Combining individuals and organizational stress interventions: An organizational development approach. *Consulting Psychology Journal: Practice and Research, 58*, 1–12.

Kotter, J. P., & Schlesinger, L. A. (1979). Choosing strategies for change. *Harvard Business Review, 57*, 106–114.

Lalonde, C. (2007). Crisis management and organizational development: Towards the conception of a learning model in crisis management. *Organizational Development Journal, 25*, 1–26.

Lindell, M. K., & Prater, C. S. (2003). Assessing community impacts of natural disasters. *Natural Hazards Review, 4*, 176–185.

Mathews, C. (2005). How to involve the business to create a solid continuity plan. *CIO Magazine*, 10. Retrieved from http://www.cio.com/article/12576

Maslow, A. H. (1998). *Maslow on management*. New York: John Wiley & Sons, Inc.

McCaslin, S. E., Jacobs, G. A., Meyer, D. L., Johnson-Jimenez, E., Metzer, T. J., & Marmar, C. R. (2005). How does negative life change following disaster response impact distress among Red Cross responders? *Professional Psychology: Research and Practice, 36*, 246–253.

Milano, C. (2005). The benefits of post-crisis counseling. *Risk Management, 52*(5), 12–17.

Miles, R. E., & Snow, C. C. (2003). Management theory linkages to organizational strategy and structure. In D. C. Hambrick (Ed.), *Organizational strategy, structure, and process* (pp. 116–138). Stanford, CA: Stanford University Press.

National Service Organization (2007). *Number of volunteers in year 2 of Katrina recovery exceeds historic year 1*. Washington DC: Special Initiatives of the Corporation for Nation and Community Service.

Neilsen, H. E. (1984). *Becoming an OD practitioner*. Englewood Cliffs, NJ: Prentice-Hall, 2–3.

Pasek, J. I. (2002). Crisis management for HR. *HR Magazine, 47*(8), 111–115.

Pearson, C., & Clair, J. (1998). Reframing crisis management, *Academy of Management Review, 23*, 59–76.

Piotrowski, C. (2006). Hurricane Katrina and organization development: Part 1. Implications of chaos theory. *Organizational Development Journal, 24*(3), 10–19.

Quarantelli, E. (2001). Another selective look at future social crises: Some aspects of which we can already see in the present. *Journal of Contingencies and Crisis Management, 9*(4), 233–237.

Quarantelli, E. L. (2005). Catastrophes are different from disasters: Some implications for crisis planning and managing drawn from Katrina. *Understanding Katrina*. Brooklyn, NY: S. S. R. Council.

Raphael, B. (1986). *When disaster strikes: A handbook for the caring professions*. London: Hyman.

Riebeek, H. (2005). The rising cost of natural disasters. *NASA Earth Observatory, March 28. Retrieved January 21, 2009, from* http://earthobservatory.nasa.gov/Features/RisingCost/

Rizzuto, T. (2008). Katrina aid and relief effort (KARE) lesson: Looking back and moving forward (Feature Article). *The Industrial-Organizational Psychologist, 45*(4), 11–26.

Rizzuto, T., & Maloney, L. (2008). Organizing chaos: Lessons from successful crisis management in the wake of Hurricane Katrina. *Professional Psychology: Research and Practice (Special Issue: Hurricane Katrina), 39*, 77–85.

Rizzuto, T., & Reeves, J. (2007) A multidisciplinary analysis of people-related barriers to technology implementation. *Consulting Psychology Journal, 59*(3), 226–240.

Robert, B, & Lajtha, C. (2002). A new approach to crisis management. *Journal of Contingencies and Crisis Management, 10*, 181–191.

Rosenthal, U., Boin, A., & Comfort, L. (2001). *Managing Crises: The management of disasters, riots, and terrorism*. Springfield, IL: Charles C. Thomas Publisher.

Runyan, R. C. (2006). Small business in the face of crisis: Identifying barriers to recovery from natural disasters. *Journal of Contingencies & Crisis Management, 14*, 12–26.

Sanchez, J. I., Korbin, W. P., & Viscarra, D. M. (1995). Corporate support in the aftermath of a natural disaster: Effects on employee strains. *The Academy of Management Journal, 38*, 504–521.

Schneider, B. (1987). The people make the place. *Personnel Psychology, 40*, 437–454.

Shrivastava, S., & Shaw, J. B (2003). Liberating HR through technology. *Human Resource Management, 42*(3), 201–222.

Senge, P. M. (1990). *The fifth discipline: The art and practice of the learning organization*. New York: Doubleday Publishing Group.

Seville, E., Brunsdon, D., Dantas, A., LeMasurier, J., Wilkinson, S., & Vargo, J. (2007). Organizational resilience: Research the reality of New Zealand organizations. *Journal of Business Continuity & Emergency Planning, 2*, 258–266.

Smith, D. (1990). Beyond contingency planning: Towards a model of crisis management. *Industrial Crisis Quarterly, 4*, 263–275.

Stock, G., & McDermott, C. (2001). Organizational and strategic predictors of manufacturing technology implementation success: An exploratory study. *Technovation, 21*(10), 625–636.

Turner, A. (2007). U.S. critical infrastructure in serious jeopardy. *CIO Online. April 19.* Retrieved January 21, 2009, from http://www.cio.com/article/107904/U.S._Critical_Infrastructure_in_Serious_Jeopardy.

Wilson J. P., & Raphael, B. (1993). Theoretical and conceptual foundations of traumatic stress syndromes. *The International Handbook of Traumatic Stress Syndromes.* New York: Plenum Press.

Yu, T., Insead, M. S., & Lester, R. H. (2008). Misery loves company: The spread of negative impacts resulting from an organizational crisis. *Academy of Management Review, 33*, 452–472.

Zotterelli, L. K. (2008). Post-Hurricane Katrina employment recovery: The interaction of race and place. *Social Science Quarterly, 89*, 592–607.

Chapter 14
Disasters and Population Health

Jennifer Johnson and Sandro Galea

Abstract Events of mass trauma are relatively common global phenomena with widespread impact on human health. We conducted this systematic literature review using the National Library of Medicine's PubMed database. We investigated the effect of disasters on six main topic areas of interest: injury and mortality, health systems and infrastructure, mental health, infectious disease, chronic disease, and health behavior. This review covers 182 articles on both natural and man-made disasters, excluding war. We present the results by topic area, across disaster type. This work highlights the scope and heterogeneity of disaster research today, providing a contextual background in which to formulate interventions and disaster planning efforts.

Introduction

The experience of mass traumatic events, or disasters, is a relatively common human experience. The Red Cross estimates nearly 500 disasters occur worldwide every year (excluding droughts and war) in which nearly 50,000 people die, 74,000 are injured, 5 million are displaced, and 80 million people are affected (cited in Norris, Baker, Murphy, & Kaniasty, 2005). Recent high-profile disasters have focused attention on disasters in the peer-reviewed scientific literature as well as in the popular press. However, attention to disasters and their influence on population health tends to be sporadic and focused on the short-term and direct consequences of these events. In many respects, understanding the full scope of the population health consequences of disasters requires an understanding of the short-term and long-term consequences of these events as well as both their direct and their indirect consequences.

S. Galea (✉)
School of Public Health Institute for Social Research, and Center for Global Health, University of Michigan, Ann Arbor MI, 48109-2029, USA
e-mail: sgalea@umich.edu

This chapter reviews the public health effects of disasters in six main areas: injury and mortality, health systems and infrastructure, mental health, infectious disease, chronic disease, and health behavior. Using a population health framework, we will use the available evidence as a springboard for a discussion about the potential full-range population effects of mass traumatic events. We will also identify opportunities for research and future directions in the area.

Method

We conducted an initial title/abstract PubMed search for terms related to our six main topic areas of interest. We limited our search to manuscripts published in the past 10 years (as of July 2008) in English using human subjects, and we excluded studies on disaster preparedness or preparedness guidelines. We limited this search to studies mentioning any study design in their title or abstract. For those main areas where our initial search results were limited (<30 articles), additional searches were conducted with less stringent limitations (e.g., no requisite mention of study design) and/or with additional search terms. Lastly, we investigated articles referenced by reviewed articles for topics not illuminated adequately by our initial search.

Results

Our initial search yielded 118 results, 93 of which were relevant to our review. Some topic areas were over-represented by this search (e.g., mental health, $n = 67$), while others were very limited (e.g., infectious disease, $n = 11$). Additional searches for more limited topics (injury and mortality, health systems and infrastructure, infectious disease, and health behavior) and for articles referenced in reviewed articles yielded 89 additional articles.

In all, our review represents 182 articles: 26 about earthquakes, 37 about storms and floods, 11 about mass fires, 48 about terrorism, 46 about technological disasters, and 14 were research across disaster types. The best-represented disasters were the September 11, 2001 terrorist attacks (35 articles), followed by the Enschede Fireworks Disaster (16 articles), the Indian Ocean Tsunami (12 articles), and the Chernobyl Disaster (12 articles). We present the results of our review below by topic type.

Injury and Mortality

We reviewed over 45 articles on the impact of disasters on injury and mortality, including cross-sectional, cohort, and case studies as well as review articles. Our article base included samples from the general population and from rescue and cleanup personnel. Original research articles on injury and mortality in the general population commonly used medical records from area hospitals and administrative death files. Much of the research on occupationally exposed groups used records from routine occupational medical assessments. Studies using questionnaires, surveys, or focus groups were rare and these instruments were distributed in camps for displaced persons or through hospitals. Review articles were rarely systematic and topics ranged from broad (e.g., all sudden impact disasters, Stratton & Tyler, 2006) to specific (e.g., lightning strike, O'Keefe Gatewood, & Zane, 2004).

We begin this section with a review of current theory regarding distribution of trauma death over time and examine its applicability to disaster settings. Next, we discuss vulnerability factors, followed by a review of disaster-specific injury and mortality patterns, and the burden of emergency response and cleanup activities. Lastly, we briefly discuss the long-term impact of disasters on injury and mortality patterns in affected populations.

Temporal distribution of trauma-related death. The temporal distribution of trauma-related death describes the timing of deaths from trauma after the occurrence of a traumatic event. Though challenging to measure in the disaster setting, the temporal distribution of trauma-related disaster deaths has important practical applications for disaster planning. In a seminal article, Baker, Oppenheimer, Stephens, Lewis, and Trunkey (1980) reviewed all trauma-related deaths in San Francisco in 1977, describing a trimodal temporal distribution (see Fig. 14.1). According to this model, the first and largest peak in deaths occurs almost immediately after trauma due to apnea from severe disruption of the nervous or cardiovascular system; the

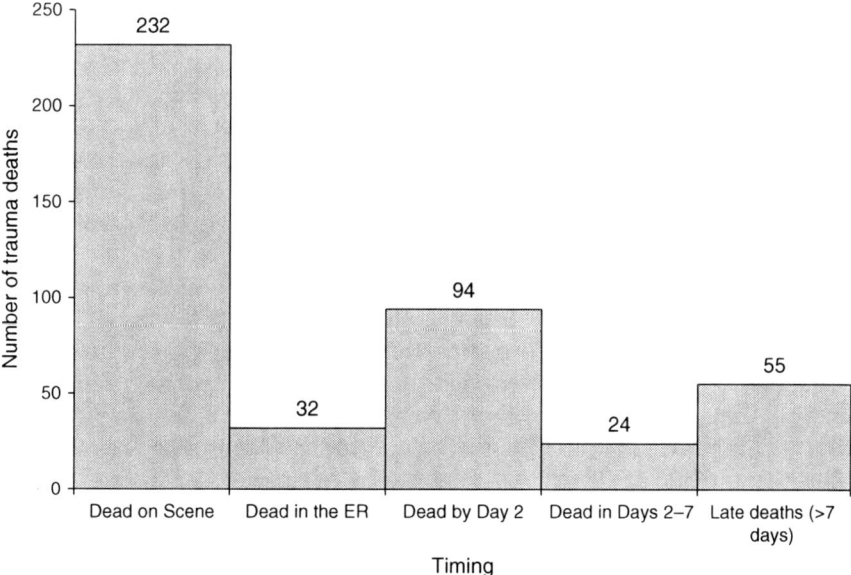

Fig. 14.1 Outcome and length of survival for 437 patients who died from trauma. Reprinted from Baker et al. (1980) with permission from Elsevier

second peak occurs minutes to hours after the trauma as a result of intracranial hematomas, ruptured abdominal organs, penetrating chest trauma, or a combination of injuries; the final peak occurs in the following weeks primarily due to sepsis or organ failure (Johnson & Travis, 2006). Since the time of Baker et al.'s report, researchers have found the temporal distribution of trauma-related deaths to be heterogeneous across different populations and varying over time (Demetriades et al., 2005; Meislin et al., 1997; Sauaia et al., 1995). Nonetheless, one can see how this model, applied on a mass scale, could be useful in disaster settings.

Following the 2004 Indian Ocean Tsunami, Johnson and Travis (2006), working at Krabi Hospital in Thailand, hypothesized a temporal distribution of tsunami-related death that is heavily biased toward the first peak, primarily due to drowning and massive physical injury, with a reduced third peak of deaths. This hypothesis is supported by Nishikiori et al. (2006a, 2006b), who found that 82% of tsunami-related deaths in Ampara district, Sri Lanka, took place within 1 day of the disaster, with an additional 18% within the following 7 days; they found no deaths reported more than 2 months thereafter. The primary causes of tsunami death were drowning, injury, and crush (Nishikiori et al., 2006a). A peak in trauma-related deaths was observed within 3 days of the 1995 Hanshin-Awaji earthquake in Japan, with a later peak in illness-related deaths (Tanaka et al., 1999).

The first peak of trauma deaths may be even greater with intentional man-made disasters, such as bombings and other terrorist attacks, which are both localized and designed specifically to take human life. Of the 168 fatalities in the Oklahoma City bombing, 163 (97%) were dead on-scene (Teague, 2004). There were very few live rescues from the rubble following the September 11, 2001 terrorist attacks (Bradt, 2003). Studies in the United States show that the majority of injuries presenting to hospitals after disaster tend to be minor (Mallonee et al., 1996; Stratton & Tyler, 2006; Teague, 2004). This may be due, in part, to the low number of live rescues after more severe disasters. Paradoxically, less severe disasters may produce far more burden of injury than more severe ones. For example, the 2003 US blackout nearly doubled the emergency medical system load in New York City during the 29 hours the city was without power, with increases in a range of call types, including difficulty breathing, injury, cardiac arrest, seizure, active labor, gunshot, and falls (Freese et al., 2006).

Certainly, there is substantial evidence that earlier rescue after disasters predicts greater probability of survival (Gautschi, Cadosch, Rajan, & Zellweger, 2008). In their review of earthquakes, Peleg, Reuveni, and Stein (2002) found that the vast majority of survivors were rescued within the first day, while those who are rescued on day 2 or beyond had a much lower probability of survival. In the 1995 Oklahoma City bombing, most of the 38 individuals requiring extrication were rescued within 45 minutes of detonation and only 3 survivors were rescued over 3 hours after the bombing (Teague, 2004). In the 2004 Indian Ocean Tsunami, Johnson and Travis (2006) noted that many victims likely perished as a result of heat and sun exposure while awaiting medical care. With increased emergency response and transportation time, those at risk of death within the first few hours of disaster will likely perish before reaching major treatment centers. This may also help explain why many studies based on medical records show that the majority of disaster-related injuries are minor (Mallonee et al., 1996; Stratton & Tyler, 2006; Teague, 2004).

Vulnerability factors. Several studies have identified demographic and circumstantial risk factors for injury and death following disasters. Demographic groups with low pre-disaster resources, mobility, and power are the most vulnerable to disaster-related injury and death (see Allen & Wayne, Chapter 8, for a related discussion). Circumstantial risk factors tend to be more disaster dependent. Nishikiori et al. (2006b) found that women, children, and the elderly were at higher risk of death due to the 2004 Tsunami in Sri Lanka. Chou et al. (2004) found that people with mental disorders, moderate physical disabilities, and recent hospitalization were more likely to die in the 1999 Taiwan earthquake. After Katrina, Brunkard, Namulanda, and Ratard (2008) found that mortality was higher among blacks and people 75 years and older. There is mixed evidence income-associated vulnerability. Chou et al. (2004) found that lower-income individuals were at higher risk of death after the tsunami, while Shoaf, Sareen, Nguyen, and Bourque (1998) found no association between income level and injury in three California earthquakes.

Lastly, for those who have poorer pre-disaster health, disasters may precipitate death, specifically with respect to cardiovascular events. Studies in Athens, Greece, and Northridge, California, both found excess cardiac mortality associated with earthquakes in these locations (Leor, Poole, & Kloner, 1996; Trichopoulos, Katsouyanni, Zavitsanos, Tzonou, & Dalla-Vorgia, 1983). In addition, the Northridge study found a decline in cardiac deaths to below baseline in the 6 days following the day of the earthquake (Leor et al., 1996). This pattern indicates that the earthquake and its associated stress may have hastened cardiac death in those who were already at risk of dying in the near future (Stalnikowicz & Tsafrir, 2002).

In an interesting comparison, Brown (1999) found no increased acute myocardial infarction (AMI) hospital admissions after the Loma Preita earthquake, which unlike the Athens or Northridge earthquakes, occurred during the daytime. Brown concludes that it was the stress of *both* earthquake and wakening that triggered the increase in cardiac death after the Northridge earthquake and that, in less vulnerable time periods (i.e., the daytime), there is no significant increase in incidence of heart attack during disasters. The literature supports the hypothesis that activities both before and after disasters may predict risk of injury or death. Glass and Zack (1979) found that cardiac deaths remained elevated for 8 days after blizzards in Massachusetts, 90% of which were due to ischemic heart disease, with an increased risk for men. The continued elevation in death suggested to the authors that activities after the storms (for example, shoveling snow and, oddly, sexual activity evidenced by excess births 9 months after a 1978 blizzard) may have resulted in the observed sustained rise in cardiac mortality.

Location at the time of disaster is another important circumstantial risk factors for death. Being indoors at the time of a tsunami or an earthquake is associated with increased risk of death (Nishikiori et al., 2006b; Peleg et al., 2002). Accordingly, factors influencing probability of being indoors at the time of earthquake, such as time of day and year, may have implications for mortality (Peleg et al., 2002). Occupation may be tied to location during disaster and thus tied to vulnerability; for example, being a fisherman was associated with tsunami death (Nishikiori et al., 2006b). The character and location of a building is especially important in the context of earthquake, including the type of ground built upon, building height and materials, quality of construction, distance to epicenter (Peleg et al., 2002), type of dwelling (Shoaf et al., 1998), and peak ground acceleration (Schultz, Koenig, & Lewis, 2007; Shoaf et al., 1998). Shoaf et al. (1998) also found that those who moved or attempted to move after an earthquake were more likely to report being injured. In a study of the Union Carbide Disaster, about one-half of those exposed to the gas cloud reported fleeing their homes – most often by walking or running and sometimes for hours – resulting in increased ventilatory rate (Dhara, Dhara, Acquilla, & Cullinan, 2002). Dhara et al. (2002) show that a total exposure index that integrates physical activity following disaster with exposure duration and location is associated with health outcomes, independent of distance to the plant.

Disaster-specific injury and mortality patterns. Because disasters are so diverse – from fires to floods to earthquakes – injury and mortality patterns cannot be adequately summarized across disaster types. This section is not meant as a comprehensive list of all possible health consequences of each disaster type, but rather as a review of the chief injuries and causes of death as supported by the literature.

In conventional weapon terrorism, the main medical concern is blast trauma injury, which may have systemic effects including effects on the lungs, abdomen, ear, eye, extremities, and other injuries (Born et al., 2007), although injuries in multiple anatomical regions are common (Kalebi & Olumbe, 2006). Gas-filled structures – namely lungs, GI tract, and the auditory system – suffer high levels of damage due to the high external pressure of an explosive wave (Crabtree, 2006). Among survivors, common injuries include soft-tissue injuries, fractures, sprains, strains, head injuries, and maxillofacial injuries, including soft-tissue injuries and eye injuries (Mallonee et al., 1996; Odhiambo, Guthua, Macigo, & Akama, 2002). Head injury may be a common cause of death (Kalebi & Olumbe, 2006). Bombings are also associated with shrapnel injuries, traumatic amputation, burns, inhalation injuries, crush syndrome, and pregnancy complications (Crabtree, 2006).

The largest concerns during fire disasters are toxic gas and smoke inhalation, as well as burns (Gewalli & Fogdestam, 2003; Meyer, 2003; van Harten et al., 2006). After electrocution, cardiopulmonary arrest is the most common cause of death; common injuries include neurologic injury, headache, burns, blunt and explosive injuries, eye and ear injuries, fetal death, hematologic abnormalities, and endocrine and sexual dysfunction (O'Keefe Gatewood & Zane, 2004).

The largest concerns for injury and mortality in floods and storms include drowning, extremity fractures, soft-tissue wounds, sprains, lacerations, near-drowning-associated aspiration pneumonias, and hypothermia (Llewellyn, 2006; Maegele et al., 2005). Primary mortality concerns after earthquake include spinal cord injury and crush syndrome (Rathore et al., 2007; Sever et al., 2002).

Chemical and radiological disasters are different from those discussed thus far in that much of the burden of injury is not immediate and may only become apparent after longer-term follow-up. Of 134 plant employees and first responders diagnosed with acute radiation sickness following the Chernobyl Disaster, there were

28 short-term (2 months) and 14 long-term (15 years) deaths, with underlying bone marrow failure and beta burns as the main contributors to early deaths (Mettler, Gus'kova, & Gusev, 2007). The action of chemical exposures depends on the chemical in question and may be system wide. For example, nosocomial exposure to Thorium X in the 1940s was associated with damage to the bone and cartilage as well as cancer of the bone, connective tissue, breast, thyroid, liver, kidney, pancreas, uterus, and bladder (Spiess, 2002), while exposure to dioxin-contaminated cooking oil in Italy in 1976 was associated with mortality from lymphoemopoietic, digestive, and respiratory cancers (Pesatori et al., 2003). Acute irritation and damage to the respiratory, ocular, and gastrointestinal systems were the main immediate effects of the Union Carbide gas leak in Bhopal, India (Beckett, 1998), although there is evidence for persistent ocular, respiratory, immunity, genetic, neurological, neurobehavioral, and reproductive effects as well as cancer (Dhara & Dhara, 2002). Many chemical exposures may be brought about as a result of other disasters, for example, rescue or cleanup workers after bombings may be exposed to damaging chemicals from collapsed buildings, or toxic gases may be released as a result of materials burning in a fire.

Lastly, many disaster-related injuries result from the breakdown of safety controls, infrastructure, and from individuals' attempts to adapt to the disaster. For example, the use of portable generators led to 47 carbon monoxide poisoning incidents during the 2004 Florida Hurricane season, leading to nearly 150 nonfatal and 6 fatal cases of carbon monoxide poisoning (Sniffen et al., 2005). Dog bite and electrocution injuries are also associated with floods and tsunamis (Llewellyn, 2006), while insect stings and bites associated with hurricanes and floods (Diaz, 2007).

Burden of emergency response and cleanup activities. Those who come to search for and rescue disaster victims are often at a high risk for injury and morbidity themselves (see Speier, Osofsky, & Osofsky, Chapter 12, for a related discussion). Cleanup activities, which may take years, also place workers at risk for toxic exposures. These groups represent secondary victims of disaster. Nowhere is this topic better documented than in the case of the September 11, 2001 terrorist attack attacks on New York City. Of the 2,801 individuals killed, 403 were fire personnel or law enforcement, together composing 14% of the dead (Bradt, 2003). After the collapse of the first tower, emergency medicine personnel on-scene were forced to stop triage and flee for their own safety (Asaeda, 2002). Rescue efforts had to contend with extreme heat and underground fires, falling hazards, dust and smoke, wind gusts, toxic substances, and waste disposal (Bradt, 2003).

Relief workers after September 11, 2001, terrorist attack suffered ocular injuries, headaches, sprains, and strains as well as symptoms of the skin, eye, nose, and throat (Bradt, 2003; Feldman et al., 2004). There is overwhelming evidence of compromised respiratory health of rescue and cleanup workers after September 11, 2001, terrorist attack and other disasters (Banauch et al., 2003; Feldman et al., 2004; Mauer, Cummings, & Carlson, 2007; Skloot et al., 2004). One report estimated that within 1 year after September 11, 2001 terrorist attack, cleanup workers suffered an average decline of lung volume equivalent to 12 years of normal age-related decline (Banauch et al., 2006). Respiratory protection measures are known to be effective in the post-disaster setting. Workers often reported using no protection, and the most common form used was a hardware store paint/dust mask (Banauch et al., 2006; Feldman et al., 2004; Mauer et al., 2007), which provides no benefit (Banauch et al., 2006). Respirators with canisters appear to provide some protection against large airway dysfunction (Skloot et al., 2004).

The evidence from the Enschede Fireworks Disaster in 2000 shows similarities to the research on September 11, 2001 terrorist attack rescue and cleanup activities. Workers involved in cleanup and rescue activities after the Enschede Fireworks Disaster showed increase in musculoskeletal, GI, respiratory, and non-specific or medically unexplained ill health (Dirkzwager, Yzermans, & Kessels, 2004; Morren, Dirkzwager, Kessels, & Yzermans, 2007).

Long-lasting impact. Injuries and deaths sustained in disasters have a longstanding impact on affected communities. Many individuals suffer permanent disability as a result of injuries sustained during disaster. For example, many survivors of the 2005 earthquake in Pakistan who suffered spinal cord injuries became paraplegic and required ongoing aggressive rehabilitation in settings where rehabilitation resources are scarce (Rathore et al., 2007; Tauqir, Mirza, Gul, Ghaffar, & Zafar, 2007). Complications of paraplegia in this setting included pressure ulcers, urinary tract infections, deep venous thromboses, bowel problems, and surgical wound infections (Rathore et al., 2007; Tauqir et al., 2007). Moreover, when these individuals return to their communities, motor problems may make original employment impossible. Gul et al. (2008) demonstrated that their training program in telemedicine effectively prepared paraplegic survivors make the transition to cognitive employment, but it is unknown whether these individuals were able to obtain and keep employment as a result of these new skills.

Kirigia, Sambo, Aldis, and Mwabu (2002) conducted a cost analysis to quantify the economic burden of disaster-associated deaths in the WHO Africa Region. They found that each death due to natural and technological disasters reduced the gross domestic product significantly by US $0.018, a substantial loss in an area where about 50% of the population lives on under US $1 per day. Keeping in mind that the Kirigia study was insensitive to the costs of injury, health care, reconstruction, and property damage among others, it may not be possible to accurately calculate the full cost of disasters.

As mentioned previously, disability from chemical exposures may be long term or permanent. A teratogenic agent is a chemical or an environmental factor that is known to cause damage to the developing fetus. For disasters involving chemical exposure, research often focuses on teratogenic outcomes, which affect communities for generations to come. The nosocomial thalidomide disaster of the 1950s and 1960s led to birth defects characterized by reduction deformities of the limbs and sensory nervous system for children whose mothers were exposed to the drug (McCredie & Willert, 1999). There is even some evidence, though inconclusive, for congenital effects of the Chernobyl Disaster throughout Europe (Hoffmann, 2001). Children with birth abnormalities and their families require additional community support and health services throughout their lives. We will cover additional evidence of chronic outcomes of disaster in the section Chronic Disease.

Health Systems and Infrastructure

We reviewed over 40 articles on the impact of disasters on health systems and infrastructure, including cross-sectional, cohort, and case studies as well as review articles. We examine both the burden of disasters on the health system and the challenges to provision of health services in the disaster setting. Studies looking at health services utilization or patient needs often used medical records, records of sick leave from work, or surveys. Studies evaluating damage to the health system or the health system response were commonly case studies or review articles utilizing administrative data; surveys and key informant interviews were used less frequently.

We begin this section with a discussion of the challenges to rescue and emergency medical operations during and immediately following disaster, followed by a review of the longer-term impact of disasters on health-care delivery. Next, we discuss emergency medical assistance teams and challenges to the provision of medical services unrelated to the disaster. We close this section by reviewing primary care and mental health-care utilization patterns in the aftermath of disaster.

Challenges to rescue and emergency medical operations. During disasters, safety of emergency and rescue workers may pose a significant challenge. While rescuing patients and providing medical attention in a timely manner is important, rescue and emergency medical workers run the risk of becoming casualties themselves if safety precautions are not followed or if the disaster takes an unexpected turn (Bradt, 2003; Teague, 2004). Rescue workers after September 11, 2001 terrorist attack had to contend with extreme heat and underground fires, falling hazards, wind gusts, and toxic substances (Bradt, 2003). Health systems must make sure that their workers have adequate prophylaxis against toxic exposures, for example, respirators to prevent pulmonary damage (Skloot et al., 2004). Rescue personnel working after the Marmara Earthquake reported their most important personal problems were health, accommodation, food, and safety (Altntas & Delooz, 2004).

Those same rescue workers after Marmara reported that their most important organization/system problems were coordination and disaster management (Altntas & Delooz, 2004). Because of their very nature, disasters pose a threat to even the best laid preparedness plans. After September 11, 2001 terrorist attack, the emergency operations centers (EOC) was first established in World Trade Center Building 7, but relocated first on September 11 because of impending building collapse, and second on September 14 due to inadequate space (Bradt, 2003). The placement of EOCs must keep safety and stability in mind.

Damage to the infrastructure, especially for non-localized disasters like earthquakes, is challenging to the provision of medical services to victims and existing patients. Existing health facilities may need to be evacuated and even condemned in the post-disaster setting (Peleg et al., 2002; Schultz et al., 2007; Sepehri & Meimandi, 2006). Where hospitals cannot be evacuated in time, they face some severe obstacles to providing care. In the days following Katrina, multiple large hospitals in New Orleans operated without power or sanitation in extreme heat (Brunkard et al., 2008). At least 70 hospital inpatients died in New Orleans hospitals and 57 victims' bodies were recovered from hospitals in the days immediately following the storm, indicating that their deaths occurred in the hospital as a result of the storm (Brunkard et al., 2008). Systems of particular concern to hospitals are oxygen supply, electricity, water, and elevators (Peleg et al., 2002). Determining hospitals' risk for damage may be difficult after sudden-onset disasters. For example, Schultz et al. (2007) showed that distance from the earthquake epicenter, the measure typically used by emergency managers, may be a less valid predictor of hospital closure than peak ground acceleration. However, peak ground acceleration data require ongoing data collection and communication in the post-disaster setting.

Another challenge to disaster-related emergency care that is nearly universal across all types of disasters is increased response time. During the New York City blackout, emergency medical response was enhanced by enlisting cross-trained firefighter and first responder companies to supplement demand; nonetheless, call-processing times within the city's September 11, 2001 terrorist attack telephone system were the rate-limiting step in emergency care – they increased fourfold during the hours of blackout (Freese et al., 2006). A challenge to both emergency transportation and patient transfer during disasters is a transportation corridor (Gautschi et al., 2008). Establishing safe and efficient transportation routes to and from the disaster site is important where roads, themselves, are damaged, but also after disasters involving mass exodus of people from buildings into the streets.

When hospitals have not been damaged, they may expect to be overwhelmed first by patients and later by families. Emergency care systems in the United States function near-capacity at times, with little elasticity for absorbing disaster-associated surge in demand (Stratton & Tyler, 2006). In the aftermath of the Gothenburg Disco Fire, misinformation and lack of communication led to the hospital's emergency disaster plan not being launched and on-scene triage not being established (Gewalli & Fogdestam, 2003). As a result, the "scoop and run" technique of patient transportation was practiced, placing major burden on receiving hospitals. Indeed, loss of communication during disasters has been reported by hospitals after many types of disasters, from earthquakes (Peleg et al., 2002; Rathore et al., 2007) to terrorist attacks (Bradt, 2003; Frank, Dewart, Schmeidler, & Demirjian, 2006), to tsunamis (Maegele et al., 2005).

Timing of patient load and arrival of outside assistance are often unfortunately mismatched. In a review of sudden impact disasters in the United States, the earliest outside assistance arrived was 24 hours (range of 24–96 hours), with peak demand occurring within 24 hours of disaster (Stratton & Tyler, 2006). After September 11, 2001 terrorist attack, the first disaster medical assistance team arrived 36 hours after the disaster (Bradt, 2003). After the Oklahoma City bombing, hospitals saw patients arriving as soon as 15 minutes post-disaster with peak arrival time of 60–120 minutes post-disaster (Teague, 2004). It is this mismatch that led Llewellyn (2006) to recommend that emergency units plan to be self-sustaining for 72 hours post-disaster, with a special emphasis on the importance of communications, supplies (especially, tetanus antitoxins, antibiotics, and insulin), and record keeping. Bradt (2003) also stressed the importance of system assets in the September 11, 2001 terrorist attack response, including action planning from incident command, GIS products, wireless technology, and workers' respite care.

Some populations may present ethical dilemmas to those providing emergency care. For example, Opium addicts suffering from a severed drug supply following the Bam Earthquake often tried to leverage rescue operations to obtain drugs and prevent withdrawal, with relative success (Movaghar et al., 2005). After September 11, 2001 terrorist attack, administrators of methadone maintenance programs in New York City faced an ethical dilemma as well: many patients reported trouble making the trek to their programs due to interrupted public transportation or chose to go to other closer clinics instead (Frank et al., 2006). Administrators were forced to make decisions about dosage for guest patients, sometimes without verification, and about take-home dosages for their own patients, given the instability of public transportation.

Challenges to health care in the post-disaster setting. Even after those directly injured have been treated, population health continues to face significant challenges after disasters. Those with chronic conditions may have been separated from their providers, their records, or their medications as a result of the disaster (Stratton & Tyler, 2006). In addition, personal care for even serious conditions may be placed on the backburner to the more pressing concerns of finding loved ones, arranging for burials, and surveying damage (Guha-Sapir, van Panhuis, & Lagoutte, 2007). Connecting these individuals to care in a timely manner is essential (see Allen & Wayne, Chapter 8, for discussion).

Disasters may result in permanent disability, with accompanying need for follow-up. Rathore et al. (2007) suggested the creation of a registry for those suffering paraplegia following earthquake to facilitate their continued contact with the medical system and rehabilitation planning. In fact, registries/lists of injured individuals or survivors have been implemented after some disasters, for example, the Oklahoma City bombing (Tucker et al., 2007), the Luby Cafeteria Shooting (North, McCutcheon, Spitznagel, & Smith, 2002), and the Enschede Fireworks Disaster (Dirkzwager, Kerssens, & Yzermans, 2006). However, these lists require high-quality data collection and collaboration during the disaster and may not be possible for more large-scale disasters where the health system itself is under fire.

Tourists and expatriate victims, residing in a country other than their upbringing, may return to their home countries to be treated, carrying with them both common and uncommon polymicrobial infections of multiple-resistant pathogens (Maegele et al., 2006; Uckay, Sax, Harbarth, Bernard, & Pittet, 2008). Although these pathogens are unlikely to spread to other patients (Uckay et al., 2008), health systems of home countries may be challenged to deal with them in the weeks to months following their return home.

Outside of rescue and medical operations, immediate public health concerns include food, clean water, sanitation, and shelter for survivors (Llewellyn, 2006). Those who have been displaced from their homes are vulnerable to insects, heat and cold, and other environmental hazards (Llewellyn, 2006). A study in a Sri Lankan relief camp 1 month after the 2004 Tsunami found that 16.1, 20.2, and 34.7% of children were wasted, stunted, and underweight, respectively, while 37% of pregnant women were undernourished (Jayatissa, Bekele, Piyasena, & Mahamithawa,

2006). Researchers in this study stressed the importance of food diversity, vitamin A megadose supplementation for children, and nutritional surveillance.

At times, the patient demand may greatly exceed the capacity of existing health systems. Cyclone-related flooding in Mozambique in 2000 led to the displacement of nearly 450,000 people; the small village of Hoke, for example, with an original population of 22,000, received approximately 33,000 displaced people, with only one local health facility (Hashizume et al., 2006). Flooding associated with the hurricanes, combined with lack of shelter, put many displaced persons at risk for malaria (Loveridge, Henner, & Lee, 2003). Where the existing health system is unequipped to diagnose patients in an efficient manner, new methods of diagnoses may be called for; the use of outside assistance is essential in areas with scarce health resources (Hashizume et al., 2006; Loveridge et al., 2003).

While the time period immediately after disaster may see an influx of support from within and outside the affected communities, that support may waver in the months to follow. Although there were excess blood donations shortly following September 11, 2001 terrorist attack (Glynn et al., 2003) and the Marmara earthquake (Sonmezoglu et al., 2005), blood donations were paradoxically short several months after Maramara.

Lastly, both administrative and individual cleanup operations place a certain burden on natural hazards and social well-being of disaster-effected areas. Cleanup operations from Ground Zero in New York City, namely, demolition activities, raised concerns about the integrity of a landfill wall on the Huron River (Bradt, 2003). Cleanup efforts may also put individuals at risk of contact with unusual hazardous substances, for example, Freon or asbestos (Bradt, 2003). After an Indian earthquake, wood used to cremate dead bodies exhausted survivors' supplies for cooking and heating (Ligon, 2006).

Emergency medical assistance teams. Because emergency medical assistance teams usually arrive on-scene within days to weeks of the disaster (Stratton & Tyler, 2006), existing emergency medical systems bear the brunt medical demands of severely injured and dying patients within the first few days of disaster (Llewellyn, 2006; also see Speier et al., Chapter 12). Nonetheless, emergency medical teams provide assistance to the much more numerous patients with minor medical conditions and those who have been displaced or evacuated as a result of disaster. Over 95% of patients seen by emergency medical teams responding to 1992 Hurricanes Andrew (Florida) and Iniki (Hawaii) were triaged to yellow (delayed care) or green (walking wounded) and around 90% of patients in each storm were sent home after their visit. The most common chief complaints of patients were wounds, musculoskeletal pain, medication refills, upper respiratory infections, rashes, and abdominal complaints (Nufer & Wilson-Ramirez, 2004). The most common pharmaceutical needs of medical assistance teams following natural disasters include tetanus vaccinations and wound care, respiratory, antibacterial, analgesic, gastrointestinal, and psychiatric medications as well as medication refills (Nufer & Wilson-Ramirez, 2004; Sepehri & Meimandi, 2006).

Medication refills are an important consideration for victims with pre-existing conditions. After a series of four hurricanes in 2004, 5.4% of Florida residents reported worsening of existing medical conditions and 13.6% reported difficulty obtaining medications (Stratton & Tyler, 2006). The first week after the establishment of a Red Cross field hospital in post-tsunami Aceh, workers saw an excess of patients with chronic conditions, which they attributed to the complete absence of health services in the previous 2 weeks, causing interruption of treatment for patients with existing conditions (Guha-Sapir et al., 2007).

Challenges to other medical services. The simultaneous relocation of facilities and patients after disaster, along with the possible destruction of medical records, may pose a challenge to re-aligning patients and their care providers. For example, Hyre, Cohen, Kutner, Alper, and Muntner (2007) studied hemodialysis patients in New Orleans, finding that nearly 45% had missed one or more treatments as a result of Hurricane Katrina, with over 15% missing three or more treatments. Again, this is not a surprising statistic given all nine hemodialysis treatment facilities in New Orleans where participants who were recruited were closed in the immediate aftermath of Katrina and two remained closed throughout the conduct of the study. Moreover, participants in the Hyre study were living in 18 states at the time of interview.

Damages to infrastructure are often inequitable. Using geographic information systems, Guidry and Margolis (2005) found that low-income schools where the majority of students were Black had twice the risk of flooding after Hurricane Floyd of 1999 as non-low-income schools with a majority of non-Black students. Damages to other infrastructure, for example, public transit, may disproportionately affect lower-income residents who may not have any other available mode of transit. As mentioned previously, problems with public transportation were sited as a major challenge to receipt of care for existing medical problems (Frank et al., 2006).

Primary health-care utilization. Victims of disaster and residents of affected communities often have increased demand for many health-care services. Care for injuries sustained may be lifelong; on the other hand, physical symptoms immediately following disaster may return to baseline levels after months or years. Primary health-care utilization for physical complaints after disaster is closely tied to psychological health both before and after disaster, as well as disaster-exposure level. The following risk factors have been identified for primary health-care contacts: (a) *direct exposure level to disaster* – witnessing the disaster, residing in a disaster-affected area (Dorn, Yzermans, Kerssens, Spreeuwenberg, & van der Zee, 2006; Remennick, 2002); (b) *indirect consequences of disaster*– loss of a child as a result of disaster (Dorn et al., 2006); (c) *participation in the disaster response*– rescuing people, supporting injured victims, identifying victims, or remains (Slottje et al., 2008); (d) *exposure to negative life events* (Boscarino, Adams, & Figley, 2006); (e) *post-disaster mental health services utilization* (den Ouden, Dirkzwager, & Yzermans, 2005) *and depression* (Boscarino, Adams, & Figley, 2006); and (f) *pre-disaster lifetime traumatic event experience* (Boscarino, Adams, & Figley, 2006).

There is strong evidence that post-disaster increases in health services utilization are mediated by psychopathology. For example, self-reported post-traumatic stress disorder 18 months after the Enshcede Fireworks disaster-predicted family practice reported vascular problems over the following 2 years (Dirkzwager et al., 2007).

The authors of this study suggest that the effects of psychopathology may operate through neurobiology, health behaviors, or heightened symptoms perception. The den Ouden study (2005) showed that individuals who visited a specialized mental health institution (MHI) after disaster presented with greater health problems to their general practitioners (GP) before the disaster, compared to survivors who did not visit the MHI; in addition, the MHI group had increased rates of GP attendance both 1 and 2 years after disaster, compared to their own baseline as well as controls (den Ouden et al., 2005). This suggests that those who are already vulnerable before disaster, with greater physical and mental health complaints, are more sensitive to the effects of disaster on their physical health.

Several studies show that primary health-care utilization in post-disaster settings is not closely tied to the severity of physical symptoms, themselves. For example, in an industrial hygiene evaluation of a workplace very close to the World Trade Center Disaster found that medical service utilization among workers in the New York City building was no different than that of workers in Dallas, TX, despite increased reports of constitutional symptoms, like headache, eye, nose, and throat irritation (Trout, Nimgade, Mueller, Hall, & Earnest, 2002). Van den Berg et al. (2007) studied a group of individuals residing in the area affected by the Enschede Fireworks Disaster; they found that the majority of self-reported physical symptoms were not presented to a general practitioner; moreover, decision to consult a GP for an individual symptom was dependent on persistence, rather than on impairment and distress.

Lastly, disaster experiences may affect the satisfaction with health-care services. Remennick (2002) found that immigrants to Israel from Chernobyl Disaster-affected areas used more health services and were less satisfied with quality of health care and their providers' attitudes than immigrants from non-affected areas in 1997. The fact that cancer-related anxiety was highly prevalent *more than a decade* after the accident reflects a unrelenting psychological toll of exposure to nuclear accidents.

Mental health services utilization. Mental health services utilization (MHSU) has been studied extensively in the post-disaster setting. Data on MHSU are closely tied to primary health-care utilization, as both physical and psychological symptoms are often presented to primary-care physicians. In one study, correlation between general practitioner-reported and self-reported psychopathology was highest for intrusive and avoidant symptoms, but much lower for depression, anxiety, and sleep symptoms (Drogendijk et al., 2007). The authors of this study suggest that some symptoms (e.g., depression) may be more likely than others to be superseded by physical symptoms when presented simultaneously to physicians.

Risk factors for MHSU after disaster include (a) *level of exposure to disaster* – being trapped even if uninjured, residence in an affected area (Boscarino, Adams, Stuber, & Galea, 2005; Dorn et al., 2006; Smith, Christiansen, Vincent, & Hann, 1999; van der Velden et al., 2006); (b) *indirect consequences of disaster* – loss of a child or relocation (Dorn et al., 2006; Soeteman et al., 2007; van der Velden, Yzermans, Kleber, & Gersons, 2007b); (c) *residence in a geographically proximate area* (Ford, Adams, & Dailey, 2006); (d) *having a perievent panic attack* (Boscarino,

Adams, Stuber, et al., 2005); (e) *access* – having private insurance, a regular doctor (Boscarino, Adams, Stuber, et al., 2005; van der Velden et al., 2007b); (f) *demographics* – female gender, single, migrant status, white race (Boscarino, Adams, Stuber, et al., 2005; van der Velden et al., 2007b); (g) *history of psychological problems* (Soeteman et al., 2007; van der Velden et al., 2007b); (h) *poor post-disaster mental health* or mental health symptomatology (Ford et al., 2006; Jordan et al., 2004; van der Velden et al., 2006, 2007b); and (i) *receiving post-disaster mental health treatment* (den Ouden et al., 2005; van der Velden et al., 2007b).

Many of the risk factors listed above for MHSU are similar to the risk factors for primary health-care utilization. There is ample evidence that both pre-disaster conditions (e.g., psychological morbidity, demographics) and disaster-related experiences (relocation, panic attack) have implications for MHSU in the post-disaster setting.

Mental Health

We reviewed 75 articles on the mental health impact of disasters, including cross-sectional, cohort, and case studies as well as review articles. Our article base included samples from the general population and from rescue and cleanup personnel. Much of the research on this topic uses cross-sectional or cohort study designs, relying on surveys, interviews and, when available, medical records.

Studies that included a comparison group did so in primarily two ways: (1) by comparing pre-disaster mental health to post-disaster mental health (e.g., time series, pre-post surveys) and (2) by assessing mental health outcomes in groups with different levels of disaster exposure/consequences (e.g., injured vs. uninjured victims, residents of affected cities vs. comparison cities). Some did not incorporate a comparison group in their study design, but explicitly asked about disaster-related mental health outcomes or increase/decrease since a disaster. Though these studies may suffer problems with information bias, they at least allow the respondent to specify whether changes in their mental health have occurred as a result of disaster (rather than as a result of other things unique to the individual such as divorce or death in the family).

Lastly, some studies did not incorporate a comparison group and did not specify disaster-specific outcomes – these studies were primarily looking at risk factors for psychopathology in the post-disaster context/setting, rather than as a result of the disaster itself. These studies are difficult to interpret in disaster research because the reader has no idea whether the distribution or prevalence of psychopathology is (a) different from normal or (b) occurred as a result of a disaster (rather than as a result of other things). We have included all types of studies in our review below; studies in this last group are marked with an asterisk (∗).

The different mental health measures summarized in this review include non-specific measures of mental health, sleep problems, somatic complaints and medically unexplained symptoms, post-traumatic stress disorder, depression, anxiety, behavioral problems (in children), adult mental health and in utero exposures, suicidality, and problems with occupational and daily functioning.

Non-specific measures of mental health. The incidence of mental health problems after disaster has been measured in a number of ways, from psychological problems presented to physician to sickness absences due to psychological problems to self-reported symptomatology in interviews or surveys. We include in this category studies that measured poor mental health status, stress, worry, grief, mental health complaints, negative affect, psychological impairment, non-specific distress, momentary moods, vitality, and health-related quality of life (HRQoL). Some studies focused on rescue and cleanup workers, while others focused on affected survivors, the general population, or special populations, like children (Dirkzwager et al., 2006), or people with chronic illness (van den Berg, van der Velden, Yzermans, Stellato, & Grievink, 2006).

Risk factors for non-specific mental health problems include (a) *direct exposure level to disaster* – degree of exposure (de Mel, McKenzie, & Woodruff, 2008; Norris et al., 2002; Wang et al., 2000), witnessing injury, death, or destruction (Ghaffari-Nejad, Ahmadi-Mousavi, Gandomkar, & Reihani-Kermani, 2007; Thomas, 2006), and direct threat of disaster (Thomas, 2006); (b) *participation in rescue and cleanup* (Dirkzwager et al., 2004; Huizink et al., 2006; Slottje et al., 2007; Spinhoven & Verschuur, 2006); (c) *media exposure* (Ford, Adams, & Dailey, 2007; Thomas, 2006; Wayment, 2004); (d) *characteristics of the disaster* – mass violence/intentional man-made event rather than an accidental or a natural disaster (Norris et al., 2002; Thomas, 2006); (e) *indirect consequences of disaster* – having a child with a severe injury (Dorn, Yzermans, Spreeuwenberg, & van der Zee, 2007), having a close one affected by disaster (Slottje et al., 2007), relocation or residential problem (Dirkzwager et al., 2006; Foster, 2002; Ghaffari-Nejad et al., 2007; Soeteman et al., 2007; Thomas, 2006), or community destruction (Thomas, 2006); (f) *proximity* – proximity to disaster (Foster, 2002; Thomas, 2006), being in the disaster-affected area/city at the time of disaster (Ghaffari-Nejad et al., 2007; Remennick, 2002; Smith et al., 1999; Soeteman et al., 2007), working near the disaster site (Trout et al., 2002); interestingly, some research has found signs of distress in geographically distant groups immediately after disaster, but with no change in ongoing moods (Whalen, Henker, King, Jamner, & Levine, 2004); (g) *alcohol problems since disaster* – alcohol dependence or problems (Adams, Bocarino, & Galea, 2006a, 2006b; Gaher, Simons, Jacobs, Meyer, & Johnson-Jimenez, 2006), or ongoing/increased alcohol use (Ford et al., 2007; Pfefferbaum et al., 2002); (h) *events since the disaster* – negative life event (Adams et al., 2006a), secondary stressors (Norris et al., 2002), post-disaster traumatic effects unrelated to disaster (Adams et al., 2006a); (i) *demographics* – female gender (de Mel et al., 2008; Dorn, Yzermans, Spreeuwenberg, et al., 2007; Ford et al., 2006; 2007; Norris et al., 2002; Thomas, 2006; Wayment, 2004), age <64 years or disability (Ford et al., 2006), minority race or ethnicity (de Mel et al., 2008; Ford et al., 2006; Norris et al., 2002; Thomas, 2006), low–medium socioeconomic status or education level (Dirkzwager et al., 2006; Ghaffari-Nejad et al., 2007), living in a developing country, middle age (Norris et al., 2002); (j) *pre-disaster psychopathology* – pre-disaster psychological problems (Dirkzwager et al., 2006; Norris et al., 2002; Soeteman et al., 2007; Wayment, 2004), pre-disaster victimization by intimate partner violence (Frasier et al., 2004), pessimism (van der Velden et al., 2007a), previous traumatic or stressful event exposure (Thomas, 2006; Wayment, 2004); (k) *social factors* – weak or deteriorating psychosocial resources (Norris et al., 2002), lower level of social support (Trout et al., 2002), less post-disaster help (Wang et al., 2000), post-disaster social strain (Wayment, 2004); (l) *other* – perceived similarity to victims (Wayment, 2004), perceived risk (Foster, 2002), having sleep problems post-disaster (Ford et al., 2006), loss of a first-degree relative during previous earthquakes (Ghaffari-Nejad et al., 2007); conversely, chronic illness was not a risk factor for mental health problems (van den Berg et al., 2006).

Many of these risk factors for mental health problems after disaster may be risk factors for mental health problems, in general. For example, van der Velden et al. (2007a) found that pessimistic victims were at higher risk for mental health symptoms after disaster than optimistic victims, but so were pessimistic non-victims. Few studies looked at protective factors for psychopathology. Protective factors include older age (>65), marriage (Ford et al., 2007), and collective helping behavior for women (Wayment, 2004). As with risk factors, some of these protective factors may be protective against mental health problems, in general, rather than in specifically in the post-disaster setting.

Some authors have attempted to quantify the contribution of each of these risk factors to psychopathology. Soeteman et al. (2007) found that pre-disaster psychological morbidity was the strongest predictor of psychological problems after the Enschede Fireworks Disaster, while Wang et al. (2000) found that post-disaster variables were as important to psychosocial outcomes as pre-disaster vulnerability after an earthquake in China. The evidence appears mixed; clearly there is support for relationships between psychopathology and pre-disaster conditions, exposure level to disaster, and events occurring after disaster.

Time appears to be the biggest contributor to recovery from mental health problems after disasters. In a study of micro-enterprise owners following the 2004 Tsunami, de Mel et al. (2008) found that mental health recovery was dependent largely on time, rather than on economic recovery. The longevity of disaster impact varies widely by study – different measurement tools and study designs may account for much of this variation. In addition, very few studies follow participants past 2 years post-event; those that do often rely on administrative records, rather than self-reported symptomatology, which may result in a reduced effect size. Moreover, one would expect longevity to vary by disaster type and severity. A recent review found that man-made disasters may have psychological impacts up to 6–14 years after disaster, while natural disasters typically have mental health impacts up to 3 years post-event (Thomas, 2006).

Sleep problems. Two studies we reviewed examined sleep problems; both involved the Enschede Fireworks Disaster. Dirkzwager et al. (2006) found exposed children aged 4–12 had larger post-disaster increases in sleep problems presented to family practitioners at both 1 and 2 years than unexposed children. Grievink et al. (2007) found much the same with self-report surveys – severe sleep problems were more than twice as likely in affected residents than controls at both 3 weeks and 18 months post-disaster; however, sleep problems did decrease in the affected group between 3 weeks and 18 months. Evidence from these two longitudinal studies both showed evidence of decline in problems over time.

Somatic complaints and medically unexplained symptoms. In disaster literature, somatic symptoms include such complaints as headaches, faintness or dizziness, pains in heart or chest, lower back pain, nausea or upset stomach, muscle soreness, dyspnea, hot or cold spells, numbness or tingling, lump in throat, feeling weak, and heavy feelings in arms or legs (Slottje et al., 2008). The implied cause of somatic symptoms is psychological – the physical manifestation of psychological distress.

Medically unexplained symptoms (MUPS) may have environmental, somatic, physical, or multiple origins, although they are commonly attributed either to the somatization of psychological disorders or to the misinterpretation of normal bodily sensations (Spinhoven & Verschuur, 2006). In the post-disaster setting, it may be difficult to disentangle the effect of environmental exposures and psychological distress in the epidemiology of these symptoms, especially for cleanup workers who may suffer toxic exposures over a prolonged period of time. We present a review below on MUPS and somatic symptoms with this limitation in mind.

There is evidence of somatic symptoms in both rescue/cleanup worker samples and the general population. Elevated physical symptoms and fatigue were reported by rescue workers after the Bijlmermeer Air Disaster (Slottje et al., 2008; Spinhoven & Verschuur, 2006; van den Berg et al., 2008), as much as 8.5 years later (Slottje et al., 2006). Almost half of those workers with physical complaints 8.5 years later attributed their symptoms to the disaster (Slottje et al., 2006).

The impact of psychopathology on somatic symptoms, even within the same disaster, is mixed. The Slottje study (2008) found symptoms to be independent of post-traumatic stress symptoms, while the Spinhoven study (2006) found elevated and persistent fatigue to be associated with higher psychopathology. Police officers and firefighters exposed to the air disaster had more physical and mental health complaints than unexposed workers, but no significant differences in lab outcomes (Hg, leukocyte, platelet), chemical outcomes (K, creatine, alanine, aminotransferase, alkaline phosphatase, gamma-glutamyl transferase, TSH, C-reactive protein, ferratin), or urinanalysis (protein) (Huizink et al., 2006). After the Enschede Fireworks Disaster, PTSD 18-month post-disaster predicted vascular problems diagnosed by a family practitioner up to 2 years later (Dirkzwager et al., 2007). Another study found anxiety and depression were associated with number of physical symptoms in survivors of the fireworks disaster (van den Berg, Grievink, Stellato, Yzermans, & Lebret, 2005). Residents of Enschede who visited a specialized mental health institution (MHI) after the fireworks disaster had more health problems, including MUPS, before the disaster and had increased health problems presented to a GP after the disaster, compared to their own baselines and non-MHI survivors (den Ouden et al., 2005). While there is likely a relationship between disaster-related psychopathology and somatic symptoms, the path of that relationship is unclear.

Risk factors for somatic symptoms/MUPS include (a) *rescue/cleanup activities* – rescuing people, supporting injured victims, searching for or identifying victims or remains, cleanup, security, or surveillance activities (Slottje et al., 2006, 2008);

(b) *direct and indirect consequences of disaster* – witnessing the disaster scene or having a close one affected by disaster (Slottje et al., 2008); (c) *pre-disaster vulnerabilities* – victimization by intimate partner violence (Frasier et al., 2004), pre-disaster psychological problems (van den Berg et al., 2008); (d) *emotional reaction to disaster* – panic attack (Adams et al., 2006a), perceiving the disaster as very bad (Slottje et al., 2006); (e) *post-disaster events* – negative life events and traumatic events (Adams et al., 2006a), lower quality of life (Spinhoven & Verschuur, 2006); (f) *demographic factors* – female gender or immigrant status (van den Berg et al., 2008); (g) *other* – tendency to be less reassured by a doctor (Spinhoven & Verschuur, 2006).

Adolescents affected by the Enschede Fireworks Disaster had significant increases in MUPS after disaster, compared to non-affected adolescents at both 1- and 2-year follow-up (Dirkzwager et al., 2006). Adult residents of Enschede also had a higher prevalence of physical symptoms than residents of an unaffected city up to 4 years after the disaster (van den Berg et al., 2005). On the other hand, rescue workers involved in the same disaster had increased non-specific ill health during the first year post-disaster, but returned to baseline levels after 3 years (Morren et al., 2007). The Slottje study above (2008) was conducted an average of 8.5 years after the Bijlmermeer Air Disaster. The literature suggests disaster-related somatic symptoms may last years to decades. A study of cleanup workers after the Chernobyl Disaster found radiation exposure level to be associated with somatic symptoms even after 18 years (Loganovsky et al., 2008).

The decision to present symptoms to a health-care provider is not dependent on impairment or distress, but rather on persistence of symptoms (van den Berg et al., 2007). Intrusions, avoidance, depression, anxiety, and sleep problems were perpetuating factors for physical symptoms (van den Berg et al., 2008), suggesting a psychopathological role in persistence of symptoms.

Post-traumatic stress disorder. As one might expect, post-traumatic stress disorder (PTSD) is the most commonly studied specific mental health outcome in disaster victims (see also Davis, Tarcza, & Munson, Chapter 5). In this section, we include studies that look at PTSD symptomatology (e.g., avoidance, intrusive thoughts, hyperarousal) and those looking at diagnoses of PTSD. Research includes samples from both rescue and cleanup workers and the general population as well as special populations, such as children (Hoven, Duarte, & Mandell, 2003) and those with chronic illness (Hyre et al., 2007).

Risk factors for PTSD after disasters include (a) *direct exposure of disaster* – direct exposure or exposure severity (Hoven et al., 2003; Neria, Nandi, & Galea, 2008), physical injury (Hoven et al., 2003; Maegele et al., 2005), and number of injuries (North et al., 2005); (b) *rescue and cleanup* – participation in rescue, recovery, or cleanup activities (Neria et al., 2008), being caught in a cloud of dust during rescue work (Mauer et al., 2007); (c) *emotional reaction to disaster* – feeling very distressed during disaster (Parslow, Jorm, & Christensen, 2006), both emotion-focused and problem-focused coping strategies (Chung, Farmer, Werrett, Easthope, & Chung, 2001), subjective appraisal at the moment of trauma (Hoven et al., 2003), and probable perievent panic attack (Pfefferbaum, Stuber, Galea, &

Fairbrother, 2006); (d) *indirect consequences of disaster* – for children, losing a family member, knowing someone who was injured or killed, living with a surviving parent with PTSD (Hoven et al., 2003), death or injury to a family member or friend (North et al., 2005), evacuation (Parslow et al., 2006), late evacuation and evacuation to a shelter or being displaced for >3 months (Hyre et al., 2007), living in an area with worse destruction (Armenian et al., 2000), family financial burden/loss (Armenian et al., 2000; F. H. Chou et al., 2007); (e) *characteristics of disaster* – human-made or technological disasters compared to natural disasters (Neria et al., 2008); PTSD prevalence after natural disaster 3–90%, man-made accidents 52–60%, shooting spree ~60.4%, war up to 87%, and terrorism ~66% (Hoven et al., 2003); (f) *behavior after disaster* – binge drinking, alcohol dependence (Adams et al., 2006b), increase in drinking post-disaster (Adams et al., 2006b; Pfefferbaum et al., 2002), alcohol consumption, hazardous alcohol consumption, change in alcohol consumption in either direction (Simons, Gaher, Jacobs, Meyer, & Johnson-Jimenez, 2005), incident drinking problems, increased use of cigarettes, or marijuana (Vlahov et al., 2002, 2006); (g) *proximity* (Foster & Goldstein, 2007; Neria et al., 2008; Smith et al., 1999); (h) *pre-disaster mental health* – pre-disaster victimization by intimate partner violence (Frasier et al., 2004), pre-disaster neuroticism (Parslow et al., 2006), pre-disaster psychiatric disorder (North et al., 2005); (i) *other mental health outcomes* – anxiety symptoms (Hoven et al., 2003), poorer mental health (Parslow et al., 2006), sleep disturbance (Chou et al., 2007); (j) *other* – media exposure (Hoven et al., 2003), for hemodialysis patients, less experience with treatment and missing three or more treatments (Hyre et al., 2007); (k) *demographics* – female gender (Hoven et al., 2003; North et al., 2005; Parslow et al., 2006), for children, younger age (Hoven et al., 2003), black race (Hyre et al., 2007), low-income level (Armenian et al., 2000), and lower education (Parslow et al., 2006).

Some researchers have tried to quantify the relative contributions of risk factors on PTSD symptomatology. Parslow et al. (2006) concluded that disaster-exposure factors were more strongly associated with PTSD symptoms than pre-trauma measures. Two recent meta-analyses of research on PTSD concluded that events occurring during or after traumatic events were more important risk factors for PTSD than pre-event characteristics (Brewin, Andrews, & Valentine, 2000; Ozer, Best, Lipsey, & Weiss, 2003). However, there is evidence that risk factors before, during, and after disaster play a role.

Other studies examined severity of PTSD symptomatology, finding similar results to the above. Post-disaster alcohol dependence (Adams et al., 2006b), death and destruction in city of residence (Goenjian et al., 2001), and radiation exposure level as a cleanup worker (Loganovsky et al., 2008) were all associated with increased severity of symptoms.

Several studies have found protective factors for PTSD symptomatology. Armenian et al. (2000) showed the importance of social factors in protection against PTSD – being with someone else at the moment of the earthquake and making new friends following the earthquake was protective for PTSD diagnosis. Victims of the Chi-Chi earthquake who had changes in their social networks after disaster were more likely to report PTSD (Chou et al., 2007). A study on the Nairobi and

Oklahoma City bombings found that victims in Nairobi who attended religious services more frequently were less likely to experience PTSD than those who attended religious services less frequently; this was not the case, however, for Oklahoma City (North et al., 2005). Risk and protective factors for psychopathology following disaster may based on culture.

As with non-specific mental health, the most important factor in the amelioration of PTSD may be time. Studies in the general population *on an average* show that PTSD prevalence decreases as time goes on (Chou et al., 2007; Grievink et al., 2007), but there is also evidence of a bifurcated path, with some individuals going into remission and others suffering sustained or worsened symptomatology as time goes on (North et al., 2002). Severe exposures may be associated with greater PTSD in the years and decades following disaster (Grievink et al., 2007; Nandi et al., 2004; Tucker et al., 2007). Loganovsky et al. (2008) found cleanup workers after the Chernobyl Disaster had greater PTSD symptomatology than controls even 18 years later. A recent review concludes that PTSD in children generally decreases over time, but without complete recovery (Hoven et al., 2003). Risk factors for persistence of PTSD symptomatology include the severity and duration of exposure (Hoven et al., 2003), functional impairment and seeking mental health treatment shortly after disaster (North et al., 2002), as well as post-disaster conditions, such as unemployment and high work stress (Nandi et al., 2004).

Depression. Depression is also commonly studied in post-disaster settings. In this section we include studies that look at depression symptomatology as well as diagnoses. Research includes samples from both rescue and cleanup workers and the general population as well as special populations, such as adolescents (Goenjian et al., 2001) or emigrants (Foster & Goldstein, 2007).

The prevalence of depression after disaster ranged from 9.4% for New York metropolitan residents (Person, Tracy, & Galea, 2006), to 18% for Pentagon employees after September 11, 2001 terrorist attack (Jordan et al., 2004), to 52% for Ministry of Health workers in an earthquake-affected region (Armenian et al., 2002). Risk factors for depression in the post-disaster setting include (a) *direct disaster exposure* – being directly affected, including being in the World Trade Center at the time of attacks, friend or relative killed, being injured, loosing possessions, property, or job, or being involved in rescue efforts (Loganovsky et al., 2008; Person et al., 2006); (b) *emotional reaction to disaster* – perceived radiation risk (Foster & Goldstein, 2007), having a perievent panic attack (Person et al., 2006); (c) *proximity* (Foster & Goldstein, 2007); (d) *indirect consequences of disaster* – living in an area with worse destruction, total material loss to family (Armenian et al., 2002); (e) *behavior since disaster* – alcohol dependence (Adams et al., 2006b), incident drinking problems, increased use of cigarettes, alcohol, or marijuana (Vlahov et al., 2002, 2006); (f) *demographics* – female gender (Armenian et al., 2002), female gender in the United States but not in Kenya (North et al., 2005), low-income, especially in neighborhoods with income inequality (Ahern & Galea, 2006); (g) *pre-disaster events* – pessimism (van der Velden et al., 2007a), experiencing multiple life stressors in the year prior, having been exposed to previous trauma (Person et al., 2006); (h) *events since disaster* – experiencing multiple secondary stressors (Person et al., 2006); (i) *other* – prior experience with earthquakes (protective, Knight, Gatz, Heller, & Bengtson, 2000), sleep disturbance (Chou et al., 2007).

As with PTSD, social factors offered protection against depression. Being with someone at the time of disaster and receiving assistance or support after disaster were protective for depression after the 1988 Armenian earthquake (Armenian et al., 2002). Interestingly, Armenian et al. (2002) found that *any* alcohol use after disaster was also protective against depression. This resonates with the findings of Simons et al. (2005), who concluded that any change in alcohol use (either positive or negative) resulted in increased risk of PTSD. Perhaps it is not alcohol use in general, but rather drastic changes in alcohol use as a result of disaster that are associated with psychopathology. It is also possible that post-disaster psychopathology, even at the sub-syndromal level, may predict changes in alcohol use in an attempt to self-medicate.

Severity of post-disaster depression was predicted by radiation risk perception and being diagnosed with a Chernobyl Disaster-related health problem (Bromet & Havenaar, 2007), as well as living in a city with worse Hurricane death and destruction (Goenjian et al., 2001). Again, depressive symptomatology is seen to decrease over time, although not to baseline levels (Grievink et al., 2007). Longevity of depression symptomatology may last years to decades (Bromet & Havenaar, 2007; Foster, 2002; Foster & Goldstein, 2007). There was still a dose–response relationship between proximity to Chernobyl and depressive symptoms 14–15 years later for immigrants to the United States (Foster & Goldstein, 2007). Eighteen years after the Chernobyl Disaster, cleanup workers showed higher rates of depression than controls (Loganovsky et al., 2008). Longevity of effects may be lower in those not directly affected by the disaster – Reijneveld, Crone, Verhulst, and Verloove-Vanhorick (2003) found that depression problems in schools affected by a café fire had returned to a control level by 12 months (Reijneveld et al., 2003).

Mental health problems associated with victimization are likely associated with biological changes in victims. Olff et al. (2006) found that survivors of the Enschede disaster with major depressive disorder had flatter salivary cortisol curves over the course of the day than healthy survivors and also tended to use more tobacco per day (Olff et al., 2006). They concluded that smoking may be an important palliative coping style and may mediate the relationship between the traumatic stress and the hypothalamic–pituitary axis.

Anxiety. One study found anxiety problems to be more prevalent than depression or PTSD after disaster; a survey of Pentagon employees that found 7.9% PTSD and 17.7% depression prevalence also found 23.1% of employees had symptoms of panic attack and 26.9% had symptoms of generalized anxiety 1–4 months after the attack (Jordan et al., 2004). Dirkzwager et al. (2006) found post-disaster increases in anxiety problems in affected adolescents were 2–3 times greater than for an unaffected group, while depressive symptoms were no different between affected and unaffected groups. Following the Chernobyl Disaster, severity of anxiety symptoms were associated with risk perception (Bromet & Havenaar, 2007; Foster & Goldstein, 2007), proximity, greater radiation exposure (Foster & Goldstein, 2007), and being diagnosed with a Chernobyl Disaster-related health problem (Bromet &

Havenaar, 2007). Like the other psychopathologies discussed, anxiety symptoms have been shown to decrease over time, sometimes to baseline levels (Reijneveld et al., 2003; Reijneveld, Crone, Schuller, Verhulst, & Verloove-Vanhorick, 2005), sometimes remaining higher than control levels (Grievink et al., 2007).

Behavioral problems. Risk factors for parent-reported behavioral problems included high-intensity exposure to September 11, 2001 terrorist attack (e.g., seeing people jumping out of windows, seeing dead people), synergistically when in combination with a previous history of trauma (Chemtob, Nomura, & Abramovitz, 2008). Reijneveld et al. (2003) also found greater behavioral problems (especially aggressive behavior) in schools affected by the Volendam café fire, compared to unaffected schools; however, they saw a decrease to control level after 12 months (Reijneveld et al., 2005). Interestingly, one study found fewer post-September 11, 2001 terrorist attack parental reports of behavioral problems 4 months after the attack, although authors hypothesized that this difference was due to decreased parental sensitivity (Stuber et al., 2005). This study was different from the Chemtob study in that it involved a community sample, rather than a sample of only children who were directly affected by the attacks. One might expect parents of directly affected children to be more sensitive than those in a sample of individuals who were largely unaffected.

Suicidality. The evidence about suicidality after disasters is mixed. Suicidality appears to be most problematic in individuals involved in cleanup work and those who were most severely affected by disaster. There is evidence for increased suicidality in cleanup workers after the Chernobyl Disaster, with Loganovsky et al. (2008) showing greater suicidal ideation in cleanup workers than controls, and Rahu et al. (1997) noting an excess death by suicide during 6.5 years of follow-up, accounting for nearly 20% of all deaths in Estonian workers. Victims of the 1999 Taiwan earthquake who lost a co-resident or family member, was injured, or had property loss were nearly 50% more likely than non-victims to commit suicide following the earthquake (Chou et al., 2003).

Daily functioning – social and occupational. Disaster-related mental illness has a significant impact on victims' ability to function in both personal and occupational capacities. Studies investigating the impact of mental illness on work often look at sickness absences – the advantage of this measure is its objectivity. Self-reports of functioning, on the other hand, may also reflect changing subjective appraisal as a result of mental health symptoms. Our results are presented below with that warning in mind.

It appears that the effects of disasters on worker productivity are high in the months following disaster, but decline to baseline or control levels thereafter. Belonging to a mental health risk group (PTSD, depression, panic attack, generalized anxiety, alcohol abuse) was correlated with reduced self-reported daily functioning for Pentagon workers 1–4 months after September 11, 2001 terrorist attack (Jordan et al., 2004). Exposure to September 11, 2001 terrorist attack was associated with both lower-quality workdays and greater workday loss for workers in New York City 1 year post-disaster, but less so at 2 years; other risk factors for productivity loss included PTSD and depression, history of traumatic events, and negative life events (Boscarino, Adams, & Figley, 2006). Similar results were shown with rescue workers involved in the Enschede Fireworks Disaster, with length of sickness absence nearly doubling in the first 6 months after disaster, but decreasing slowly thereafter (Dirkzwager et al., 2004). Morren et al. (2007) show the prevalence of absences specifically due to psychological problems among rescue workers increased in the first 18 months after the Enschede Fireworks Disaster, compared to control group, and declined thereafter.

Around 40% of survivors of the Oklahoma City and Nairobi bombings reported impairment of functioning with family, friends, or work 6–10 months after the bombing. Coping mechanisms may be socially influenced. Survivors of the Nairobi bombing were more likely to report turning to family and friends, participating in a support group, or relying on religious support to cope with their experience, while survivors of the Oklahoma City bombing were more likely to report taking medication, drinking alcohol, and seeing a psychiatrist (North et al., 2005). For older adults exposed to the 1993 Midwest floods, higher levels of pre-flood social support were associated with having received and provided social support within the first 60 days after the floods (Tyler, 2006). Like many psychological outcomes, impairment following disaster is related to pre-disaster, post-disaster, and disaster-exposure variables.

The relationship between mental illness and functional impairment may be mediated by coping mechanisms. In a sample of Oklahoma City bombing victims receiving support services, increased alcohol use was associated with functional impairment (Pfefferbaum & Doughty, 2001). Worksite crisis interventions may have a beneficial effect on both mental health and functional outcomes, including reduced risk for binge drinking and alcohol dependence, PTSD symptoms, major depression, somatization, anxiety, and global impairment (Boscarino, Adams, & Figley, 2005).

Infectious Disease

The literature on infectious disease outcomes after disaster is limited. We found very little original research in the area, in stark contrast to an abundance of preparedness guidelines, editorials, and commentary. This dearth of published research may be due, in part, to the focus of published literature on disasters occurring in high-income or developed nations, specifically the United States (Norris et al., 2002; Uckay et al., 2008), where infectious diseases may be less problematic due to extensive public health infrastructure and health system resources. Original research in this area commonly uses medical records or administrative data. The majority of articles we reviewed deal with floods and storms, which makes legitimate sense given the nature of infection.

Below we briefly discuss the evidence for epidemics following disaster and the contribution of infectious disease to disaster mortality. Next, we review the impact of infectious disease on the health system. We close the chapter by discussing the different sources of infection in a post-disaster setting and particular species and conditions of concern.

Epidemics. A recent review indicates that there is little evidence for epidemics of disease following geophysical disasters (Floret, Viel, Mauny, Hoen, & Piarroux, 2006). No severe outbreaks occurred in the aftermath of the 2004 Tsunami or Hurricane Katrina, where the majority of the peer-reviewed literature lies. Yet infections are a frequent consequence of disasters – primarily skin, wound, and respiratory infections (Uckay et al., 2008). Diarrheal diseases are a common indirect result of disasters that disrupt sanitation or water quality (Watson, Gayer, & Connolly, 2007).

Infectious disease mortality. Baker et al.'s trimodal model (1980) of trauma deaths predicts an excess of "late stage" deaths after mass trauma due, in part, to sepsis; however, there was little evidence of this after 2004 Tsunami (Nishikiori et al., 2006a). A recent review of geophysical disasters indicates that epidemics rarely contribute significantly to the death toll after disaster (Floret et al., 2006).

Respiratory and wound infections after disaster may be implicated in deaths, although the mortality rate varies greatly by pathogen. For instance, none of the presentations for "cold" led to death following the Hanshin-Awaji Earthquake, while 80 of 619 cases (13%) of pneumonia resulted in death (Tanaka et al., 1999). Of 14 cases of wound infections of *Vibro vulnificus* following Hurricane Katrina, there were five deaths; the cause of these deaths, however, is not reported and underlying conditions were implicated in increased risk of severe *Vibro* infection in the majority of these patients (Engelthaler et al., 2005). In other situations, disaster-related outbreaks have shown far lower mortality than is usual for the pathogen. A tetanus outbreak following the 2004 Tsunami in Aceh, Indonesia, showed a 17% mortality rate, compared to a usual expected mortality of 50% for adults and 80% for children in developing countries (Jeremijenko, McLaws, & Kosasih, 2007).

Impact on health system. The impact of infectious disease visits on health systems following disasters varies widely. Respiratory diseases, in particular, may represent a significant proportion of hospital visits. Hospitals in Japan saw an increase in illness-related admissions over the 15 days after the Hanshin-Awaji earthquake – a third of which were for respiratory disease (including pneumonia, cold, asthma, and other; Tanaka et al., 1999). Infectious disease represented 8.4% of diagnoses at the Red Cross Field Hospital after the 2004 Tsunami (Guha-Sapir et al., 2007). Another study showed infectious diseases were detected in 85% of hospital patients after flooding in Mozambique (Kondo et al., 2002). Respiratory illnesses represented 15% of emergency department visits following Hurricane Floyd, according to the CDC (cited in Llewellyn, 2006). Especially in natural and unintentional manmade disasters, risk of infectious disease will be somewhat dependent on chance in terms of disaster timing, location, and severity of damage.

Demand for infectious agent-related supplies is often high after disasters. The National Disaster Medical System Special Operations Response following Hurricane Andrew reported supplies of tetanus antitoxin and antibiotics were depleted within 24 hours of the Hurricane (Llewellyn, 2006). Following Hurricane Iniki and Andrew, tetanus vaccination and antibiotics were in the top five drugs prescribed (Nufer & Wilson-Ramirez, 2004). After the Bam earthquake, top prescriptions by emergency medical assistance teams included cold preparations (8%) and anti-bacterials (11.2%) (Sepehri & Meimandi, 2006).

Blood donations have been shown to increase after disasters (Glynn et al., 2003; Sonmezoglu et al., 2005). However, the number of donations confirmed positive for HIV, Hepatitis C, and Hepatitis B has been shown to increase in some circumstances (Glynn et al., 2003), largely explained by an excess of first time and lapsed repeat donors, but not in others (Sonmezoglu et al., 2005).

Sources of Infection

Soil and water. Watson et al. (2007) summarize the convincing evidence for diarrheal disease outbreak/clustering due to contaminated water after disasters, with reports from Bangladesh, West Bengal, Mozambique, Indonesia, Pakistan, the United States, Mumbai, Argentina, Russia, Rio de Janeiro, and Taiwan following floods, an earthquake, and storms. Kondo et al. (2002) reported a spike in diarrheal illnesses with simultaneous deterioration in drinking water quality after major flooding in Mozambique.

In another review, Uckay et al. (2008) found frequent reports of infections with gram-negative bacteria, such as *Aeromonas* and *Vibrio* species, after the Indian Ocean Tsunami, indicating a marine source of infection; moreover, atypical fungal and mycobacterial infections in immunocompetent patients suggest traumatic inoculation at the disaster site. After Hurricane Katrina, wounds infected with *Vibrio* species were also noted, with 6 of 24 cases resulting in death (Todd, 2006). Unusual fungal infection due to airborne dust has been documented following an earthquake in southern California (Watson et al., 2007). Lastly, a tetanus outbreak was noted after the 2004 Tsunami in Aceh, Indonesia, likely due to immersion of superficial wounds during the tsunami (Jeremijenko et al., 2007).

Vector borne disease. Outbreaks of malaria following flooding have been seen in Costa Rica, Peru, Mozambique, Sudan, Haiti, but not in Indonesia following the 2004 Tsunami (Ivers & Ryan, 2006; Kondo et al., 2002; Morgan, 2004; Watson et al., 2007). Dengue outbreaks are documented after monsoon rains and flooding in India, Thailand, Brazil, Indonesia, and Venezuela; heavy rain and flooding may be associated with arboviral diseases and lymphatic filariasis around the world (Ivers & Ryan, 2006). Lastly, an increase in triatomine bugs, the vector for Chagas disease, was documented in the 6 months following Hurricane Isadore in Mexico, where the maximum increase was along the path of the hurricane (Guzman-Tapia, Ramirez-Sierra, Escobedo-Ortegon, & Dumonteil, 2005).

Hospital-acquired disease. Evidenced for hospital-acquired infections includes the presence of multiply-drug-resistant species and multi-methicillin-resistant *Staphylococcus aureus* (MRSA) following the 2004 Tsunami and Hurricane Katrina, as well as correlation of multi-drug-resistant bacteria frequency with hospital stay duration (Uckay et al., 2008). On the other hand, Todd (2006) reported that the pattern of MRSA infections found in displaced children after Hurricane Katrina indicated a community source, rather than more invasive hospital strains. Resistant infections are likely acquired from both hospital and community environments.

Person-to-person/crowding. There is evidence for disease outbreaks or clusters due to crowding of displaced populations. The only true outbreak after Hurricane Katrina was a norovirus outbreak at a temporary shelter in Texas (Todd, 2006), which is spread through person-to-person or fomite contact. Measles clusters have been found in the Philippines, Aceh Indonesia, and Pakistan, after tsunami, volcano eruption, and earthquake; meningitis infections among displaced persons in Aceh Indonesia and Pakistan have also been documented (Watson et al., 2007). Moreover, food shortages and malnutrition in temporary shelters may increase vulnerability to infection (Kondo et al., 2002). Dead bodies, on the other hand, pose little risk of infection or epidemic following disasters (Ligon, 2006; Morgan, Ahern, & Cairncross, 2005; Watson et al., 2007), nonetheless workers handling dead animal and human remains should use precautions (Ligon, 2006).

Conditions and species of concern. Wound infections are a serious concern for those suffering injury during disaster (Ligon, 2006; Llewellyn, 2006). Common diseases of concern include tetanus (Jeremijenko et al., 2007; Ligon, 2006; Uckay et al., 2008; Watson et al., 2007), *Aeromonas* and *Vibrio* species (Ligon, 2006; Llewellyn, 2006), necrotizing fasciitis, and mycobacterium infections (Llewellyn, 2006). Microbiological assessment of 17 seriously injured tourists returning home identified common and uncommon multi-resistant pathogens (Maegele et al., 2005). Gram-negative bacteria were common in this group, as well as victims after tornadoes in Georgia and the United States (Uckay et al., 2008).

Acute respiratory infections (ARI) are another concern in the post-disaster setting (Ligon, 2006). ARI may be a major cause of illness in displaced populations especially, with increases in ARI seen in Nicaragua following Hurricane Mitch, in Aceh following the tsunami, and in Pakistan following an earthquake (Watson et al., 2007). One study found over two-thirds of children in a post-tsunami relief camp had an ARI (Jayatissa et al., 2006). Upper respiratory tract infections in those same 17 injured tourists returning home were found to contain a high rate of multiply-resistant species (Maegele et al., 2005). Maegele (2006) found that all of those tourists suffered near drowning involving aspiration of immersion fluids, marine, and soil debris; all patients displayed signs of pneumonitis and pneumonia, while several had severe sinusitis. Upper respiratory infection was in the top five chief complaints and top five diagnoses following Hurricanes Andrew and Iniki (Nufer & Wilson-Ramirez, 2004), and respiratory viral diseases were common after Hurricane Katrina (Uckay et al., 2008).

Diarrheal diseases are an important consequence of disasters. One study showed 17.9% of children in a post-tsunami relief camp had diarrhea (Jayatissa et al., 2006). Cholera, *Escherichia coli*, Salmonella, *Cryptosporidium parvum*, leptospirosis, and Hepatitis A and E are all possible causes of diarrheal disease after disasters (Ligon, 2006; Llewellyn, 2006; Morgan et al., 2005; Sur, Dutta, Nair, & Bhattacharya, 2000; Watson et al., 2007). Many diarrheal outbreaks may not be due to one specified pathogen (Uckay et al., 2008).

Chronic Disease

We reviewed nearly 40 articles on the impact of disasters on chronic diseases, including cross-sectional, cohort, and case studies as well as review articles. Our article base included samples from the general population and from rescue and cleanup personnel. By the very nature of chronic disease, studies often had longer follow-up than many other topic areas. As a result, the longitudinal cohort is a common design. Because many of these studies involve self-reported symptomatology, this area may represent the effects of long-term mental health as well as physical outcomes of disaster exposure. Where possible, we try to tease apart these effects.

In this section, we investigate the health effects of disasters across organ systems. We begin by reviewing the impact of disaster on cardiovascular health, followed by a brief discussion of diabetes and arthritis. Next, we discuss respiratory health, kidney and urinary health, and neurological effects. We review reproductive and developmental health effects of disasters, followed by musculoskeletal problems and cancer. Lastly, we discuss specific problems and conditions caused by particular exposures. Again, this is not an exhaustive list of all research on these topics, but rather an overview of the common areas of research.

Cardiovascular health outcomes. In this section, we include both cardiovascular outcomes (incident disease and death) and risk factors for cardiovascular disease, including hypertension, cholesterol, blood pressure, heart rate, vascular problems, and autonomic reactivity. Some studies examine self-reported symptomatology as well as objective measures. For example, over 8 years after the Amsterdam Air Disaster, exposed police and fireworkers were more likely to report cardiovascular complaints than unexposed workers; however, they had no significant differences in blood count or chemical values, with the exception of increased monocytes (Huizink et al., 2006).

The impact of disasters on cardiovascular health may depend on exactly what is being measured. For example, one study found no correlation between earthquake-related experiences and blood pressure or cholesterol; however, disaster experiences did predict resting heart rate (Bland et al., 2000). Autonomic reactivity (heart rate, diastolic/systolic and mean arterial blood pressure) and development of new vascular problems were both sensitive to disaster exposure, even years later (Dirkzwager et al., 2007; Tucker et al., 2007).

The relationship between cardiovascular health and disaster exposure may also be mediated partially by stress. Risk factors for cardiovascular problems are primarily related to indirect consequences of disasters, including having a child who was burned (Dorn, Yzermans, Guijt, & van der Zee, 2007); disaster damage, loss of possessions, or total loss (Armenian, Melkonian, & Hovanesian, 1998); financial loss, increased distance from family and friends, and decreased visiting due to relocation (Bland et al., 2000). Some demographic factors predicted vascular problems, including lower SES and female gender (Dorn, Yzermans, Guijt, et al., 2007). Bland et al. (2000) did not find support for mediation of the relationship between earthquake experience and resting heart rate by psychological stress.

There may be a life-course effect of stress on cardiovascular risk – all the way back to fetal development. Adults who were exposed to a Dutch Famine in late gestation had reduced glucose tolerance; those exposed in early gestation had a more atherogenic lipid profile, higher fibrinogen concentrations, lower factor VII concentrations, a higher BMI, and more often rated their health as poor; those exposed in mid gestation had increased obstructive airway disease (Roseboom et al., 2001).

Diabetes. There is some evidence that disaster-exposed individuals have higher rates of diabetes later in life (Armenian et al., 1998; Pesatori et al., 2003). Risk factors for diabetes after earthquake included loss of possessions and disaster-related damage (Armenian et al., 1998). Endocrine effects may, however, be sex specific. For example, female victims of dioxin exposures (but not men) were more likely to develop diabetes in the 20-year follow-up (Pesatori et al., 2003).

Arthritis. Earthquake victims with new arthritis diagnoses in the 4 years after earthquake were more likely to sustain greater loss of possessions and disaster-related damage than those without arthritis, matched for age and sex, controlling for education, and body mass index (Pesatori et al., 2003). Although this finding would seem to imply mediation by emotional problems and/or somatization, one might imagine additional confounding variables, as well.

Respiratory health. Respiratory problems represent one of the most studied chronic health effects of disasters. Much of this information comes from rescue and cleanup workers, who often sustain more severe exposure to airborne particulates and other lung irritants for a more prolonged period of time than the general population. Following September 11, 2001 terrorist attack, workers involved in rescue, cleanup, and recovery suffered reduced pulmonary function (Banauch et al., 2006), increased respiratory symptoms (Tao et al., 2007), cough, and lung function abnormalities (Skloot et al., 2004). Following the Enschede Fire Disaster, rescue and cleanup workers suffered increased respiratory symptoms (Dirkzwager et al., 2004) and excess sick leave due to respiratory problems (Morren et al., 2007).

Respiratory problems have been reported in civilian populations as well. Ten years after the Union Carbide gas leak, respiratory symptoms were more common and lung function more reduced who were living closer to the plant (Beckett, 1998). A review of the health effects of this disaster found evidence for radiological changes to the lungs, respiratory symptomatology and impairment, with progressive decline in lung function over 2 years of follow-up. This same disaster was found to have respiratory and mucous membrane symptoms 9 years after the explosion by Dhara et al. (2002); risk factors for these symptoms included proximity to the plant, duration of exposure, and physical activity following exposure.

For disasters with a more time-limited exposure, respiratory damage may be more reparable. After the Volendam café fire, adolescent survivors had increased respiratory symptoms 1 year after the fire, but not after 4 years (Dorn, Yzermans, Spreeuwenberg, Schilder, & van der Zee, 2008).

Kidney and urinary health. The evidence on kidney and urinary problems as a result of disaster varies by disaster type. Workers exposed to the Amsterdam Air Disaster showed had similar kidney function parameters as unexposed workers 8 years later (Bijlsma et al., 2008) and no differences in urinanalysis 8.5 years later (Huizink et al., 2006). Exposure to the Union Carbide industrial accident, on the other hand, was associated with urinary burn 9 years later (Dhara et al., 2002).

Neurological problems. Neurological health of those directly exposed to disaster, particularly chemical exposures, may suffer. Neurological and neurobehavioral problems have been associated with exposure to the Union Carbide gas leak (Dhara & Dhara, 2002), in rescue workers after the Enschede Fireworks Disaster (Morren et al., 2007), and in those exposed to the Tokyo Sarin attack (Nishiwaki et al., 2001). Specifically, backward digit memory span tests acted in a dose–response manner with exposure to Sarin gas (Nishiwaki et al., 2001). In a review of the health effects of the Chernobyl Disaster, Dhara and Dhara (2002) report evidence of impaired auditory and visual memory, attention response speed, associate learning, and motor speed and precision, with some tests showing a dose–response effect.

Reproductive and developmental health. In our review, reproductive health problems were reported by two articles, both investigating industrial accidents. Dhara and Dhara (2002) found evidence for menstrual cycle disruption, leukorrhea, dysmenorrhea, miscarriage, and both perinatal and neonatal mortality for women affected by the disaster; furthermore, animal experiments show that MIC has fetotoxic effects in mice. After the Seveso accident, men with greater blood-dioxin levels fathered significantly more girls than boys up to 20 years after the accident (Mocarelli et al., 2000).

The research on reproductive health behavior following disasters is limited and largely restricted to displaced women. Poverty, isolation, overcrowding, and the arrival of military, relief, construction, and transport personnel may contribute to increased risk of STI transmission in the aftermath of disaster (Carballo, Hernandez, Schneider, & Welle, 2005). A study in the country of Georgia found that women with PID were more likely to be internally displaced (due to conflict) than not, even after controlling for their lifetime sexual partners, IUD or condom use, induced abortion history, gynecological exam history, and STI history (Doliashvili & Buckley, 2008). After Hurricane Katrina, women were less likely to have multiple sex partners and less likely to be attending family planning services or using birth control, compared to before (Kissinger, Schmidt, Sanders, & Liddon, 2007). Kissinger et al. (2007) also found that nearly 20% of young women in a local family planning study had difficulty accessing necessary family planning care in the 5–6 months following Hurricane Katrina (Kissinger et al., 2007). This is not surprising given over 85% of these women had lived in three or more places in that time span and both of the family planning clinics where subjects were recruited were flooded and either moved or closed down completely.

Research on the developmental impact of disasters focuses on two main routes of effect – in utero chemical or radiological exposures and the effects of maternal stress on the developing fetus (sometimes acting in concert). Researchers have found no evidence of cognitive impairments in children exposed in utero or at a young age to the Chernobyl Disaster (Bromet & Havenaar, 2007; Taormina et al., 2008). Nor was there evidence of increased under-five mortality in the 5 years following the disaster (Gruber et al., 2005). Zichittella et al. (2004) also found no additional infant or post-neonatal mortality after the Chernobyl Disaster. Interestingly, evacuee mothers in the Taormina study were almost three times as likely to report their children having memory problems as controls, stressing the need for objective measures of chronic health.

The Quebec Ice Storms in 1998, on the other hand, had a negative impact on cognitive and language development of children exposed in utero as well as perinatal outcomes, infant temperament, and physical development, specifically for those exposed in the second trimester (King & Laplante, 2005). This is in contrast with the Roseboom study (2001) on cardiac outcomes, which showed exposure in late gestation to be most important; this difference is reflective of different developmental programming periods for different organ systems.

Though the evidence is still mixed, there is some support for the impact of in utero disaster exposure on adult mental health. One study looked at disaster-associated antisocial personality disorder (ASPD), examining the effects of prenatal nutritional deficiency due to an intentional man-made famine during World War II. Neugebauer, Hoek, & Susser (1999) found that men exposed to severe nutritional deficiency in the first or second trimester had 2.5 odds of ASPD as men unexposed to nutritional deficiency. Neugebauer did not find any effect of third-trimester exposure, suggesting fetal programming at specific points in time.

Another study in our review looked at non-affective psychosis and maternal flood-related stress (Selten, van der Graaf, van Duursen, Gispen-de Wied, & Kahn, 1999). Unfortunately, psychotic disorders are fairly rare and they did not separate their sample by trimester of exposure, which the Neugebauer study (1999) showed to be important. They found that those exposed to maternal flood stress in utero were 1.8 times as likely to have non-affective psychosis disorders in adulthood, however, the difference did not achieve statistical significance at the 95% confidence level (95% CI: 0.9–3.5).

Given the power of disaster-related stress to alter the sex ratio of children born in months following disaster, likely through excess fetal death (Catalano, Bruckner, Gould, Eskenazi, & Anderson, 2005), the concept of fetal-determined vulnerability for adult mental illness is not implausible. None of our reviewed articles examined biological mechanisms for observed effects.

Musculoskeletal problems. Chronic musculoskeletal problems have been reported following the Enscede Fireworks Disaster (den Ouden et al., 2005; Dirkzwager et al., 2004; Morren et al., 2007), the Amsterdam Air Disaster (Deeg, Huizink, Comijs, & Smid, 2005), the Volendam Café Fire (Dorn et al., 2008), and the Union Carbide Accident (Dhara & Dhara, 2002; Dhara et al., 2002).

Survivors of the Enschede Fireworks Disaster who visited a mental health institution after disaster (possibly a proxy for exposure status) had an increase in musculoskeletal problems presented to GPs in the year following crash, compared to before, but returned to baseline by 2 years (den Ouden et al., 2005). Rescue workers in the Enscede Disaster had greater musculoskeletal problems presented to an occupational physician up to 2 years after disaster compared to before; they also had greater absences from work during the first year post-disaster, but had returned to baseline by before year 2 (Dirkzwager et al., 2004). Morren et al. (2007) found rescue workers had greater sick leave for musculoskeletal problems in the first year post-disaster and remaining higher than controls until 3 years post-disaster.

Older persons living closest to the Bijlmer Air Disaster were experienced health decline above normal aging-associated decline; the effect was most obvious in interview-rated mobility (Deeg et al., 2005). Adolescent survivors of the Volendam Café Fire had increased GP-reported musculoskeletal problems in the first year after disaster, but not in later years (Dorn et al., 2008). Exposure to the Union Carbide Accident was associated with musculoskeletal problems, including muscle pain, joint pain, and bone pain (Dhara et al., 2002); the neuromuscular-toxic property of MIS is supported by animal studies (Dhara & Dhara, 2002).

Cancer. Chemical and radiological exposures are of particular interest to cancer researchers. Patients who received 224Ra injections for bone tuberculosis and ankylosing spondylitis in the 1940s and 1950s suffered increased risk of cancers system wide (including cancers of the bone, connective tissue, breast, thyroid, liver, kidney, pancreas, uterus, and bladder) in the 12–21 years following "treatment" (Spiess, 2002). Exposure to the dioxin TCDD following the Seveso Accident was associated with increased risk of morbidity and mortality from lymphoemopoietic neoplasm and cancers of the digestive and respiratory systems (Pesatori et al., 2003). A cancer incidence study from 1987 to 1992, 8 years after the Union Carbide Accident, found no evidence of increased risk for cancer of the lung, oropharynx, or oral cavity due to gas exposures; however, the authors note that more time may be necessary for the effect to show (Dikshit & Kanhere, 1999).

Specific problems and conditions. Exposure to Union Carbide incident associated with persistent respiratory and ocular problems (Dhara & Dhara, 2002). Bhopal Eye Syndrome, coined by Andersson et al. (1990), includes full resolution of the initial interpalpebral superficial erosion, increased risk for eye infections, hyperresponsive phenomena, and possibly cataracts.

Spanish Toxic Oil Syndrome (TOS) is a condition caused by ingestion of rapeseed oil denatured with aniline – a disaster taking place in Spain in 1981 – characterized by fever, rash, eosinophilia, pulmonary edema, and myalgia. Recent research has shown that impaired acetylation, and the genetic polymorphisms associated with it, mediated susceptibility to TOS (Ladona et al., 2001; McCredie & Willert, 1999). This may have implications for other disasters as well – genetic vulnerability may play a role in both occurrence and severity of symptoms after disaster.

Health Behavior

We reviewed over 25 articles on the impact of disasters on health behavior, including cohort, case-control, cross-sectional, ecological, and other study designs (e.g., key informant interviews). Our article base included samples from the general population and from disaster relief personnel. Surveys were by far the most common data sources for studies looking at most health behaviors, with the exception of child abuse for which administrative data were used. Much of the research in this area examines short-term effects of disasters. In this section, we review findings related to substance use, including alcohol, drug abuse, and tobacco. We also discuss the impact of disasters on child abuse and domestic violence.

Alcohol. Alcohol use and misuse after disasters has been widely studied with mixed results. Outcomes of interest included alcohol consumption, change in use, alcohol problems, alcohol dependence, hazardous alcohol consumption, and binge drinking. Much of the research we reviewed was in the United States with a focus on September 11, 2001 terrorist attack. Moreover, research on this topic is often cross-sectional, which does not allow researchers to determine the temporality of "cause" and "effect" – this is particularly problematic with the association between mental health status and alcohol use. Some authors refer to alcohol use/misuse as a risk factor for mental health problems after disaster, while others postulate that alcohol use/misuse is a coping mechanism brought on by poor mental health. It is likely that causality operates in both directions, in concert with mediating and moderating factors.

There is evidence for increased prevalence of alcohol problems after disaster. Researchers have shown a disaster effect on excessive alcohol consumption, increased alcohol use, and increased prevalent drinking problems after the Volendam Café Fire (Reijneveld et al., 2005), Oklahoma City bombing (Smith et al., 1999), and September 11, 2001 terrorist attack (Vlahov et al., 2006), respectively. Various measures of alcohol use/misuse were associated with (a) *exposure factors* – greater exposure (Boscarino, Adams, & Galea, 2006); injury, peritraumatic reaction, worry about safety (Pfefferbaum et al., 2002); degree of exposure for women (Vetter, Rossegger, Rossler, Bisson, & Endrass, 2008); grief and PTSD symptoms (Pfefferbaum & Doughty, 2001); conversely, sensory exposure and interpersonal exposure were not associated with increased alcohol intake (Pfefferbaum et al., 2002); (b) *proximity* – attending school where many students were affected (Reijneveld et al., 2003, 2005), living in the affected city (Smith et al., 1999); (c) *post-disaster mental health* – partial PTSD, sub-syndromal PTSD, PTSD severity, depression, and poor mental health status (Adams et al., 2006b); negative affect, mediated by coping motives (Gaher et al., 2006); grief, post-traumatic stress, trouble functioning (Pfefferbaum et al., 2002); receipt of peer support (protective, (Ford et al., 2006)); hyperarousal and intrusion symptoms (Simons et al., 2005); symptoms of PTSD and depression (Vetter et al., 2008; Vlahov et al., 2002, 2006); endorsement of emotional reactions and functional difficulties (Pfefferbaum et al., 2008).

The bulk of the research in this topic investigates the association between poor mental health and alcohol use/misuse. Some researchers have found mental health symptoms to be more strongly associated with alcohol use/misuse outcomes than disaster-exposure characteristics (Pfefferbaum & Doughty, 2001; Pfefferbaum et al., 2002), while others have found a lack of association between psychopathology and alcohol, after controlling for exposure level (Boscarino, Adams, & Galea, 2006). Interestingly, poor mental health may be associated with not just increased alcohol use (Adams et al., 2006b; Pfefferbaum et al., 2002; Vlahov et al., 2002), but also decreased use (Pfefferbaum et al., 2008), or both (Simons et al., 2005). Increased alcohol use was also protective for physical health, in the Adams study (2006b). As with the mental health section, many of these proposed risk factors may, in fact, apply to substance use in general, rather than only in a post-disaster context.

Drug abuse. Research on drug abuse after disasters is a bit more diverse than that on alcohol use, with research taking place following September 11, 2001 terrorist attack and the Oklahoma City bombing, the Chi-Chi and Bam Earthquakes, and the 2004 Indian Ocean Tsunami. Outcomes of interest include substance use, abuse, and dependence as well as cannabis use, specifically. There was one study on recovering substance users.

Evidence for a disaster effect on drug abuse is mixed, with researchers finding and increase (near doubling) on drug abuse/dependence following the Chi-Chi Earthquake (Chou et al., 2007), but not following the Volendam Café Fire (Reijneveld et al., 2003, 2005). Reineveld et al. did, however, find a disaster effect on alcohol use, indicating that alcohol may be more sensitive to the impact of disasters than drug abuse, for obvious reasons (e.g., accessibility, social acceptability, cost, etc.). Risk factors for substance use after disasters include degree of exposure, PTSD symptomatology (Vetter et al., 2008), PTSD, and depression (Vlahov et al., 2002). As with alcohol use, both exposure characteristics and post-disaster mental health have been supported as potential "risk factors" for substance use.

The effect of disasters on drug abuse is most prominent in the immediate time frame. During the 29 hours of the New York City Blackout, 911 emergency calls for drug- or alcohol-related emergencies actually decreased (Freese et al., 2006). In the days following September 11, 2001 terrorist attack, patients in recovery programs reported difficulty getting to their treatment due to interrupted public transport (Frank et al., 2006). In this same study, one of two residential recovery programs, half of the methadone programs, and over half of the drug-free outpatient programs reported an increase in positive urine toxicology following September 11, 2001 terrorist attack. Over half of opium abusers in and around the city during the Bam earthquake reported withdrawal symptoms due to a disturbed supply and half of these reported their symptoms to a medical provider, asking for morphine or another analgesic (Movaghar et al., 2005).

In short, to the degree that disasters disturb normal life for the average person, they also disturb normal life for drug users and those in recovery – sometimes by restricting use, but other times putting them at a greater risk of relapse. We did not see any research dealing with incidence of new drug problems after disaster, which would be of interest.

Tobacco. As with alcohol use, smoking has been posited as both a coping mechanism to deal with mental health problems following disaster and a contributor to worsening mental health. Directionality of association is as much a problem with tobacco as it is with alcohol.

There is evidence for increased smoking and additional initiation up to 18 months following disasters (Smith et al., 1999). Risk factors for increased tobacco consumption include traumatic disaster experience (Parslow & Jorm, 2006), denial of emotional reactions and functional difficulties (Pfefferbaum et al., 2008), peritraumatic reaction, grief, worry about safety, and trouble functioning (Pfefferbaum et al.,

2002). Pfefferbaum et al. (2002) also found that sensory exposure and interpersonal exposure were not associated with increased tobacco intake after the Oklahoma City bombing.

Evidence on the effect of PTSD on tobacco consumption is mixed, with Parslow and Jorm (2006) finding no independent effect of PTSD, beyond disaster traumatic experience in bushfire-exposed young adults, while Pfefferbaum et al. (2002) found that post-traumatic stress was associated with increased smoking after the Oklahoma City bombing. Vetter et al. (2008) found that severity of PTSD symptoms increased odds of tobacco consumption, and Vlahov et al. (2002) found a smoking association with both PTSD and depression. The directionality of this relationship between post-disaster psychopathology and tobacco consumption is unclear.

In one of the few studies looking at the biology behind disaster stress and addiction, Olff et al. (2006) found that survivors of the Enschede Fireworks Disaster with depression tended to use more tobacco per day and also tended to have a flatter diurnal cortisol curve than health controls of survivors with PTSD. The authors conclude that smoking may actually mediate the relationship between the post-disaster depression and the hypothalamic–pituitary axis.

Child abuse and domestic violence. Child and spousal abuse have serious consequences for population health and well-being. Tragically, there is evidence that disasters may cause an increase in child abuse. The evidence in this field of research is mainly ecological – from administrative records – rather than etiologic. Child abuse reports in affected counties were disproportionately higher 3–6 months after Hurricane Hugo and the Loma Prieta Earthquake, compared to other years; however, there was no significant difference after Hurricane Andrew (Curtis, Miller, & Berry, 2000). Likewise, hospital admissions for inflicted traumatic brain injury in young children (shaken baby syndrome) increased 6 months after Hurricane Floyd in affected regions, compared to pre-disaster, with no corresponding increase in counties less affected by the disaster; levels returned to baseline thereafter (Keenan, Marshall, Nocera, & Runyan, 2004).

The evidence on intimate partner violence (IPV) following disasters is mixed. Frasier et al. (2004) found no significant increase in IPV after Hurricane Floyd, although the study did have some non-response issues (with nearly 1/3 of their sample refusing response to a question about lifetime IPV). Another study conducted 7–9 months after Hurricane Katrina found IPV rate was three times the United States baseline for displaced persons living in group trailer parks in Mississippi and Louisiana (Larrance, Anastario, & Lawry, 2007).

Conclusion

We have reviewed the literature about the range of public health consequences of disasters here. As is clear from this review, collectively experienced traumatic events influence the health of populations across a range of health indicators. The literature about the scope of these consequences is vast. Yet there remain substantial gaps in our understanding of the consequences of these events, with the literature about particular health indicators often providing conflicting evidence. Some of this lack of clarity may be due to the complexity of mass traumatic events, with the impact of these events being heterogeneous across groups comprising populations. While we can draw general inference about the population health consequences of disasters, such inference must be drawn cautiously with due recognition that the net result of one mass traumatic event may be different than other comparable disasters in different contexts. Future work in this field may fruitfully consider this complexity, developing models that can help predict how the interplay between the mass traumatic event and the context that is affected contribute to changes in population health. Such work may provide guidance for intervention that can mitigate the consequences of future events.

References

Adams, R. E., Boscarino, J. A., & Galea, S. (2006a). Social and psychological resources and health outcomes after the World Trade Center Disaster. *Social Science & Medicine, 62* (1), 176–188.

Adams, R. E., Boscarino, J. A., & Galea, S. (2006b). Alcohol use, mental health status and psychological well-being 2 years after the World Trade Center attacks in New York City. *The American Journal of Drug and Alcohol Abuse, 32* (2), 203–224.

Ahern, J., & Galea, S. (2006). Social context and depression after a disaster: The role of income inequality. *Journal of Epidemiology and Community Health, 60,* (9), 766–770.

Altntas, K. H., & Delooz, H. (2004). The problems faced by three government disaster response teams of Ankara City during the Marmara earthquake – 1999 response. *European Journal of Emergency Medicine, 11* (2), 95–101.

Andersson, N., Ajwani, M. K., Mahashabde, S., Tiwari, M. K., Muir, M. K., Mehra, V., et al. (1990). Delayed eye and other consequences from exposure to methyl isocyanate: 93% follow up of exposed and unexposed cohorts in Bhopal. *British Journal of Industrial Medicine, 47* (8), 553–558.

Armenian, H. K., Melkonian, A. K., & Hovanesian, A. P. (1998). Long term mortality and morbidity related to degree of damage following the 1998 earthquake in Armenia. *American Journal of Epidemiology, 148* (11), 1077–1084.

Armenian, H. K., Morikawa, M., Melkonian, A. K., Hovanesian, A., Akiskal, K., & Akiskal, H. S. (2002). Risk factors for depression in the survivors of the 1988 earthquake in Armenia. *Journal of Urban Health, 79* (3), 373–382.

Armenian, H. K., Morikawa, M., Melkonian, A. K., Hovanesian, A. P., Haroutunian, N., Saigh, P. A., et al. (2000). Loss as a determinant of PTSD in a cohort of adult survivors of the 1988 earthquake in Armenia: Implications for policy. *Acta Psychiatrica Scandinavica, 102* (1), 58–64.

Asaeda, G. (2002). The day that the START triage system came to a STOP: Observations from the World Trade Center Disaster. *Academic Emergency Medicine: Official Journal of the Society for Academic Emergency Medicine, 9* (3), 255–256.

Baker, C. C., Oppenheimer, L., Stephens, B., Lewis, F. R., & Trunkey, D. D. (1980). Epidemiology of trauma deaths. *American Journal of Surgery, 140* (1), 144–150.

Banauch, G. I., Alleyne, D., Sanchez, R., Olender, K., Cohen, H. W., Weiden, M., et al. (2003). Persistent hyperreactivity and reactive airway dysfunction in firefighters at the World Trade Center. *American Journal of Respiratory and Critical Care Medicine, 168* (1), 54–62.

Banauch, G. I., Hall, C., Weiden, M., Cohen, H. W., Aldrich, T. K., Christodoulou, V., et al. (2006). Pulmonary function after exposure to the World Trade Center collapse in the New York City fire department. *American Journal of Respiratory and Critical Care Medicine, 174* (3), 312–319.

Beckett, W. S. (1998). Persistent respiratory effects in survivors of the Bhopal disaster. *Thorax, 53* (Suppl. 2), S43–6.

Bijlsma, J. A., Slottje, P., Huizink, A. C., Twisk, J. W., van der Voet, G. B., de Wolff, F. A., et al. (2008). Urinary uranium and kidney function parameters in professional assistance workers in the epidemiological study air disaster in Amsterdam (ESADA). *Nephrology, Dialysis, Transplantation: Official Publication of the European Dialysis and Transplant Association – European Renal Association, 23* (1), 249–255.

Bland, S. H., Farinaro, E., Krogh, V., Jossa, F., Scottoni, A., & Trevisan, M. (2000). Long term relations between earthquake experiences and coronary heart disease risk factors. *American Journal of Epidemiology, 151* (11), 1086–1090.

Born, C. T., Briggs, S. M., Ciraulo, D. L., Frykberg, E. R., Hammond, J. S., Hirshberg, A., et al. (2007). Disasters and mass casualties: II. Explosive, biologic, chemical, and nuclear agents. *The Journal of the American Academy of Orthopaedic Surgeons, 15* (8), 461–473.

Boscarino, J. A., Adams, R. E., & Figley, C. R. (2005). A prospective cohort study of the effectiveness of employer-sponsored crisis interventions after a major disaster. *International Journal of Emergency Mental Health, 7* (1), 9–22.

Boscarino, J. A., Adams, R. E., & Figley, C. R. (2006). Worker productivity and outpatient service use after the September 11th attacks: Results from the New York City terrorism outcome study. *American Journal of Industrial Medicine, 49* (8), 670–682.

Boscarino, J. A., Adams, R. E., & Galea, S. (2006). Alcohol use in New York after the terrorist attacks: A study of the effects of psychological trauma on drinking behavior. *Addictive Behaviors, 31* (4), 606–621.

Boscarino, J. A., Adams, R. E., Stuber, J., & Galea, S. (2005). Disparities in mental health treatment following the World Trade Center Disaster: Implications for mental health care and health services research. *Journal of Traumatic Stress, 18* (4), 287–297.

Bradt, D. A. (2003). Site management of health issues in the 2001 World Trade Center Disaster. *Academic Emergency Medicine, 10* (6), 650–660.

Brewin, C. R., Andrews, B., & Valentine, J. D. (2000). Meta-analysis of risk factors for posttraumatic stress disorder in trauma-exposed adults. *Journal of Consulting and Clinical Psychology, 68* (5), 746–766.

Bromet, E. J., & Havenaar, J. M. (2007). Psychological and perceived health effects of the chernobyl disaster: A 20-year review. *Health Physics, 93* (5), 516–521.

Brown, D. L. (1999). Disparate effects of the 1989 Loma Prieta and 1994 Northridge earthquakes on hospital admissions for acute myocardial infarction: Importance of superimposition of triggers. *American Heart Journal, 137* (5), 830–836.

Brunkard, J., Namulanda, G., & Ratard, R. (2008). Hurricane Katrina deaths, Louisiana, 2005. *Disaster Medicine and Public Health Preparedness*, EPub August 27.

Carballo, M., Hernandez, M., Schneider, K., & Welle, E. (2005). Impact of the tsunami on reproductive health. *Journal of the Royal Society of Medicine, 98* (9), 400–403.

Catalano, R., Bruckner, T., Gould, J., Eskenazi, B., & Anderson, E. (2005). Sex ratios in California following the terrorist attacks of September 11, 2001. *Human Reproduction, 20* (5), 1221–1227.

Chemtob, C. M., Nomura, Y., & Abramovitz, R. A. (2008). Impact of conjoined exposure to the World Trade Center attacks and to other traumatic events on the behavioral problems of preschool children. *Archives of Pediatrics & Adolescent Medicine, 162* (2), 126–133.

Chou, F. H., Wu, H. C., Chou, P., Su, C. Y., Tsai, K. Y., Chao, S. S., et al. (2007). Epidemiologic psychiatric studies on post-disaster impact among chi-chi earthquake survivors in Yu-Chi, Taiwan. *Psychiatry and Clinical Neurosciences, 61* (4), 370–378.

Chou, Y. J., Huang, N., Lee, C. H., Tsai, S. L., Chen, L. S., & Chang, H. J. (2004). Who is at risk of death in an earthquake? *American Journal of Epidemiology, 160* (7), 688–695.

Chou, Y. J., Huang, N., Lee, C. H., Tsai, S. L., Tsay, J. H., Chen, L. S., et al. (2003). Suicides after the 1999 Taiwan earthquake. *International Journal of Epidemiology, 32* (6), 1007–1014.

Chung, M. C., Farmer, S., Werrett, J., Easthope, Y., & Chung, C. (2001). Traumatic stress and ways of coping of community residents exposed to a train disaster. *The Australian and New Zealand Journal of Psychiatry, 35* (4), 528–534.

Crabtree, J. (2006). Terrorist homicide bombings: A primer for preparation. *Journal of Burn Care & Research, 27* (5), 576–588.

Curtis, T., Miller, B. C., & Berry, E. H. (2000). Changes in reports and incidence of child abuse following natural disasters. *Child Abuse & Neglect, 24* (9), 1151–1162.

de Mel, S., McKenzie, D., & Woodruff, C. (2008). Mental health recovery and economic recovery after the tsunami: High-frequency longitudinal evidence from Sri Lankan small business owners. *Social Science & Medicine (1982), 66* (3), 582–595.

Deeg, D. J., Huizink, A. C., Comijs, H. C., & Smid, T. (2005). Disaster and associated changes in physical and mental health in older residents. *European Journal of Public Health, 15* (2), 170–174.

Demetriades, D., Kimbrell, B., Salim, A., Velmahos, G., Rhee, P., Preston, C., et al. (2005). Trauma deaths in a mature urban trauma system: Is "trimodal" distribution a valid concept? *Journal of the American College of Surgeons, 201* (3), 343–348.

den Ouden, D. J., Dirkzwager, A. J., & Yzermans, C. J. (2005). Health problems presented in general practice by survivors before and after a fireworks disaster: Associations with mental health care. *Scandinavian Journal of Primary Health Care, 23* (3), 137–141.

Dhara, V. R., & Dhara, R. (2002). The Union Carbide Disaster in Bhopal: A review of health effects. *Archives of Environmental Health, 57* (5), 391–404.

Dhara, V. R., Dhara, R., Acquilla, S. D., & Cullinan, P. (2002). Personal exposure and long-term health effects in survivors of the Union Carbide Disaster at Bhopal. *Environmental Health Perspectives, 110* (5), 487–500.

Diaz, J. H. (2007). The impact of hurricanes and flooding disasters on hymenopterid-inflicted injuries. *American Journal of Disaster Medicine, 2* (5), 257–269.

Dikshit, R. P., & Kanhere, S. (1999). Cancer patterns of lung, oropharynx and oral cavity cancer in relation to gas exposure at Bhopal. *Cancer Causes & Control: CCC, 10* (6), 627–636.

Dirkzwager, A. J., Kerssens, J. J., & Yzermans, C. J. (2006). Health problems in children and adolescents before and after a man-made disaster. *Journal of the American Academy of Child and Adolescent Psychiatry, 45* (1), 94–103.

Dirkzwager, A. J., van der Velden, P. G., Grievink, L., & Yzermans, C. J. (2007). Disaster-related posttraumatic stress disorder and physical health. *Psychosomatic Medicine, 69* (5), 435–440.

Dirkzwager, A. J., Yzermans, C. J., & Kessels, F. J. (2004). Psychological, musculoskeletal, and respiratory problems and sickness absence before and after involvement in a disaster: A longitudinal study among rescue workers. *Occupational and Environmental Medicine, 61* (10), 870–872.

Doliashvili, K., & Buckley, C. J. (2008). Women's sexual and reproductive health in post-socialist Georgia: Does internal displacement matter? *International Family Planning Perspectives, 34* (1), 21–29.

Dorn, T., Yzermans, C. J., Guijt, H., & van der Zee, J. (2007). Disaster-related stress as a prospective risk factor for hypertension in parents of adolescent fire victims. *American Journal of Epidemiology, 165* (4), 410–417.

Dorn, T., Yzermans, C. J., Kerssens, J. J., Spreeuwenberg, P. M., & van der Zee, J. (2006). Disaster and subsequent healthcare utilization: A longitudinal study among victims, their family members, and control subjects. *Medical Care, 44* (6), 581–589.

Dorn, T., Yzermans, C. J., Spreeuwenberg, P. M., Schilder, A., & van der Zee, J. (2008). A cohort study of the long-term impact of a fire disaster on the physical and mental health of adolescents. *Journal of Traumatic Stress, 21* (2), 239–242.

Dorn, T., Yzermans, C. J., Spreeuwenberg, P. M., & van der Zee, J. (2007). Physical and mental health problems in parents of adolescents with burns – a controlled, longitudinal study. *Journal of Psychosomatic Research, 63* (4), 381–389.

Drogendijk, A. N., Dirkzwager, A. J., Grievink, L., van der Velden, P. G., Marcelissen, F. G., & Kleber, R. J. (2007). The correspondence between persistent self-reported post-traumatic problems and general practitioners' reports after a major disaster. *Psychological Medicine, 37* (2), 193–202.

Engelthaler, D., Lewis, K., Anderson, S., Snow, S., Gladden, L., Hammond, R. M., et al. (2005). Vibrio illnesses after Hurricane Katrina – multiple states, August – September 2005. *Morbidity and Mortality Weekly Report, 54* (37), 928–931.

Feldman, D. M., Baron, S. L., Bernard, B. P., Lushniak, B. D., Banauch, G., Arcentales, N., et al. (2004). Symptoms, respirator use, and pulmonary function changes among New York City firefighters responding to the World Trade Center Disaster. *Chest, 125* (4), 1256–1264.

Floret, N., Viel, J. F., Mauny, F., Hoen, B., & Piarroux, R. (2006). Negligible risk for epidemics after geophysical disasters. *Emerging Infectious Diseases, 12* (4), 543–548.

Ford, J. D., Adams, M. L., & Dailey, W. F. (2006). Factors associated with receiving help and risk factors for disaster-related distress among Connecticut adults 5–15 months after the September 11th terrorist incidents. *Social Psychiatry and Psychiatric Epidemiology, 41* (4), 261–270.

Ford, J. D., Adams, M. L., & Dailey, W. F. (2007). Psychological and health problems in a geographically proximate population time-sampled continuously for three months after the September 11th, 2001 terrorist incidents. *Anxiety, Stress, and Coping, 20* (2), 129–146.

Foster, R. P. (2002). The long-term mental health effects of nuclear trauma in recent Russian immigrants in the United States. *The American Journal of Orthopsychiatry, 72* (4), 492–504.

Foster, R. P., & Goldstein, M. F. (2007). Chernobyl disaster sequelae in recent immigrants to the United States from the Former Soviet Union (FSU). *Journal of Immigrant and Minority Health, 9* (2), 115–124.

Frank, B., Dewart, T., Schmeidler, J., & Demirjian, A. (2006). The impact of 9/11 on New York City's substance abuse treatment programs: A study of program administrators. *Journal of Addictive Diseases, 25* (1), 5–14.

Frasier, P. Y., Belton, L., Hooten, E., Campbell, M. K., DeVellis, B., Benedict, S., et al. (2004). Disaster down east: Using participatory action research to explore intimate partner violence in eastern North Carolina. *Health Education & Behavior, 31* (Suppl. 4), 69–84.

Freese, J., Richmond, N. J., Silverman, R. A., Braun, J., Kaufman, B. J., & Clair, J. (2006). Impact of a citywide blackout on an urban emergency medical services system. *Prehospital and Disaster Medicine, 21* (6), 372–378.

Gaher, R. M., Simons, J. S., Jacobs, G. A., Meyer, D., & Johnson-Jimenez, E. (2006). Coping motives and trait negative affect: Testing mediation and moderation models of alcohol problems among American Red Cross disaster workers who responded to the September 11, 2001 terrorist attacks. *Addictive Behaviors, 31* (8), 1319–1330.

Gautschi, O. P., Cadosch, D., Rajan, G., & Zellweger, R. (2008). Earthquakes and trauma: Review of triage and injury-specific, immediate care. *Prehospital and Disaster Medicine, 23* (2), 195–201.

Gewalli, F., & Fogdestam, I. (2003). Triage and initial treatment of burns in the Gothenburg Fire Disaster 1998: On-call plastic surgeons' experiences and lessons learned. *Scandinavian Journal of Plastic and Reconstructive Surgery and Hand Surgery, 37* (3), 134–139.

Ghaffari-Nejad, A., Ahmadi-Mousavi, M., Gandomkar, M., & Reihani-Kermani, H. (2007). The prevalence of complicated grief among Bam earthquake survivors in Iran. *Archives of Iranian Medicine, 10* (4), 525–528.

Glass, R. I., & Zack, M. M., Jr. (1979). Increase in deaths from ischaemic heart-disease after blizzards. *Lancet, 1* (8114), 485–487.

Glynn, S. A., Busch, M. P., Schreiber, G. B., Murphy, E. L., Wright, D. J., Tu, Y., et al. (2003). Effect of a national disaster on blood supply and safety: The September 11 experience. *The Journal of the American Medical Association, 289* (17), 2246–2253.

Goenjian, A. K., Molina, L., Steinberg, A. M., Fairbanks, L. A., Alvarez, M. L., Goenjian, H. A., et al. (2001). Posttraumatic stress and depressive reactions among Nicaraguan adolescents after Hurricane Mitch. *The American Journal of Psychiatry, 158* (5), 788–794.

Grievink, L., van der Velden, P. G., Stellato, R. K., Dusseldorp, A., Gersons, B. P., Kleber, R. J., et al. (2007). A longitudinal comparative study of the physical and mental health problems of affected residents of the Firework Disaster Enschede, the Netherlands. *Public Health, 121* (5), 367–374.

Gruber, L. E., Mahoney, M. C., Lawvere, S., Chunikovskiy, S. P., Michalek, A. M., Khotianov, N., et al. (2005). Patterns of childhood mortality in a region of Belarus, 1980–2000. *European Journal of Pediatrics, 164* (9), 544–551.

Guha-Sapir, D., van Panhuis, W. G., & Lagoutte, J. (2007). Short communication: Patterns of chronic and acute diseases after natural disasters – a study from the international committee of the Red Cross field hospital in Banda Aceh after the 2004 Indian Ocean Tsunami. *Tropical Medicine & International Health, 12* (11), 1338–1341.

Guidry, V. T., & Margolis, L. H. (2005). Unequal respiratory health risk: Using GIS to explore hurricane-related flooding of schools in eastern North Carolina. *Environmental Research, 98* (3), 383–389.

Gul, S., Ghaffar, H., Mirza, S., Fizza Tauqir, S., Murad, F., Ali, Q., et al. (2008). Multitasking a telemedicine training unit in earthquake disaster response: Paraplegic rehabilitation assessment. *Telemedicine Journal and e-Health, 14* (3), 280–283.

Guzman-Tapia, Y., Ramirez-Sierra, M. J., Escobedo-Ortegon, J., & Dumonteil, E. (2005). Effect of Hurricane Isidore on *triatoma dimidiata* distribution and Chagas disease transmission risk in the Yucatan Peninsula of Mexico. *The American Journal of Tropical Medicine and Hygiene, 73* (6), 1019–1025.

Hashizume, M., Kondo, H., Murakami, T., Kodama, M., Nakahara, S., Lucas, M. E., et al. (2006). Use of rapid diagnostic tests for malaria in an emergency situation after the flood disaster in Mozambique. *Public Health, 120* (5), 444–447.

Hoffmann, W. (2001). Fallout from the Chernobyl nuclear disaster and congenital malformations in Europe. *Archives of Environmental Health, 56* (6), 478–484.

Hoven, C. W., Duarte, C. S., & Mandell, D. J. (2003). Children's mental health after disasters: The impact of the World Trade Center attack. *Current Psychiatry Reports, 5* (2), 101–107.

Huizink, A. C., Slottje, P., Witteveen, A. B., Bijlsma, J. A., Twisk, J. W., Smidt, N., et al. (2006). Long term health complaints following the Amsterdam Air Disaster in police officers and firefighters. *Occupational and Environmental Medicine, 63* (10), 657–662.

Hyre, A. D., Cohen, A. J., Kutner, N., Alper, A. B., & Muntner, P. (2007). Prevalence and predictors of posttraumatic stress disorder among hemodialysis patients following Hurricane Katrina. *American Journal of Kidney Disease, 50* (4), 585–593.

Ivers, L. C., & Ryan, E. T. (2006). Infectious diseases of severe weather-related and flood-related natural disasters. *Current Opinion in Infectious Diseases, 19* (5), 408–414.

Jayatissa, R., Bekele, A., Piyasena, C. L., & Mahamithawa, S. (2006). Assessment of nutritional status of children under five years of age, pregnant women, and lactating women living in relief camps after the tsunami in Sri Lanka. *Food and Nutrition Bulletin, 27* (2), 144–152.

Jeremijenko, A., McLaws, M. L., & Kosasih, H. (2007). A tsunami related tetanus epidemic in Aceh, Indonesia. *Asia-Pacific Journal of Public Health, 19* Spec No, 40–44.

Johnson, L. J., & Travis, A. R. (2006). Trimodal death and the injuries of survivors in Krabi Province, Thailand, post-tsunami. *ANZ Journal of Surgery, 76* (5), 288–289.

Jordan, N. N., Hoge, C. W., Tobler, S. K., Wells, J., Dydek, G. J., & Egerton, W. E. (2004). Mental health impact of 9/11 Pentagon attack: Validation of a rapid assessment tool. *American Journal of Preventive Medicine, 26* (4), 284–293.

Kalebi, A. Y., & Olumbe, A. K. (2006). Forensic findings from the Nairobi U.S. Embassy terrorist bombing. *East African Medical Journal, 83* (7), 380–388.

Keenan, H. T., Marshall, S. W., Nocera, M. A., & Runyan, D. K. (2004). Increased incidence of inflicted traumatic brain injury in children after a natural disaster. *American Journal of Preventive Medicine, 26* (3), 189–193.

King, S., & Laplante, D. P. (2005). The effects of prenatal maternal stress on children's cognitive development: Project ice storm. *Stress, 8* (1), 35–45.

Kirigia, J. M., Sambo, L. G., Aldis, W., & Mwabu, G. M. (2002). The burden of natural and technological disaster-related mortality on gross domestic product (GDP) in the WHO African region. *African Journal of Health Sciences, 9* (3–4), 169–180.

Kissinger, P., Schmidt, N., Sanders, C., & Liddon, N. (2007). The effect of the Hurricane Katrina disaster on sexual behavior and access to reproductive care for young women in New Orleans. *Sexually Transmitted Diseases, 34* (11), 883–886.

Knight, B. G., Gatz, M., Heller, K., & Bengtson, V. L. (2000). Age and emotional response to the Northridge earthquake: A longitudinal analysis. *Psychology and Aging, 15* (4), 627–634.

Kondo, H., Seo, N., Yasuda, T., Hasizume, M., Koido, Y., Ninomiya, N., et al. (2002). Post-flood–infectious diseases in Mozambique. *Prehospital and Disaster Medicine, 17* (3), 126–133.

Ladona, M. G., Izquierdo-Martinez, M., Posada de la Paz, M. P., de la Torre, R., Ampurdanes, C., Segura, J., et al. (2001). Pharmacogenetic profile of xenobiotic enzyme metabolism in survivors of the Spanish toxic oil syndrome. *Environmental Health Perspectives, 109* (4), 369–375.

Larrance, R., Anastario, M., & Lawry, L. (2007). Health status among internally displaced persons in Louisiana and Mississippi travel trailer parks. *Annals of Emergency Medicine, 49* (5), 590–601, 601, e1–12.

Leor, J., Poole, W. K., & Kloner, R. A. (1996). Sudden cardiac death triggered by an earthquake. *The New England Journal of Medicine, 334* (7), 413–419.

Ligon, B. L. (2006). Infectious diseases that pose specific challenges after natural disasters: A review. *Seminars in Pediatric Infectious Diseases, 17* (1), 36–45.

Llewellyn, M. (2006). Floods and tsunamis. *The Surgical Clinics of North America, 86* (3), 557–578.

Loganovsky, K., Havenaar, J. M., Tintle, N. L., Guey, L. T., Kotov, R., & Bromet, E. J. (2008). The mental health of clean-up workers 18 years after the Chernobyl accident. *Psychological Medicine, 38* (4), 481–488.

Loveridge, B. W., Henner, J. R., & Lee, F. C. (2003). Accurate clinical diagnosis of malaria in a postflood epidemic: A field study in Mozambique. *Wilderness & Environmental Medicine, 14* (1), 17–19.

Maegele, M., Gregor, S., Steinhausen, E., Bouillon, B., Heiss, M. M., Perbix, W., et al. (2005). The long-distance tertiary air transfer and care of tsunami victims: Injury pattern and microbiological and psychological aspects. *Critical Care Medicine, 33* (5), 1136–1140.

Maegele, M., Gregor, S., Yuecel, N., Simanski, C., Paffrath, T., Rixen, D., et al. (2006). One year ago not business as usual: Wound management, infection and psychoemotional control during tertiary medical care following the 2004 Tsunami Disaster in Southeast Asia. *Critical Care, 10* (2), R50.

Mallonee, S., Shariat, S., Stennies, G., Waxweiler, R., Hogan, D., & Jordan, F. (1996). Physical injuries and fatalities resulting from the Oklahoma City bombing. *The Journal of the American Medical Association, 276* (5), 382–387.

Mauer, M. P., Cummings, K. R., & Carlson, G. A. (2007). Health effects in New York state personnel who responded to the World Trade Center Disaster. *Journal of Occupational and Environmental Medicine, 49* (11), 1197–1205.

McCredie, J., & Willert, H. G. (1999). Longitudinal limb deficiencies and the sclerotomes. An analysis of 378 dysmelic malformations induced by thalidomide. *The Journal of Bone and Joint Surgery British Volume, 81* (1), 9–23.

Meislin, H., Criss, E. A., Judkins, D., Berger, R., Conroy, C., Parks, B., et al. (1997). Fatal trauma: The modal distribution of time to death is a function of patient demographics and regional resources. *The Journal of Trauma, 43* (3), 433–440.

Mettler, F. A., Jr, Gus'kova, A. K., & Gusev, I. (2007). Health effects in those with acute radiation sickness from the Chernobyl accident. *Health Physics, 93* (5), 462–469.

Meyer, H. J. (2003). The Kaprun cable car fire disaster – aspects of forensic organisation following a mass fatality with 155 victims. *Forensic Science International, 138* (1–3), 1–7.

Mocarelli, P., Gerthoux, P. M., Ferrari, E., Patterson, D. G., Jr, Kieszak, S. M., Brambilla, P., et al. (2000). Paternal concentrations of dioxin and sex ratio of offspring. *Lancet, 355* (9218), 1858–1863.

Morgan, O. (2004). Infectious disease risks from dead bodies following natural disasters. *Pan American Journal of Public Health, 15* (5), 307–312.

Morgan, O., Ahern, M., & Cairncross, S. (2005). Revisiting the tsunami: Health consequences of flooding. *PLoS Medicine, 2* (6), e184.

Morren, M., Dirkzwager, A. J., Kessels, F. J., & Yzermans, C. J. (2007). The influence of a disaster on the health of rescue workers: A longitudinal study. *Canadian Medical Association Journal, 176* (9), 1279–1283.

Movaghar, A. R., Goodarzi, R. R., Izadian, E., Mohammadi, M. R., Hosseini, M., & Vazirian, M. (2005). The impact of Bam earthquake on substance users in the first 2 weeks: A rapid assessment. *Journal of Urban Health, 82* (3), 370–377.

Nandi, A., Galea, S., Tracy, M., Ahern, J., Resnick, H., Gershon, R., et al. (2004). Job loss, unemployment, work stress, job satisfaction, and the persistence of posttraumatic stress disorder one year after the September 11 attacks. *Journal of Occupational and Environmental Medicine, 46* (10), 1057–1064.

Neria, Y., Nandi, A., & Galea, S. (2008). Post-traumatic stress disorder following disasters: A systematic review. *Psychological Medicine, 38* (4), 467–480.

Neugebauer, R., Hoek, H. W., & Susser, E. (1999). Prenatal exposure to wartime famine and development of antisocial personality disorder in early adulthood. *The Journal of the American Medical Association, 282* (5), 455–462.

Nishikiori, N., Abe, T., Costa, D. G., Dharmaratne, S. D., Kunii, O., & Moji, K. (2006a). Timing of mortality among internally displaced persons due to the tsunami in Sri Lanka: Cross sectional household survey. *British Medical Journal Clinical Research Edition, 332* (7537), 334–335.

Nishikiori, N., Abe, T., Costa, D. G., Dharmaratne, S. D., Kunii, O., & Moji, K. (2006b). Who died as a result of the tsunami? Risk factors of mortality among internally displaced persons in Sri Lanka: A retrospective cohort analysis. *BMC Public Health, 6*, 73.

Nishiwaki, Y., Maekawa, K., Ogawa, Y., Asukai, N., Minami, M., Omae, K., et al. (2001). Effects of sarin on the nervous system in rescue team staff members and police officers 3 years after the Tokyo subway sarin attack. *Environmental Health Perspectives, 109* (11), 1169–1173.

Norris, F. H., Baker, C. K., Murphy, A. D., & Kaniasty, K. (2005). Social support mobilization and deterioration after Mexico's 1999 flood: Effects of context, gender, and time. *American Journal of Community Psychology, 36* (1–2), 15–28.

Norris, F. H., Friedman, M. J., Watson, P. J., Byrne, C. M., Diaz, E., & Kaniasty, K. (2002). 60,000 disaster victims speak: Part I. An empirical review of the empirical literature, 1981–2001. *Psychiatry, 65* (3), 207–239.

North, C. S., McCutcheon, V., Spitznagel, E. L., & Smith, E. M. (2002). Three-year follow-up of survivors of a mass shooting episode. *Journal of Urban Health, 79* (3), 383–391.

North, C. S., Pfefferbaum, B., Narayanan, P., Thielman, S., McCoy, G., Dumont, C., et al. (2005). Comparison of post-disaster psychiatric disorders after terrorist bombings in Nairobi and Oklahoma City. *The British Journal of Psychiatry, 186*, 487–493.

Nufer, K. E., & Wilson-Ramirez, G. (2004). A comparison of patient needs following two hurricanes. *Prehospital and Disaster Medicine, 19* (2), 146–149.

Odhiambo, W. A., Guthua, S. W., Macigo, F. G., & Akama, M. K. (2002). Maxillofacial injuries caused by terrorist bomb attack in Nairobi, Kenya. *International Journal of Oral and Maxillofacial Surgery, 31* (4), 374–377.

O'Keefe Gatewood, M., & Zane, R. D. (2004). Lightning injuries. *Emergency Medicine Clinics of North America, 22*(2), 369–403.

Olff, M., Meewisse, M. L., Kleber, R. J., van der Velden, P. G., Drogendijk, A. N., van Amsterdam, J. G., et al. (2006). Tobacco usage interacts with postdisaster psychopathology on circadian salivary cortisol. *International Journal of Psychophysiology, 59* (3), 251–258.

Ozer, E. J., Best, S. R., Lipsey, T. L., & Weiss, D. S. (2003). Predictors of posttraumatic stress disorder and symptoms in adults: A meta-analysis. *Psychological Bulletin, 129* (1), 52–73.

Parslow, R. A., & Jorm, A. F. (2006). Tobacco use after experiencing a major natural disaster: Analysis of a longitudinal study of 2063 young adults. *Addiction, 101* (7), 1044–1050.

Parslow, R. A., Jorm, A. F., & Christensen, H. (2006). Associations of pre-trauma attributes and trauma exposure with screening positive for PTSD: Analysis of a community-based study of 2,085 young adults. *Psychological Medicine, 36* (3), 387–395.

Peleg, K., Reuveni, H., & Stein, M. (2002). Earthquake disasters – lessons to be learned. *The Israel Medical Association Journal, 4* (5), 361–365.

Person, C., Tracy, M., & Galea, S. (2006). Risk factors for depression after a disaster. *The Journal of Nervous and Mental Disease, 194* (9), 659–666.

Pesatori, A. C., Consonni, D., Bachetti, S., Zocchetti, C., Bonzini, M., Baccarelli, A., et al. (2003). Short- and long-term morbidity and mortality in the population exposed to dioxin after the "Seveso Accident". *Industrial Health, 41* (3), 127–138.

Pfefferbaum, B., & Doughty, D. E. (2001). Increased alcohol use in a treatment sample of Oklahoma City bombing victims. *Psychiatry, 64* (4), 296–303.

Pfefferbaum, B., North, C. S., Pfefferbaum, R. L., Christiansen, E. H., Schorr, J. K., Vincent, R. D., et al. (2008). Change in smoking and drinking after September 11, 2001, in a national sample of ever smokers and ever drinkers. *The Journal of Nervous and Mental Disease, 196* (2), 113–121.

Pfefferbaum, B., Stuber, J., Galea, S., & Fairbrother, G. (2006). Panic reactions to terrorist attacks and probable posttraumatic stress disorder in adolescents. *Journal of Traumatic Stress, 19* (2), 217–228.

Pfefferbaum, B., Vinekar, S. S., Trautman, R. P., Lensgraf, S. J., Reddy, C., Patel, N., et al. (2002). The effect of loss and trauma on substance use behavior in individuals seeking support services after the 1995 Oklahoma City bombing. *Annals of Clinical Psychiatry, 14* (2), 89–95.

Rahu, M., Tekkel, M., Veidebaum, T., Pukkala, E., Hakulinen, T., Auvinen, A., et al. (1997). The Estonian study of Chernobyl cleanup workers: II. Incidence of cancer and mortality. *Radiation Research, 147* (5), 653–657.

Rathore, M. F., Rashid, P., Butt, A. W., Malik, A. A., Gill, Z. A., & Haig, A. J. (2007). Epidemiology of spinal cord injuries in the 2005 Pakistan earthquake. *Spinal Cord, 45* (10), 658–663.

Reijneveld, S. A., Crone, M. R., Schuller, A. A., Verhulst, F. C., & Verloove-Vanhorick, S. P. (2005). The changing impact of a severe disaster on the mental health and substance misuse of adolescents: Follow-up of a controlled study. *Psychological Medicine, 35* (3), 367–376.

Reijneveld, S. A., Crone, M. R., Verhulst, F. C., & Verloove-Vanhorick, S. P. (2003). The effect of a severe disaster on the mental health of adolescents: A controlled study. *Lancet, 362* (9385), 691–696.

Remennick, L. I. (2002). Immigrants from Chernobyl-affected areas in Israel: The link between health and social adjustment. *Social Science & Medicine, 54* (2), 309–317.

Roseboom, T. J., van der Meulen, J. H., Ravelli, A. C., Osmond, C., Barker, D. J., & Bleker, O. P. (2001). Effects of prenatal exposure to the Dutch famine on adult disease in later life: An overview. *Molecular and Cellular Endocrinology, 185* (1–2), 93–98.

Sauaia, A., Moore, F. A., Moore, E. E., Moser, K. S., Brennan, R., Read, R. A., et al. (1995). Epidemiology of trauma deaths: A reassessment. *The Journal of Trauma, 38* (2), 185–193.

Schultz, C. H., Koenig, K. L., & Lewis, R. J. (2007). Decision making in hospital earthquake evacuation: Does distance from the epicenter matter? *Annals of Emergency Medicine, 50* (3), 320–326.

Selten, J. P., van der Graaf, Y., van Duursen, R., Gispen-de Wied, C. C., & Kahn, R. S. (1999). Psychotic illness after prenatal exposure to the 1953 Dutch Flood Disaster. *Schizophrenia Research, 35* (3), 243–245.

Sepehri, G., & Meimandi, M. S. (2006). Pattern of drug prescription and utilization among Bam residents during the first six months after the 2003 Bam earthquake. *Prehospital and Disaster Medicine, 21* (6), 396–402.

Sever, M. S., Erek, E., Vanholder, R., Ozener, C., Yavuz, M., Kayacan, S. M., et al. (2002). Lessons learned from the Marmara Disaster: Time period under the rubble. *Critical Care Medicine, 30* (11), 2443–2449.

Shoaf, K. I., Sareen, H. R., Nguyen, L. H., & Bourque, L. B. (1998). Injuries as a result of California earthquakes in the past decade. *Disasters, 22* (3), 218–235.

Simons, J. S., Gaher, R. M., Jacobs, G. A., Meyer, D., & Johnson-Jimenez, E. (2005). Associations between alcohol use and PTSD symptoms among American Red Cross disaster relief workers responding to the 9/11/2001 attacks. *The American Journal of Drug and Alcohol Abuse, 31* (2), 285–304.

Skloot, G., Goldman, M., Fischler, D., Goldman, C., Schechter, C., Levin, S., et al. (2004). Respiratory symptoms and physiologic assessment of ironworkers at the World Trade Center Disaster Site. *Chest, 125* (4), 1248–1255.

Slottje, P., Smidt, N., Twisk, J. W., Huizink, A. C., Witteveen, A. B., van Mechelen, W., et al. (2006). Attribution of physical complaints to the air disaster in Amsterdam by exposed rescue workers: An epidemiological study using historic cohorts. *BMC Public Health, 6*, 142.

Slottje, P., Twisk, J. W., Smidt, N., Huizink, A. C., Witteveen, A. B., van Mechelen, W., et al. (2007). Health-related quality of life of firefighters and police officers 8.5 years after the air disaster in Amsterdam. *Quality of Life Research, 16* (2), 239–252.

Slottje, P., Witteveen, A. B., Twisk, J. W., Smidt, N., Huizink, A. C., van Mechelen, W., et al. (2008). Post-disaster physical symptoms of firefighters and police officers: Role of types of exposure and post-traumatic stress symptoms. *British Journal of Health Psychology, 13* (Pt 2), 327–342.

Smith, D. W., Christiansen, E. H., Vincent, R., & Hann, N. E. (1999). Population effects of the bombing of Oklahoma City. *The Journal of the Oklahoma State Medical Association, 92* (4), 193–198.

Sniffen, J. C., Cooper, T. W., Johnson, D., Blackmore, C., Patel, P., Harduar-Morano, L., et al. (2005). Carbon monoxide poisoning from hurricane-associated use of portable generators – Florida, 2004. *Morbidity and Mortality Weekly Report, 54* (28), 697–700.

Soeteman, R. J., Yzermans, C. J., Kerssens, J. J., Dirkzwager, A. J., Donker, G. A., ten Veen, P. M., et al. (2007). Health problems presented to family practices in the Netherlands 1 year before and 1 year after a disaster. *Journal of the American Board of Family Medicine, 20* (6), 548–556.

Sonmezoglu, M., Kocak, N., Oncul, O., Ozbayburtlu, S., Hepgul, Z., Kosan, E., et al. (2005). Effects of a major earthquake on blood donor types and infectious diseases marker rates. *Transfusion Medicine, 15* (2), 93–97.

Spiess, H. (2002). Peteosthor – a medical disaster due to radium-224A personal recollection. *Radiation and Environmental Biophysics, 41* (3), 163–172.

Spinhoven, P., & Verschuur, M. (2006). Predictors of fatigue in rescue workers and residents in the aftermath of an aviation disaster: A longitudinal study. *Psychosomatic Medicine, 68* (4), 605–612.

Stalnikowicz, R., & Tsafrir, A. (2002). Acute psychosocial stress and cardiovascular events. *The American Journal of Emergency Medicine, 20* (5), 488–491.

Stratton, S. J., & Tyler, R. D. (2006). Characteristics of medical surge capacity demand for sudden-impact disasters. *Academic Emergency Medicine, 13* (11), 1193–1197.

Stuber, J., Galea, S., Pfefferbaum, B., Vandivere, S., Moore, K., & Fairbrother, G. (2005). Behavior problems in New York City's children after the September 11, 2001 terrorist attacks. *The American Journal of Orthopsychiatry, 75* (2), 190–200.

Sur, D., Dutta, P., Nair, G. B., & Bhattacharya, S. K. (2000). Severe cholera outbreak following floods in a northern district of west Bengal. *The Indian Journal of Medical Research, 112*, 178–182.

Tanaka, H., Oda, J., Iwai, A., Kuwagata, Y., Matsuoka, T., Takaoka, M., et al. (1999). Morbidity and mortality of hospitalized patients after the 1995 Hanshin-Awaji earthquake. *The American Journal of Emergency Medicine, 17* (2), 186–191.

Tao, X. G., Massa, J., Ashwell, L., Davis, K., Schwab, M., & Geyh, A. (2007). The World Trade Center clean up and recovery worker cohort study: Respiratory health amongst cleanup workers approximately 20 months after initial exposure at the disaster site. *Journal of Occupational and Environmental Medicine, 49* (10), 1063–1072.

Taormina, D. P., Rozenblatt, S., Guey, L. T., Gluzman, S. F., Carlson, G. A., Havenaar, J. M., et al. (2008). The Chernobyl accident and cognitive functioning: A follow-up study of infant evacuees at age 19 years. *Psychological Medicine, 38* (4), 489–497.

Tauqir, S. F., Mirza, S., Gul, S., Ghaffar, H., & Zafar, A. (2007). Complications in patients with spinal cord injuries sustained in an earthquake in northern Pakistan. *The Journal of Spinal Cord Medicine, 30* (4), 373–377.

Teague, D. C. (2004). Mass casualties in the Oklahoma City bombing. *Clinical Orthopaedics and Related Research, 422*, 77–81.

Thomas, C. R. (2006). Psychiatric sequelae of disasters. *Journal of Burn Care & Research, 27* (5), 600–605.

Todd, B. (2006). Infection control and Hurricane Katrina. What nurses can learn in the aftermath of the disaster. *The American Journal of Nursing, 106* (3), 29–31.

Trichopoulos, D., Katsouyanni, K., Zavitsanos, X., Tzonou, A., & Dalla-Vorgia, P. (1983). Psychological stress and fatal heart attack: The Athens (1981) earthquake natural experiment. *Lancet, 1* (8322), 441–444.

Trout, D., Nimgade, A., Mueller, C., Hall, R., & Earnest, G. S. (2002). Health effects and occupational exposures among office workers near the World Trade Center Disaster site. *Journal of Occupational and Environmental Medicine, 44* (7), 601–605.

Tucker, P. M., Pfefferbaum, B., North, C. S., Kent, A., Burgin, C. E., Parker, D. E., et al. (2007). Physiologic reactivity despite emotional resilience several years after direct exposure to terrorism. *The American Journal of Psychiatry, 164* (2), 230–235.

Tyler, K. A. (2006). The impact of support received and support provision on changes in perceived social support among older adults. *International Journal of Aging & Human Development, 62* (1), 21–38.

Uckay, I., Sax, H., Harbarth, S., Bernard, L., & Pittet, D. (2008). Multi-resistant infections in repatriated patients after natural disasters: Lessons learned from the 2004 Tsunami for hospital infection control. *The Journal of Hospital Infection, 68* (1), 1–8.

van den Berg, B., Grievink, L., Stellato, R. K., Yzermans, C. J., & Lebret, E. (2005). Symptoms and related functioning in a traumatized community. *Archives of Internal Medicine, 165* (20), 2402–2407.

van den Berg, B., Grievink, L., van der Velden, P. G., Yzermans, C. J., Stellato, R. K., Lebret, E., et al. (2008). Risk factors for physical symptoms after a disaster: A longitudinal study. *Psychological Medicine, 38* (4), 499–510.

van den Berg, B., van der Velden, P. G., Yzermans, C. J., Stellato, R. K., & Grievink, L. (2006). Health-related quality of life and mental health problems after a disaster: Are chronically ill survivors more vulnerable to health problems? *Quality of Life Research, 15* (10), 1571–1576.

van den Berg, B., Yzermans, C. J., van der Velden, P. G., Stellato, R. K., Lebret, E., & Grievink, L. (2007). Are physical symptoms among survivors of a disaster presented to the general practitioner? A comparison between self-reports and GP data. *BMC Health Services Research, 7*, 150.

van der Velden, P. G., Grievink, L., Kleber, R. J., Drogendijk, A. N., Roskam, A. J., Marcelissen, F. G., et al. (2006). Post-disaster mental health problems and the utilization of mental health services: A four-year longitudinal comparative study. *Administration and Policy in Mental Health, 33* (3), 279–288.

van der Velden, P. G., Kleber, R. J., Fournier, M., Grievink, L., Drogendijk, A., & Gersons, B. P. (2007a). The association between dispositional optimism and mental health problems among disaster victims and a comparison group: A prospective study. *Journal of Affective Disorders, 102* (1–3), 35–45.

van der Velden, P. G., Yzermans, C. J., Kleber, R. J., & Gersons, B. P. (2007b). Correlates of mental health services utilization 18 months and almost 4 years postdisaster among adults with mental health problems. *Journal of Traumatic Stress, 20* (6), 1029–1039.

van Harten, S. M., Bierens, J. J., Welling, L., Patka, P., Kreis, R. W., & Boers, M. (2006). The Volendam fire: Lessons learned from disaster research. *Prehospital and Disaster Medicine, 21* (5), 303–309.

Vetter, S., Rossegger, A., Rossler, W., Bisson, J. I., & Endrass, J. (2008). Exposure to the Tsunami Disaster, PTSD symptoms and increased substance use – an internet based survey of male and female residents of Switzerland. *BMC Public Health, 8,* 92.

Vlahov, D., Galea, S., Ahern, J., Rudenstine, S., Resnick, H., Kilpatrick, D., et al. (2006). Alcohol drinking problems among New York City residents after the September 11 terrorist attacks. *Substance Use & Misuse, 41* (9), 1295–1311.

Vlahov, D., Galea, S., Resnick, H., Ahern, J., Boscarino, J. A., Bucuvalas, M., et al. (2002). Increased use of cigarettes, alcohol, and marijuana among Manhattan, New York, residents after the September 11 terrorist attacks. *American Journal of Epidemiology, 155* (11), 988–996.

Wang, X., Gao, L., Zhang, H., Zhao, C., Shen, Y., & Shinfuku, N. (2000). Post-earthquake quality of life and psychological well-being: Longitudinal evaluation in a rural community sample in northern China. *Psychiatry and Clinical Neurosciences, 54* (4), 427–433.

Watson, J. T., Gayer, M., & Connolly, M. A. (2007). Epidemics after natural disasters. *Emerging Infectious Diseases, 13* (1), 1–5.

Wayment, H. A. (2004). It could have been me: Vicarious victims and disaster-focused distress. *Personality and Social Psychology Bulletin, 30* (4), 515–528.

Whalen, C. K., Henker, B., King, P. S., Jamner, L. D., & Levine, L. (2004). Adolescents react to the events of September 11, 2001: Focused versus ambient impact. *Journal of Abnormal Child Psychology, 32* (1), 1–11.

Zichittella, L. J., Mahoney, M. C., Lawvere, S., Michalek, A. M., Chunikhovskiy, S. P., & Khotianov, N. (2004). Infant mortality trends in a region of Belarus, 1980–2000. *BMC Pediatrics, 4,* 3.

Subject Index

A

Acute respiratory infections (ARI), 307
Adjustment
    child, outcomes following trauma events, 83
    children and adolescents' self-reports of their overall, 83
    disaster-exposed children/adolescents displaying high levels of, 45
    meaning making in, to loss and trauma, 115
    and resilience following traumatic events, 45–47
Adolescent/youth emotional development during disaster (Hurricane Katrina), 27–28
    ecological-needs-based perspective, 28–30
    research on effects of Katrina
        exosystem influences, 33–34
        macrosystem influences, 30–33
        mesosystem influences, 34–36
        microsystem influences, 36–37
        ontogenic influences, 37–40
Adults, psychological impact of hurricanes/storms, 97–98
    diagnostic considerations, 98–99
    findings from previous hurricanes/storms, 101–103
    Hurricane Katrina
        effects of displacement from Gulf Coast, 105–106
        effects of exposure to, 105
        findings from young adults, 104
        mental illness, prevalence rates, and associated findings, 103–104
    racial differences and resulting psychological impact, 106
    disruption to service and treatment, 107–108
    effects on those with pre-hurricane storm fears, 106–107
    risk and resiliency, 100–101
Aftermath of natural disaster, helping others in, 233
    association with faith community, 234–235
    bridging belief-to-behavior gap, 236–237
    good intentions, noble phrases, and ethics, 236
    reports of "being helped," 234
"Agentic" model, 100–101
Age-related change, older adult population, natural disasters and, 173–175
    in cognition, 174
    in physical health, 173–174
    in social relations, 174–175
Aggression, as reaction to disaster, 37–38, 72
Aging, successful, 176
Alcohol, disasters and, 313–314
Ameliorative coping, 58
ARI, *see* Acute respiratory infections (ARI)
Arthritis, disasters and, 309

B

Behavioral health activities, in response to catastrophic event, 249–251
Bioecological model, 114
Bronfenbrenner's ecological systems theory, 28
"Burnout," *see* "vicarious traumatization"

C

Cancer, disasters and, 312
Cardiovascular health outcomes, disasters and, 308–309
CERT, *see* Community Emergency Response Teams (CERT)
Child abuse, disasters and, 315

327

Child adaptation, disasters affecting
  exosystem influences on, 33
  microsystem influences on, 36
Child mental health
  exosystem influences on, 33–34
  parent–child separations during trauma, 34
Chronic disease, disasters and, 308–312
  arthritis, 309
  cancer, 312
  cardiovascular health outcomes, 308–309
  diabetes, 309
  kidney and urinary health, 309–310
  musculoskeletal problems, 311–312
  neurological problems, 310
  reproductive and developmental health, 310–311
  respiratory health, 309
  specific problems and conditions, 312
Cognition, 174
Cognitive–behavioral treatment, 72–73
Cognitive development, very young *vs.* older children, 7
Cognitive restructuring, 47
Communication, older children *vs.* very young children, 7
Community Emergency Response Teams (CERT), 155
Competence, 84
Conservation of resources model, 28–29
Coping, 48, 75
  and adjustment, 48–50
    parental, 49–50
    youth, 49
  before and after storms, 186
  ameliorative coping, 58
  approaches to, 204–207
  destructive coping, 59
  diversion, 58
  issues, after Katrina, 197–198
  and resilience in late adulthood, 176
    determinants of adaptive behavior in older adults, 178–180
    review of coping, 178
    review of resilience, 176–178
  self-efficacy, 100–101
Cost–reward model, 225–227
Crisis, 197
  issues, after Katrina, 196–197
Cultural competence and disaster behavioral health, 67
  focus groups, objectives, 67–68

D

Dark humor, *see* survival humor
Death, trauma-related, 283–285
Diabetes, disasters and, 309
Diathesis–stress model, 74–75
Disaster behavioral health, cultural competence and, 67
Disaster humor, *see* survival humor
Disaster mental health response to catastrophic event, 241–242
  assistance to children and schools, 254–255
  behavioral health activities, 250–251
  first-responder intervention, 248–249
    emergency response and employee stress management, 249
    first-responder crisis counseling, 248–249
  first wave of emergency responding, 244–247
    extended community mental health center hours, 248
    general needs shelters and mobile crisis teams, 248
    medical special needs shelters, 246–247
    SARBO – I-10 & causeway Blvd and TIMOSA – New Orleans Airport, 247–248
    TMOSA-Baton Rouge, 247
  initial response, 251–252
  mass casualty identification, 249–250
  preparation and response, 242–244
  work on cruise ships with first responders and their families, 252–254
  work with re-opening schools, 255–257
Disaster recovery in workplace organizations, 261–262
  guide for disaster prevention, preparation, and recovery process, 276
  OD in extraordinary circumstances, 264
    developmental stages of disaster response, 265–266
    restoring human, operational, and technical organizational structures, 267–274
  ordinary disaster and typical approaches to OD
    ordinary disasters *versus* catastrophic disasters, 263
    typical OD in normal circumstances, 263–264
  organizational recovery needs after Hurricane Katrina, 273

practical and scientific suggestions for
workplace disaster recovery
research directions, 275–276
workplace preparation and planning,
274–275
workplace recovery in overview, 262
Disaster response, developmental stages of,
265–266
during-stage emergency, 265–266
post-stage disaster, 266
pre-stage crisis, 265
Disasters
benefit finding, families and
improved relationships, 118–119
prioritization and planning, 119
reappraisal, 119
child adaptation, 36
child interviews, 17–20
See also Narrative story stem technique
(NSST)
children's emotional responses to, drawing
roofs, 22
developmental adaptation to, 38
early childhood education and, 8–10
effects on young children, 7–8
exposure to natural, 75
humor, families and, 122–123
internalizing reactions to, 37
leading to emotional dysregulation, 37
mediating factors, effects of, 7–8
optimism, families and, 121–122
ordinary *versus* catastrophic disasters, 263
post-traumatic stress, effects on older
children, 7
preparation, social work perspective
disaster planning teams and
partnerships, 163
emergency preparedness, 160–162
identifying high-risk elders, 163–164
older persons' resilience and exposure
to hurricanes, 162–163
social work roles and risks – freelancing
and credentialing issues, 164–166
role of educators following, 9
sense making, families and
attribution to higher power, 120–121
general acceptance, 121
old adages survive, 121
order in social environment, 119–120
social support and discrimination, 31–32
stages exhibited in play and conversations,
17

young children knowledge before, during,
and after, 9
Disasters and population health, 281–282
chronic disease, 308–312
arthritis, 309
cancer, 312
cardiovascular health outcomes,
308–309
diabetes, 309
kidney and urinary health, 309–310
musculoskeletal problems, 311–312
neurological problems, 310
reproductive and developmental health,
310–311
respiratory health, 309
specific problems and conditions, 312
health behavior, 312–315
alcohol, 313–314
child abuse and domestic violence, 315
drug abuse, 314
tobacco, 314–315
health systems and infrastructure, 289–295
challenges to health care in post-disaster
setting, 291–292
challenges to other medical services,
293
challenges to rescue and emergency
medical operations, 289–291
emergency medical assistance teams,
292–293
mental health services utilization,
294–295
primary health-care utilization,
293–294
infectious disease, 304–307
epidemics, 305
impact on health system, 305–306
infectious disease mortality, 305
sources of infection, 306–307
injury and mortality, 282–288
burden of emergency response and
cleanup activities, 287–288
disaster-specific injury and mortality
patterns, 286–287
long-lasting impact, 288
temporal distribution of trauma-related
death, 283–285
vulnerability factors, 285–286
mental health, 295–304
anxiety, 302–303
behavioral problems, 303
daily functioning – social and
occupational, 303–304

Disasters and population health (*cont.*)
    depression, 301–302
        non-specific measures of mental health, 296–297
        post-traumatic stress disorder, 299–301
        sleep problems, 297–298
        somatic complaints and medically unexplained symptoms, 298–299
        suicidality, 303
    method, 282
Disaster services with frail older persons, 153–154
    disaster preparation from social work perspective
        disaster planning teams and partnerships, 163
        emergency preparedness, 160–162
        identifying high-risk elders, 163–164
        older persons' resilience and exposure to hurricanes, 162–163
        social work roles and risks – freelancing and credentialing issues, 164–166
    hurricane aftereffects and elderly, 154–156
        effects of evacuation and transfer, 156–157
        hurricanes of 2008: Gustav and Ike, 158–160
        special needs shelters and transportation issues, 157–158
Disaster Technical Assistance Cadre (DTAC), 66
Diversion, 58–59
Domestic violence, disasters and, 315
Drug abuse, disasters and, 314
DTAC, *see* Disaster Technical Assistance Cadre (DTAC)

E
Early childhood education
    developmental and educational needs, 5–6, 21
    and disasters, 8–10
Ecological-needs-based perspective of adolescent/youth emotional development in disaster, 28–30
Ecological systems theory, 28
Ecologies
    and Bronfenbrenner's ecological systems theory, 28
    and needs influencing youth adaptation following disaster, 29
Emotional development
    community peer groups, microsystem, 36
    very young *vs.* older children, 7
Emotional development of adolescent/youth during disaster, 27–28
    ecological-needs-based perspective, 28–30
    research on effects of Katrina
        exosystem influences, 33–34
        macrosystem influences, 30–33
        mesosystem influences, 34–36
        microsystem influences, 36–37
        ontogenic influences, 37–40
Empathy, 223
Empathy–altruism hypothesis, 223–224
    vs. relief of negative state view, 224
Ethnicity, 80
Exosystem, 28, 29
    child adaptation and, 33
    child mental health and, 33–34
    Katrina (Hurricane), research on effects of, 33–34
Exposure, 75
    level of, 75–76
Expression of knowledge, development, and learning, children's, 6–7

F
Faith, crisis, coping, and meaning making after Katrina, 195–196
    approaches to coping, 204–207
    crisis as tragedy/opportunity/"part of life," 201–204
    discussion, 212–213
    issues
        coping, 197–198
        crisis, 196–197
        meaning making, 198–199
    meaning making, 207–212
    method
        analysis and coding, 199–200
        reflexivity, 200–201
        sample and interview procedures, 199
Families and disasters, 113–114
    description of targeted study site and data collection, 116–117
        benefit finding, 118–119
        discussion, 123–124
        humor, 122–123
        method, 117
        optimism, 121–122
        results, 117–118
        sense making, 119–121
    recommendations and future directions, 125–127
    theoretical background and related literature, 114–115

Subject Index

Family Relations (FR), 113
Family Support Scale (FSS), 32
Federal Emergency Management Agency (FEMA), 32
FEMA, *see* Federal Emergency Management Agency (FEMA)
Financial strain, impact of disaster on child and, 34
"Frail elderly," 155

G

Gallows humor, *see* survival humor
Geographic differences in language/literacy/play and disasters
    conversations, 16–17
    drawing hurricane experiences, 15–16
    hurricane stories, 13–15
    play, 16
    using books about hurricanes, 16
    writing about hurricanes, 15

H

Health and quality of life before and after storms, 182
Health behavior, disasters and, 312–315
    alcohol, 313–314
    child abuse and domestic violence, 315
    drug abuse, 314
    tobacco, 314–315
Health outcomes following traumatic events, 84–85
Health status, medications, and life circumstances, changes in, 183
Health systems and infrastructure, disasters and, 289–295
    challenges to health care in post-disaster setting, 291–292
    challenges to other medical services, 293
    challenges to rescue and emergency medical operations, 289–291
    emergency medical assistance teams, 292–293
    mental health services utilization, 294–295
    primary health-care utilization, 293–294
Healthy emotional adaptation, 28
Helping in aftermath of natural disaster, 233
    association with faith community, 234–235
    bridging belief-to-behavior gap, 236–237
    good intentions, noble phrases, and ethics, 236
    reports of "being helped," 234
Hurricanes
    aftereffects and elderly, 154–156

    effects of evacuation and transfer, 156–157
    hurricanes of 2008: Gustav and Ike, 158–160
    special needs shelters and transportation issues, 157–158
children about, 9–10
children's cognitive processing of, 6
children's demonstrated knowledge on effects of, 20
conversations, 16–17
drawing experiences, 15–16
experienced related to psychological symptoms, 31
spontaneous student-initiated activities, 12
stories, 13–15
    differences in classroom activities across states, 14
teacher's responses to, 11
using books about, 16
writing about, 15
young children's understanding of, assessment, 10

I

Infectious disease, disasters and, 304–307
    Acute respiratory infections (ARI), 307
    diarrheal diseases, 307
    epidemics, 305
    impact on health system, 305–306
    infectious disease mortality, 305
    sources of infection, 306–307
        conditions and species of concern, 307
        hospital-acquired disease, 306–307
        person-to-person/crowding, 307
        soil and water, 306
        vector borne disease, 306
Injury and mortality, disaster and, 282–288
    burden of emergency response and cleanup activities, 287–288
    disaster-specific injury and mortality patterns, 286–287
    long-lasting impact, 288
    outcome and length of survival for patients who died from trauma, 283
    temporal distribution of trauma-related death, 283–285
    vulnerability factors, 285–286

J

Journal of Marriage and Family (JMF), 113

K

Katrina Aid and Relief Effort (KARE), 271
Katrina (Hurricane), 65–66
　challenges psychologists encountered post, 85
　educate school teachers/administrators on needs of students impacted by, 67
　impact on residents, 97
　impacts in Louisiana and Mississippi
　　children displaced by, 7
　　decrease in student population, 4
　　no counseling/instructions regarding hurricanes, 9
　　psychological distress in children, 4
　　schools, 3, 5
　　statistics, 4
　mother's psychopathology on her child's distress following, 71
　profound effects on child/adolescent emotional development, 27
　psychological impact of, 68–69
　regional differences in psychosocial impact of, 31
　research on effects of
　　exosystem influences, 33–34
　　macrosystem influences, 30–33
　　mesosystem influences, 34–36
　　microsystem influences, 36–37
　　ontogenic influences, 37–40
　young children's cognitive reactions to, 69
Katrina (Hurricane), impact on children and adolescents, 65–66
　challenges, 85
　　African–American Church and community-based organizations preparedness, 88
　　breach, 87–88
　　cultural sensitivity for psychologists working in disaster relief, 86
　　disaster and relief issues, 87
　　getting back into field/profession, 85–86
　　lessons learned and recommendations, 85–87
　　public policy issues, 88
　　recommendations for interventions, 88–89
　　restoration issues, 87–88
　　safety, general well-being, and vicarious traumatization, 86
　　social sciences, 86–87
　children's functioning following traumatic experiences, 74–82
　clinical initiatives, 66
　deployments to Gulf Coast, 66–68
　complimentary models, 82–85
　impact 15 months post-disaster, 69, 73
　impact of stress on low-income families, 70
　impact on adolescents in Mississippi, Marsee, 72
　literature on reactions to, 68
　　assessment, 68–72
　　interventions, 72–74
　　shortcoming of assessment and intervention, 74
　parent–child interaction, 81–82
　psychological impact on children from New Orleans area, 71
　role of ethnicity, 80
Kidney and urinary health, disasters and, 309–310
Kin selection theory, 221–222

L

Language development, very young vs. older children, 7
Learning technique, connecting between prior knowledge and new knowledge, 6
Louisiana Health Aging Study (LHAS), 172, 180, 189, 220, 233

M

Macrosystem, 28, 29
　Katrina (Hurricane), research on effects of, 30–33
Meaning making, 207–212
　issues, after Katrina, 198–199
Mental health
　impacts of storm on children/adults, 68
　post-traumatic stress disorder, 299–301
Mesosystem, 28, 29
　Katrina (Hurricane), research on effects of, 34–36
　severed ties in children's lives, 34
Microsystem, 28, 29
　Katrina (Hurricane), research on effects of, 36–37
Moral development, very young vs. older children, 7
Musculoskeletal problems, disasters and, 311–312

N

Narrative story stem technique (NSST), 18, 23
　typical scene created by a child regarding hurricane, 19

Subject Index

Natural disasters and oldest-old adults, 171–173
  coping with Katrina and Rita: LHAS hurricane study, 180
    overview of method, 181
    results and discussion, 181–187
  implications, 187
    practical, 189
    psychological, 187–188
  older adult population, 173
    developmental implications, 175–176
    three domains of age-related change, 173–175
  resilience and coping in late adulthood, 176
    determinants of adaptive behavior in older adults, 178–180
    review of coping, 178
    review of resilience, 176–178
Negating, 208
Negative state relief hypothesis, 225
Neurological problems, disasters and, 310
NSST, see narrative story stem technique (NSST)

O

OD, see organizational development (OD)
Older adult population, natural disasters and, 173
  developmental implications, 175–176
  three domains of age-related change, 173–175
    age-related changes in cognition, 174
    age-related changes in physical health, 173–174
    age-related changes in social relations, 174–175
Older adults in aftermath of Katrina (Hurricane), 136
  coding and analyses, 138
  help and support received from individuals and community services, 140
  immediacy of support: days following Hurricane Katrina, 139–140
  informal support, 141–144
    ambivalent relationships, 141–142
    negative relationships, 144
    neutral relationships, 143–144
    positive relationships, 142–143
  journey out of New Orleans, 138–139
  perceptions of source of support, 147
  perceptions of support, 146
  procedures, 136–137
  questions and measures, 137–138
  rebuilding relationships, 145–146
Oldest-old adults, natural disasters and, 171–173
  coping with Katrina and Rita: LHAS hurricane study, 180
    overview of method, 181
    results and discussion, 181–187
  implications, 187
    practical, 189
    psychological, 187–188
  older adult population, 173
    developmental implications, 175–176
    three domains of age-related change, 173–175
  resilience and coping in late adulthood, 176
    determinants of adaptive behavior in older adults, 178–180
    review of coping, 178
    review of resilience, 176–178
Ontogenic level, 28, 29
  Katrina (Hurricane), research on effects of, 37–40
Organizational development (OD), 263
  in circumstances of disaster, 261
  classical practices, 263–264
  in extraordinary circumstances, 264
    developmental stages of disaster response, 265–266
    restoring human, operational, and technical organizational structures, 267–274
  ordinary disaster and typical approaches to ordinary disasters *versus* catastrophic disasters, 263
  typical OD in normal circumstances, 263–264

P

Parent–child separations
  during trauma and child mental health, 34
PFA, see Psychological First Aid (PFA)
Physical and language development, children, 6
Positive adjustment in youth post-Katrina, 45–47
  coping and adjustment, 48–50
  current study and hypotheses, 50–54
  discussion, 57–59
    additional findings, 60
    study strengths and limitations, 60
  results
    descriptive statistics, 54–55
    regression analyses, 55–57
  social support and adjustment, 47–48

Post-disaster, positive outcomes for youth, 50
  demographic characteristics, 53
  descriptive statistics
    community violence, 55
    Hurricane exposure, 54–55
    positive adjustment and adaptive skills, 55
    youth and parent coping, 55
    youth and parent social support, 55
  maternal/youth risk and protective factors, 53–54
  measures used, 51–52
  regression analyses, 55–56
    child-reported personal adjustment, 56
    parent-reported child adaptive skills, 57
    predicting child-reported personal adjustment, 56
    predicting parent-reported adaptive skills, 57
  See also Social support, parent-provided
Post-traumatic growth (PTG), 46–47, 58
  vs. resilience, 47
Post-traumatic stress
  disasters' effects on older children, 7
Post-traumatic stress disorder (PTSD), 266
  age effects in, 80–81
  assessment in preschool-aged children, 39
  during disasters, 7, 8
  effects on child and adolescent emotional development, 27
  as impact of Katrina
    children diagnosed with, 68–69
    mediating effect between exposure and somatic symptoms, 85
    moderational role of competence and, 84
    reduction in, test anxiety reduction intervention, 35
  risk factors of developing, 100
  sense of control or calmness and developing, 88
  trait anxiety and, 38–39
Presocialization, 229
Project SERV, see School Emergency Response to Violence (Project SERV)
Prosocial behaviors, 220
Protective factors, 177–178
Psychological adjustment
  of children and adolescents following trauma, 83
Psychological First Aid (PFA), 258
Psychology behind helping and prosocial behaviors, 219–220
  crossing barrier from intention to action
    disaster helping literature, 231–233
    life span development view, 228–231
  helping others in aftermath of natural disaster, 233
    bridging belief-to-behavior gap, 236–237
    pride through association with faith community, 234–235
    reports of "being helped," 234
    road paved with good intentions, noble phrases, and ethics, 236
  purpose of helping, 220–221
    belief in just world, 227–228
    cost–reward model, 225–227
    empathy–altruism hypothesis and relief of negative state, 223–225
    kin selection view of prosocial behavior, 221–223
PTSD, see post-traumatic stress disorder (PTSD)

R

Reciprocal altruism, 222–223
Reflexivity, after Katrina, 200–201
Relief of negative state view, 224–225
  vs. empathy–altruism hypothesis, 223–224
Reproductive and developmental health, disasters and, 310–311
Resilience, 45–46, 84, 176–177
  areas of functioning in youth that reflect, 46
  and coping in late adulthood, 176
    determinants of adaptive behavior in older adults, 178–180
    review of coping, 178
    review of resilience, 176–178
  families and, 114
  pathways leading to, 100
  stress and, 176
  vs. PTG, 47
Resilience model, 84
Resiliency, 100
Resource loss, 78–79
Respiratory health, disasters and, 309
Respiratory protection measures, 287–288
Response, 258
Restoring human, operational, and technical organizational structures, 267–274
  recovering human structure of organization, 267–270
  recovering operational structure of organization, 270–273

Subject Index

recovering technical structure of organization, 273–274
Risk and resilience model, 28
Rita (Hurricane), impacts on Louisiana and Mississippi
  school, 5
  decrease in student population, 4
  statistics, 4

S

SAMHSA, *see* Substance Abuse and Mental Health Services Administration (SAMHSA)
SAMHSA Crisis Counseling Program, 33
SARBO, *see* Search and Rescues Operations Bases (SARBO)
School Emergency Response to Violence (Project SERV), 255
Search and Rescues Operations Bases (SARBO), 244, 246
Seniors Without Families Triage (SWiFT), 164
Social support, 47, 76–77
  and adjustment, 47–48
    maternal, 48
    youth, 48
  and mental health, 70
  parent-provided, 58–59
Social support networks, dynamics of older adults, 133–134
  implications, 146–150
  older adults in aftermath of Hurricane Katrina, 136
    coding and analyses, 138
    immediacy of support: days following Hurricane Katrina, 139–140
    informal support: relationships and interactions, 141–144
    journey out of New Orleans, 138–139
    perceptions of support, 146
    procedures, 136–137
    questions and measures, 137–138
    rebuilding relationships, 145–146
  social support in late life, 134–135
    support for older adults in times of disasters, 135–136
Social work perspective, disaster preparation from
  disaster planning teams and partnerships, 163
  emergency preparedness, 160–162
  identifying high-risk elders, 163–164
  older persons' resilience and exposure to hurricanes, 162–163

social work roles and risks – freelancing and credentialing issues, 164–166
Special needs, 157
Special Needs Shelters (SNS), 157
Stafford Disaster Relief and Emergency Assistance Act, 32–33
Storms' aftermath, assessing children's needs, 9
Stress in young children due to uncertainty and change, 10
Substance Abuse and Mental Health Services Administration (SAMHSA), 32–33
  See also Federal Emergency Management Agency (FEMA)
Survival humor, 122
SWiFT, *see* Seniors Without Families Triage (SWiFT)

T

Temporary Medical Observation Staging Areas (TMOSA), 244, 245
TMOSA, *see* Temporary Medical Observation Staging Areas (TMOSA)
Tobacco, disasters and, 314–315
Transactional stress and coping model (TSC), 82–83
Trauma
  adjustment and resilience following, 45–47
  child adjustment outcomes following, 83
  children's functioning following, 74–82
  health outcomes following, 84–85
  leading to negative health outcomes, 84–85
  loss, 115
  parent–child separations, 34
  psychological adjustment of children and adolescents following, 83

V

VIA Inventory of Strengths (VIA-IS), 232
"Vicarious traumatization," 86
Vulnerability analysis, 163
Vulnerability–stress model, 74–75

W

Workplace, disaster recovery in, 261–262
  OD in extraordinary circumstances, 264
  developmental stages of disaster response, 265–266
  restoring human, operational, and technical organizational structures, 267–274

Workplace, disaster recovery in (*cont.*)
    ordinary disaster and typical approaches to OD
        ordinary disasters *versus* catastrophic disasters, 263
        typical OD in normal circumstances, 263–264
    practical and scientific suggestions for workplace disaster recovery
        research directions, 275–276
        workplace preparation and planning, 274–275
    workplace recovery in overview, 262

X

Young children's demonstrated understanding of hurricanes, 3–4
    child interviews, 17–20
    destruction of schools and effects on developing children, 4–5
    development of young children, 5–7
    early childhood education and disasters, 8–10
    young children and disasters, 7–8
    future directions, 22–23
    geographic differences in language, literacy, and play
        conversations, 16–17
        drawing hurricane experiences, 15–16
        hurricane stories, 13–15
        play, 16
        using books about hurricanes, 16
        writing about hurricanes, 15
    stages of disasters exhibited in play and conversations, 17
    study, 10–11
        discussion, 20–22
        teacher survey, 11–13